University Casebook Series

April, 1992

ACCOUNTING AND THE LAW, Fourth Edition (1978), with Problems Pamphlet (Successor to Dohr, Phillips, Thompson & Warren)

George C. Thompson, Professor, Columbia University Graduate School of Business.
Robert Whitman, Professor of Law, University of Connecticut.
Ellis L. Phillips, Jr., Member of the New York Bar.
William C. Warren, Professor of Law Emeritus, Columbia University.

ACCOUNTING FOR LAWYERS, MATERIALS ON (1980)

David R. Herwitz, Professor of Law, Harvard University.

ADMINISTRATIVE LAW, Eighth Edition (1987), with 1989 Case Supplement and 1983 Problems Supplement (Supplement edited in association with Paul R. Verkuil, Dean and Professor of Law, Tulane University)

Walter Gellhorn, University Professor Emeritus, Columbia University.
Clark Byse, Professor of Law, Harvard University.
Peter L. Strauss, Professor of Law, Columbia University.
Todd D. Rakoff, Professor of Law, Harvard University.
Roy A. Schotland, Professor of Law, Georgetown University.

ADMIRALTY, Third Edition (1987), with 1991 Statute and Rule Supplement

Jo Desha Lucas, Professor of Law, University of Chicago.

ADVOCACY, see also Lawyering Process

AGENCY, see also Enterprise Organization

AGENCY—PARTNERSHIPS, Fourth Edition (1987)

Abridgement from Conard, Knauss & Siegel's Enterprise Organization, Fourth Edition.

AGENCY AND PARTNERSHIPS (1987)

Melvin A. Eisenberg, Professor of Law, University of California, Berkeley.

ANTITRUST: FREE ENTERPRISE AND ECONOMIC ORGANIZATION, Sixth Edition (1983), with 1983 Problems in Antitrust Supplement and 1991 Case Supplement

Louis B. Schwartz, Professor of Law, University of Pennsylvania.
John J. Flynn, Professor of Law, University of Utah.
Harry First, Professor of Law, New York University.

BANKRUPTCY, Second Edition (1989), with 1991 Case Supplement

Robert L. Jordan, Professor of Law, University of California, Los Angeles.
William D. Warren, Professor of Law, University of California, Los Angeles.

BANKRUPTCY AND DEBTOR–CREDITOR LAW, Second Edition (1988)

Theodore Eisenberg, Professor of Law, Cornell University.

UNIVERSITY CASEBOOK SERIES—Continued

BUSINESS ASSOCIATIONS, AGENCY, PARTNERSHIPS, AND CORPORATIONS (1991)

William A. Klein, Professor of Law, University of California, Los Angeles.
Mark Ramseyer, Professor of Law, University of California, Los Angeles.

BUSINESS CRIME (1990), with 1991 Case Supplement

Harry First, Professor of Law, New York University.

BUSINESS ORGANIZATION, see also Enterprise Organization

BUSINESS PLANNING (1991)

Franklin Gevurtz, Professor of Law, McGeorge School of Law.

BUSINESS PLANNING, Temporary Second Edition (1984)

David R. Herwitz, Professor of Law, Harvard University.

BUSINESS TORTS (1972)

Milton Handler, Professor of Law Emeritus, Columbia University.

CHILDREN IN THE LEGAL SYSTEM (1983), with 1990 Supplement (Supplement edited in association with Elizabeth S. Scott, Professor of Law, University of Virginia)

Walter Wadlington, Professor of Law, University of Virginia.
Charles H. Whitebread, Professor of Law, University of Southern California.
Samuel Davis, Professor of Law, University of Georgia.

CIVIL PROCEDURE, see Procedure

CIVIL RIGHTS ACTIONS (1988), with 1991 Supplement

Peter W. Low, Professor of Law, University of Virginia.
John C. Jeffries, Jr., Professor of Law, University of Virginia.

CLINIC, see also Lawyering Process

COMMERCIAL AND DEBTOR–CREDITOR LAW: SELECTED STATUTES, 1991 EDITION

COMMERCIAL LAW, Third Edition (1992)

Robert L. Jordan, Professor of Law, University of California, Los Angeles.
William D. Warren, Professor of Law, University of California, Los Angeles.

COMMERCIAL LAW, Fourth Edition (1985), with 1991 Case Supplement

E. Allan Farnsworth, Professor of Law, Columbia University.
John Honnold, Professor of Law, University of Pennsylvania.

COMMERCIAL PAPER, see also Negotiable Instruments

COMMERCIAL PAPER, Third Edition (1984), with 1991 Case Supplement

E. Allan Farnsworth, Professor of Law, Columbia University.

COMMERCIAL PAPER AND BANK DEPOSITS AND COLLECTIONS (1967), with Statutory Supplement

William D. Hawkland, Professor of Law, University of Illinois.

COMMERCIAL TRANSACTIONS—Principles and Policies, Second Edition (1991)

Alan Schwartz, Professor of Law, Yale University.
Robert E. Scott, Professor of Law, University of Virginia.

UNIVERSITY CASEBOOK SERIES—Continued

COMPARATIVE LAW, Fifth Edition (1988)
Rudolf B. Schlesinger, Professor of Law, Hastings College of the Law.
Hans W. Baade, Professor of Law, University of Texas.
Mirjan P. Damaska, Professor of Law, Yale Law School.
Peter E. Herzog, Professor of Law, Syracuse University.

COMPETITIVE PROCESS, LEGAL REGULATION OF THE, Revised Fourth Edition (1991), with 1991 Selected Statutes Supplement
Edmund W. Kitch, Professor of Law, University of Virginia.
Harvey S. Perlman, Dean of the Law School, University of Nebraska.

CONFLICT OF LAWS, Ninth Edition (1990), with 1992 Supplement
Willis L. M. Reese, Professor of Law, Columbia University.
Maurice Rosenberg, Professor of Law, Columbia University.
Peter Hay, Professor of Law, University of Illinois.

CONSTITUTIONAL LAW, Eighth Edition (1989), with 1991 Case Supplement
Edward L. Barrett, Jr., Professor of Law, University of California, Davis.
William Cohen, Professor of Law, Stanford University.
Jonathan D. Varat, Professor of Law, University of California, Los Angeles.

CONSTITUTIONAL LAW, CIVIL LIBERTY AND INDIVIDUAL RIGHTS, Second Edition (1982), with 1991 Supplement
William Cohen, Professor of Law, Stanford University.
John Kaplan, Professor of Law, Stanford University.

CONSTITUTIONAL LAW, Twelfth Edition (1991), with 1991 Supplement (Supplement edited in association with Frederick F. Schauer, Professor, Harvard University)
Gerald Gunther, Professor of Law, Stanford University.

CONSTITUTIONAL LAW, INDIVIDUAL RIGHTS IN, Fifth Edition (1992), (Reprinted from CONSTITUTIONAL LAW, Twelfth Edition), with 1991 Supplement (Supplement edited in association with Frederick F. Schauer, Professor, Harvard University)
Gerald Gunther, Professor of Law, Stanford University.

CONSUMER TRANSACTIONS, Second Edition (1991), with Selected Statutes and Regulations Supplement
Michael M. Greenfield, Professor of Law, Washington University.

CONTRACT LAW AND ITS APPLICATION, Fourth Edition (1988)
Arthur Rosett, Professor of Law, University of California, Los Angeles.

CONTRACT LAW, STUDIES IN, Fourth Edition (1991)
Edward J. Murphy, Professor of Law, University of Notre Dame.
Richard E. Speidel, Professor of Law, Northwestern University.

CONTRACTS, Fifth Edition (1987)
John P. Dawson, late Professor of Law, Harvard University.
William Burnett Harvey, Professor of Law and Political Science, Boston University.
Stanley D. Henderson, Professor of Law, University of Virginia.

CONTRACTS, Fourth Edition (1988)
E. Allan Farnsworth, Professor of Law, Columbia University.
William F. Young, Professor of Law, Columbia University.

CONTRACTS, Selections on (statutory materials) (1988)

UNIVERSITY CASEBOOK SERIES—Continued

CONTRACTS, Second Edition (1978), with Statutory and Administrative Law Supplement (1978)

Ian R. Macneil, Professor of Law, Cornell University.

COPYRIGHT, PATENTS AND TRADEMARKS, see also Competitive Process; see also Selected Statutes and International Agreements

COPYRIGHT, PATENT, TRADEMARK AND RELATED STATE DOCTRINES, Third Edition (1990), with 1991 Selected Statutes Supplement and 1981 Problem Supplement

Paul Goldstein, Professor of Law, Stanford University.

COPYRIGHT, Unfair Competition, and Other Topics Bearing on the Protection of Literary, Musical, and Artistic Works, Fifth Edition (1990), with 1991 Statutory and Case Supplement

Ralph S. Brown, Jr., Professor of Law, Yale University.
Robert C. Denicola, Professor of Law, University of Nebraska.

CORPORATE ACQUISITIONS, The Law and Finance of (1986), with 1991 Supplement

Ronald J. Gilson, Professor of Law, Stanford University.

CORPORATE FINANCE, Third Edition (1987)

Victor Brudney, Professor of Law, Harvard University.
Marvin A. Chirelstein, Professor of Law, Columbia University.

CORPORATION LAW, BASIC, Third Edition (1989), with Documentary Supplement

Detlev F. Vagts, Professor of Law, Harvard University.

CORPORATIONS, see also Enterprise Organization and Business Organization

CORPORATIONS, Sixth Edition—Concise (1988), with 1991 Case Supplement and 1991 Statutory Supplement

William L. Cary, late Professor of Law, Columbia University.
Melvin Aron Eisenberg, Professor of Law, University of California, Berkeley.

CORPORATIONS, Sixth Edition—Unabridged (1988), with 1991 Case Supplement and 1991 Statutory Supplement

William L. Cary, late Professor of Law, Columbia University.
Melvin Aron Eisenberg, Professor of Law, University of California, Berkeley.

CORPORATIONS AND BUSINESS ASSOCIATIONS—STATUTES, RULES, AND FORMS (1991)

CORRECTIONS, SEE SENTENCING

CREDITORS' RIGHTS, see also Debtor-Creditor Law

CRIMINAL JUSTICE ADMINISTRATION, Fourth Edition (1991), with 1991 Supplement

Frank W. Miller, Professor of Law, Washington University.
Robert O. Dawson, Professor of Law, University of Texas.
George E. Dix, Professor of Law, University of Texas.
Raymond I. Parnas, Professor of Law, University of California, Davis.

CRIMINAL LAW, Fifth Edition (1992)

Andre A. Moenssens, Professor of Law, University of Richmond.
Fred E. Inbau, Professor of Law Emeritus, Northwestern University.
Ronald J. Bacigal, Professor of Law, University of Richmond.

UNIVERSITY CASEBOOK SERIES—Continued

CRIMINAL LAW AND APPROACHES TO THE STUDY OF LAW, Second Edition (1991)

John M. Brumbaugh, Professor of Law, University of Maryland.

CRIMINAL LAW, Second Edition (1986)

Peter W. Low, Professor of Law, University of Virginia.
John C. Jeffries, Jr., Professor of Law, University of Virginia.
Richard C. Bonnie, Professor of Law, University of Virginia.

CRIMINAL LAW, Fourth Edition (1986)

Lloyd L. Weinreb, Professor of Law, Harvard University.

CRIMINAL LAW AND PROCEDURE, Seventh Edition (1989)

Ronald N. Boyce, Professor of Law, University of Utah.
Rollin M. Perkins, Professor of Law Emeritus, University of California, Hastings College of the Law.

CRIMINAL PROCEDURE, Fourth Edition (1992)

James B. Haddad, late Professor of Law, Northwestern University.
James B. Zagel, Chief, Criminal Justice Division, Office of Attorney General of Illinois.
Gary L. Starkman, Assistant U. S. Attorney, Northern District of Illinois.
William J. Bauer, Chief Judge of the U.S. Court of Appeals, Seventh Circuit.

CRIMINAL PROCESS, Fourth Edition (1987), with 1991 Supplement

Lloyd L. Weinreb, Professor of Law, Harvard University.

DAMAGES, Second Edition (1952)

Charles T. McCormick, late Professor of Law, University of Texas.
William F. Fritz, late Professor of Law, University of Texas.

DECEDENTS' ESTATES AND TRUSTS, See also Family Property Law

DECEDENTS' ESTATES AND TRUSTS, Seventh Edition (1988)

John Ritchie, late Professor of Law, University of Virginia.
Neill H. Alford, Jr., Professor of Law, University of Virginia.
Richard W. Effland, late Professor of Law, Arizona State University.

DISPUTE RESOLUTION, Processes of (1989)

John S. Murray, President and Executive Director of The Conflict Clinic, Inc., George Mason University.
Alan Scott Rau, Professor of Law, University of Texas.
Edward F. Sherman, Professor of Law, University of Texas.

DOMESTIC RELATIONS, see also Family Law

DOMESTIC RELATIONS, Second Edition (1990), with 1992 Supplement

Walter Wadlington, Professor of Law, University of Virginia.

EMPLOYMENT DISCRIMINATION, Second Edition (1987), with 1990 Supplement

Joel W. Friedman, Professor of Law, Tulane University.
George M. Strickler, Professor of Law, Tulane University.

EMPLOYMENT LAW, Second Edition (1991), with Statutory Supplement and 1991 Case Supplement

Mark A. Rothstein, Professor of Law, University of Houston.
Andria S. Knapp, Visiting Professor of Law, Golden Gate University.
Lance Liebman, Professor of Law, Harvard University.

UNIVERSITY CASEBOOK SERIES—Continued

ENERGY LAW (1983), with 1991 Case Supplement

Donald N. Zillman, Professor of Law, University of Utah.
Laurence Lattman, Dean of Mines and Engineering, University of Utah.

ENTERPRISE ORGANIZATION, Fourth Edition (1987), with 1987 Corporation and Partnership Statutes, Rules and Forms Supplement

Alfred F. Conard, Professor of Law, University of Michigan.
Robert L. Knauss, Dean of the Law School, University of Houston.
Stanley Siegel, Professor of Law, University of California, Los Angeles.

ENVIRONMENTAL POLICY LAW, Second Edition (1991)

Thomas J. Schoenbaum, Professor of Law, University of Georgia.
Ronald H. Rosenberg, Professor of Law, College of William and Mary.

EQUITY, see also Remedies

EQUITY, RESTITUTION AND DAMAGES, Second Edition (1974)

Robert Childres, late Professor of Law, Northwestern University.
William F. Johnson, Jr., Professor of Law, New York University.

ESTATE PLANNING, Second Edition (1982), with 1985 Case, Text and Documentary Supplement

David Westfall, Professor of Law, Harvard University.

ETHICS, see Legal Ethics, Legal Profession, Professional Responsibility, and Social Responsibilities

ETHICS OF LAWYERING, THE LAW AND (1990)

Geoffrey C. Hazard, Jr., Professor of Law, Yale University.
Susan P. Koniak, Professor of Law, University of Pittsburgh.

ETHICS AND PROFESSIONAL RESPONSIBILITY (1981) (Reprinted from THE LAWYERING PROCESS)

Gary Bellow, Professor of Law, Harvard University.
Bea Moulton, Legal Services Corporation.

EVIDENCE, Seventh Edition (1992)

John Kaplan, Late Professor of Law, Stanford University.
Jon R. Waltz, Professor of Law, Northwestern University.
Roger C. Park, Professor of Law, University of Minnesota.

EVIDENCE, Eighth Edition (1988), with Rules, Statute and Case Supplement (1990)

Jack B. Weinstein, Chief Judge, United States District Court.
John H. Mansfield, Professor of Law, Harvard University.
Norman Abrams, Professor of Law, University of California, Los Angeles.
Margaret Berger, Professor of Law, Brooklyn Law School.

FAMILY LAW, see also Domestic Relations

FAMILY LAW, Third Edition (1992)

Judith C. Areen, Professor of Law, Georgetown University.

FAMILY LAW AND CHILDREN IN THE LEGAL SYSTEM, STATUTORY MATERIALS (1981)

Walter Wadlington, Professor of Law, University of Virginia.

UNIVERSITY CASEBOOK SERIES—Continued

FAMILY PROPERTY LAW, Cases and Materials on Wills, Trusts and Future Interests (1991)

Lawrence W. Waggoner, Professor of Law, University of Michigan.
Richard V. Wellman, Professor of Law, University of Georgia.
Gregory Alexander, Professor of Law, Cornell Law School.
Mary L. Fellows, Professor of Law, University of Minnesota.

FEDERAL COURTS, Eighth Edition (1988), with 1991 Supplement

Charles T. McCormick, late Professor of Law, University of Texas.
James H. Chadbourn, late Professor of Law, Harvard University.
Charles Alan Wright, Professor of Law, University of Texas, Austin.

FEDERAL COURTS AND THE FEDERAL SYSTEM, Hart and Wechsler's Third Edition (1988), with 1992 Case Supplement, and the Judicial Code and Rules of Procedure in the Federal Courts (1991)

Paul M. Bator, Professor of Law, University of Chicago.
Daniel J. Meltzer, Professor of Law, Harvard University.
Paul J. Mishkin, Professor of Law, University of California, Berkeley.
David L. Shapiro, Professor of Law, Harvard University.

FEDERAL COURTS AND THE LAW OF FEDERAL–STATE RELATIONS, Second Edition (1989), with 1991 Supplement

Peter W. Low, Professor of Law, University of Virginia.
John C. Jeffries, Jr., Professor of Law, University of Virginia.

FEDERAL PUBLIC LAND AND RESOURCES LAW, Second Edition (1987), with 1990 Case Supplement and 1990 Statutory Supplement

George C. Coggins, Professor of Law, University of Kansas.
Charles F. Wilkinson, Professor of Law, University of Oregon.

FEDERAL RULES OF CIVIL PROCEDURE and Selected Other Procedural Provisions, 1991 Edition

FEDERAL TAXATION, see Taxation

FIRST AMENDMENT (1991)

William W. Van Alstyne, Professor of Law, Duke University.

FOOD AND DRUG LAW, Second Edition (1991), with Statutory Supplement

Peter Barton Hutt, Esq.
Richard A. Merrill, Professor of Law, University of Virginia.

FUTURE INTERESTS (1970)

Howard R. Williams, Professor of Law, Stanford University.

FUTURE INTERESTS AND ESTATE PLANNING (1961), with 1962 Supplement

W. Barton Leach, late Professor of Law, Harvard University.
James K. Logan, formerly Dean of the Law School, University of Kansas.

GENDER DISCRIMINATION, see Women and the Law

GOVERNMENT CONTRACTS, FEDERAL, Successor Edition (1985), with 1989 Supplement

John W. Whelan, Professor of Law, Hastings College of the Law.

GOVERNMENT REGULATION: FREE ENTERPRISE AND ECONOMIC ORGANIZATION, Sixth Edition (1985)

Louis B. Schwartz, Professor of Law, Hastings College of the Law.
John J. Flynn, Professor of Law, University of Utah.
Harry First, Professor of Law, New York University.

UNIVERSITY CASEBOOK SERIES—Continued

HEALTH CARE LAW AND POLICY (1988)

Clark C. Havighurst, Professor of Law, Duke University.

HINCKLEY, JOHN W., JR., TRIAL OF: A Case Study of the Insanity Defense (1986)

Peter W. Low, Professor of Law, University of Virginia.
John C. Jeffries, Jr., Professor of Law, University of Virginia.
Richard C. Bonnie, Professor of Law, University of Virginia.

IMMIGRATION LAW AND POLICY (1992)

Stephen H. Legomsky, Professor of Law, Washington University.

INJUNCTIONS, Second Edition (1984)

Owen M. Fiss, Professor of Law, Yale University.
Doug Rendleman, Professor of Law, College of William and Mary.

INSTITUTIONAL INVESTORS (1978)

David L. Ratner, Professor of Law, Cornell University.

INSURANCE, Second Edition (1985)

William F. Young, Professor of Law, Columbia University.
Eric M. Holmes, Professor of Law, University of Georgia.

INSURANCE LAW AND REGULATION (1990)

Kenneth S. Abraham, University of Virginia.

INTERNATIONAL LAW, see also Transnational Legal Problems, Transnational Business Problems, and United Nations Law

INTERNATIONAL LAW IN CONTEMPORARY PERSPECTIVE (1981), with Essay Supplement

Myres S. McDougal, Professor of Law, Yale University.
W. Michael Reisman, Professor of Law, Yale University.

INTERNATIONAL LEGAL SYSTEM, Third Edition (1988), with Documentary Supplement

Joseph Modeste Sweeney, Professor of Law, University of California, Hastings.
Covey T. Oliver, Professor of Law, University of Pennsylvania.
Noyes E. Leech, Professor of Law Emeritus, University of Pennsylvania.

INTRODUCTION TO LAW, see also Legal Method, On Law in Courts, and Dynamics of American Law

INTRODUCTION TO THE STUDY OF LAW (1970)

E. Wayne Thode, late Professor of Law, University of Utah.
Leon Lebowitz, Professor of Law, University of Texas.
Lester J. Mazor, Professor of Law, University of Utah.

JUDICIAL CODE and Rules of Procedure in the Federal Courts, Students' Edition, 1991 Revision

Daniel J. Meltzer, Professor of Law, Harvard University.
David L. Shapiro, Professor of Law, Harvard University.

JURISPRUDENCE (Temporary Edition Hardbound) (1949)

Lon L. Fuller, late Professor of Law, Harvard University.

JUVENILE, see also Children

UNIVERSITY CASEBOOK SERIES—Continued

JUVENILE JUSTICE PROCESS, Third Edition (1985)
    Frank W. Miller, Professor of Law, Washington University.
    Robert O. Dawson, Professor of Law, University of Texas.
    George E. Dix, Professor of Law, University of Texas.
    Raymond I. Parnas, Professor of Law, University of California, Davis.

LABOR LAW, Eleventh Edition (1991), with 1991 Statutory Supplement
    Archibald Cox, Professor of Law, Harvard University.
    Derek C. Bok, President, Harvard University.
    Robert A. Gorman, Professor of Law, University of Pennsylvania.
    Matthew W. Finkin, Professor of Law, University of Illinois.

LABOR LAW, Second Edition (1982), with Statutory Supplement
    Clyde W. Summers, Professor of Law, University of Pennsylvania.
    Harry H. Wellington, Dean of the Law School, Yale University.
    Alan Hyde, Professor of Law, Rutgers University.

LAND FINANCING, Third Edition (1985)
    The late Norman Penney, Professor of Law, Cornell University.
    Richard F. Broude, Member of the California Bar.
    Roger Cunningham, Professor of Law, University of Michigan.

LAW AND MEDICINE (1980)
    Walter Wadlington, Professor of Law and Professor of Legal Medicine, University of Virginia.
    Jon R. Waltz, Professor of Law, Northwestern University.
    Roger B. Dworkin, Professor of Law, Indiana University, and Professor of Biomedical History, University of Washington.

LAW, LANGUAGE AND ETHICS (1972)
    William R. Bishin, Professor of Law, University of Southern California.
    Christopher D. Stone, Professor of Law, University of Southern California.

LAW, SCIENCE AND MEDICINE (1984), with 1989 Supplement
    Judith C. Areen, Professor of Law, Georgetown University.
    Patricia A. King, Professor of Law, Georgetown University.
    Steven P. Goldberg, Professor of Law, Georgetown University.
    Alexander M. Capron, Professor of Law, University of Southern California.

LAWYERING PROCESS (1978), with Civil Problem Supplement and Criminal Problem Supplement
    Gary Bellow, Professor of Law, Harvard University.
    Bea Moulton, Professor of Law, Arizona State University.

LEGAL ETHICS (1992)
    Deborah Rhode, Professor of Law, Stanford University.
    David Luban, Professor of Law, University of Maryland.

LEGAL METHOD (1980)
    Harry W. Jones, Professor of Law Emeritus, Columbia University.
    John M. Kernochan, Professor of Law, Columbia University.
    Arthur W. Murphy, Professor of Law, Columbia University.

LEGAL METHODS (1969)
    Robert N. Covington, Professor of Law, Vanderbilt University.
    E. Blythe Stason, late Professor of Law, Vanderbilt University.
    John W. Wade, Professor of Law, Vanderbilt University.
    Elliott E. Cheatham, late Professor of Law, Vanderbilt University.
    Theodore A. Smedley, Professor of Law, Vanderbilt University.

UNIVERSITY CASEBOOK SERIES—Continued

LEGAL PROFESSION, THE, Responsibility and Regulation, Second Edition (1988)
Geoffrey C. Hazard, Jr., Professor of Law, Yale University.
Deborah L. Rhode, Professor of Law, Stanford University.

LEGISLATION, Fourth Edition (1982) (by Fordham)
Horace E. Read, late Vice President, Dalhousie University.
John W. MacDonald, Professor of Law Emeritus, Cornell Law School.
Jefferson B. Fordham, Professor of Law, University of Utah.
William J. Pierce, Professor of Law, University of Michigan.

LEGISLATIVE AND ADMINISTRATIVE PROCESSES, Second Edition (1981)
Hans A. Linde, Judge, Supreme Court of Oregon.
George Bunn, Professor of Law, University of Wisconsin.
Fredericka Paff, Professor of Law, University of Wisconsin.
W. Lawrence Church, Professor of Law, University of Wisconsin.

LOCAL GOVERNMENT LAW, Second Revised Edition (1986)
Jefferson B. Fordham, Professor of Law, University of Utah.

MASS MEDIA LAW, Fourth Edition (1990)
Marc A. Franklin, Professor of Law, Stanford University.
David A. Anderson, Professor of Law, University of Texas.

MUNICIPAL CORPORATIONS, see Local Government Law

NEGOTIABLE INSTRUMENTS, see Commercial Paper

NEGOTIABLE INSTRUMENTS AND LETTERS OF CREDIT (1992) (Reprinted from Commercial Law) Third Edition (1992)
Robert L. Jordan, Professor of Law, University of California, Los Angeles.
William D. Warren, Professor of Law, University of California, Los Angeles.

NEGOTIATION (1981) (Reprinted from THE LAWYERING PROCESS)
Gary Bellow, Professor of Law, Harvard Law School.
Bea Moulton, Legal Services Corporation.

NEW YORK PRACTICE, Fourth Edition (1978)
Herbert Peterfreund, Professor of Law, New York University.
Joseph M. McLaughlin, Dean of the Law School, Fordham University.

OIL AND GAS, Sixth Edition (1992)
Richard C. Maxwell, Professor of Law, Duke University.
Stephen F. Williams, Judge of the United States Court of Appeals.
Patrick Henry Martin, Professor of Law, Louisiana State University.
Bruce M. Kramer, Professor of Law, Texas Tech University.

ON LAW IN COURTS (1965)
Paul J. Mishkin, Professor of Law, University of California, Berkeley.
Clarence Morris, Professor of Law Emeritus, University of Pennsylvania.

PENSION AND EMPLOYEE BENEFIT LAW (1990), with 1991 Supplement
John H. Langbein, Professor of Law, University of Chicago.
Bruce A. Wolk, Professor of Law, University of California, Davis.

PLEADING AND PROCEDURE, see Procedure, Civil

POLICE FUNCTION, Fifth Edition (1991), with 1991 Supplement
Reprint of Chapters 1–10 of Miller, Dawson, Dix and Parnas's CRIMINAL JUSTICE ADMINISTRATION, Fourth Edition.

UNIVERSITY CASEBOOK SERIES—Continued

PREPARING AND PRESENTING THE CASE (1981) (Reprinted from THE LAWYERING PROCESS)

Gary Bellow, Professor of Law, Harvard Law School.
Bea Moulton, Legal Services Corporation.

PROCEDURE (1988), with Procedure Supplement (1991)

Robert M. Cover, late Professor of Law, Yale Law School.
Owen M. Fiss, Professor of Law, Yale Law School.
Judith Resnik, Professor of Law, University of Southern California Law Center.

PROCEDURE—CIVIL PROCEDURE, Sixth Edition (1990), with 1991 Supplement

Richard H. Field, late Professor of Law, Harvard University.
Benjamin Kaplan, Professor of Law Emeritus, Harvard University.
Kevin M. Clermont, Professor of Law, Cornell University.

PROCEDURE—CIVIL PROCEDURE, Successor Edition (1992)

A. Leo Levin, Professor of Law Emeritus, University of Pennsylvania.
Philip Shuchman, Professor of Law, Rutgers University.
Charles M. Yablon, Professor of Law, Yeshiva University.

PROCEDURE—CIVIL PROCEDURE, Fifth Edition (1990), with 1991 Supplement

Maurice Rosenberg, Professor of Law, Columbia University.
Hans Smit, Professor of Law, Columbia University.
Rochelle C. Dreyfuss, Professor of Law, New York University.

PROCEDURE—PLEADING AND PROCEDURE: State and Federal, Sixth Edition (1989), with 1991 Case Supplement

David W. Louisell, late Professor of Law, University of California, Berkeley.
Geoffrey C. Hazard, Jr., Professor of Law, Yale University.
Colin C. Tait, Professor of Law, University of Connecticut.

PROCEDURE—FEDERAL RULES OF CIVIL PROCEDURE, 1991 Edition

PRODUCTS LIABILITY AND SAFETY, Second Edition (1989), with 1989 Statutory Supplement

W. Page Keeton, Professor of Law, University of Texas.
David G. Owen, Professor of Law, University of South Carolina.
John E. Montgomery, Professor of Law, University of South Carolina.
Michael D. Green, Professor of Law, University of Iowa

PROFESSIONAL RESPONSIBILITY, Fifth Edition (1991), with 1992 Selected Standards on Professional Responsibility Supplement

Thomas D. Morgan, Professor of Law, George Washington University.
Ronald D. Rotunda, Professor of Law, University of Illinois.

PROPERTY, Sixth Edition (1990)

John E. Cribbet, Professor of Law, University of Illinois.
Corwin W. Johnson, Professor of Law, University of Texas.
Roger W. Findley, Professor of Law, University of Illinois.
Ernest E. Smith, Professor of Law, University of Texas.

PROPERTY—PERSONAL (1953)

S. Kenneth Skolfield, late Professor of Law Emeritus, Boston University.

PROPERTY—PERSONAL, Third Edition (1954)

Everett Fraser, late Dean of the Law School Emeritus, University of Minnesota.
Third Edition by Charles W. Taintor, late Professor of Law, University of Pittsburgh.

UNIVERSITY CASEBOOK SERIES—Continued

PROPERTY—INTRODUCTION, TO REAL PROPERTY, Third Edition (1954)

Everett Fraser, late Dean of the Law School Emeritus, University of Minnesota.

PROPERTY—FUNDAMENTALS OF MODERN REAL PROPERTY, Third Edition (1992)

Edward H. Rabin, Professor of Law, University of California, Davis.
Roberta Rosenthal Kwall, Professor of Law, DePaul University.

PROPERTY, REAL (1984), with 1988 Supplement

Paul Goldstein, Professor of Law, Stanford University.

PROSECUTION AND ADJUDICATION, Fourth Edition (1991), with 1991 Supplement

Reprint of Chapters 11–26 of Miller, Dawson, Dix and Parnas's CRIMINAL JUSTICE ADMINISTRATION, Fourth Edition.

PSYCHIATRY AND LAW, see Mental Health, see also Hinckley, Trial of

PUBLIC UTILITY LAW, see Free Enterprise, also Regulated Industries

REAL ESTATE PLANNING, Third Edition (1989), with Revised Problem and Statutory Supplement (1991)

Norton L. Steuben, Professor of Law, University of Colorado.

REAL ESTATE TRANSACTIONS, Revised Second Edition (1988), with Statute, Form and Problem Supplement (1988)

Paul Goldstein, Professor of Law, Stanford University.

RECEIVERSHIP AND CORPORATE REORGANIZATION, see Creditors' Rights

REGULATED INDUSTRIES, Second Edition (1976)

William K. Jones, Professor of Law, Columbia University.

REMEDIES, Third Edition (1992)

Edward D. Re, Professor of Law, St. John's University.
Stanton D. Krauss, Professor of Law, University of Bridgeport.

REMEDIES (1989)

Elaine W. Shoben, Professor of Law, University of Illinois.
Wm. Murray Tabb, Professor of Law, Baylor University.

SALES, Third Edition (1992)

Marion W. Benfield, Jr., Professor of Law, Wake Forest University.
William D. Hawkland, Professor of Law, Louisiana State Law Center.

SALES (1992) (Reprinted from Commercial Law) Third Edition (1992)

Robert L. Jordan, Professor of Law, University of California, Los Angeles.
William D. Warren, Professor of Law, University of California, Los Angeles.

SALES AND SALES FINANCING, Fifth Edition (1984)

John Honnold, Professor of Law, University of Pennsylvania.

SALES LAW AND THE CONTRACTING PROCESS, Second Edition (1991) (Reprinted from Commercial Transactions) Second Edition (1991)

Alan Schwartz, Professor of Law, Yale University.
Robert E. Scott, Professor of Law, University of Virginia.

UNIVERSITY CASEBOOK SERIES—Continued

SECURED TRANSACTIONS IN PERSONAL PROPERTY, Third Edition (1992) (Reprinted from COMMERCIAL LAW, Third Edition (1992))

Robert L. Jordan, Professor of Law, University of California, Los Angeles.
William D. Warren, Professor of Law, University of California, Los Angeles.

SECURITIES REGULATION, Seventh Edition (1992), with 1992 Selected Statutes, Rules and Forms Supplement

Richard W. Jennings, Professor of Law, University of California, Berkeley.
Harold Marsh, Jr., Member of California Bar.
John C. Coffee, Jr., Professor of Law, Columbia University.

SECURITIES REGULATION, Second Edition (1988), with Statute, Rule and Form Supplement (1991)

Larry D. Soderquist, Professor of Law, Vanderbilt University.

SECURITY INTERESTS IN PERSONAL PROPERTY, Second Edition (1987)

Douglas G. Baird, Professor of Law, University of Chicago.
Thomas H. Jackson, Dean of the Law School, University of Virginia.

SECURITY INTERESTS IN PERSONAL PROPERTY (1985) (Reprinted from Sales and Sales Financing, Fifth Edition)

John Honnold, Professor of Law, University of Pennsylvania.

SELECTED STANDARDS ON PROFESSIONAL RESPONSIBILITY, 1992 Edition

SELECTED STATUTES AND INTERNATIONAL AGREEMENTS ON UNFAIR COMPETITION, TRADEMARK, COPYRIGHT AND PATENT, 1991 Edition

SELECTED STATUTES ON TRUSTS AND ESTATES, 1992 Edition

SOCIAL RESPONSIBILITIES OF LAWYERS, Case Studies (1988)

Philip B. Heymann, Professor of Law, Harvard University.
Lance Liebman, Professor of Law, Harvard University.

SOCIAL SCIENCE IN LAW, Second Edition (1990)

John Monahan, Professor of Law, University of Virginia.
Laurens Walker, Professor of Law, University of Virginia.

TAXATION, FEDERAL INCOME (1989)

Stephen B. Cohen, Professor of Law, Georgetown University

TAXATION, FEDERAL INCOME, Second Edition (1988), with 1991 Supplement (Supplement edited in association with Deborah H. Schenk, Professor of Law, New York University)

Michael J. Graetz, Professor of Law, Yale University.

TAXATION, FEDERAL INCOME, Seventh Edition (1991)

James J. Freeland, Professor of Law, University of Florida.
Stephen A. Lind, Professor of Law, University of Florida and University of California, Hastings.
Richard B. Stephens, late Professor of Law Emeritus, University of Florida.

TAXATION, FEDERAL INCOME, Successor Edition (1986), with 1991 Legislative Supplement

Stanley S. Surrey, late Professor of Law, Harvard University.
Paul R. McDaniel, Professor of Law, Boston College.
Hugh J. Ault, Professor of Law, Boston College.
Stanley A. Koppelman, Professor of Law, Boston University.

UNIVERSITY CASEBOOK SERIES—Continued

TAXATION, FEDERAL INCOME, OF BUSINESS ORGANIZATIONS (1991), with 1991 Supplement

    Paul R. McDaniel, Professor of Law, Boston College.
    Hugh J. Ault, Professor of Law, Boston College.
    Martin J. McMahon, Jr., Professor of Law, University of Kentucky.
    Daniel L. Simmons, Professor of Law, University of California, Davis.

TAXATION, FEDERAL INCOME, OF PARTNERSHIPS AND S CORPORATIONS (1991), with 1991 Supplement

    Paul R. McDaniel, Professor of Law, Boston College.
    Hugh J. Ault, Professor of Law, Boston College.
    Martin J. McMahon, Jr., Professor of Law, University of Kentucky.
    Daniel L. Simmons, Professor of Law, University of California, Davis.

TAXATION, FEDERAL INCOME, OIL AND GAS, NATURAL RESOURCES TRANSACTIONS (1990)

    Peter C. Maxfield, Professor of Law, University of Wyoming.
    James L. Houghton, CPA, Partner, Ernst and Young.
    James R. Gaar, CPA, Partner, Ernst and Young.

TAXATION, FEDERAL WEALTH TRANSFER, Successor Edition (1987)

    Stanley S. Surrey, late Professor of Law, Harvard University.
    Paul R. McDaniel, Professor of Law, Boston College.
    Harry L. Gutman, Professor of Law, University of Pennsylvania.

TAXATION, FUNDAMENTALS OF CORPORATE, Third Edition (1991)

    Stephen A. Lind, Professor of Law, University of Florida and University of California, Hastings.
    Stephen Schwarz, Professor of Law, University of California, Hastings.
    Daniel J. Lathrope, Professor of Law, University of California, Hastings.
    Joshua Rosenberg, Professor of Law, University of San Francisco.

TAXATION, FUNDAMENTALS OF PARTNERSHIP, Third Edition (1992)

    Stephen A. Lind, Professor of Law, University of Florida and University of California, Hastings.
    Stephen Schwarz, Professor of Law, University of California, Hastings.
    Daniel J. Lathrope, Professor of Law, University of California, Hastings.
    Joshua Rosenberg, Professor of Law, University of San Francisco.

TAXATION OF CORPORATIONS AND THEIR SHAREHOLDERS (1991)

    David J. Shakow, Professor of Law, University of Pennsylvania.

TAXATION, PROBLEMS IN THE FEDERAL INCOME TAXATION OF PARTNERSHIPS AND CORPORATIONS, Second Edition (1986)

    Norton L. Steuben, Professor of Law, University of Colorado.
    William J. Turnier, Professor of Law, University of North Carolina.

TAXATION, PROBLEMS IN THE FUNDAMENTALS OF FEDERAL INCOME, Second Edition (1985)

    Norton L. Steuben, Professor of Law, University of Colorado.
    William J. Turnier, Professor of Law, University of North Carolina.

TORT LAW AND ALTERNATIVES, Fifth Edition (1992)

    Marc A. Franklin, Professor of Law, Stanford University.
    Robert L. Rabin, Professor of Law, Stanford University.

TORTS, Eighth Edition (1988)

    William L. Prosser, late Professor of Law, University of California, Hastings.
    John W. Wade, Professor of Law, Vanderbilt University.
    Victor E. Schwartz, Adjunct Professor of Law, Georgetown University.

UNIVERSITY CASEBOOK SERIES—Continued

TORTS, Third Edition (1976)
Harry Shulman, late Dean of the Law School, Yale University.
Fleming James, Jr., Professor of Law Emeritus, Yale University.
Oscar S. Gray, Professor of Law, University of Maryland.

TRADE REGULATION, Third Edition (1990)
Milton Handler, Professor of Law Emeritus, Columbia University.
Harlan M. Blake, Professor of Law, Columbia University.
Robert Pitofsky, Professor of Law, Georgetown University.
Harvey J. Goldschmid, Professor of Law, Columbia University.

TRADE REGULATION, see Antitrust

TRANSNATIONAL BUSINESS PROBLEMS (1986)
Detlev F. Vagts, Professor of Law, Harvard University.

TRANSNATIONAL LEGAL PROBLEMS, Third Edition (1986), with 1991 Revised Edition of Documentary Supplement
Henry J. Steiner, Professor of Law, Harvard University.
Detlev F. Vagts, Professor of Law, Harvard University.

TRIAL, see also Evidence, Making the Record, Lawyering Process and Preparing and Presenting the Case

TRUSTS, Sixth Edition (1991)
George G. Bogert, late Professor of Law Emeritus, University of Chicago.
Dallin H. Oaks, President, Brigham Young University.
H. Reese Hansen, Dean and Professor of Law, Brigham Young University.
Claralyn Martin Hill, J.D. Brigham Young University.

TRUSTS AND ESTATES, SELECTED STATUTES ON, 1992 Edition

TRUSTS AND WILLS, See also Decedents' Estates and Trusts, and Family Property Law

UNFAIR COMPETITION, see Competitive Process and Business Torts

WATER RESOURCE MANAGEMENT, Third Edition (1988), with 1992 Supplement
The late Charles J. Meyers, formerly Dean, Stanford University Law School.
A. Dan Tarlock, Professor of Law, IIT Chicago-Kent College of Law.
James N. Corbridge, Jr., Chancellor, University of Colorado at Boulder, and Professor of Law, University of Colorado.
David H. Getches, Professor of Law, University of Colorado.

WOMEN AND THE LAW (1992)
Mary Joe Frug, late Professor of Law, New England School of Law.

WILLS AND ADMINISTRATION, Fifth Edition (1961)
Philip Mechem, late Professor of Law, University of Pennsylvania.
Thomas E. Atkinson, late Professor of Law, New York University.

WRITING AND ANALYSIS IN THE LAW, Second Edition (1991)
Helene S. Shapo, Professor of Law, Northwestern University.
Marilyn R. Walter, Professor of Law, Brooklyn Law School.
Elizabeth Fajans, Writing Specialist, Brooklyn Law School.

University Casebook Series

EDITORIAL BOARD

DAVID L. SHAPIRO
DIRECTING EDITOR
Professor of Law, Harvard University

EDWARD L. BARRETT, Jr.
Professor of Law, University of California, Davis

ROBERT C. CLARK
Dean of the School of Law, Harvard University

OWEN M. FISS
Professor of Law, Yale Law School

GERALD GUNTHER
Professor of Law, Stanford University

THOMAS H. JACKSON
Dean of the School of Law, University of Virginia

HARRY W. JONES
Professor of Law, Columbia University

HERMA HILL KAY
Professor of Law, University of California, Berkeley

PAGE KEETON
Professor of Law, University of Texas

ROBERT L. RABIN
Professor of Law, Stanford University

CAROL M. ROSE
Professor of Law, Yale University

CASS R. SUNSTEIN
Professor of Law, University of Chicago

SAMUEL D. THURMAN
Professor of Law, Hastings College of the Law

CASES, PROBLEMS AND MATERIALS

ON

SALES TRANSACTIONS: DOMESTIC AND INTERNATIONAL LAW

By

JOHN O. HONNOLD
William A. Schnader Professor of Commercial Law Emeritus
University of Pennsylvania Law School

and

CURTIS R. REITZ
Algernon Sydney Biddle Professor of Law
University of Pennsylvania Law School

Westbury, New York
THE FOUNDATION PRESS, INC.
1992

COPYRIGHT © 1992 By THE FOUNDATION PRESS, INC.
615 Merrick Ave.
Westbury, N.Y. 11590

All rights reserved
Printed in the United States of America

Library of Congress Cataloging-in-Publication Data

Honnold, John.
    Cases, problems and materials on sales transactions : domestic and international law / John O. Honnold and Curtis R. Reitz.
      p.   cm. — (University casebook series)
    Includes index.
    ISBN 1-56662-004-X
    1. Sales—United States—Cases. 2. Sales—Cases. I. Reitz, Curtis R. II. Title. III. Series.
KF914.H58 1992
346.73'072—dc20
[347.30672]   92–19841

H. & R. Sales Transactions UCB

*To the students
who for four decades
have shared the exploration
that led to this book*

*

PREFACE

Through the fifth edition of Honnold, Sales and Sales Financing, the Sales materials appeared only as Part I of that book. Recent law school curricular patterns indicate that it may be useful to have the Sales materials available separately. As those familiar with Sales and Sales Financing will discover, this book, while the first edition under this title, is a continuation and revision of Part I of the prior work.

The principal role of a course on Sales is to build upon the first-year course in Contracts.[1] A course in Contracts typically introduces students to the matters of contract formation, validity, breach, and remedies. Contracts casebooks now commonly incorporate some provisions of Article 2 of the Uniform Commercial Code. Contracts courses, however, remain broadly eclectic in the types of transactions covered.

The editors envision a course based on this book as a sequel to the course in Contracts. These materials center on the performance of agreements for the sale of goods. The cases and problems, focused on one generic type transaction, permit sustained examination of the significance of context to give meaning to contract obligations and rights.[2]

This book is also intended to permit broad and deep consideration of major United States commercial statutes and an important new and widely-adopted international convention providing uniform law for the international sale of goods.

Study of Article 2, the fundamental article of the Uniform Commercial Code, with the overlay of federal laws, is an excellent way to develop understanding of the nature and sources of domestic United States law in this sphere. In this course, we hope that students will get a sense of the Article as a whole and begin to understand how such codes are used, and should be used, in shaping commercial transactions and in resolving commercial disputes.[3] The materials are concerned with techniques of statutory construction for this special kind of uniform legislation. This involves intelligent attention to statutory text, in light of legislatively defined terms. It involves appreciation of the value and limitations of the "official comments" to the Commercial Code. Beyond these textual

---

[1] A course in Sales might also be an extension of the first-year course in Property. Property courses, however, tend to give dominant consideration to the law of real property and may treat personal property or personalty only in passing. Thus, students in Sales may be meeting the law of personal property afresh.

[2] This tends to offset one of the drawbacks of typical first-year Contracts courses. A hallmark of the basic course in Contracts is the relentlessly doctrinal structure of the tradition syllabus.

[3] The introduction to the Uniform Commercial Code that students receive in Contracts may lead them to see Article 2 as a repository of discrete provisions on offer and acceptance, remedies for breach, and so forth—more like a restatement of the common law than a code with an overall style and philosophy.

concerns, these materials inquire into the legislative purposes and the intended social benefits of this kind of statute.

Commercial transactions in the modern world are increasingly international in character. The United States is a huge consumer of products produced abroad and a huge producer of products for export. Nearly half (by value) of all goods bought and sold by persons in this country involve imports or exports, and the percentage is rising steeply. For transactions of this nature, the world community is establishing a growing body of international private law, notably for our purposes the Convention on Contracts for the International Sale of Goods. This Convention, now part of the law of the United States and more than 30 other nations, must be considered in comparison with, and in contrast to the Uniform Commercial Code, which governs in domestic or intranational sales. The Convention is vitally important for its own substance and the methods of its construction and implementation. Further, however, the Convention represents an emerging body of international private laws that will be fundamental to tomorrow's professional work of today's law students. In every chapter, and in almost every section, these materials address the commercial issues under the Convention as well as under the domestic law of the United States.

As with previous editions of Honnold's Sales and Sales Financing, the principal cases have been chosen on the ground that they are worthy of classroom discussion. The cases tend to be recent for the good reason that they arise from current commercial practices and reflect the types of legal issues that are being adjudicated or arbitrated today. (A table of the cases by types of goods follows the table of contents.) Extensive notes on the centuries-long development of commercial law, including legislative history of certain provisions of the Uniform Commercial Code and the Convention on International Sales of Goods, give students a background for understanding the contrasting strands of continuity and change that mark this subject.

Problems are included throughout the materials to focus students' attention on the provisions of relevant laws and their application to common transactional patterns. Some Problems are introductory, providing students with a preliminary view of an area. Others develop further the issues considered by courts or arbitration panels in the principal cases.

In Chapter 5, two complex commercial transactions are presented in full detail, with specimen documents and forms. These prototypical documentary transactions, one domestic in context, the other international, which appeared in prior editions of this book, give students a detailed picture of how these matters are structured and the reasons that underlie the commercial patterns.

We wish to thank our colleagues and the many law librarians and students whose encouragement and support have made this edition possible. Special thanks are due to those law teachers, users of the prior

PREFACE

edition, who suggested revisions for this work. Mrs. Margaret Ulrich provided invaluable assistance in manuscript preparation.

This edition is a collaborative effort of Professors Honnold and Reitz. The latter took primary responsibility for producing this edition and is responsible for any errors or omissions.

JOHN O. HONNOLD
CURTIS R. REITZ

Philadelphia, Pa.
June, 1992

*

SUMMARY OF CONTENTS

	Page
Preface	v
Table of Cases by Types of Goods	xxvii
Table of Cases	xxix
Table of Statutes	xxxiii

CHAPTER 1. GENERAL INTRODUCTION 1
- (A) Development of Commercial Law 1
- (B) Scope and Approach of Article 2 of the Commercial Code 9
  - (1) Scope 9
  - (2) General Legal Principles and the Code 22
  - (3) Interpretation of the Code 25
- (C) Scope and Approach of the Convention on Contracts for the International Sale of Goods 30
  - (1) Scope 30
  - (2) General Legal Principles and the Convention 32
  - (3) Interpretation of the Convention 35

CHAPTER 2. TITLE: SELLERS' RESPONSIBILITY AND BUYERS' RIGHTS 37
- (A) Domestic United States Law 37
  - (1) Warranty of Title 38
  - (2) Good Faith Purchase of Goods 44
  - (3) "Entrusting" and "Buyers in Ordinary Course" 48
- (B) International Sales Law 52

CHAPTER 3. QUALITY: SELLERS' RESPONSIBILITY AND BUYERS' RIGHTS 54
- Section 1. Introduction 54
- Section 2. Warranties of Quality: Express and Implied 58
  - (A) Domestic United States Law 58
  - (B) International Sales Law 96
- Section 3. Warranty Disclaimers and Limitation of Damages Clauses 104
  - (A) Domestic United States Law 104
  - (B) International Sales Law 142
- Section 4. Legal Bars to Actions for Breach of Warranty 143
  - (A) Domestic United States Law 143
  - (B) International Sales Law 159
- Section 5. Consumer Protection Laws 163
  - (A) Consumer Health: Product Liability 164
  - (B) Magnuson-Moss Warranty Act (MMWA) 167
  - (C) Strict Liability for Economic Loss 177

SUMMARY OF CONTENTS

	Page
Section 6. Privity Between Owner or User and Warrantor	185
(A) Domestic United States Law	185
(B) International Sales Law	207

CHAPTER 4. BUYERS' RESPONSIBILITY FOR THE PRICE 208
- (A) Domestic United States Law 208
- (B) International Sales Law 210

CHAPTER 5. EXECUTION OF SALES CONTRACTS: MANNER, TIME AND PLACE 213

Section 1. Introduction 213
- (A) Domestic United States Law 214
  - (1) Two-Party Transactions 215
  - (2) Transactions Using Carriers to Deliver Goods 218
  - (3) Transactions in Goods Not to be Moved 222
- (B) International Sales Law 223

Section 2. Acceptance, Rejection, and Cure; Avoidance 226
- (A) Domestic United States Law 226
  - (1) Acceptance and Rejection 226
  - (2) Rightful Rejection 235
  - (3) Wrongful Rejection 260
- (B) International Sales Law 276
  - (1) Buyers' Avoidance for Sellers' Breach 276
  - (2) Sellers' Avoidance for Buyers' Breach 278

Section 3. Revocation of Acceptance 278
- (A) Domestic United States Law 278
- (B) International Sales Law 287

Section 4. Performance and the Credit Risk 290
- (A) Domestic United States Law 291
  - (1) The Situation of Buyers 305
  - (2) The Situation of Sellers 307
  - (3) Sellers' Power to Reclaim Goods 308
- (B) International Sales Law 310
  - (1) Ball Bearings for Brazil: A Prototype Export Transaction 311
  - (2) Responsibility of Buyers and Sellers who Agree to Documentary Sales Using Letters of Credit 340
  - (3) Responsibility of Banks Under Their Letters of Credit 343
  - (4) "Standby" (or "Guaranty") Letters of Credit 368

CHAPTER 6. RISK OF LOSS 375
Section 1. Introduction 375
Section 2. Casualty in Two-Party Transactions 378
- (A) Domestic United States Law 378
- (B) International Sales Law 397

SUMMARY OF CONTENTS

	Page
Section 3. Casualty During Shipment	398
(A) Domestic United States Law	398
(B) International Sales Law	407
APPENDIX: FEDERAL BILLS OF LADING ACT	415
INDEX	417

DETAILED TABLE OF CONTENTS

	Page
PREFACE	v
TABLE OF CASES BY TYPES OF GOODS	xxvii
TABLE OF CASES	xxix
TABLE OF STATUTES	xxxiii

CONTRACT FOR SALE	1
CHAPTER 1. GENERAL INTRODUCTION	1
(A) Development of Commercial Law	1
Scope of the Course	1
Development of Commercial Law	1
(1) Mercantile Custom and Nationalization	1
(2) Nineteenth Century Codification	2
(3) Federal Courts and the "General Commercial Law"	3
(4) Specialized Statutes in Britain and America	3
(5) The Uniform Commercial Code	4
(6) Special Legislation to Protect Consumers	6
(7) Uniform Laws for International Transactions	7
Sales	7
Negotiable Instruments and Credit Transfers	8
Other Fields	8
(8) Reference Materials	8
(B) Scope and Approach of Article 2 of the Commercial Code	9
(1) Scope	9
Goods and Services	10
Advent Systems Limited v. Unisys Corp. (3d Cir. 1991)	11
Notes	19
(1) Uniform Commercial Code: Which Version?	19
(2) Domestic Law: Which Nation's?	20
(3) Computer Systems as "Goods"	20
(4) Contract Formation; Statute of Frauds	20
(5) Professional Responsibility	21
Goods and Real Property	21
(2) General Legal Principles and the Code	22
Introduction	22
Sales Codifications and Contract Law	22
The Code and the General Body of Law	23
Section 1–103. Supplementary General Principles of Law Applicable	23
Course of Dealing and Usage of Trade	23
"Good Faith"	24

xiii

DETAILED TABLE OF CONTENTS

	Page
(B) Scope and Approach of Article 2 of the Commercial Code—Continued	
Unconscionability	24
(3) Interpretation of the Code	25
(1) Two Polar Approaches to Statutory Interpretation	25
(2) Pre–UCC Commercial Law Codifications	26
(3) Approaching Article 2 of the Uniform Commercial Code	26
(4) The Comments to the Code: Uses and Hazards	28
(5) Definitions	30
(C) Scope and Approach of the Convention on Contracts for the International Sale of Goods	30
(1) Scope	30
Place of Business	31
Goods, Seller and Buyer	31
Goods and Services	31
Problem 1	31
Problem 2	32
Goods and Real Property	32
(2) General Legal Principles and the Convention	32
Introduction	32
The Convention and the General Body of Law	33
"Good Faith" and "Fair Dealing"	34
The Convention and Party Autonomy	34
Contract Interpretation	35
(3) Interpretation of the Convention	35
Introduction	35
International Character of the Convention	36
The Need to Promote Uniformity	36
The Need to Promote the Observance of Good Faith in International Trade	36
CHAPTER 2. TITLE: SELLERS' RESPONSIBILITY AND BUYERS' RIGHTS	37
(A) Domestic United States Law	37
Introduction	37
(1) Warranty of Title	38
Introduction	38
Wright v. Vickaryous (Alaska 1980)	38
Notes	40
(1) Inventory Finance	40
(2) Clouds on Title	41
Problem 1	41
Problem 2	42
Problem 3	42
Problem 4	42

DETAILED TABLE OF CONTENTS

	Page
(A) Domestic United States Law—Continued	
Lease Transactions: Lessor's Warranty	43
(2) Good Faith Purchase of Goods	44
The Two Party Setting	44
Sales by Agents	44
Crimes and Torts	44
Problem 5	45
Problem 6	45
Problem 7	45
Problem 8	45
Good Faith Purchase of Goods: The Basic Rules in Three Party Setting	45
Problem 9	47
Problem 10	48
Lease Transactions: "Good Faith Lessee"	48
(3) "Entrusting" and "Buyers In Ordinary Course"	48
Prefatory Note	48
Porter v. Wertz (N.Y. 1981)	49
Note	52
Lease Transaction: "Entrusting" and Lessees "In Ordinary Course"	52
(B) International Sales Law	52
Sellers' Responsibility	52
Good Faith Purchasers	53
CHAPTER 3. QUALITY: SELLERS' RESPONSIBILITY AND BUYERS' RIGHTS	54
Section 1. Introduction	54
Historical Background	54
Types of Warranties	56
Commercial and Consumer Parties	57
Buyers' Monetary Remedies	57
Section 2. Warranties of Quality: Express and Implied	58
(A) Domestic United States Law	58
T. J. Stevenson & Son v. 81,193 Bags of Flour (5th Cir. 1980)	58
Notes	63
(1) Contract Interpretation	63
(2) Inspection, Shipment and Payment	63
Sidco Products Marketing, Inc. v. Gulf Oil Corp. (5th Cir. 1988)	63
Notes	67
(1) Merchantable Quality: Ordinary Purposes	67
(2) Merchantable Quality: Fitness for Purpose	67
Problem 1	67

DETAILED TABLE OF CONTENTS

	Page
(A) Domestic United States Law—Continued	
(3) Merchantable Quality: Pass Without Objection in the Trade	67
(4) Merchantable Quality: Fair Average Quality	68
Integrated Circuits Unlimited, Inc. v. E.F. Johnson (2d Cir. 1989)	68
(5) Merchantable Quality: Contract Description	69
(6) Merchantable Quality of Manufactured Goods: Design Standards	69
Problem 2	70
Royal Business Machines v. Lorraine Corp. (7th Cir. 1980)	70
Notes	75
(1) Sellers' Talk; Affirmations of Fact	75
(2) "Opinion," "Value," "Commendation," and Express Warranties	75
(3) Relationship to the Goods	76
(4) Part of the Basis of the Bargain	76
(5) Reliance and Basis of the Bargain	76
Cipollone v. Liggett Group, Inc. (3d Cir. 1990)	77
(6) Other "Fields" of Law	78
Problem 3	79
Problem 4	80
Chatlos Systems v. National Cash Register Corp. (3d Cir. 1982	80
Notes	88
(1) Benefit of the Bargain: What Was the Bargain?	88
(2) Parol Evidence Rule	88
Problem 5	88
(3) Lease Transactions	89
(4) Consequential Damages	89
Advent Systems Limited v. Unisys Corp. (3d Cir. 1991)	90
Carnation Company v. Olivet Egg Ranch (Cal. App. 1986)	92
(B) International Sales Law	96
(1) Sellers' Obligations	96
(2) Buyers' Remedies	96
Award in Case No. 3779 (ICC 1981)	96
Notes	101
(1) International Commercial Arbitration	101
(2) Comparing Arbitration and Adjudication	101
Award in Case No. 3880 (ICC 1983)	102
(3) Other "Fields" of Law	104
Section 3. Warranty Disclaimers and Limitation of Damages Clauses	104
(A) Domestic United States Law	104
Introduction	104

DETAILED TABLE OF CONTENTS

Page

(A) Domestic United States Law—Continued
Insurance Co. of North America v. Automatic Sprinkler Corp.
(Ohio 1981) 105
Notes 109
    (1) Bargain in Fact 109
    (2) Construction of UCC 2–316(2) 109
    (3) Legislative History 109
Universal Drilling Co. v. Camay Drilling Co. (10th Cir. 1984) 110
Notes 114
    (1) Contract Interpretation: UCC 2–316(1) 114
        Problem 1 114
    (2) Commercial Sophistication of Buyers 114
    (3) Oral Warranties and Written Negations: Parol Evidence
        and UCC 2–202 114
Western Industries, Inc. v. Newcor Canada Limited (7th Cir. 1984) 115
Notes 119
    (1) Battle of the Forms 119
    (2) Implied Warranty Disclaimers or Limitation of Damages 119
Kunststoffwerk Alfred Huber v. R.J. Dick, Inc. (3d Cir. 1980) 119
Note 123
    Choice of Forum 123
Milgard Tempering, Inc. v. Selas Corp. (9th Cir. 1990) 123
Notes 128
    (1) Repair or Replace Clauses 128
    (2) Failure of Essential Purpose 129
    (3) Failure of Purpose and Consequential Damages 129
        S. M. Wilson & Co. v. Smith International, Inc. (9th
        Cir.1978) 129
        Chatlos Systems, Inc. v. National Cash Register (3d Cir.
        1980) 130
        Fiorito Bros., Inc. v. Fruehauf Corp. (9th Cir. 1984) 131
    (4) Unconscionability and Consequential Damages 132
        A & M Produce Co. v. FMC Corp. (Cal. App. 1982) 132
Hill v. BASF Wyandotte Corp. (4th Cir. 1982) 134
Notes 139
    (1) Sales to Farmers 139
    (2) Warranties by Manufacturers' Representatives 139
    (3) Manufacturers' Warranties on Labels 140
    (4) Post-purchase Disclaimers 140
        Problem 2 140
    (5) Consequential Damages Clauses in Farm Supply Sales;
        Unconscionability 141
        Durham v. Ciba-Geigy Corp. (S. Dak. 1982) 141

DETAILED TABLE OF CONTENTS

	Page
(B) International Sales Law	142
Problem 3	143
Problem 4	143

Section 4. Legal Bars to Actions for Breach of Warranty ... 143
- (A) Domestic United States Law ... 143
  - Introduction ... 143
    - (1) Notice of breach ... 144
  - M.K. Associates v. Stowell Products, Inc. (D. Me. 1988) ... 144
  - Notes ... 147
    - (1) UCC 2–607(3): Rationale and History ... 147
    - (2) Statute of Limitations ... 149
  - Tittle v. Steel City Oldsmobile GMC Truck, Inc. (Ala. 1989) ... 149
  - Notes ... 157
    - (1) Magnuson-Moss Warranty Act ... 157
    - (2) Construction of UCC 2–725(2) ... 157
      - Moorman Manufacturing Co. v. National Tank Co. (Ill. 1982) ... 158
      - Moore v. Puget Sound Plywood (Neb. 1983) ... 159
    - (3) Limitation Period for Implied Warranties ... 159
- (B) International Sales Law ... 159
  - (1) Notice of Breach ... 159
    - Final Award in Case No. 5713 (ICC 1989) ... 160
  - (2) Period of Limitations ... 163

Section 5. Consumer Protection Laws ... 163
- Introduction ... 163
- International Sales Law ... 164
- (A) Consumer Health: Product Liability ... 164
- (B) Magnuson-Moss Warranty Act (MMWA) ... 167
  - (1) Scope ... 167
    - Problem 1 ... 168
    - Problem 2 ... 168
    - Problem 3 ... 168
  - (2) "Truth in Warranting" ... 169
  - (3) Implied Warranty Disclaimers ... 170
    - Problem 4 ... 170
  - (4) Clauses Limiting Damages ... 171
    - Problem 5 ... 171
    - Problem 6 ... 171
  - (5) Limited Duration of Implied Warranties ... 171
  - (6) Recovery of Attorneys' Fees and Costs ... 172
  - (7) Federal Forum for Warranty Litigation ... 172
  - Skelton v. General Motors Corp. (7th Cir. 1981) ... 173
  - Notes ... 177

DETAILED TABLE OF CONTENTS

	Page
(B) Magnuson-Moss Warranty Act (MMWA)—Continued	
(1) Federal Court Diversity Jurisdiction	177
(2) Construction of MMWA 110(d)(1)(B)	177
(C) Strict Liability for Economic Loss	177
(1) Ordinary Consumer Buyers	177
(2) Commercial Buyers	178
East River S.S. Corp. v. Transamerica Delaval Inc. (U.S. 1986)	178
Notes	185
(1) Hazardous Risks and Strict Tort Liability	185
(2) Disclaimers of Strict Tort Liability	185
Section 6. Privity Between Owner or User and Warrantor	185
(A) Domestic United States Law	185
(1) Introduction	185
(2) Manufacturers' Advertisements as Express Warranties	186
Problem 1	186
(3) Assignment and Third Party Beneficiary Law	187
Problem 2	187
Problem 3	187
(4) Manufacturers' Implied Warranties	187
Morrow v. New Moon Homes (Alaska 1976)	188
Notes	196
(1) Sequential Actions or Direct Action	196
(2) Contract Description and Merchantability	196
(3) Change in Condition of the Goods After Manufacture	196
(4) Measure of Ordinary Damages for Economic Loss	197
(5) Consequential Economic Losses	197
(6) Warranty Disclaimers and Clauses Limiting Damages	197
(7) Notice of Breach to Remote Manufacturers	197
(8) Statute of Limitations on Manufacturers' Liability	197
(9) Fitness for Particular Purpose	198
Problem 4	198
(10) Components Suppliers	198
(11) Remote Sellers of Primary Goods	198
Szajna v. General Motors Corp. (Ill. 1986)	198
Notes	202
(1) Rationale	202
(2) UCC 2–318; Non-Uniform Variations	202
Collins Company, Ltd. v. Carboline Company (Ill. 1988)	202
Notes	206
(1) Horizontal or Vertical Privity; UCC 2–318	206
(2) Express and Implied Assignments	206
(3) Warranty to Original Owner Only	206

DETAILED TABLE OF CONTENTS

	Page
(B) International Sales Law	207
Problem 5	207

CHAPTER 4. BUYERS' RESPONSIBILITY FOR THE PRICE 208
(A) Domestic United States Law 208
    Amount of the Price; "Open" Price Terms 208
    Price Terms in Long-Term Supply Contracts 208
    Problem 1 208
    Problem 2 209
    Quality of the Money; "Legal Tender" 210
(B) International Sales Law 210
    "Open" Price Terms 210
    Choice of Currency 210
    Restricted Convertibility; "Hard" and "Soft" Currencies 211

CHAPTER 5. EXECUTION OF SALES CONTRACTS: MANNER, TIME AND PLACE 213

Section 1. Introduction 213
    Agreed Terms and Default Rules 213
    Two-Party Execution 213
    Execution Through Third Parties: Carriers and Banks 214
    Remedies for Non-Execution or Improper Execution 214
(A) Domestic United States Law 214
    (1) Two-Party Transactions 215
        Manner of Sellers' Tender of Delivery of Goods 215
        Place of Sellers' Tender 215
        Time of Sellers' Tender 215
        Manner of Buyers' Tender of Payment 215
        Time and Place of Tender of Payment 216
        Tender of Delivery in "Lots" 216
        Problem 1 216
        Problem 2 217
        Problem 3 217
        Problem 4 218
        Problem 5 218
    (2) Transactions Using Carriers to Deliver Goods 218
        F.O.B. or Free on Board 219
        "At a Particular Destination" Contracts 219
        "The Place of Shipment" Contracts 219
        Time of Sellers' Tender 221
        Manner, Time and Place of Buyers' Tender 221
        Problem 6 222
        Problem 7 222
    (3) Transactions in Goods Not to be Moved 222

DETAILED TABLE OF CONTENTS

	Page
(B) International Sales Law	223
Manner and Place of Delivery	224
Time of Delivery	225
Problem 8	225
Nachfrist Provisions	225
Buyers' Tender of Payment	226
Time and Place of Buyers' Tender	226
Inspection of Goods Before Payment	226
Section 2. Acceptance, Rejection, and Cure; Avoidance	226
(A) Domestic United States Law	226
(1) Acceptance and Rejection	226
Buyers' Duty to Accept Goods	226
Buyers' Right to Reject Goods	227
Significance of Acceptance or Rejection	227
Manner of Buyers' Acceptance of Goods	228
Time of Acceptance: Inspection of Goods Before Acceptance	228
Zabrieskie Chevrolet, Inc. v. Smith (N.J. Super. 1968)	228
Plateq Corp. v. Machlett Laboratories (Conn. 1983)	229
Acceptance or Rejection of Goods Delivered by Carrier	233
Manner and Time of Buyers' Rejection of Goods	233
Effective Rejection and Transfer of Possession	233
Problem 1	233
Problem 2	234
(2) Rightful Rejection	235
The "Perfect Tender Rule"	235
Moulton Cavity & Mold v. Lyn-Flex Industries (Me. 1979)	235
Notes	240
(1) Substantial Performance	240
(2) History of the Perfect Tender Rule	240
(3) Retention of the Perfect Tender Rule in the Code	241
(4) Installment Sales: A Different Set of Standards	241
Problem 3	242
Problem 4	242
T.W. Oil, Inc. v. Consolidated Edison Co. (N.Y. 1982)	242
Notes	247
(1) Sellers' Right to Cure Non-Conforming Tenders	247
(2) Repair as Cure	247
(3) Cure and Warranty Service	248
(4) Price Adjustment as Cure	248
Mendelson-Zeller Co. v. Joseph Wedner & Son Co. (U.S. Dep't Agric. 1970)	248
Notes	251
(1) Delay in Sellers' Tender of Delivery	251
(2) Contract Interpretation	251

DETAILED TABLE OF CONTENTS

Page

(A) Domestic United States Law—Continued
- (3) Construction of UCC 2–309 — 251
- (4) Buyer's Rejection and Resale — 251
- Problem 5 — 252
- Fertico Belgium S.A. v. Phosphate Chemicals Export Association, Inc. (N.Y. 1987) — 252
- Notes — 259
  - (1) Anticipating Breach — 259
  - (2) Rejection of Goods Already Paid For; Buyers' "Security Interest" — 259
  - (3) Construction of UCC 2–711(3) — 259
- (3) Wrongful Rejection — 260
- Sellers' Remedies — 260
- Apex Oil Co. v. The Belcher Co. of New York, Inc. (2d Cir. 1988 — 260
- Notes — 269
  - (1) Commodities Futures — 269
  - (2) Construction of UCC 2–707 and 2–708 — 269
- Problem 6 — 269
- R.E. Davis Chemical Corp. v. Diasonics, Inc. (7th Cir. 1987) — 270
- Notes — 275
  - (1) Subsequent Decision — 275
  - (2) Construction of 2–708(2) — 275
  - (3) Revision of Article 2 — 276

(B) International Sales Law — 276
- (1) Buyers' Avoidance for Sellers' Breach — 276
- Avoidance for Sellers' Late Performance — 277
- Time of Avoidance — 277
- Manner of Avoidance — 277
- Effect of Avoidance — 277
- Problem 7 — 277
- (2) Sellers' Avoidance for Buyers' Breach — 278

Section 3. Revocation of Acceptance — 278
(A) Domestic United States Law — 278
- McCullough v. Bill Swad Chrysler-Plymouth (Ohio 1983) — 278
- Notes — 283
  - (1) Substantial Impairment; Measure of Conforming Goods and Identity of Warrantor — 283
  - (2) Manner and Time of Buyers' Revocation of Acceptance — 284
  - (3) Cure After Revocation — 284
  - (4) Buyers' Legal Actions Following Revocation — 284
  - (5) Actions Against Manufacturers — 285
  - (6) Actions Against Lenders — 285
  - (7) Use After Revocation and the Code — 286

DETAILED TABLE OF CONTENTS

	Page
(A) Domestic United States Law—Continued	
(8) Compensation for Use After Revocation	286
(9) Magnuson-Moss "Full" Warranties; "Lemon Laws"	287
(B) International Sales Law	287
Avoidance for Fundamental Breach	287
Manner of Avoiding	287
Time of Avoidance	287
Effect of Avoidance	288
Cure of Non-Conforming Deliveries	288
Problem 1	289
Problem 2	289
Problem 3	289
Problem 4	290
Section 4. Performance and the Credit Risk	290
Introduction	290
(A) Domestic United States Law	291
(1) Simultaneous Exchanges	291
(2) Sequential Exchanges	291
(3) Documentary Transactions	291
Negotiable Bills of Lading	292
Negotiable Drafts	292
Banks' Services	292
Negotiation; Rights of Holders	293
Diagram of a Documentary Transaction	294
(1) The Situation of Buyers	305
Problem 1	305
Rejection of Tender of Documents	306
Contracting for Documentary Transactions	306
Inspection by Third Party	306
Inspection by Carrier	306
(2) The Situation of Sellers	307
Problem 2	307
Problem 3	307
Problem 4	308
Sellers' Use of Drafts to Obtain Credit	308
(3) Sellers' Power to Reclaim Goods	308
Introduction	308
Problem 5	309
Problem 6	309
Problem 7	309
(B) International Sales Law	310
Introduction	310
(1) Ball Bearings for Brazil: A Prototype Export Transaction	311

DETAILED TABLE OF CONTENTS

	Page
(B) International Sales Law—Continued	
(2) Responsibility of Buyers and Sellers Who Agree to Documentary Sales Using Letters of Credit	340
Sales Contracts' Provisions for Letters of Credit	340
Problem 8	341
Revocable Letters of Credit	341
Bankers' Acceptances and Letters of Credit	342
"Back-to-Back" Credits	342
(3) Responsibility of Banks Under Their Letters of Credit	343
The ICC Uniform Customs and Practice for Documentary Credits (UCP)	343
UCC Article 5; New York Exclusion	344
Permanent Editorial Board Comment	344
Reasons for Rejection	344
Petra Int'l Banking Corp. v. First Amer. Bank of Va. (E.D.Va. 1991)	347
Notes	356
(1) Nature of Terms of Conditioning Banks' Obligations	356
(2) Bills of Lading: "Clean" and "Foul"	356
Problem 9	357
(3) Bills in a Set	357
Union Export Co. v. N.I.B. Intermarket, A.B. (Tenn. 1990)	358
Notes	363
(1) "Holder in Due Course" Protection for Collecting Banks	363
(2) Attachment of Proceeds of Letters of Credit	364
Andina Coffee, Inc. v. National Westminster Bank, USA (N.Y.App. Div. 1990)	364
(4) "Standby" (or "Guaranty") Letters of Credit	368
New Wine in Old Bottles	368
Ground Air Transfer, Inc. v. Westates Airlines, Inc. (1st Cir.1990)	368
Notes	374
(1) Independence From Underlying Transactions	374
(2) General References	374
CHAPTER 6. RISK OF LOSS	**375**
Section 1. Introduction	375
The Problem	375
Historical Background; Early Common Law	375
"Property" and Risk in the Sale of Goods Act and the Uniform Sales Act	377
Difficulty with the "Property" Concept; The Code	377
1980 Convention on International Sales of Goods	378

DETAILED TABLE OF CONTENTS

	Page
Section 2. Casualty in Two-Party Transactions	378
(A) Domestic United States Law	378
Introduction	378
Problem 1	379
Martin v. Melland's Inc. (N. Dak. 1979)	379
Notes	383
(1) Insurance Coverage	383
(2) Effect of Casualty on Parties' Contract Obligations: UCC 2–613	383
(3) Insurance Carrier Subrogation	384
(4) Insurance at Less Than Market Value	384
(5) Risk of Loss in Non-Merchant Seller Transactions	384
Problem 2	385
United Air Lines v. Conductron Corp. (Ill. App. 1979)	385
Notes	390
(1) Risk of Loss After Buyers Have Received Goods	390
(2) Alternative Analysis Under UCC2–711(1)	390
Problem 3	390
Problem 4	391
Ron Mead T.V. & Appliance v. Legendary Homes, Inc. (Okla. App.1987)	391
Notes	392
(1) Basis of the Decision: Analytical Confusion	392
(2) Proposed Repeal of UCC 2–510	393
(3) Sellers' Price Action	393
Multiplastics v. Arch Industries (Conn. 1974)	394
(B) International Sales Law	397
Problem 5	398
Section 3. Casualty During Shipment	398
(A) Domestic United States Law	398
Introduction	398
Shipment and Destination Contracts	398
Problem 1	399
Pestana v. Karinol Corp. (Fla. App. 1979)	399
Notes	403
(1) Allocation of Freight Costs as Allocation of Risk of Loss	403
(2) Policy Considerations Relevant to Risk Allocation Rules	403
Problem 2	404
Problem 3	404
Problem 4	404
Note: Liability of Domestic U.S. Carriers	405
Rail and Truck	405
Air Carriers	406

DETAILED TABLE OF CONTENTS

	Page
(A) Domestic United States Law—Continued	
Note: Insurers v. Carriers	406
Claims Against Common Carriers	406
(B) International Sales Law	407
Introduction	407
Problem 5	407
Problem 6	408
Precision in Defining the Moment of Risk Passing	409
Rheinberg-Kelleri GMBH v. Vineyard Wine Co. (N.C. App. 1981)	409
Note: Liability of Carriers in International Transport	410
Liability of Ocean Carriers	410
The Hague Rules	410
The Hamburg Rules	411
Marine Insurance	412
Liability of Air Carriers	412
APPENDIX: FEDERAL BILLS OF LADING ACT	415
INDEX	417

TABLE OF CASES BY TYPES OF GOODS

Students may be aided by the following list of the types of goods involved in the principal and note cases included in these materials.

	Page
Aircraft	369
Appliances, household	391
Automobile accessories	101
Automobile, Chevrolet	228
Automobiles, 1976–1979 GM cars	172
Automobile, 1976 Pontiac	198
Automobile, 1978 Chrysler	278
Automobile, 1981 Oldsmobile	149
Belting, nylon cord	119
Cattle	38
Chemical for fire protection system	105
Chemicals, calcium chloride	358
Chicken feed	92
Cigarettes	77
Coffee	364
Computer system	11, 80, 89, 130
Copy machines	70
Diagnostic equipment	270
Dowels, ash	144
Dump truck bodies	131
Fertilizer	252
Flight simulator	385
Glass tempering furnace	123
Grain storage tank	158
Haystack mover	379
Herbicide, Basalin	134
Herbicide, Milogard	141
Micro processors	68
Middle layer emulsion	63
Mobile house	188
Molds for shoe innersoles	236
Oil drilling rigs	110
Oil, fuel-oil	242
Oil, heating oil	260
Oil refining by-product: middle layer emulsion	63
Painting by Utrillo	49
Plastic pellets	394
Plywood siding	159
Produce, perishable	248

xxvii

TABLE OF CASES BY TYPES OF GOODS

	Page
Roofing system	202
Steel tanks, lead-covered	229
Supertankers	178
Tomato weight-sizing machine	132
T–shirts	347
Tunnel boring machine	129
Unspecified	160
Watches, electronic	399
Welding machines	115
Wheat flour	58
Whey powder	96
Women's boots	102

TABLE OF CASES

Principal cases are in italic type. Non-principal cases are in roman type. References are to Pages.

Advent Systems Ltd. v. Unisys Corp., 11, 19, 20, 21, 22, 24, 31, 32, 76, *90*
Alderman Bros. Co. v. New York, N. H. & H. R. Co., 308
Allen v. G.D. Searle & Co., 166
Aluminum Co. of America v. Essex Group, Inc., 209
A & M Produce Co. v. FMC Corp., 132
Andina Coffee, Inc. v. National Westminster Bank, United StatesA, 364
Andover Air Ltd. Partnership v. Piper Aircraft Corp., 285
Apex Oil Co. v. The Belcher Co. of New York, Inc., 260, 269
Asciolla v. Manter Oldsmobile–Pontiac, Inc., 285
Askco Engineering Corp. v. Mobil Chemical Corp., 252

Bagel v. American Honda Motor Co., Inc., 206
Bank of Newport v. First Nat. Bank, 374
Baxter v. Ford Motor Co., 186
Best Buick v. Welcome, 80
Boelens v. Redman Homes, Inc., 172
Bogestad v. Anderson, 42
Bowes v. Shand, 240
Boysen v. Antioch Sheet Metal, Inc., 234
British Imex Industries Limited v. Midland Bank Limited, 356
Bunge v. First Nat. Bank of Mt. Holly Springs, 308
Butts v. Glendale Plywood Co., 310

California and Hawaiian Sugar Co. v. Sun Ship, Inc., 10
Campbell Soup Co. v. Wentz, 25
Carlill v. Carbolic Smoke Ball Co., 186
Carnation Co. v. Olivet Egg Ranch, 92
Catania v. Brown, 198
Chandelor v. Lopus, 54
Chatlos Systems, Inc. v. National Cash Register Corp., 670 F.2d 1304, pp. *80,* 88, 89
Chatlos Systems, Inc. v. National Cash Register Corp., 635 F.2d 1081, p. 130
Cipollone v. Liggett Group, Inc., 77
Cline v. Prowler Industries of Maryland, Inc., 166
Codling v. Paglia, 166
Collins Co., Ltd. v. Carboline Co., 202
Commonwealth Petroleum Co. v. Petrosol Intern., Inc., 223

Compagnie Commerciale Sucres et Denrees v. C. Czarnikow Ltd., 225
Consolidated Data Terminals v. Applied Digital Data Systems, Inc., 114
Conte v. Dwan Lincoln–Mercury, Inc., 285

Descalzi Fruit Co. v. William S. Sweet & Son, 252
Dixon, Irmaos & Cia, Ltda v. Chase Nat. Bank of City of New York, 358
Duffee v. Judson, 22
Durfee v. Rod Baxter Imports, Inc., 285
Durham v. Ciba–Geigy Corp., 141

East River S.S. Corp. v. Transamerica Delaval, Inc., 178
E. Clemens Horst Co. v. Biddle Bros., 311
Economy Forms Corp. v. Kandy, Inc., 234
Edelstein v. Toyota Motors Distributors, 285
Erie R. Co. v. Tompkins, 3
Ex parte (see name of party)

Farrell v. Manhattan Market Co., 164
Fertico Belgium S.A. v. Phosphate Chemicals Export Ass'n, Inc., 252, 277, 278
Filley v. Pope, 240
Fiorito Bros., Inc. v. Fruehauf Corp., 131
Flynn v. Bedell Co. of Massachusetts, 164
Ford Motor Credit Co. v. Harper, 285
Frankel v. Foreman & Clark, 241
Friend v. Childs Dining Hall Co., 164

Gasque v. Mooers Motor Car Co., Inc., 285
Geo. C. Christopher & Son, Inc. v. Kansas Paint & Color Co., Inc., 141
Gochey v. Bombardier, Inc., 285
Goldstein v. G. D. Searle & Co., 166
Golsen v. ONG Western, Inc., 209
Greenman v. Yuba Power Products, Inc., 165, 187
Ground Air Transfer, Inc. v. Westates Airlines, Inc., 368

Hadley v. Baxendale, 89, 165
Hawkins v. Pemberton, 55, 80
Heller v. United States Suzuki Motor Corp., 197
Henningsen v. Bloomfield Motors, Inc., 165, 187
Hill v. BASF Wyandotte Corp., 134, 140, 186, 197

TABLE OF CASES

Ian Stach, Ltd. v. Baker Bosly, Ltd., 341
Insurance Co. of North America v. Automatic Sprinkler Corp. of America, 105, 110
Integrated Circuits Unlimited, Inc. v. E.F. Johnson Co., 68
International Milling Co. v. Hachmeister, Inc., 63
Iowa Elec. Light and Power Co. v. Atlas Corp., 209

Jacob & Youngs, Inc. v. Kent, 240
Jeanneret v. Vichey, 43, 52, 53
Johnson v. General Motors Corp., 207
Johnson v. General Motors Corp., Chevrolet Motors Div., 286
Jones v. Ballard, 42
Jones v. Just, 55
Julian v. Laubenberger, 164

Keystone Aeronautics Corp. v. R. J. Enstrom Corp., 185
Kunststoffwerk Alfred Huber v. R. J. Dick, Inc., 119, 123, 143

Legal Tender Cases, The, 210
Levi v. Booth, 48
L. Gillarde Co. v. Joseph Martinelli & Co., Inc., 252
Liberty Nat. Bank & Trust Co. v. Bank of America Nat. Trust & Sav. Ass'n, 356
Lobianco v. Property Protection, Inc., 22
Long Island Lighting Co. v. Transamerica Delaval, Inc., 10
Louis Sherry Ice Cream Co., Inc. v. Harlem River Consumers' Co-op, Inc., 234
Lucien Bourque, Inc. v. Cronkite, 10

Manchester Pipeline Corp. v. Peoples Natural Gas. Co., a Div. of Internorth, Inc., 21
Martin v. Melland's Inc., 379, 383, 384, 385
Massey-Ferguson, Inc. v. Laird, 140
McCullough v. Bill Swad Chrysler–Plymouth, Inc., 278, 283, 284, 285, 286
McFarland v. Newman, 55
Mendel v. Pittsburgh Plate Glass Company, 166, 167
Mendelson-Zeller Co., Inc. v. Joseph Wedner & Son Co., 248, 251
Milgard Tempering, Inc. v. Selas Corp. of America, 123, 129
Missouri Public Service Co. v. Peabody Coal Co., 209
M.K. Associates v. Stowell Products, Inc., *144*, 147, 159
Moore v. Puget Sound Plywood, Inc., 159
Moorman Mfg. Co. v. National Tank Co., 158
Morrison's Cafeteria v. Haddox, 70
Morrow v. New Moon Homes, Inc., 188, 196, 197, 198, 202

Moulton Cavity & Mold, Inc. v. Lyn–Flex Industries, Inc., 235, 240
Mowrey v. Walsh, 46
Mullan v. Quickie Aircraft Corp., 166
Multiplastics, Inc. v. Arch Industries, Inc., 217, 394
Murray v. Holiday Rambler, Inc., 285

National Heater Co., Inc. v. Corrigan Co. Mechanical Contractors, Inc., 222
Neilson Business Equipment Center, Inc. v. Italo V. Monteleone, M.D., P.A., 11
Nisky v. Childs Co., 164
Norrington v. Wright, 240
Northern Indiana Public Service Co. v. Carbon County Coal Co., 209

Pacific Reliant Industries, Inc. v. Amerika Samoa Bank, 340
Parker v. Patrick, 46
Pavia & Co. v. Thurmann–Nielsen, 341
Peevyhouse v. Garland Coal & Min. Co., 58
Pennsylvania Glass Sand Corp. v. Caterpillar Tractor Co., 185
Pestana v. Karinol Corp., 222, 399
Petra Intern. Banking Corp. v. First American Bank of Virginia, 347, 356
Plante v. Jacobs, 58
Plateq Corp. of North Haven v. Machlett Laboratories, Inc., 229
Porter v. Wertz, 49
Powers v. Coffeyville Livestock Sales Co., Inc., 42
Prentis v. Yale Mfg. Co., 166

Randall v. Newson, 57
Rayner & Co. v. Hambros Bank, 357
R.E. Davis Chemical Corp. v. Diasonics, Inc., 270, 275
Resources Inv. Corp. v. Enron Corp., 209
Rheinberg-Kellerei GMBH v. Vineyard Wine Co., Inc., 409
Roman Ceramics Corp. v. Peoples Nat. Bank, 374
Ron Mead T.V. & Appliance v. Legendary Homes, Inc., 218, *391, 393*
Royal Business Machines, Inc. v. Lorraine Corp., 70, 76, 78, 88, 89, 119

SA Discount Bank v. Teboul, Recueil, 364
Santor v. A & M Karagheusian, Inc., 178
Schafer v. Chrysler Corp., 172
Schenectady Steel Co., Inc. v. Bruno Trimpoli General Const. Co., Inc., 10
Seekings v. Jimmy GMC of Tucson, Inc., 285
Seely v. White Motor Co., 178
Seixas v. Woods, 55
Sidco Products Marketing, Inc. v. Gulf Oil Corp., 63, 69, 89
Singer Co., Link Simulation Systems Div. v. Baltimore Gas and Elec. Co., 10
Skelton v. General Motors Corp., *172*, 177

TABLE OF CASES

Smith v. Navistar Intern. Transp. Corp., 286
S. M. Wilson & Co. v. Smith Intern., Inc., 129
Southland Mobile Home Corp. v. Chyrchel, 390
Swartz v. General Motors Corp., 166
Swift v. Tyson, 3
Szajna v. General Motors Corp., 198, 202

Tarling v. Baxter, 376, 377
Taterka v. Ford Motor Co., 67
Temple–Eastex Inc. v. Addison Bank, 357
Tittle v. Steel City Oldsmobile GMC Truck, Inc., 149, 157
T. J. Stevenson & Co., Inc. v. 81,193 Bags of Flour, 58, 63, 67, 218, 227, 306
T.W. Oil, Inc. v. Consolidated Edison Co. of New York, Inc., 242, 247, 248

Union Export Co. v. N.I.B. Intermarket, A.B., 358, 363, 364
United Air Lines, Inc. v. Conductron Corp., 385, 390, 397
United States Roofing, Inc. v. Credit Alliance Corp., 284

Universal Drilling Co. v. Camay Drilling Co., 110, 114, 186

Valley Farmers' Elevator v. Lindsay Bros. Co., 22
Ventura v. Ford Motor Corp., 172
Volkswagen of America, Inc. v. Novak, 285
Volvo of America Corp. v. Wells, 285
Voytovich v. Bangor Punta Operations, Inc., 285

Wagmeister v. A. H. Robins Co., 166
Ward v. Great Atlantic & Pacific Tea Co., 164, 165
Wat Henry Pontiac Co. v. Bradley, 58
Western Industries, Inc. v. Newcor Canada Ltd., 115, 119, 143
White v. Garden, 46
William F. Wilke, Inc. v. Cummins Diesel Engines, Inc., 391
Woodward v. Row, 2
Wright v. Vickaryous, 38, 41, 44, 227

Zabriskie Chevrolet, Inc. v. Smith, 228, 247

TABLE OF STATUTES

UNITED STATES

UNITED STATES CODE ANNOTATED
7 U.S.C.A.—Agriculture

Sec.	This Work Page
499a—499s	251

15 U.S.C.A.—Commerce and Trade

Sec.	This Work Page
2301—2312	167
Ch. 50	167

28 U.S.C.A.—Judiciary and Judicial Procedure

Sec.	This Work Page
1332	177

31 U.S.C.A.—Money and Finance

Sec.	This Work Page
5103	210

46 U.S.C.A.—Shipping

Sec.	This Work Page
190—195	410
1300—1315	410

49 U.S.C.A.App.—Transportation

Sec.	This Work Page
81 to 124	220
88	292
88(b)	220
	308
89	220
89(c)	305
	307
90	220
	292
	308
91	220
	308
100	307
102	307
108	293
111(b)	293

POPULAR NAME ACTS

MAGNUSON–MOSS WARRANTY ACT

Sec.	This Work Page
101—112	167
101(1)	167
101(3)	167
101(6)	168
	173
101(6)(A)	174
101(7)	170
101(8)	168
102	167
102(a)	169
103(a)	169
103(a)(1)	169
103(a)(2)	169
104(a)(3)	171
104(a)(4)	287
104(e)	169
106(a)	169
108(a)	170
	171
108(b)	171
108(c)	170
110(d)	174
	175
110(d)(1)	172
110(d)(1)(B)	172
	177
110(d)(2)	172
110(d)(3)(B)	172
111(b)	171
111(b)(1)	168

SALE OF GOODS ACT

Sec.	This Work Page
17	377
18	377
20	377

UNIFORM SALES ACT

Sec.	This Work Page
12	55
	56
	76
	77
22	377
41	22
49	148

xxxiii

TABLE OF STATUTES

UNIFORM SALES ACT

Sec.	This Work Page
63(1)	377
64	275
	276
64(2)	275
64(3)	275
64(4)	275
	276
66	377
73	22

UNIFORM COMMERCIAL CODE

Sec.	This Work Page
Art. 1	4
	23
	24
	29
	30
1–102	29
1–102(1)	26
1–102(2)(a)	27
1–102(2)(b)	27
	346
1–102(3)	27
	29
	104
	391
1–102(3)(f)	29
1–102(c)	27
1–103	23
	24
	42
	44
	45
	76
	78
	79
	139
	291
	346
1–103, Comment 3	23
1–103, Comment g	79
1–104	26
1–105	20
1–106	275
1–109	390
1–201	30
1–201(3)	67
	89
1–201(9)	49
1–201(10)	107
1–201(11)	67
	89
	213
1–201(17)	68
1–201(19)	24
	49
	364
1–201(30)	178

UNIFORM COMMERCIAL CODE

Sec.	This Work Page
1–201(32)	48
	49
1–201(33)	48
	49
1–201(37)	391
1–201(42)	89
1–201(44)	49
1–201(45)	223
1–203	24
	34
1–205	23
	346
1–205(2)	24
	67
1–205(3)	24
1–206	21
Art. 2	4
	5
	9
	10
	11
	20
	21
	22
	23
	24
	26
	27
	28
	30
	42
	45
	48
	149
	164
	222
	241
	276
	284
	286
	309
	358
	385
	393
2–102	9
2–103	30
	42
	390
	393
2–103(1)(a)	9
	49
	52
2–103(1)(b)	24
	34
2–103(1)(c)	379
2–103(1)(d)	9
2–104(1)	43
	114
	379

xxxiv

TABLE OF STATUTES

UNIFORM COMMERCIAL CODE

Sec.	This Work Page
2–104(1) (Cont'd)	384
2–105(1)	10
	21
2–105(5)	216
2–106	208
2–106(1)	9
	20
	37
	69
2–106, Comment 2	235
2–107(1)	21
2–201	21
2–201(1)	21
2–202	35
	88
	89
	96
	114
	115
	139
	140
2–203—2–207	20
2–204	90
2–205	23
2–206	23
	214
2–207	23
	119
	143
	214
2–209	23
	140
2–210	23
	187
2–210(2)	343
2–210(4)	308
Art. 2, pt. 3	214
2–301	23
	214
	227
	308
2–302	24
	25
	115
	141
	190
	194
2–302, Comment 1	25
2–304	381
2–304(1)	384
2–305	208
	210
2–305(1)	208
2–306	21
2–307	216
	241
2–308(a)	215
2–308(c)	292
2–309	251

UNIFORM COMMERCIAL CODE

Sec.	This Work Page
2–309(1)	215
	221
2–310	214
	306
2–310(a)	216
	221
2–310(b)	221
	305
2–310, Comment 4	306
2–311	217
2–311(1)	213
2–311(2)	220
2–312	41
	43
	52
2–312(1)	42
2–312(1)(a)	38
2–312(1)(b)	38
2–312(2)	38
	42
2–312(3)	38
2–313	56
	78
	80
	114
	139
	140
	192
2–313(1)	104
2–313(1)(a)	56
	76
	77
2–313(1)(b)	69
2–313(1)(c)	114
2–313(2)	56
	76
	137
2–313, Comment 3	76
	77
2–314	56
	63
	109
	114
	191
	193
2–314(1)	70
	164
2–314(2)	69
2–314(2)(a)	67
	69
	80
2–314(2)(b)	68
	69
2–314(2)(c)	196
2–314(2)(d)	69
2–314(2)(e)	69
2–314(f)	140
2–314, Comment 7	68

TABLE OF STATUTES

UNIFORM COMMERCIAL CODE

Sec.	This Work Page
2–315	6
	56
	191
	193
	195
2–316	25
	109
	110
	142
	166
	190
	194
	197
2–316(1)	104
	114
	115
2–316(2)	104
	107
	108
	109
	143
2–316(3)	143
2–316(3)(a)	107
2–316(3)(b)	80
	104
2–316(3)(c)	104
	119
2–316(4)	108
2–316, Comment 3	110
2–316, Comment 4	110
2–316, Comment 5	110
2–317	57
2–318	166
	187
	191
	202
	206
	207
2–319	219
	398
2–319(1)	219
2–319(1)(a)	398
2–319(1)(b)	219
	398
2–319(1)(c)	219
2–319(2)	219
	317
	398
2–319(4)	306
	311
2–319, Comment 1	219
2–320	219
	317
	405
	408
2–320(2)	398
2–320(2)(a)	220
2–320(2)(c)	399
2–320(3)	398

UNIFORM COMMERCIAL CODE

Sec.	This Work Page
2–320(4)	306
	311
2–321	219
	306
	408
2–321(3)	311
2–322	219
	306
	399
2–323(1)	220
2–323(2)	358
2–325	320
2–325(1)	341
2–325(3)	342
2–326(1)	129
2–327	129
2–401	27
	380
2–401(1)	380
2–401(2)	37
	380
2–403	49
2–403(1)	44
	45
	48
	49
2–403(2)	48
	49
	52
2–403, Comment 1	48
Art. 2, pt. 5	214
2–501(1)	22
2–503	218
	221
	379
2–503(1)	215
	382
	384
2–503(1)(a)	215
2–503(1)(b)	215
2–503(2)	218
2–503(3)	218
	219
	251
2–503(4)	222
	223
2–503(4)(a)	223
2–503(4)(b)	223
2–503(5)	221
	292
	306
2–503, Comment 4	215
2–503, Comment 5	222
	403
2–504	218
	221
	233
	292
	399

TABLE OF STATUTES

UNIFORM COMMERCIAL CODE

Sec.	This Work Page
2–504 (Cont'd)	409
2–504(a)	219
	223
2–504(b)	221
	306
2–504(c)	219
	221
	409
	410
2–504, Comment 1	218
2–505	391
2–507	308
2–507(1)	214
	217
	227
	291
	392
2–507(2)	45
	308
	309
2–507, Comment 3	309
2–508	227
	284
2–508(1)	247
2–509	379
	380
	381
	383
	390
	399
	405
2–509(1)	382
	398
	403
	407
2–509(1)(a)	391
	398
	404
2–509(1)(b)	398
2–509(2)	381
2–509(3)	379
	383
	384
	385
	390
	393
2–509, Comment 3	383
2–510	379
	390
	393
	405
	407
2–510(1)	234
	384
	390
	404
2–510(3)	384
2–511	215

UNIFORM COMMERCIAL CODE

Sec.	This Work Page
2–511(1)	214
	291
	384
2–511(2)	215
2–512(2)	305
2–513(1)	216
	228
	233
	306
2–513(2)	218
2–513(3)	306
2–513(3)(b)	305
2–513(4)	306
2–601	227
	235
	241
	242
	259
	305
	306
	405
2–602	280
2–602(1)	228
	233
	234
2–602(2)(a)	280
	286
2–602(2)(b)	228
	286
2–602(2)(c)	228
2–603	252
2–603(1)	228
	251
2–603(3)	228
2–604	228
2–605	233
2–606	234
2–606(1)	228
2–606(1)(a)	228
	404
2–606(1)(b)	228
	233
	234
2–606(1)(c)	228
	286
2–607	195
	252
2–607(1)	234
2–607(2)	227
	235
2–607(3)	147
	148
	165
	172
	227
2–607(3)(a)	144
	147
	148
	190

TABLE OF STATUTES

UNIFORM COMMERCIAL CODE

Sec.	This Work Page
2-607(3)(a) (Cont'd)	227
	233
	234
2-607(4)	227
2-607(5)	41
	196
2-607(5)(b)	38
2-607, Comment 4	147
	233
2-608	227
	278
	280
	284
	285
2-608(2)	284
2-608(3)	278
	280
	284
	286
2-609	259
2-609(1)	217
2-610	217
	259
2-612(1)	241
2-612(2)	227
	242
	259
	306
2-612(3)	259
2-612, Comment 1	241
2-612, Comment 2	241
2-613	383
	384
2-613, Comment 1	383
2-615	209
	384
2-702(2)	309
2-703	260
2-704(2)	276
2-705	310
2-705(2)(c)	310
2-706	259
	260
	265
	269
	270
	275
2-706(6)	259
2-706, Comment 2	269
2-708	269
	275
	276
2-708(1)	260
	269
	270
	275
2-708(2)	260
	269
	275

UNIFORM COMMERCIAL CODE

Sec.	This Work Page
2-708(2) (Cont'd)	276
2-709	45
	234
2-709(1)	384
2-709(1)(a)	227
	393
	399
	405
2-709(1)(b)	260
2-709(2)	260
2-711	227
2-711(1)	227
	278
	285
	390
2-711(3)	259
	282
	284
2-712	227
	278
2-713	227
	278
2-714	58
	96
	227
	234
2-714(1)	58
2-714(2)	57
	58
	130
	197
2-715	194
	227
2-715(1)	58
2-715(2)	58
	89
	96
2-716	288
2-718	25
	104
2-719	25
	104
	109
	110
	119
	138
	142
	166
	190
	194
	197
2-719(1)(a)	105
	129
2-719(2)	129
	138
2-719(3)	105
	108
	114
	132

TABLE OF STATUTES

UNIFORM COMMERCIAL CODE

Sec.	This Work Page
2–719(3) (Cont'd)	141
	166
	171
2–722	251
2–725	144
	163
	167
	195
	197
	227
2–725(1)	149
	167
2–725(2)	149
	157
	158
	159
Art. 2A	4
	5
2A–103(1)(g)	89
2A–103(1)(j)	43
2A–103(1)(v)	48
2A–209(1)	89
2A–210	89
2A–211	43
2A–212	89
2A–213	89
2A–304(2)	52
Art. 3	4
	5
	27
	292
	293
	363
	364
3–104	216
	292
3–302(a)(2)(ii)	364
3–303	364
3–305	293
	363
3–111	293
3–409	293
	308
3–410	293
3–413	308
	363
3–414	308
3–414(b)	308
3–501(b)(1)	293
3–502(c)	293
	307
Art. 4	4
	5
	293
4–103(e)	308
4–105(5)	293
4–105(6)	293
4–201	293
4–202	293

UNIFORM COMMERCIAL CODE

Sec.	This Work Page
4–202(a)	308
4–202(a)(1)	293
4–202(c)	308
4–202, Comment 4	308
4–212	293
4–213	308
4–403(1)	307
4–501	293
4–503	293
4–503(1)	293
4–503(2)	307
Art. 4A	5
Art. 5	4
	344
5–102(3)	346
5–102(4)	344
	346
5–105	344
5–113	358
5–114	363
5–114(2)(a)	363
	364
5–114(2)(b)	374
5–116(1)	343
Art. 6	5
Art. 7	4
	220
	223
	293
7–104(1)(a)	292
7–202	223
7–301(1)	307
7–301(2)	307
7–303	310
7–304	357
7–304(3)	357
7–304(5)	357
7–305(1)	293
7–403	220
	308
	310
7–403(1)	220
	308
7–403(3)	220
7–403(4)	220
7–404	220
	307
7–501	293
7–501(1)	305
7–502	293
7–507	308
7–508	308
Art. 8	5
Art. 9	5
	38
	259
9–104	346
9–203(2)	346
9–302(1)(d)	163

xxxix

TABLE OF STATUTES

UNIFORM COMMERCIAL CODE

Sec.	This Work Page
9–306(2)	41
	44
9–318(4)	343
9–504(2)	259
9–505	163
9–507(1)	163

FEDERAL RULES OF CIVIL PROCEDURE

Sec.	This Work Page
14	41
	196

CASES, PROBLEMS AND MATERIALS

ON

SALES TRANSACTIONS: DOMESTIC AND INTERNATIONAL LAW

*

THE CONTRACT FOR SALE

Chapter 1

GENERAL INTRODUCTION

(A) DEVELOPMENT OF COMMERCIAL LAW

Scope of the Course. The dominant theme of this book is the distribution of goods. The fascination of the subject results in part from its astonishing variety: complex contracts negotiated between economic giants and clauses signed by unsuspecting consumers; face-to-face deals and cabled arrangements for imports and exports; sales "cash on the barrelhead" (facilitated by sophisticated banking devices) and sales on long-term credit. Such wild variations place heavy strain on the rules of law and on the ingenuity of counsellors.

This book centers on the performance of sales contracts. What quality of goods must the seller supply? How must shipment and delivery be handled? At what point must buyer pay for the goods? The goods are destroyed: can the seller recover the price from the buyer or must he take the loss? If there is insurance, who gets the proceeds of the policy? One party becomes insolvent: can the other party get the goods? Goods obtained by fraud or theft are resold: who bears the loss? In dealing with hazards such as these, we need to take into account not only legal rules but also relevant commercial practices. Throughout, we must consider ways in which counselling may avoid some of these difficulties.

Development of Commercial Law. In spite of recent reformulations of the law, it would be crippling to know nothing of the roots from which this branch of the law has grown. As we shall see, old issues keep coming back. The following outline may help some students probe more deeply into the origins of commercial law.

(1) Mercantile Custom and Nationalization. Until the seventeenth century a large share of commercial law was merchants' law—a body of customs made and administered by the merchants themselves. Some of the rules were international in scope: maritime insurance policies still bear the marks of the Genoese and Antwerp customs. Courts of merchants also decided controversies that developed at the fairs which were the centers for much of early trade; important staple commodities (such as wool) were governed by specialized courts with a jury of merchants presided over by a "mayor of the staple," skilled in mercantile practice.[1]

In the seventeenth century the merchants' courts were shouldered to one side by the King's judges who in 1666 proclaimed that "the law of merchants is the law of the land"[2]—a hollow claim that was in part fulfilled by the work of a renowned Scotsman, William Murray, who in 1756 was made Chief Justice of the King's Bench and was given the title of Lord Mansfield. In controversies between merchants, Mansfield made it a point to ascertain and apply the customs of the trade. One of his tools for this work was a special group of merchants who acted as a jury in commercial cases and gave him advice on commercial practice.[3] But, as Karl Llewellyn noted in "Across Sales on Horseback,"[4] mercantile custom was not fully imported into the law of sales. Llewellyn contended that this was an accident: the decisive sales cases did not come to Mansfield but to judges of a different bent who were content to decide mercantile transactions on the basis of concepts developed for a static land economy. And it may be that most of the mercantile customs within the wide field of sales are too varied to be frozen into general rules of law. At any rate, a body of common-law doctrine developed to govern sales of goods; the rules were systematized in the treatises of Blackburn (1st ed. 1845) and Benjamin (1st ed. 1868).[5]

(2) Nineteenth Century Codification. In the nineteenth century codification was in the air. In 1804, in the aftermath of revolution and under Napoleon's firm hand, conflicting local rules and customs in France were supplanted by the Civil Code. Napoleon carried the Code to much of Europe; even after his armies were driven out the Code

---

1. See Honnold, "The Influence of the Law of International Trade on the Development and Character of English and American Commercial Law," in Sources of the Law of International Trade (Schmitthoff ed. 1964) 70. Further material on *pie poudre* (dusty foot) courts—merchants could hardly keep a shine—may be found in Holdsworth, The Development of the Law Merchant and its Courts, 1 Select Essays in Anglo-American Legal History 289—331 (1907). For additional information on the law merchant, see: Stoecker, The *Lex Mercatoria*: To What Extent Does It Exist?, 7 J. Int'l Arb., March 1990, at 101; Berman, The Law of International Commercial Transactions (*Lex Mercatoria*), 2 J. Int'l Dispute Resolution 235 (1988); L. Trakman, The Law Merchant: The Evolution of Commercial Law (1983); Thayer, Comparative Law and the Law Merchant, 6 Brook.L.Rev. 139 (1936); MacKinnon, Origins of Commercial Law, 52 Law Q.Rev. 30 (1936); Sanborn, Origins of the Early English Maritime and Commercial Law 335 (1930); L. Goldschmidt, Universalgeschicte des Handelsrechts (1891).

2. Woodward v. Row, 2 Keb. 132, 84 Eng.Rep. 84 (1666).

3. A brief and readable account of Mansfield's work may be found in Holdsworth, Some Makers of English Law (1938), 160—175. For more detail, see Fifoot, Lord Mansfield (1936). Chapter IV (82—117) is devoted to commercial law. Mansfield's Scottish background is not irrelevant, for it may explain his receptiveness to civil law doctrines prevalent in Scotland.

4. 52 Harv.L.Rev. 725 (1939). This article, in spite of its title, is no pony for sales law. There is a sequel called The First Struggle to Unhorse Sales in 52 Harv. L.Rev. 873 (1939) which calls for the same comment.

5. Students interested in personalities behind the law may enjoy exploring the career of Judah P. Benjamin. A member of Jefferson Davis' cabinet, on the fall of the Confederacy he emigrated to England. Success there followed swiftly the publication of his outstanding treatise on Sales. See Meade, Judah P. Benjamin (1943); E. Evans, Judah P. Benjamin, The Jewish Confederate (1988).

remained, and also was followed in most of Latin America and in substantial parts of Africa and Asia.

Jeremy Bentham argued the case for codification in England, and in 1811 he wrote to President Madison volunteering personally to write a code of law for the new world. In New York the constitution of 1846 called for the codification of the entire body of law of the state. Under the leadership of David Dudley Field, New York adopted the first Code of Civil Procedure and prepared a code of substantive law which, although rejected in New York, was adopted in 1872 in California, and in the Dakotas, Idaho and Montana. But proposals for general codification were, for the most part, rejected.[6]

(3) Federal Courts and the "General Commercial Law." Maintaining uniformity of commercial law among the settled states of the Eastern seaboard was difficult enough; the problem became wholly unmanageable as new states were carved out of the wilderness. Frontier law was rough and ready, marked by a shortage of law books and legal education, and a cheerful willingness to improvise.[7] The rapidly developing commerce of the new world lacked uniform or even predictable rules of law.

In 1821 Joseph Story, speaking in his home state of Massachusetts, called for codification of aspects of commercial law. This call was not answered, and in 1842 Story wrote the opinion in Swift v. Tyson holding that federal courts, unhampered by divergent state court decisions, could declare uniform rules for "general commercial law." Indeed the opinion opened up wider vistas: Lord Mansfield and Cicero were cited for the proposition that commercial law was "in a great measure, not the law of a single country only, but of the commercial world." [8] The federal courts continued to declare rules of "general commercial law," in a sporadic manner and with decreasing effectiveness, until 1938 when such federal law-making was held unconstitutional in Erie Railroad Co. v. Tompkins.[9]

(4) Specialized Statutes in Britain and America. A development like Swift v. Tyson was not needed in England: royal judges had established a common law.[10] But towards the end of the century

6. For materials and further references on the codification movement see Honnold, The Life of the Law: Readings on the Growth of Legal Institutions (1964) 100–122, 494–496.

7. Pound, The Formative Era of American Law 7–12 (1938).

8. Swift v. Tyson, (41 U.S.) 16 Pet. 1, 18 (1842). See Gilmore, Commercial Law in the United States: Its Codification and Other Misadventures, in Aspects of Comparative Commercial Law, 449, 452–457 (Ziegel and Foster 1969).

9. Erie Railroad Co. v. Tompkins, 304 U.S. 64, 58 S.Ct. 817, 82 L.Ed. 1188 (1938). See Heckman, Uniform Commercial Law in the Nineteenth Century Federal Courts: The Decline and Abuse of the Swift Doctrine, 27 Emory L.J. 45 (1978).

10. Scotland, however, held to Roman law. In 1855, a Royal Commission brought in an important and fascinating report on ways in which "the Mercantile Laws in the different parts of the United Kingdom of Great Britain and Ireland may be advantageously assimilated." Second Report of the Commissioners on Mercantile Laws of the United Kingdom, 354 Parliamentary Papers (1855). In 1856 Parliament enacted legislation to deal with some of these divergencies. Mercantile Law Amendment Act, Scotland, 1856, 19 & 20 Vict. c. 60; Mer-

pressure for certainty led to statutory enactments in specific fields of commercial law. Parliament in 1882 enacted the Bills of Exchange Act and in 1893 enacted the Sale of Goods Act—laws which still are in force in various parts of the world as part of the legacy of empire.

Enactment of these two important laws in Britain was soon followed by similar legislation in the United States. The National Conference of Commissioners on Uniform State Laws in 1895 requested John J. Crawford to draft a Uniform Negotiable Instruments Law (NIL). Within one year the NIL was completed and by 1924 had been enacted by every state. By 1906 the Uniform Sales Act (USA) had been drafted by Professor Williston and approved by the Commissioners. The USA was eventually adopted in over thirty states; the principal exceptions were in the South. The NIL and the USA were patterned closely after the British Bills of Exchange Act and Sale of Goods Act; these Acts had been based on case-law doctrine developed in the nineteenth century. The legislative goals were stability, clarity and uniformity, rather than reform. The NIL and the USA were followed by more specialized uniform laws: on warehouse receipts (1906), bills of lading (1909), conditional sales (1918), and trust receipts (1933).

(5) The Uniform Commercial Code. In 1936, the New York Merchants' Association launched a movement to modernize sales law, and proposed the adoption by Congress of a Federal Sales Act to govern foreign and interstate trade. To avoid the problems which would be posed by separate federal law, the National Conference of Commissioners on Uniform State Laws in 1940 started work on a Revised Sales Act to supplant the Uniform Sales Act; this project, under joint sponsorship by the Commissioners and the American Law Institute, grew into the Uniform Commercial Code. The Chief Reporter and supervising architect of the Code project was Professor Karl Llewellyn; the Associate Chief Reporter was Professor (later Dean) Soia Mentschikoff.

The Code's rules are set forth in eleven Articles; two additional articles deal with effective dates and related matters. Article 1 has general rules that are applicable throughout the Code. Articles 2 and 3 supplant the Uniform Sales Act and the Negotiable Instruments Law. Other prior uniform laws are supplanted by other parts of the Code. A quick overview as to the Code's scope can best be gained by examining its Table of Contents; background for specific parts of the Code will be presented later in these materials.

The part of the Code most important for the first part of these materials is Article 2 (Sales).[11] In Chapter 5 of this book we shall meet the Code's Article 3 (Negotiable Instruments), Article 4 (Bank Deposits and Collections), Article 5 (Letters of Credit) and Article 7 (Documents of Title).

cantile Law Amendment Act, 1856, 19 & 20 Vict. c. 97.

11. Cross references are made to the newest addition to the Commercial Code, Article 2A (Leases).

By 1968 the Code had been adopted by all states except Louisiana, where integration with the Civil Code presented difficulties.[12] The Code has also been enacted by Congress for the District of Columbia and by the Legislature of the Virgin Islands.

The legislative history of the Code is complex. For now it should suffice to note that the first version of the Code was released in 1952 and was promptly enacted in Pennsylvania. Studies by the New York Law Revision Commission led to substantial revisions that were embodied in the 1957 and 1958 Official Texts.[13] Then, for over a decade, the Code sponsors held the line against proposals for change; only glaring errors were corrected in the Official Texts of 1962 and 1966.[14]

The Official Text of 1972 made substantial revisions, centering on Article 9 (Secured Transactions); in 1978 there were important changes centering on Article 8 (Investment Securities).

In the late 1980's, the Code's sponsors, the Conference of Commissioners on Uniform State Laws and the American Law Institute, launched a program of major additions and revisions. Two new articles have been added—Article 2A on Leases (1987 with 1990 amendments) and Article 4A on Funds Transfers (1989). In 1988, the sponsors of the Code recommended that states either repeal or substantially revise Article 6 (Bulk Sales).

A major revision of Article 3 on Negotiable Instruments, with related changes in Article 4 (Bank Deposits and Collections), was concluded in 1991. Meanwhile a drafting committee to revise Article 8 (Investment Securities) began working in August 1991 with the expectation that it will complete its task in 1992 or 1993.

The Uniform State Laws Conference and the American Law Institute have turned next to Article 2 (Sales) and Article 9 (Secured Transactions). In 1991, a drafting committee was authorized to revise Article 2. This step followed the completion of a major report by a study committee on that Article. In 1990 a study committee began reviewing Article 9; it is safe to predict that this Article will be revised substantially in the 1990's.

Students studying commercial law while these important changes are in progress have an obvious problem and a significant opportunity. For parts of the Code, two versions of the text and comments must be considered;[15] since uniform enactment of revisions and additions takes

---

12. Louisiana adopted Articles 1, 3, 4 and 5, effective January 1, 1975.

13. For further details and references see the senior editor's account in New York Law Revision Commission, Study of Uniform Commercial Code, Vol. 1, 348 (1955). (Herein cited N.Y.L.Rev.Comm., Study of UCC.) The analysis of Article 2 on Sales is set forth in N.Y.L.Rev.Comm., Study of UCC, Vol. 1, pages 347 et seq.

14. Revealing and amusing comments on the making of the UCC appear in Symposium: Origins and Evolution: Drafters Reflect Upon the Uniform Commercial Code, 43 Ohio St.L.J. 537–642 (1982).

15. Current statutory supplements of the Code published for student use put superseded versions of the text and comments in appendices to the most recent Official Text promulgated by the Uniform

several years to complete, both the new and old versions of the Code will be in force in some states. Inevitably, the Commercial Code will not be "uniform" for some years.[16] For other parts of the Code, students can know that changes are forthcoming but cannot know what the new texts and comments will be. This may be unsettling to someone looking merely to learn what the law "is." But considering a major body of statutory law in flux is a unique opportunity to gain the deeper understanding that comes from evaluating the perceived weaknesses in older texts and considering whether the proposed changes will be better.[17]

A practicing lawyer must, of course, work from the version enacted in his or her state. Judicial decisions, including every case in these materials, are governed by that version of the Commercial Code in the jurisdiction whose law governs the transaction in question.

(6) Special Legislation to Protect Consumers. In many countries the "Commercial Code" is applicable only when one (or both) of the parties is a merchant. Lawyers schooled in such a legal setting are startled to learn that the "Uniform Commercial Code" extends to transactions among ordinary consumers and that (with a few exceptions) the rules are the same for both commercial and consumer transactions.

It must quickly be added that these general rules may lead to different results in commercial and in consumer settings. One example is the rule of UCC 2–315 which gives the buyer special protection when she relies "on the seller's skill or judgment"; similar flexibility is inherent in the Code's rules on "good faith" and "unconscionability." The point is that the application of these rules does not depend on placing the parties or the transaction in a "commercial" or "consumer" category.

One of the striking legal developments of recent years has been the enactment of legislation designed to give special protection to "consumers." With respect to general rules of commercial law, like those of the UCC, Congress has usually played a subsidiary role; in the field of consumer protection Congress has taken the lead. Sweeping regulation of sellers' warranties in the interests of consumers first became effective on July 4, 1975, under the federal Magnuson–Moss Warranty Act. (The impact of this legislation will be considered in Chapter 3.)

In 1960 Senator Paul Douglas introduced his first legislative proposal for "Truth in Lending." This proposal stimulated counter-measures for state enactment, including the preparation by the National

States Laws Conference and the American Law Institute.

16. The Commercial Code as proposed after 1967 was not adopted uniformly by state legislatures. Hundreds of changes (usually minor) were made by various states in enacting the Code.

17. Current students may find that their up-to-date knowledge of the emerging Commercial Code is an asset that prospective employers will value, as happened three decades ago when very few practicing lawyers had studied the Commercial Code as initially promulgated.

Conference of Commissioners on Uniform State Laws of a Uniform Consumer Credit Code (the "U3C"). The U3C, as promulgated in 1968, provided the basis for legislation in a number of states; a revised version was issued in 1974. But these proposals for uniform state legislation did not divert the Congress from Senator Douglas' proposals: In 1968 Congress passed the Consumer Credit Protection Act; Title I is the Truth in Lending Act. More recently, the Federal Trade Commission has issued important regulations for the protection of consumers.

(7) Uniform Laws for International Transactions. Important steps have been taken to unify the law applicable to international trade. Trade with the larger part of the world—the continent of Europe, the American republics to the south and much of Asia and Africa—carries the parties to sales contracts and their lawyers into legal systems which stem from unfamiliar roots; the differences in legal concepts are, of course, complicated by linguistic barriers.

Sales. One field for unification is the law applicable to the international sale of goods. As early as 1930 work toward this goal was under way in Europe, and in April 1964 a diplomatic conference at The Hague finalized conventions establishing a Uniform Law on the International Sale of Goods (ULIS) and a Uniform Law on the Formation of Contracts for the International Sale of Goods (ULF). By 1972 sufficient ratifications, primarily by countries of western Europe, had occurred to bring these conventions into force.

These two conventions broke the ground for international unification, but the lack of world-wide collaboration in their preparation stood in the way of general adoption. In 1966 the General Assembly of the United Nations provided for the creation of the United Nations Commission on International Trade Law (UNCITRAL). UNCITRAL's membership, limited to 36 States, is allocated among the regions of the world: Africa, 9; Asia, 7; Eastern Europe, 5; Latin America, 6; Western Europe and Others, 9. This last region (the industrial West) extends to Australia, Canada, and the United States. The United States has been a member from the outset, and has played an active role in UNCITRAL's work.

UNCITRAL promptly created a Working Group (a cross-section of the Commission's world-wide membership) to prepare new international rules that would meet objections to the 1964 conventions on international sales. By 1978 the Working Group and the full Commission had unanimously approved a new draft Convention. In 1980 a diplomatic conference of 62 States, at the end of five weeks of intensive work, approved the United Nations Convention on Contracts for the International Sale of Goods. The Convention went into force on January 1, 1988 following ratification (or similar implementation) by eleven States. The United States was one of those nations. By 1991 the Convention had been ratified by over 30 States, including nations on each continent and with diverse legal and economic systems.

Negotiable Instruments and Credit Transfers. A second field for unification involves the rules governing important instruments used in international payments—bills of exchange, promissory notes, checks. In this field, UNCITRAL developed uniform rules which led in 1988 to the United Nations Convention on International Bills of Exchange and Promissory Notes; an unusual feature of this Convention is that its rules apply only to a special international instrument that states it is issued under the Convention. See G. Herrmann, 10 U. Pa. J. Intl. Bus. L. 517–577 (1988). More recently, the Commission has been developing a Model Law on International Credit Transfers.

Other Fields. Because of the vital part that sea transport plays in international trade, UNCITRAL decided to examine the rules that govern the responsibility of ocean carriers for cargo. (Problems of risk of loss in this area are examined in Chapter 6). The Commission found that these rules, developed under the strong influence of the carriers, gave inadequate protection to cargo and developed new rules that were submitted in 1978 to diplomatic conference at Hamburg that finalized the United Nations Convention on Carriage of Goods by Sea (the "Hamburg Rules"). In spite of active opposition on behalf of the carriers, in 1991 the Convention received (primarily from developing countries) the twenty ratifications required to bring the Convention into force, which occurs on November 1, 1992. Countries that have indicated interest in the Convention by becoming signatories but have not yet ratified include Brazil, France, Germany, the four Scandinavian nations and the United States.[18]

Other examples of the rapidly growing body of uniform law for international commerce include the 1976 UNCITRAL Arbitration Rules, which become effective by a reference in a contractual arbitration clause, and the 1985 UNCITRAL Model Law on International Commercial Legislation. See A. Broches in ICCA, International Handbook on Commercial Arbitration (Arb. Supp. 11, Jan. 1990); H. Holtzmann & J. Neuhaus, Guide to the UNCITRAL Model Law (1989); A. Redfern & M. Hunter, Law and Practice of International Commercial Arbitration 360–404, 416–430 (text of the UNCITRAL Rules), 435–449 (text of the Model Law) (1986).

(8) Reference Materials. A most useful tool for intensive research on the Code is the Uniform Commercial Code Reporting Service. This service includes the UCC and Comments—including local variations. It also includes cases that cite the UCC and a digest of decided cases arranged by topic. Another helpful research guide is Uniform Laws Annotated. Useful insights into the drafting history of the UCC are provided by the twenty-three volumes of Uniform Commercial Code Drafts (E. Kelly ed. 1984).

---

18. Growing use of large steel containers has stimulated arrangements linking different modes of transport—road, rail, air and sea. Desire for uniform international rules led to the 1980 International Convention on Multimodal Transport, based on the 1978 Hamburg Rules.

On the Code as a whole, see J. White and R. Summers, Uniform Commercial Code (3d ed. 1988); R. Alderman, A Transactional Guide to the Uniform Commercial Code (2d ed. 1983). On sales, see G. Wallach, The Law of Sales Under the Uniform Commercial Code (1981). The myriad intersections between the UCC and other laws are thoroughly developed in R. Hillman, J. McDonnell, & S. Nickles, Common Law and Equity Under the UCC (1984 & Supp.1990). In view of the rapid evolution of laws regarding consumer protection, loose-leaf services are useful. See CCH: Trade Regulation Reporter; Consumer Credit Guide.

Several commentaries have been published on the International Sales Convention. See C.M. Bianca & M.J. Bonell (eds.), Commentary on the International Sales Law (1987); P. Schlechtriem, Uniform Sales Law (1986); J. Honnold, Uniform Law for International Sales Under the 1980 United Nations Convention (2d ed. 1991). For cross reference between the Convention and the Commercial Code, see A. Kritzer, Guide to Practical Applications of the United Nations Convention on Contracts for the International Sale of Goods (1989). Legislative history of the Convention is compiled in J. Honnold, Documentary History of the Uniform Law for International Sales (1989). See also Pfund, International Unification of Private Law: A Report on U.S. Participation—1987–88, 22 Int. Law. 1157 (1988).

(B) SCOPE AND APPROACH OF ARTICLE 2 OF THE COMMERCIAL CODE

(1) SCOPE

Uniform Commercial Code Article 2 declares that it "applies to transactions in goods." UCC 2–102. The principal transaction, reflected in the title of Article 2, is "sales." [19] The principal actors are "buyers," defined somewhat tautologically in UCC 2–103(1)(a), and "sellers," similarly defined in (1)(d). A "sale" is "the passing of title [to goods] from the seller to the buyer for a price." UCC 2–106(1). "Sales" result from "contracts for sale," defined in the same section and divided into "present sales" and "future sales." For the most part, these elementary concepts have clear meanings that do not often blur at the edges.

That cannot be said of "goods," the object of "sales," which has a clear core of meaning but bristles with difficulties in many settings. The Code defines "goods" as "all things (including specially manufactured goods) which are movable at the time of identification to the contract for sale other than the money in which the price is to be paid,

---

19. Language purists might wonder why the simplified nomenclature is a noun derived from the sellers' side of transactions that are necessarily two-sided. The transactions could have been denominated "purchases" or, even handedly, "purchases and sales." Under much weight of history,

investment securities (Article 8) and things in action." UCC 2–105(1).[20]

Query: Are contracts between a utility and its customers for supply of electric power contracts for the sale of goods? See Singer Co. v. Baltimore Gas and Electric Co., 79 Md.App. 461, 558 A.2d 419 (1989).

Goods and Services. Article 2 applies to transactions in goods but does not govern transactions in services, which remain essentially common-law contracts. Obviously, many familiar transactions require one party to deliver goods and render services for a single price. Would UCC Article 2 or common law govern? Should the contracts be divided, with different law governing its parts, or should transactions treated by the parties as indivisible be placed entirely under or outside Article 2? The Code gives no guidance to the parties or the courts.[21] Not surprisingly, the result has been much unsatisfactory litigation.

Consider, for example, a contract to supply and install the structural steel necessary for a bridge. In one such case, three levels of the New York courts struggled inconclusively with the question of characterization; in the end, the Court of Appeals bypassed the issue on the view that the questions presented in that case would be decided the same way whether or not Article 2 applied. Schenectady Steel Co. v. Bruno Trimpoli General Construction Co., 34 N.Y.2d 939, 359 N.Y.S.2d 560, 316 N.E.2d 875 (1974).

Not all difficult cases can be so finessed. Driven to solve the problem, courts may treat contracts as divisible if that is feasible and, if not, tend to choose the governing law by measuring whether the goods or the services component is economically more dominant.[22] Compare Long Island Lighting Co. v. Transamerica Delaval, Inc., 646 F.Supp. 1442 (S.D.N.Y.1986), with Lucien Bourque, Inc. v. Cronkite, 557 A.2d

the short form title, however, is simply "sales."

20. See Annot., What constitutes "goods" within the scope of UCC Article 2, 4 ALR 4th 912.

21. The Code does address transactions in which sellers perform services in contracts to manufacture goods to buyers' specifications. The definition of "goods" in UCC 2–105(1) expressly includes specially manufactured goods. In special-order contracts, typically the services would be performed at seller's place of business before the goods were tendered to buyer. See, e.g., California and Hawaiian Sugar Co. v. Sun Ship, Inc., 794 F.2d 1433 (9th Cir.1986)(construction of ocean-going barge).

22. Determining the relative value of the elements of sales/service transactions is more difficult than might first appear. Increasingly, the value of the physical elements of goods has diminished relative to the value of the technology or information needed to manufacture or process them. Consider the ubiquitous semi-conductor chip, essential for so many high-tech products. The raw materials in these chips have almost no economic value; value comes from the intelligence embedded in the chips. The value of the raw materials in a modern automobile, sold for many thousands of dollars, is a few hundred dollars. For many goods, it is not a mistake to say that their value represents "congealed services." Would it be feasible or desirable to make the applicability of Article 2 depend upon weighing manufacturers' costs of materials and labor?

One macroeconomic effect of the diminishing value of materials used to make goods has been a long term decline in the market value of primary commodities like copper, tin, iron, aluminum, rubber, etc. Economies of nations that depend upon extractive industries have suffered significantly.

193 (Me.1989); see also Annot., Applicability of UCC Article 2 to mixed contracts for sale of goods and services, 5 ALR 4th 501.

Query: Is a contract for sale of a "turn-key" computer system that includes hardware, software, installation and post-installation service governed by Article 2? See Neilson Business Equipment Center, Inc. v. Italo V. Monteleone, M.D., P.A., 524 A.2d 1172 (Del.1987). Is a contract to design and install a computer program in the buyer's existing hardware governed by Article 2?

If these matters were to be resolved by statute, what would be a good Code solution?

ADVENT SYSTEMS LIMITED v. UNISYS CORP.

United States Court of Appeals, Third Circuit, 1991.
925 F.2d 670.

OPINION by WEIS, C.J.

In this diversity case we conclude that computer software is a good within the Uniform Commercial Code; in the circumstances here a nonexclusive requirements contract complies with the statute of frauds; and expert testimony on future lost profits based on prior projections is suspect when actual market performance data are available. Because the district court ruled that the Code did not apply, we will grant a new trial on a breach of contract claim. ...

Plaintiff, Advent Systems Limited, is engaged primarily in the production of software for computers. As a result of its research and development efforts, by 1986 the company had developed an electronic document management system (EDMS), a process for transforming engineering drawings and similar documents into a computer data base.

Unisys Corporation manufactures a variety of computers. As a result of information gained by its wholly-owned United Kingdom subsidiary during 1986, Unisys decided to market the document management system in the United States. In June 1987 Advent and Unisys signed two documents, one labeled "Heads of Agreement" (in British parlance "an outline of agreement") and, the other, "Distribution Agreement."

In these documents, Advent agreed to provide the software and hardware making up the document systems to be sold by Unisys in the United States. Advent was obligated to provide sales and marketing material and manpower as well as technical personnel to work with Unisys employees in building and installing the document systems. The agreement was to continue for two years, subject to automatic renewal or termination on notice.

During the summer of 1987, Unisys attempted to sell the document system to Arco, a large oil company, but was unsuccessful. Nevertheless, progress on the sales and training programs in the United States was satisfactory, and negotiations for a contract between Unisys (UK) and Advent were underway.

The relationship, however, soon came to an end. Unisys, in the throes of restructuring, decided it would be better served by developing its own document system and in December 1987 told Advent their arrangement had ended. Unisys also advised its UK subsidiary of those developments and, as a result, negotiations there were terminated.

Advent filed a complaint in the district court alleging ... breach of contract.... The district court ruled at pretrial that the Uniform Commercial Code did not apply because although goods were to be sold, the services aspect of the contract predominated.

A jury ... awarded damages to Advent in the sum of $4,550,000 on the breach of contract claim....

On appeal ... Unisys contends that the relationship between it and Advent was one for the sale of goods and hence subject to the terms of the statute of frauds in the Uniform Commercial Code. Because the agreements lacked an express provision on quantity, Unisys insists that the statute of frauds bans enforcement. In addition, Unisys contends that the evidence did not support the damage verdict.

* * *

II.

SOFTWARE AND THE UNIFORM COMMERCIAL CODE

The district court ruled that as a matter of law the arrangement between the two parties was not within the Uniform Commercial Code and, consequently, the statute of frauds was not applicable. As the district court appraised the transaction, provisions for services outweighed those for products and, consequently, the arrangement was not predominantly one for the sale of goods.

In the "Heads of Agreement" Advent and Unisys purported to enter into a "joint business collaboration." Advent was to modify its software and hardware interfaces to run initially on equipment not manufactured by Unisys but eventually on Unisys hardware. It was Advent's responsibility to purchase the necessary hardware. "In so far as Advent has successfully completed [some of the processing] of software and hardware interfaces," Unisys promised to reimburse Advent to the extent of $150,000 derived from a "surcharge" on products purchased.

Advent agreed to provide twelve man-weeks of marketing manpower, but with Unisys bearing certain expenses. Advent also undertook to furnish an experienced systems builder to work with Unisys personnel at Advent's prevailing rates, and to provide sales and support training for Unisys staff as well as its customers.

The Distribution Agreement begins with the statement, "Unisys desires to purchase, and Advent desires to sell, on a non-exclusive basis, certain of Advent hardware products and software licenses for resale worldwide." Following a heading "Subject Matter of Sales," appears this sentence, "(a) Advent agrees to sell hardware and license software to Unisys, and Unisys agrees to buy from Advent the products listed in Schedule A." Schedule A lists twenty products, such as computer cards, plotters, imagers, scanners and designer systems.

Advent was to invoice Unisys for each product purchased upon shipment, but to issue separate invoices for maintenance fees. The cost of the support services was set at 3% "per annum of the prevailing Advent user list price of each software module for which Unisys is receiving revenue from a customer." Services included field technical bulletins, enhancement and maintenance releases, telephone consultation, and software patches, among others. At no charge to Unisys, Advent was to provide publications such as installation manuals, servicing and adjustment manuals, diagnostic operation and test procedures, sales materials, product brochures and similar items. In turn, Unisys was to "employ resources in performing marketing efforts" and develop "the technical ability to be thoroughly familiar" with the products.

In support of the district court's ruling that the U.C.C. did not apply, Advent contends that the agreement's requirement of furnishing services did not come within the Code. Moreover, the argument continues, the "software" referred to in the agreement as a "product" was not a "good" but intellectual property outside the ambit of the Uniform Commercial Code.

Because software was a major portion of the "products" described in the agreement, this matter requires some discussion. Computer systems consist of "hardware" and "software." Hardware is the computer machinery, its electronic circuitry and peripheral items such as keyboards, readers, scanners and printers. Software is a more elusive concept. Generally speaking, "software" refers to the medium that stores input and output data as well as computer programs. The medium includes hard disks, floppy disks, and magnetic tapes.

In simplistic terms, programs are codes prepared by a programmer that instruct the computer to perform certain functions. When the program is transposed onto a medium compatible with the computer's needs, it becomes software. ...

The increasing frequency of computer products as subjects of commercial litigation has led to controversy over whether software is a "good" or intellectual property. The Code does not specifically mention software.

In the absence of express legislative guidance, courts interpret the Code in light of commercial and technological developments. The Code is designed "to simplify, clarify and modernize the law governing commercial transactions" and "to permit the continued expansion of commercial practices." 13 Pa. Cons. Stat. Ann. § 1102 (Purdon 1984). As the Official Commentary makes clear:

> This Act is drawn to provide flexibility so that, since it is intended to be a semi-permanent piece of legislation, it will provide its own machinery for expansion of commercial practices. It is intended to make it possible for the law embodied in this Act to be developed by the courts in the light of unforeseen and new circumstances and practices.

Id. comment 1.

The Code "applies to transactions in goods." 13 Pa. Cons. Stat. Ann. § 2102 (Purdon 1984). Goods are defined as "all things (including specially manufactured goods) which are movable at the time of the identification for sale." Id. at § 2105. The Pennsylvania courts have recognized that " 'goods' has a very extensive meaning" under the U.C.C. Duffee v. Judson, 251 Pa.Super. 406, 380 A.2d 843, 846 (1977); see also Lobianco v. Property Protection, Inc., 292 Pa.Super. 346, 437 A.2d 417 (1981) ("goods" under U.C.C. embraces every species of property other than real estate, choses in action, or investment securities.).

Our Court has addressed computer package sales in other cases, but has not been required to consider whether the U.C.C. applied to software per se. See Chatlos Systems, Inc. v. National Cash Register Corp., 635 F.2d 1081 (3d Cir.1980) (parties conceded that furnishing the plaintiff with hardware, software and associated services was governed by the U.C.C.); see also Carl Beasley Ford, Inc. v. Burroughs Corporation, 361 F.Supp. 325 (E.D.Pa.1973) (U.C.C. applied without discussion), aff'd, 493 F.2d 1400 (3d Cir.1974). Other Courts of Appeals have also discussed transactions of this nature. RRX Industries, Inc. v. Lab–Con, Inc., 772 F.2d 543 (9th Cir.1985) (goods aspects of transaction predominated in a sale of a software system); Triangle Underwriters, Inc. v. Honeywell, Inc., 604 F.2d 737, 742–43 (2d Cir.1979) (in sale of computer hardware, software, and customized software goods aspects predominated; services were incidental).

Computer programs are the product of an intellectual process, but once implanted in a medium are widely distributed to computer owners. An analogy can be drawn to a compact disc recording of an orchestral rendition. The music is produced by the artistry of musicians and in itself is not a "good," but when transferred to a laser-readable disc becomes a readily merchantable commodity. Similarly, when a professor delivers a lecture, it is not a good, but, when transcribed as a book, it becomes a good.

That a computer program may be copyrightable as intellectual property does not alter the fact that once in the form of a floppy disc or other medium, the program is tangible, movable and available in the marketplace. The fact that some programs may be tailored for specific purposes need not alter their status as "goods" because the Code definition includes "specially manufactured goods."

The topic has stimulated academic commentary [2] with the majority espousing the view that software fits within the definition of a "good" in the U.C.C.

Applying the U.C.C. to computer software transactions offers substantial benefits to litigants and the courts. The Code offers a uniform body of law on a wide range of questions likely to arise in computer software disputes: implied warranties, consequential damages, disclaimers of liability, the statute of limitations, to name a few.

The importance of software to the commercial world and the advantages to be gained by the uniformity inherent in the U.C.C. are strong policy arguments favoring inclusion. The contrary arguments are not persuasive, and we hold that software is a "good" within the definition in the Code.

The relationship at issue here is a typical mixed goods and services arrangement. The services are not substantially different from those generally accompanying package sales of computer systems consisting of hardware and software. See Chatlos Systems, Inc. v. National Cash Register Corp., 479 F.Supp. 738, 741 (D.N.J.1979); Beasley Ford, 361 F.Supp. at 328.

Although determining the applicability of the U.C.C. to a contract by examining the predominance of goods or services has been criticized, we see no reason to depart from that practice here. As we pointed out in De Filippo v. Ford Motor Co., 516 F.2d 1313, 1323 (3d Cir.), cert. denied, 423 U.S. 912 (1975), segregating goods from non-goods and insisting "that the Statute of Frauds apply only to a portion of the contract, would be to make the contract divisible and impossible of performance within the intention of the parties."

We consider the purpose or essence of the contract. Comparing the relative costs of the materials supplied with the costs of the labor may be helpful in this analysis, but not dispositive. Compare RRX, 772 F.2d at 546 ("essence" of the agreement) with Triangle, 604 F.2d at 743 ("compensation" structure of the contract).

In this case the contract's main objective was to transfer "products." The specific provisions for training of Unisys personnel by Advent were but a small part of the parties' contemplated relationship.

The compensation structure of the agreement also focuses on "goods." The projected sales figures introduced during the trial demonstrate that in the contemplation of the parties the sale of goods clearly

---

2. Among the articles and notes that have reviewed extant caselaw are: Boss & Woodward, Scope of the Uniform Commercial Code; Survey of Computer Contracting Cases, 43 Bus. Law. 1513 (1988); Owen, The Application of Article 2 of the Uniform Commercial Code To Computer Contracts, 14 N. Kentucky L. Rev. 277 (1987); Rodau, Computer Software: Does Article 2 of the Uniform Commercial Code Apply, 35 Emory L.J. 853 (1986); Holmes, Application of Article Two of the Uniform Commercial Code to Computer System Acquisitions, 9 Rutgers Computer & Technology L.J. 1 (1982); Note, Computer Software As A Good Under the Uniform Commercial Code: Taking a Byte Out of the Intangibility Myth, 65 B. U.L. Rev. 129 (1985); Note, Computer Programs as Goods Under the U.C.C., 77 Mich.L.Rev. 1149 (1979).

predominated. The payment provision of $150,000 for developmental work which Advent had previously completed, was to be made through individual purchases of software and hardware rather than through the fees for services and is further evidence that the intellectual work was to be subsumed into tangible items for sale.

We are persuaded that the transaction at issue here was within the scope of the Uniform Commercial Code and, therefore, the judgment in favor of the plaintiff must be reversed.

III.

THE STATUTE OF FRAUDS

This brings us to the Unisys contention that the U.C.C. statute of frauds bars enforcement of the agreement because the writings do not contain a quantity term.

Section 2–201(a) provides that a contract for the sale of goods of $500 or more is not enforceable unless in writing. "[A] contract ... is not enforceable ... unless there is some writing sufficient to indicate that a contract for sale has been made.... A writing is not insufficient because it omits ... a term agreed upon but the contract is not enforceable ... beyond the quantity of goods shown in such writing." 13 Pa. Cons. Stat. Ann. § 2201(a) (Purdon 1984). The comment to this section states that although the required writing need not contain all the material terms there are "three definite and invariable requirements as to the memorandum," one of which is that "it must specify a quantity." Id. comment 1.

* * *

The circumstances here do not require us to adopt an open-ended reading of the statute but permit us to apply a narrower holding. Nothing in the Code commands us to ignore the practicality of commercial arrangements in construing the statute of frauds. Indeed, the Code's rule of construction states that the language "shall be liberally construed and applied to promote its underlying purposes and policies." 13 Pa. Cons. Stat. Ann. § 1102(a). As noted earlier, Comment 1 to that section observes that the Code promotes flexibility in providing "machinery for expansion of commercial practices." Following this guidance, we look to the realities of the arrangement between the parties.

In the distribution agreement, Unisys agreed to engage in the business of selling identified document systems during the two-year term of the contract and to buy from Advent on stated terms the specified products necessary to engage in that venture. The detailed nature of the document, including as it does, such provisions as those for notice of breach, opportunity for cure, and termination leaves no doubt that the parties intended to create a contract.

The parties were obviously aware that they were entering a new, speculative market and some uncertainty was inevitable in the amount of sales Unisys could make and the orders it would place with Advent.

Consequently, quantity was not stated in absolute terms. In effect, the parties arrived at a non-exclusive requirements contract, a commercially useful device. We do not consider that in the circumstances here the arrangement raises the statute of frauds bar.

The Code recognizes exclusive requirements contracts in section 2–306, and imposes on the parties to such agreements a duty of good faith. For present purposes, the salient factor is that exclusive requirements contracts satisfy the quantity requirements of the statute of frauds, albeit no specific amount is stated. . . .

The reasons for excepting exclusive requirements contracts from the strictures of the statute of frauds are strong. The purchasing party, perhaps unable to anticipate its precise needs, nevertheless wishes to have assurances of supply and fixed price. The seller, on the other hand, finds an advantage in having a steady customer. Such arrangements have commercial value. To deny a enforceability through a rigid reading of the quantity term in the statute of frauds would run contrary to the basic thrust of the Code—to conform the law to business reality and practices.

By holding that exclusive requirements contracts comply with the statute of frauds, courts have decided that indefiniteness in the quantity term is acceptable. If the agreement here does not satisfy the statute of frauds because of indefiniteness of a quantity term, then neither does an exclusive requirements contract. We find no reason in logic or policy to differentiate in the statute of frauds construction between the contract here and an exclusive requirements arrangement.

The same reasons that led courts to dispense with a specific and certain quantity term in the exclusive requirements context apply equally when a continuing relationship is non-exclusive. The same regulating factor—good faith performance by the parties—applies and prevents the contracts from being illusory. The writings here demonstrate that the parties did not articulate a series of distinct, unrelated, simple buy and sell arrangements, . . . but contemplated what resembles in some respects a joint venture or a distributorship.

A construction of the statute of frauds which does not recognize the quite substantial difference between a simple buy and sell agreement and what occurred here is unduly restrictive. Section 2–306 in recognizing exclusive requirements and output contracts does not purport to treat them as the only permissible types of open quantity agreements. We do not read section 2–306 as an exclusionary measure, but rather as one capable of enlargement so as to serve the purposes of the Code.

* * *

In sum, we hold that the writings here satisfy the statute of frauds.

IV.
ENFORCEABILITY

Having concluded that the statute of frauds is not a bar, we now confront the issue of enforceability.

Section 2–204 provides that a contract does not fail for indefiniteness even though one or more terms have been left open if the parties intended to make a contract and there is a reasonably certain basis for giving an appropriate remedy. 13 Pa. Cons. Stat. Ann. § 2204(c) (Purdon 1984). As Professor Murray has explained:

> Rather than focusing upon what parties failed to say, the Code and RESTATEMENT 2d focus upon the overriding question of whether the parties manifestly intended to make a binding arrangement. If that manifestation is present, the only remaining concern is whether the terms are definite enough to permit courts to afford an appropriate remedy. The second requirement assists courts to determine the degree of permissible indefiniteness.

J. Murray, Murray On Contracts § 38, at 85 (3d ed. 1990).

Unlike the statute of frauds issue discussed earlier, the definiteness required to provide a remedy rests on a very solid foundation of practicality. A remedy may not be based on speculation and an award cannot be made if there is no basis for determining if a breach has occurred.

Unisys argues that since there are specific non-exclusive stipulations in the agreement, they negate the implication found in most exclusive requirements contracts that a "best efforts clause" is included. That may be so, but that does not nullify the obligation of the parties to deal in good faith.

Section 1–203 of the Code provides that contracts require a "good faith performance." This requires the parties to observe "reasonable commercial standards of fair dealing in the trade."

The Pennsylvania Superior Court has concluded that in the absence of any express language, the law will imply an agreement by the parties to do those things that "according to reason and justice they should do in order to carry out the purposes for which the contract was made and to refrain from doing anything that would destroy or injure the other party's right to receive the fruits of the contract." Slater v. Pearle Vision Center, Inc., 376 Pa.Super. 580, 546 A.2d 676, 679 (1988). See Restatement (Second) of Contracts § 205 (1979). ....

The terms of the agreement between Unisys and Advent lend themselves to imply a good faith obligation on the parties of at least some minimal effort: "A fundamental assumption of both parties is that throughout the term of this agreement, Unisys will employ resources in performing marketing efforts involving Advent Products and will develop the technical capability to be thoroughly familiar with these products."

On remand, Advent may be able to show that it was inconsistent with good faith for a party that has committed itself to engage in particular business for a specified period of time to cease devoting any resources to that venture prior to the end of the stated period. ... We leave open the possibility that the performance of the parties following signing of the documents and perhaps pre-contractual expectations will provide evidence to satisfy the requirements of section 2–204. See §§ 2–208, 1–205 (course of performance, usage of trade).

On the other hand, it may be that the reason Unisys decided to devote no resources to the project of selling document systems is relevant to whether the standard of fair dealing in the trade was breached. Simply because no resources were devoted, does not mean in and of itself that there was a breach of the covenant of good faith. See, e.g., Angelica Uniform Group, Inc. v. Ponderosa Systems, Inc., 636 F.2d 232, 232 (8th Cir.1980); R.A. Weaver & Assoc., Inc. v. Asphalt Construction, Inc., 587 F.2d 1315, 1321–22 (D.C.Cir.1978); Southwest Natural Gas Co. v. Oklahoma Portland Cement Co, 102 F.2d 630, 632–33 (10th Cir.1939); 1 J. White & R. Summers, Uniform Commercial Code § 3–8, at 169 (3d ed. 1988).

Whether Advent can establish the definiteness required to sustain a remedy is a serious question. The record before us consists of evidence submitted on the basis of the pretrial ruling denying application of the U.C.C. Our contrary holding will require the parties to reassess the proofs necessary to meet the Code. We are in no position to anticipate the evidence that may appear in further proceedings and, thus, at this juncture cannot rule whether the agreement between Unisys and Advent is enforceable.

V.
DAMAGES *
* * *

The judgment in favor of the defendant on the tortious interference claim will be affirmed. The judgment in favor of the plaintiff on the breach of contract claim will be reversed and the case will be remanded for further proceedings.

Notes

(1) Uniform Commercial Code: Which Version? For pedagogical purposes, we refer in this course to the Uniform Commercial Code in the latest version promulgated by its sponsors, the Uniform State Laws Conference and the American Law Institute. Neither organization is a legislature empowered to create positive law. The Commercial Code takes effect only when enacted as a state or federal statute. In that process, legislatures may, and sometimes do modify the text in a non-uniform way. A practicing lawyer or judge, applying the Code, must use a version duly enacted into law and in force when the disputed transaction occurred. In *Advent Systems,* note that the courts cited and applied the Pennsylvania version of the Code. Throughout the course, you will see citations to state-enacted versions of the Code.

---

* [This part of the court's opinion is reserved for Chapter 3, Section 2. Eds.]

When variations in the state-enacted versions of the Code exist, it may be necessary to identify which state's version governs the issue arising in a dispute. The Commercial Code includes a choice of law provision. UCC 1–105.

(2) **Domestic Law: Which Nation's.** The seller in *Advent Systems,* a United Kingdom company, contracted with a United States company, whose headquarters is in Pennsylvania. The courts applied Pennsylvania law to the contract dispute.[23] The probable explanation is that the contract had a specific choice of law clause to that effect. In bargaining for contracts, how important are the terms of a choice-of-law clause likely to be to the representatives of the parties? Would a party be likely to use much of its bargaining leverage, e.g., give up something of economic value, to prevail on this clause?

(3) **Computer Systems as "Goods."** Is the rationale of the Court of Appeals persuasive? What "substantial benefits" may result from applying the Code to computer software transactions? Who are the potential beneficiaries? Was the seller in *Advent Systems* a beneficiary?

Should the scope of a statute's coverage be decided on the basis of "policy arguments" weighed by courts?

The Commercial Code was drafted and enacted before advances in physics and engineering produced the marvels of data processing by computer. In all probability, no draft of Article 2 was ever done on a word processor. Would the standards of Article 2 be likely to fit a "product" like computer software with its unique combination of intellectual property, design and performance services, and relatively inexpensive tangible components?

Commonly, owners of software copyright the program and "license" others to use it; licensees may not sell or transfer the program, and may not decompile or reverse engineer it or modify it without permission of the owner. To this extent, the transaction does not fit the "passing of title" element in the UCC 2–106(1) definition of "sale."

In its August 1991 authorization of a drafting committee to revise Article 2, the Uniform State Laws Conference instructed the committee to address the possible needs for special treatment of computer systems transactions.

(4) **Contract Formation; Statute of Frauds.** These materials examine only a few problems of contract formation. Article 2 of the Commercial Code has a number of provisions on this topic, primarily UCC 2–203 through 2–207, which are usually studied in a course on Contracts.

The Commercial Code continues the requirement, first established in England in 1677, that contracts for sales of goods, worth more than a

---

23. The Convention on Contracts for the International Sale of Goods did not take effect until after the events giving rise to this dispute. Even in 1991, the United Kingdom had not yet ratified the Convention.

low threshold of value, cannot be enforced unless evidenced by a writing. UCC 2–201(1). Provisions introduced into the Code's Statute of Frauds in subparagraphs (2) and (3) attenuate or eliminate the traditional requirement of a writing signed by the party to be charged.

Buyer's litigation strategy in *Advent Systems* was successful in persuading the court that the transaction was governed by Article 2, but unsuccessful in arguing that the documentation failed to meet the quantity-shown-in-the-writing requirement of UCC 2–201. Note how the court used another provision of the Code, 2–306, as its basis for construing 2–201.

If the court had held the transaction to be outside of Article 2, it would not follow that the transaction was free of a possible statute of frauds defense. The Code has another provision which requires a writing to indicate that a contract for the sale of personal property (other than goods) has been made. UCC 1–206. Would this provision have been useful to the buyer? [24]

The statute of frauds for sales of goods may be eliminated from the Commercial Code. The Permanent Editorial Board Article 2 Study Group "strongly recommends" consideration of repeal of UCC 2–201 in the ongoing revision of that article. Preliminary Report, p. 52 (1990).

(5) Professional Responsibility. Assuming that the purpose of a statute of frauds is, as its name indicates, to bar fraudulent claims that contracts exist, may a professionally responsible lawyer assert the statute of frauds as an affirmative defense on behalf of a client who does not deny the existence of the alleged agreement? See ABA Model Rules of Professional Conduct 3.1, 4.1; ABA Code of Professional Conduct EC 7–1 to 7–9, DR 7–101(B), 7–102(A)(2) and (B).

Goods and Real Property. The line between real property and goods is necessarily somewhat artificial. Movability, the essential characteristic of things defined to be goods, is not uncharacteristic of land. Rocks and soil can be moved; top soil, gravel and "fill" are regularly bought and sold. The Code brings into Article 2 some things that are, by the terms of a contract, to be severed by the seller, including specifically minerals, growing crops, and timber. UCC 2–107(1). See, e.g., Manchester Pipeline Corp. v. Peoples Natural Gas Co., 862 F.2d 1439 (10th Cir.1988).

The Code is also helpful in characterizing transactions that go the other way, goods that are, by terms of a contract, to be affixed to realty. So long as the things are movable at the time of identification to a contract for sale, they are "goods" under UCC 2–105(1). The time of

---

24. The traditional statute of frauds contains a provision applicable to contracts not to be performed within one year. This provision is not limited to contracts concerning transactions in property. Would this provision have been useful to the buyer in *Advent Systems*?

"identification" is set forth in UCC 2–501(1). Under this provision, a thing to be affixed to real estate is almost certain to be identified to the goods contract while still movable. The two Pennsylvania cases relied upon by the court in concluding that Article 2 applied in *Advent Systems* arose out of transactions of this kind. Duffee v. Judson, 251 Pa.Super. 406, 380 A.2d 843 (1977) (sale of mobile home to be installed on buyer's foundation); Lobianco v. Property Protection, Inc., 292 Pa.Super. 346, 437 A.2d 417 (1981) (sale and installation of burglar alarm system). See also Valley Farmers' Elevator v. Lindsay Brothers Co., 398 N.W.2d 553 (Minn.1987).

Contracts may involve transfer of both real estate and goods for a single price, the analogue of transactions in goods and services. Consider, for example, the sale of a new house in which the builder-developer has installed a stove, a refrigerator, other appliances and fixtures. Real estate sales are governed by common law.[25] Should Article 2 apply to any part of the contract?

Query: Suppose the owner of a business, such as a jewelry store, contracts to sell all of the assets of the business, including the inventory, the display cases, the accounts receivable, the trade name under which the store has operated and other "goodwill," and the balance of a lease on the building. Is the contract governed by Article 2?

(2) GENERAL LEGAL PRINCIPLES AND THE CODE

Introduction. One system for organizing the distribution of goods is to require economic units to produce and distribute in accordance with a state economic plan. Under such a system there are rules dealing with the sale of goods but their character is profoundly influenced by the underlying economic system. By the same token, in a market economy the law of sales is shaped by the premise that distribution is organized by myriads of private contracts. A seller's obligation to supply or deliver goods and a buyer's obligation to accept and pay arise only because of an agreement, and depend on its legal effect. Sales law, consequently, is in large measure a specialized branch of contract law, although problems often have a "property" dimension because of the parties' concern for control over the goods to which the agreement relates.

Sales Codifications and Contract Law. The Uniform Sales Act for the most part did not restate the basic "contract" rules. Section 41 laid down the general although self-evident rule: "It is the duty of the seller to deliver the goods, and of the buyer to accept and pay for them, *in accordance with the terms of the contract* to sell or sale." In addition Section 73 incorporated the whole body of basic law. Thus, under the Uniform Sales Act, sales transactions were governed by the state's basic

---

25. The Commissioners on Uniform State Laws promulgated a Uniform Land Transactions Act in 1977. No state has adopted this act.

law of contracts, including the rules governing offer and acceptance, consideration, assignment, and the like.

The Code's Article 2 on Sales starts from the same contractual premise as the Uniform Sales Act. Section 2–301 provides: "The obligation of the seller is to transfer and deliver and that of the buyer is to accept and pay in accordance with the contract." The Code, however, dips much more deeply into contract law than did the Uniform Sales Act. The Code states rules for offer and acceptance (2–206, 2–207), consideration (2–205), modification (2–209), delegation and assignment (2–210); in some respects these provisions deviate from traditional contract rules.

The Code and the General Body of Law. Does the Uniform Commercial Code set forth all of the rules for transactions that fall within its scope? One answer is provided in Article 1 by a provision that is applicable throughout the Code.

Section 1–103 Supplementary General Principles of Law Applicable

Unless displaced by the particular provisions of this Act, the principles of law and equity, including the law merchant and the law relative to capacity to contract, principal and agent, estoppel, fraud, misrepresentation, duress, coercion, mistake, bankruptcy, or other validating or invalidating cause shall supplement its provisions.

Comment 3 to this section emphasizes that the listing of particular fields of law "is merely illustrative" of the total body of "law and equity."

One notes that this underlying body of law is available only to the extent that it has not been "displaced by the particular provisions" of the Code. The Code is long and complex. Do its provisions so thoroughly occupy the field that there will be little occasion to look beyond? The answer to this question is shaped by the interplay of factors such as these: (1) The extent to which the Code, in addition to length, has depth and breadth; (2) The variety and complexity of the world, its people, and their problems; (3) The richness of the general body of law. We can begin to evaluate these factors only as we get deeper into the course; the answers will not be the same for all parts of the Code. At this stage one can offer only a general, Polonius-like precept: As one digs into the Code, be on guard lest it narrow one's legal horizons: there is a wide world beyond.

Course of Dealing and Usage of Trade. Another provision in Article 1, applicable throughout the Code, is Section 1–205, which gives effect to the "course of dealing between the parties" and to "usage of trade." The significance of these provisions can best be appreciated in their application to specific problems. Lawyers, it seems, have not yet made full use of these pervasive rules; one reason may be hesitation about ways to solve the evidentiary problems inherent in proof of "usage of trade." It seems likely that this is a frontier of the law that awaits further development.

"Good Faith." Another provision that is applicable throughout the Code is Section 1–203: "Every contract or duty within this Act imposes an obligation of good faith in its performance or enforcement."

We already met the requirement of "good faith" in *Advent Systems,* supra, and we shall see it throughout the materials. In some settings, "good faith" is an integral part of specific rules on the special status of good faith purchasers. The general requirement of "good faith" in Article 1 is much broader and deeper; UCC 1–203 imposes an affirmative obligation of "good faith" for each step of the "performance or enforcement" of every "contract or duty" that falls within the broad reach of the Code.

The pervasive character of this requirement makes it important to understand the nature of the "obligation of good faith." Article 1(1–201(19)) restricts "good faith" to "honesty in fact in the conduct or transaction concerned." Article 2, however, contains a more elastic definition: Section 2–103(1)(b) provides: " 'Good faith' in the case of a merchant means honesty in fact and the observance of reasonable commercial standard of fair dealing in the trade."

The statement that merchants must observe "*reasonable* commercial standards of *fair dealing* in the trade" reaches significantly beyond the requirement of Section 1–205(3) that usages of trade in the vocation or trade in which the parties are engaged give "particular meaning to and supplement or qualify terms of an agreement." In defining "usage of trade," 1–205(2) injects no normative requirement of reasonableness: "A usage of trade is any practice or method of dealing having such regularity of observance in a place, vocation or trade as to justify an expectation that it will be observed with respect to the transaction in question." Literally, this language would incorporate practices of chicane that regularly are observed in a thieves' market. On the other hand, the Comment states that Section 1–205(2) provides for full recognition "for new usages and usages currently observed by the great majority of *decent* dealers, even though dissidents *ready to cut corners* do not agree." The Comment, with a little effort, can be squared with the statutory language that usage of trade gives "particular meaning" to an agreement; in most settings a contracting party will assume that the other party is one of the "great majority of decent dealers" and not one of the few "dissidents ready to cut corners."

It is evident that the "good faith" requirement is susceptible of wide possibilities of interpretation. And the Comments, usually so generous, at this point are strangely silent.

Unconscionability. Students of the law of contracts probably have met the striking provision of UCC 2–302 that authorizes courts to deny enforcement to "unconscionable" agreements. The foregoing provisions of Article 1 (1–103, 1–203) are applicable throughout the Code; UCC 2–302 is literally applicable only within the scope of Article 2 on

Sales. However, there is reason to suppose that this broad and appealing idea will not be confined within narrow limits; we shall meet this concept in various settings.

The most difficult (and intriguing) problem is the lack of any definition in the Code of the key concept of "unconscionability." Comment 1 to UCC 2–302 seeks to meet this gap. At one point the Comment refers to the "basic test" of whether the clause is "onesided"; at another the Comment states that "the principle is one of the prevention of oppression and unfair surprise (cf. Campbell Soup Co. v. Wentz, 172 F.2d 80, 3d Cir.1948), and not of disturbance of allocation of risks because of superior bargaining power." (Can these two comments be reconciled?) The Comment in addition states that "the underlying basis of the section is illustrated by the results in cases such as the following. . . ." The Comment then summarizes the holdings of ten cases. Five of these involved narrow construction of clauses disclaiming implied warranties of quality; the Code deals with this problem specifically in Section 2–316. The remaining five cases limited the impact of clauses restricting remedies for breach, a problem covered in Section 2–719. Cf. 2–718 (agreements for unreasonably large liquidated damage are void as a penalty). Thus, even if these Comments are influential in construing the Code, the possible scope of Section 2–302, in areas not duplicated by Sections 2–316, 2–718 and 2–719, is left for case-law development. Experience under similarly broad provisions of civil law codes may suggest possible lines of development. See Schlesinger, Comparative Law 232–3, 495 et seq. (3d ed.1970); Schlesinger, The Uniform Commercial Code in the Light of Comparative Law, 1 Inter–Am.L.Rev. 11 (1959). Recent vigorous applications of 2–302's ban on "unconscionable" clauses in the setting of disclaimers of warranties will be examined in Chapter 3, Section 3.

(3) INTERPRETATION OF THE CODE

This course requires examination and interpretation of the texts of state statutory law, primarily the Uniform Commercial Code. Our objective is to find the meaning of the text as applied to factual circumstances found in reported decisions or posed in problem situations, many of which are set out in these materials. Given the central importance of this task, it is useful at the outset to consider how to go about it.

(1) Two Polar Approaches to Statutory Interpretation. Four hundred years ago, during the reign of Elizabeth I, one of the greatest common-law judges, Lord Coke, proposed a maxim for statutory interpretation: Identify the "mischief . . . for which the common law did not provide [a remedy]," and then identify precisely the "remedy the Parliament hath resolved."[26] Lord Coke's maxim posits that statutes are corrective measures, enacted from time to time to overcome particu-

---

26. Heydon's Case, 3 Co. Rep. 7a, 7b, 76 Eng.Rep. 637, 638 (1584).

lar deficiencies in the common law. On this view, each statute is only a patch on the broad cloth of common law and its meaning can be ascertained by examining the nature of the hole the legislature sought to mend.

When the statute to be construed is a large, integrated work, such as a code, a quite different approach is to seek the meaning of its various provisions in light of the overarching purposes and policies that animate the whole work. A piecemeal mischief-correction reading would not take adequate account of the greater set of principles envisioned by the legislature. Gaps in the text of a code can be filled by interpolating provisions that serve the code's general policies.

(2) Pre–UCC Commercial Law Codifications. Neither approach fits the first codification of commercial law, a century ago, in the United Kingdom (the Bills of Exchange Act and the Sale of Goods Act). The avowed purpose of the principal drafter, Mackensie Chalmers, was to celebrate the perfection of common law by writing it down for all to see more clearly. To convince Parliament to accept his proposals, Chalmers assured the legislators that the codifications made no change in the law.

Nor does Coke's maxim fit the reason for transplanting Chalmers' codes to the United States. Major impetus for commercial law codification here was the desire to create uniformity among the laws of the states. With the same statutory text enacted in all states, and with courts admonished to construe the text to achieve uniformity, parties to commercial transactions did not need to be much concerned that the law might change as their dealings crossed state boundaries.[27]

On this view of the statutes' purpose, substantive law reform, small-scale or large-scale, was not important.[28] Codifications of this kind would serve an objective that places value on the law being certain and predictable, an objective that some have thought to be especially appropriate in the field of commercial law.[29]

(3) Approaching Article 2 of the Uniform Commercial Code. Drafters of the Commercial Code declared that it is "a general act intended as a unified coverage of its subject matter," UCC 1–104, and the comment describes it as "carefully integrated" to cover "an entire 'field' of law." The Code's first substantive provision states: "This Act shall be liberally construed and applied to promote its underlying purposes and policies." UCC 1–102(1). Thus, Coke's maxim would not be a useful way to approach the Commercial Code in general, nor

---

27. The Uniform Sales Act was a disappointment in the quest for uniformity. At its peak of adoptions, only 23 of 53 possible jurisdictions had enacted it.

28. This gave rise to an interesting question of the continued vitality of common-law precedents as authoritative sources of interpretation of the statutory texts.

29. The Chalmers codes resemble the 20th-century restatements of the law promulgated by the American Law Institute. Restatements, however, are not positive law enacted by legislatures and binding as authorities that must be implemented by courts.

Article 2 in particular. But how did the Code's purposes and policies for Article 2 differ from those of the pre-UCC codifications?[30] Echoes of Chalmers' limited objective of setting down the law appear in the Code's purpose to simplify and clarify the law,[31] but the Code's drafters, notably Karl Llewellyn, put great emphasis on the need to "modernize" commercial law.[32] UCC 1–102(2)(a).

Modernization of sales law meant at least two changes. First, the basic conceptual framework of the Sales Act was jettisoned. Under the Sales Act, a series of difficult and diverse issues turned on a single legal abstraction: the location of the "property" or ownership of the goods. This idea was totally scrapped, UCC 2–401, in favor of the view that independent normative standards be stated for issues "irrespective of title."[33]

Second, the Code expressly adopted a policy and purpose to free the marketplace to develop its own normative standards: "to permit the continued expansion of commercial practices through custom, usage and agreement of the parties." UCC 1–102(2)(b); see also UCC 1–102(3). The stated policy appears to favor considerable private autonomy in the marketplace, in effect conferring normative power on "the actual."

One commentator found that the drafters of Article 2 had followed the view that moral or economic judgments about the good society should not be made by legislative decisions; rather these matters

---

30. Other articles of the Commercial Code are very different from Article 2 in approach and relationships with pre-UCC law. For example, Article 9 fundamentally recast the law of secured transactions while Article 3 (Negotiable Instruments) hewed very close to prior law.

31. Uniformity of law among the states continues to be a stated objective, evident in both the title of the Code and as one of its stated purposes. UCC 1–102(c). In this respect, the Code has succeeded well beyond its predecessors.

32. The 1906 Sales Act particularly was condemned as an anachronism:

In nineteenth-century commerce, the prototypical sales transaction was the face-to-face sale in which the buyer paid cash and took her goods home. [The picture of a commercial transaction in the Sales Act ... is typified "by the horseman who stops at the saddler's door to buy a new saddle."] ... In the modern world of sales, ... most commercial sellers and buyers ... contract for a sale in the future; their agreement is usually on the buyer's or seller's printed form; their sale is on credit; and their relationship has just begun. In addition, there may be one or more middlemen between the seller-manufacturer and the buyer, who may be buying for resale or use. Both the commercial structure of a sale and the needs of the parties to it will vary markedly depending on whether it is a sale to a business buyer for resale or use, or to a consumer.

By the late 1930s, Llewellyn was not alone in seeing problems of obsolescence in the Uniform Sales Act. Indeed, the merchants were the first to complain, followed by the academic community and the commercial bar.

Wiseman, The Limits of Vision: Karl Llewellyn and the Merchant Rules, 100 Harv.L.Rev. 465, 475–477 (1987).

33. The principal drafter of the Sales Act, Samuel Williston, urged rejection of Article 2 because of its elimination of the touchstone of title. Williston, The Law of Sales in the Proposed Uniform Commercial Code, 63 Harv.L.Rev. 561 (1950).

The lack of conceptual unity in Article 2 led a French commentator, Denis Tallon, to say the Code is not a *code* at all, but only "a collection of practical solutions" to particular problems. See Diamond, Codification of the Law of Contracts, 31 Modern L. Rev. 361, 379 (1968).

should be delegated to courts. He concluded that this view of a limited legislative function appeared to be premised on what he termed a triad of dubious assumptions:

> [1] that self-evident ideal resolutions of situational problems exist [and need not be declared by the legislature], [2] that they can be discovered by careful scrutiny of actual situations [in case-by-case litigation], and [3] that once articulated they will be widely accepted.

Danzig, A Comment on the Jurisprudence of the Uniform Commercial Code, 27 Stan.L.Rev. 621, 635 (1975).

Another commentator took a different view. He posited that Article 2 requires courts to give particular meaning to very broad legislative norms, that the Code permits and requires courts to support and regulate the marketplace, and concluded that the drafters had done their work well:

> One critic characterizes Article 2 as a direction to discover the law—the standards and morality of commercial law—in the practices of the market place. But what if those practices—at least as pursued by the majority of traders in a given industry—are unfair, inequitable or unjust? ... The overriding standards of commercial reasonableness, honesty-in-fact, conscionability and, yes, decency, are the ultimate principles which may not be overcome in any application of Article 2. ... In this effort, Article 2 not only enables but directs courts to impose their understanding of commercial morality on the market place.

Murray, The Article 2 Prism: The Underlying Philosophy of Article 2 of the Uniform Commercial Code, 21 Washburn L.J. 1, 19–20 (1981).[34]

(4) The Comments to the Code: Uses and Hazards. A hazard for the lazy mind, and a help for the responsible lawyer, are the Comments of the draftsmen which follow each section of the Code.

---

34. Another commentator offered a more sympathetic view of Llewellyn's personal vision:

> Llewellyn ... was not entirely uncritical in his acceptance of mercantile reality. His vision also encompassed a normative belief that the law should encourage the better practices and control the worst abuses of the market. ... [H]e recognized the potential unfairness of applying merchant standards to individuals who lacked knowledge of these standards and experience with them. ...
>
> Llwellyn's vision of the possibility of Grand Style judging in sales litigation was ... based on his assessment of the ... institutional organization of those groups affected by the Sales Act. He frequently asserted that sales law was "nonpolitical." Llwewllyn's idiosyncratic use of the term meant that sales law was noncontroversial in the sense that no organized constituency of those affected would see itself as having a vested interest in outcomes tilted in a particular direction. An organized consumer movement did not yet exist. Merchants were both sellers and buyers; and for that reason a consensus existed among the "better' merchants that fair and balanced rules as between merchant sellers and buyers were desirable.

Wiseman, The Limits of Vision: Karl Llewellyn and the Merchant Rules, 100 Harv.L.Rev. 465, 492, 540 (1987).

Professor Wiseman concluded, however, that a large part of Llewellyn's personal vision, encapsulated in his proposals for a considerable number of "merchant rules," was lost as the these proposals were dropped from the Code or their content was diluted in the lengthy drafting process.

Some of the troublesome problems about their place in the Code system need to be faced at the outset.

The most obvious point about the Comments is the one which, curiously enough, is most often overlooked: The text to the Code was enacted by the legislature; the Comments were not. One is tempted to ignore this point because the Comments, written in an explanatory and non-statutory style, are easier to read. *Facilis est descensus Averno.*

But the tempter will whisper: The drafters wrote these Comments, didn't they? If they say what the Code does, that's bound to be right, isn't it? Why bother then with this prickly statutory language? (You may find it easier to resist these temptations if you put yourself, in your mind's eye, in the role of a judge to whom this argument has been made and then imagine your comments to that hapless attorney.)

The problem of the force of the Comments is sufficiently important to justify some background. Versions of the Code prior to 1957 included a significant provision about the Comments in the general provisions of Article 1, which is applicable to the Code as a whole. Section 1–102, *Purposes; Rules of Construction,* stated in subsection (3):

> (f) The Comments of the National Conference of Commissioners on Uniform State Laws and the American Law Institute may be consulted in the construction and application of this Act but if text and comment conflict, text controls.

In 1956 the sponsoring organizations released a document entitled "1956 Recommendations of the Editorial Board for the Uniform Commercial Code," recommending wide-spread revisions which, for the most part, are reflected in the current version of the Code. These "1956 Recommendations" called for the deletion of the above-quoted provision of Section 1–102(3)(f), and did not substitute any new provision on the status of the Comments. The question immediately arises: Does this deletion imply the rejection of the idea behind the deleted provision so that reference to the Comments has become illegitimate?

An answer appears in the Comments to the 1956 Recommendations. The reasons for this and other changes were only briefly stated; the explanation for this change was as follows: "paragraph (3)(f) was deleted because the old comments were clearly out of date and it was not known when new ones could be prepared."[35]

Revised comments accompanied the 1957 and subsequent versions of the Code, but without any statutory provision referring to them. Embarrassing questions arise if one subjects the Comments to the standards often imposed for recourse to legislative history. In some states the revised Comments had not yet been drafted at the time of the Code's adoption. In others it is highly doubtful that the Comments

---

35. 1956 Recommendations, page 3. Perhaps we face here an engineering problem: How high can the comments lift themselves by their own bootstraps? Are the editors violating their own principles in quoting this comment? See Braucher, The Legislative History of the Uniform Commercial Code, 58 Colum.L.Rev. 798, 808–809 (1958).

were laid before the legislators in the form of a committee report explaining the legislation which the legislators were asked to adopt.

It would be very wrong, however, to conclude that the Comments are without value to lawyers and to courts. Professor Williston's treatise on Sales has been given heavy weight by courts in construing the Uniform Sales Act on the ground that it reflected the intent of the draftsman, although it was written subsequent to the drafting of the Act; courts have repeatedly quoted the Comments in construing the Code. We shall read many opinions in which the Comments are given substantial weight in the reasoning of the courts.

Surely the Comments may be given at least as much weight as an able article or treatise construing the Code. It is equally clear that the Comments do not approach the weight of legislation; if the statutory provisions adopted by the legislature contradict or fail to support the Comments, the Comments must be rejected.

The point is significant, for we shall see instances, easily understood in the light of the Comments' bulk and the many successive revisions of the Code, where the Comments contradict the statute. More frequent are instances of enthusiastic discussion of significant problems on which the statute is silent.

A thorough job construing the Code calls for using the Comments to make sure one has found the pertinent language of the statute, as a double-check on a tentative construction, and as a secondary aid where the language of the statute is ambiguous. However, the editors warn students that they sternly reject any reference to Comments until *after* the pertinent statutory language has been carefully examined in the light of the statutory definitions and the statutory structure.

(5) Definitions. The Code has a large number of definitions and contains ingenious devices to aid in finding them. A fast and easy way to find many of these definitions is by the list of "Definitional Cross References" at the end of the Comments. However, a careful lawyer will not rely on the completeness of these references in the Comments. For a thorough job, one will check Article 1, which contains important provisions applicable to the Code as a whole; Section 1–201 contains the definitions of forty-six terms used throughout the Code. In addition, one will check the definitions specially applicable to Article 2; Section 2–103 provides a unique and helpful device: an "index of definitions" inserted in the text of the statute.

(C) SCOPE AND APPROACH OF THE CONVENTION ON CONTRACTS FOR THE INTERNATIONAL SALE OF GOODS

(1) SCOPE

The Convention on Contracts for the International Sale of Goods (CISG) "applies to contracts of sale of goods between parties whose places of business are in different States ... when the States are Contracting States," but does not apply to sales of goods "bought for personal, family or household use." CISG 1(a)[36] and 2(a).[37]

A nation becomes a Contracting State by ratification, acceptance, approval or accession. (We must adapt to the international usage of "state" to mean nation.) The nuances of these terms are not important for our purposes. The United States became a Contracting State when the Senate gave its advice and consent to the President's signing of the Convention. As of 1991, 32 nations are Contracting States.

Place of Business. Some parties to international sales contracts may have only one place of business, but many have more than one. When a party to a contract has more than one place of business, CISG refers to the place "which has the closest relationship to the contract and its performance." CISG 10(a).[38]

Goods, Seller and Buyer. CISG offers no definition of "goods." Indeed, the Convention defines none of the terms used in it. Although ships, vessels, hovercraft or aircraft are probably "goods," the Convention excludes sales of them from its scope. CISG 2(e). While investment securities, negotiable instruments and money are unlikely to be deemed "goods," sales of these are also expressly excluded by CISG 2(d).

The Convention defines neither "seller" nor "buyer," but sales by auction, on execution or otherwise by authority of law are expressly excluded from its scope. CISG 2(b) and (c).

Goods and Services. Unlike the Commercial Code, the Convention expressly recognizes contracts for mixed goods and services. CISG provides that it does not apply if "the preponderant part of the obligations of the party who furnishes the goods consists in the supply of labour and other services." CISG 3(2). Like the Commercial Code, CISG includes within its scope contracts for the supply of goods to be manufactured or produced, with a proviso that excludes any contract in which the buyer supplies a substantial part of the materials necessary for such manufacture or production. CISG 3(1).

Problem 1. Assume that the contract in *Advent Systems,* between United Kingdom and United States companies, lacked a choice-of-law clause. Assume further (contrary to the facts) that both the United States and the United Kingdom had ratified CISG before the transaction occurred. Would a United States or a United Kingdom court properly conclude that the transaction was governed by CISG?

36. The Convention may apply to contracts when only one party's place of business is in a Contracting State if the choice of law rules of private international law lead to the application of the law of a Contracting State. CISG 1(b). Nations are permitted to ratify the Convention without agreeing to be bound by Article 1(b), and the United States has done so.

37. Contracts for consumer goods may be governed by the Convention if the seller neither knew nor ought to have known that they were bought for that purpose.

38. If a party has no place of business, applicability is determined by the party's "habitual residence." CISG 10(b).

Problem 2. Assume that the contract in *Advent Systems* was made in 1988, after the United States but not the United Kingdom had ratified CISG. Assume further that the parties inserted a clause in their agreement that the contract was to be governed by CISG. Would a United States or a United Kingdom court properly conclude that this clause should be given effect? The Convention does not deal with this question. What body of law is relevant?

Goods and Real Property. The Convention is silent on contracts for extraction or severance of property from real estate or for affixing property to real estate.

(2) GENERAL LEGAL PRINCIPLES AND THE CONVENTION

Introduction. The Convention on Contracts for the International Sale of Goods does not purport to legislate a regulatory system for the global marketplace. Its objective, stated in a Preamble, was to articulate a set of uniform rules which took into account the different social, economic and legal systems that exist among the nations of the world and thus to contribute to the removal of legal barriers in international trade. The Preamble added that "the development of international trade on the basis of equality and mutual benefit is an important element in promoting friendly relations among States." The diversity of domestic legal systems spanned different kinds of common-law, civil-law, and socialist systems. When the Convention was prepared, the world was sharply divided politically and economically between East and West and, in different ways, to a lesser degree, between North and South.[39]

The drafters faced the Herculean task of preparing legal rules understandable to individuals regardless of their legal heritages.[40] Beyond producing a comprehensible set of rules, the drafters had to produce a Convention acceptable politically to a sufficient number of nations to achieve the objective of uniformity.

No international effort to legislate on a subject of this breadth had ever succeeded before. The Convention thus represents a breakthrough

---

39. The Convention's Preamble also mentions "the broad objectives in the resolutions adopted by the sixth special session of the General Assembly of the United Nations on the establishment of a New International Economic Order." The Preamble does not reiterate those objectives. Inclusion of a reference to the New International Economic Order was done at the instance of representatives of certain developing nations who seek a legal regime that will stimulate economic growth in their countries. The Preamble was drafted at the end of the diplomatic conference after the substantive provisions of the Convention had been debated and approved. Does this affect the weight of the Preamble in interpreting the Convention? See J. Honnold, Uniform Law for International Sales § 475 (2d ed. 1991).

40. Among other things, this required the drafters to create legal language that avoided use of words and phrases that, while apparently simple in meaning, had taken on special and often complex meaning familiar to lawyers trained in a particular legal system, but frustratingly opaque to lawyers not grounded in that system. Particularly insidious are words and phrases that are used in several legal systems but with significant difference in meaning; the French refer to these as "false friends."

of enormous significance, not only within its own scope, but for the possible future development of private international law.

The Convention and the General Body of Law. Unlike the Commercial Code and its predecessors, the Convention does not rest on a base of an established body of international law. Like the Commercial Code, the Convention, while long and complex, does not purport to state legal rules that cover all issues that might arise in international sales transactions. How are questions not expressly addressed by the Convention to be answered?

The Convention declares that answers should be sought first in the penumbra of the Convention:

> Questions concerning matters governed by this Convention which are not expressly settled in it are to be settled in conformity with the general principles on which it is based.... (CISG 7(2)).

The Convention's approach to gap-filling reflects that established for civil law codes which were designed to displace an entire body of pre-existing law. Some representatives objected that, since these general principles had not been articulated, reference to them in the Convention injected a high degree of uncertainty as to its meaning. This objection was met with the argument that filling gaps by turning to the domestic law of some nation, the only alternative, was a worse solution that would produce even greater uncertainty and, further, undermine the effort to produce a body of uniform law.

Proponents of a "general principles" statement prevailed in the provision of CISG 7(2) quoted above, but the objectors prevailed in seeking a subordinate reference to some nation's domestic law if a needed general principle cannot be found. Article 7(2) continues:

> ... or, in the absence of such principles, in conformity with the law applicable by virtue of the rules of private international law.

The "rules of private international law" are the choice-of-law rules which exist apart from the Convention and which designate the domestic law that governs any particular contract dispute.

While only future litigation will reveal authoritatively how the two facets of CISG 7(2) will be applied, the views of respected commentators will be important to that outcome. One of us has outlined an approach to implementation of this provision. He first discusses three problem areas to illustrate how the Convention's "general principles" may be ascertained: reliance on representations of the other party, the duty to communicate information needed by the other party, and the obligation to take steps to avoid unnecessary hardship for the other party. He then propounds a general approach:

> This approach responds to the reference in Article 7(2) to the principles on which the Convention "is based" by requiring that general principles to deal with new situations be moored to premises that underlie specific provisions of the Convention. Thus, like the inductive approach employed in case law development, the first

step is the examination of instances regulated by specific provisions of the Convention. The second step is to choose between these two conclusions: (a) The Convention deliberately rejected the extension of these specific provisions; (b) The lack of a specific provision to govern the case at hand results from a failure to anticipate and resolve the issue. If the latter alternative applies, the third step is to consider whether the case governed by the specific provisions of the Convention and the case at hand are so analogous that a lawmaker would not have deliberately chosen discordant results for the group of similar situations. In this event, it seems appropriate to conclude that the general principle embracing these situations is authorized by Article 7(2).

See J. Honnold, Uniform Law for International Sales § 102 (2d ed. 1991).

"Good Faith" and "Fair Dealing." In the course of drafting the Convention, some delegates supported inclusion of a general rule obligating the parties to sales transactions to observe the principles of good faith and fair dealing. Although this principle exists in some common-law and civil-law countries,[41] the proposal was ultimately rejected. A different good faith concept was adopted in regard to interpretation of the Convention, which is discussed in (3) below.

The Convention and Party Autonomy. An important general principle of the Convention is the sweeping scope of its acceptance of the power of parties to sales contracts to derogate from or vary the effect of virtually every article and, indeed, to exclude the application of the Convention altogether. CISG 6.[42] This provision signals unmistakably that the drafters of the Convention did not intend to fashion a regulatory system restricting private behavior in the marketplace.

For the near future at least, lawyers who advise clients engaged in international sales face the challenging professional task of considering what advice they should give concerning utilization of the power recognized under CISG 6. If you were asked to advise a trading company, what factors would you deem important? How would you weigh them?

A related question arises for counsel advising clients engaged in international sales transactions that lie outside the scope of CISG 1(1).

---

41. E.g., the Uniform Commercial Code contains a general good faith provision regarding performance and enforcement of contracts, UCC 1–203, which imposes on merchant sellers and merchant buyers the duty to observe reasonable commercial standards of fair dealing in the trade. UCC 2–103(1)(b). The German Civil Code (§ 242) states: "The debtor is bound to effect performance according to the requirements of good faith, giving consideration to common usage."

42. The CISG 6 exception to party autonomy relates to a possible requirement, that may be added to the Convention by ratifying nations, that sales contracts must be concluded in or evidenced by a writing. Article 11 negates such a requirement, but that was so offensive to some nations that the Final Provisions permit a Contracting State to declare that CISG 11 does not apply where any party has its place of business in that State. CISG 96. Similar provision is made regarding modification of contracts. See CISG 29.

Suppose, for example, you were counsel of a United States company selling goods to a buyer in a nation that has not ratified the Convention. (Recall that the United States exercised the right under CISG 95 to exclude the application of CISG 1(1)(b).) Would you advise inserting a contract provision that elects the Convention as the parties' choice of law for some or all questions that may arise under the contract? If the other side presses strongly for choice of its own domestic law, would choosing the Convention be an attractive compromise?

Contract Interpretation. In furtherance of a system of party autonomy, the Convention includes a number of important provisions regarding the ascertainment of the meaning of contracts. Article 8 contains basic rules of contract interpretation that seek to give binding force to the parties' common intentions or expectations, CISG 8(1), but, where that cannot be found, to protect each party's reasonable understanding of the statements and conduct of the other. CISG 8(2).

For these purposes, a tribunal interpreting a sales contract is instructed to give due consideration "to the circumstances of the case including the negotiations, any practices which the parties have established between themselves, usages and any subsequent conduct of the parties." CISG 8(3). (The rules on trade usage are expanded in CISG 9.)

Contrast the provisions in CISG 8 with the common-law parol evidence rule and its statutory formulation in UCC 2–202. CISG 11 adds: "[A contract] may be proved by any means, including witnesses."

(3) INTERPRETATION OF THE CONVENTION

Introduction. Despite the remarkable drafting achievement of the sponsors of the Convention on Contracts for the International Sale of Goods, issues will inevitably arise as to the meaning of some of its provisions. Earlier we discussed the approach to interpretation of the Commercial Code, a difficult question even within the ordinary principles of statutory interpretation of a single nation. The Convention is not a body of positive law added to an existing corpus with established principles of statutory construction. In many respects, it is a *sui generis* legal document, to be interpreted in the first instance by the parties to sales contracts (and their lawyers) in shaping their own conduct and, if disputes require tribunals for resolution, to be interpreted by those tribunals. If those tribunals are courts, they will be the ordinary courts of the nations empowered to try contract cases. (In the United States, these may be either federal or state courts.) There are, for now, no international courts before whom private parties can try such cases.

Recognizing the daunting problems facing interpretation of the international Convention in national courts, the drafters included a provision on how the Convention should be interpreted. Article 7(1) provides:

> In the interpretation of this Convention, regard is to be had to its international character and to the need to promote uniformity in its application and the observance of good faith in international trade.

International Character of the Convention. The first point made by CISG 7(1) puts in positive form the principle that courts should not approach the Convention as if it were comparable to the domestic legislation of their own countries. Whatever the general approach of courts to interpretation of the statutes of their own legislatures, the Convention admonishes courts to take an independent approach to the Convention and its "international character."

> To read the words of the Convention with regard for their "international character" requires that they be projected against an international background. With time, a body of international experience will develop through international case law and scholarly writing. In the meantime, the only international setting for the Convention's words is its legislative history—its genetic background.

J. Honnold, Uniform Law for International Sales § 88 (2d ed. 1991).

The Need to Promote Uniformity. The Convention's second principle of interpretation stresses the obvious objective of seeking to have the Convention uniform not only in text, but in the gloss placed on the text by courts construing its words. Among other things, this instructs courts to give weight to prior decisions of other tribunals, whether in the same or different countries, so that differences in interpretation are minimized or avoided. This principle should not require courts to make mechanical repetitions of perceived errors, but rather to be sensitive and responsive to the Convention's objective of uniformity of interpretations wherever made.

The Need to Promote the Observance of Good Faith in International Trade. As previously mentioned, the drafters of the Convention rejected a broad good faith requirement addressed to the parties to international sales contracts, but in the process of so doing they accepted the principle that the need to promote good faith in international trade was appropriate for the limited purpose of interpreting the Convention. This can be illustrated by reference to CISG 19(2) and 21(2), which require a party to inform another who is known to be subject to a misapprehension. These articles, which deal with the process of contract formation, could be interpreted narrowly or liberally. Professor Honnold suggests that a liberal reading would promote the observance of good faith in international trade. J. Honnold, Uniform Law for International Sales §§ 94–95 (2d ed. 1991). Another commentator, Professor Schlectriem, states that the good faith principle could be usefully applied in the interpretation of numerous Convention provisions which use the term of reasonableness. P. Schlectriem, Uniform Sales Law—The UN Convention on Contracts for the International Sale of Goods 39 (1986).

Chapter 2

TITLE: SELLERS' RESPONSIBILITY AND BUYERS' RIGHTS

(A) DOMESTIC UNITED STATES LAW

Introduction. This chapter introduces the duality of property ("title") and contract in sales transactions. Under the Commercial Code, "a 'sale' consists in the passing of title from the seller to the buyer for a price." UCC 2–106(1).[1] For present purposes, the legal significance of having, or not having title to goods is largely a matter of excluding ownership claims of other persons to those goods. The person with title to goods is entitled to possess, use, or dispose of them.

Title to goods passes under contracts for sale. A "present sale" is a sale "which is accomplished by the making of the contract." Id. Title passes when the contract is made. A contract for sale may also be "a contract to sell goods at a future time." Id. When title passes in a contract to sell goods at a future time is largely within the control of the contracting parties. "Unless otherwise explicitly agreed, title passes to the buyer at the time and place at which the seller completes his performance with respect to the physical delivery of the goods... ." UCC 2–401(2).

In this chapter we consider first the meaning of "title" and "passing of title" and a seller's contractual responsibility to make title "pass" to the buyer. A seller who fails to meet this responsibility may be held accountable for damages in a warranty action by the buyer.

Buyers aggrieved by sellers' breach of the warranty of title may be entitled to protection other than recovery of damages from their sellers. They may be entitled to keep the goods even though their sellers lacked title. If the buyer is a "good faith purchaser" or a "buyer in the ordinary course of business," the buyer may be able to fend off a previous owner's claim to regain possession and control of the goods. After the materials on warranty of title, we will introduce the law of good faith purchase.

1. The Uniform Sales Act used the passing of title ("property") as the fulcrum for resolving a number of legal issues that may arise during the performance of sales contracts. The Commercial Code's rules on performance and remedies are not based on title passing. However, passing of title continues to be of primary importance to the parties to sales contracts because legal rights and duties not governed by the Code may turn upon the question of ownership. For example, tax obligations may fall upon the owner of property. In this chapter, we are concerned primarily with the role of title to resolve conflicting ownership claims to the goods.

(1) WARRANTY OF TITLE

Introduction. Buyers of goods ordinarily expect to obtain "good" or "clean" title to the goods they have purchased. Two types of cases may defeat that expectation: sales of stolen goods and sales of encumbered goods.[2]

Having bought and paid for goods, a buyer will be surprised and disappointed to learn that the seller did not own the goods sold and did not have authority to sell them on behalf of the true owner. If there was a thief in the seller's "chain of title," the rightful owner who finds the goods may demand their return from anyone whose claim to them derives from the thief.

Encumbrances on the title to goods (often called "liens") arise sometimes through the voluntary action of an owner, who creates or consents to the creation of an interest in the property. The principal example of this form of encumbrance is a "security interest" under UCC Article 9. Other times, an encumbrance arises by action of a third party, usually against the will of the owner. Thus, a judgment creditor may obtain a lien on property of the judgment debtor by the process of attachment or judgment execution. Alternatively, liens may arise by operation of law without a judgment. Examples are the liens that may be obtained by the Internal Revenue Service for unpaid federal taxes ("tax liens") or by repairers of goods for their services ("mechanics' liens").

A seller's responsibility to the buyer who is compelled to surrender goods to the rightful owner is stated in UCC 2–312(1)(a). A seller warrants that "the title conveyed shall be good, and its transfer rightful." The warranty against encumbrances is set forth in UCC 2–312(1)(b): "the goods shall be delivered free from any security interest or other lien or encumbrance of which the buyer at the time of contracting has no knowledge." Sellers' warranty can be excluded or modified "by specific language" in the agreement of sale or by certain "circumstances." UCC 2–312(2).

WRIGHT v. VICKARYOUS
Supreme Court of Alaska, 1980.
611 P.2d 20.

MATTHEWS, JUSTICE.

On January 8, 1977, Vickaryous bought forty-five head of cattle from Wright at an auction sale. His bid was $13,032.50. Unknown to Vickaryous at the time, the Farmer's Home Administration, the Northwest Livestock Production Credit Association, and the State of Alaska

---

2. For property subject to a patent or trademark or other form of intellectual property, a seller may sell the goods without conveying the right to use them without infringement of the rights of the owner of the intellectual property. Intellectual property law often separates the physical thing from the right to use it. Rights to use are commonly conveyed by license by the patent holder or owner of the intellectual property right. Sellers' warranty with respect to infringement of intellectual property rights is found in UCC 2–312(3). See also UCC 2–607(5)(b).

Revolving Loan Fund each held perfected and filed security interests on the cattle. However, they had consented to the auction sale of the cattle in conversations with Wright. Thus, under the terms of section 9–306(2) of the Uniform Commercial Code as enacted in Alaska, their security interests were released by the sale.

Shortly after the auction, and on the same day that it was held, Wright and Vickaryous modified the sale contract to provide that Vickaryous would pay $1,000.00 down with the balance of the purchase price to be paid on or before delivery, no later than January 14th. Vickaryous then was told by a third party that there were liens on the cattle. The next day, an employee of Wright tendered delivery of the cattle to Vickaryous. He told the employee that he would not accept them because of the liens. On Monday, January 10th, Vickaryous contacted an attorney and asked him to determine whether the cattle were encumbered; the attorney discovered the filed security interests and advised Vickaryous of their existence. Vickaryous then stopped payment on the $1,000.00 check he had given as a down payment.

On Tuesday, January 11th, Wright served Vickaryous with a notice of intent to resell the cows and hold Vickaryous responsible for any deficiency. An auction resale was conducted on January 15th at which $3,166.00 was received. The expenses of resale were $1,025.00.

Wright brought this action to recover the difference between the contract price with Vickaryous and the resale price plus costs.

Trial was to the court. The court determined that although the security interests were released as a matter of law against Vickaryous, they remained of record and constituted "a substantial shadow" over the title to the cattle, sufficient to breach the warranty of freedom from encumbrances provided by section 2–312 of the U.C.C. The court found that since Wright made no effort to cure the uncertainty which constituted the breach of warranty he was not entitled to hold Vickaryous liable for breach of the sale contract.

Wright's main point on appeal is that there was no breach of the warranty of freedom from encumbrances since he had obtained the consent to sale of the secured parties and, therefore, their security interests were discharged as a matter of law. Vickaryous counters, and the court held, that the existence of apparently valid security interests on file constituted a cloud on the title and therefore a breach of warranty in the absence of an explanation by Wright that the security interests had been discharged.

Unless explicitly excluded, or the circumstances are such as to indicate otherwise, there is in every contract for the sale of goods a warranty that the title is good, and that the goods will be delivered free from encumbrances. This warranty is expressed in U.C.C. § 2–312(1) (AS 45.05.092(a)) which provides:

> Subject to (b) of this section there is in a contract for sale a warranty by the seller that

(1) the title conveyed shall be good, and its transfer rightful; and

(2) the goods shall be delivered free from a security interest or other lien or encumbrance of which the buyer at the time of contracting has no knowledge.

The official commentary to section 2–312 states:

Subsection (1) makes provision for a buyer's basic needs in respect to a title which he in good faith expects to acquire by his purchase, namely, that he receive a good, clean title transferred to him also in a rightful manner *so that he will not be exposed to a lawsuit in order to protect it.* [emphasis added]

Uniform Commercial Code § 2–312, Comment 1. The emphasized language makes it clear that a marketable title concept is intended, for otherwise it would not be important whether a buyer was merely exposed to a lawsuit, but rather whether he could win it.

Cases decided in other jurisdictions confirm our view that section 2–312 expresses a concept of marketable title. In American Container Corp. v. Hanley Trucking Corp., 111 N.J.Super. 322, 268 A.2d 313, 318 (1970) the court stated the following with respect to the section 2–312 warranty:

The purchaser of goods warranted as to title has a right to rely on the fact that he will not be required, at some later time, to enter into a contest over the validity of his ownership. The mere casting of a substantial shadow over his title, regardless of the ultimate outcome, is sufficient to violate a warranty of good title.

Accord, Ricklefs v. Clemens, 216 Kan. 128, 531 P.2d 94, 100 (1975). Other authorities involving the sale of personal property, not decided under the Uniform Commercial Code, likewise have concluded that a buyer need not complete a purchase which apparently will require a lawsuit to protect that which is acquired....

Under the facts of this case Wright could easily have saved the transaction by explaining that the sale was made with the consent of the secured parties and that their liens were discharged. Remarkably, he chose not to do so, and thus his breach stands.

. . .

Affirmed.

Notes

(1) **Inventory Finance.** Merchants and farmers commonly borrow money to finance their activities. Lenders often secure their loans with security interests in the goods to be sold. Seldom will any buyer knowingly take goods subject to a pre-sale encumbrance. Lenders' release of encumbrances on merchants' and farmers' inventory at the time of retail sale is routine commercial practice. Financers want the inventory sold (they get repaid from the proceeds of the sales) and

therefore authorize the merchants or farmers to sell the goods to buyers free of security interests. This commercial practice is reflected in UCC 9–306(2), which provides that a security interest does not "continue" upon authorized sale of the goods.³ In *Wright*, the court found that the secured parties had consented to the sale free of the encumbrances, but found further that the buyer was unaware of the release of security interests. The court treats the buyer as a surprised recipient of an intermeddler's report that encumbrances existed. How likely is it that an auction buyer of 45 head of cattle would be so unsophisticated in that marketplace as to be surprised by the information? How likely is it that such a buyer would not expect that encumbrances created by the seller would be released?

After buyer refused to accept them, the cattle were resold, in an apparently similar auction, one week after the first auction, but the price obtained in the second auction was sharply lower. Does this suggest that the buyer may have overbid in the first auction and, having realized this, wanted a way to escape the obligation to pay the contract price? If this were buyer's motive, would buyer's action be consistent with the obligation to act in good faith in the performance of the contract?

(2) Clouds on Title. The *Wright* court held that seller was in breach of the obligation under UCC 2–312 even though no third party ever pressed a claim against the buyer's title. Is this conclusion supported by the *text* of the section? Is it supported by the Comment? Is the Comment authorized to go beyond the text?

Third party claims of title to goods or claims of encumbrances on goods can range from being clearly plausible to quite fanciful. Where on this spectrum does sellers' responsibility end?

Should it matter whether the issue is raised before, or after, the buyer has accepted the goods and paid the price? After payment and acceptance, would a buyer have a right to damages under UCC 2–312 on the basis of an unsubstantiated concern that there was an encumbrance on the goods?

Problem 1. After a sale of goods, a third party (X) contends that it holds a security interest that survived the sale from S to B; S contends that the security interest was invalid. If X brings an action against B, may B transfer some of the costs and risks of litigation to S by a third-party action (impleader) against S? See Rule 14, Federal Rules of Civil Procedure. If S is not subject to the jurisdiction of the court where B is sued, a "vouching" letter under UCC 2–607(5) may induce S to take over the defense—or at least provide B with a claim against S that could be vindicated without retrial of issues raised in the action by X v. B. But this is far from "quiet possession." Should B be subjected to the

---

3. This matter is considered more fully in materials on secured transactions.

uncertainties and costs of even a disputed claim of title? How should the problem be solved?

Problem 2. The Hammer Auction Company operates a sales barn at which livestock are sold regularly at auction. Hammer sells the livestock on commission for many cattlemen. Buyers are aware that Hammer is not the owner and acts as the agent of some unnamed principal. William Buyer made the high bid on three heifers which had been left with Hammer by Sam Theft. After the purchase, Buyer learned that the heifers were stolen and had to return them to the true owner. Buyer sues Hammer to recover the amount of his bid.

What argument may be made for the defendant, Hammer, based on UCC 2–312(1)? Was Hammer "the seller" of the livestock? See UCC 2–103. Under common-law agency doctrine, one who contracts as agent for another without disclosing the identity of the principal is not merely an agent, but is deemed a "party to the contract." Restatement (Second) of Agency §§ 321–322. See Jones v. Ballard, 573 So.2d 783 (Miss.1990) (warranty of title); cf. Powers v. Coffeyville Livestock Sales Co., 665 F.2d 311 (10th Cir.1981) (warranty of quality). Does this doctrine from common law apply to transactions under UCC Article 2. Recall UCC 1–103.

What argument may be made for the defendant, Hammer, under UCC 2–312(2)? Does the statute displace the common-law of agency? Is "the seller" in 2–312(1) the same as "the person selling" in 2–312(2)? Should 2–312(2) be read to create an immunity for auctioneers and other agents of partially disclosed or undisclosed principals? See Comment 5.

Problem 3. Charles Creditor held a judgment against Daniel Debtor, and sued out a writ of attachment to levy on Debtor's property. Pursuant to the writ of attachment, Samuel Sheriff seized a tractor in Debtor's possession and sold it at an execution sale; Buyer bought the tractor for $500. Unknown to all parties, the tractor was subject to a mortgage held by Leo Lean to secure a $300 debt which Debtor owed Lean. Lean's mortgage was binding after the sale, and Lean threatens to seize the tractor from Buyer unless Debtor's debt is satisfied. Has Buyer any recourse against Sheriff or Creditor? See UCC 2–312(2); Bogestad v. Anderson, 143 Minn. 336, 173 N.W. 674 (1919). Has Buyer any recourse against Debtor?

Problem 4. Marie Louise Jeanneret, a citizen of Switzerland, is a well-known art dealer in Geneva. Defendants Anna and Luben Vichey, wife and husband, are citizens of the United States. Anna's father, Carlo Frua DeAngeli, had an extensive and internationally recognized private collection of paintings in Milan, Italy. One of these was a painting, Portrait sur Fond Jaune, by the renowned French post-impressionist, Henri Matisse, who was born in 1869 and died in 1954. Title to the Matisse painting ultimately vested in Anna Vichey. In 1970 the Matisse painting was brought to the Vicheys' apartment in New York City. In January 1973 Mme. Jeanneret began negotiations for the purchase of the painting, and an agreement was reached for its sale for 700,000 Swiss francs, then equivalent to approximately $230,-000. Luben Vichey delivered the painting to plaintiff in Geneva in March 1973.

Mme. Jeanneret included the Matisse painting in a large exhibit of 20th century masters at her gallery in Geneva. In November 1974, Mme. Jeanneret encountered Signora Bucarelli, superintendent in charge of the export of paintings from Italy, who declared she had been looking for the Matisse painting because she suspected its illegal exportation from Italy under laws designed to protect that nation's cultural heritage. Subsequently, the Assistant Minister of Culture issued a notification declaring the painting "an important work" of "particular artistic and historical interest" within the meaning of Italian law.

Mme. Jeanneret brought suit against the Vicheys for breach of warranty of title. At trial, John Tancock, a vice-president of Sotheby Parke Bernet auction house and head of its Department of Impressionist and Modern Painting and Sculpture, testified that, but for the question of illegal exportation, he would appraise the painting at $750,000. On the other hand, if the painting lacked "the necessary export documents from any country where it had been located," his opinion was that it would be impossible to sell the painting since "[n]o reputable auction house or dealer would be prepared to handle it." Hence "on the legitimate market its value is zero."

What should be the result of this action under UCC 2–312? Does Italy's cultural heritage law affect the owners' title to objects possessed in Italy that are restricted as to export? Would the 2–312 provision on infringement be invoked by an export restriction? Were sellers "merchants"? See UCC 2–104(1). If the trade usage of the reputable art dealers is self-imposed, in that they would incur no liability to the Italian government if they did handle such works, should that affect determination of Mme. Jeanneret's claim under 2–312? See Jeanneret v. Vichey, 693 F.2d 259 (2d Cir.1982).

Lease Transactions: Lessor's Warranty. The supplier of goods in a lease transaction does not contract to pass title to the goods. Under the Commercial Code, " 'lease' means a transfer of the right to possession and use of the goods for a term in return for consideration...." UCC 2A–103(1)(j). The related warranty of a lessor is found in UCC 2A–211:

> (1) There is in a lease contract a warranty that for the lease term no person holds a claim or interest in the goods that arose from an act or omission of the lessor ... which will interfere with the lessee's enjoyment of its leasehold interest.

(2) GOOD FAITH PURCHASE OF GOODS

Buyers confronted with claims that they lack good title to purchased goods or that their property is subject to a security interest or other lien may contest the claims of the third parties. In doing so, buyers are assisted by a set of legal rules that fall under the general heading of good faith purchaser protections. Sometimes used is the Latin formulation: *bona fide* purchase. The legal effect of this set of rules is to give some buyers better title than their sellers had. Thus, in some circumstances sellers who lack "good" title may be able nonetheless to sell goods to buyers whose title is "clear."

The Two Party Setting

Before we take up the good faith purchase rules in a three-party setting, it is helpful to review some fundamental principles of law as they affect the rights of buyers and sellers.

Sales by Agents. Generally, the law assures owners of property of security in their ownership, but the law also recognizes that owners may dispose of their property through the actions of others. Owners of property or of an interest in property may authorize someone else, an agent, to dispose of their interests. We saw two examples in *Wright v. Vickaryous.* The owner of the cattle authorized an auctioneer to sell them and the holders of the security interests authorized the owner to sell the cattle free of their interests. The common law of "principal and agent" expressly undergirds the Commercial Code. UCC 1–103. Agents' common-law powers to transfer these property interests are reflected in UCC 2–403(1) (purchaser acquires all title which his transferor "had power to transfer" and 9–306(2) (security interest continues notwithstanding sale "unless the disposition was authorized by the secured party").

Crimes and Torts. Owners of property may be deprived of possession by theft or fraud. These actions violate the principle of security of ownership of property. This principle of property law only partially intersects sales law. Thieves, of course, are not buyers. In criminal law, they commit larceny, robbery and burglary. Sales law is not germane to the legal relationship between thief and victim. However, some fraudulent transactions that induce owners to surrender possession of their goods occur in the form of credit sales to "buyers" who have no intention to pay the contract price.

The most practical form of relief for such victims of crime or fraud is to recover their property. Theoretically, the victims have claims for damages under the tort theory of conversion; moreover, defrauded owners could "ratify" the fraud-tainted transactions and sue the cheats for the agreed price. Collecting money judgments in these circumstances is highly unlikely.[4] The law permits rightful owners specific

---

4. Criminal law has been reformed in recent years to increase victims' rights. One aspect of this reform has been to order restitution and reparation as a part of offenders' sentences.

relief, usually in the form of an action for replevin, that will result in restoration of the goods to the rightful owners if the goods are found in the possession of the wrongdoers.

Problem 5. A owned a large quantity of cotton, worth $25,000, which was stored in its warehouse. B broke into the warehouse and stole the cotton. The police arrested B and found the cotton in B's truck. Can A recover the cotton from B? Is A's right to relief based on the UCC? What law governs?

Problem 6. A delivered a large quantity of cotton to B upon B's promise to pay $25,000 in 30 days. A delivered the goods to B on credit as a result of B's cunning misrepresentation that he was Y, a reputable and credit-worthy merchant. At the end of that period, B failed to pay. Can A recover the cotton from B? UCC 2–403(1) refers to persons with "voidable title," but the UCC does not define that term or provide the remedy for avoiding a voidable title. What law does govern the rights of A and B? See UCC 1–103.

Problem 7. B ordered a large quantity of cotton from A with payment to be made 30 days after delivery. A expressed reluctance to accept the order because of doubt that B could pay. To induce A to accept the order, B delivered a statement, purportedly from B's bank, attesting to B's credit-worthiness. After A delivered the cotton, he discovered that the bank statement was a forgery. B has not paid for the cotton. Can A recover the cotton from B? Does UCC Article 2 apply?

Problem 8. (a) A delivered a large quantity of cotton to B upon B's promise to pay $25,000 in 30 days. At the end of that period, B failed to pay. Can A recover the cotton from B? Does UCC Article 2 apply? See UCC 2–507(2)? Was payment "due and demanded on delivery"? What remedy does A have? See UCC 2–709. What policy grounds might explain the absence of a remedy that restores the cotton to A?

(b) Should A be entitled to a court order that the cotton be returned if A could prove that, at the time the contract was made, B intended not to pay? Did B, by silence, falsely imply an intent to pay? Is B's conduct comparable to misrepresentation of his identity or credit-worthiness? See Keeton, Fraud–Statements of Intention, 15 Tex.L.Rev. 185 (1937).

Good Faith Purchase of Goods: The Basic Rules in Three Party Setting

We turn now to the three-party situation. The goods are no longer in the possession of a thief or cheat. A typical sequence of events is as follows: A is the owner of goods. B acquires the goods by theft or fraud such that A has the right to recover the goods from B. B resells the goods to C who is unaware of how B obtained the goods. A seeks to replevy the goods from C, or to hold C liable in damages for conversion.

The traditional legal rule is this: If B did not acquire "title" or "property" in the goods, he cannot confer property on C: *Nemo dat quod non habet.* This rule is still dominant in Anglo–American law where the goods were stolen from A. On the other hand, for cases where A was induced to deliver the goods to B by fraud, a second rule was developed. Where A sold the goods because of B's fraud, A could rescind the transaction and recover his property, but B had "voidable title" and A's right to rescind could be "cut off" by resale of the goods to a *bona fide* purchaser.[5]

Professor Gilmore summarized the historical development:

> The initial common law position was that equities of ownership are to be protected at all costs; an owner may never be deprived of his property rights without his consent. That worked well enough against a background of local distribution where seller and buyer met face to face and exchanged goods for cash. But as the marketplace became first regional and then national, a recurrent situation came to be the misappropriation of goods by a faithless agent in fraud of his principal. Classical theory required that the principal be protected and that the risks of agency distribution be cast on the purchaser. The market demanded otherwise.
>
> The first significant breach in common law property theory was the protection of purchasers from such commercial agents. The reform was carried out through so-called Factor's Acts, which were widely enacted in the early part of the 19th century. Under these Acts any person who entrusted goods to a factor—or agent— for sale took the risk of the factor's selling them beyond his authority; anyone buying from a factor in good faith, relying on his possession of the goods, and without notice of the limitations on his authority, took good title against the true owner. In time the Acts were expanded to protect people, i.e., banks, who took goods from a factor as security for loans made to the factor to be used in operating the factor's own business. The Factor's Acts, as much in derogation of the common law as it is possible for a statute to be, were restrictively construed and consequently turned out to be

---

5. The seminal case in the voidable title area is the English case of Parker v. Patrick, 101 Eng. Rep. 99 (K.B. 1793), which was followed in Mowrey v. Walsh, 8 Cowen 238 (N.Y.Sup.Ct.1828). The only reason mentioned by the New York court for distinguishing fraud and theft was the one given by the English court in its one sentence, per curiam opinion—the existence of a statute as to theft. By the time of White v. Garden, 10 Common Bench, 919, 138 Eng. Rep. 364 (Q.B. 1851), however, doctrine had developed to the point that the court could write that where fraud was involved, "the transaction is not absolutely void, except at the option of the seller; that he may elect to treat it as a contract, and he must do the contrary before the buyer has acted as if it were such, and resold the goods to a third party." See Weinberg, Markets Overt, Voidable Titles, and Feckless Agents: Judges and Efficiency in the Antebellum Doctrine of Good Faith Purchase, 56 Tul. L. Rev. 1, 23–32 (1981).

considerably less than the full grant of mercantile liberty which they had first appeared to be. Other developments in the law gradually took the pressure off the Factor's Acts, which came to be confined to the narrow area of sales through commission merchants, mostly in agricultural produce markets.

Even while they were cutting the heart out of the Factor's Acts, the courts were finding new ways to shift distribution risks. Their happiest discovery was the concept of "voidable title"—a vague idea, never defined and perhaps incapable of definition, whose greatest virtue, as a principle of growth, may well have been its shapeless imprecision of outline. The polar extremes of theory were these: if B buys goods from A, he gets A's title and can transfer it to any subsequent purchaser; if B steals goods from A, he gets no title and can transfer none to any subsequent purchaser, no matter how clear the purchaser's good faith. "Voidable title" in B came in as an intermediate term between the two extremes: if B gets possession of A's goods by fraud, even though he has no right to retain them against A, he does have the power to transfer title to a good faith purchaser.

The ingenious distinction between "no title" in B (therefore true owner prevails over good faith purchaser) and "voidable title" in B (therefore true owner loses to good faith purchaser) made it possible to throw the risk on the true owner in the typical commercial situation while protecting him in the noncommercial one. Since the law purported to be a deduction from basic premises, logic prevailed in some details to the detriment of mercantile need, but on the whole voidable title proved a useful touchstone.

The contrasting treatment given to sales on credit and sales for cash shows the inarticulate development of the commercial principle. When goods are delivered on credit, the seller becomes merely a creditor for the price: on default he has no right against the goods. But when the delivery is induced by buyer's fraud—buyer being unable to pay or having no intention of paying—the seller, if he acts promptly after discovering the facts, may replevy from the buyer or reclaim from buyer's trustee in bankruptcy. The seller may not, however, move against purchasers from the buyer, and the term "purchaser" includes lenders who have made advances on the security of the goods. By his fraudulent acquisition the buyer has obtained voidable title and purchasers from him are protected.

Gilmore, The Commercial Doctrine of Good Faith Purchase, 63 Yale L.J. 1057–60 (1954).[6]

Problem 9. A owned a large quantity of cotton, worth $25,000, which was stored in its warehouse. B broke into the warehouse and stole the cotton. Unaware of the theft, C entered into a contract to buy the cotton from B for $25,000.

6. Reproduced with permission of the Yale Law Journal.

(a) After payment to B had occurred, the police discovered that C had possession of the cotton that had been stolen from A. B has disappeared with the $25,000. A institutes legal action to replevy the cotton from C. What result? Is the answer found in the Commercial Code?

(b) Before the police traced the cotton to C, C sold and delivered the cotton to D who paid $27,000. A institutes legal action against C for conversion? What result? Does A have a cause of action against D? Is the answer found in the Commercial Code?

Problem 10. A delivered a large quantity of cotton to B upon B's promise to pay $25,000 in 30 days. A delivered the goods to B on credit as a result of B's misrepresentation that he was X, a reputable and credit-worthy merchant. At the end of that period, B failed to pay. Meanwhile B sold and delivered the cotton to C who paid B $27,000. A institutes legal action to replevy the cotton from C. What result? Is the answer found in the Commercial Code? See UCC 2–403(1).

Note that the drafters of the Commercial Code did not merely restate the traditional rule based on "voidable title." They added a sentence to 2–403(1) that results in protection of good faith purchasers, without using the "voidable title" phrase, in four kinds of transactions. Comment 1 refers to these as "specific situations which have been troublesome under prior law." What is the common element or elements of these situations?

Lease Transaction: "Good Faith Lessee." Assume that C in Problem 10 was a lessee rather than a buyer. Would C's leasehold interest be protected under UCC 2–403(1)? See definitions of "purchase" and "purchaser" in UCC 1–201(32) and (33). Compare the definition of "purchase" in UCC 2A–103(1)(v). For the purpose of Article 2, does a lease create in a lessee an "interest in property"?

(3) "ENTRUSTING" AND "BUYERS IN ORDINARY COURSE"

Prefatory Note. The Code's sharpest break with the traditional law of good faith purchase is found in UCC 2–403(2). Suppose an owner (A) leaves his diamond ring for repair with a jeweler (B) who both repairs and sells jewelry. The jeweler wrongfully sells the ring to a good faith purchaser (C). Who has the right to the ring—the original owner or the good faith purchaser?

The common law favored the original owner. Merely entrusting possession to a dealer was not sufficient to clothe the dealer with the authority to sell. "If it were otherwise people would not be secure in sending their watches or articles of jewelry to a jeweler's establishment to be repaired or cloth to a clothing establishment to be made into garments." Levi v. Booth, 58 Md. 305, 315 (1882).

During the nineteenth century, however, many states enacted "Factor's Acts" under which an owner of goods who entrusted them to an agent (or "factor") with limited authority to sell took the risk that the agent might sell them beyond the authority. A good faith purchaser, relying on the agent's possession of the goods and having no notice that it was exceeding the authority, took good title against the original owner. But the Factor's Acts did not protect the good faith purchaser where, as in the example of the diamond ring, the owner entrusted the goods to another for some purpose other than that of sale. A mere bailee could not pass good title to a good faith purchaser.

Here UCC 2–403(2) goes well beyond the Factor's Acts, since it applies to "[a]ny entrusting," i.e., "any delivery" under (3), regardless of the purpose, to a "merchant who deals in goods of that kind." Who is entitled to the diamond ring under the Code? Note that the protection of 2–403 is extended to a "buyer in the ordinary course of business," a category significantly narrower than "good faith purchaser for value." Compare the scope of "buyer" under UCC 2–103(1)(a) with the definitions of "purchase" and "purchaser" under UCC 1–201(32) and (33). Compare also the specific requirements and limitations of "ordinary course of business" in UCC 1–201(9) with the broader meaning of "good faith" and "value" in UCC 1–201(19) and (44).

PORTER v. WERTZ

Court of Appeals of New York, 1981.
53 N.Y.2d 696, 439 N.Y.S.2d 105, 421 N.E.2d 500.

[Samuel Porter, an art collector, owned Utrillo's painting "Chateau de Lion–sur–Mer." Harold Von Maker, who identified himself to Porter as Peter Wertz, an art dealer, approached Porter and expressed an interest in the Utrillo. Porter, unaware of Von Maker's real identity or his background of illegal activities, permitted Von Maker to hang the Utrillo temporarily in Von Maker's home pending a decision as to purchase. Von Maker delivered the painting to the real Peter Wertz, a delicatessen employee, with instruction to try to sell it to a gallery. After unsuccessful efforts at other galleries, Peter Wertz sold the Utrillo to Richard Feigen, an art dealer (Feigen Galleries). Feigen in turn sold the painting to Brenner, who resold it to a third party who took the painting to South America.

Porter, who had no knowledge of these transactions at the time, discovered what Von Maker, Wertz, and Feigen had done and brought action for conversion against Feigen. Feigen argued that Porter had "entrusted" the painting to Von Maker and as a consequence: (1) Feigen was protected under UCC 2–403(2) as a "buyer in ordinary course of business," or (2) Porter's claim was barred by equitable estoppel under UCC 2–403(1). The trial court rejected Feigen's defense under 2–403(2), but upheld the claim of estoppel. The Appellate Division reversed and Feigen appealed to the Court of Appeals.]

MEMORANDUM

The judgment appealed from and order of the Appellate Division brought up for review should be affirmed, 68 A.D.2d 141, 416 N.Y.S.2d 254, with costs. We agree with the Appellate Division's conclusion that subdivision (2) of section 2–403 of the Uniform Commercial Code does not insulate defendants from plaintiff Porter's lawful claim to the Utrillo painting. Subdivision (2) of section 2–403 of the Uniform Commercial Code provides: "Any entrusting of possession of goods to a merchant who deals in goods of that kind gives him power to transfer all rights of the entruster to a buyer in ordinary course of business." The "entruster provision" of the Uniform Commercial Code is designed to enhance the reliability of commercial sales by merchants (who deal with the kind of goods sold on a regular basis) while shifting the risk of loss through fraudulent transfer to the owner of the goods, who can select the merchant to whom he entrusts his property. It protects only those who purchase from the merchant to whom the property was entrusted in the ordinary course of the merchant's business.

While the Utrillo painting was entrusted to Harold Von Maker, an art merchant, the Feigen Gallery purchased the painting not from Von Maker, but from one Peter Wertz, who turns out to have been a delicatessen employee acquainted with Von Maker. It seems that Von Maker frequented the delicatessen where Peter Wertz was employed and that at some point Von Maker began to identify himself as Peter Wertz in certain art transactions. Indeed, Von Maker identified himself as Peter Wertz in his dealings with Porter.

Defendants argued that Feigen reasonably assumed that the Peter Wertz who offered the Utrillo to him was an art merchant because Feigen had been informed by Henry Sloan that an art dealer named Peter Wertz desired to sell a Utrillo painting. Feigen therefore argues that for purposes of subdivision (2) of section 2–403 of the Uniform Commercial Code it is as though he purchased from a merchant in the ordinary course of business. Alternatively, he claims that he actually purchased the Utrillo from Von Maker, the art dealer to whom it had been entrusted, because Peter Wertz sold the painting on Von Maker's behalf. Neither argument has merit.

Even if Peter Wertz were acting on Von Maker's behalf, unless he disclosed this fact to Feigen, it could hardly be said that Feigen relied upon Von Maker's status as an art merchant. It does not appear that the actual Peter Wertz ever represented that he was acting on behalf of Von Maker in selling the painting.

As to the argument that Feigen reasonably assumed that Peter Wertz was an art merchant, it is apparent from the opinion of the Appellate Division that the court rejected the fact finding essential to this argument, namely, that Peter Wertz had been introduced to Feigen by Henry Sloan as an art merchant. The court noted that in his examination before trial Richard Feigen had testified that he could not recall whether Henry Sloan had described Peter Wertz as an art dealer and concluded that this substantially weakened the probative force of Feigen's trial testimony on this point. Indeed, Peter Wertz testified that Von Maker had not directed him to the Feigen Gallery but had simply delivered the painting to Wertz and asked him to try to find a buyer for the Utrillo. Wertz had been to several art galleries before he approached the Feigen Gallery. Thus, the Appellate Division's finding has support in the record.

Because Peter Wertz was not an art dealer and the Appellate Division has found that Feigen was not duped by Von Maker into believing that Peter Wertz was such a dealer, subdivision (2) of section 2–403 of the Uniform Commercial Code is inapplicable for three distinct reasons: (1) even if Peter Wertz were an art merchant rather than a delicatessen employee, he is not the same merchant to whom Porter entrusted the Utrillo painting; (2) Wertz was not an art merchant; and (3) the sale was not in the ordinary course of Wertz' business because he did not deal in goods of that kind (Uniform Commercial Code, § 1–201, subd. [9]).

Nor can the defendants-appellants rely on the doctrine of equitable estoppel. It has been observed that subdivision (1) of section 2–403 of the Uniform Commercial Code incorporates the doctrines of estoppel, agency and apparent agency because it states that a purchaser acquires not only all title that his transferor had, but also all title that he had power to transfer (White & Summers, Uniform Commercial Code, § 3–11, p. 139).

An estoppel might arise if Porter had clothed Peter Wertz with ownership of or authority to sell the Utrillo painting and the Feigen Gallery had relied upon Wertz' apparent ownership or right to transfer it. But Porter never even delivered the painting to Peter Wertz, much less create apparent ownership in him; he delivered the painting to Von Maker for his own personal use. It is true, as previously noted, that Von Maker used the name Peter Wertz in his dealings with Porter, but the Appellate Division found that the Feigen Gallery purchased from the actual Peter Wertz and that there was insufficient evidence to establish the claim that Peter Wertz had been described as an art dealer by Henry Sloan. Nothing Porter did influenced the Feigen Gallery's decision to purchase from Peter Wertz a delicatessen employee. Accordingly, the Feigen Gallery cannot protect its defective title by a defense of estoppel.

The Appellate Division opined that even if Von Maker had duped Feigen into believing that Peter Wertz was an art dealer, subdivision (2) of section 2–403 of the Uniform Commercial Code would still not protect his defective title because as a merchant, Feigen failed to purchase in good faith. Among merchants good faith requires not only honesty in fact but observance of reasonable commercial standards. (Uniform Commercial Code, § 2–103, subd. [1], par. [b]). The Appellate Division concluded that it was a departure from reasonable commercial standards for the Feigen Gallery to fail to inquire concerning the title to the Utrillo and to fail to question Peter Wertz' credentials as an art dealer. On this appeal we have received *amicus* briefs from the New York State Attorney–General urging that the court hold that good faith among art merchants requires inquiry as to the ownership of an *objet d'art,* and from the Art Dealers Association of America, Inc., arguing that the ordinary custom in the art business is not to inquire as to title and that a duty of inquiry would cripple the art business which is centered in New York. In view of our disposition we do not reach the good faith question.

Judgment appealed from and order of the Appellate Division brought up for review affirmed with costs, in a memorandum.

NOTE

Lease Transaction: "Entrusting" and Lessees "In Ordinary Course." Consider a sale of a power shovel by M, a merchant who deals in goods of that kind, to B who pays for the equipment. With M's consent, B leaves the power shovel with M pending B's need for it on a construction project that is expected to begin shortly. Before B returns to take possession of the power shovel, M leases it to L. B discovers that L has the power shovel and demands that L surrender it to B.

Is L's right to possession protected under UCC 2–403(2)? See the definition of "buyer" in UCC 2–103(1)(a). Is L's right to possession protected under UCC 2A–304(2)? Is L a "subsequent lessee"? The comment to this section provides:

> Section 2A–307(2) resolves the potential dispute between B, M and L. By virtue of B's entrustment of the goods to M and M's lease of the goods to L, B has a cause of action against M under the common law.... Thus, B is a creditor of M.... Section 2A–307(2) provides that B, as M's creditor, takes subject to M's lease to L. Thus, if L does not default under the lease, L's enjoyment and possession of the goods should be undisturbed.

Query: Is there legal slight of hand in characterizing B as merely a creditor of M?

(B) INTERNATIONAL SALES LAW

Sellers' Responsibility. The Convention on Contracts for the International Sale of Goods provides that, absent agreement otherwise, a seller must deliver goods that are "free from any right or claim of a third party." CISG 41. The Convention does not use the word "title." Does the Convention's formulation of the sellers' obligation differ from UCC 2–312 in any substantial way?[7]

The parties in *Jeanneret* were from different nations: United States sellers and a Swiss buyer. The buyer was a dealer who pur-

---

7. The Convention's provision on sellers' obligation with respect to intellectual property is found in Article 42.

chased the Matisse painting for resale. Would this transaction be within the scope of CISG? See CISG 2(a). Assuming that the Convention were applied in a case like *Jeanneret,* what would be the outcome?

Good Faith Purchasers. Article 4(b) declares that the Convention "is not concerned with the effect which the contract may have on the property in the goods sold." Given CISG 4(b)'s disclaimer of concern with property rights in the goods even between sellers and buyers, not surprisingly the CISG has no provision on the property or ownership rights of third parties. When such issues arise in relation to sales transactions otherwise governed by CISG, what law would apply to resolve conflicting claims to the goods?

Chapter 3

QUALITY: SELLERS' RESPONSIBILITY AND BUYERS' RIGHTS

SECTION 1. INTRODUCTION

Historical Background. The scope of sellers' responsibility to buyers has passed through a remarkable evolution of a curiously cyclical character. In the Middle Ages the authority of the Church and of guilds combined to impose heavy standards of quality upon sellers.[1] Thereafter, as we shall see, English law came to afford but little protection to buyers: *caveat emptor!* This outlook, in turn, has been reversed in modern law, but quaint language in current statutes cannot be understood without some appreciation of this development.

The law of sales is here, as at so many points, enmeshed with the larger body of contract law. Students of the development of contracts will recall the reluctance of early courts to enforce simple promises; in a static land economy, legal obligations were not to be assumed lightly. Although the specific undertakings in a document bearing the maker's seal received early legal protection, less formal undertakings had to wait for the ancient action "on the case" to develop beyond its tort ancestry into its contractual descendant, the action of special assumpsit.

The reluctance to give legal effect to simple informal statements is illustrated by the famous 1625 decision of Chandelor v. Lopus [2] in which a buyer brought an action on the case against a goldsmith for affirming that a stone he sold the buyer was a "bezoar" (or "bezar"), a stone found in the alimentary organs of goats and supposed to have remarkable medicinal qualities. (How the plaintiff proved that this was not a "true" bezoar does not appear.) The Exchequer Chamber ruled, after verdict for the plaintiff, that the declaration based on this affirmation was insufficient: " ... the bare affirmation that it was a bezar stone, without warranting it to be so is no cause of action." [3] Just how far the seller had to go to "warrant" was not stated; apparently he had to make an explicit statement like "I warrant that ..." or "I agree to be bound that...."

It is striking to find this curious decision dominating the New York

---

1. Hamilton, The Ancient Maxim Caveat Emptor, 40 Yale L.J. 1133 (1931).
2. Cro. Jac. 4, 79 Eng. Rep. 3 (1625).
3. In view of the peculiar nature of the commodity, it may be worthwhile to record the further statement of the judges that, " ... every one in selling wares will affirm that his wares are good, or the horse which he sells is sound."

court's thinking in the 1804 commercial case of Seixas v. Woods.[4] A dealer advertised and sold wood as "brazilletto," a wood valuable for manufacturing a chemical used in making dye; in fact the wood was worthless "peachum." A judgment for the buyer was reversed. Chancellor Kent's concurring opinion stated: "The mentioning the word, as Brazilletto wood, in the bill of parcels, and in the advertisement some days previous to the sale, did not amount to a warranty to the plaintiffs. To make an affirmation at the time of the sale, a warranty, it must appear by evidence to be so *intended,* and not to have been a mere matter of judgment and opinion, and of which the defendant had no particular knowledge. Here it is admitted, the defendant was equally ignorant with the plaintiffs, and could have had no such intention."[5]

Before many decades passed, cases like these were overturned. The *Seixas* ("brazilletto") case was rejected in New York in a 1872 case involving a dealer who bought barrels of "blue vitriol" and innocently resold them as such: when the material proved to be "salzburger vitriol" (a less valuable commodity) the dealer was held liable to the purchaser.[6] The opinions in such cases usually did not discuss the reasons of policy that produced the change in approach, but one may surmise that a greater volume and speed of trade called for firmer protection for contractual expectations. True, the dealer who resold may have been misled by its supplier; but the rule of law that made the dealer liable for its representations would normally give the dealer recourse against the supplier; certainly it would be difficult for the ultimate purchaser to recover from the dealer's supplier.[7]

When Professor Williston came to draft the Uniform Sales Act, one of his principal targets was the emphasis which some cases placed on the seller's "intent"—an offensive manifestation of a "subjective" view of contracts.[8] To obliterate this approach, Section 12 of the Uniform Sales Act provided: "Any affirmation of fact or any promise by the seller relating to the goods is an express warranty if the *natural tendency* of such affirmation or promise is to induce the buyer to purchase the goods, and if the buyer purchases the goods *relying*

---

4. 2 Caines 48 (1804).

5. Chief Justice Gibson, of Pennsylvania, used characteristically salty (and extreme) language to similar effect in McFarland v. Newman, 9 Watts 55 (Pa.1839). Gibson also drew a questionable analogy between a sale of goods and the deed for real estate. "A sale is a contract executed, on which, of course, no action can be directly founded." [Why not?] He added that warranty is "no more a part of the sale than the covenant of warranty in a deed is part of the conveyance." [Is it possible at the same time to convey property and undertake contractual obligations?]

6. Hawkins v. Pemberton, 51 N.Y. 198 (1872).

7. This practical point was emphasized in Jones v. Just, L.R. 3 Q.B. 197 (1868). Defendant sellers argued that they had relied on the selection of the goods by a supplier in Singapore; Mellor, J., replied that defendant sellers "had recourse against [the supplier] for not supplying an article reasonably merchantable."

8. The Commissioners' Note to USA 12 referred to the "intent" concept and stated that " ... the fundamental basis for liability on warranty is the justifiable reliance on the seller's assertions."

thereon."⁹ This language was well chosen to focus attention on the crucial question of reasonable reliance by the buyer on the seller's statements. This formulation also foreclosed difficult (and unprofitable) litigation over whether the seller's statement was a "promise" or an "affirmation of fact."

The Code in Section 2–313(1)(a) closely follows the above provision of the Uniform Sales Act. However, there is one puzzling change: There is no reference to reliance by the buyer; instead, an affirmation or a promise is an express warranty if it "becomes part of the basis of the bargain." The meaning of this phrase will be explored later.

Types of Warranties. It is orthodox learning, carried forward by the Uniform Sales Act and the Uniform Commercial Code, that warranties come in various "types." "Express" warranties (UCC 2–313) are to be distinguished from warranties that are "implied." Implied warranties of quality fall in two statutory categories: "merchantable quality" (UCC 2–314), and "fitness for particular purpose" (UCC 2–315).

Consider a simple example of each of the three types of warranties. *Case 1:* B and S, a Chevrolet dealer, sign an agreement of sale for a "new Corvair." After delivery, B discovers that the car had been used as a demonstrator with the odometer disconnected. *Case 2:* A car purchased by B has a defective crankshaft that promptly breaks. *Case 3:* B tells S, a paint dealer, that he wants paint for the outside of his house. S puts on the counter a can of "Lustro" which B buys. This paint is good for interior walls but is washed from exterior walls by the first rain. *Case 1* involves an express warranty (UCC 2–313), *Case 2* the warranty of merchantable quality (UCC 2–314), and *Case 3* the warranty of fitness for particular purpose (UCC 2–315).

In spite of the complexity and diversity of these statutory provisions it may help to consider whether they may be related—and possibly inspired by a common principle. For example, suppose that, just before the purchase, the seller had been asked these questions: In *Case 1,* "Has anyone been driving this car before?" In *Case 2,* "Is the crankshaft sound?" In *Case 3,* "Will the paint stand up under a rain?" Would the seller normally have given the undertakings requested by the buyer? If the seller had refused, would the buyer have purchased the goods?

Do buyers normally articulate such questions? If not, why not? Because they are unimportant? Or because the answers "go without saying"?¹⁰ As we watch the *results* (as contrasted with the language) of the cases it will be useful to analyze the degree of kinship between the

---

9. USA 12 also included a sentence dealing with statements as to "value" or "opinion." This troublesome provision, and its overgrown offspring in UCC 2–313(2) will be considered later.

10. Are there analogous situations, outside the law of sale, where legal effect is given to understandings and expectations that are real, but normally are not fully expressed?

terms of the contract (including "express" warranties) and the various "types" of "implied" warranties?[11]

These seemingly simple-minded questions have larger impact than might be evident at first glance, for the answers may be relevant not only in defining the scope of a seller's undertaking but also in determining the effectiveness of contract terms purporting to disclaim and limit "warranties." These questions may even be relevant to the border warfare between the "fields" of sales (contract) and tort.

Commercial and Consumer Parties. With few exceptions, warranty law emerged historically in transactions between merchant buyers and merchant sellers, such as the "brazilletto" wood and the "blue vitriol" cases. (The most notable exception was horse trading, perhaps one of the earliest consumer goods transactions.) The commercial aspect of the cases explains the use of "merchantable" in the basic implied warranty of quality. Transactions between business sellers and business buyers, usually corporations, continue to be important in warranty law. Also important are warranties in sales of consumer products sold by retail dealers and bought by individuals for personal, family or household use. Consumer product warranties emerged initially on the same legal principles fashioned for commercial goods, but, increasingly, laws protective of ordinary consumers have become a special subpart of warranty law. The most litigated consumer product transactions involve retail sales of new cars, the modern counterpart of horse trading.[12]

Buyers' Monetary Remedies. The basic remedial principle of contract law applies in warranty cases. Aggrieved buyers are entitled to the benefit of their bargains. In simplest terms, this means that buyers' monetary recovery for breach of warranty is measured by the value of goods that would have met sellers' obligation. Since buyers commonly have received goods of *some* value and keep those goods, their value must be subtracted from the value of goods as warranted. One finds this formula in UCC 2–714(2).[13]

---

11. Randall v. Newson 2 Q.B. 102 (Court of Appeal, 1877) held a seller liable on the sale of a defective carriage pole. Lord Justice Brett, after referring to various types of warranties that had been mentioned in earlier opinions, stated: "The governing principle ... is that the thing offered and delivered under a contract of purchase and sale must answer the description of it which is contained in words in the contract, or which would be so contained if the contract were accurately drawn out." This unified approach, however, was not sufficiently dominant in the English cases to be reflected in the drafting of the Sale of Goods Act. As a result, the different "types" of warranties, developed in the typical case-law process of distinguishing unwanted precedents, were cast into statutory form, and were carried into the Uniform Sales Act and on into the Sales article of the Code. The Code does provide, however, that "warranties whether express or implied shall be construed as consistent with each other and as cumulative...." UCC 2–317.

12. Consumers are also frequent sellers, as occurs when a consumer "trades in" an existing car (or other "durable" good) on purchase of a new car (or good).

13. "Value" in this formulation means "market value" or "market price," the amounts that informed sellers and buyers have set or would have set for goods of the different levels of quality. In active markets for goods of the kind, "market price" is a statistical compilation of many actual

The market-oriented formula of UCC 2–714(2) is not an exclusive measure of buyers' damages. Buyers may seek recovery measured "in any manner which is reasonable." UCC 2–714(1). If the quality non-conformity is correctable, a buyer may seek to recover the cost of repairing the defect.[14]

Buyers who accepted goods with non-conformities may not be "made whole" by monetary recovery measured only by the value of goods as warranted or by the cost of repair. The Code authorizes buyers, "in a proper case," to recover "incidental damages" (UCC 2–715(1)) and "consequential damages." UCC 2–715(2). Potential liability for consequential damages is a major risk that faces buyers and sellers in some sales transactions. Sellers frequently seek to "contract out" of this potential liability. We will return to that subject later in this chapter.[15]

SECTION 2. WARRANTIES OF QUALITY: EXPRESS AND IMPLIED

(A) DOMESTIC UNITED STATES LAW

T.J. STEVENSON & Co. v. 81,193 BAGS OF FLOUR

United States Court of Appeals, Fifth Circuit, 1980.
629 F.2d 338, rehearing denied 651 F.2d 77 (5th Cir.1981).

BROWN, C.J.

With this decision we hopefully end, in all but a minor respect, an amphibious imbroglio and commercial law practitioner's nightmare involving three shiploads of enriched wheat flour. By a coincidence in this confusing case, each shipload of flour became infested, to varying degrees, with confused (*triboleum confusam*) and red rust (*triboleum casteneum*) flour beetles (sometimes called weevils). None of the parties involved—seller, buyer, and carrier—acted faultlessly over the course of the transaction. All brought their differences to the able District Judge for resolution. The District Judge carefully considered

---

contract prices. Where no active market of the precise goods exists, "value" must be determined by extrapolation from other transactions. Sometimes this is done by expert appraisers.

14. See, e.g., Wat Henry Pontiac Co. v. Bradley, 202 Okl. 82, 210 P.2d 348 (1949) (pre-Code case). The reasonableness limitation no doubt precludes recovery of repair costs that greatly exceed the value added to a non-conforming product. Students may recall studying this as a common-law principle of damages in cases like Peevyhouse v. Garland Coal & Mining Co., 382 P.2d 109 (Okl. 1962); Plante v. Jacobs, 10 Wis.2d 567, 103 N.W.2d 296 (1960).

15. Section 2–714 provides measures of recovery for buyers in regard to accepted goods, goods that belong to the buyers. A quite different measure of recovery is needed when goods have not been accepted by a buyer or, if accepted, are returned to the seller. Warranty law is deeply involved in such transactions, but we shall defer consideration of them until later chapters on performance of sales contracts.

five weeks of testimony presented by the parties, their numerous pleadings, motions, briefs and arguments, scores of interlocking mixed law-fact issues, and difficult questions of federal civil procedure, state commercial, and admiralty law. The Judge's careful and lengthy opinion, 449 F.Supp. 84 (S.D.Ala.1976), resolved the imbroglio but failed to fully convince the parties. The District Judge convinced us, however, and we affirm in almost all respects. Without pause to reflect on the complications that simple insects—confused flour beetles or otherwise—can create in the lives of men and Courts, we proceed to explain our decision.

I. The Life–Cycle of This Appeal: Inception, Growth, and Development

A. The Documents

In April 1974 the Republic of Bolivia entered into two contracts for the purchase of 28,618 metric tons of American enriched wheat flour from ADM Milling Co. ADM owns a number of mills throughout the Midwest. Bolivia sought the flour for distribution to her citizens. The contracts were prepared on ADM's standard form, with quantity, chemical specifications, price, mode of shipment, payment terms, and delivery details filled in. The contracts required packing the flour in 100 pound capacity cotton bags and delivering it to Mobile, Alabama. Railcar shipment was contemplated to Mobile, followed by ocean carriage to South America. This was to take place from May to September 1974. The contracts contained the following delivery terms: "F.A.S. MOBILE, ALABAMA, for export;" and "Delivery of goods by SELLER to the carrier at point of shipment shall constitute delivery to BUYER. ..." Upon satisfactory delivery, the price was payable by irrevocable letter of credit.

Each contract contained an express warranty of merchantability:

Except as provided on the reverse side, SELLER MAKES NO WARRANTY, EXPRESS OR IMPLIED, THAT EXTENDS BEYOND THE DESCRIPTION ON THE FACE HEREOF, except that the product sold hereunder shall be of merchantable quality. ...

[The contracts of sale contained explicit specifications as to protein, ash and moisture content of the flour. There were no specifications as to insect infestation. The buyer agreed to pay the $6.6 million purchase price by a letter of credit, which was payable upon seller's presentation of documents, including an independent firm's certificate of quality concerning the protein, ash and moisture content of the flour immediately prior to loading on ships in Mobile. Seller engaged the services of an inspection firm to sample and evaluate the flour and to prepare certificates of quality.

[Full performance of the contract required eight shiploads of flour to be transported from Mobile to South America. No major problems arose with the first five shipments, which were shipped and paid for.

[As the sixth and seventh shipments were being loaded, the inspection firm noticed signs of infestation. The flour loaded on these vessels was fumigated to kill live insects and both ships sailed to South America. The inspection firm issued certificates stating that the flour complied with the contractual requirements and seller obtained payment under the letter of credit (approximately $1.7 million) for these two shiploads. As the flour was being unloaded at the port in Chile, buyer discovered live and dead weevils. Buyer refused to take possession of the flour. Buyer and seller subsequently agreed that buyer would take possession and sell the infested flour through a salvage broker in Bolivia. The net proceeds of this resale were $326,000 less than the contract price.

[Meanwhile, the eighth shipment was being loaded in Mobile. The inspection firm noticed that some of this flour was infested and these lots were fumigated before loading. After loading, the shipping company, on its own initiative, engaged an inspector to determine whether the cargo was infested. The buyer learned the results of that inspection report and declared it would not accept the shipment; the buyer also blocked the seller from obtaining payment under the letter of credit of the contract price ($850,000) for this final shipment. The shipment never went to South America. Seller eventually took it off the ship and sold it for $454,000 to a United States manufacturer of ceiling tiles.

[The District Court, sitting without a jury, found that the sixth, seventh and eighth shipments of flour had become infested either at the plants where it had been milled or on the rail cars used to transport the flour to Mobile. The court concluded that the flour in these shipments was unmerchantable and that buyer, therefore, had rightfully rejected them. On buyer's claim for damages for the sixth and seventh shipments, judgment was entered for buyer in the amount of $325,960.51. On seller's claim for the price of the eighth shipment, judgment was for the buyer.]

B. The Warranty

The District Judge held that the flour in each of the three shipments failed to meet the express warranty provisions of the contracts. ADM expressly warranted that the bagged flour would be "of merchantable quality" and that it would "comply with all of the applicable provisions of the Federal Food, Drug and Cosmetic Act ['FDA']." The District Judge decided that the infested flour breached both warranties. We, however, pretermit analysis of the FDA warranty since it is difficult to interpret and unnecessary to our resolution of this case. Instead we examine only ADM's warranty of merchantability.

The Code defines the minimum standards required of "merchantable" goods:

Goods to be merchantable must be at least such as ...

(c) are fit for the ordinary purposes for which such goods are used....

UCC § 2–314(2) (emphasis supplied). Like the District Judge we consider only the subsection (c) portion of that definition, and do not reach the arguably applicable standards of subsections (a) and (b). The question is therefore whether the flour at various critical points in time was "fit for the ordinary purposes for which such goods are used."

Official Comments 2 and 8 provide helpful clues to divining the parties' intent (emphasis supplied):

2. The question when the warranty is imposed turns basically on the meaning of the terms of the agreement as recognized in the trade. Goods delivered under an agreement made by a merchant in a given line of trade *must be of a quality comparable to that generally acceptable in that line of trade under the description or other designation of the goods used in the agreement.*

. . .

8. Fitness for the ordinary purposes for which goods of the type are used is a fundamental concept of the present section and is covered in paragraph (c). As stated above, merchantability is also a part of the obligation owing to the purchaser for use. Correspondingly, protection, under this aspect of the warranty, of the person buying for resale to the ultimate consumer is equally necessary, and *merchantable goods must therefore be "honestly" resalable in the normal course of business because they are what they purport to be.*

These comments amplify what is implicit in the statute: "fit for ordinary purposes" merchantability is an ambiguous phrase which has little meaning unless trade usage and other extrinsic evidence is considered. A substantial amount of extrinsic evidence was accordingly admitted and considered by the District Judge in evaluating ADM's warranty of merchantability.

Before reviewing the facts, we observe that finding what the parties meant by "merchantability" requires some evaluation of standards in the commercial market and the state of the art in flour manufacturing. The merchantability of infested flour to be sold to consumers is a question of degree and kind. We have often recognized that no food is completely pure.[23] The FDA has long permitted very small amounts of insect fragments and other *dead* infestation in food products. To declare that any contamination of flour—even by small

---

23. "A scientist with a microscope could find its filthy, putrid, and decomposed substances in almost any canned food we eat." United States v. 484 Bags, More or Less, supra, 423 F.2d at 841 (quoting United States v. 1,500 Cases, More or Less, 236 F.2d 208, 211 (7th Cir.1956)).

amounts of insect fragments, renders the flour unmerchantable would no doubt be out of step with commercial reality and would wreak havoc on food manufacturers and distributors while affording little or no additional protection to the consumer. What this case involves, however, is significant amounts of *live* infestation, by flour beetle eggs, larvae, pupae, and adults. Here the question is: How much live infestation renders consumer-destined flour unfit for the ordinary purposes for which it is used?

The record in this case contains a number of relatively undisputed facts that shed light on the meaning of "merchantable" flour. First, flour beetle infestation in flour mills is an ever present and difficult to eliminate problem. Some flour buyers, such as the United States Government, have however been able to keep infestation problems in their flour to a bare minimum by using their own inspectors to test the flour during its manufacture and at various points thereafter. Also, the relatively stringent precautions taken in ADM-operated mills have reduced infestation problems in their flour to a very great degree. The record further shows that flour containing live infestation, though possibly not dead remains, must be completely fumigated before it can be sold to consumers. Such fumigation is, however, not a normal preparation undertaken by flour buyers. In this context, the fact that the flour involved in the instant case had to be fumigated takes on great significance. Cf. UCC § 1–205(1). As the District Judge stated, "Clearly, if wheat flour found to be infested with beetles would have passed the above [merchantable quality] test . . ., there would have been no need for the flour to have been fumigated. . . ." 449 F.Supp. at 126. We believe that the District Judge's observation closely tracks the Official Comments' statement that goods intended for resale to consumers, as here, are not merchantable unless " 'honestly' resalable in the normal course of business." The evidence in sum indicates that consumer-intended flour containing substantial amounts of live infestation is not merchantable under prevailing standards.

We are not aware of any precedent, in Illinois or elsewhere, which considers the issue of merchantability under circumstances similar to the instant case. . . .

Judicial interpretation, trade usage, and course of dealing point to but one conclusion as to flour infested with significant amounts of live flour beetles: although the flour may be "fit for human consumption" in the sense that it can be eaten without causing sickness, it is nonetheless not of merchantable quality. Such flour is not what is normally expected in the trade. It is not what ADM agreed to supply to Bolivia. Our holding is a narrow one. We do not say, for example, that one live beetle egg in a batch of 10,000 bags of flour renders that flour unmerchantable. Nor do we decide the merchantability of flour containing dead infestation in large or small amounts. Furthermore, we construe only the merchantability standard for flour which will be resold to consumers, not for flour sold directly to consumers. Finally, we emphasize that merchantability is an evolving standard, so that what is unmerchantable at one time and on one record may not be so in another case. In sum, we conclude that the District Judge was not erroneous in finding that the infested flour was not in conformity with ADM's warranty of merchantability.

. . .

[Judgment affirmed.]

Notes

(1) **Contract Interpretation.** (a) The court's legal task was to interpret the express undertaking that the wheat flour would be "merchantable." The court turns to the Commercial Code, UCC 2–314, to search for the meaning of the contract term. Was this justifiable? The court relies particularly on Comments to 2–314. Is it likely that the representatives of the Bolivian government or of ADM Milling Co. were familiar with the Code or the Comments when the contract was drawn?

(b) The court also adverted to "standards in the commercial market" and "the state of the art in flour manufacturing." Did the court see these as significant to the meaning of UCC 2–314? The court noted that some buyers send their own inspectors to their sellers' plants to test flour being processed. Is this indicative of the quality standards in the marketplace?

(c) The court found that seller used relatively stringent precautions in its own mills and that this reduced infestation problems to a very great degree. The trial court opinion revealed that this was the flour in the first five shipments. ADM Milling Co. lacked capacity to mill the entire amount of the contract and contracted to buy the remainder from other milling companies. Is this relevant to determination of the seller's responsibility?

(d) Within the United States, the required degree of purity of flour sold is often the subject of trade association standards. For an interesting contract dispute that involved the differing standards of both the Millers' National Federation and the American Bakers' Association, see International Milling Co. v. Hachmeister, Inc., 380 Pa. 407, 110 A.2d 186 (1955).

(2) **Inspection, Shipment and Payment.** The *T.J. Stevenson* case reveals common commercial practices regarding performance of sales contracts when parties are at a distance from each other. Performance problems are taken up in Chapter 5.

SIDCO PRODUCTS MARKETING, INC. v. GULF OIL CORP.
United States Court of Appeals, Fifth Circuit, 1988.
858 F.2d 1095.

EDITH H. JONES, CIRCUIT JUDGE:

At issue here is the grant of summary judgment for the defendant [Gulf] concerning claims for breach of express and implied warranties

... in the sale [by Gulf to Sidco] of a material called "middle layer emulsion" (MLE). Texas law applies in this diversity case. Concluding essentially that Gulf did not misrepresent the nature or qualities of MLE to the ultimate purchaser Sidco, we affirm.

I. BACKGROUND

According to Sidco, this is the story of a pig in a poke. On December 15, 1983, Gulf published a Bid Inquiry in which it invited bids from a selected group of purchasers for a product called "middle layer emulsion." One company on the bid list was Chemwaste, Inc. Several portions of the Bid Inquiry are relevant to our discussion. First, the product was defined as Middle Layer Emulsion [MLE], "a mixture of oil, water and particulate matter." Second, paragraph 10 of the Bid Inquiry afforded any prospective purchaser the opportunity to "inspect the tanks containing MLE and ... obtain a reasonable sample therefrom for testing." The bid price was to be gauged by the value of recoverable hydrocarbons estimated to be contained in the MLE. Third, a cautionary environmental note appeared as paragraph 14 of the Bid Inquiry:

> The solids in the middle layer emulsion are listed by the United States Environmental Protection Agency in 40 CFR Part 261 as a "Hazardous Waste from Specific Sources, Slop Oil emulsion solids from the petroleum refining industry" with an EPA hazardous waste number of K049. If the solids are removed from the middle layer emulsion, then the disposal of these solids are regulated by the Federal Government as well as many state and local governments. It will be the responsibility of the successful bidder to dispose of these solids and any waste water generated in accordance with all applicable Federal, State and local rules and regulations.

Sidco became interested in purchasing MLE for processing and resale of the oil in it when its president, Dirk Stronck, obtained and read a copy of the Bid Inquiry, including paragraph 14. Because Gulf was selling the product only to authorized bidders, Stronck contacted Romero Brothers Oil Exchange, Inc., which acquired from Chemwaste the right to sell MLE. Sidco availed itself of the opportunity to examine MLE chemically and engaged E.W. Saybolt & Company, Inc. for this purpose. Upon receipt of what it believed were satisfactory test results from Saybolt, Sidco signed a contract to purchase the MLE from Romero. The Romero contract was executed for Sidco by Ron Bougere, its then vice-president.

The sale from Gulf to Chemwaste, thence to Romero and Sidco, occurred January 24, 1984. Sidco paid $394,482 for MLE estimated to yield 28,077 barrels of recoverable hydrocarbons. Sidco then entered into a processing agreement with Texas Oil and Chemical Terminal, Inc. [TOCT] for "slop oil" without showing TOCT the Bid Inquiry or advising it that the product was MLE. TOCT's attempts to process

MLE encountered serious difficulty—the product first plugged a pump screen and damaged TOCT's heater and later clogged a processing tower.

After further testing, Sidco was led to inquire of the Texas Department of Water Resources whether MLE might be a "hazardous waste" regulated by federal environmental law. The department answered affirmatively. [Sidco] protested this decision, but was ordered to and did remove the MLE from the TOCT refinery, which was not licensed to process hazardous waste, and paid for repairs to TOCT's heater. Nevertheless, hydrocarbon products were eventually extracted and sold by Sidco for gross revenue exceeding $400,000.

Sidco claims to have sustained over $13 million in damages, including $60,000 out-of-pocket costs, over $360,000 in lost revenues, the loss of $5 million in financial backing for proposed slop oil activities, and foregone business opportunities exceeding $8.6 million.

Sidco's lawsuit against Gulf alleged the following causes of action:

1. Gulf breached an express warranty regarding the nature and quality of MLE, in violation of Tex. Bus. & Com. Code Ann. § 2.313;

2. Gulf breached the implied warranty of merchantability in that MLE was not fit for the purpose for which slop oil is ordinarily sold, violating Tex. Bus. & Com. Code Ann. § 2.314.

* * *

II. DISCUSSION

The determination most critical to the success of Sidco's position is the nature of the misrepresentations or omissions by Gulf in its Bid Inquiry. Sidco concedes that the Bid Inquiry constitutes the only relevant communication between Gulf and Sidco's representatives prior to Sidco's purchase of MLE. Sidco charges that Gulf misrepresented three characteristics of the MLE: that it formed an unusually tight emulsion which was not susceptible to ordinary processing methods; that the product was not "ordinary slop oil," and that the product in its totality was a hazardous waste under applicable environmental regulations. Sidco alleges that all of its damages flowed from these misrepresentations. Sidco's breach of warranty claims, and its alleged breach of the DTPA founded on warranty and misrepresentation claims, depend upon the existence of these pleaded and vigorously argued misrepresentations of MLE's qualities.

Try as we may, we are unable to discern in the bare simplicity of Gulf's Bid Inquiry the false representations that Sidco asserts. The pertinent portions of the Bid Inquiry were quoted above. MLE is there described as an emulsion, which the dictionary alerts us is an "intimate mixture" of two incompletely miscible liquids, such as water and oil, or of a semisolid or solid dispersed in a liquid. Webster's Third New Int'l Dictionary. The MLE is defined to contain water, hydrocarbons and particulate matter. Prospective purchasers are offered the opportunity to sample a sufficient quantity of the MLE to determine its qualities. Finally, there is a cautionary note about the hazardous waste nature of solids contained in the MLE. There is, however, no affirmation of fact concerning the susceptibility of MLE to any particular hydrocarbon processing or refining technique. There is no representation that MLE is "ordinary slop oil." The term slop oil appears only once in the Bid Inquiry, as a descriptive term (in paragraph 14) in the title of the EPA regulation governing the nature of the solids. MLE itself is not represented in the Bid Inquiry as either environmentally hazardous or non-hazardous. The Bid Inquiry did, however, put the would-be purchaser on notice that he should sample and test the MLE in order to determine the nature and quantity of its hydrocarbon content and to calculate his bid price. To put the matter briefly, the Bid Inquiry described MLE much as would a want-ad for a "truck," in that it described the product generically and left the rest of the characteristics to be discerned by the purchaser in his test-drive or at his mechanic's shop.

A warranty is a promise or affirmation of fact concerning a product or a description of the product to which the product is represented to conform. Tex. Bus. & Com. Code Ann. §§ 2.313(a)(1) and (2). Gulf's Bid Inquiry made no promise or description of MLE with regard to its processability or its status as either "ordinary slop oil" or an EPA-regulated hazardous waste. Where there is no such representation, promise, or affirmation that becomes part of the basis of the parties' bargain, there is no express warranty to be breached. La Sara Grain Co. v. First National Bank, 673 S.W.2d 558, 565 (Tex.1984).

Sidco responds to this conclusion in two ways, which we believe are but versions of the same argument. Gulf, it says, "by its conduct" as well as by the Bid Inquiry, "acted as if" MLE was ordinary slop oil. Alternatively, the essence of Gulf's duplicitous conduct, Sidco contends, is that Gulf *omitted* to disclose that MLE could not be processed by ordinary refinery means, that it was not ordinary slop oil and that it was, irrespective of the solids it contained, a hazardous waste. Omissions, however, are not affirmative representations of any sort and thus cannot support a warranty claim, because express warranties must be explicit. ... On the record before us, it appears that Gulf's Bid Inquiry embodied no express warranty concerning the processability of MLE or its status as "ordinary slop oil" or a non-hazardous material.

Sidco also contends that MLE was sold under an implied warranty of merchantability or fitness for the purposes for which "ordinary slop oil" is used. Gulf moved for summary judgment on this issue, asserting that slop oil is bought and sold so that it can be processed to yield valuable petroleum products. Since the MLE did eventually produce $400,000 of such products for Sidco, the implied warranty of merchantability was fulfilled. This argument suffers from the lack of record evidence demonstrating that, if MLE were to be equated to "ordinary slop oil" for implied warranty purposes, the revenue earned for its petroleum contents represented a "quality comparable to that generally acceptable in that line of trade ..." Official Comment 2 to Tex. Bus. & Com. Code Ann. § 2.314. Alternatively, however, Gulf asserts that there can be no implied warranty of merchantability as requested by Sidco, because Gulf nowhere expressly represented MLE as "ordinary slop-oil." We find this latter rationale convincing and consistent with our previous discussion.

* * *

For these reasons, the summary judgment granted by the district court is AFFIRMED.

Notes

(1) Merchantable Quality: Ordinary purposes. Goods may be useful for more than one purpose. Flour may be useful for human consumption, but can also be used in the manufacture of ceiling tiles. Sidco believed erroneously that the middle layer emulsion could be used as "slop oil," but the goods could be used as a source of hydrocarbons. Cows may be used as dairy animals, for breeding purposes, or for slaughter. What should determine the "ordinary purposes" of goods that have multiple uses? Can the answer be found in the words of the contract of the parties? Are there other sources?

(2) Merchantable Quality: Fitness for Ordinary Purpose. Once purposes are identified, how good must goods be to be deemed "fit"? The Fifth Circuit said in *T.J. Stevenson* that it would not decide generally how much infestation could exist in flour that was still fit for human consumption. It declared that merchantability is an "evolving standard." What should determine the minimum standard of "fitness" of goods?

Problem 1. Buyer purchased a new Mustang automobile from a Ford dealer. After 30 months, during which Buyer had driven the car 75,000 miles, Buyer discovered that the way the taillight assembly gaskets had been installed permitted water to enter and cause severe rust damage. Did Seller breach the warranty of merchantability? On these facts, the Wisconsin Supreme Court held that the rust problem did not render the car unfit for the purpose of driving. "When a car can provide safe, reliable transportation it is generally considered merchantable." Taterka v. Ford Motor Co., 86 Wis.2d 140, 271 N.W.2d 653 (1978). If the car had been a Mercedes, would the same ruling be appropriate?

(3) Merchantable Quality: Pass Without Objection in the Trade. Section 2–314(2)(a) defines merchantability by reference to trade standards. The Code provides that trade usage (UCC 1–205(2)) becomes, by implication, part of the parties' bargain in fact (UCC 1–201(3) ("agreement") which results in defining their legal obligations (UCC 1–201(11) ("contract"). If goods of a certain quality are regularly accepted without objection by buyers in the trade, this provides a contractual standard against which to measure the objection of a particular buyer in the same trade. See Comment 7 to UCC 2–314. Does this suggest that the issue of sellers' responsibility should be decided as a matter of contract interpretation?

(4) Merchantable Quality: Fair Average Quality. UCC 2–314(2)(b) specifies that goods must be such as "in the case of fungible goods, are of fair average quality within the description." Comment 7 implies a limited scope for this provision: " 'Fair average' is a term directly appropriate to *agricultural* bulk products ..." (emphasis added). The statute, of course, extends to non-agricultural fungible goods; "fungible" goods, as defined in UCC 1–201(17), comprise not only various bulk products (like ores) but also most manufactured goods where "any unit is, by nature or usage of trade, the equivalent of any other like unit."

Comment 7 to UCC 2–314 seeks to shed light on the standard by stating that "fair average" means "goods centering around the middle belt of quality, not the least or the worst that can be understood in the particular trade by the designation, but such as can pass 'without objection.' Of course a fair percentage of the least is permissible but the goods are not 'fair average' if they are all of the least or worst quality possible under the description."

Does the text of the statute support the implication that goods fail to be of "merchantable quality" if they are below average quality but are "within the description"? Suppose that buyers had been accepting shipments of sugar which ranged in polarization between 75 and 80, with the various shipments averaging out at 77 1/2. Would the shipment in that case which polarized at 75 3/8 fail to meet the statutory standard? If buyers started rejecting shipments below 77 1/2, so that the average quality of acceptable sugar rose to 79, would this in turn justify rejection of sugar below a polarization of 79? Can independent meaning be given to paragraph (b)? See 1 N.Y.L.R.C., Study of the Uniform Commercial Code 400–01 (1955). Are similar problems latent in paragraph (d)?

INTEGRATED CIRCUITS UNLIMITED, INC. v. E.F. JOHNSON CO., 691 F.Supp. 630 (E.D.N.Y.1988), aff'd, 875 F.2d 1040 (2d Cir.1989).

Manufacturer of two-way taxi radios contracted to buy 2500 microprocessors to be used as components in the radios to be delivered in installments. After 1900 had been delivered, buyer notified seller that these items were unsatisfactory. The buyer asserted that it had had 130 (some 8%) of the microprocessors tested by an independent laboratory which reported that 2.6% of those tested had failed to perform. Buyer asserted that its acceptable quality level—the number of devices which can be defective without rendering the entire shipment unacceptable—was 1%.

Seller sued buyer for the unpaid price; buyer sought refund of the price paid.[1] After a bench trial, the court preliminarily accepted seller's expert witness' testimony that a defect rate of less than 5% was sufficient to make the goods conforming and rejected testimony of buyer's technicians who lacked industry-wide experience. On further reflection, the trial court observed that, in products containing only five components, a 5% failure rate for each part would result in a probability that one in four of the products had an inadequate component. The court held that credible evidence had shown an industry standard requiring a failure rate much lower than 1%. The court found for the buyer.

The trial court also addressed the adequacy of action based upon sampling of only 8% of the microprocessors. The court noted that the tests were expensive. While the sample had not been selected randomly, the court found that selection for sampling sufficed because it had been made without bias. The court concluded that the statistical probabilities were high enough and sufficiently reliable to warrant the buyer's action.

(5) Merchantable Quality: Contract Description. In *Sidco*, the advocate for the MLE buyer described the contract as a purchase of "a pig in a poke." Sales in which the parties use no description of the goods are not likely to occur. Normally, the goods would be described verbally.[2] "Any description of the goods which is made part of the basis of the bargain creates an express warranty that the goods shall conform to the description." UCC 2–313(1)(b). What is added to the idea of *express* warranty by the provisions in UCC 2–314(2) that define an *implied* warranty on the basis of the "contract description" (UCC 2–314(2)(a) and (b)) or "the agreement" (UCC 2–314(2)(d) and (e))? A satisfactory answer is not easy to find.

Section 2–314(2)(c) does not refer on its face to "contract description" or "agreement," but it declares sellers responsible for the ordinary utility of "such goods." To what antecedent could "such" goods refer? The goods described in the agreement or contract? The goods delivered?

(6) Merchantable Quality of Manufactured Goods: Design Standards. Manufacturers determine their own quality-control standards. Such standards, which may be high or low, are used to decide whether the manufacturer will sell a finished product in the marketplace. (Manufacturers of some goods, e.g., glass crystal or clothing, market some products that do not meet the firms' standards as "seconds.") If a manufacturer fails to detect that a product does not conform to its quality-control standards and, without notice of that fact,

---

1. Buyer contended it had not accepted the goods in question. Much of the legal analysis of the courts addressed the question whether buyer's rejection was rightful. On some microprocessors, the court found for the seller. As to materials rightly rejected, the buyer did not seek damages for seller's breach.

2. In a "present sale" (UCC 2–106(1)) words may be considerably less important than the parties' focus on the thing itself. So, too, in a sale by sample or model.

sells the product to a buyer, is the product, for that reason, unmerchantable?

Problem 2. A restaurant patron ordered and was served a platter that includes a portion of fish almondine. While eating, the patron choked on a fishbone, which lodged in his esophagus. The patron was rushed to a hospital where a bone, one centimeter long, was removed. Patron sues Restaurant for breach of the implied warranty of merchantability. (Note that serving food in a restaurant is a sale under UCC 2–314(1).) What result? See Morrison's Cafeteria v. Haddox, 431 So.2d 975 (Ala.1983)(jury verdict for patron reversed; as a matter of law, a one-centimeter bone in a fish fillet does not make the food unmerchantable). We consider sellers' liability for buyers' personal injuries further in Section 5 infra.

ROYAL BUSINESS MACHINES, INC. v. LORRAINE CORP.
United States Court of Appeals, Seventh Circuit, 1980.
633 F.2d 34.

BAKER, D.J.

This is an appeal from a judgment of the district court entered after a bench trial awarding ... [Booher] $1,171,216.16 in compensatory and punitive damages against ... [Royal]. The judgment further awarded Booher attorneys' fees of $156,800.00. ... The judgment also granted Royal a set-off of $12,020.00 for an unpaid balance due on computer typewriters.

The case arose from commercial transactions extending over a period of 18 months between Royal and Booher in which Royal sold and Booher purchased 114 RBC I and 14 RBC II plain paper copying machines. [Booher bought the machines for the purpose of leasing them to its customers.] In mid-August 1976, Booher filed suit against Royal in the Indiana courts claiming breach of warranties and fraud. ...

The issues in the cases arise under Indiana common law and under the U.C.C. as adopted in Indiana, Ind.Code § 26–1–102 et seq. (1976). ...

EXPRESS WARRANTIES

We first address the question whether substantial evidence on the record supports the district court's findings that Royal made and breached express warranties to Booher. The trial judge found that Royal Business Machines made and breached the following express warranties:

(1) that the RBC Model I and II machines and their component parts were of high quality;

(2) that experience and testing had shown that frequency of repairs was very low on such machines and would remain so;

(3) that replacement parts were readily available;

(4) that the cost of maintenance for each RBC machine and cost of supplies was and would remain low, no more than 1/2 cent per copy;

(5) that the RBC machines had been extensively tested and were ready to be marketed;

(6) that experience and reasonable projections had shown that the purchase of the RBC machines by Mr. Booher and Lorraine Corporation and the leasing of the same to customers would return substantial profits to Booher and Lorraine;

(7) that the machines were safe and could not cause fires; and

(8) that service calls were and would be required for the RBC Model II machine on the average of every 7,000 to 9,000 copies, including preventive maintenance calls.

Substantial evidence supports the court's findings as to Numbers 5, 7, 8, and the maintenance aspect of Number 4, but, as a matter of law, Numbers 1, 2, 3, 6, and the cost of supplies portion of Number 4 cannot be considered express warranties.

Paraphrasing U.C.C. § 2–313 as adopted in Indiana, an express warranty is made up of the following elements: (a) an affirmation of fact or promise, (b) that relates to the goods, and (c) becomes a part of the basis of the bargain between the parties. When each of these three elements is present, a warranty is created that the goods shall conform to the affirmation of fact or to the promise.

The decisive test for whether a given representation is a warranty or merely an expression of the seller's opinion is whether the seller asserts a fact of which the buyer is ignorant or merely states an opinion or judgment on a matter of which the seller has no special knowledge and on which the buyer may be expected also to have an opinion and to exercise his judgment. ... General statements to the effect that goods are "the best," ..., or are "of good quality," ... or will "last a lifetime" and be "in perfect condition," ... are generally regarded as expressions of the seller's opinion or "the puffing of his wares" and do not create an express warranty.

No express warranty was created by Royal's affirmation that both RBC machine models and their component parts were of high quality. This was a statement of the seller's opinion, the kind of "puffing" to be expected in any sales transaction, rather than a positive averment of fact describing a product's capabilities to which an express warranty could attach. ...

Similarly, the representations by Royal that experience and testing had shown that the frequency of repair was "very low" and would remain so lack the specificity of an affirmation of fact upon which a warranty could be predicated. These representations were statements of the seller's opinion.

The statement that replacement parts were readily available is an assertion of fact, but it is not a fact that relates to the goods sold as required by Ind.Code § 26–1–2–313(1)(a) and is not an express warranty to which the goods were to conform. Neither is the statement about the future costs of supplies being 1/2 cent per copy an assertion of fact that relates to the goods sold, so the statement cannot constitute the basis of an express warranty.

It was also erroneous to find that an express warranty was created by Royal's assurances to Booher that purchase of the RBC machines would bring him substantial profits. Such a representation does not describe the goods within the meaning of U.C.C. § 2–313(1)(b), nor is the representation an affirmation of fact relating to the goods under U.C.C. § 2–313(1)(a). It is merely sales talk and the expression of the seller's opinion. See Regal Motor Products v. Bender, 102 Ohio App. 447, 139 N.E.2d 463, 465 (1956) (representation that goods were "readily saleable" and that the demand for them would create a market was not a warranty). ...

On the other hand, the assertion that the machines could not cause fires is an assertion of fact relating to the goods, and substantial evidence in the record supports the trial judge's findings that the assertion was made by Royal to Booher. The same may be said for the assertion that the machines were tested and ready to be marketed. ...

As for findings 8 and the maintenance portion of Number 4, Royal's argument that those statements relate to predictions for the future and cannot qualify as warranties is unpersuasive. An expression of future capacity or performance can constitute an express warranty. In Teter v. Shultz, 110 Ind.App. 541, 39 N.E.2d 802, 804 (1942), the Indiana courts held that a seller's statement that dairy cows would give six gallons of milk per day was an affirmation of fact by the seller relating to the goods. It was not a statement of value nor was it merely a statement of the seller's opinion. The Indiana courts have also found that an express warranty was created by a seller's representation that a windmill was capable of furnishing power to grind 20 to 30 bushels of grain per hour in a moderate wind and with a very light wind would pump an abundance of water. Smith v. Borden, 160 Ind. 223, 66 N.E. 681 (1903). Further, in General Supply and Equipment Co. v. Phillips, [490 S.W.2d 913 (Tex.App.1972)], the Texas courts upheld the following express warranties made by a seller of roof panels: (1) that tests show no deterioration in 5 years of normal use; (2) that the roofing panels won't turn black or discolor ... even after years of exposure; and (3) that the panels will not burn, rot, rust, or mildew. ...

Whether a seller affirmed a fact or made a promise amounting to a warranty is a question of fact reserved for the trier of fact. General Supply and Equip. Co. v. Phillips, supra. Substantial evidence in the record supports the finding that Royal made the assertion to Booher that maintenance cost for the machine would run 1/2 cent per copy and that this assertion was not an estimate but an assertion of a fact of performance capability.

Finding Number 8, that service calls on the RBC II would be required every 7,000 to 9,000 copies, relates to performance capability and could constitute the basis of an express warranty. There is substantial evidence in the record to support the finding that this assertion was also made.

While substantial evidence supports the trial court's findings as to the making of those four affirmations of fact or promises, the district court failed to make the further finding that they became part of the basis of the bargain. Ind.Code § 26–1–2–313(1) (1976). While Royal may have made such affirmations to Booher, the question of his knowledge or reliance is another matter.[7]

This case is complicated by the fact that it involved a series of sales transactions between the same parties over approximately an 18-month period and concerned two different machines. The situations of the parties, their knowledge and reliance, may be expected to change in light of their experience during that time. An affirmation of fact which the buyer from his experience knows to be untrue cannot form a part of the basis of the bargain. ... Therefore, as to each purchase, Booher's expanding knowledge of the capacities of the copying machines would have to be considered in deciding whether Royal's representations were part of the basis of the bargain. The same representations that could have constituted an express warranty early in the series of transactions might not have qualified as an express warranty in a later transaction if the buyer had acquired independent knowledge as to the fact asserted.

The trial court did not indicate that it considered whether the warranties could exist and apply to each transaction in the series. Such an analysis is crucial to a just determination. Its absence renders the district court's findings insufficient on the issue of the breach of express warranties.

Since a retrial on the questions of the breach of express warranties and the extent of damages is necessary, we offer the following observations. The court must consider whether the machines were defective upon delivery. Breach occurs only if the goods are defective upon delivery and not if the goods later become defective through abuse or neglect. ...

---

7. The requirement that a statement be part of the basis of the bargain in order to constitute an express warranty "is essentially a reliance requirement and is inextricably intertwined with the initial determination as to whether given language may constitute an express warranty since affirmations, promises and descriptions tend to become a part of the basis of the bargain. It was the intention of the drafters of the U.C.C. not to require a strong showing of reliance. In fact, they envisioned that all statements of the seller become part of the basis of the bargain unless clear affirmative proof is shown to the contrary. See Official Comments 3 and 8 to U.C.C. § 2–313." Sessa v. Riegle, 427 F.Supp. 760, 766 (E.D.Pa.1977), aff'd without op. 568 F.2d 770 (3d Cir.1978). ...

In considering the promise relating to the cost of maintenance, the district court should determine at what stage Booher's own knowledge and experience prevented him from blindly relying on the representations of Royal. A similar analysis is needed in examining the representation concerning fire hazard in the RBC I machines. The court also should determine when that representation was made. If not made until February 1975, the representation could not have been the basis for sales made prior to that date.

FRAUD AND MISREPRESENTATION

The district court found that beginning in April or May of 1974 and continuing throughout most of 1975, Royal, by and through its agents and employees acting in the course and scope of their employment, persuaded Booher to buy RBC I and RBC II copiers by knowingly making material oral misrepresentations which were relied upon by Booher to his injury.

Under Indiana law, the essential elements of actionable fraud are representations, falsity, scienter, deception, and injury.... A fraud action must be predicated upon statements of existing facts, not promises to perform in the future. ... Nor do expressions of opinion qualify as fraudulent misrepresentations. The district court made no specific findings as to which of the alleged representations it relied upon in finding fraud. If the court held all eight to be fraudulent misrepresentations, the court erred as to Numbers 1, 2, and 6 because, as discussed above, these were merely expressions of the seller's opinion rather than statements of material fact upon which a fraud action could be based. Numbers 3, 4, 5, 7, and 8, on the other hand, readily qualify as material factual representations. ...

The trial court, however, is silent on the remaining question, that of deception or reasonable reliance by Booher on the representations in the various transactions. ... This issue is virtually identical to the basis of the bargain question remanded under the express warranty theory.

The district court's finding of fraud, therefore, must be set aside, and the cause remanded for retrial on the questions of the specific misrepresentations relied upon by Booher in each transaction and the reasonableness of that reliance.

With regard to rescission as a remedy for fraud, rescission would be available only for those specific sales to which fraud attached. ...

IMPLIED WARRANTIES

The district court found that Royal breached the implied warranties of merchantability and of fitness for a particular purpose. We cannot agree that the record supports the court's findings.

A warranty of merchantability is implied by law in any sale where the seller is a merchant of the goods. To be merchantable, goods must, *inter alia,* pass without objection in the trade under the contract description, be of fair average quality, and be fit for the ordinary purposes for which such goods are used. Ind.Code § 26–1–2–314 (1976). They must "conform to ordinary standards, and ... be of the same average grade, quality and value as similar goods sold under similar circumstances." ... It was Booher's burden to prove that the copying machines were not merchantable. ... Booher failed to satisfy his burden of proof as to standards in the trade for either the RBC I or RBC II machine. No evidence supports the trial court's findings of a breach of the implied warranty of merchantability.

An implied warranty of fitness for a particular purpose arises where a seller has reason to know a particular purpose for which the goods are required and the buyer relies on the seller's skill or judgment to select or furnish suitable goods. Ind.Code § 26–1–2–315 (1976). The court found that Royal knew the particular purpose for which all the RBC machines were to be used and, in fact, that Royal had taken affirmative steps to persuade Booher to become its dealer and that occasionally its employees even accompanied Booher on calls to customers. ...

The district court, however, failed to distinguish between implied warranties on the RBC I and on the RBC II machines. Nor did the court differentiate among the different transactions involving the two machines. On remand the district court should make further findings on Booher's actual reliance on Royal's skill or judgment in each purchase of the RBC I and RBC II machines. We view it as most unlikely that a dealer who now concedes himself to be an expert in the field of plain paper copiers did not at some point, as his experience with the machines increased, rely on his own judgment in making purchases.

...

[Judgment reversed. Cause remanded for a new trial.]

Notes

(1) **Sellers' Talk; Affirmations of Fact.** The court considers six statements which were the basis of buyer's claim for breach of express warranty. Were any of the six statements "promises" of the seller? If a person makes a promise, which is supported by consideration, and does not perform the promise, is the person liable for breach of contract? Is there a difference between breach of contract and breach of warranty? Note that the Code defines an express warranty as either promises or affirmations of fact. In general contract law, does an affirmation of fact serve as the basis of liability for breach of contract?

(2) **"Opinion," "Value," "Commendation," and Express Warranties.** Professor Page Keeton outlined the wide variations in the impact of statements which might fall under the heading of "opinion." Quoting words of Learned Hand, Keeton observed that some statements are like the claims of campaign managers before election: "rather designed to allay the suspicion that would attend their absence than to be understood as having any relation to objective truth." Keeton, The

Rights of Disappointed Purchasers, 32 Tex.L.Rev. 1, 8 (1953). On the other hand, some statements of opinion may be expected to produce reliance.

In a slightly different connection, Keeton illustrated the effect of the nature of the recovery on the framing of the legal rule. A misrepresentation which is innocent ordinarily will not support an action for damages for deceit. But such a misrepresentation may more readily provide a defense to an action to enforce the agreement which it induced and even, in some cases, a basis for rescission of a completed transaction. Id. at 10. Is such shaping of the rule to the remedy feasible under current statutory structures?

The Code provides that "an affirmation" that is "merely of the value of the goods" or "a statement purporting to be merely the seller's opinion or commendation of the goods" does not create a warranty. UCC 2–313(2). Sales pitches of this genre are very common; would sellers continue this practice if it did not influence buyers? Are there reasons of public policy for negating buyers' protection if sellers' affirmations or statements are not true?

Does the exception in 2–313(2) apply to sellers' promises as to future value of goods?

(3) Relationship to the Goods. Under UCC 2–313(1)(a), an affirmation of fact or promise is not an express warranty unless it "relates to the goods." The court in *Royal Business Machines* found that three of seller's statements lacked this characteristic. Were any of these statements promises? In *Advent Systems,* chapter 1 supra, the seller promised, inter alia, to train buyer's personnel. Did that promise relate to the goods? Assuming that seller refused to provide the training and buyer sued for breach, could seller defend on the ground that the promise did not relate to the goods? Did the Code drafters mislead by including "or promise" in UCC 2–313(1)(a) without cross-reference to UCC 1–103?

(4) Part of the Basis of the Bargain. Under UCC 2–313(1)(a), an affirmation of fact or promise is not an express warranty unless it "becomes part of the basis of the bargain." Insofar as this applies to promises, is it consistent with general contract law? The Official Comment addressed to this phrase, Comment 3, does not refer to sellers' promises, but only to affirmations of fact. Is that indicative of the scope of the limiting concept of "part of the basis of the bargain"? Is there more justification for applying that limiting concept to affirmations of fact?

(5) Reliance and Basis of the Bargain. The Uniform Sales Act provision limited express warranty to an affirmation (or promise) that had "the natural tendency ... to induce the buyer to purchase the goods, and the buyer purchases the goods relying thereon." USA 12. The Code drafters deliberately dropped these elements and substituted the term, "part of the basis of the bargain." Comment 3 declares: no particular reliance need be shown. Nonetheless, courts like *Royal*

Business Machines seek the meaning of "part of the basis of the bargain" in the idea of buyer reliance. See the court's footnote 7. In light of the deliberate legislative choice to drop a reliance requirement from the text of the law, can the reasoning of the courts in reliance terms be explained? What is the meaning of the penultimate sentence in Comment 3?

Is the underlying problem different from any general contract inquiry seeking to find the nature of the parties' reasonable expectations? See Murray, Basis of the Bargain, Transcending Classical Concepts, 66 Minn.L.Rev. 283 (1982).

CIPOLLONE v. LIGGETT GROUP, INC., 893 F.2d 541 (3d Cir.1990), cert. granted, ___ U.S. ___, 111 S.Ct. 1386, 113 L.Ed.2d 443 (1991).
[In a case brought on behalf of a woman whose illness and death allegedly had resulted from years of smoking cigarettes manufactured by the Liggett Group, Inc., plaintiff contended that the manufacturer had made certain express warranties in its advertisements and that those warranties had been breached.]

We turn now to another major area of dispute between the parties, one that implicates the conceptual basis of express warranty law. . . . With respect to this issue, the district court gave the following instructions to the jury:

> [Plaintiff] must prove . . . that Liggett, prior to 1966, made one or more of the statements claimed by the plaintiff and that such statements were affirmations of fact or promises by Liggett . . . [and] that such statements were part of the basis of the bargain between Liggett and consumers like Rose Cipollone. . . .
>
> The law does not require plaintiff to show that Rose Cipollone specifically relied on Liggett's warranties.
>
> Ordinarily a guarantee or promise in an advertisement or other description of the goods becomes part of the basis of the bargain if it would naturally induce the purchase of the product and no particular reliance by the buyer on such statement needs to be shown. However, if the evidence establishes that the claimed statement cannot fairly be viewed as entering into the bargain, that is, that the statement would not naturally induce the purchase of a product, then no express warranty has been created.

* * *

The history of section 2–313(1)(a), although informative, fails to give a clear answer as to whether reliance is required. Section 2–313(1)(a) is an adaptation of section 12 of the Uniform Sales Act. A comparison of the two sections reveals that they are substantially the same except for the replacement of section 12's express reliance requirement with section 2–313(1)(a)'s basis of the bargain requirement.

* * *

... Comment 4 states that "the whole purpose of the law of warranty is to determine what it is that the seller has in essence agreed to sell." ... Reliance is irrelevant to what a seller agrees to sell.[28]

... We hold that once the buyer has become aware of the affirmation of fact or promise, the statements are presumed to be part of the "basis of the bargain" unless the defendant, by "clear affirmative proof," shows that the buyer knew that the affirmation of fact or promise was untrue. ...

Applying our interpretation of section 2–313 to the case at bar, we conclude that the district court's jury instructions were erroneous for two reasons. First, they did not require the plaintiff to prove that Mrs. Cipollone had read, seen, or heard the advertisements at issue. Second, they did not permit the defendant to prove that although Mrs. Cipollone had read, seen, or heard the advertisements, she did not believe the safety assurances contained therein. We must therefore reverse and remand for a new trial on this issue.

(6) Other "Fields" of Law. UCC 1–103 provides that the principles of law and equity, including the law relative to "fraud, misrepresentation ... [and] mistake" supplement the Code unless displaced by particular provisions of it.

As *Royal Business Machines* demonstrates, factual situations giving rise to express warranty claims are likely to give rise as well to claims of fraud or misrepresentation. The Restatement (Second) of Torts (1977) provides:

> § 525. Liability for Fraudulent Misrepresentation
>
> One who fraudulently makes a misrepresentation of fact, opinion, intention or law for the purpose of inducing another to act or to refrain from action in reliance on it, is subject to liability to the other in deceit for pecuniary loss caused to him by his justifiable reliance upon the misrepresentation.

An illustration to § 525 reveals the close relationship between the tort and the law of express warranty:

---

28. For example, imagine a tire merchant describing a tire to three different prospective purchasers, each listening to his sales talk at the same time. The seller guarantees that the tire will (1) be safe for use even in heavily loaded vehicles; (2) last at least 20,000 miles; and (3) be the same style tire sold with a Rolls Royce. The first purchaser buys the tire relying on the seller's safety warranty. The second buys the tire relying on the seller's durability warranty. The third buys the tire relying on the seller's style warranty. None of the purchasers communicates to the seller the reason why he or she is purchasing one of the tires, although the reason for the purchase is communicated to the buyer's spouse, who will later come forward to testify truthfully regarding what the buyer relied on when making the purchase. It is implausible that each buyer has a different warranty, and that the second buyer, but not the first or third buyers, can sue if the tire wears out before 20,000 miles. [Footnote by court]

A, in order to induce B to buy a heating device, states that it will give a stated amount of heat while consuming only a stated amount of fuel. B is justified in accepting A's statement as an assurance that the heating device is capable of giving the services that A promises.

The Restatement, § 526, defines "fraudulently" in broad terms. The Restatement adds a provision for "negligent misrepresentation," § 552, and a special provision for "innocent misrepresentation" in certain transactions, including sales or rental of goods:

§ 552C. Misrepresentation in Sale, Rental or Exchange Transaction

(1) One who, in a sale, rental or exchange transaction with another, makes a misrepresentation of a material fact for the purpose of inducing the other to act or to refrain from acting in reliance upon it, is subject to liability to the other for pecuniary loss caused to him by his justifiable reliance upon the misrepresentation, even though it is not made fraudulently or negligently.

"Misrepresentation," as a part of general contract law, permits a party who has been misled by a fraudulent *or* material misrepresentation in the negotiation of a contract to avoid it. Restatement (Second) of Contracts § 164 (1981). See also E. Farnsworth, Contracts §§ 4.10—4.15 (2d ed. 1990).

Another "field" mentioned in UCC 1–103 is the law of mistake. The Restatement (Second) of Contracts provides:

§ 152. When Mistake of Both Parties Makes a Contract Voidable

(1) Where a mistake of both parties at the time a contract was made as to a basic assumption on which the contract was made has a material effect on the agreed exchange of performances, the contract is voidable by the adversely affected party unless he bears the risk of the mistake under the rule stated in § 154.

Comment *g* describes the "close relationship" between this principle and the law governing warranties.[3] See also E. Farnsworth, Contracts §§ 9.2, 9.3 (2d ed. 1990).

Problem 3. Seller, a dealer in chemicals, told Buyer, "I've just received a shipment from Ace Chemical Co. in response to my order for Blue Vitriol. I can sell it to you at $60 per barrel." Buyer purchased 100 barrels. The barrels were sealed and it was not feasible or

---

3. General contract law further provides relief, in limited circumstances, for unilateral mistake if the other party had reason to know of the mistake. See Restatement (Second) of Contracts § 153(b). In recent years, some courts have granted contract relief in limited circumstances even though one party's mistake was not palpable to the other. See also E. Farnsworth, Contracts § 9.4 (2d ed. 1990).

customary for Seller or Buyer to open the barrels before delivery. Seller had no reason to believe that the shipment from Ace did not conform with his order. When Buyer opened the barrels and tested the material it proved to be "Salzburger Vitriol," an inferior product.

Has Buyer a claim against Seller under UCC 2–313? (See Hawkins v. Pemberton, the 1872 Blue Vitriol decision discussed in Section 1, supra.) Has Buyer any alternative ground for recovery? See UCC 2–314(2)(a).

Problem 4. Seller, a car dealer, showed Buyer a car on display in the showroom. While Buyer was examining the car, Seller described the car as a "Model 57–V." Buyer agreed to buy the car for $3,000. The contract of sale described the car as a "Model 57–V." After the purchase, Buyer found that the car was a "Model 57–J." The two models were the same except that Model 57–V had four doors, chrome trim and a rug on the floor, while Model 57–J had two doors, no chrome trim and a rubber mat in place of a rug.

Has Buyer a claim under UCC 2–313? Under UCC 2–314(2)(a)? See UCC 2–316(3)(b). Cf. Best Buick v. Welcome, 18 UCC Rep.Serv. 75 (Mass.Div.App.Div.1975) (1968 Mercedes, traded in on new car, described as "1970" model).

CHATLOS SYSTEMS, INC. v. NATIONAL CASH REGISTER CORP.

United States Court of Appeals, Third Circuit, 1982.
670 F.2d 1304.

[Chatlos Systems, Inc. (Chatlos) designed and manufactured cable pressurization equipment for the telecommunications industry. In the spring of 1974, Chatlos decided to buy a computer system and contacted several manufacturers, including National Cash Register Corp. (NCR). NCR recommended its 399/656 disc system. NCR's representative said that the equipment would provide Chatlos with six accounting functions: accounts receivable, payroll, order entry, inventory deletion, state income tax, and cash receipts. The representative also told Chatlos that the system would solve inventory problems, result in direct savings of labor costs, and be programmed to be in full operation in six months. On July 24, 1974, Chatlos signed a written agreement in which NCR warranted the equipment "for 12 months after delivery against defects in material, workmanship and operational failure from ordinary use."

[NCR installed the equipment, but never succeeded in making it fully operational. In November 1976, Chatlos instructed NCR to remove the equipment. NCR refused.]

Per Curiam

This appeal from a district court's award of damages for breach of warranty in a diversity case tried under New Jersey law presents two questions: whether the district court's computation of damages under N.J.Stat.Ann. § 12A:2–714(2) was clearly erroneous, and whether the district court abused its discretion in supplementing the damage award with pre-judgment interest. We answer both questions in the negative and, therefore, we will affirm.

Plaintiff-appellee Chatlos Systems, Inc., initiated this action in the Superior Court of New Jersey, alleging, *inter alia,* breach of warranty regarding an NCR 399/656 computer system it had acquired from defendant National Cash Register Corp. The case was removed under 28 U.S.C. § 1441(a) to the United States District Court for the District of New Jersey. Following a nonjury trial, the district court determined that defendant was liable for breach of warranty and awarded $57,152.76 damages for breach of warranty and consequential damages in the amount of $63,558.16. Chatlos Systems, Inc. v. National Cash Register Corp., 479 F.Supp. 738 (D.N.J.1979), aff'd in part, remanded in part, 635 F.2d 1081 (3d Cir.1980). Defendant appealed and this court affirmed the district court's findings of liability, set aside the award of consequential damages, and remanded for a recalculation of damages for breach of warranty. Chatlos Systems, Inc. v. National Cash Register Corp., 635 F.2d 1081 (3d Cir.1980). On remand, applying the "benefit of the bargain" formula of N.J.Stat.Ann. § 12A:2–714(2) (Uniform Commercial Code § 2–714(2)), the district court determined the damages to be $201,826.50, to which it added an award of pre-judgment interest. Defendant now appeals from these damage determinations, contending that the district court erred in failing to recognize the $46,020 contract price of the delivered NCR computer system as the fair market value of the goods as warranted, and that the award of damages is without support in the evidence presented. Appellant also contests the award of pre-judgment interest.

... The district court relied ... on the testimony of plaintiff-appellee's expert, Dick Brandon, who, without estimating the value of an NCR model 399/656, presented his estimate of the value of a computer system that would perform all of the functions that the NCR 399/656 had been warranted to perform. Brandon did not limit his estimate to equipment of any one manufacturer; he testified regarding manufacturers who could have made systems that would perform the functions that appellant had warranted the NCR 399/656 could perform. He acknowledged that the systems about which he testified were not in the same price range as the NCR 399/656. Appellant likens this testimony to substituting a Rolls Royce for a Ford, and concludes that the district court's recomputed damage award was therefore clearly contrary to the evidence of fair market value—which in NCR's view is the contract price itself.

Appellee did not order, nor was it promised, merely a specific NCR computer model, but an NCR computer system with specified capabilities. The correct measure of damages, under N.J.Stat.Ann. § 12A:2–714(2), is the difference between the fair market value of the goods accepted and the value they would have had if they had been as warranted. Award of that sum is not confined to instances where there has been an increase in value between date of ordering and date of delivery. It may also include the benefit of a contract price which, for whatever reason quoted, was particularly favorable for the customer. Evidence of the contract price may be relevant to the issue of fair market value, but it is not controlling. ... Appellant limited its fair market value analysis to the contract price of the computer model it actually delivered.[3] Appellee developed evidence of the worth of a computer with the capabilities promised by NCR, and the trial court properly credited the evidence.[4]

Appellee was aided, moreover, by the testimony of Frank Hicks, NCR's programmer, who said that he told his company's officials that the "current software was not sufficient in order to deliver the program that the customer [Chatlos] required. They would have to be rewritten or a different system would have to be given to the customer." Appendix to Brief for Appellee at 2.68. Hicks recommended that Chatlos be given an NCR 8200 but was told, "that will not be done." Id. at 2.69. Gerald Greenstein, another NCR witness, admitted that the 8200 series was two levels above the 399 in sophistication and price. Id. at 14.30. This testimony supported Brandon's statement that the price of the hardware needed to perform Chatlos' requirements would be in the $100,000 to $150,000 range.

Essentially, then, the trial judge was confronted with the conflicting value estimates submitted by the parties. Chatlos' expert's estimates were corroborated to some extent by NCR's supporters. NCR, on the other hand, chose to rely on contract price. Credibility determinations had to be made by the district judge. Although we might have come to a different conclusion on the value of the equipment as warranted had we been sitting as trial judges, we are not free to make our own credibility and factual findings. We may reverse the district

---

[3]. At oral argument, counsel for appellant responded to questions from the bench, as follows:

Judge Rosenn: Your position also is that you agree, number one, that the fair market value is the measure of damages here.

Counsel for Appellant: Yes, sir.

Judge Rosenn: The fair market value you say, in the absence of other evidence to the contrary that is relevant, is the contract price. That is the evidence of fair market value.

Counsel: That's right.

Judge Rosenn: Now seeing that had the expert or had the plaintiff been able to establish testimony that there were other machines on the market that were similar to your machine—

Counsel: Yes.

Judge Rosenn: That the fair market value of those was $50,000, that would have been relevant evidence but it had to be the same machine—same type machine.

Counsel: Well, I would say that the measure of damages as indicated by the statute requires the same machine—"the goods"—in an operable position.

[4]. We find the following analogy, rather than the Rolls Royce–Ford analogy submitted by appellant, to be on point:

Judge Weis: If you start thinking about a piece of equipment that is warranted to lift a thousand pounds and it will only lift 500 pounds, then the cost of something that will lift a thousand pounds gives you more of an idea and that may be—

Counsel for Appellee: That may be a better analogy, yes.

Judge Weis: Yes.

court only if its factual determinations were clearly erroneous. Krasnov v. Dinan, 465 F.2d 1298 (3d Cir.1972).[5]

Upon reviewing the evidence of record, therefore, we conclude that the computation of damages for breach of warranty was not clearly erroneous. We hold also that the district court acted within its discretion in awarding pre-judgment interest, Chatlos Systems, Inc. v. National Cash Register Corp., 635 F.2d at 1088.

The judgment of the district court will be affirmed.

ROSENN, CIRCUIT JUDGE, dissenting.

The primary question in this appeal involves the application of Article 2 of the Uniform Commercial Code as adopted by New Jersey in N.J.S.A. 12A:2–101 et seq. (1962) to the measure of damages for breach of warranty in the sale of a computer system. I respectfully dissent because I believe there is no probative evidence to support the district court's award of damages for the breach of warranty in a sum amounting to almost five times the purchase price of the goods. The measure of damages also has been misapplied and this could have a significant effect in the marketplace, especially for the unique and burgeoning computer industry.[1]

In July 1974, National Cash Register Corporation (NCR) sold Chatlos Systems, Inc. (Chatlos), a NCR 399/656 disc computer system (NCR 399) for $46,020 (exclusive of 5 percent sales tax of $1,987.50). The price and system included:

The computer (hardware)	$40,165.00
Software (consisting of 6 computer programs)[2]	5,855.00
	$46,020.00

NCR delivered the disc computer to Chatlos in December 1974 and in March 1975 the payroll program became operational. By March of the following year, however, NCR was still unsuccessful in installing an operational order entry program and inventory deletion program. Moreover, on August 31, 1976, Chatlos experienced problems with the payroll program. On that same day and the day following NCR installed an operational state income tax program, but on September 1,

---

5. The dissent essentially is based on disagreement with the estimates provided by Chatlos' expert, Brandon. The record reveals that he was well qualified; the weight to be given his testimony is the responsibility of the factfinder, not an appellate court.

1. Plaintiff's expert, Brandon, testified that generally 40 percent of all computer installations result in failures. He further testified that successful installations of computer systems require not only the computer companies' attention but also the attention of the customers' top management.

2. The six basic computer programs were: (1) accounts receivable, (2) payroll, (3) order entry, (4) inventory deletion, (5) state income tax, and (6) cash receipts. The contract price also included installation.

1976, Chatlos demanded termination of the lease [3] and removal of the computer.

When this case was previously before us, we upheld the district court's liability decision but remanded for a reassessment of damages, instructing the court that under the purchase contract and the law consequential damages could not be awarded. Consequential damages, therefore, are no longer an issue here.

On remand, the district court, on the basis of the previous record made in the case, fixed the fair market value of the NCR 399 as warranted at the time of its acceptance in August 1975 at $207,826.50. It reached that figure by valuing the hardware at $131,250.00 and the software at $76,575.50, for a total of $207,826.50. The court then determined that the present value of the computer hardware, which Chatlos retained, was $6,000. Putting no value on the accepted payroll program, the court deducted the $6,000 and arrived at an award of $201,826.50 plus pre-judgment interest at the rate of 8 percent per annum from August 1975.

Chatlos contends before this court, as it had before the district court on remand, that under its benefit of the bargain theory the fair market value of the goods as warranted was several times the purchase price of $46,020. ...

[T]he sole issue before us now is whether the district court erred in fixing the fair market value of the computer system as warranted at the time of the acceptance in August 1975 at $207,826.50.

II.

A.

I believe that the district court committed legal error. ...

There are a number of major flaws in the plaintiff's attempt to prove damages in excess of the contract price. I commence with an analysis of plaintiff's basic theory. Chatlos presented its case under a theory that although, as a sophisticated purchaser, it bargained for several months before arriving at a decision on the computer system it required and the price of $46,020, it is entitled, because of the breach of warranty, to damages predicated on a considerably more expensive system. Stated another way, even if it bargained for a cheap system, i.e., one whose low cost reflects its inferior quality, because that system did not perform as bargained for, it is now entitled to damages measured by the value of a system which, although capable of performing the identical functions as the NCR 399, is of far superior quality and accordingly more expensive.

---

3. Chatlos decided to lease the system rather than purchase it outright. To permit this arrangement, NCR sold the system to Mid Atlantic National Bank in July 1975 for $46,020, which leased the system to Chatlos. Chatlos made monthly payments to Mid Atlantic in amounts which would have totaled $70,162.09 over the period of the lease.

The statutory measure of damages for breach of warranty specifically provides that the measure is the difference at the time and place of acceptance between the value "of the goods accepted" and the "value they would have had if they had been as warranted." The focus of the statute is upon "the goods accepted"—not other hypothetical goods which may perform equivalent functions. "Moreover, the value to be considered is the reasonable market value of the *goods delivered,* not the value of the goods to a particular purchaser or for a particular purpose." KLPR–TV, Inc. v. Visual Electronics Corp., 465 F.2d 1382, 1387 (8th Cir.1972) (emphasis added). The court, however, arrived at value on the basis of a hypothetical construction of a system as of December 1978 by the plaintiff's expert, Brandon. The court reached its value by working backward from Brandon's figures, adjusting for inflation.

. . .

Although NCR warranted performance, the failure of its equipment to perform, absent any evidence of the value of any NCR 399 system on which to base fair market value, does not permit a market value based on systems wholly unrelated to the goods sold. Yet, instead of addressing the fair market value of the NCR 399 had it been as warranted, Brandon addressed the fair market value of another system that he concocted by drawing on elements from other major computer systems manufactured by companies such as IBM, Burroughs, and Honeywell, which he considered would perform "functions identical to those contracted for" by Chatlos. He conceded that the systems were "[p]erhaps not within the same range of dollars that the bargain was involved with" and he did not identify specific packages of software. Brandon had no difficulty in arriving at the fair market value of the inoperable NCR equipment but instead of fixing a value on the system had it been operable attempted to fashion a hypothetical system on which he placed a value. The district court, in turn, erroneously adopted that value as the fair market value for an operable NCR 399 system. NCR rightly contends that the "comparable" systems on which Brandon drew were substitute goods of greater technological power and capability and not acceptable in determining damages for breach of warranty under section 2–714. Furthermore, Brandon's hypothetical system did not exist and its valuation was largely speculation.

B.

A review of Brandon's testimony reveals its legal inadequacy for establishing the market value of the system Chatlos purchased from NCR. Brandon never testified to the fair market value which the NCR 399 system would have had had it met the warranty at the time of acceptance. . . .

Thus, the shortcomings in Brandon's testimony defy common sense and the realities of the marketplace. First, ordinarily, the best evi-

dence of fair market value is what a willing purchaser would pay in cash to a willing seller. ... In the instant case we have clearly "not ... an unsophisticated consumer," ... who for a considerable period of time negotiated and bargained with an experienced designer and vendor of computer systems. The price they agreed upon for an operable system would ordinarily be the best evidence of its value. The testimony does not present us with the situation referred to in our previous decision, where "the value of the goods rises between the time that the contract is executed and the time of acceptance," in which event the buyer is entitled to the benefit of his bargain. ... On the contrary, Chatlos here relies on an expert who has indulged in the widest kind of speculation. Based on this testimony, Chatlos asserts in effect that a multi-national sophisticated vendor of computer equipment, despite months of negotiation, incredibly agreed to sell an operable computer system for $46,020 when, in fact, it had a fair market value of $207,000.
...

Fourth, the record contains testimony which appears undisputed that computer equipment falls into one of several tiers, depending upon the degree of sophistication. The more sophisticated equipment has the capability of performing the functions of the least sophisticated equipment, but the less sophisticated equipment cannot perform all of the functions of those in higher levels. The price of the more technologically advanced equipment is obviously greater.

It is undisputed that in September 1976 there were vendors of computer equipment of the same general size as the NCR 399/656 with disc in the price range of $35,000 to $40,000 capable of providing the same programs as those required by Chatlos, including IBM, Phillips, and Burroughs. They were the very companies who competed for the sale of the computer in 1974 in the same price range. On the other hand, Chatlos' requirements could also be satisfied by computers available at "three levels higher in price and sophistication than the 399 disc." Each level higher would mean more sophistication, greater capabilities, and more memory. Greenstein, NCR's expert, testified without contradiction that equipment of Burroughs, IBM, and other vendors in the price range of $100,000 to $150,000, capable of performing Chatlos' requirements, was not comparable to the 399 because it was three levels higher. Such equipment was more comparable to the NCR 8400 series.

...

III.

The purpose of the N.J.S.A. 12A:2–714 is to put the buyer in the same position he would have been in if there had been no breach. See Uniform Commercial Code 1–106(1). The remedies for a breach of warranty were intended to compensate the buyer for his loss; they were not intended to give the purchaser a windfall or treasure trove. The buyer may not receive more than it bargained for; it may not obtain the value of a superior computer system which it did not purchase even though such a system can perform all of the functions the inferior system was designed to serve. ...

...

VI.

On this record, therefore, the damages to which plaintiff is entitled are $46,020 less $6,000, the fair market value at time of trial of the retained hardware, and less $1,000, the fair market value of the payroll program, or the net sum of $39,020.

Accordingly, I would reverse the judgment of the district court and direct it to enter judgment for the plaintiff in the sum of $39,020 with interest from the date of entry of the initial judgment at the rate allowed by state law.

SUR PETITION FOR REHEARING

The petition for rehearing filed by appellant in the above entitled case having been submitted to the judges who participated in the decision of this court and to all the other available circuit judges of the circuit in regular active service, and no judge who concurred in the decision having asked for rehearing, and a majority of the circuit judges of the circuit in regular active service not having voted for rehearing by the court in banc, the petition for rehearing is denied. Judges Adams, Hunter and Garth would grant the petition for rehearing.

ADAMS, CIRCUIT JUDGE, dissents from the denial of rehearing, and makes the following statement:

Ordinarily, an interpretation of state law by this Court, sitting in diversity, is not of sufficient consequence to warrant reconsideration by the Court sitting in banc. One reason is that if a federal court misconstrues the law of a state, the courts of that state have an opportunity, at some point, to reject the federal court's interpretation. See Chuy v. Philadelphia Eagles Football Club, 595 F.2d 1265, 1286–87 (3d Cir.1979) (in banc) (Aldisert, J., dissenting). In this case, however, the majority's holding, which endorses a measure of damages that is based on what appears to be a new interpretation of New Jersey's commercial law, involves a construction of the Uniform Commercial Code as well. Rectification of any error in our interpretation is, because of the national application of the Uniform Commercial Code, significantly more difficult than it would be if New Jersey law alone were implicated. Moreover, the provision of the Uniform Commercial Code involved here is of unusual importance: the measure of damages approved by this Court may create large monetary risks and obligations in a wide range of commercial transactions, including specifically the present burgeoning computer industry. Because there would appear to be considerable force to the dissenting opinion of Judge Rosenn and because I believe that the principle articulated by the majority should be reviewed by the entire Court before it is finally adopted, I would grant the petition for rehearing in banc.

JAMES HUNTER, III and GARTH, CIRCUIT JUDGES join in this statement.

Notes

(1) Benefit of the Bargain: What Was the Bargain? Was it reasonable for Chatlos to expect to receive goods worth five times the contract price? Should the price term be part of the "contract description" of goods sold? Consider Comment 7 to UCC 2–314: "In cases of doubt as to what quality is intended, the price at which a merchant closes a contract is an excellent index of the nature and scope of his obligation under the present section." Would it have been appropriate to probe more deeply into the probable expectations of the parties as to seller's obligation and buyer's remedy in the event that the computer system failed to perform? Should expectations as to (A) performance and (B) redress be considered in relation to each other? Are implied expectations as to redress less permissible that implied expectations as to performance, such as implied warranties of quality? Note that the court, in its earlier decision, gave full effect to the contract provision denying recovery for consequential damages. Does this shed light on the parties' allocation of the risks and benefits of the agreement?

(2) Parol Evidence Rule. In *Chatlos* and, apparently, in *Royal Business Machines*, sellers were charged with liability for breach of oral statements made by their representatives. When contracts of sale are reduced to writing, frequently sellers include in the document a declaration that the document contains the complete agreement of the parties and that there are no promises or representations not contained therein. These "integration" clauses are meant to invoke the parol evidence rule, which for sales contracts is codified in UCC 2–202. In addition to barring evidence that would *contradict* a writing intended as a final expression of a sales agreement, paragraph (b) bars "consistent additional terms" if the court finds "the writing to have been intended also as a complete and exclusive statement of the terms of an agreement." The parol evidence rule, and its codified sales version, are complex legal issues normally studied in the course on Contracts.

What might explain the absence of final written expressions with integration clauses in *Royal Business Machines* and *Chatlos?*

Problem 5. An agreement was signed for the sale of air conditioning equipment to Buyer. The written contract contained detailed specifications concerning the type of equipment, the horsepower of the motors and the tons of refrigeration to be produced. The machinery met the contract specifications, but it was not sufficiently large or powerful to cool Buyer's building. Seller refused to take back the equipment, and pointed out that Buyer received an efficiently operating unit of precisely the size called for in the contract.

Buyer tells his attorney that Seller had recommended the model and size, and had assured Buyer that it would cool Buyer's building. In preparing for trial, Buyer's attorney is concerned that Buyer's testimony with respect to the foregoing statements by Seller would be excluded under the parol evidence rule. The attorney asks you to develop a line of questions that would minimize this danger.

Examine carefully the language of UCC 2–202. Note that "Term" is defined (UCC 1–201(42)) as "that portion of an agreement which relates to a particular matter." Compare UCC 1–201(3) ("agreement" is defined as "the bargain of the parties in fact as found in their language or *by implication from other circumstances* ...") with UCC 1–201(11) ("contract" means "the total legal obligation which results from the parties' agreement as affected by this Act and any other applicable rules of law"). Does UCC 2–202 exclude the above evidence if offered to establish an *implied* warranty?

(3) Lease Transactions. The "buyer" in *Chatlos* was actually a lessee. Because Chatlos lacked sufficient credit to purchase the computer system on an installment basis, an intermediary company bought the system from NCR and leased it to Chatlos. The courts treated Chatlos as a buyer for purposes of the litigation. In 1987, Article 2A on Leases was added to the Code. Under UCC 2A–209(1), seller's warranties to a lessor extend to the lessee if the lease is a "finance lease" (UCC 2A–103(1)(g). This provision codifies the result in *Chatlos*.

The buyer of the copying machines in *Royal Business Machines* was an ordinary equipment lessor, not a financing lessor. As to its lessees, such a lessor's warranties of quality are provided in UCC 2A–210, –212, and –213. These sections parallel the warranty provisions in Article 2.

(4) Consequential Damages. A problem of large importance in sales transactions is the scope of sellers' liability for buyers' consequential damages. The legal issue is related to general contract law growing out of *Hadley v. Baxendale*.[4] The common-law principle is codified in the Code at UCC 2–715(2).

Within the context of sales transactions, buyers may suffer many types of consequential damages resulting from non-conformity of goods purchased. However, certain categories of damages tend to arise regularly. Merchants buying inventory may suffer consequential damages in the form of lost revenues. Such a claim was advanced in *Sidco* and may explain the large amount of the compensatory damages awarded by the trial court in *Royal Business Machines*. Persons buying business equipment may incur expenses coping with the fall-out of the equipment's failure. Such a claim was advanced in *Chatlos*. Farmers buying seeds or herbicides may suffer damages in crop failures. We will see such cases later in this chapter.

A quite different set of consequential losses arises when buyers suffer personal injuries as a result of defects in the goods. This branch of warranty law has become integrally related to the law of strict tort

---

4. A remarkable study of *Hadley v. Baxendale* discloses that the case, as decided, was not a contract case. See Danzig, *Hadley v. Baxendale:* A Study in the Industrialization of the Law, 4 J. Legal Studies 249 (1975).

ADVENT SYSTEMS LIMITED v. UNISYS CORP.

United States Court of Appeals, Third Circuit, 1991.
925 F.2d 670.

WEIS, C.J.

[The main part of this decision appeared in Chapter 1. Having held that the transaction was governed by the Uniform Commercial Code that the claim for relief was not barred by the statute of frauds, and that the agreement was enforceable under UCC 2–204, the court discussed whether the buyer might recover for lost profits resulting from the seller's breach. That discussion follows.]

Under Pennsylvania law, loss of profits may be recovered in a contract action if there is (1) evidence to establish the damages with reasonable certainty; (2) they were the proximate consequence of the wrong; (3) they were reasonably foreseeable. ... Proof of damages need not be mathematically precise, but the evidence must establish the fact "with a fair degree of probability." ...

The Pennsylvania Supreme Court has been skeptical of claims for loss of profits by a "new and untried business." ... An award, however, may be made "where such a loss was reasonably foreseeable to the parties at the time that the contract was entered and where those damages are capable of proof of reasonable certainty." ...

In addressing proof of damages in National Controls Corp. v. National Semiconductor Corp., 833 F.2d 491, 496 (3d Cir.1987) we pointed out that it is necessary to consider the fact that the "damages sought must be a proximate consequence of the breach, not merely remote or possible. ... The element of causation defines the range of socially and economically desirable recovery and requires not only 'but-for' causation in fact but also that the conduct be a substantial factor in bringing about the harm."

In that case the Court vacated an award for loss of profits based on the theory that one of plaintiff's customers would have purchased certain products from plaintiff. "An award of lost profits required speculation by the jury on the likelihood that, absent [defendant's] breaches, [a third-party] would have proceeded with the project and on the likelihood that [the third-party] would have chosen [plaintiff] as a supplier." Id. at 498.

National Controls emphasizes the need for evidence sufficiently concrete to provide a reasonable degree of certainty that the verdict is more than the result of a lottery or emotional reaction. Predicting the results of business dealings that might have, but never did, occur is of course a difficult matter of proof.

When a business has become established, the Pennsylvania Supreme Court has mentioned several methods of proof to establish prospective loss profits: (1) evidence of past profits; (2) profits made by others or by similar contract where the facts were not greatly different; (3) testimony of experts if based on anything more than individual opinions or conjecture. ...

Advent's profits depended on Unisys' efforts and ability to resell the document systems. These were comparatively new products in a market in which Unisys had high hopes, but little, if any, share. Significantly, Arco, one of the companies both Unisys and Advent had hoped to capture as a customer, decided instead to look to IBM, although that company had not yet developed a comparable product. Other businesses such as Southwestern Bell, originally thought to be a prospective customer of Unisys, eventually bought Advent systems marketed through another company and, thus, cannot be the basis for any claim of loss here.

Advent's case on loss of profits rested primarily on the testimony of its expert, Dr. Alfred Kuehn. He relied heavily on industry projections prepared by Frost & Sullivan in 1986 and a market analysis published by the Yankee Group in 1987. These studies both predicted dramatic increases in sales of document systems.

When the trial took place in August 1989, the two year period for which the court ruled that damages could be awarded had already expired. At the time the expert testified, actual results in the marketplace during the pertinent two years, 1987–89, did not support the rosy predictions made earlier. Nevertheless he based his opinion on those outdated projections. For example, he forecast total industry sales in the United States in 1987 of $77 million dollars. But according to defendant's expert, actual sales that year were $12 million dollars. In 1988 plaintiff's forecast was $255 million, but the actual figure was approximately $10 million dollars.

When questioned whether he thought data of what actually occurred was more valuable than past projections, Dr. Kuehn said "Both were important along with other things that are equally important." He did not elaborate further, but apparently his reasoning was that because Unisys had not entered the market, the actual total sales figure in the United States were lower than they would have been otherwise. On this record that explanation is unconvincing at best.

* * *

In Olympia Equipment Leasing Co. v. Western Union Telegraph Co., 797 F.2d 370, 382 (7th Cir.1986), cert. denied, 480 U.S. 934 (1987), the Court referred to the "old problem of expert witnesses" and criticized testimony on prospective lost profits. The Court observed that, "[t]he expert in this case dazzled the jury with an array of figures conveying a delusive impression of exactness'—delusive because the figures had no relation to reality." We too have serious reservations about the validity of expert testimony based on prior predictions of sales for a given period when actual performance data for that same time span are available.

The jury's verdict must also have been based to some extent on the defendant's own contemporaneous sales projections described by the trial judge as "wildly optimistic." The same difficulty about the validity of those projections exists because apparently to some extent they too were based on the same studies cited by Dr. Kuehn.

We have serious doubts that the evidence in this record is adequate to support the award for lost profits. ... We, of course, cannot anticipate what proof on damages will be produced on remand.

CARNATION COMPANY v. OLIVET EGG RANCH

California Court of Appeal, First District, 1986.
First Appellate District, Division Two.
189 Cal.App.3d 809, 229 Cal.Rptr. 261.

KLINE, J.

Olivet Egg Ranch [Olivet] ... appeal[s] following jury trial on [its] claims of fraud and breach of various warranties arising out of [its] purchase and use of chicken feed produced by the Albers Milling Division of the Carnation Company [Albers].

* * *

[Olivet] ... controlled and managed an egg producing operation in Northern California.

For approximately five years, Olivet or its predecessors in interest purchased chickenfeed from Albers, which operated a mill in Santa Rosa. After unsuccessfully seeking payment of its bills, Carnation advised appellants they would no longer be allowed to purchase on credit. Appellants executed a note for the $606,382 balance owed to Carnation. When appellants defaulted on the note Carnation commenced this litigation. Appellants cross-complained on various theories, all premised on their assertion that the feed sold them was 'misformulated, mis-produced and nutritionally substandard' and, therefore, breached a variety of express and implied warranties made to appellants by Carnation and its employees. Appellants alleged that the feed's nutritional deficiencies had caused a decrease in Olivet's egg production revenues and sought to offset such losses against the amount due Carnation on the note.

After lengthy pretrial discovery, jury trial commenced in October 1979. Because the execution and terms of the note were uncontested, appellants proceeded as if plaintiffs and presented their case first. At the conclusion of Olivet's case Carnation successfully moved for nonsuit as to the loss of goodwill portion of Olivet's damage claim. The court granted a nonsuit on goodwill damages as to the breach of warranty causes of action only on the theory appellants had not met their burden of proving, under California Uniform Commercial Code section 2715, that they had made reasonable efforts to mitigate the damages flowing from the loss of their retail egg marketing accounts.

At the close of evidence Carnation was granted a directed verdict as to a portion of the damages suffered by Olivet's predecessor in interest in 1970.

The jury found that Carnation had breached its warranties and damaged Olivet in the amount of $225,000, but that the claim of fraudulent misrepresentation had not been established.

Separate judgments for both parties were entered and Olivet moved for a new trial on various grounds. ... The court denied the motion for new trial, granted a motion to vacate the two previously entered judgments and ordered nunc pro tunc entry of the net judgment after verdict. This appeal followed.

I.

Burden of Proof Under California Uniform Commercial Code Section 2715, subdivision (2)(a)

The nonsuit as to the $309,000 loss in goodwill appellants claimed due to their inability to service their egg marketing accounts [3] was granted upon the theory that California Uniform Commercial Code section 2715, subdivision (2)(a) places on the aggrieved party the burden of showing it took reasonable steps to mitigate its consequential damages. In granting nonsuit the court necessarily determined that, as a matter of law, Olivet failed to present evidence sufficient to meet its burden. It will be necessary to consider whether Olivet presented evidence sufficient to withstand nonsuit on this issue only if we first determine that the court's imposition of the burden on Olivet was legally correct. Olivet could not be penalized for failing to meet a burden which actually rested with Carnation. Thus, we are squarely faced with a question of first impression in California: which party bears the burden of proving the adequacy or inadequacy of efforts to mitigate consequential damages under California Uniform Commercial Code section 2715, subdivision (2)(a)?

---

3. Olivet had an arrangement with several large supermarket chains pursuant to which the markets invested in the ranch partnership and purchased all of their requirements directly from the ranch at a retail price. Olivet was thereby provided with an assured outlet for its eggs and was to derive a profit for the processing and marketing, as well as the egg sale. Due to Olivet's shortfall in egg production, it ultimately was unable to keep up with the requirements of its market accounts and Olivet transferred the accounts to Olson Egg Farms. Appellants claimed the loss of the goodwill value of the retail marketing arm of its operation as an additional element of damages.

The nonsuit was granted only as to the loss of goodwill attributable to the claimed breach of warranty. Because the burden of proof on mitigation as to the fraud cause of action is on the party asserting the defense, the court ruled that the issue remained in the case as to that claim.

Section 2715, subdivision (2)(a), which was adopted without change from the Uniform Commercial Code (UCC), simply declares that "[c]onsequential damages resulting from the seller's breach include ... [a]ny loss resulting from general or particular requirements and needs of which the seller at the time of contracting had reason to know and which could not reasonably be prevented by cover or otherwise."

The official comment to the parallel provision of the UCC does not shed much light on allocation of the burden of proof. Paragraph 2 of the pertinent UCC comment provides in material part that: "The 'tacit agreement' test for the recovery of consequential damages is rejected. Although the older rule at common law which made the seller liable for all consequential damages of which he had 'reason to know' in advance is followed, the liberality of that rule is modified by refusing to permit recovery unless the buyer could not reasonably have prevented the loss by cover or otherwise. Subparagraph (2)[of the statute] carries forward the provision of the prior uniform statutory provision as to consequential damages resulting from breach of warranty, but modifies the rule by requiring first that the buyer attempt to minimize his damages in good faith, either by cover or otherwise." This comment does not demonstrate, as respondent asserts, that section 2715, subdivision (2)(a) was intended to act as "a restraint on the liberality of the common law."

Paragraph 4 of the UCC comment makes specific reference to the UCC's section on the liberal administration of remedies, indicating that the right to consequential damages should be broadly, not narrowly, construed. Furthermore, while paragraph 4 states that "[t]he burden of proving the extent of loss incurred by way of consequential damage is on the buyer ..." this statement does not determine the allocation of the burden of proof on the mitigation issue. It is entirely possible for the injured party to bear the burden of proving the extent of consequential damages while the breaching party has the duty of proving those items which limit the award of consequential damages.

The UCC's failure to allocate unambiguously the burden of proving mitigation has resulted in conflicting interpretations among those jurisdictions that have considered the question. Unfortunately, these cases are of little value to us since they do not analyze the problem nor explain why the burden should rest with one party or the other. By and large the cases merely state the unembellished conclusion that one or the other party has the burden of proof on this issue.

* * *

While the commentators do not unanimously support allocating the burden to the breaching party, there is substantial support among them for this position. Corbin, for example, declares that "[t]he burden of proving that losses could have been avoided by reasonable effort and expense must always be borne by the party who has broken the contract." (5 Corbin on Contracts (1964) § 1039 ...) White and Summers state that "consequential damages that the *defendant* proves the buyer could have avoided will not be allowed ..." (J. White and R. Summers, Uniform Commercial Code (2d ed. 1980) §§ 6–7, p. 250, italics added.) ...

Placing on the party who breaches the burden of showing that consequential losses could have been avoided is intuitively attractive, since proof that there has been a failure to mitigate adequately will reduce the damages awarded and, therefore, seems more in the nature of a defense than an element of the plaintiff's affirmative case. In this sense, proof of failure to mitigate is analogous to evidence showing comparative negligence in tort law, which must be alleged and proved by the defendant.... Moreover, it is sensible to require the defendant to prove those items which go to reduce the plaintiff's recovery, as plaintiffs would have little incentive to do so.

Respondent maintains that "[i]t makes more sense to place the burden of proving efforts to mitigate on the party best able to adduce evidence of such efforts." While this argument is on its surface appealing it does not stand up to closer scrutiny. As has been noted "[v]ery often one must plead and prove matters as to which his adversary has superior access to the proof. Nearly all required allegations of the plaintiff in actions for tort or breach of contract relating to the defendant's acts or omissions describe matters peculiarly in the defendant's knowledge. Correspondingly, when the defendant is required to plead contributory negligence, he pleads facts specially known to the plaintiff." (McCormick on Evidence (3d ed. 1984) ch. 36, § 337 at p. 950.)

Moreover, in cases such as this defendants do not genuinely lack the ability to ascertain the pertinent facts. A carefully drafted set of interrogatories could have provided Carnation with all the information it required about Olivet's efforts to mitigate its consequential damages. Since it therefore had access to the relevant evidence we see no reason why this consideration should prevent allocation to Carnation of the burden of showing that appellants failed to adequately mitigate their consequential damages.

For the foregoing reasons, we hold that while the burden of proving the extent of loss incurred by way of consequential damages rests with the injured party, section 2715, subdivision (2)(a) imposes upon the allegedly breaching party the burden of proving the inadequacy of efforts to mitigate consequential damages. Thus, Carnation, not Olivet, properly had the burden of proof on the issue of Olivet's mitigation of the consequential damages arising from Carnation's breach. Olivet therefore had no duty to present evidence of mitigation and the granting of the nonsuit on the basis of Olivet's asserted failure to produce such evidence was error. The nonsuit removed from the jury's consideration a $309,000 damage claim. Since Carnation never presented evidence on this issue there is no way of knowing whether appellants likely would have prevailed if the court had placed the burden of proof on Carnation. Accordingly, the judgment must be reversed.

* * *

Rouse, J., and Smith, J., concurred.

(B) INTERNATIONAL SALES LAW

Having considered sellers' obligations for the quality of their goods under domestic United States law, we turn briefly to consider the analogous provisions of the Convention on International Sales. The first case studied in this chapter, an international sale of flour from a United States milling company to the Bolivian government, arose before the Convention existed and was decided under the UCC. Would this case, and other cases and problems, be analyzed or decided differently if the law governing the matter is the CISG?

(1) Sellers' Obligations. The Convention sets forth sellers' quality obligations in Section II of Chapter II. The primary standards, in Article 35, resemble the warranty provisions of the UCC, but there are substantial differences. The CISG does not use the term "warranty." Compare carefully the provisions in Article 2(b) with their counterparts in the UCC and consider the UCC provisions for which no counterparts exist in the CISG. What conclusions can be drawn from these comparisons? Are the quality obligations of sellers under CISG greater or less than their obligations under the UCC?

The CISG does not contain a parol evidence provision comparable to UCC 2–202. Article 11 provides that a contract "need not be ... evidenced by writing" and "may be proved by any means, including witnesses." See also CISG 8(3). However, the parties by agreement may derogate from CISG 11 by an "integration clause" (CISG 6) or may agree that modification of a written agreement must be in writing (CISG 29(2)).

(2) Buyers' Remedies. Buyers' remedies under CISG are stated broadly in Article 45, which cross refers to Articles 74 to 77. How does the basic formula in the first sentence of Article 74 compare with UCC 2–714? What is the meaning of "loss ... suffered"? Does this permit a buyer to recover damages determined by the value the goods would have had if they had been conforming, the so-called "benefit of the bargain"? How does the formula in the second sentence of Article 74 compare with UCC 2–715(2)?

AWARD IN CASE NO. 3779 OF 1981
Collection of ICC Arbitral Awards 1974–85, p. 138

Arbitrator: Prof. Jacques H. Herbots (Belgium)
Parties: Claimant: Swiss seller
Respondent: Dutch buyer
Published: Not (yet) published

* * *

[FACTS]

Three contracts were concluded in 1979 between the parties, all three concerning the same type of merchandise [whey powder] of which the quality was described in detail.

The merchandise, coming from a Canadian factory was to be delivered C.I.F. Rotterdam. The contracts were made in French and all contained—except for quantities—the same conditions, including an arbitral clause referring disputes to arbitration under the Arbitration Rules of the ICC. However, only the first two contracts were signed by the parties and executed. The third contract was not signed and before shipment from Canada took place, it was cancelled by the Respondent who complained that the merchandise delivered under the first two contracts was not in accordance with the quality prescribed in the contract.

The Canadian Factory sent one of its technicians, Dr. E., to the Netherlands and samples were taken and examined in an independent laboratory. It appeared that they were in accordance with the contractual requirements when analyzed under the North American method, but not when the European analytic method was used.

Arbitration followed in which the Swiss seller claimed US $55,000 (including *inter ali* a $37,500 paid to the Canadian factory) in respect of the cancellation of the third contract. The Dutch buyer introduced a counterclaim of Hfl. 181,645.—covering losses in respect of the first two contracts.

[EXTRACT]

I. *Competence of Arbitrator*

The clause attributing jurisdiction to the ICC occurs in two preceding and similar contracts that were signed by both parties, as well as in the third contract, that, although it was not signed, was not protested against within a reasonable delay either.

Although the contracts are independent from one another from a juridical point of view, the three contracts form a group from an economic point of view.

If, in principle, silence does not mean acceptance, this meaning is, however, attributed to it in view of the circumstances, in particular, the previous business relations of the parties.

Consequently, within the context of their juridical relation and according to their obligations of good faith, the exception of incompetence does not apply.

II. *Law Applicable to the Contract*

* * *

In an international sale of goods, when the parties remain silent, the domestic law of the country in which the seller has his place of residence is to be applied (see the Hague Convention on the International Sale of Goods of June 15, 1955); Kahn, J., Rep.Dall., Dr. internat., V° Vente commerciale; Lunz, Cours Acad. Dr. Internat. 1965, I, 1; Federal Court of Switzerland, 12th February 1952, R 1953, 390, note Flattet).

The chosen language, the place where the contract was entered into by correspondence together with applying the theory of reception, and the way of payment, all point in the same direction.

Consequently, Swiss law is applicable to the contract in dispute.

* * *

IV. *With Respect to the Merits of the Dispute*

* * *

3. *The misunderstanding*

Both parties seem to have acted in good faith.

Actually, the Claimant had immediately declared his willingness to submit samples drawn by both parties to a test by a competent laboratory to be chosen by both parties, and to accept cancellation of the remaining contracts if this analysis proved that the Respondent's allegations had been well-founded.

The Respondent, on his part, also immediately reported the quality problems encountered, asked for an expert and sent samples to the Canadian factory. He agreed to pay for the goods that had already arrived in Rotterdam and he restricted himself to refusing to give any forwarding-instructions or to receive the goods ordered, but not yet loaded on board.

The dispute essentially arises from a misunderstanding.

The following conclusion is essential for understanding the matter: "The main conclusion of Dr. E. during his visit to the Dutch buyer was that the goods sent were not the product the Dutch buyer believed to have bought; the Dutch buyer maintains that, when the Swiss seller initially gave a description of the goods, no mention was made of a method of analysis. The Dutch buyer supposed that, since the description was given by a European firm, the European methods were to be applied ..." (quotation from document 24). To this the Claimant replies: "It goes without saying that the methods to be used should be those of the country of origin or those that are universally accepted, such as the (North American) method" (document 3).

It was only when the quality problems emerged that the Claimant announced the method of analyzing, *inter alia,* the solubility index, viz. the (North American) method that, according to him, is intentionally accepted (document 6 bis).

The Canadian factory was willing to send a technician but made the condition that first agreement should be reached on the method of analysis (document 7).

It is certain that the goods are in accordance with the contractual description, provided that the samples are analyzed according to the (North American) method.

It appears from the proceedings that, although it is not a sale on sample, a sample had been sent to the Respondent prior to the conclusion of the contracts.

The first deliveries were in accordance with this quality, the latter not, although they remained in accordance with the contractual description of the goods, which explains why it was only at a late stage that the misunderstanding came to light.

The misunderstanding is essentially about the solubility degree of the powder delivered.

The method of analysis must be carefully specified in order to be able to determine the solubility degree of the powder.

In Switzerland, methods of analysis are used that are incorporated in the Swiss Manual on Foods, of which Manual the chapter on goods like this particular powder has, unfortunately, not been published yet.

Although the North American method (actually designed for a different type of powder) is better known in the international powder industry involved than a French method, it cannot be considered, however, to be implicitly understood, at least, not on the European market.

The French method differs from the (North American) method with respect to the temperature during the dissolution and the technique of dissolution. The two methods are particularly different with respect to the method of expressing the result in a figure (the solubility index). The Canadian factory took this into account when it was too late, notably, when the Respondent complained about the quality of the goods and the question of analyzing the samples was raised.

4. *Shared responsibilities with respect to the origin of the misunderstanding*

From a telex from the Canadian factory to the Claimant ... it appears that the factory claims to have been clear as to the description of the goods and the methodology, and that the contractual (possibly insufficient) description of the goods, given by the Claimant to his own clients, does not concern him at all, from which it can be deduced that the factory leaves the total contractual responsibility to the Claimant in the case he had not done likewise with his own principal, that is to say, the Respondent.

The Claimant should have known that there was a possibility of error on the European market with respect to the appreciation of the description of the powder.

One cannot presume that there is agreement on the (North American) method between a Swiss seller and a Dutch buyer.

The Claimant should have mentioned that the contractual description was to be interpreted according to the (North American) method, as the Canadian supplier had done in his contract with the Claimant.

The Claimant should have informed the buyer of the conditions on which he contracted (see T.G.I., Argentan, 15th October 1970, D.S., 1971, p. 718, note of M. Ghestin, quoted by Lucas de Leyssac, *L'obligation de renseignements dans les contrats*, in: *L'information en droit privé*, L.G.D., J., 1978, p. 316).

With respect to the interpretation of the contract, the (also in Swiss law) traditional rule can be applied as well: "*in dubio, contra proferentem*".

As Loysel wrote: "qui vend le pot, dit le mot".

The seller is obliged to state clearly what obligations he is undertaking.

The Respondent, on the other hand, knew very well that the goods were of Canadian origin, because he had had contact with the supplier.

Consequently, the error is equally due to his negligence, for he should have asked about the meaning of the symbols used in the contractual description of the powder of North American origin.

The dialectics between the right of being informed, and the obligation of informing oneself is thus at the heart of the problem in the present dispute.

The error of the Respondent is due to a negligence shared with the Claimant (in Swiss law one can find the following instances of shared negligence: A and B have concluded a sale, for which the price has been fixed on the basis of a tariff, the rectification of which has been published many times. A and B conclude a contract without informing themselves about the provisions of clearing that are applicable to their deal—see ENGEL, Pierre, *Traité des obligations en droit Suisse*, Neuchatel, 1973, p. 257).

The (North American) method being more frequently used than the other methods, the negligence of the Claimant as to the information seems less than that of the Respondent.

* * *

THEREFORE:

We, Arbitrator, deciding in accordance with the provisions of the ICC Rules of Conciliation and Arbitration, within the limits of our mission, that was extended by decision of the Court of Arbitration;

> observe in the commercial relations of the parties the existence of an arbitration clause to settle the present dispute and consequently declare ourselves competent to decide and award with respect to the claim and the counterclaim;

With respect to the claim

condemn the Respondent to pay to the Claimant the amount of $27,000 as indemnification for the invalidation (that is to say cancellation) of the third contract.

With respect to the counterclaim

reject the claim of the Respondent for indemnification because of the non-conformity of the goods delivered under the two preceding contracts.

Order that the costs of the arbitration, including costs and fee of the arbitrator, being $8,300, will be borne by the Claimant for 2/5 and by the Respondent for 3/5.

Notes

(1) International Commercial Arbitration. Many parties to international sales contracts elect by a clause in those contracts to have disputes resolved by arbitration. (The same is true for other kinds of international contracts.) One type of arbitration that may be chosen is arbitration pursuant to rules and procedures of the International Chamber of Commerce, which established in 1923 what is now called the International Court of Arbitration. Since its founding, the ICC Court has handled more than 6,700 cases. Most of those are unreported. However, since 1974, selected arbitral awards have been published. The initial collection, spanning eleven years, contained the whey powder determination. Since 1976, the International Council for Commercial Arbitration has been publishing Yearbooks of Commercial Arbitration which contain a selection of arbitral awards and other materials. These sources make it possible to compare commercial arbitration, its results and its method of dispute resolution, with the more familiar results and methods of adjudication.

Commercial arbitration is also widely used in the United States and elsewhere for the resolution of commercial disputes not involving international transactions. Domestic commercial arbitration tends to be done with high concern for privacy of the parties and the arbitrators in the United States are not expected to write reasoned awards. We lack even selected reports of arbitration awards of this kind.

(2) Comparing Arbitration and Adjudication. What aspects of the arbitrator's reasoning and award in the whey powder case are peculiar to the arbitration mode of dispute resolution? If this controversy had been submitted to a United States or other national court for disposition, would the court's reasoning have been the same? Would the outcome probably be the same?

AWARD MADE IN CASE NO. 2129 IN 1972, Collection of ICC Arbitral Awards 1974–1985, p. 23. A German seller contracted to deliver motor car accessories to a United States buyer. Buyer claimed relief for expenses incurred in altering the goods to make them usable on United States automobiles, which were larger than German automobiles. The arbitrator, applying the Ohio Commercial Code, found for the United States buyer:

> The defendant's equipment had to be fit for the ordinary purposes for which it was to be used. Thus, the equipment manufactured for the German market had to be modified to service the U.S. market. At the time of contracting the defendant knew the purpose for which the equipment was required and the buyer relied upon him to furnish suitable machines.... This warranty of merchantability and fitness applies to sales for use as well as to sales for resale and can be invoked by the plaintiff as well as by his customers. The plaintiff is therefore entitled to be reimbursed for the money he spent repairing or altering the defendant's equipment pursuant to an implied warranty of merchantability and fitness.

AWARD OF SEPTEMBER 27, 1983, CASE NO. 3880
(Original in French)

Arbitrators: Dr. Werner Wenger; Prof. Lucien Simont; Prof. Marcel Storme

Parties: Claimant: Belgian buyer A
Defendant: Belgian seller B

Published in: 110 *Journal du droit international (Clunet)* 1983, p. 897, with note Y. Derains and S. Jarvin, pp. 897–899.

[FACTS]

On January 26, 1979, claimant A and defendant B entered into a contract whereby B undertook to supply A with 150,000 pairs of ladies' boots between April and August 1979. On the same date, B entered into an identical contract (differing only in relation to the price) with a Romanian State trading enterprise C, who was to supply the same quantity of boots to B. When the Romanian enterprise C defaulted, arbitration proceedings were commenced by A who sought damages for late delivery and defective goods. The arbitrators rejected a request by defendant B to join the claim with an arbitration it had commenced separately against its supplier, the Romanian enterprise C, based on that company's default in delivery. Claimant A was successful as to 75% of its claim.

[EXTRACT]

[On *force majeure:*]

... [D]efendant B contends ... that to the extent that the contract obliged it to supply boots made at the factory D in Romania, the source proposed by its supplier, the Romanian enterprise C, the default of the latter constituted an insurmountable obstacle and an extraneous cause relieving it of any liability towards Claimant A.

* * *

It follows that, B's obligations being in the nature of obligations of result, their non-fulfilment places B in default and involves it in liability vis-à-vis A, except for those cases where the latter company cancelled orders without justification....

[On the mitigation of damages:]

B argues, however, that A could have offered its clients in sufficient time merchandise equivalent to the subject-matter of the contract between the parties, in conformity with its obligation to take all appropriate steps to limit its damage and reduce its losses.

The boots which were the subject-matter of the contract have a seasonal character and could not be sold and delivered to A's client except at the beginning of the winter season at the latest. B, on the basis of promises made by its own supplier, had led A to believe, up to August 1979 and, at least for the major part of the order, even up to the first half of September 1979, that it would be in a position to deliver the goods, admittedly late, but before the last moment. Its failure to fulfil these promises only became apparent after it was too late to obtain the merchandise elsewhere. In effect, having regard to the changing fashions to which this type of product is subject, suppliers keep very little in stock. B omits to identify the sources to which A could have turned at the end of September 1979, to obtain merchandise equivalent to that described in the Contract.

In these circumstances it is not appropriate to reduce the compensation for damages suffered by reason of a violation of the creditor to observe its obligation to mitigate its damages.

[On loss of goodwill:]

Having regard to the fact that, out of a total of about 127,000 pairs of boots ordered by A from B, a significant number, 45,509 pairs, or about 35%, were the subject of justifiable complaints about failure to meet delivery dates and defects in quality. This percentage considerably exceeds what would normally be expected to be tolerated. Having regard to the seasonal character of the merchandise, A was only able to satisfy its clients from other sources to a limited extent. One's commercial reputation would seem to be affected when a business finds itself in the position of not being able to fulfil a significant proportion of its orders.

The nature of the effect on its reputation is such as to make it impossible, in the absence of precise criteria, to determine the exact extent of the damage caused by it; that such damage cannot be evaluated. In these circumstances, it appears that for the reasons stated above, and taking all aspects of the case into consideration, particularly the net margin of A and the trading figures with the clients mentioned above from 1980–1982 in comparison with previous years, A's claim can only be deemed to be partly founded, and the sum of Bfrs. 200,000 must be allowed to it as damages for any prejudice to its commercial reputation.

(3) Other "Fields" of Law. The Convention (CISG 4) "governs only" the "obligations of the seller and the buyer arising from [the international sales] contract." Does the CISG displace rules of law that deal with defective goods under rubrics other than "contract"? To what extent is an international sales contract subject to law of fraud, misrepresentation or mistake, like those referred to earlier in United States law? Consider CISG 4(a). What issues are excluded from the CISG as going to the "validity of the contract"? The problems regarding the relationship between the Convention and domestic law are important and difficult. See J. Honnold, Uniform Law for International Sales §§ 64–67, 232–237 (2d ed. 1991).

SECTION 3. WARRANTY DISCLAIMERS AND LIMITATION OF DAMAGES CLAUSES

(A) DOMESTIC UNITED STATES LAW

Introduction. Neither the warranty provisions nor the provisions defining buyers' remedies, as set forth in the UCC, preclude the parties from entering into contracts that provide otherwise.[1] Since the law of the United States and the United Kingdom took shape in the 19th century, sellers and buyers have regularly included contract terms on the extent of warranty obligation or damages recovery. In many kinds of sales transactions, patterns of warranty disclaimers or limitation of damages clauses have become so common that their absence in a given transaction would be remarkable.

Under the Code, express warranties arise only if sellers' words or conduct become "part of the basis of the bargain." UCC 2–313(1). When words or conduct tending to create an express warranty are found in the parties' agreements, but other words or conduct tend to negate such a warranty, the Code provides a standard for contract construction. UCC 2–316(1).

Both implied warranty provisions in the Code contain the conditioning language: "unless excluded or modified," which expressly permits the parties to agree that these warranties have been negated. As we will see, the Code further imposes certain *formal* requirements on sellers who seek to do so. UCC 2–316(2). An *implied disclaimer* of implied warranties is provided in the circumstances of a present sale. UCC 2–316(3)(b). Implied warranties can also be excluded or modified by course of dealing, course of performance, or usage of trade. UCC 2–316(3)(c).

The Code's treatment of clauses limiting sellers' liability for damages is found in UCC 2–718 and 2–719. The latter provides that the

---

1. UCC 1–102(3) provides the basic principle of contract autonomy. Only a few legal standards may not be varied by agreement.

parties may agree to "limit or alter the measure of damages recoverable under this Article, as by limiting the buyer's remedies to return of the goods and repayment of the price or to repair and replacement of non-conforming goods or parts." UCC 2–719(1)(a). Consequential damages may be limited or excluded unless the limitation or exclusion is unconscionable. UCC 2–719(3).

In the marketplace for goods, would you expect that clauses limiting the damages that aggrieved buyers may recover and clauses disclaiming warranties are equally important? Do these clauses deal with the same or different economic risks? Which clause is more likely to cause a potential buyer to forego a purchase?

INSURANCE CO. OF NORTH AMERICA v. AUTOMATIC SPRINKLER CORP.

Supreme Court of Ohio, 1981.
67 Ohio St.2d 91, 423 N.E.2d 151.

Appellee, Automatic Sprinkler Corporation of America ("Automatic Sprinkler"), purchased the components of a dry chemical fire protection system from appellant, The Ansul Company ("Ansul"). Both parties understood that Automatic Sprinkler would install this system in a building occupied by Youngstown Steel and Alloy Corporation ("Youngstown Steel").

A representative of Ansul signed a "Proposal," dated February 13, 1970. No one signed the proposal on behalf of Automatic Sprinkler. This document is five pages long. The front of each page includes typewritten or printed information which either describes the goods or states the price. Only the fifth and last page has printing on the back including:

> "This sale is subject to the following terms and conditions:
>
> " . . .
>
> "9. The Ansul extinguisher is warranted to the original purchaser for five years from date of delivery against defects in workmanship and material. The Ansul Company will replace or repair any metal parts which in its opinion are defective and have not been tampered with or subjected to misuse, abuse or exposed to highly corrosive conditions. This warranty is *in lieu of* all other warranties express or implied. The Ansul Company assumes no liability for *consequential* or other loss or *damage* whatsoever arising out of injuries to or death of persons and damages to or destruction of property in any manner caused by, incident to, or connected with the use of the equipment, and the Buyer shall *indemnify* and save harmless the Seller from and against all such claims, loss, cost or damage. In addition, unless the Ansul equipment is maintained per Ansul's recommendations, Ansul hereby disclaims all liability whatsoever, including, but not limited to, any

liability otherwise attaching under the warranty provisions of this paragraph." (Emphasis added.)

There are 15 paragraphs in all—each without a heading, each without extraordinary capitalization.

Ansul delivered the goods under a "Purchase Order," dated April 14, 1970, "per Ansul Quotation 8674 signed 2–13–70."

A fire occurred on September 9, 1974, at the building occupied by Youngstown Steel. The Ansul fire extinguisher system did not discharge.

None of the aforementioned facts is disputed. Two lawsuits did result, however.

Insurance Company of North America ("INA"), subrogee to the building owner, complained against Automatic Sprinkler and Ansul (case No. 80–619). Automatic Sprinkler ultimately cross-claimed against Ansul. Youngstown Steel and its insurer sued Automatic Sprinkler (case No. 80–620) Automatic Sprinkler then filed a third-party complaint against Ansul. In both cases, the claims alleged breach of warranty and negligence.

Later, the Court of Common Pleas consolidated these cases. The trial judge granted Ansul's motion for summary judgment and dismissed Automatic Sprinkler's claims against Ansul in both cases because (1) Ansul had disclaimed all warranties on sale and limited Automatic Sprinkler's remedies to repair and replacement of defective parts and (2) Automatic Sprinkler agreed to indemnify Ansul and hold it harmless from all claims. The Court of Appeals reversed the trial court, holding that the disclaimer and exclusion of consequential damages fail because they are not conspicuous.

The Court of Appeals also held that "there is no basis for summary judgment in favor of the Ansul Company on the indemnity provision question at this stage of the case," because paragraph 9 is not conspicuous. The court reversed and remanded the cause to the trial court for further proceedings on this issue.

The cause is now before this court pursuant to the allowance of motions to certify the record.

. . .

LOCHER, JUSTICE.

This case presents three issues: (1) whether Ansul has effectively disclaimed all implied warranties with Automatic Sprinkler; (2) whether Ansul has effectively excluded all liability for consequential damages; and (3) whether Automatic Sprinkler must indemnify Ansul against all claims arising in this litigation. Resolving each of these issues requires an interpretation of paragraph 9.

We hold that Ansul has neither disclaimed its liability for implied warranties nor excluded its liability for consequential damages.

I.

Ansul attempted to disclaim all liability to Automatic Sprinkler for breach of implied warranties by including the following language in paragraph 9: "This warranty is in lieu of all other warranties express or implied." Automatic Sprinkler argues that this language fails as a disclaimer because it does not mention merchantability and is not conspicuous as required by [UCC 2–316(2)]. Ansul, on the other hand, suggests that the "in lieu of" language is similar to "as is" under [UCC 2–316(3)(a)]. Under Ansul's view, the disclaimer is effective regardless of whether it is conspicuous or whether it mentions merchantability.

We hold that the "in lieu of" language is not similar to "as is".... The effort to disclaim liability for all implied warranties fails because paragraph 9 is not conspicuous and because the disclaimer does not mention merchantability.

"As is" language describes the *quality of the goods* sold. As an example of "as is" language, [UCC 2–316(3)(a)] expressly includes "with all faults." ... Official Comment 7 ... further explains the intent of the drafters:

> "Paragraph [(a)] deals with general items such as 'as is,' 'as they stand,' 'with all faults,' and the like. Such terms in ordinary commercial usage are understood to mean that the buyer takes the entire risk as to the *quality of the goods* involved. ..." (Emphasis added.)

...

We recognize that the courts have held that "in lieu of" language eliminates implied warranties. ... We reject this conclusion.

Under [2–316(3)(a)] "other language which, in common understanding, calls the buyer's attention to the exclusion of warranties and makes plain that there is no implied warranty" must be language which is consistent with the intention of the drafters and the General Assembly. This language must describe the *quality of the goods.*

Accordingly, the "in lieu of" language in paragraph 9 falls outside [2–316(3)(a)].

This "in lieu of" provision does not qualify, therefore, as a disclaimer of implied warranties under [2–316(2)]. There is no mention of merchantability. In addition, we have held that paragraph 9 is inconspicuous.

[UCC 1–201(10)] defines "conspicuousness" as follows:

> " 'Conspicuous': A term or clause is conspicuous when it is so written that a reasonable person against whom it is to operate ought to have noticed it. A printed heading in capitals (as: NON-NEGOTIABLE BILL OF LADING) is conspicuous. Language in the body of a form is 'conspicuous' if it is in larger or other contrasting type or color. But in a telegram any stated term is

'conspicuous.' Whether a term or clause is 'conspicuous' or not is for decision by the court."

Paragraph 9 appears among 15 other paragraphs on the back of the last page of the Proposal. This is the only page with writing on the back and is unnumbered. None of these paragraphs has a heading, extraordinary capitalization or contrasting type. Furthermore, Ansul alone executed the Proposal which contained paragraph 9 approximately two months before Automatic Sprinkler submitted its purchase order. In light of all these circumstances, therefore, it is clear that paragraph 9 is inconspicuous.

Accordingly, we hold that the "in lieu of" provision in paragraph 9 does not disclaim all implied warranties.

II.

Ansul argues that, even if the purported disclaimer fails, paragraph 9 excludes "liability for consequential or other loss or damage...." We disagree.

[UCC 2–719(3) and 2–316(4)] permit parties to exclude consequential damages without expressly requiring that the exclusion be conspicuous. Nevertheless, courts and commentators have read U.C.C. 2–719[3] and U.C.C. 2–316[4] *in pari materia.* See e.g., Avenell v. Westinghouse Electric Corp. (Cuyahoga Cty., 1974), 41 Ohio App.2d 150, 324 N.E.2d 583; Zicari v. Joseph Harris Co., Inc. (1969), 33 App.Div.2d 17, 304 N.Y.S.2d 918; Nordstrom, Law of Sales, at 276; Special Project—Article Two Warranties in Commercial Transactions, 64 Cornell L.Rev. 30, 224. Nordstrom, supra, explains why these two statutes should be read together, as follows:

> "The requirement that the agreement contain the alteration of basic Code remedies brings into play those ideas discussed in the prior section of this text [dealing with disclaimers of implied warranties]. The limitation [or exclusion of remedies] must be a part of the parties' bargain in fact. If it is contained in a printed clause which was not conspicuous or brought to the buyer's attention, the seller had no reasonable expectation that the buyer understood that his remedies were being restricted to repair and replacement. As such, the clause cannot be said to be a part of the bargain (or agreement) of the parties." (Citation omitted.)

Any other reading of these provisions would permit inconspicuous provisions excluding or limiting damage recovery to circumvent the protection for buyers in [2–316(2)]. ...

Paragraph 9 is inconspicuous in its entirety. The attempt to exclude liability for consequential damages, therefore, is also inconspicuous. Accordingly, Automatic Sprinkler may recover consequential damages from Ansul.

...

Notes

(1) Bargain in Fact. Could Automatic Sprinkler Corporation of America contend persuasively that the language in the "Proposal" that disclaimed "all other warranties" was unclear to the buyer as a disclaimer of the warranty of merchantability? Could Automatic Sprinkler contend persuasively that it was reasonably unaware of the clause on Ansul's liability for consequential damages? Do you think it likely or unlikely that corporations like Automatic Sprinkler use such contractual clauses in transactions in which they are sellers?

(2) Construction of UCC 2–316(2). Why did the drafters of the Commercial Code include 2–316(2)? What did they intend by the requirement that a seller must "mention merchantability" to disclaim the 2–314 warranty?

The Ohio Supreme Court made no effort to resolve the controversy on the bargain in fact, but rather decided the case on the basis of Ansul's compliance with the "mention" clause in UCC 2–316(2) and with the court's implication of a statutory "conspicuousness" requirement in UCC 2–719. What is the public policy rationale of those *formal* requirements? Is it arguable that the legislation was designed to protect consumer buyers and not buyers like Automatic Sprinkler? Could a court properly exclude buyers who are large corporations?

(3) Legislative History. Consider the history of UCC 2–316. In the initial drafts of the Code, from 1940 to 1952, subsection (2) provided:

> (2) Exclusion or modification of the implied warranty of merchantability or of fitness for a particular purpose must be in specific language and if the inclusion of such language creates an ambiguity in the contract as a whole it shall be resolved against the seller; except that [the three subparagraphs now in (3) followed as exceptions].

Comments to the 1952 draft provided:

> 3. Disclaimer of the implied warranties of merchantability and of fitness for particular purpose is permitted under subsection (2), but with the safeguard that such disclaimers must be in specific terms and that any ambiguity must be resolved against the seller.
>
> 4. Implied warranties may not be excluded merely by the use of a clause disclaiming "all warranties express or implied." On the other hand, a clause such as "We assume no responsibility that the goods concerned in this contract are fit for any particular purpose for which they are being bought outside of the general purposes of goods of the description," would normally be sufficient to satisfy the requirement that the disclaimer be in "specific terms."
>
> 5. The provision of subsection (2) that an ambiguity arising from the co-existence of words of disclaimer and evidence showing the creation of the implied warranties of merchantability or fitness for a particular purpose must be resolved against the seller is intended to pose the true issue in such cases. This section rejects

that line of approach which presupposes the original existence of warranty and then attempts to deal with the question of whether it has been disclaimed by language in the agreement. ...

In 1955, after the Code had been adopted in Pennsylvania and was under consideration in a number of states, the Code was revised. The language above was deleted and the current provision substituted, with the exceptions set off in a new paragraph (3). The Editorial Board, which proposed the revision, gave this brief explanation:

> **Reason.** The purpose of this change is to relieve the seller from the requirement of disclaiming a warranty of fitness in specific language and yet afford the buyer an adequate warning of such disclaimer.

No explanation was given for adding the requirements (i) that a valid disclaimer must "mention merchantability," (ii) that a disclaimer of the warranty of fitness for particular purpose must be in writing and conspicuous, or (iii) that a disclaimer of warranty of merchantability, if in a writing, must be conspicuous. Comments to take account of the 1955 (and 1956) text changes were published in 1957. Comments 3, 4 and 5, in their present form, replaced the earlier comments.

Does the history shed light on the drafters' intention with regard to the necessary form of a disclaimer of the implied warranty of merchantability? What weight should a court place on such history in construing the Code as adopted by a particular legislature, such as the construction of the Ohio version of the Commercial Code in the *Insurance Company* case?

(4) Construction of UCC 2–719. In what sense is the *Insurance Company* decision a construction of 2–719? Is it conceivable that the drafters of the Code were unaware of the differences in the formulations of 2–316 and 2–719? Does the court's approach trespass on the legislature's prerogative?

UNIVERSAL DRILLING CO. v. CAMAY DRILLING CO.
United States Court of Appeals, Tenth Circuit, 1984.
737 F.2d 869.

McKay, Circuit Judge.

The parties to this lawsuit are "experienced, sophisticated, intelligent business[men] with vast education and experience in petroleum engineering, ... oil and gas exploration, and ... [the] makeup and operation of oil drilling rigs and equipment." ... In June 1977 they entered into negotiations for the purchase and sale of two drilling rigs referred to by the parties as the Marthens Rig and Rig 10.

The negotiations resulted in a contract dated July 1, 1977, [which contained the following clauses:

> 18.01 The assets being purchased and sold hereunder are being sold by [defendant] in an "as-is" condition and without any warranty of operability or fitness.

* * *

26.01 This Agreement and the exhibits hereto and the agreements referred to herein set forth the entire agreement and understanding of the parties in respect of the transactions contemplated hereby and supersede all prior agreements, arrangements and understanding relating to the subject matter hereof. No representation, promise inducement or statement of intention has been made by [defendant] or [plaintiffs] which is not embodied in this Agreement or in the documents referred to herein, and neither [defendant] nor [plaintiffs] shall be bound by or liable for any alleged representation, promise, inducement or statements of intention not so set forth.] *

... The contract defines the property to be sold as the personal property listed in Exhibits A, B and C to the contract. Rig 10 is defined as the property in Exhibit A and the Marthens Rig is defined as the property in Exhibits B and C. [The purchase price was $2,925,000.]

Subsequent to the delivery of the property, plaintiffs complained that the property they received did not conform to the contract alleging that they were to receive two used but nevertheless operable drilling rigs. Defendant, however, relying on the contract, argued that it delivered all of the property listed in the specific exhibits. This diversity lawsuit resulted.

At trial, [t]he trial court ... rejected plaintiffs' theory that there were breaches of express warranties based on the description of the goods contained in the contract. Plaintiffs appeal... .

* * *

Breach of Express Warranties by Description

Approaching this issue it must again be remembered that the parties to this suit are experienced in the field of oil and gas exploration and drilling. Furthermore, none of the parties allege that they were in an inferior bargaining position.

Plaintiffs do not dispute the trial court's finding that the contract, specifically paragraph 18.01, effectively disclaimed all implied warranties. Plaintiffs do allege, however, that the description of the assets contained in the contract created an express warranty that the assets would conform to that description. In addition, plaintiffs argue that such an express warranty of description cannot be disclaimed, ... or at least was not effectively disclaimed.

Section 2–316 of the Uniform Commercial Code as adopted in Colorado provides for the modification and exclusion of warranties. Colo. Rev. Stat. § 4–2–315 (1973). In particular it provides that

[w]ords or conduct relevant to the creation of an express warranty and words or conduct tending to negate or limit warranty

* [The court reproduced the contract in a footnote. Eds.]

shall be construed wherever reasonable as consistent with each other; but subject to the provisions of this article on parol or extrinsic evidence (section 4–2–202), negation or limitation is inoperative to the extent such construction is unreasonable.

Id. § 4–2–316(1). Accordingly, the initial inquiry must be whether express warranties were created under section 4–2–313 and if so how they are affected by section 18.01 of the contract.

Plaintiff argues that this case is controlled by Section 4–2–313(b) which provides that "[a]ny description of the goods which is made part of the basis of the bargain creates an express warranty that the goods shall conform to the description." Colo. Rev. Stat. § 4–2–313(b). The principles underlying section 4–2–313 are set out in comment four to that section:

> 4. In view of the principle that the whole purpose of the law of warranty is to determine what it is that the seller has in essence agreed to sell, the policy is adopted of those cases which refuse except in unusual circumstances to recognize a material deletion of the seller's obligation. Thus, a contract is normally a contract for a sale of something describable and described. A clause generally disclaiming "all warranties, express or implied" cannot reduce the seller's obligation with respect to such description and therefore cannot be given literal effect under Section 2–316.
>
> This is not intended to mean that the parties, if they consciously desire, cannot make their own bargain as they wish. But in determining what they have agreed upon in good faith is a factor and consideration should be given to the fact that the probability is small that a real price is intended to be exchanged for a pseudo-obligation.

Id. § 4–2–313 comment 4.

Similarly, Professors White and Summers argue that a seller should not be able to disclaim a warranty created by description.

> We hope courts will reach similar conclusions and strike down attempted disclaimers in cases in which the seller includes a description of the article which amounts to a warranty and then attempts to disclaim all express warranties. To illustrate further: assume that the sales contract describes machinery to be sold as a "haybaler" and then attempts to disclaim all express warranties. If the machine failed to bale hay and the buyer sued, we would argue that the disclaimer is ineffective. In our judgment, the description of the machine as a "haybaler" is a warranty that the machine will bale hay and, in the words of 2–316, a negation or limitation ought to be "inoperative" since it is inconsistent with the warranty.

J. White & R. Summers, Handbook of the Law Under the Uniform Commercial Code § 12–3 at 433 (2d ed. 1980).

Plaintiff relies principally on two cases that follow this rationale. Century Dodge Inc. v. Mobley, 155 Ga.App. 712, 272 S.E.2d 502, 504 (1980)(cert. denied); Blankenship v. Northtown Ford, Inc., 95 Ill.App. 3d 303, 420 N.E.2d 167, 170–71 (1981). In both cases automobile dealers had sold "new" cars which for various reasons did not meet the description of a "new" car. Consequently the courts held that the boilerplate disclaimer provisions of the consumer sales contracts did not relieve the dealers of their responsibility to deliver a "new" car.

We do not question the rationale of the above authorities. Nonetheless, we find them not controlling the instant case. If in this case we were dealing with a consumer transaction, as in the cases just cited, we would be more inclined to follow those authorities. However, as noted in subsequent cases, "the courts are less reluctant to hold educated businessmen to the terms of contracts to which they have entered than consumers dealing with skilled corporate sellers." ...

Furthermore, both sections 4–2–313 and 4–2–316 express the policy of the statutory scheme to allow parties to make any bargain they wish. Comment four to section 4–2–313 states that if parties consciously desire they can disclaim whatever warranties they wish. Colo. Rev. Stat. § 4–2–313 comment 4 (1973). In addition, comment one to section 4–2–316 explains that its purpose is to "protect a buyer from unexpected and unbargained language of disclaimer." Id. § 4–2–316 comment 1. Consequently, we will not rewrite the contract in this case. The exhibits to the contract which described the goods must be read in conjunction with the contract itself. The contract states that the goods are used and there is no guarantee that they are fit or even *operable*.

If we were to hold the contract in the instant case created undisclaimable express warranties by description, we cannot think of alternative language that would memorialize the intent of the parties—to purchase and sell used "as is" equipment which has value but which may need repairs or additional parts to be fit and operable.

Our holding on this issue does not leave plaintiffs in general without remedy in similar contexts or the plaintiffs in this case with an "empty bargain." If the goods delivered do not meet the description in the contract there is a breach of the contract. In short, if no mast were delivered or if what was delivered was junk metal which in no way resembled a mast, plaintiffs would have a cause of action for breach of the contract.

Finally, plaintiffs did not receive an empty bargain. An appraisal which plaintiffs commissioned valued the goods received at an amount in excess of $3,000,000. ... The purchase price for the assets was $2,925,000.

The trial court did not err in excluding plaintiffs' evidence regarding breach of warranty.

* * *

AFFIRMED.

Notes

(1) Contract Interpretation: UCC 2–316(1). Buyer apparently argued, under UCC 2–316(1), that the words of negation of warranty in ¶ 18.01 were "inoperative" in light of the words of description. Could buyer have made its essential point differently? Could buyer have argued that the "operability" language in ¶ 18.01 referred to future performance of the rigs, but was not intended to declare that the rigs were presently not in operating condition?

Problem 1. In negotiations that led to the purchase of a mobile home, the seller showed a model mobile home to the buyer. The contract stated in capital letters that the sale was "AS IS." The buyer asserts that the mobile home delivered to him was not like the model. What result? See UCC 2–313(1)(c), 2–316(1); Consolidated Data Terminals v. Applied Digital Data Systems, Inc., 708 F.2d 385 (9th Cir.1983).

(2) Commercial Sophistication of Buyers. On the surface of the Uniform Commercial Code provisions defining sellers' responsibility for quality, the Code does not differentiate among buyers who are seasoned veterans in buying goods of the kind, buyers who are commercially naive, and buyers in between.[2] Nor does the Code's provision on exclusion or modification of warranties. What, then, explains the emphasis that the *Universal Drilling* court put on the experience and sophistication of the parties? The buyer relied principally on two decisions involving consumer retail sales of new automobiles. The Tenth Circuit expressed no question about the rationale of those decisions, but found them not controlling. Does the Code permit such different treatment for consumer retail sales and sales of business equipment?

The Code provision on contractual limitation or exclusion of consequential damages sets forth two standards, one for "injury to the person in the case of consumer goods" and another for "loss [that] is commercial." UCC 2–719(3). Is this provision sensitive to market levels of sales transactions?

(3) Oral Warranties and Written Negations: Parol Evidence and UCC 2–202. Cases frequently arise in which buyers and sellers executed contract documents containing clauses negating the existence of any warranties, particularly express warranties not contained in the documents, but buyers later contend that the sellers (or their sales personnel) had made oral affirmations or promises that would constitute warranties under UCC 2–313. A clause commonly inserted in writings of this kind, sometimes in the boilerplate of a printed form, asserts that the writing is a complete and exclusive statement.

Words in such documents cannot be construed as reasonably consistent with the words allegedly spoken. In providing a rule of contract

---

2. The Code does differentiate among sellers on the basis of commercial experience in UCC 2–314. Only a seller who is "a merchant with respect to [the] goods" sold makes an implied warranty of merchantability. "Merchant" is defined in UCC 2–104(1).

construction for this type of case, UCC 2–316(1) cites the Code's parol evidence provision, UCC 2–202. Under the latter provision, if the words of negation of warranty are in a writing that a court finds to have been intended as the final expression of their agreement, those terms of negation may not be "contradicted by evidence of any prior agreement or of a contemporaneous oral agreement." This may exclude evidence of words or conduct relevant to the creation of an express warranty. Even if a buyer's evidence does not "contradict" a term in the written final expression, that evidence may be excluded if a court finds that the writing was intended by the parties to have been a complete and exclusive statement of the terms of the agreement.

Consider the following concern expressed about UCC 2–202: "To what extent should a 'merger' clause in a standard form contract be permitted to accomplish indirectly what cannot be done directly, e.g., the disclaimer of an express warranty. See 2–316(1). Other than § 2–302, there is no explicit control over the risk of unfair surprise [in the Commercial Code]. A possible solution is to require that a 'merger' clause in a standard form contract be 'separately signed' by the party against whom the clause operates. See § 2–205." Permanent Editorial Board Study Group on UCC Article 2 p. 60 (1990). Would you support the proposed solution?

For further reading, see E. Farnsworth, Contracts § 7.3 (2d ed. 1990); J. White & R. Summers, Uniform Commercial Code §§ 2–9 to 2–12 (3d ed. 1988).

WESTERN INDUSTRIES, INC. v. NEWCOR CANADA LIMITED
United States Court of Appeals, Seventh Circuit, 1984.
739 F.2d 1198.

POSNER, CIRCUIT JUDGE.

Western Industries purchased several custom-built welding machines from Newcor Canada for use in manufacturing microwave oven cavities. The machines did not work right and Western brought this breach of contract action against Newcor, basing federal jurisdiction on diversity of citizenship. Newcor counterclaimed for the unpaid portion of the purchase price of the machines. The jury awarded Western damages of $1.3 million dollars and Newcor about half that (the full unpaid balance of the purchase price of the machines) on its counterclaim. Separate judgments were entered on the two claims and both parties have appealed. The appeals raise a variety of interesting substantive and procedural issues, the former being controlled (the parties agree) by the law of Wisconsin, including the Uniform Commercial Code, which Wisconsin has adopted.

The contract between Western and Newcor grew out of Western's contract with a Japanese manufacturer of microwave ovens, Sharp, to supply Sharp with cavities for microwave ovens. Sharp wanted Western to weld the cavities by a process known as projection welding, because that is how microwave oven cavities are made in Japan; and Western agreed. The projection method is not used in the United States to weld thin metal, such as the cavities of microwave ovens are made of; spot welding is the method used here. So when Western went to Newcor, a leading manufacturer of specialty welding machines, to explore the possibility of buying machines for use in fulfilling its contract with Sharp, it had to ask Newcor to design and build a type of welding machine that Newcor was unfamiliar with. Newcor agreed to do this, however, and after further discussions Western's director of engineering placed a purchase order by phone for eight machines with Newcor's sales engineer on May 17, 1979. According to the memoranda that both men made of the conversation, no specific terms other than the date of delivery were discussed; price was not discussed, for example. On May 23 Newcor delivered to Western a formal written quotation of terms for the sale. On the back of one page a number of standard contract terms were printed, including one disclaiming all liability for consequential damages. Western did not reply immediately, but in mid July it sent Newcor a formal purchase order, mysteriously pre-dated to May 15, that included on the back a set of printed terms one of which stated that the buyer (Western) was entitled to general as well as special damages in the event of a breach of the seller's warranties. On July 20 Newcor sent Western an acknowledgement form stating, "In conformity with our conditions of sale appearing in [the written quotation ...] furnished to you by us, this approves and accepts your order." Western did not respond. The parties never discussed any of the printed terms contained in the contract forms that they had exchanged. Three machines were bought later through a similar exchange of forms. The parties treat the sale of all 11 machines as one contract, as shall we.

The machines were built and delivered but turned out to be unusable for making microwave oven cavities. Newcor took the machines back and rebuilt them as spot welding machines, redelivering them to Western a year after the delivery date called for in the contract. As a result of the delay in getting machines that it could use, Western incurred unforeseen expenses in fulfilling its commitment to Sharp; for example, it had to manufacture cavities manually at much higher cost than it would have incurred if it has had proper machines. These expenses are the basis of its damage claim against Newcor.

Newcor's first ground of appeal is that the district judge improperly excluded evidence that the custom of the specialty welding machine trade is not to give a disappointed buyer his consequential damages but just to allow him either to return the machines and get his money back or (for example if the breach consists in delivering them late) keep the machines and get the purchase price reduced to compensate for the costs of delay. ... Newcor contends that it is not liable for any damages above the purchase price, however those damages are described; and if this is right, then even if Newcor had a contract with

Western that it broke it is not liable for any of the damages that Western was awarded.

Although trade custom or usage is a question of fact, see UCC 1-205(2) and Official Comments 4 and 9; ... the district judge refused to allow Newcor's three principal witnesses on the existence of the alleged trade custom to testify, on the ground that they were incompetent to give such testimony; and having done this the judge later instructed the jury that there was no issue of trade custom in the case. Two of the three witnesses whom Newcor wanted to call were experienced executives of companies that manufacture specialty welding machines (one of them was also the president of those manufacturers' trade association), and between them the two had almost 75 years of experience in selling such machines. The third witness was a former executive of Western and had long experience in buying such machines. These witnesses were prepared to testify that consequential damages were unheard of in their trade. When a machine did not work the manufacturer would spend his own money to fix it or would take it back and refund the purchase price to the buyer, but he would not compensate the buyer for the disruption to the buyer's business caused by the defect.

* * *

Although we are in no position to determine whether the custom alleged by Newcor actually exists, we think it relevant to note that the hypothesis that it exists is certainly not so incredible that testimony on the subject could be excluded by analogy to the principle that excludes testimony in contradiction of the laws of nature. The relevant trade is the manufacture of a particular kind of custom-built machinery. A custom-built machine is quite likely either not to be delivered on time or not to work (not at first, anyway) when it is delivered; anyone who has ever had a house built for him knows the perils of custom design. If a custom-built machine is delivered late, or does not work as the buyer had hoped and expected it would, the buyer's business is quite likely to suffer, and may even be ruined; and as the buyers of these welding machines are substantial manufacturers to whose businesses the machines are essential, the potential costs of defective design or late delivery are astronomical.

... [A]ll we need find in order to conclude that Newcor's evidence of trade custom was admissible is that a rational jury could have concluded that, yes, it was the custom for manufacturers of specialty welding machines not to be liable for consequential damages. That contractual liability for such damages (in the absence of special notice) is of relatively recent vintage, that many breaches of contract are (as here) involuntary, that only the sky would be the limit to the amount of consequential damages that manufacturers of machinery indispensable to their customers' businesses might run up, that those manufacturers not only have a better idea of what the potential injury to them might be but also might be able to avert it more easily than their supplier—

all these things make it not at all incredible that a custom might have evolved in this industry against a buyer's getting consequential damages in the event of a breach.

If there was such a custom, it would not take the manufacturers of specialty welding machines off the financial hook completely. When they have to take back and resell custom-built machines they face the prospect of a heavy loss. A machine custom-designed to one manufacturer's specifications may not fit any other's. That is no doubt why Newcor spent hundreds of thousands of dollars to rebuild these machines as spot-welding machines that Western could use. That is also why we reject Newcor's argument that Western should be estopped to claim damages because it induced Newcor to rebuild the machines. Newcor rebuilt them in its own interest, to mitigate the loss it would have incurred if it had had to take back the machines and refund the purchase price; if it had taken back the machines it would have had to rebuild them in order to be able to resell them.

But a disclaimer of liability for consequential damages would place some limit on the exposure of the manufacturers of specialty welding machines. It would also give buyers incentives to take their own precautions, which might be efficacious, against the disasters that might befall them if the machines did not work. ... There was much evidence that Western made a serious mistake in agreeing with Sharp (rather casually as it appears) to build microwave oven cavities by projection welding, a process which, it turned out, American safety standards made infeasible. Western would have been less likely to make such mistakes if it had known with certainty that it would not be able to get consequential damages if the machines didn't work.

* * *

Newcor has a second ground of appeal. It wanted to put before the jury not only the theory that trade custom had supplied a silent contractual term excluding liability for consequential damages, but also the theory that the explicit terms of the contract excluded such liability.... .

* * *

As a practical matter, however, Newcor's alternative theory is not very different from its main theory—that the custom of the trade excluded liability for consequential damages. Given an exchange of inconsistent forms, Newcor would have to present a reason why its form disclaiming liability for consequential damages should be accepted over Western's form asserting such liability; and the reason would have to be the custom of the trade, as that is the only substantial ground that Newcor has for claiming precedence for its disclaimer. ...

* * *

The parties raise some other issues, which we have considered but find to have no merit. The judgment in favor of Western on its claim and the judgment in favor of Newcor on its counterclaim are reversed

Sec. 3   *WARRANTY DISCLAIMERS*   119

and the case is remanded for a new trial on both claims, with no costs in this court.

REVERSED AND REMANDED.

CUDAHY, CIRCUIT JUDGE, concurring. * * *

Notes

(1) Battle of the Forms. The facts in *Western Industries* illustrate a familiar process in which the representatives of the two contracting firms doing the actual negotiation communicate with each other by inserting the details of the particular deal on their firm's printed forms. Who writes the terms that are printed on such forms? How can the drafters design terms that will fit the unknown particular agreements in which the forms may be used?

The portion of the court's opinion addressed to the battle of the forms has been omitted. Most students study this topic in the course on Contracts. The governing law for domestic United States transactions is the infamous UCC 2–207.

(2) Implied Warranty Disclaimers or Limitation of Damages. The Commercial Code expressly declares that implied warranties can be excluded or modified by course of dealing, course of performance, or usage of trade. UCC 2–316(3)(c). Recall the decision in *Royal Business Machines*, Section 2, supra. No similar provision is found in 2–719. Is the omission significant?

KUNSTSTOFFWERK ALFRED HUBER v. R.J. DICK, INC.
United States Court of Appeals, Third Circuit, 1980.
621 F.2d 560.

WEIS, CIRCUIT JUDGE.

In this diversity case, the district court concluded that under the Uniform Commercial Code the buyer has the burden of establishing that the seller agreed to pay consequential damages when goods proved defective. We hold that to avoid such liability the seller must prove an agreement that limits damages, and, in this instance, the course of dealing between the parties was not adequate to demonstrate such an understanding. Accordingly, we modify a judgment in favor of the plaintiff-seller for goods sold to allow credits for losses on resale incurred by the defendant-buyer.

The plaintiff brought suit in the United States District Court for the Eastern District of Pennsylvania to recover the cost of nylon industrial belting it sold to the defendant. Counterclaims asserted that some of the belting had been defective. After a bench trial, the district court entered judgment for the plaintiff, deducting from the requested damages portions of the amounts sought by two of the defendant's counterclaims.

The defendant, R.J. Dick, Inc., distributes nylon cord belting throughout the United States. Its principal place of business is in Iowa, and it maintains a warehouse in King of Prussia, Pennsylvania. The plaintiff is a sole proprietorship that manufactures nylon cord belting in Offenburg, West Germany under the trade name "Vis."

In September 1967 plaintiff's export manager, Alfred Ziegler, sent a letter to the defendant's president, quoting prices on belting and enclosing terms for delivery and payment. Included in the correspondence was a form entitled "General Terms of Sales II." One paragraph in the form limited the plaintiff's liability for defective merchandise to replacement or price reduction and excluded damages of any kind:

> [Reclamations must be made within 10 days after receipt of merchandise and prior to processing or use. Our guaranty is limited to replacement or price reduction and excludes damages of any kind. Also, we do not give a guaranty for specific utilization. Minor deviations do not provide grounds for reclamations.] *

In the following month, Ziegler and Vis's owner, Alfred Huber, visited King of Prussia and arranged for sale of their product to the Dick Company. At no time were the Vis general terms of sale discussed, and, consequently, Dick did not agree to be bound by the provisions of the form, including the limitation on damages recoverable for defective merchandise.

During the period from 1967 to 1974 there were occasions when the plaintiff's product did not meet the defendant's standards, either on initial inspection or after a period of use by defendant's customers. When the defendant issued a credit to a customer for belting that had manufacturing defects, a claim was made to the plaintiff for replacement or credit. If a difference arose between the parties over whether the defect was attributable to the manufacturer, the claim would be compromised.

In late 1973, Dick's problems with the belting increased, the most frequent being delamination, which made the product unusable. Beginning at that time and continuing through 1974, Ziegler complained about Dick's delay in payments. This suit followed the parties' inability to resolve these difficulties.

At trial, the plaintiff asserted that after making allowances for various credits to which it was agreeable, the defendant owed $30,910.29. Against this figure, however, the defendant asserted four counterclaims.

* * *

The court did allow partial recovery on the third and fourth counterclaims. The defendant contended in the third claim that it was entitled to $7,300.69, the amount it had credited its customers for defective material supplied by the plaintiff in 1974. The Court, how-

---

* [The court reproduced the contract clause in a footnote. Eds.]

ever, awarded $3,398.25, a sum representing the price the defendant paid plaintiff. ... The fourth claim was for defective belting that one of Dick's distributors sold to a company called Wesco. Dick issued a credit of $7,092.80 on that transaction, but again the court allowed only the amount the defendant had paid plaintiff for the goods, $3,301.95. ... The defendant appeals.

* * *

The issue underlying the remaining two claims is straightforward: Was the defendant entitled to recover the credits granted customers when the product proved defective? In other words, was the defendant entitled to the profits it would have made on those sales? The parties agree that Pennsylvania law applies, particularly Article 2 of the Uniform Commercial Code.

* * *

There is no dispute that plaintiff was aware of the nature of defendant's business, i.e., that the goods were to be resold. In these circumstances, we conclude that under § 715(2)(a) the credits that defendant was obliged to extend to customers are proper consequential damages. ...

The plaintiff does not dispute this proposition but argues that the parties agreed to exclude recovery of such damages under U.C.C. § 2–719(1)(a). That section provides that the agreement between the parties may provide for limiting the measure of damages, as by restricting the buyer's remedy to return of the goods and repayment of the price or to repair and replacement nonconforming goods. Pa. Stat. Ann. tit. 12A, § 2–719(1)(a) (Purdon 1970).

There is insufficient evidence in the record to establish an express agreement to limit damages. The trial judge found that the only communication between the parties bearing on the subject was the form sent by plaintiff to defendant in September 1967. He stated that "Dick never expressly consented to the Huber contract" and therefore could not be held subject to it. Nevertheless, the trial judge reasoned that the form had put the defendant on notice that Huber did not intend to assume liability for consequential damages and that Dick therefore had the burden, which it failed to carry, of informing plaintiff that such damages might be demanded.

* * *

The plaintiff argues ... that there was a "course of performance" under U.C.C. § 2–208(1) which established an agreement to forgo consequential damages. Since there was no single contract between the parties, but rather a series of separate sales, we believe it more accurate to characterize the conduct as a "course of dealing," defined in U.C.C. § 1–205(1). The plaintiff's argument is not weakened by adopting the course of dealing route because the Code specifically permits a course of dealing or a usage of trade, unlike a course of performance, to "give particular meaning to and supplement or qualify terms of an agreement." U.C.C. § 1–205(3), Pa. Stat. Ann. tit. 12A, § 1–205(3) (Purdon 1970) (emphasis added).[6] In Posttape Associates v. Eastman Kodak Co., 537 F.2d 751 (3d Cir.1976), we concluded that a limitation of damages could be imposed by a trade usage; it follows that a course of dealing is a circumstance that may establish this term as part of the bargain of the parties in fact. U.C.C. § 1–201(3), Pa. Stat. Ann. tit. 12A, § 1–201(3) (Purdon 1970).

The inquiry then is whether the record establishes the course of dealing the plaintiff suggests. Initially we observe that the burden is on the plaintiff to prove the limitation agreement, ... especially where it is to be found in a course of dealing.[7]

In its findings the district court did not set out facts that would constitute a course of dealing establishing defendant's agreement to forgo consequential damages. On appeal, the plaintiff does not point to specific parts of the record where such facts may be found, nor has our independent review disclosed such evidence. It is not enough that the defendant accepted replacement or credits for the purchase price in many instances. Obviously, if the defects were detected before resale and supplies of belting were available to fill outstanding orders, the defendant might not have had a claim for lost profits. In other instances it may well be that even after resale, the defendant's customers were content to accept replacement rather than demand a refund. Moreover, the record does show that the parties compromised many of the claims for defects in workmanship.

We find no instances in which the defendant had made a claim for loss of profits on resale transactions other than those underlying the counterclaims. If such claims had been made and then been denied by the plaintiff without protest from the defendant, the argument that a course of dealing established such a limitation might have some force. Cf. U.C.C. § 2–208(1), Pa. Stat. Ann. tit. 12A, § 2–208(1) (Purdon 1970) ("any course of performance accepted or acquiesced in without objection shall be relevant to determine the meaning of the agreement").... Absent such circumstances, however, we cannot say that the plaintiff has met the burden of proving a limitation agreement. Accordingly, the defendant is entitled to recover on the two counterclaims for loss of profits on actual sales.

---

6. By its own terms, a course of performance goes no further than being "relevant to determine the meaning of the agreement." U.C.C. § 2–208(1), Pa. Stat. Ann. tit. 12A, § 2–208(1) (Purdon 1970). Nevertheless, courts have generally allowed a course of performance to supplement and qualify the terms of an agreement as well. J. White & R. Summers, Uniform Commercial Code § 3–3 (1972).

7. In discussing terms supplied by a course of dealing, a usage of trade, and a course of performance, Professors White and Summers observed:

"Who has the burden of proof? The Code does not say. Yet courts are likely to impose the burden of proof on the party who seeks to benefit from evidence of course of dealing, trade usage, or course of performance."

J. White & R. Summers, Uniform Commercial Code § 3–3, at 88 (1972)(footnote omitted).

The total of the two counterclaims is $14,393.49. The parties agree that the increases sought by the defendant and contained in this figure accurately reflect the loss on sales. That total will therefore be deducted from the amount which plaintiff claimed to be due—$30,910.29—thus resulting in an award to the plaintiff of $16,516.80. The case will be remanded to the district court so that it may modify its judgment accordingly.

Note

Choice of Forum. The German seller in *Kunststoffwerk* was litigating in a foreign court, the "home" court of the U.S. buyer. What led to this choice of forum? In counselling German or other non-U.S. sellers or buyers dealing with U.S. firms, would you recommend structuring transactions to obtain a more familiar or at least a neutral forum? How could this be done?

MILGARD TEMPERING, INC. v. SELAS CORP.
United States Court of Appeals, Ninth Circuit, 1990.
902 F.2d 703.

HALL, CIRCUIT JUDGE:

This appeal marks the end of nearly seven years of litigation over a "sure fire" glass tempering furnace purchased over ten years ago. The seller, Selas Corporation of America ("Selas") appeals the judgment of the district court awarding the buyer, Milgard Tempering, Inc. ("Milgard"), damages resulting from its failure to repair serious defects in the furnace.... We have jurisdiction under 28 U.S.C. § 1291 (1988) and affirm.

I

... On June 11, 1979, [Milgard] entered into a carefully-negotiated contract with appellant/cross-appellee Selas to purchase a horizontal batch tempering furnace. ... Under the contract, Selas agreed to design and manufacture the furnace for $1.45 million. Its design was complex, and in Selas' eyes, experimental. However, Selas marketed it as a working piece of equipment. The contract provided a $50,000 bonus if Selas delivered all the major components before January 31, 1980. It also provided a penalty of $5,000 per week (not to exceed a total of $25,000) for every week of late delivery after March 31, 1980. Selas failed to meet either deadline, having completed delivery of major components in November, 1982.

Selas agreed to assemble the furnace at Milgard's plant and to assist in a "debugging period" that both parties expected would end June or July 1980. The contract also required Selas, in a series of preacceptance tests, to demonstrate that the furnace was capable of achieving designated yield and cycle rates. Section 28.5 of the contract limited Selas' liability for breach of warranty to repair or replacement of the furnace and barred liability for consequential damages. The parties modified the contract and agreed to forego the preacceptance tests and instead place the furnace in commercial production in July, 1980, thus making glass available for the "debugging" process.

By January 1982, Selas continued work on the furnace, but failed to achieve yield and cycle rates that substantially conformed with the contract specifications. Milgard then filed suit against Selas for breach of contract. In March 1982, the parties, without counsel, attempted to enter into a contractual agreement to settle the dispute. Under the proposed agreement, Selas would take over the tempering operation for 60 days to demonstrate the furnace's ability to achieve a 90 yield rate. It would also pay any operating losses Milgard incurred during that period. Then, if Milgard operated the furnace for six months without incident, Selas would "finetune" the furnace to achieve a 95 rate. Selas did the work and paid Milgard's operating losses. Milgard dismissed the suit without prejudice. However, during the six-month period, the furnace failed to perform to the specifications of either the contract or the attempted settlement agreement.

Milgard initiated a second lawsuit on March 4, 1983, alleging breach of contract and breach of warranty. On June 29, 1984, Judge Tanner in the district court granted summary judgment in favor of Selas. ... This court, in Milgard Tempering, Inc. v. Selas Corp. of America, 761 F.2d 553 (9th Cir.1985)[hereinafter Milgard I], reversed and remanded for trial. ...

On remand, after a five-week bench trial, Judge Bryan in the district court found that the furnace had never lived up to the specifications in the contract. He held that the limited repair remedy failed of its essential purpose and that Selas' default was sufficiently severe to expunge the cap on consequential damages. He awarded Milgard $1,076,268 in net damages. ...

Selas appeals the judgment and denial of its motion for new trial.... . We affirm.

II

Selas ... argues that the district court erred in ruling that the limited repair remedy failed of its "essential purpose" and that such failure lifted the contractual cap on consequential damages.

A

Section 28.5 of the contract limited Milgard's remedies in the event of breach of warranty to repair or replacement of the defective equipment.

> [In the event of a breach of any warranty, express, implied or statutory, or in the event the equipment is found to be defective in workmanship or material or fails to conform to the specifications thereof, *[Selas'] liability shall be limited to the repair or replace-*

ment of such equipment as is found to be defective or non-conforming, provided that written notice of any such defect or non-conformity must be given to Selas within 1 year from the date of acceptance, or 15 months from completion of shipment, whichever first occurs. In the event that acceptance is delayed through the fault of Selas, then the Selas 1 year warranty shall be applicable and not begin until the date of acceptance. *Selas assumes no liability for no [sic] consequential or incidental damages of any kind (including fire or explosion in the starting, testing, or subsequent operation of the equipment), and the Purchaser assumes all liability for the consequences of its use or misuse by the Purchaser or his employees. In no event will Selas be liable for damages resulting from the non-operation of Purchaser's plant, loss of product, raw materials or production as a result of the use, misuse or inability to use the equipment covered by this proposal* or from injury to any person or property alleged to be caused by or resulting from the use of the product produced with the equipment to be supplied to Purchaser by Selas pursuant to this proposal whether the customer or Purchaser is mediate or immediate. Purchaser hereby releases [Selas] of and from and indemnifies [it] against, all liability not specifically assumed by [it] hereunder. (Emphasis added).] *

Such limitations on a party's remedies are permitted by Washington's version of the U.C.C., Wash.Rev.Code § 62A.2–719(1)(a) (West Supp. 1989).

An exclusive or limited remedy ... must be viewed against the background of § 62A.2–719(2).... . This section requires a court to examine the contract in general and the remedy provision in particular to determine what the remedy's essential purpose is and whether it has failed.

A limited repair remedy serves two main purposes. First, it serves to shield the seller from liability during her attempt to make the goods conform. Second, it ensures that the buyer will receive goods conforming to the contract specifications within a reasonable period of time. . . . .

A contractual provision limiting the remedy to repair or replacement of defective parts fails of its essential purpose within the meaning of § 62A.2–719(2) if the breaching manufacturer or seller is unable to make the repairs within a reasonable time period.... It is not necessary to show negligence or bad faith on the part of the seller, for the detriment to the buyer is the same whether the seller's unsuccessful efforts were diligent, dilatory, or negligent. ...

The district court in this case found that the furnace had never lived up to the specifications of the contract. ... Moreover, the court found that the few successful improvements were not made within a reasonable period of time, taking over two and one-half years. We

* [The court reproduced the contract in a footnote. Eds.]

agree that under these circumstances, the unreasonable delay and ultimate failure in repair made the repair remedy ineffective; thus, the remedy failed of its essential purpose.

Although the contract did not guarantee a specific time for completion of debugging, the court found that the writing was not completely integrated. . . . . Looking at the commercial context, the court found that both parties implicitly agreed that the complete period for start up and "debugging" would take about eight weeks. . . . .

B

Washington courts have not addressed the issue of whether failure of a limited repair remedy may serve to invalidate a consequential damages exclusion. Therefore, it is our responsibility to determine how the state's supreme court would resolve it. In undertaking this task, we may draw upon recognized legal sources including statutes, treatises, restatements, and published opinions. . . . . We may also look to "well-reasoned decisions from other jurisdictions." . . .

1

We begin our analysis with Fiorito Bros., Inc. v. Fruehauf Corp., 747 F.2d 1309, 1314–15 (9th Cir.1984). In that case, we held that under Washington law, the failure of a repair remedy does not automatically remove a cap on consequential damages. We predicted that Washington courts would take a case-by-case approach and examine the contract provisions to determine whether the exclusive remedy and damage exclusions are either "separable elements of risk allocation" or "inseparable parts of a unitary package of risk-allocation." Id. at 1315 (quoting district court).

If the exclusions are inseparable, we reasoned, a court's analysis should track the Official Washington Comments to § 62A.2–719(2) [hereinafter Washington Comments], which explain that the subsection "relates to contractual arrangements which become oppressive by change of circumstances. . . ." 747 F.2d at 1315. We then affirmed the district court's ruling that the seller's arbitrary and unreasonable refusal to live up to the limited repair clause "rendered the damages limitation clause oppressive and invalid." Id.

Fiorito relied heavily on this circuit's analysis . . . in [S.M. Wilson & Co. v. Smith Int'l, Inc.,] 587 F.2d 1363. Wilson involved a contract between commercially sophisticated parties for a tunnel boring machine. The contract contained both a limited repair clause and a cap on consequential damages. After concluding that the repair remedy failed of its essential purpose within § 2719(2), this court held that the bar to consequential damages remained enforceable. We explained:

> Parties of relatively equal bargaining power negotiated an allocation of their risks of loss. Consequential damages were assigned to the buyer, Wilson. The machine was a complex piece of equipment designed for the buyer's purposes. The seller Smith did not ignore

his obligation to repair; he simply was unable to perform it. This is not enough to require that the seller absorb losses the buyer plainly agreed to bear. Risk shifting is socially expensive and should not be undertaken in the absence of a good reason. An even better reason is required when to so shift is contrary to a contract freely negotiated. The default of the seller is not so total and fundamental as to require that its consequential damage limitation be expunged from the contract.

Id. at 1375 (emphasis added). However this court in Wilson quickly pointed out that its holding was limited to the facts and was in no way intended to state that consequential damages caps always survive failure of limited repair remedies. Id. at 1375–76.

2

The district court in the instant case found Selas' default "fundamental, but not total." Nonetheless, it found the breach sufficiently fundamental to remove the cap on consequential damages. Selas claims that the court misunderstood the legal standard and that consequential damages may be allowed only when the seller's breach is both total and fundamental.

We agree that the district court's characterization of the case law was flawed. However, the analysis it employed was not. This court has found nothing magical about the phrase "total and fundamental" default in relation to U.C.C. 2–719(2). In Fiorito we eschewed such wooden analysis, leaving "[e]ach case [to] stand on its own facts." Id., 747 F.2d at 1314 (quoting Wilson, 587 F.2d at 1376). We further expressed our distaste for talismanic analysis in Milgard I, finding the "oppressive circumstances" analysis utilized by Fiorito and the Washington Comments and the "total and fundamental" default analysis in Wilson in accord with each other. 761 F.2d at 556.

The task before the district court was to examine the remedy provisions and determine whether Selas' default caused a loss which was not part of the bargained-for allocation of risk. .... This was the analysis that the district court actually employed.

We agree with the district court's decision to lift the cap on consequential damages. Milgard did not agree to pay $1.45 million in order to participate in a science experiment. It agreed to purchase what Selas represented as a cutting-edge glass furnace that would accommodate its needs after two months of debugging. Selas' inability to effect repair despite 2.5 years of intense, albeit injudicious,[9] effort

---

9. Selas exacerbated the repair problem by not providing a qualified process engineer during the initial debugging period and stubbornly refusing to replace the unproven ircon transfer system with more reliable methods that were available. We therefore agree with the district court's conclusion that "Selas did not make a completely open and honest effort to bring the furnace into compliance with the contract requirements." .... However, as noted earlier, the question of Selas' good faith is not dispositive of this appeal.

caused Milgard losses not part of the bargained-for allocation of risk. Therefore, the cap on consequential damages is unenforceable.

III

Next, Selas challenges the district court's determination of damages. The court had found that for 21 months (April 1, 1980 to December 31, 1982), the furnace was incapable of reaching any of the yield rates outlined in the contract. Thereafter, the furnace could reach a few with some regularity. Accordingly, the district court calculated damages for two time periods. First, it calculated Milgard's lost profits during the 21-month "damage" period. Second, it calculated losses Milgard did and would incur after December 31, 1982.

* * *

All three tests for loss of profits have been met in this case. First, the district judge made the factual finding that the parties contemplated the possibility of lost profits. Because § 28.5 of the contract refers to such profits, this finding is not clearly erroneous.

Second, the district court found that the failure of the machine to conform to the contract specifications proximately caused Milgard to lose profits. Selas does not challenge this finding and we do not disturb it.

Third, the district court had a sufficient factual basis upon which to make its computation of lost profits. ... Milgard's sole source of evidence in this area was its expert witness, Dr. Finch. Although the district judge found some of Dr. Finch's figures difficult to swallow, he pointed out that that did not negate them. ... [T]he court discounted the damage award in accordance with the weight of Finch's testimony. Therefore, we find no error.

* * *

VIII

For these reasons, the judgment of the district court is AFFIRMED.

Notes

(1) Repair or Replace Clauses. Agreements in which sellers undertake to repair or replace the goods sold are very common in sales of business equipment and consumer goods. What do sellers seek to gain by use of such clauses? Are such clauses advantageous or disadvantageous to buyers?

How do repair or replace clauses relate to quality warranties? Did Selas purport to disclaim any warranties in the contract of sale? Why not? Even if a seller purports to disclaim all warranties, a repair or replace clause must contain some quality standard; typically that is found in the terms of the condition that activates seller's duty to repair or replace.[3] A condition frequently used in such clauses activates seller's duty "if the goods suffer defect in materials or workmanship." How does this standard compare with the criteria of merchantability? Does "defect" mean something different than "non-conformity"?

How do repair or replace clauses relate to contractual limitations of damages? Recall UCC 2–719(1)(a). In what sense is a seller's undertaking to repair or replace a "remedy" for the buyer?

(2) Failure of Essential Purpose. While a seller's repair or replace undertaking may be additive to buyer's other remedies, ordinarily agreements provide that the undertaking is in substitution for those remedies. What language in the furnace sale contract had that effect? The Code provides that statutory remedies become available to a buyer if an exclusive or limited remedy fails of its essential purpose. UCC 2–719(2).[4] What economic value is protected by repair or replacement? What statutory remedy is most analogous to the remedy of repair or replacement?

(3) Failure of Purpose and Consequential Damages. The terse language of UCC 2–719(2) gives little guidance on the issue decided in *Milgard*. "Remedy ... as provided in this Act" does not necessarily mean consequential damages. Comment 1 refers to occurrence of circumstances that "deprive either party of the substantial value of the bargain." Is the Ninth Circuit's approach consistent with seeking to protect the value of the bargain struck between seller and buyer?

S. M. WILSON & CO. v. SMITH INTERNATIONAL, INC., 587 F.2d 1363 (9th Cir.1978). Buyer purchased a tunnel boring machine which the buyer needed to construct mine shafts. Seller agreed to design, build and deliver the machine for a price of $550,000. Seller warranted that the machine was free from defects in materials and workmanship, but that is obligation under the warranty was limited to repair or replacement of defective parts returned to seller not later than 90–days after commencement of drilling operations using the machine. The sales document provided further that seller "shall not be liable for any loss or damage resulting, directly or indirectly, from the use or loss of use of the machine. Without limiting the generality of the foregoing this exclusion from liability embraces the purchaser's expenses for downtime or for making up downtime.... ."

---

3. In sales of consumer goods, some sellers undertake to replace some products if the customer requests. Customer satisfaction is the quality criterion. Similarly, some merchants sell consumer goods on "unconditional" money-back terms, the only condition being the buyer's return of the goods and request for the price paid. Merchants sometimes buy inventory from suppliers on terms that permit return of unsold goods. See UCC 2–326(1), 2–327.

4. Readers of UCC 2–719(2) may be puzzled by the notion that a "remedy" might have a "purpose." Human beings have objectives, abstractions do not. If the Code is referring to someone's purpose in an agreement for an exclusive or limited remedy, is it the buyer's purpose, or the seller's, or both parties'?

As delivered, the machine performed at a rate much slower than seller had promised. Apparently ignoring the 90-day clause in its warranty, seller tried but failed, for a substantial time after delivery, to repair the machine. Eventually, the defect was found and corrected. Because of problems with the machine, a drilling project expected by buyer to be completed in 80 days took 210 days to complete. Substantial consequential losses, alleged by buyer to have been $1.8 million, were sought by buyer. The trial court, making no finding of the amount of buyer's damages, held that such damages were precluded by the no-consequential damages clause in the contract of sale. The Court of Appeals, affirming, held that even though the replace/repair remedy had failed of its essential purpose, the contract provision barring recovery of consequential damages was enforceable. 587 F.2d 1363 (9th Cir.1978).

The Court of Appeals said:

> The issue remains whether the failure of the limited repair remedy to serve its purpose requires permitting the recovery of consequential damages as sections 2714(3) and 2715 permit. We hold it does not. In reaching this conclusion we are influenced heavily by the characteristics of the contract.... Parties of relatively equal bargaining power negotiated an allocation of their risks of loss. ... The seller ... did not ignore his obligation to repair; he simply was unable to perform it. This is not enough to require that the seller absorb losses the buyer plainly agreed to bear. ... The default of the seller was not so total and fundamental as to require that its consequential damage limitation be expunged from the contract.

CHATLOS SYSTEMS, INC. v. NATIONAL CASH REGISTER CORP., 635 F.2d 1081 (3d Cir.1980). Buyer, manufacturer of telecommunications equipment, purchased a computer system for its accounting needs. The contract price for the entire system was $46,000. The contract contained the following clause: "In no event shall NCR [the seller] be liable for special or consequential damages from any cause whatsoever." Eighteen months after the system was supposed to be operational, seller had been unable to make the system work properly and buyer asked seller to remove the computer. We previously considered this case in connection with the measure of the buyer's damages under 2–714(2). Another issue in that case was the enforceability of the clause excluding consequential damages.

At a bench trial, the court awarded buyer consequential damages in the amount of $63,500. The Court of Appeals for the Third Circuit reversed. The court said:

> Whether the preclusion of consequential damages should be effective in this case depends upon the circumstances involved.

The repair remedy's failure of essential purpose, while a discrete question, is not completely irrelevant to the issue of the conscionability of enforcing the consequential damages exclusion. ... Recognizing this, the question here narrows to the unconscionability of the buyer retaining the risk of consequential damages upon the failure of the essential purpose of the exclusive repair remedy.

... It is ... important that the claim is for commercial loss and the adversaries are substantial business concerns. We find no great disparity in the parties' bargaining power or sophistication. Apparently, Chatlos [the buyer], a manufacturer of complex electronic equipment, had some appreciation of the problems that might be encountered with a computer system. Nor is there a "surprise" element present here. The limitation was clearly expressed in a short, easily understandable sales contract. ...

... Some disruption of normal business routines, expenditure of employee time, and impairment of efficiency cannot be considered highly unusual or unforeseeable in a faulty computer installation. Moreover, although not determinative, it is worth mentioning that even though unsuccessful in correcting the problems within an appropriate time, NCR continued its efforts. Indeed, on the date of termination NCR was still actively working on the system at the Chatlos plant.

... We conclude, therefore, that the provision of the agreement excluding consequential damages should be enforced.... .

FIORITO BROS., INC. v. FRUEHAUF CORP., 747 F.2d 1309 (9th Cir.1984). Buyer, a heavy construction company, purchased thirteen dump truck bodies for use in carrying wet concrete to highway construction sites for the price of $66,600. Before the purchase agreement, seller's representative had assured buyer that the bodies were suitable for this purpose. The agreement was documented on seller's standard-form sales order, in which seller warranted that the goods were free from defects in materials and workmanship with the "sole remedy" of buyer being seller's five-year repair/replace promise. The form further provided that: "Seller and Customer agree that Seller shall have no liability for any cargo loss, loss of use or other incidental or consequential damages arising out of this order or which are alleged to have been caused by any of the goods delivered hereunder." None of the truck bodies was able to handle wet concrete. On buyer's complaint, seller's representative declared that the problems were not covered by the warranty. Later, seller wrote to buyer that its investigation had revealed that the product had been misused. Seller never acted to repair or replace the truck bodies. At trial, seller admitted that it had not conducted any investigation of buyer's use of the product. The jury awarded buyer $130,000 in damage. How much of this was for consequential damages does not appear in the opinion.

Affirming the judgment of the trial court, the Court of Appeals for the Ninth Circuit held that seller's repair/replace remedy had failed of its essential purpose. The court held further that the no-consequential-damages clause was unenforceable. 747 F.2d 1309 (9th Cir.1984).

The appellate court quoted with approval the trial court's opinion:

> In the current case, it does not make sense to view the exclusive-remedy and consequential-damage provisions independently. The purpose of the parties in agreeing to this exclusive-remedy provision was to [i]nsure that the Plaintiff would not suffer from down time and other such consequential harms that follow from defective conditions in the trucks.... *It cannot be maintained that it was the parties' intention that Defendant be enabled to avoid all consequential liability for breach by first agreeing to an alternative remedy provision designed to avoid consequential harms, and then scuttling that alternative remedy through its recalcitrance in honoring the agreement.* (Emphasis added by Court of Appeals).

The Court of Appeals further upheld the trial judge's findings that the consequential-damages clause was not oppressive when the agreement was made, that the parties had relatively equal bargaining positions and sophistication, but that circumstances during performance rendered the damages limitation clause oppressive and invalid.

(4) Unconscionability and Consequential Damages. Would it be preferable to address the question of consequential damages limitation clauses in terms of unconscionability rather than failure of essential purpose? Does UCC 2–719(3) invite analysis of such clauses under the rubric of unconscionability? Which standard is more comprehensible to the parties and the courts? Consider the following case:

A & M PRODUCE CO. v. FMC CORP., 135 Cal.App.3d 473, 186 Cal.Rptr. 114 (1982). An experienced farmer, who operated as a corporation, decided to grow tomatoes for the first time and shopped for a weight-sizing machine to process his crop. After discussions with representatives of FMC, farmer ordered two machines for $32,000.00. The parties executed a contract document on a printed one-page FMC form, which provided on the back that seller warranted the machines to be free from defects in materials and workmanship under normal use and service for 12 months and, further, disclaimed all other express or implied warranties. The terms on the back of the document continued:

> [Seller's] obligation under this warranty is limited to repairing or replacing any part of the equipment which is found to be defective.... .

SELLER IN NO EVENT SHALL BE LIABLE FOR CONSEQUENTIAL DAMAGES ARISING OUT OF OR IN CONNECTION WITH THIS AGREEMENT.... CONSEQUENTIAL DAMAGES FOR PURPOSES HEREOF SHALL INCLUDE, WITHOUT LIMITATION, LOSS OF USE, INCOME OR PROFIT....

FMC delivered and installed the equipment. When the tomato crop ripened, the machines failed to work properly. Tomatoes piled up in front of the singulator belt and overflow tomatoes had to be sent through the machines again, causing damage to the crop. An FMC representative managed to control the overflow problem by stopping and starting the machine, but this significantly reduced the processing speed. After several weeks, the farmer ceased processing because the income from the tomatoes—some of which had been damaged—was inadequate to cover his costs.

The farmer offered to return the machines upon refund of his $5,000.00 down payment. FMC rejected this proposal and sued for the balance of the purchase price. The trial court held that it would be unconscionable to enforce the warranty disclaimer and limitation of consequential damages clauses and entered judgment upon a verdict for the farmer in excess of $260,000.00. The Court of Appeal affirmed.

As to the exclusion of consequential damages, several factor combine to suggest that the exclusion was unreasonable on the facts of this case. Consequential damages are a commercially recognized type of damage actually suffered by A & M due to FMC's breach. ... If the seller's warranty was breached, consequential damages were not merely "reasonably foreseeable": they were explicitly obvious. All parties were aware that once the tomatoes began to ripen, they all had to be harvested and packed within a relatively short period of time. ...

Another factor supporting the trial court's determination involves the avoidability of the damages and relates directly to the allocation of risks which lies at the foundation of the contractual bargain. It has been suggested that "[r]isk shifting is socially expensive and should not be undertaken in the absence of a good reason. An even better reason is required when to so shift is contrary to a contract freely negotiated." (S.M. Wilson & Co. v. Smith Intern., Inc. (9th Cir.1978) 587 F.2d 1363, 1375.) But ... FMC was the only party reasonably able to prevent this loss by not selling A & M a machine inadequate to meet its expressed needs. ...

In summary, our review of the totality of circumstances in this case, including the business environment within which the contract was executed, supports the trial court's determination that the disclaimer of warranties and the exclusion of consequential damages in FMC's form contract were unconscionable and therefore unenforceable. When non-negotiable terms on preprinted form agreements combine with disparate bargaining power, resulting in the allocation of commercial risks in a socially or economically unreasonable manner, the concept of unconscionability as codified in Uniform Commercial Code sections 2–302 and 2–719, subdivision (3), furnishes legal justification for refusing enforcement of the offensive result.

A concurring opinion contained this:

> Facts fly as "thick as autumnal leaves that strow the brooks of Vallombrose," in support of the trial court's conclusion that these contract clauses were oppressive, contrary to oral representations made to induce the purchase, and unreasonably favorable to the party with a superior bargaining position. No experienced farmer would spend $32,000 for equipment which could not process his tomatoes before they rot and no fair and honest merchant would sell such equipment with representations negated in its own sales contract.

HILL v. BASF WYANDOTTE CORP.
United States Court of Appeals, Fourth Circuit, 1982.
696 F.2d 287.

PHILLIPS, CIRCUIT JUDGE:

In this diversity case controlled by South Carolina law BASF Wyandotte Corp. (BWC), manufacturer of Basalin, an agricultural herbicide, appeals from a judgment in favor of Hill, a farmer who bought Basalin from a retailer and used it with allegedly injurious consequences to his soybean crop. A jury, finding breach of warranty running from BWC as manufacturer to Hill as ultimate purchaser under relevant provisions of the state's version of the Uniform Commercial Code (U.C.C.), awarded Hill substantial direct and consequential damages.

Concluding that BWC was bound by no warranty save that expressed in writing on the cans of herbicide purchased by Hill and that under its terms Hill's remedy for breach was limited to direct damages, we vacate the judgment and remand for a new trial limited to the issues of liability and damages for breach of the express warranty on the herbicide cans.

I

In 1977, Hill was an experienced farmer with extensive farming operations in Richland County, South Carolina. Along with other crops he grew a substantial amount of soybeans. In recent years he had used a herbicide called Treflan, produced by a manufacturing rival of BWC's, to control weeds in producing this crop. In late January or early February of 1977 he met with a man named Pennington, who was a sales agent for BWC. They discussed the properties of BWC's herbicide, Basalin, which was then selling at a lower price than Treflan's. In the course of their discussions, in response to questioning by Hill,

Pennington told Hill that "if you used Treflan, you [use Basalin] the same way ... the entire same way"; that "it would control the same weeds that Treflan will"; that "it would do the same way as Treflan, but it is cheaper"; "to put it down the same way, you don't have to change a thing, do it the same way."

Relying, according to his later testimony, upon these statements by Pennington, Hill decided to buy and use considerable quantities of Basalin in growing his 1977 soybean crop. BWC did not have a direct retail outlet in the area, and Hill made his purchases of Basalin from Kerr–McGee Chemical Corporation, a local agricultural chemical retailer. He made four separate purchases, the first on February 14, and the other three during April. In all he bought 365 gallons, all in 5-gallon cans, for a total purchase price of $8,382.35 which he paid in two separate installments.

On each of the cans of Basalin purchased there appeared a label containing a warranty and certain conditions of sale that included an allocation of risk, a disclaimer of any warranties other than the one expressly stated, and a limitation of remedies for breach of that warranty.

CONDITIONS OF SALE AND WARRANTY *

The Directions for Use of this product reflect the opinion of experts based on field use and tests. The directions are believed to be reliable and should be followed carefully. However, it is impossible to eliminate all risks inherently associated with use of this product. Crop injury, ineffectiveness or other unintended consequences may result because of such factors as weather conditions, presence of other materials, or the manner of use or application all of which are beyond the control of BASF WYANDOTTE CORPORATION ("BWC") or the seller. All such risks shall be assumed by the Buyer.

"BWC" warrants that this product conforms to the chemical description on the label and is reasonably fit for the purpose referred to in the Directions for Use subject to the inherent risks referred to above. "BWC" MAKES NO OTHER EXPRESS OR IMPLIED WARRANTY OF FITNESS OF MERCHANTABILITY OR ANY OTHER EXPRESS OR IMPLIED WARRANTY. In no case shall "BWC" or the Seller be liable for consequential, special or indirect damages resulting from the use or handling of this product. "BWC" and the Seller offer this product and the Buyer and user accept it, subject to the foregoing Conditions of Sale and Warranty which may be varied by agreement in writing signed by a duly authorized representative of "BWC." The purchase price of Basalin includes a royalty for a non-transferable license to practice the method of U.S. 3,854,927.

* [The court reproduced the text of the label in a footnote. Eds.]

> Read the entire label. Use only according to label instructions. Read "CONDITIONS OF SALE AND WARRANTY" before buying or using. If terms are not acceptable, return product at once, unopened.

After reading the label, Hill applied the herbicide to 1,450 acres of soybeans. He applied Treflan to approximately another 200 acres of soybeans. Following planting of this crop in May and June, Hill began in July to notice weed problems—particularly pig weed—in the Basalin fields. No corresponding problem was noted then or later in the Treflan fields. Efforts of various kinds were made to control the weed problem, but none were successful.

In the Basalin-treated fields, Hill had a bad crop, with lower yield than he had had in other years and a poorer quality that required greater-than-ordinary expense in harvesting. Ascribing this result to Basalin's failure to control weeds as warranted, Hill brought this action against BWC alleging breach of warranty and misrepresentation, and seeking $48,257.35 in direct and consequential damages.

BWC defended on several grounds: *inter alia,* that Hill's use of Basalin was not the proximate cause of any crop loss sustained; that BWC's sole warranty was that expressed on the label and that it was not breached; and that, in any event, under terms of the warranty, Hill's remedy was limited to recovery of the purchase price.

The case was first tried to Judge Chapman and a jury. On trial the evidence of causation was substantially conflicting. Hill's evidence indicated a significant difference in the yields on the Basalin-treated and Treflan-treated crops, and included testimony suggesting that Treflan in general was rated by experts as a better product and that other farmers in the area had had similar problems with Basalin during the same crop year. On the other hand, BWC's evidence included, *inter alia,* testimony that the two products were essentially identical in chemical composition and were rated of equal quality by experts; that the 1977 crop year had been a bad one generally in the area, with a drought at the critical time that might well have caused any diminished yield experienced; and that a significant portion of the Basalin-treated crop involved a seed variety more vulnerable to the drought conditions than was the variety used in Hill's smaller Trefland-treated crop.

Judge Chapman ruled as a matter of law that the only warranties in issue were the express warranties on the Basalin can which, by virtue of the applicable state U.C.C. provision ... 2–318 extended BWC's warranty beyond the retailer to Hill as a consumer; and that if breach of that warranty was proven, Hill's remedy was limited by its terms to direct damages as measured by the purchase price. On that basis the case was submitted to the jury which was then unable to reach a verdict, resulting in the declaration of a mistrial.

The case was then retried to Judge Anderson and a jury on substantially the same evidence. At the conclusion of the retrial,

Judge Anderson, in direct disagreement with Judge Chapman's earlier critical rulings, instructed the jury that it might find BWC liable on the oral warranty of Pennington as well as any express warranty on the cans of Basalin, and that it might award consequential as well as direct damages if it found breach of warranty and damages proximately caused by the breach. This jury returned a general verdict for Hill of $209,725.

Following the denial of various post-trial motions by BWC, this appeal was taken.

II

BWC's contentions on appeal are essentially that Judge Anderson erred in his two rulings by which, in specific disagreement with those earlier made by Judge Chapman, he allowed the jury to treat Pennington's oral representations as an oral express warranty binding on BWC and to award consequential as well as direct damages for any breach found. We agree that there was error of law in both respects.

A

BWC contends that Pennington's oral representation did not amount to a warranty binding upon BWC for two reasons. First, as a matter of law, that the representation amounted to no more than sales puffing, as Judge Chapman had ruled on the first trial. Second, that in any event, BWC's express disclaimer of any express or implied warranties other than those expressed on the label was binding as a matter of law upon Hill as purchaser.

While we would be disposed to agree that under [UCC 2–313(2)] ... Pennington's representation was simply a "statement purporting to be merely the seller's opinion or commendation of the goods [that did] not create a warranty," we rest decision primarily on the conclusion that, in any event, Hill was bound by the disclaimer on the label of any warranties but those expressly stated there. Though on trial Hill attempted to discount the subjective effect of the label's contents upon him as he read them, he conceded that he did read the label before using any of the Basalin. There is, therefore, no question of either his actual notice of the disclaimer's existence as an express condition of the sale or that he was invited by another provision of the label to repudiate by return of the product if unwilling to accept the sale conditions.

Under controlling provisions of the U.C.C. as enacted in South Carolina, S.C.Ann.Code § 36–2–202 (Law.Co-op.1976) (parol or extrinsic evidence), and of the express conditions of the particular sale, the Pennington oral statements could not, as a matter of law, be allowed to vary the terms of the conditions of sale and warranty on the product label ... which alone controlled the legal relations of the parties to the executed sale.

Hill seeks to avoid the controlling effect of these statutory provisions by characterizing the disclaimer on the product label as a unilateral attempt by a seller following execution of a contract of sale or a consummated sale to disclaim express warranties made in conjunction with the sale or contract. The cases he cites in support of this proposition, e.g., Klein v. Asgrow Seed Co., 246 Cal.App.2d 87, 54 Cal.Rptr. 609 (Cal.Ct.App.1966), do support it, but they and that proposition are simply inapposite to the facts of this case. They deal with the effect of a post-contract or post-sale attempt unilaterally to avoid, by a later disclaimer, warranties embodied in or arising from an executory contract of sale or a completed sale. That is simply not the situation here in issue.

B

The district court also erred in allowing the jury to award consequential damages in the face of the express limitation of remedies on the label.

[UCC 2–719] ... authorizes remedy limitations such as that expressed here on the Basalin label unless those limitations are determined to be unconscionable, or not intended to be exclusive, or to have failed of their essential purpose. Id. Judge Anderson, as had Judge Chapman in the original trial, held the limitation in issue not to be unconscionable. Hill does not challenge that ruling on appeal. This leaves only the possibilities that the limitation expressed was not intended to be exclusive, or that the exclusive remedy as limited failed of its essential purpose within the meaning of the statute.

Hill urges that he never agreed that the limitation expressed should make the remedy as limited an exclusive one. He accepted, however, a product with a label proclaiming that damages in no case would exceed those contemplated on the label. The label extends to purchaser-users the privilege of returning Basalin cans unopened if the purchaser does not agree to the terms and conditions on the label. Hill read the label and chose not to return the product but to use it. He cannot defeat the warrantor's expressed intention to limit remedy by a privately held intention not to accept the limitation while accepting and using the product.

Hill's argument that such a limited remedy necessarily "fails of its essential purpose" [UCC 2–719(2)] is equally unavailing. The argument seems to be that because Hill *claims* damages in the amount by which his crop yield was allegedly reduced and cannot *obtain* such damages if the limitation on remedy is enforced, then the remedy "fails of its essential purpose." This would of course turn the provision on its head since it would always prevent imposition of any limitation that might prevent recovery of particular relief sought. The "fail of essential purpose" exception to the general right of sellers to limit liability under the U.C.C. applies most obviously to those situations where the limitation of remedy involves repair or replacement that cannot return the goods to their warranted condition. ... This exception does not apply here.

III

It is not possible to determine from the general verdict whether the jury found liability based solely upon breach of the Pennington oral "warranty" or of both that "warranty" and the express warranty on the label. It is therefore necessary to vacate the judgment in its entirety and remand for a new trial limited to the issues of whether BWC is liable for breach of the express warranty on the label and, if so, the amount of damages to which Hill is entitled for the breach under the limitation of remedies that we have held was validly imposed in the conditions of sale on the label.

It is so ordered.

Notes

(1) Sales to Farmers. The Uniform Commercial Code does not have special provision for sales of goods to farmers. Farmers who grow crops commonly purchase seed, fertilizer, and herbicides. Non-conformity of any of these supplies can result in substantial loss of the expected crops. The market value of each of these supplies tends to be a very small fraction of the value of the expected crops. In this setting, not surprisingly, suppliers try to avoid potential liability for the consequential damages of crop failure. Should the law provide specially for allocation of this risk between farmers and their suppliers? What would be the optimal legal standard? How significant is the fact that Hill was "an experienced farmer with extensive farming operations"?

(2) Warranties by Manufacturers' Representatives. Hill purchased the herbicide from a retailer, who is not a party to the litigation. Hill sued the manufacturer, BWC, and based his case in part on statements made by Pennington, a representative of the manufacturer. Putting aside for the moment the parol evidence exclusion, would a statement about the goods by someone who is not "the seller" be an express warranty under UCC 2–313? Could the statement become "part of the basis of the bargain"? If 2–313 does not apply, is there any other basis on which to find a warranty obligation?[5] Consider UCC 1–103.

The Fourth Circuit denied recovery on the claim based on Pennington's statements under UCC 2–202. If, as appears, Hill and BWC had no agreement between themselves, and certainly never adopted a writing as the final expression of an agreement, was the court correct

---

5. In the marketing of consumer goods, a familiar transaction is the endorsement of goods given the Good Housekeeping Seal of Approval. The publisher of the magazine promises a remedy to consumers who buy endorsed products that turn out to be defective. Some credit card issuers, similarly, promise a remedy to consumers who, by use their credit cards, purchase products that turn out to be defective. Would such endorsements be enforceable under the UCC?

in applying 2–202 to exclude Hill's claims based on Pennington's statements?

(3) Manufacturers' Warranties on Labels. BWC placed what purported to be a warranty on the labels of each can of Basalin. Conceivably Hill first saw and read the label after he had bought the goods from the retailer. Was the manufacturer's statement on the label a warranty by BWC under UCC 2–313? See Massey–Ferguson, Inc. v. Laird, 432 So.2d 1259 (Ala.1983)(buyer of combine knew that manufacturer made a standard warranty, but did not examine the specific terms before contracting to purchase).

Note that a manufacturer's statement on the label would be a warranty by a retailer under UCC 2–314(f). As to retailers and their customers, the Code characterizes such statements as *implied* warranties.

(4) Post-Purchase Disclaimers. If a seller makes an express or implied warranty before or at the time of a contract of sale, does the seller have the power thereafter to limit or exclude the warranty? The parties have the power, by agreement, to modify a contract, UCC 2–209, but neither party has the unilateral power to decrease its contractual obligations to the other.

Was the purported disclaimer in the label in *Hill* a unilateral post-contract disclaimer? Could Hill seek to recover on basis of the express warranty in the label and not be bound by the disclaimer in the label?

The Basalin labels purport to disclaim implied warranties of merchantability and fitness for particular purpose. Hill apparently made no claim that either implied warranty existed or had been breached? What might explain that omission in plaintiff's case? What might explain the inclusion of disclaimers of these warranties in the labels?

Problem 2. Supreme Paint Company is a manufacturer of paint products. In response to an inquiry from Boyer Construction Co. about the price for a quantity purchase of ZX paint, Supreme wrote to Boyer:

> "Can quote you attractive price of $14 per gallon, freight prepaid to construction site, for immediate order for shipments of 100 gallons or more."

On September 10, Boyer replied:

> "Please ship 100 gallons of your ZX Paint for delivery at the construction site by November 1; unless we advise you to the contrary, make similar shipments to arrive December 1 and January 1."

The first shipment arrived on October 20. The invoice, which was received on the same day at Boyer's headquarters, noted the delivery of 100 gallons of ZX paint at a total price of $1400. The invoice bore at the bottom the following clearly printed statement:

> "Our paint products are prepared under carefully controlled manufacturing conditions, but if any of our products should be

defective, we will gladly replace the product or refund the purchase price. We shall not be responsible for any other warranties, express or implied, including the warranty of merchantable quantity which extend beyond the description on the face hereof, and in no event shall be responsible for any special or consequential damages."

Boyer promptly paid for this shipment and for the two subsequent shipments that were made pursuant to the original schedule, and Boyer applied the paint to his construction job. The paint proved to be defective and peeled off. Early in January the November application began to peel, and the same developed for the later applications. Consequently Owner rejected Boyer's construction work, with the result that Boyer had to remove some of the siding for the building, clean off the original coat of paint by sand blasting and apply new paint. This extra work cost Boyer $150,000.

Did the disclaimer on the invoice become part of the contract with respect to some, or all, of the shipments? Is the disclaimer of consequential damages effective? See Geo. C. Christopher & Sons v. Kansas Paint & Color Co., 215 Kan. 185, 523 P.2d 709 (1974), modified on other grounds, 215 Kan. 510, 525 P.2d 626 (1974).

(5) Consequential Damages Clauses in Farm Supply Sales; Unconscionability. In the trial court, Hill contended that the limited remedy provided by BWC, pursuant to the terms of the Basalin labels, was unconscionable, but the contention was abandoned on appeal. How would you support an argument on this point for the farmer-buyer? See UCC 2–302, 2–719(3).

DURHAM v. CIBA–GEIGY CORP., 315 N.W.2d 696 (S.D.1982). Farmer purchased a herbicide, "Milogard," to control the growth of weeds in his milo crop. Due to a foxtail weed problem, the crop yield was low. An action was brought against the Milogard manufacturer on the basis of the labels on the cans, which stated: "Milogard 4L controls annual morningglory, carpetweed, lambsquarter, pigweed, ragweed, foxtail, smartweed, and velvetleaf." The labels also contained a warranty, disclaimer, and limitation of damages clause substantially identical to the label on the Basalin cans. The trial court held the limitation of damages clause unconscionable and the supreme court affirmed:

> [T]he label represents that foxtail will be controlled by the pesticide but the user subsequently discovers that the pesticide is ineffective to control foxtail. To permit the manufacturer of the pesticide to escape all consequential responsibility for the breach of contract by inserting a disclaimer of warranty and limitation of consequential damage clause, such as was used herein, would leave the pesticide user without any substantial recourse for his loss. One-sided agreements whereby one party is left without a remedy for another

party's breach are oppressive and should be declared unconscionable. . . .

In this case, loss of the intended crop due to the ineffectiveness of the herbicide is inevitable and potential plaintiffs should not be left without a remedy. Furthermore, the purchasers of pesticides are not in a position to bargain with chemical manufacturers for contract terms more favorable than those listed on the pre-printed label, nor are they in a position to test the effectiveness of the pesticide prior to purchase. . . .

The legislature of this state has spent considerable time and effort in establishing the law of warranty in South Dakota, and the damages that are recoverable for a breach of that warranty. Appellant seeks to restrict and abolish this established law on the label of the product to the point where there is no actionable warranty for the consumer. This is not acceptable.

We agree with the trial court's determination that appellant's disclaimer of warranty and limitation of consequential damages clause is invalid as unconscionable and contrary to the public policy of this state.

(B) INTERNATIONAL SALES LAW

The Convention on Contracts for the International Sale of Goods does not contain regulatory provisions comparable to UCC 2–316 and 2–719. Under CISG 6, the parties may "derogate from or vary the effect of" any of the Convention's provisions. Article 6 permits parties to agree to disclaimers of a quality warranty under CISG 35(2)[6] or to clauses limiting damages otherwise provided by the Convention, particularly by CISG 74. On the surface, therefore, it appears that the regulatory provisions of domestic law, like those of the Commercial Code, would not apply to international sales contracts.

However, the Convention does not purport to exclude application of all domestic laws to international sales contracts. Thus, Article 4(a) declares that the Convention is not concerned with "the validity of the contract or any of its provisions." Should CISG 4 be construed to permit challenge of warranty disclaimers or clauses limiting damages in international sales contracts as "invalid" under United States domestic law?[7]

"The answer should be No. . . . It would be awkward to require [an international sales] contract to 'mention merchantability' in order

---

6. CISG 35(2) also contains a provision that the parties may agree otherwise.

7. CISG 7(2) refers to the rules of private international law for choice of law on questions not settled by the Convention. Since questions of "validity" are expressly not governed by the Convention, the law governing such questions would be found by application of the choice of law rules under private international law. In an appropriate case, United States domestic law might be chosen as the governing law.

to disclaim an implied obligation under [CISG] 35(2) that ... does not itself refer to 'merchantability.' ...

"The argument [that CISG 4(a) incorporates UCC 2–316(2) and (3)] proves too much for it leads to the conclusion that any domestic rule that denied full literal effect to a contract provision on the ground that it does not accurately represent the parties' understanding would constitute a rule of 'validity.' The reference to domestic rules of 'validity' in Article 4(a) cannot be carried this far without intruding on the Convention's rules for interpreting international sales contracts. More specifically, Article 8 addresses a basic question of interpretation in a manner somewhat similar to the rules of domestic law in UCC 2–316. ... The point is not, of course, that Article 8 of the Convention and UCC 2–316 are identical but rather that both address the same issue. It follows that the reference to 'validity' in Article 4(a) of the Convention may not be read so broadly as to import domestic rules that would supplant articles of the Convention such as Article 8." J. Honnold, Uniform Law for International Sales §§ 233–234 (2d ed. 1991). *Contra:* Note, 53 Fordham L. Rev. 863 (1985).

Whether or not CISG 4(a) incorporates regulatory provisions of the Uniform Commercial Code, counsel for sellers engaged in international sales transactions to which United States law may apply would be prudent to advise their clients to contract in accordance with the disclosure requirements of the UCC. However, an international sales contract drafter should not rely on the UCC rules that a disclaimer clause is sufficient if it mentions "merchantability" or uses the phrase "as is." A non-U.S. buyer, relying on CISG 8, could reasonably argue that the full import of these provisions had not been made clear to it.

Problem 3. The parties in *Western Industries* were a United States buyer and a Canadian seller. The transaction occurred prior to the CISG taking effect. If the case had been governed by the CISG, how would the battle of the forms be treated? See Art. 19. Is the CISG provision an improvement on the UCC 2–207? If the CISG had applied, would the outcome have changed?

Problem 4. The parties in *Kunststoffwerk* were a United States buyer and a German seller. The transaction occurred before the CISG took effect. If the CISG had applied, would the outcome have changed?

SECTION 4. LEGAL BARS TO ACTIONS FOR BREACH OF WARRANTY

(A) DOMESTIC UNITED STATES LAW

Introduction. A buyer may be barred from litigation of the merits of a warranty claim if the buyer fails to give the seller timely notice of the seller's breach. Even if a buyer's notice is timely, the buyer may be barred from relief if the buyer has not commenced a law suit within the statutory period of limitations. The notice-to-seller requirement is found in UCC 2–607(3)(a). The statute of limitations for transactions in goods is UCC 2–725.

(1) Notice of breach. Lawyers representing sellers in warranty litigation must be drawn to the "slam dunk" provision that results in buyers' being "barred from any remedy." 2–607(3)(a). A buyer is subject to this result if, after acceptance of goods,[1] the buyer fails to notify seller of breach within a reasonable time after the buyer discovered or should have discovered the breach.

M.K. ASSOCIATES v. STOWELL PRODUCTS, INC.
United States District Court, for the District of Maine, 1988.
697 F. Supp. 20.

CARTER, DISTRICT JUDGE

I. Introduction

M.K. Associates, a seller of wood products, has brought an action to recover the remainder of the purchase price due from a sale of ash dowels to the defendant Stowell Products, Inc. The defendant claims that the plaintiff breached the contract because the dowels were defective. The defendant argues that it is entitled to set off the remaining amount due as damages caused by the defective goods.

The case was tried before the court on September 19, 1988. For the reasons set forth below, the court finds for the plaintiff. The findings of fact and conclusions of law follow.

II. Findings of Fact

From December, 1986 through February, 1987, Stowell Products, through its purchasing manager, Wayne Curley, made a series of offers for ash dowels from M.K. Associates. The dowels were delivered during the period from December, 1986 to March, 1987. Stowell Products intended to use the dowels to manufacture products to fill a contract with another company, Mirro/Foley Corp., due in late August, 1987. Although Stowell Products made periodic payments to M.K. Associates on these orders up through the fall of 1987, it was substantially in arrears as early as March, 1987. The parties have stipulated that the amount still due for the purchase and delivery of the ash dowels is $10,518.40.

---

1. "Acceptance" of goods is defined in UCC 2–606. What conduct constitutes "acceptance" can be a difficult question. We will consider that subject in Chapter 5, Section 2, infra. Cases in which buyers claim sellers' breach of warranty typically involve problems not detected by buyers for some time after delivery of the goods, by which time "acceptance" will have occurred under 2–606. Sometimes, however, warranty problems surface before "acceptance." Of the cases studied, the *T.J. Stevenson* case (sale of flour to Bolivia), Section 2, supra, is a notable example of pre-acceptance warranty litigation.

The employee who received the orders from M.K. Associates noticed that some of the dowels were defective because they were "out of round," and he reported this defect to Wayne Curley, the purchasing manager. The factory foreperson, Virginia Johnson, found she was unable to use the dowels because of the defects. From June to September, 1987, Johnson ran the dowels through a "seavey" machine in order to correct the defects. This corrective process enabled Stowell Products to use the dowels for the Mirro/Foley order, although the order was not shipped until September 25, 1987, about a month late.

In the spring of 1987, Wayne Curley, purchasing manager of Stowell Products, and Doug Bucy, general manager, had a series of conversations with M.K. Associates. These conversations discussed the fact that Stowell Products was behind on its payments for the order. Only one conversation, however, made any mention of problems with the dowels. This conversation occurred between Curley and Marshall Kates, owner of M.K. Associates, in March, 1987. At this time, Curley asked Kates if one of the orders could be cancelled because of problems in running the dowels through the production process. Kates answered that he couldn't cancel. They did not discuss the issue further.

Stowell Products made no other attempts to raise the issue of defects in the dowels to M.K. Associates. On September 2, 1987, M.K. Associates filed a complaint in this court for the remainder due from Stowell Products on the dowel order.

III. Conclusions of Law

The issue in this case is whether Stowell Products is entitled to deduct damages for defects in the dowels purchased from M.K. Associates against the amount owed for the orders. The defendant does not dispute that Stowell Products accepted the dowels from M.K. Associates, and that it did not revoke this acceptance. Instead, the defendant decided to keep the dowels and use them in its business. . . .

Nonetheless, accepting defective goods does not preclude a buyer from pursuing remedies for breach of contract due to defects in goods. 11 M.R.S.A. § 2–607(2). "The buyer on notifying the seller of his intention so to do may deduct all or any part of the damages resulting from any breach of the contract from any part of the price still due under the same contract." 11 M.R.S.A. § 2–717. A buyer claiming a breach of contract after accepting goods must, however, notify the seller of the breach within a reasonable time after discovery of the breach, or the buyer will be barred from any breach of contract remedy. 11 M.R.S.A. § 2–607(3)(a).

The critical question in this case, therefore, is whether the defendant gave timely notice of the breach of contract claim. What constitutes reasonable time depends on the particular circumstances of a case. 11 M.R.S.A. § 1–204. The policies underlying the requirement of timely notice are first, to enable the seller to cure or replace, second, to give the seller an opportunity to prepare for negotiation and litigation, and third, to ensure finality. J. White & R. Summers, Uniform Commercial Code 421–22 (2d ed. 1980). See also In Re Morweld Steel Products Corp., 8 Bankr. 946, 951 (W.D.Mich.1981) (quoting Steel & Wire Corp. v. Thyssen Inc., 20 U.C.C. Rep. 892 (E.D.Mich.1976)). To further these purposes, "reasonable time" for notice is interpreted strictly for commercial buyers. See 11 M.R.S.A. § 2–607, Uniform Commercial Code (U.C.C.) Comment 4.

The defendant argues that notice of the breach was given by Wayne Curley, purchasing manager for Stowell Products, to Marshall Kates, owner of M.K. Associates, in their conversation in March, 1987. In this conversation, Curley told Kates that defects in some dowels were causing production problems, and Kates said he could not cancel the order. The defendant argues that Curley's conversation with Kates was sufficient notice. It is true that "no formality of notice is required." 11 M.R.S.A. § 2–717, U.C.C. Comment 2. "The content of the notification need merely be sufficient to let the seller know that the transaction is still troublesome and must be watched." 11 M.R.S.A. § 2–607, U.C.C. Comment 4. Nevertheless, after Kates responded that he would not be able to cancel the order, Curley let the matter rest and gave Kates no indication that Stowell Products pursued it further. Therefore, the defendant did not give adequate notice that the transaction was still troublesome.

Moreover, the U.C.C. Comments emphasize that notice of a claim of breach is crucial. "The notification which saves the buyer's rights under this Article need only be such as informs the seller that the transaction is claimed to involve a breach, and thus opens the way for normal settlement through negotiation." 11 M.R.S.A. § 2–607, U.C.C. Comment 4. Even if the seller knows of defects in the goods, the buyer must notify the seller of the buyer's claim that the defects constitute a breach. In Re Morweld Steel Products Corp., supra at 952 (quoting Standard Alliance Industries Inc. v. The Black Clawson Co., 587 F.2d 813 (6th Cir.1978), cert. denied, 441 U.S. 923 (1979)). The requirement that a commercial buyer's notice must include an indication that the buyer considers the contract breached is consistent with the policies behind the notice requirement, which include ensuring finality for transactions and allowing the seller to prepare for negotiation and settlement. In the conversation with Kates, however, Curley did not clearly let Kates know that Stowell Products considered the contract breached.

Finally, U.C.C. Comment 2 to 11 M.R.S.A. § 2–717 states that "any language which reasonably indicates the buyer's reason for holding up his payment is sufficient." Despite repeated conversations concerning late payments, no one from Stowell Products suggested to M.K. Associates that payments were being withheld to cover the costs of defects in the dowels.

Therefore, Stowell Products' only notice of the breach was in its answer to the plaintiff's complaint, filed on October 13, 1987, more than five months after the dowels were received and more than three months after the defendant began processing the dowels. The defendant argues that it was reasonable to wait until the Mirro/Foley order was completed in order to determine the total amount of damages.

The U.C.C. does not require, however, that the buyer give notice of the exact amount of damages that will be incurred. See Custom Automated Machinery v. Penda Corp., 537 F.Supp. 77, 86 (N.D.Ill.1982) (buyer not required to tell seller amount of damages as long as seller on notice of reason for withholding payment). At least by June, 1987, the defendant knew of significant costs that would be incurred by correcting the defective dowels. The defendant has given no reason to justify letting several months go by while it used the defective goods for its own business purposes before warning M.K. Associates that it considered the contract breached.

The defendant also claims that the delay was reasonable in light of the purposes of the notice requirement, since ample time for settlement remained after the plaintiff began this litigation. Courts have held, however, that waiting until the seller sues for the purchase price to claim a breach of contract fails to satisfy the requirement of timely notice. In Re Morweld Steel Products Corp., supra at 951–53; Pace v. Sagebrush Sales Co., 114 Ariz. 271, 560 P.2d 789 (1977).

IV. Conclusion

The defendant accepted and used the dowels from M.K. Associates despite any defects it found. The defendant failed to notify the plaintiff of any claim of a breach of contract until the plaintiff began this litigation. This delay was unreasonable, and therefore the defendant is barred from deducting damages for breach of contract.

Accordingly, the Court hereby ORDERS that judgment in this action be entered for the plaintiff in the amount of Ten Thousand Five Hundred Eighteen Dollars and Forty Cents ($10,518.40), plus interest and costs as provided by law.

Notes

(1) **UCC 2–607(3): Rationale and History.** Comment 4 states that "the rule of requiring notification is designed to defeat commercial bad faith... ." The court in *M.K. Associates* gives three quite different policies said to underlie the requirement. Does the *text* of 2–607(3)(a) support the positions in the comment or the opinion? What purpose could be important enough to justify totally barring a buyer's claim without regard to the degree of injury, if any, to the interest of the seller? Comment 4 declares that the necessary content of a buyer's notice is minimal: "merely sufficient to let the seller know that the transaction is still troublesome and must be watched ..., [not] a clear statement of all the objections that will be relied upon by the buyer ..., and [not] a claim for damages or of any threatened litigation or other

resort to a remedy."[2] Can the extreme consequence be reconciled with that minimal information requirement?

As indicated in the comment (Prior Uniform Statutory Provision), 2–607(3) has an antecedent in USA 49, which also barred buyers who failed to give sellers timely notice of breach. But USA 49 had no counterpart in the Sale of Goods Act. Why did the drafters of the United States statute add this element? See S. Williston, The Law Governing Sales of Goods at Common Law and Under the Uniform Sales Act § 488 (1909). See also John C. Reitz, Against Notice: A Proposal to Restrict the Notice of Claims Rule in UCC § 2–697(a)(3), 73 Cornell L. Rev. 534, 540–541 (1988).

Some civil law jurisdictions impose a requirement of buyers' prompt notice of default. Some nations provide very short periods within which actions must be brought (statutes of limitation or "prescription") or notices given to sellers. G. Treitel, Remedies for Breach of Contract: A Comparative Account 141 (1988). Another technique is used in the German Commercial Code, §§ 377–378. In the case of commercial sales, buyers are required to examine goods promptly after delivery and to give notice of any discernible lack of conformity discovered; if a buyer fails to give such notice, goods are deemed to be in conformity with the contract. Id.

Could UCC 2–607(3)(a), in its present form, be construed to provide relief only if a seller can show that buyer's delay has prejudiced the seller and limiting the bar to recovery to the extent necessary to overcome the prejudice shown? One commentator argues for an affirmative answer:

> Many courts have in effect interpreted the "reasonable time" standard of the rule to reflect a rough balance of the interests of the buyer in obtaining a remedy against the interests [of the seller] served by the notice rule. Because the legislatures have not provided any guidance on the policy goals underlying the notice rule, the courts are free to construe them as broadly or narrowly as they think proper. ...
>
> The prejudice least likely to justify barring all of the buyer's claim is loss of opportunity to cure [the nonconformity]. When the seller demonstrates such a loss, the court might use the mitigation principle to justify barring only the costs that the seller could have avoided.
>
> [For the prejudice resulting from seller's loss of the opportunity to gather evidence of the goods conformity, courts should employ an evidentiary presumption in seller's favor.] Traditionally, courts place the burden of production of evidence on the party with the best access to the relevant evidence. Courts should also be free to

---

2. Would a notice be sufficient if it stated in entirety: "Your delivery was nonconforming"?

Sec. 4 *ACTIONS FOR BREACH OF WARRANTY* 149

employ presumptions to prevent the careless or deliberate behavior of one litigant from prejudicing the opposing litigant's defense or prosecution.

John C. Reitz, supra, 588–589. Do you agree with this analysis?

The Permanent Editorial Board UCC Article 2 Study Group stated in its Preliminary Report (pp. 168–169):

Literal interpretation of the notice requirement should be rejected. Either the text of § 2–607(3)(a) or the comments should be revised to require only that the notice inform the seller that problems have arisen or continue to exist with regard to the accepted goods. Also, the comments should clarify that the buyer has no obligation to notify for breaches of which it has no knowledge.

Do you agree?

(2) Statute of Limitations. The UCC generally shortened the period of limitations for warranty actions. The usual contract period is about six years. Section 2–725(1) provides a four-year period.[3] The period begins to run when a buyer's cause of action accrues, defined for most transactions as the date of tender of delivery. UCC 2–725(2). Buyer's knowledge or lack of knowledge of the breach is not material.

When does the period of limitations begin to run on seller's breach of implied warranty of merchantability? Of fitness for particular purpose? Could the period expire before a buyer has learned of the breach?

Determining when the period of limitations begin to run on seller's breach of an express warranty is more difficult. If a seller has provided a repair/replace type of express warranty, when does a buyer's cause of action accrue? Among other issues to be considered is the meaning of the exception clause in the second sentence of 2–725(2). That issue is presented in the case that follows.

TITTLE v. STEEL CITY OLDSMOBILE GMC TRUCK, INC.

Supreme Court of Alabama, 1989.
544 So.2d 883.

SHORES, JUSTICE.

The plaintiff, Rodney K. Tittle, appeals a summary judgment entered in favor of defendants, Steel City Oldsmobile GMC Truck, Inc. (hereinafter "Steel City"), and General Motors Corporation (hereinafter "General Motors").

Tittle purchased a 1981 Oldsmobile automobile from Steel City on October 9, 1981, and accepted delivery of it the same day. With the purchase of his automobile, General Motors provided Tittle with a

---

[3] The section also permits parties to a contract of sale to reduce the period (with a one-year minimum) but not to extend it.

document entitled "1981 Oldsmobile New Car Warranty." This writing provided that Steel City, as Tittle's Oldsmobile dealer, would repair and adjust defects in material or workmanship that occurred during the first 12 months or first 12,000 miles in which the car was in use. The document provided, further, that the warranty period would begin on the date the car was first delivered or placed in service. In addition to this warranty, Tittle purchased from General Motors Acceptance Corporation (hereinafter "GMAC"), the company with whom he financed the purchase of the car, a supplemental warranty that extended coverage of the original warranty to 36 months or 36,000 miles.

After Tittle accepted the automobile, he discovered numerous defects in it and repeatedly asked Steel City and GMAC to cure the problems. When Steel City proved unable, after a number of attempts, to repair the vehicle, Tittle met with the zone representative for GMAC, Don Ackerman. Tittle alleges that Mr. Ackerman, as agent for GMAC, offered to extend the existing warranty on the vehicle for an additional 12 months or 12,000 miles if Tittle would allow Steel City another opportunity to repair the defects in the vehicle. Tittle agreed, but following several unsuccessful attempts to repair the vehicle, Tittle returned the car to Steel City.

Tittle sued on January 29, 1986, in Jefferson County Circuit Court, alleging that Steel City, GMAC, and General Motors had breached their respective express warranties as well as implied warranties of merchantability and fitness. Tittle founded his claims upon the federal Consumer Product Warranty Act, known commonly as the Magnuson-Moss Act, 15 U.S.C. § 2301 et seq., and upon Alabama's version of the Uniform Commercial Code (hereinafter "U.C.C."), § 7-1-101 et seq., Ala. Code (1975). In their answers to the plaintiff's complaint, both Steel City and General Motors specifically pleaded the statute of limitations as an affirmative defense.

Steel City and General Motors filed motions for summary judgment based upon the statute of limitations defense. During the hearing on the motions, the trial judge asked the parties to present the court with additional authorities supporting their respective positions. The court requested that the parties submit these authorities on or before April 1, 1988. General Motors responded to the trial court's request by providing it with four cases. Tittle, however, filed both a supplemental brief opposing the defendants' motion for summary judgment and an affidavit containing facts not alleged at the time the court heard the summary judgment motions.

On April 4, 1988, the trial court entered summary judgment in favor of Steel City and General Motors. The court found that Tittle's claims were barred by the statute of limitations at the time his complaint was filed. The trial court specifically noted that the plaintiff's case remained pending as to defendant GMAC, but made its order final with respect to Steel City and General Motors. See, Ala. R. Civ. P. 54(b). It is from this summary judgment that the plaintiff appeals.

Apparently anticipating Tittle's argument on appeal, General Motors filed a motion to strike the plaintiff's affidavit from the record, on June 20, 1988.

The issue presented this Court for review is whether the trial court erred in entering summary judgment for these two defendants on the ground that Tittle's claim for breach of an express warranty was barred by the statute of limitations. In arguing this issue, the parties raise five questions this Court must address: first, what statute of limitations applies in cases brought under the Magnuson–Moss Act or the breach of warranty claims brought under Alabama's version of the U.C.C.?; second, does Ala. Code (1975), § 8–20–12, toll the statute of limitations for breach of warranty in consumer cases until the breach is discovered?; third, does the warranty issued by General Motors explicitly extend to the future performance of the vehicle?; fourth, is a repair and replacement warranty breached upon tender of the car or upon refusal or failure to repair an alleged defect?; and fifth, was Mr. Tittle's affidavit properly submitted to the trial court and included in the record on appeal, and, if so, did the affidavit present a genuine issue of material fact precluding the trial court's summary judgment?

I.

The Magnuson–Moss Act authorizes civil actions by consumers in state or federal court when suppliers, warrantors, or service contractors violate its provisions. 15 U.S.C. § 2310(d)(1). The Act, however, does not provide a statute of limitations for claims that arise under this legislation. Where a federal statute grants a cause of action, but does not include a statute of limitations governing the scope of that statute's application, federal common law requires that the court apply the state statute of limitations governing the state action most closely analogous to the federal claim. DelCostello v. International Brotherhood of Teamsters, 462 U.S. 151 (1983). The state law action most analogous to Tittle's Magnuson–Moss warranty claim is an action for breach of warranty in a contract for sale. Thus, the statute of limitations that appropriately applies to Tittle's state breach of warranty action is the same statute of limitations that appropriately applies to his federal Magnuson–Moss claim. Under Alabama's version of the U.C.C., the statute of limitations that applies to an action for breach of any contract for sale is found in § 7–2–725, Ala. Code (1975).

* * *

III.

Under § 7–2–725(2), a cause of action for breach of warranty accrues when the seller tenders to the buyer the goods made the basis of the warranty. Once the cause of action accrues, the statute provides a four-year limitations period in which the buyer may file suit, subject to two exceptions. First, a cause of action will not accrue, in the case of consumer goods, on a claim for damages for injury to the person until the injury occurs.* And, second, where the seller of consumer goods gives the buyer an express warranty that extends to the future performance of the goods, a cause of action will not accrue until the buyer discovers or should have discovered the defect in the goods.

Tittle argues that the trial court erred in entering summary judgment in this case even if the limitations period contained in § 7-2-725 is the one that appropriately applies to his cause of action, because, he says, the warranties given him by Steel City and General Motors explicitly extended to the future performance of his automobile. Consequently, Tittle claims that his cause of action did not accrue until he discovered or should have discovered the breach of the Steel City and General Motors warranties.

While Tittle's argument has been addressed in other jurisdictions, the question of whether a so-called "repair and replacement" warranty extends to the future performance of goods, so as to fall within the limited exception set out in § 7-2-725(2), is a case of first impression for this Court. Therefore, a brief analysis of the case law interpreting this section is appropriate. Before we analyze case law, however, it is critical that we consider exactly what the warranties given Tittle purport to guarantee.

Page 2 of Tittle's warranty is entitled, "1981 Oldsmobile New Car Limited Warranty." This document provides that "Oldsmobile Division, General Motors Corporation, warrants each new 1981 car," that "this warranty covers any repairs and needed adjustments to correct defects in material or workmanship," and that "the warranty period begins on the date the car is first delivered or put in use." The warranty further provides, "your Oldsmobile dealer will make the repairs or adjustments, using new or remanufactured parts." The warranty stipulates on page 3 that "it is our intent to repair under the warranty, without charge, anything that goes wrong during the warranty period that is our fault." The warranty then distinguishes the term "defects," which "are covered [under the warranty] because we, the manufacturer, are responsible," from the term "damages," which are not covered by the warranty because the manufacturer has "no control over damage caused by such things as collision, misuse and lack of maintenance which occurs after the car is delivered." Page 4 of the warranty, under the separate heading "Emission Components Defect Warranty, further provides:

> Oldsmobile ... warrants to owners of 1981 Oldsmobile passenger cars that the car (1) was designed, built, and equipped so as to conform at the time of sale with applicable regulations of the Environmental Protection Agency, and (2) is free from defects in materials and workmanship which cause the car to fail to conform with applicable Federal Environmental Protection Agency regula-

---

* [The Alabama version of § 2-725 contains a non-uniform amendment that establishes the date of a personal injury as the date on which the period of limitations begins to run with respect to such claims. Eds.]

tions for a period of use of 50,000 miles or 5 years, whichever occurs first.

In 1976, in the leading case of Voth v. Chrysler Motor Corp., 218 Kan. 644, 545 P.2d 371 (1976), the Supreme Court of Kansas spoke to Tittle's argument. The warranty in Voth read in pertinent part:

> Chrysler Corporation warrants this vehicle to the first registered owner only against defects in material and workmanship in normal use as follows: (1) the entire vehicle (except tires) for 12 months or 12,000 miles of operation after the vehicle is first placed in service, whichever occurs first, from the date of sale or delivery thereto; and (2) the engine block, head and all internal engine parts, water pump, intake manifold, transmission case and all internal transmission parts, torque converter (if so equipped), drive shaft universal joints, rear axle and differential, and rear wheel bearings for 5 years or 50,000 miles of operation after the vehicle is first placed in service, whichever occurs first, from the date of such sale or delivery. Any part of this vehicle found defective under the conditions of this warranty will be repaired or replaced, at Chrysler's option, without charge at an authorized Imperial, Chrysler, Plymouth, or Dodge dealership.

Voth, 218 Kan. at 647, 545 P.2d at 374–75 (quoting Chrysler's warranty from the record).

This warranty is similar to the warranty issued by General Motors in this case. The Kansas Supreme Court held that the Chrysler warranty did not explicitly extend to the future performance of the vehicle. Moreover, the court found that the warranty did not guarantee performance without malfunction during the term of the warranty, but warranted only that the manufacturer would repair or replace defective parts in the event the car malfunctioned. Voth, 218 Kan. at 648, 545 P.2d at 375. The Kansas court explains its rationale through a quotation from Owens v. Patent Scaffolding Co., 77 Misc.2d 992, 354 N.Y.S.2d 778 (Sup.Ct.1974), rev'd on other grounds, 50 A.D.2d 866, 376 N.Y.S.2d 948 (1975), in which an argument similar to Tittle's was rejected:

> In this case the warranty does not go to performance of the equipment. To warrant to make needed repairs to leased equipment is not a warranty extending to its future performance. All that the supplier promises is that if the equipment needs repairs he will make them. It does not promise that in the future the goods will not fall into disrepair or malfunction, but only that if it does, the supplier will repair it. [Underlying] the warranty to make needed repairs is the assumption that the goods may fall into disrepair or otherwise malfunction. No warranty that the goods will not is to be inferred from the warranty to make needed repairs.

Voth, 218 Kan. at 651, 545 P.2d at 378 (quoting Owens, supra, 77 Misc.2d at 999, 354 N.Y.S.2d at 785).

In articulating the distinction between a warranty to repair and a warranty extending to future performance, the court in Owens said:

> A promise to repair is an express warranty that the promise to repair will be honored [citations omitted]. The seller's warranty ... that ... [goods] "will give satisfactory service at all times" is distinguishable from the supplier's warranty to "make modifications, alterations or repairs to the component parts of the equipment" when necessary. [The words in the former warranty] go to the performance of the goods; that it "will give satisfactory service at all times." When the time came that the [goods] did not give satisfactory service, the warranty was breached. [The former warranty] explicitly extended to future performance of the goods, and its breach could only be discovered at the time of such performance.

77 Misc.2d at 998, 354 N.Y.S.2d at 784.

In Ontario Hydro v. Zallea Systems, Inc. 569 F.Supp. 1261 (D.Del. 1983), Chief Judge Latchum expressed the distinction between these two types of warranties in this manner:

> [T]he key distinction between these two kinds of warranties is that a repair or replacement warranty merely provides a *remedy* if the product becomes defective, while a warranty for future performance *guarantees the performance* of the product itself for a stated period of time. In the former case, the buyer is relying upon the warranty merely as a method by which a defective product can be remedied which has no effect upon his ability to discover his breach. In the latter instance, the buyer is relying upon the warranty as a guarantee of future performance and therefore has no opportunity to discover the breach until the future performance has been tested. (Emphasis in original.)

Ontario Hydro, at 1266.

Other courts and authorities support the same conclusion: a promise to repair is not necessarily a promise of future performance.... See also, W. D. Hawkland, Uniform Commercial Code Service, § 2–725:02 at 480 (the hardship to the buyer that may sometimes be created by the four-year limitations period as measured from tender of delivery is thought to be outweighed by the commercial benefit derived from an established limitations period).

Tittle, in response to the foregoing cases, proffers two cases that he suggests represent substantial authority from other jurisdictions directly contrary to Voth and similar cases. In the first case, Standard Alliance Industries, Inc. v. Black Clawsen Co., 587 F.2d 813 (6th Cir.1978), cert. denied, 441 U.S.923, 99 S.Ct. 2032, 60 L.Ed.2d 396 (1979), the seller of a forging machine, in addition to warranting specific performance levels for the operation of the machine, warranted that "the equipment manufactured by it would be free from defects in workmanship and material" for a period of one year. 587 F.2d at 816–

17 (emphasis added). When the manufacturer failed, after numerous attempts, to repair the defective machinery, the buyer brought an action against the seller alleging breach of his express warranty. The Standard Alliance court held that the warranty at issue in the case extended to the future performance of the machine for a period of one year and that the buyer's cause of action accrued when the purchaser discovered or should have discovered that the machine was defective. Id., at 817.

In the second case, R. W. Murray Co. v. Shatterproof Glass Corp., 697 F.2d 818 (8th Cir.1983), the manufacturer's warranty provided:

> Vision and spandrel glass shall be guaranteed by the glass manufacturer for a period of ten (10) years from the date of acceptance of the project to furnish and replace any unit which develops material destruction of vision between the interglass surfaces. This guarantee is for material and labor costs for replacing.

697 F.2d at 821–22 n. 2.

> Shatterproof Glass Corporation warrants its insulating glass units for a period of twenty (20) years from the date of manufacture against defects in material or workmanship that result in moisture accumulation, film formation or dust collection between the interior surfaces, resulting from failure of the hermetic seal. Purchaser's exclusive remedy and Shatterproof's 'total' liability under this warranty shall be limited to the replacement of any lite failing to meet the terms of this warranty. Such replacement will be made F.O.B. Detroit to the shipping point nearest the installation.

697 F.2d 822 n. 3. The court construed these warranties as extending to the future performance of the goods for periods of 10 years and 20 years, respectively, and held that the purchaser's cause of action for breach of warranty accrued when the breach was, or should have been, discovered.

Despite the language used in the Shatterproof Glass warranties, guaranteeing for a specified period of time that a product is "free" from defects, as in Standard Alliance, seems to us altogether different from guaranteeing that product "against" defects, as in Voth. In the first instance, the manufacturer guarantees that the product possesses no defect whatsoever, while in the second instance the manufacturer guarantees that where defects emerge, he will remedy them, generally by repairing or replacing the defective part. While Shatterproof Glass used the term "against" in its warranty, we reconcile the holding in that case with Voth and Standard Alliance by noting the explicit nature of the remaining language in the warranty. Had the Shatterproof Glass court held that the warranties fell outside the U.C.C. § 2–725(2) "extends to future performance" exception, then despite the 10– and 20–year periods set out in the warranties, § 2–725(1) would have terminated the plaintiff's right of action four years after tender of the goods. (Section 2–725(1) provides in pertinent part, "By the original agreement the parties may reduce the period of limitation to not less than one year but may not extend it [beyond four years from the date of tender].")

In the present case, the warranty under which Tittle pursued his claim is even more free of ambiguity than that found in Voth and the other cases. The activating language of that warranty provides: "This warranty covers any repairs and needed adjustments to correct defects in material or workmanship." This language clearly does not guarantee that the car will perform free of defects for the term of the agreement. In fact, as the court in Voth recognized, the language of the guarantee anticipates that defects will occur. We, therefore, hold that the warranty provided Tittle upon the purchase of his car did not extend to the car's future performance.

We recognize that, under the analysis adopted by this Court, one might reasonably suggest that the language of the "Emission Components Defect Warranty" places it within our definition of a warranty that extends to future performance, at least within the limited scope of that separate provision. The emissions warranty provides: "Oldsmobile ... warrants ... that the car ... is free from defects in material and workmanship which cause the car to fail to conform with applicable Federal Environmental Protection Agency regulations for a period of use of 50,000 miles or 5 years, whichever comes first." We note, however, that although he enumerates an exhaustive list of defects, Tittle never alleged in his complaint or elsewhere that his vehicle failed to conform to EPA emissions standards. Hence, this provision is not applicable to the case before us.

IV.

Tittle next contends that even if the General Motors and Steel City warranties do not extend to the future performance of the vehicle, the cause of action does not accrue until there is a refusal or failure to repair. This contention, however, directly contradicts the plain meaning of the language in § 7–2–725, which states that a cause of action for breach of any contract for sale accrues when the breach occurs and that the breach occurs upon tender of delivery, regardless of the buyer's knowledge of the breach, unless the warranty explicitly extends to future performance. We have earlier determined that Tittle's warranty does not extend to the future performance of his car. The trial court, therefore, correctly determined that Tittle's cause of action, by statute and by the express terms of his warranty, accrued at the time Steel City delivered the vehicle to him.

V.

Finally, Tittle argues that even if we affirm the lower court's rulings regarding interpretation of § 7–2–725, the trial court still erred in granting summary judgment because, he says, a material issue of fact exists as to whether the defendants are estopped to assert the statute of limitations based upon their agent's representations.

* * *

... General Motors and Steel City argue that they should not be estopped from raising the statute of limitations defense because, they say, no evidence exists that the misrepresentations made by Mr. Ackerman were intentional or fraudulent, or that Tittle, relying on these representations, was induced not to file a lawsuit. ...

Tittle states in his affidavit that in 1984 a General Motors representative, Mr. Don Ackerman, represented that Steel City would repair the defects in his vehicle; that Mr. Ackerman indicated that if Tittle would allow Steel City another opportunity to repair the car, then Ackerman would extend the warranty 12 months or 12,000 miles; and that based on Mr. Ackerman's representations, he continued to attempt to have the car repaired rather than returning the car to the appellees. We find that a jury might conceivably construe Mr. Ackerman's statements as a promise to make repairs in return for a promise not to sue.

In reviewing a disposition of a motion for summary judgment, we use the same standard as that of the trial court in determining whether the evidence before the court made out a genuine issue of material fact. ... We do not here decide whether these defendants are estopped as a matter of law from asserting the statute of limitations as a defense; rather, we hold that a fact issue exists as to whether Ackerman acted as an agent for General Motors and Steel City and made a statement that Tittle reasonably relied on in delaying the filing of this lawsuit.

We, therefore, reverse the summary judgment in favor of General Motors and Steel City.

REVERSED AND REMANDED.

Notes

(1) Magnuson–Moss Warranty Act. The buyer in *Tittle* based his claim in part on the Magnuson–Moss Warranty Act. The court found nothing in that act that affected the statute of limitations issue. We will take up the Magnuson–Moss Act in the next section.

(2) Construction of UCC 2–725(2). The second sentence of UCC 2–725(2) poses obvious difficulties for interpretation. In a sense, all warranties of quality extend to performance of goods after tender of delivery, but the second sentence cannot be read properly as an exception that swallows the rule that the period of limitations ordinarily runs from the date of tender of delivery.

> Consider the case in which the manufacturer promises to repair any defect in a car's drivetrain that occurs within two years or 24,000 miles, whichever occurs first. ... [M]any courts would interpret this as a warranty that extends to future performance and would therefore grant four years from the time of the occurrence of the defect. On the other hand, one might read the agreement to mean simply that the seller will repair any defect that comes to light within that period irrespective of its cause, but

that the seller's liability ends at the earlier [of two years or] 24,000 miles and does not extend for four years beyond that time. The seller (and buyer if the truth be known) may construe such agreement not as a warranty at all but as an agreement to repair unrelated to any defect in the goods (as, for example, a wheel that breaks when it hits a pothole).

J. White & R. Summers, Uniform Commercial Code 479 (3d ed. 1988). Do you agree with the authors' analysis?

MOORMAN MANUFACTURING CO. v. NATIONAL TANK CO., 91 Ill.2d 69, 61 Ill.Dec. 746, 435 N.E.2d 443 (1982). In 1966 Moorman purchased a large grain-storage tank from National. The contract of sale contained the following:

Tank designed to withstand 60 lbs. per bushel grain and 100 m.p.h. winds.

In 1976 a crack developed in the tank; Moorman brought suit against National in 1977. One count of the complaint, based on the quoted language, alleged breach of express warranty. National contended that the claim was barred by the statute of limitations. The trial court, relying on the exception in 2–725(2), held that Moorman's claim was not time-barred. The Illinois Supreme Court reversed.

> The final issue is whether count IV, based upon breach of express warranty, was barred by the statute of limitations. ...
>
> Several appellate court decisions in this State have held that merely because it is reasonable to expect that a warranty of merchantability extends for the life of a product does not mean that such a warranty "explicitly extends to future performance." ...
>
> In Binkley Co. v. Teledyne Mid–America Corp. (E.D.Mo.1971), 333 F.Supp. 1183, aff'd (8th Cir. 1972), 460 F.2d 276, the seller of a welding machine expressly warranted that a welder would weld at a rate of 1,000 feet per 50–minute hour, which it never did. The court defined "explicit" under 2–725(2) as " ' "[n]ot implied merely, or conveyed by implication; distinctly stated; plain in language; clear; not ambiguous; express; unequivocal." ' " (333 F.Supp. 1183, 1186.) Although the warranty expressly stated that the welder would weld at 1,000 feet per hour, the court found that the statute had lapsed because there was no reference to future time in the warranty and, thus, no explicit warranty of future performance. In response to the buyer's argument that he was unable to test the product until after delivery the court pointed to the clear language of section 2–725(2) which provides that the breach occurs at the time of delivery "regardless of the aggrieved party's lack of knowledge."

We agree with the decision in that case as well as the appellate decisions in this State adhering to the clear language of the statute.

[Justice Simon concurred specially.]

MOORE v. PUGET SOUND PLYWOOD, INC., 214 Neb. 14, 332 N.W.2d 212 (1983). In 1970 the Moores purchased plywood for siding on their house. Problems in the siding developed in 1977; the Moores sued Plywood in 1981. The Nebraska Supreme Court held that the claim was not time-barred.

> ... England v. Leithoff, 212 Neb. 462, 323 N.W.2d 98 (1982), ... foreshadows the outcome of this case. We held therein that an oral representation concerning the origin of goods, made in the course of a sale, constitutes an express warranty under § 2-313(1)(b), which provides, among other things, that any description of goods which becomes a part of the basis of the bargain creates an express warranty that the goods shall conform to the description. According to the parties the description of the goods as "siding" carried with it the representation that it would last the lifetime of the house. Therefore, the requisite elements of § 2-313(1)(b) are present; that is, the description of the goods became a part of the bargain and created in the minds of the parties the expectation that the siding would last the lifetime of the house. Section 2-725(2) provides in part: ... The instant breach did not occur upon tender of delivery since, in light of the expectations of the parties, the warranty herein necessarily extended explicitly to future performance.

(3) Limitation Period for Implied Warranties. On what date does the period of limitations begin to run on a buyer's potential claim that the goods are unmerchantable? On a potential claim that the goods are not fit for the buyer's particular purpose? Could the second sentence UCC 2-725(2) be construed to apply to any implied warranty claims?

(B) INTERNATIONAL SALES LAW

(1) Notice of breach. Assume that *M.K. Associates* had been an international sales transaction governed by CISG. Would the result have been the same or different? See CISG 39(1). The answer seems reasonably clear. Like the UCC, CISG imposes a notice requirement with comparable elements of "reasonable time" and buyer's discovery. Instead of "barred from any remedy" CISG uses "loses the right to rely on a lack of conformity." Is there a different meaning?

A perceptive reader of CISG 39(1), familiar with the UCC, would observe that the CISG demands more in the content of a buyer's notice than "of breach." How much factual detail must buyers include to "specify ... the nature of the lack of conformity"? If multiple non-conformities are discovered, must each be detailed? When a second non-conformity surfaces after a notice has been given, must another notice be sent?

Having worked through the CISG provision and made comparison to the UCC, one might stop the legal analysis. To do so would be to commit a grave error. See CISG 44. What could explain drafting in this style? [4]

The danger continues beyond noticing that CISG 44 modifies CISG 39(1). On the face of CISG 44, a reader might conclude that relief from loss of the right to rely on a lack of conformity is available only if a buyer has not yet paid the full price. "[T]he buyer may reduce the price in accordance with article 50...." When one turns to CISG 50, however, one learns that a buyer can "reduce" a price "whether or not the price has already been paid." In short, a buyer who is excused under CISG 44 has not only the right to set off damages against the unpaid price, but also has an affirmative right to recover some or all of the price paid.

Fortunately these "traps" are not typical of the drafting of the CISG. However, they should alert those who use the Convention to the need for great care in its application.

The CISG imposes an outside limit on the time for a buyer's notice to the seller specifying the nature of the lack of non-conformity. Buyers must give notice within two years from the date the goods were "actually handed over" to them, whether or not the buyers discovered or ought to have discovered the non-conformities ("in any event"). CISG 39(2). An exception exists if this time limit is "inconsistent with a contractual period of guarantee." Note that the CISG 44 excuse provision is not available against the CISG 39(2) time bar.

The UCC has no provision comparable to CISG 39(2).

FINAL AWARD IN CASE NO. 5713 of 1989
International Chamber of Commerce
15 Y.B. Comm. Arb. 70 (1990)

Parties: Claimant/counterdefendant: Seller
Defendant/counterclaimant: Buyer

Place of
arbitration: Paris, France
Published in: Unpublished
Subject matters: — applicable law

---

[4]. In the last days of the diplomatic conference that produced the Convention, there was a major inter-regional disagreement regarding the notice requirement in CISG 39. Proposals by developing countries to relax the requirement had not been adopted. The proponents of modifying CISG 39 were sufficiently dissatisfied that the necessary two-thirds vote in favor of the Convention was in jeopardy. A compromise solution was proposed and became CISG 44. It was made a separate article so that the added provision would apply also to the notice requirements of CISG 43(1). J. Honnold, Uniform Law for International Sales § 261 (2d ed. 1991).

Sec. 4　　ACTIONS FOR BREACH OF WARRANTY　　161

— Art. 13(3) and (5) ICC Rules
— Hague Convention of 1955 on the Law Applicable to the International Sales of Goods
— Vienna Sales Convention of 1980
— International trade usages
— set-off
— Art. 70 French New Code of Civil Procedure

Facts

In 1979, the parties concluded three contracts for the sale of a product according to certain contract specifications. The buyer paid 90% of the price payable under each of the contracts upon presentation of the shipping documents, as contractually agreed.

The product delivered pursuant to the first and third contracts met the contract specifications. The conformity of the second consignment was disputed prior to its shipment. When the product was again inspected upon arrival, it was found that it did not meet the contract specifications. The product was eventually sold by the buyer to third parties at considerable loss, after having undergone a certain treatment to make it more saleable.

The seller initiated arbitration proceedings to recover the 10% balance remaining due under the contracts. The buyer filed a counterclaim alleging that the seller's claim should be set off against the amounts which the buyer estimates to be payable to the buyer by the seller, i.e., the direct losses, financing costs, lost profits and interest.

Excerpt

I. Applicable Law

The contract contains no provisions regarding the substantive law. Accordingly that law has to be determined by the Arbitrators in accordance with Art. 13(3) of the ICC rules.[1] Under that article, the Arbitrators will "apply the law designated as the proper law by the rule of conflicts which they deem appropriate".

The contract is between a Seller and a Buyer [of different nationalities] for delivery [in a third country]. The sale was f.o.b. so that the transfer of risks to the Buyer took place in [the country of the Seller]. [The country of the Seller] accordingly appears as being the jurisdiction to which the sale is most closely related.

---

1. Art. 13 of the ICC Rules of 1975 (Not amended by the 1988 amendments) reads in relevant part:

"3. The parties shall be free to determine the law to be applied by the arbitrator to the merits of the dispute. In the absence of any indication by the parties as to the applicable law, the arbitrator shall apply the law designated as the proper law by the rule of conflict which he deems appropriate.

(....)

5. In all cases the arbitrator shall take account of the provisions of the contract and the relevant trade usages."

The Hague Convention on the law applicable to international sales of goods dated 15 June 1955 (Art. 3) regarding sales contracts, refers as governing law to the law of the Seller's current residence.... [2] [The country of the Buyer] has adhered to the Hague Convention, not [the country of the Seller]. However, the general trend in conflicts of law is to apply the domestic law of the current residence of the debtor of the essential undertaking arising under the contract. That debtor in a sales contract is the Seller. Based on those combined findings, [the law of the country of the Seller] appears to be the proper law governing the Contract between the Seller and the Buyer.

As regards the applicable rules of [the law of the country of the Seller], the Arbitrators have relied on the Parties' respective statements on the subject and on the information obtained by the Arbitrators from an independent consultant.... The Arbitrators, in accordance with the last paragraph of Art. 13 of the ICC rules, will also take into account the "relevant trade usages".

II. Admissibility of the Counterclaim

  (a) Under [the law of the country of the Seller]

* * *

  (b) Under the international trade usages prevailing in the international sale of goods

The Tribunal finds that there is no better source to determine the prevailing trade usages than the terms of the United Nations Convention on the International Sale of Goods of 11 April 1980, usually called "the Vienna Convention". This is so even though neither [the country of the Buyer] nor [the country of the Seller] are parties to that Convention. If they were, the Convention might be applicable to this case as a matter of law and not only as reflecting the trade usage.

The Vienna Convention, which has been given effect to in 17 countries, may be fairly taken to reflect the generally recognized usages regarding the matter of the non-conformity of goods in international sales. Art. 38(1) of the Convention puts the onus on the Buyer to "examine the goods or cause them to be examined promptly". The Buyer should then notify the Seller of the non-conformity of the goods within a reasonable period as of the moment he noticed or should have noticed the defect; otherwise he forfeits his right to raise a claim based on the said non-conformity. Art. 39(1) specifies in this respect that:

> In any event the buyer shall lose the right to rely on a lack of conformity of the goods if he has not given notice thereof to the seller within a period of two years from the date on which the

---

2. Art. 3 of the Hague Convention on the Law Applicable to the International Sales of Goods reads in pertinent part: "In default of a law declared applicable by the parties under the conditions provided in the preceding article, a sale shall be governed by the domestic law of the country in which the vendor has his habitual residence at the time when he received the order...."

goods were handed over, unless the lack of conformity constituted a breach of a guarantee covering a longer period.

In the circumstances, the Buyer had the shipment examined within a reasonable time-span since [an expert] was requested to inspect the shipment even before the goods had arrived. The Buyer should also be deemed to have given notice of the defects within a reasonable period, that is eight days after the expert's report had been published.

Tribunal finds that, in the circumstances of the case, the Buyer has complied with the above-mentioned requirements of the Vienna Convention. These requirements are considerably more flexible than those provided under [the law of the country of the Seller]. This law, by imposing extremely short and specific time requirements in respect of the giving of the notices of defects by the Buyer to the Seller appears to be an exception on this point to the generally accepted trade usages.

In any case, the Seller should be regarded as having forfeited its right to invoke any non-compliance with the requirements of Arts. 38 and 39 of the Vienna Convention since Art. 40 states that the Seller cannot rely on Arts. 38 and 39, "if the lack of conformity relates to facts of which he knew, or of which he could not have been unaware, and which he did not disclose". Indeed, this appears to be the case, since it clearly transpires from the file and the evidence that the Seller knew and could not be unaware [of the non-conformity of the consignment to] contract specifications.

* * *

---

(2) Period of Limitations. CISG contains no period of limitations. That is found in an entirely separate convention, the United Nations Convention on the Limitation Period of the International Sale of Goods. A sufficient number of nations had ratified this Convention for it to take effect in 1988. As of January 1992, the Convention was pending ratification by the Senate of the United States. Like UCC 2–725, the Convention sets a four-year limitation period. A convention is required to replace the greatly diverse limitation ("prescription") periods and subordinate rules, such as rules on "tolling," among various nations' domestic laws.

SECTION 5. CONSUMER PROTECTION LAWS

Introduction. The Sales Article of the Uniform Commercial Code and its predecessor, the Uniform Sales Act, provided little, if any, special protection for consumers buying goods for ordinary personal, family or household purposes.[1] Consumer protection law has developed nonetheless, and the sales statutes have been substantially involved in

---

1. By contrast, the UCC article on secured transactions provides particularly for credit transactions in consumer goods. See, e.g., 9–302(1)(d); 9–505; 9–507(1).

those developments. One concern has been for the health of consumers. A second concern has focused on consumers' economic interest, particularly the concern that the value of goods purchased be commensurate with the price paid.

International Sales Law. The Convention on International Sales of Goods is explicitly not concerned with sales of ordinary consumer goods. CISG 2(a). Further, the Convention does not apply to a seller's liability for death or personal injury caused by the goods to any person. CISG 5.

(A) CONSUMER HEALTH: PRODUCT LIABILITY

Owners of products sometimes suffer traumatic injuries when they use or consume the goods they have bought. If a product poses a higher than expected risk of injuring someone, we are likely to say that that product has a "defect." For some time, injured persons have had a possible cause of action in negligence, but to prevail in such an action a plaintiff must prove, inter alia, that the defendant (or someone for whom the defendant is vicariously responsible) acted with a lack of due care.

Advocates of consumer protection, seeking a legal theory that did not require proof of defendants' fault, turned to warranty law. The prototypical injured plaintiff was a buyer who had consumed spoiled or adulterated food. In cases decided in the late 19th century and early 20th century, courts implied warranties in ordinary retail sales,[2] even in transactional settings where sellers of canned or packaged goods did not know, and had no practical way of finding out the true quality of the goods.[3] Once a warranty was breached, courts had no difficulty in

---

2. The British Sale of Goods Act and its United States counterpart, the Uniform Sales Act, posed a problem for buyers: the basic warranty of quality, merchantability, was not "implied" in ordinary retail sales of food or other goods. Caselaw codified by these statutes had found the warranty of merchantability arising in situations where sellers had contracted to supply goods that would fit contract descriptions; Mackensie Chalmers "restated" the cases by limiting merchantability to sales "by description." Protection had to be found under the rubric of fitness for particular purpose.

The change is well illustrated by developments in Massachusetts. Farrell v. Manhattan Market Co, 198 Mass. 271, 84 N.E. 481 (1908) (buyer suffered ptomaine poisoning from a fowl: buyer denied relief); Ward v. Great Atlantic & Pacific Tea Co., 231 Mass. 90, 120 N.E. 225 (1918) (buyer broke a tooth on a stone in a can of baked beans: buyer recovered); Flynn v. Bedell Co., 242 Mass. 450, 136 N.E. 252 (1922) (buyer contracted skin disease from dyed fur collar of coat: verdict for buyer upheld).

Consumers injured by unwholesome food or beverages served by a restaurant or hotel faced an additional legal hazard. At common law, some courts considered such transactions a service ("uttering") rather than a sale and, therefore, not transactions in which a warranty of quality applied. Compare Friend v. Childs Dining Hall Co., 231 Mass. 65, 120 N.E. 407 (1918), with Nisky v. Childs Co., 103 N.J.L. 464, 135 Atl. 805 (1927). The Commercial Code declares that such transactions are sales under Article 2. UCC 2–314(1).

3. Compare Julian v. Laubenberger, 16 Misc. 646, 38 N.Y.S. 1052 (1896) (sale of can of salmon: since both parties knew that seller had not prepared the food, had not inspected it, and was entirely ignorant of the contents of the can, it would be unreasonable to say that the buyer had relied upon the superior knowledge of the

broadening the classes of injury compensable as consequential damages from commercial losses, as in *Hadley v. Baxendale,* to personal injuries and property damage.

The move toward greater consumer protection did not end with establishment of retailers' warranty liability. Injured consumers needed, and eventually were allowed to obtain warranty relief directly from remote manufacturers of certain defective consumer goods that caused personal injuries. The list of such goods was confined to food, beverages, and other items of "intimate bodily use." In 1960, the New Jersey Supreme Court held that the owner of an automobile, injured when the steering failed, should have a warranty claim against the manufacturer. Henningsen v. Bloomfield Motors, Inc., 32 N.J. 358, 161 A.2d 69 (1960).

Two years later, the California Supreme Court created a new tort to protect the consumer-owner of a lathe injured by a piece of wood ejected from the equipment. Greenman v. Yuba Power Products, Inc. 59 Cal.2d 57, 27 Cal.Rptr. 697, 377 P.2d 897 (1963).[4] During this period, the American Law Institute was preparing a second edition of the Restatement of Torts. The new tort was inserted into the revision as § 402A, Special Liability of Seller of Product for Physical Harm to User or Consumer. More commonly, the tort is known as strict tort liability. As "restated," it is formulated as follows:

(1) One who sells any product in a defective condition unreasonably dangerous to the user or consumer or to his property is subject to liability for physical harm thereby caused to the ultimate user or consumer, or to his property, if

(a) the seller is engaged in the business of selling such a product, and

(b) it is expected to and does reach the user or consumer without substantial change in the condition in which it is sold.

(2) The rule stated in Subsection (1) applies although

(a) the seller has exercised all possible care in the preparation and sale of his product, an

(b) the user or consumer has not bought the product from or entered into any contractual relation with the seller.

---

seller), with Ward v. Great Atlantic & Pacific Tea Co., 231 Mass. 90, 120 N.E. 225 (1918) (sale of can of baked beans and pork: even though seller is not the manufacturer, seller is in a better position to ascertain the reliability of the manufacturer; the principle of retailers' liability may work apparent hardship in some instances, but that is no reason to change it).

4. Greenman had been tried on a warranty theory. The California Supreme Court found that it could not sustain the trial court judgment because the plaintiff had not given seller timely notice of the breach of warranty. See UCC 2-607(3)(a similar provision existed in the Sales Act). Rather than reverse on this "intricacy" of sales law, the California court held that the judgment could be affirmed on the new tort theory.

Reception of § 402A as new common law was rapid and widespread. Only a small number of state supreme courts have rejected strict tort liability.[5]

Judicial acknowledgment of the new tort did not displace consumers' warranty claims arising out of the same facts. What has emerged, therefore, is that consumer buyers in most states have substantially overlapping theories of possible recovery for personal injuries.[6]

For a number of reasons, consumers and their lawyers prefer to rely primarily upon strict tort liability. Suits can be brought directly against the manufacturers of the goods. The essential elements of the tort were derived entirely from earlier warranty cases, with the omission, of course, of the notice requirement of warranty law.[7] Proof of a defendant's liability on a strict tort theory is therefore less difficult than the proof under a warranty theory. The strict tort theory is also more protective of consumers with regard to contractual disclaimers or clauses limiting damages. Comment *m* to § 402A states that the "consumer's" cause of action "is not affected by any disclaimer or other agreement."[8] A major difference in the two theories lies in the measure of recovery: plaintiffs proceeding in a tort theory ordinarily are permitted to recover damages for pain and suffering and, in extraordinary cases, may be permitted to recover punitive damages.

Moreover, a consumer who suffers an injury some considerable time after the good was sold may be unable to proceed successfully on a warranty theory while the strict tort theory is still available. The period of the tort statute of limitations does not commence until the

---

5. E.g., Cline v. Prowler Industries of Md., Inc., 418 A.2d 968 (Del.1980); Swartz v. General Motors Corp., 375 Mass. 628, 378 N.E.2d 61 (1978); Prentis v. Yale Manufacturing Co., 421 Mich. 670, 365 N.W.2d 176 (1984). In New York, the Court of Appeals initially rejected the new tort. Mendel v. Pittsburgh Plate Glass Co., 25 N.Y.2d 888, 251 N.E.2d 143 (1969). However, the New York court quickly joined the majority of states. Codling v. Paglia, 32 N.Y.2d 330, 298 N.E.2d 622 (1973).

6. Section 402A is not limited to consumer-buyer plaintiffs, but rather extends to the "ultimate user or consumer" whether or not one who bought the product. A caveat attached to § 402A notes that the Institute expresses no opinion on whether the section should apply to persons other than users or consumers, typically casual bystanders. Contrast the Restatement's scope of protected persons with the scope of such persons under a warranty theory. The Commercial Code originally limited recovery for personal injuries to members of the family or household or house guests of the buyer. UCC 2–318 (now Alternative A). In 1966, drafters of the Code offered state legislatures two broader alternatives. We will consider § 2–318 more fully later in this chapter, in the section on privity, *infra*.

7. Some states relax the notice requirement in cases of buyers claiming damages for personal injuries under a breach of warranty theory. In Illinois, for example, the notice requirement can be satisfied in some cases by pleadings in the litigation with sellers. E.g., Goldstein v. G.D. Searle & Co., 62 Ill.App.3d 344, 378 N.E.2d 1083 (1978); but see Wagmeister v. A.H. Robins Co., 64 Ill.App.3d 964, 382 N.E.2d 23 (1978); Allen v. G.D. Searle & Co., 708 F.Supp. 1142 (D.Or.1989). Retail buyers are aided if dispute over the notice requirement is treated as an issue of fact to be decided by juries. E.g., Mullan v. Quickie Aircraft Corp., 797 F.2d 845 (10th Cir. 1986).

8. The Commercial Code permits use of warranty disclaimers (UCC 2–316) and of damage limitation clauses (UCC 2–719), with the exception that clauses limiting or excluding recovery for personal injuries are prima facie unconscionable (UCC 2–719(3)).

injury, while the warranty statute of limitations begins to run at the time of delivery of the goods. UCC 2–725(1). If an injury occurs some years after delivery, the tort statute may be more favorable to plaintiffs.[9]

Personal injury claims, whether based on strict tort or warranty theory, give rise to an array of complex and difficult legal questions that we cannot explore in these materials. Private litigation of this type has become interrelated with federal and state regulatory laws on consumer product safety. In the remainder of this section, we will focus on issues of economic loss rather than personal injuries.

(B) MAGNUSON–MOSS WARRANTY ACT (MMWA)

The law of strict tort liability, together with warranty law, provided considerable relief for consumers who suffer personal injuries or property damage, but did little or nothing for consumers who bought and paid for goods that turned out to be disappointing in economic value. Many consumer goods were marketed under contracts that gave little or no effective relief to consumer buyers. This led to the 1975 enactment of a federal statute, the Magnuson–Moss Warranty Act. The federal statute does not displace state warranty law. The federal act is a partial overlay on state law. Whenever the MMWA applies to a transaction, determination of a seller's responsibility will be governed basically by the UCC warranty provisions, with which we are now familiar, but modified by the provisions of the federal statute. Both the UCC and the MMWA must be considered in every transaction to which the MMWA applies.

The MMWA appears in Title 15, Chapter 50 of the U.S. Code, §§ 2301–2312. For purposes of this course, however, we will use the Act's section numbers, MMWA 101–112. The MMWA is interpreted and supplemented by Federal Trade Commission Regulations. For an overall review of MMWA, see C. Reitz, Consumer Product Warranties Under Federal and State Laws (2d ed. 1987).[10]

(1) **Scope.** The MMWA does *not* apply to all consumer purchases of consumer goods. While the Act has broad definitions of "consumer" (MMWA 101(3)) and "consumer product" (MMWA 101(1)), the federal statute applies only to transactions in which the seller has made a

---

9. The claim of the plaintiff in *Mendel*, the early New York case that declined to recognize strict tort liability (note 5 *supra*), was held to be time barred under the four-year statute of limitations applicable to sales of goods. See UCC 2–725. New York's tort statute of limitations, however, would not have barred the claim.

The warranty statute of limitations may be more favorable to a plaintiff who suffers injury shortly after goods have been delivered but fails to institute legal proceedings within the one- or two-year limitation period generally provided for tort claims. Even though the tort claim is time-barred, the warranty period may not have elapsed as of the filing of suit.

10. Some parts of the MMWA have no counterparts in the Commercial Code. Federal law requires sellers to make warranty information available to potential buyers in advance of sale and in a way prescribed by law. (MMWA 102 and FTC Regs. 701 and 702). See C. Reitz, chapters 3 and 4.

"written warranty" (MMWA 101(6) and FTC Reg. § 700.3) or "service contract" (MMWA 101(8)). These terms, particularly "written warranty," are of the utmost importance to understanding the effective scope of the MMWA.

Even without a close reading of the statute and regulations, note that the MMWA does not apply if the *only* warranty obligation of a seller is an implied warranty. Implied warranties cannot be a "written warranty" or "service contract." To bring a transaction within the Act, a seller must make an express warranty or undertake an express obligation with respect to the goods. However, again it is quite evident that not all express warranties would meet the definition of "written warranty." Express *oral* warranties are excluded regardless of the content of the seller's undertaking. The threshold question in all MMWA cases is whether an express warranty, in writing, meets the *content* elements of the Act's definitions.[11]

Problem 1. Eckstein purchased a new car from Maumee Valley Autos, Inc. The purchase order form, signed by the dealer and the buyer, declared that the dealer, at its option, would repair or replace any part that proved defective in materials or workmanship within twelve months from the date of purchase or 12,000 miles of use, whichever occurred first.

(a) If Eckstein's car were to prove defective, would he have the benefit of protection under the MMWA? See MMWA 101(6). The UCC?

(b) If Eckstein seeks only to enforce the dealer's repair/replace undertaking, does the MMWA provide him with more warranty protection than would be available under the UCC?

Problem 2. Seller sold a used car to Buyer. Seller's salesman told Buyer that the car had gone only 60,000 miles, that the motor had been carefully checked out, and that the piston rings and brake linings had just been replaced. The only writing was a bill of sale transferring title to Buyer. The car proved to be in very bad shape, and the brakes failed, causing serious injury to Buyer and to the car.

(a) Has Buyer any rights under the MMWA? See MMWA 101(6), 102(b)(2).

(b) Has the Buyer any rights? See MMWA 111(b)(1).

Problem 3. Seller sold and installed a furnace in Buyer's home. The only writing was an agreement of sale, signed by Seller and Buyer, which read:

Seller agrees to deliver to Buyer and install one Cozy Furnace, for a total of $2,500. It is agreed that the Seller shall not be respon-

---

11. "Certain representations, such as energy efficiency ratings for electrical appliances, care labeling of wearing apparel, and other product information disclosures may be express warranties under the Uniform Commercial Code. However, these disclosures alone are not written warranties under this Act." FTC Reg. § 700.3.

sible to Buyer for any special or consequential damages resulting from the operation or malfunction of the furnace.

Three months after installation, the furnace exploded and soot was blown throughout the house, with the result that the house had to be redecorated at a cost of $3,000.

Has Buyer any rights under the MMWA or under the UCC?

(2) "Truth in Warranting." The perceptive reader may now be asking: why did Congress pass the MMWA? Many (if not most) express warranties are excluded from the Act's coverage, seller's are permitted under the Act to sell without any warranty at all, and the Act adds nothing to the substance of seller's voluntary undertakings in a "written warranty" or "service contract." What consumer benefits *are* provided by this Act?

A partial answer is that Congress focused on certain transaction types in which it found need for reform. These were transactions in consumer durable goods, notably new automobiles, in which consumers received less warranty protection than they had been led to expect.

The MMWA objective was to create a marketplace in which there was "truth in warranting." In part, this explains the Act's requirement that every "written warranty" must be designated "clearly and conspicuously" as either a "limited" warranty or a "full" warranty (MMWA 103(a)). Moreover, if a warranty is designated as "full," the designation must also contain a "statement of duration" (MMWA 103(a)(1)). The FTC, by regulation, requires that the designations appear as a caption or prominent title, clearly separated from the text of the warranty. FTC Reg. § 700.6.[12]

The MMWA further provided that, for a "written warranty" to qualify as "full," it must meet "Federal minimum standards" provided in MMWA 104 (MMWA 103(a)(1)). Any "written warranty" that fails to meet all of these minimum standards must be designated as a "limited warranty" (MMWA 103(a)(2)).[13]

Congress no doubt expected that "written warranties" would continue to be made on consumer durables. The definitions of the MMWA covered the printed warranties, often bordered in handsome filigree, that manufacturers of consumer durable goods tended to provide. In this expectation, Congress was correct. Congress may also have expected that consumers would come to understand the difference between "full" and "limited" warranties and, by exercise of market power,

---

12. Pursuant to MMWA 102(a), the FTC regulation adds that the body of a "written warranty" must contain nine categories of specified information, must be in a "single document," and the language used must be "simple and readily understood." FTC Reg. § 701.3(a).

Neither the MMWA nor the FTC regulations have comparable provisions on the designation or content of "service contracts." But see MMWA 106(a).

13. If a warrantor designates a warranty as "full," the MMWA declares that this designation incorporates the "Federal minimum standards" (MMWA 104(e)), whether or not those standards are explicitly contained in the warranty document.

would induce sellers to avoid the pejoratively titled "limited warranty." In this expectation, Congress was incorrect. Only a few sellers ever offered "full" warranties on high-priced goods.[14]

(3) Implied Warranty Disclaimers. "The most dramatic provisions of the Magnuson–Moss Warranty Act may be those that unveil the implied warranties of quality, particularly the implied warranty of merchantability, with respect to consumer [durable] goods. For decades prior to the Act, manufacturers and dealers routinely marketed goods with contract language disclaiming all implied warranties of quality. [The MMWA] bars those disclaimers by any supplier who makes a *written warranty* or who, contemporaneously with sale, enters into a *service contract*." C. Reitz, supra, at 73–74. See MMWA 108(a).

If a disclaimer is improperly included in a contract of sale, notwithstanding MMWA 108(a), the Act declares it ineffective. MMWA 108(c).

The disclaimer preclusion provision in MMWA 108(a) applies to all "written warranties." The same rule applies, whether the warranty is "full" or "limited."

The MMWA does not speak to the content of the implied warranties of quality. The Act incorporates whatever meaning those warranties have under state law. MMWA 101(7).

Problem 4. Seller manufactures and installs central air conditioning systems. Buyer came into Seller's shop and described the size of his home to the salesman. The salesman drew Buyer's attention in Seller's catalog to the "HOMAIR," a unit that delivered 35,000 BTU of refrigeration. Buyer agreed to purchase the HOMAIR. The one-page sales contract stated at the bottom:

LIMITED WARRANTY

Seller expressly warrants against defects in materials, workmanship and installation if, and only if, such defects are brought to Seller's attention within one year of installation, whereupon Seller, at Seller's option, will repair or replace the defective part or parts. THERE ARE NO WARRANTIES, EITHER EXPRESS OR IMPLIED, INCLUDING THE WARRANTY OF MERCHANTABILITY, WHICH EXTEND BEYOND THE DESCRIPTION ON THE FACE HEREOF. IN NO EVENT SHALL SELLER BE LIABLE FOR SPECIAL OR CONSEQUENTIAL DAMAGES.

(a) The air conditioning unit broke down eighteen months after the date of installation. Seller informed Buyer that a new motor was required, and that the cost to Buyer for the motor and installation would be $350. What are Buyer's rights? See MMWA 108(a).

---

14. A notable exception was American Motors Co., which offered "full" warranties on its new cars. The manufacturer did not survive. "Full" warranties are more prevalent in sales of relatively low-priced consumer goods if sellers are willing to undertake to replace a defective product or refund the price.

(b) After the system was installed and began to function, Buyer discovered that the system did not generate enough cold air to cool his house. He also learned that the problem was not due to any defect in parts or operation, but was because the system was inadequate for the size of his house. What rights does Buyer have against Seller for breach of implied warranty of fitness for purpose? See MMWA 108(a).

(4) Clauses Limiting Damages. The position of the MMWA on clauses limiting damages is explicit only in the Act's treatment of "full" warranties. Section 104(a)(3) permits a "full" warrantor to exclude or limit consequential damages if the clause appears conspicuously on the face of the warranty.[15] The position with respect to "limited" warranties must be inferred.

Problem 5. Consider again the transaction in Problem 4. Suppose that a system of adequate size had been installed. A defect in the tubing caused a leak of condensed moisture which damaged a wall of the house; the repairs cost $1500. May Buyer recover from Seller for this cost? See MMWA 108(a).

Is it reasonable to infer that Congress would require more consumer protection under a "limited" warranty than is required under a "full" warranty? Must the formalities of conspicuousness and on-the-face placement be met in a "limited" warranty?

Problem 6. Seller sold a new car to Buyer under a FULL (ONE YEAR) WARRANTY which included on the face of the warranty a conspicuous provision disclaiming responsibility for consequential damages. See MMWA 104(a)(3). Six months after the purchase the brakes failed. The car was demolished and Buyer was seriously injured. May Buyer recover (a) for the damage to the car and (b) for his personal injuries? See MMWA 111(b) and UCC 2–719(3).

(5) Limited Duration of Implied Warranties. "In a most perplexing provision, the [MMWA] permits "limited" warrantors to limit the duration of implied warranties of quality [MMWA 108(b)] ... The notion of limiting duration connotes the shortening of a period of time. Implied warranties of quality do not have any period of existence. An implied warranty is breached or is not breached in the scintilla of time that marks tender of delivery of the goods. A time period begins to run from that moment, the period of the statute of limitations. But plainly an implied warranty is not some kind of continuing promise ...

"At least five possible meanings might be ascribed to terms limiting the duration of implied warranties.

 1. [S]hortening of the statute of limitations period.

 2. [L]engthening the statute of limitations period.

---

15. Even for "full" warranties, this conclusion is a matter of inference. The Act's formulation, "may not ... unless," must be read to mean "may ... if". Is this is a plausible interpretation of the statute?

3. [Defining] the time within which a buyer must give notice of breach or be barred from any remedy under [UCC 2–607(3)].

4. [Defining] a period of time after which a buyer cannot complain of non-conformities that later come to light even though they could not reasonably have been discovered earlier.

5. [Defining] a time during which buyer's remedy is to seek seller's repair or other promised post-delivery relief. . . .

"None of the suggested meanings . . . is entirely satisfactory as a matter of statutory construction. . . . In my view, the fifth meaning comes closest to the spirit of the . . . Act. It also makes sense in the marketplace." C. Reitz, supra, pp. 82, 86, 95.

(6) Recovery of Attorneys' Fees and Costs. The MMWA authorizes prevailing plaintiffs to recover, over and above other monetary remedies, an additional amount for attorneys' fees and costs. MMWA 110(d)(2). Allowance of fees and costs is not a matter of right; recovery lies in the discretion of the trial court. Courts may allow fees and costs only if actions are "brought" under MMWA 110(d)(1). Whether that condition has been met can be a difficult question. See C. Reitz, supra, pp. 134–143. In an ordinary breach of warranty case, the answer appears to turn on when and how plaintiff first mentions the MMWA.

A New Jersey case, which resulted in the consumer recovering damages in the amount of $6,745.59, concluded with an award of attorneys' fees of $5,165.00. Ventura v. Ford Motor Corp., 180 N.J. Super. 45, 433 A.2d 801 (1981). Similar awards have been made in other cases. See C. Reitz, supra, pp. 141–143. The largest recovery of fees and costs to date, nearly $2.5 million, occurred in the engine interchange class action against General Motors Corp. Id. at 140–141.

(7) Federal Forum for Warranty Litigation. The MMWA permits certain plaintiffs to bring warranty actions in federal courts. MMWA 110(d)(1)(B). This provision has limited usefulness to a single-plaintiff case because the amount in controversy must be at least $50,000.00 (MMWA 110(d)(3)(B)), and courts have held that amounts claimed for personal injuries are not counted for this purpose for this purpose. See Boelens v. Redman Homes, Inc., 748 F.2d 1058 (5th Cir.1984), reh'g denied, 759 F.2d 504 (1985); but see C. Reitz, supra, pp. 144–146.[16]

The amount in controversy in a class action may easily exceed the statutory threshold, but an odd formulation of MMWA 110(d)(1) may still foreclose jurisdiction in federal court. The following case illustrates.

---

16. One district court allowed a claim for punitive damages to be counted toward the $50,000.00 threshold. Schafer v. Chrysler Corp., 544 F.Supp. 182 (N.D.Ind. 1982); C. Reitz, supra, pp. 147–148.

SKELTON v. GENERAL MOTORS CORP.
United States Court of Appeals, Seventh Circuit, 1981.
660 F.2d 311.

CUDAHY, CIRCUIT JUDGE.

Section 110(d) of Title I of the Magnuson–Moss Warranty–Federal Trade Commission Improvements Act ("Magnuson–Moss" or the "Act") creates a federal private cause of action for consumers damaged by the failure of a warrantor "to comply with any obligation under ... a written warranty." 15 U.S.C. § 2310(d)(1) (1976). The issue on this interlocutory appeal is whether a "written warranty" actionable under § 110(d) is limited to the particular promises, undertakings or affirmations of fact expressly defined as "written warranties" by Congress in the Act. The district court held that § 110(d) provides a federal cause of action not merely for breach of a "written warranty" as defined in the Act but also for breach of "all written promises presented in connection with the sale of a formally warranted product." 500 F.Supp. 1181, 1190 (N.D.Ill.1980). We reverse.

I.

Plaintiffs, purchasers of automobiles manufactured by defendant General Motors Corporation ("GM"), brought this action as a nationwide class action on behalf of all purchasers of GM automobiles manufactured from 1976 through 1979. In Count I of their amended complaint, plaintiffs allege that GM, through its "brochures, manuals, consumer advertising and other forms of communications to the public generally and to members of plaintiffs' class specifically," warranted and represented that 1976 through 1979 GM automobiles contained THM 350(M38) transmissions, or "transmissions of similar quality and performance. ... and that [such transmissions] would meet a specified level of performance." Plaintiffs charge in Count I that, contrary to these warranties and representations, GM substituted inferior THM 200(M29) transmissions for THM 350(M38) transmissions in GM automobiles manufactured from 1976 through 1979. This undisclosed substitution is alleged to constitute a violation of written ... warranties under § 110(d) of Magnuson–Moss. ...

General Motors moved to dismiss ... plaintiffs' complaint for failure to state a claim upon which relief could be granted. On October 1, 1980, the district court ... denied GM's motion to dismiss the "written warranty" claim in Count I. 500 F.Supp. 1181 (N.D.Ill.1980). ...

II.
* * *

[The plaintiffs did not deny that GM had given the buyer a formal warranty that was a "written warranty" as defined in § 101(6) of the Act. This written warranty did not refer to the type of transmission used in the automobile. The District Court concluded that the brochures and manuals that stated that the automobiles had THM 350(M38) transmissions were not "written warranties" under § 101(6)(A) since this written material did not relate "to the material or workmanship *and* [affirm] ... that such material or workmanship is *defect free* or will meet a specified level of performance *over a specified period of time.*"

[The District Court, however, concluded that since GM had made a formal "express warranty" with the statements specified in § 101(6)(A), the Act should be construed to allow a federal remedy under the Act for misstatements made in written material other than "the paper with the filagree border." The substantial matters at stake included the Act's provisions in § 110(d), providing for private actions, class actions in the federal courts and the recovery of attorney's fees.]

Section 110(d) creates a private cause of action for breach of "written warranty," subject to the requirements that: (1) the consumer must have an individual claim of at least $25; (2) the total amount in controversy must equal or exceed $50,000; and (3) if brought as a class action, the complaint must name at least one hundred plaintiffs. 15 U.S.C. § 2310(d)(3) (1976). Section 110 also makes any failure to comply with the requirements of the Act a violation of § 5(a)(1) of the Federal Trade Commission Act (15 U.S.C. § 45(a)(1) (1976)), and empowers the FTC and the Attorney General to seek injunctive relief against (1) failure to comply with any obligation under the Act, and (2) written warranties which may be "deceptive" to a reasonable individual. 15 U.S.C. § 2310(c) (1976).

III.

The scope of the private action for breach of "written warranty" created by § 110(d) is the issue presented to us for resolution. Section 110(d) provides in part that:

> [A] consumer who is damaged by the failure of a supplier, warrantor, or service contractor to comply with any obligation under this title, or a written warranty, implied warranty, or service contract, may bring suit for damages and other legal and equitable relief [in any state court of competent jurisdiction or in an appropriate federal district court].

15 U.S.C. § 2310(d)(1) (1976).

The district court properly rejected plaintiffs' argument that the Act's draftsmen intended in § 110(d) to create a federal private cause of action for breach of all written express warranties. None of the legislative history offered by plaintiffs in this record provides the clear evidence of Congressional intent necessary to overcome the "familiar principle governing the interpretation of statutes ... that if a statutory definition of a word is given, that definition must prevail, regardless of what other meaning may be attributable to the word." ... Indeed, we are less than confident that it is possible to distill any unambiguous

Congressional intent from the Act's legislative history. As the district court noted:

> [A review of the Act's legislative history] is the legal equivalent of an archaeological dig. Various consumer warranty bills were pending before the House and Senate for four years, during which each body defined, discarded, reintroduced and redefined concepts which in some fashion or another are related to the enacted legislation. Some provisions of the Act are vestigial reminders of concepts buried but not totally forgotten during the on-going legislative process. Both proponents and opponents of an expansive interpretation have cited compelling, to them, legislative history only dimly related to the language which finally emerged as law.
>
> . . .
>
> [The opinion included an extended discussion of the Act's legislative history, and concluded that this material did not support departure from a strictly literal construction of the provisions defining the scope of private actions under § 110(d).]

IV.

Although the district court properly declined to adopt plaintiffs' interpretation of § 110(d), it also rejected GM's argument that the only written warranties actionable under § 110(d) are those promises, representations or undertakings defined as "written warranties" in § 101(6). In its view:

> Congress . . . indicated that although the Magnuson–Moss Act only regulates transactions involving written warranties as the term is narrowly defined in § 101(6), once a consumer is involved in such a transaction there is a policy of providing federal remedies beyond the four corners of the formal warranty.

500 F.Supp. at 1191. Thus, the district court concluded that, whenever a manufacturer elects to extend a "written warranty" to a consumer, "[o]ther written promises presented in connection with the same transaction should also be enforceable as part of the 'written warranty.'" 500 F.Supp. at 1190.

The district court's determination that "written warranty" in § 110(d) means something more than it was defined to mean in § 101(6) has two aspects. First, the court found that the "Act itself suggests several different possible meanings of the phrase 'written warranty'" and is therefore ambiguous. 500 F.Supp. at 1187. Second, because of this ambiguity, the district court looked to the purposes of the Act, as derived from its legislative history, and concluded that § 110(d) should be construed to provide "a remedy for all written promises presented in connection with the sale of a formally warranted product." 500 F.Supp. at 1190.

We believe that the three ambiguities identified by the district court, which we shall consider individually, are not sufficiently real or substantial to warrant rejection of the definition of "written warranty" provided by Congress in the Act. Moreover, as already discussed, we do not find in the Act's legislative history a clear Congressional intention that the term "written warranty" was meant to have different meanings in different sections of the Act. *See* Part III, supra. And, if anything is apparent from the statutory scheme, it is the importance of providing a clear, carefully circumscribed meaning to the term "written warranty." ...

There is no clear evidence that Congress intended for written warranty in § 102 to mean something different than the definition it ascribed to the term in § 101(6), and we consequently presume that Congress intended for "written warranty" to have the same meaning in both sections. We therefore decline to accept the position that "written warranty" means both a particular class of representations and some undefined "document" containing those representations. It is more appropriate to read the inconsistent phrase "inclusion in the written warranty" [emphasis supplied] to mean "inclusion *with* the written warranty" or "inclusion in *the document containing* the written warranty."

The term "written warranty" serves a central function in the Act of identifying the particular representations that are subject to the Act's disclosure and content requirements. Because of the function it serves, it is important that the term have a single, precise meaning. The § 101(6) definition provides that unambiguous meaning, and that definition is used (all things considered) with commendable aptness by the draftsmen in the forty-odd appearances of the term "written warranty" in every section of the Act. We cannot agree that syntactical slips such as the use of the preposition "in" in § 102, create ambiguities in the statutory scheme of sufficient weight to justify discarding the meticulously worded definition of "written warranty" in § 101(6) in favor of an undefined "document," or "pile of written documents," as urged by the district court. See 500 F.Supp. at 1190.

V.

In sum, we are constrained to interpret "written warranty" in § 110(d) in accordance with the definition of "written warranty" provided by Congress in § 101(6).

Reversed.

HARLINGTON WOOD, JR., CIRCUIT JUDGE, dissenting.

This is a close case of statutory interpretation, but I respectfully dissent from the majority's conclusion that the Act must be so strictly and rigidly read as to exclude coverage of the alleged transmission substitution by General Motors.

Judge Moran, in the trial court, carefully pondered the arguments and concluded that the act was broader than General Motors argued, but not so broad as plaintiffs' urged. I generally agree with his interpretation.

As Judge Moran noted, 500 F.Supp. at 1184, he was not the first one to have some difficulty interpreting the Act. Others before him have characterized it as serving as no exemplar of legislative clarity. I would, therefore, not begin and end by viewing the Act's definition provisions in such isolation as to conclude that the beneficial consumer protection purposes of the Act are thereby completely limited. Were this a criminal statute, I might be bound to resolve the question in favor of General Motors, but it is not.

This Act needs some limited judicial first aid in order to be able to accomplish its remedial purposes. Therefore, I would interpret the Act to mean that those written documents of General Motors which made specific representations of substance about the product, not just advertising ballyhoo, and which were introduced by General Motors into the transaction became, as a practical matter, inferentially incorporated into the written warranty. The written warranty would then more fully deserve its gold filigree frame.

Notes

(1) Federal Court Diversity Jurisdiction. The Magnuson–Moss Warranty Act creates a new head of federal jurisdiction, which plaintiffs in *Skelton* sought to use. Without regard to that act, however, warranty litigation is often litigated in federal courts under diversity-of-citizenship jurisdiction, 28 U.S.C. § 1332. Diversity jurisdiction, however, is generally not available in warranty litigation arising out of retail sales because of the high level of the required amount in controversy, raised in 1988 to $50,000. (The federal courts' opinions we read before *Skelton* involved controversies over business goods of considerable value.)

(2) Construction of MMWA 110(d)(1)(B). The Court of Appeals concluded that the statute's omission of claims based on express warranties other than "written warranties" reflected a deliberate Congressional choice. Do you see any other explanation for the structure of MMWA 110(d)(1)(B)?

If a seller provided a "written warranty" to a buyer, may the buyer bring an action in federal court under MMWA 110(d)(1)(B) solely for breach of an implied warranty?

If a seller provided a "written warranty" and that document included warranty provisions in addition to those necessary to meet the definition of "written warranty," may the buyer sue for breach of the "definitional" terms and the additional terms in federal court under MMWA 110(d)(1)(B)?

(C) STRICT TORT LIABILITY FOR ECONOMIC LOSS

(1) Ordinary Consumer Buyers. We noted earlier that strict tort liability emerged principally to protect individuals who had suffered personal injuries caused by defective and unsafe products, but the drafters of Restatement (Second) of Torts § 402A added the possibility of recovery for "physical harm ... to ... property." As state courts fashioned their versions of this new tort, the scope of liability for economic losses became a matter of controversy. Most state courts have held that strict tort liability does not extend to claims for the economic value of the product itself. In Restatement terminology, the "property" for which recovery may be had is property other than the allegedly defective product. Some courts disagree.

Genesis of the disagreement is a 1965 New Jersey decision, based on breach of warranty, in which the buyer of carpet was permitted to recover damages when a buyer discovered a latent flaw in carpet after its installation. Affirming judgment for the buyer, the New Jersey Supreme Court added, in dictum, that buyer could have cast the seller's liability "in simpler form," namely strict tort liability. Santor v. A & M Karagheusian, Inc., 44 N.J. 52, 207 A.2d 305 (1965).

Immediately thereafter, the California Supreme Court, the court which created strict tort liability, declared the New Jersey position to be an improper extension of the new tort. Seely v. White Motor Co., 63 Cal.2d 9, 403 P.2d 145 (1965).

The ensuing controversy echoes down the years as state after state chooses sides and academics and others comment.

(2) Commercial Buyers. While strict tort liability arose in the cases about products purchased by individuals for personal, family or household use, the doctrinal formulation of the new tort did not restrict it to ordinary retail transactions. Products purchased for commercial purposes are also consumed or used. If the buyer is a corporation, that "person" [17] cannot suffer personal injuries. But an organization can suffer property damage. Moreover, if property damage compensable in tort includes loss of value of the product purchased, an organization would be a likely plaintiff in a strict tort liability suit. Even buyers of $125 million supertankers might try to recover on a strict tort liability theory.

EAST RIVER S.S. CORP. v. TRANSAMERICA DELAVAL, INC.

Supreme Court of the United States, 1986.
476 U.S. 858, 106 S.Ct. 2295, 90 L. Ed. 2d 865.

BLACKMUN, J., delivered the opinion for a unanimous Court.

In this admiralty case, we must decide whether a cause of action in tort is stated when a defective product purchased in a commercial transaction malfunctions, injuring only the product itself and causing purely economic loss. The case requires us to consider preliminarily

---

17. "Person" is commonly defined to mean an individual or an organization. See UCC 1–201(30).

whether admiralty law, which already recognizes a general theory of liability for negligence, also incorporates principles of products liability, including strict liability. Then, charting a course between products liability and contract law, we must determine whether injury to a product itself is the kind of harm that should be protected by products liability or left entirely to the law of contracts.

I

In 1969, Seatrain Shipbuilding Corp. (Shipbuilding), a wholly owned subsidiary of Seatrain Lines, Inc. (Seatrain), announced it would build the four oil-transporting supertankers in issue.... Each tanker was constructed pursuant to a contract in which a separate wholly owned subsidiary of Seatrain engaged Shipbuilding. Shipbuilding in turn contracted with respondent, now known as Transamerica Delaval Inc. (Delaval), to design, manufacture, and supervise the installation of turbines (costing $1.4 million each ...) that would be the main propulsion units for the 225,000–ton, $125 million ... supertankers. When each ship was completed, its title was transferred from the contracting subsidiary to a trust company (as trustee for an owner), which in turn chartered the ship to one of the petitioners, also subsidiaries of Seatrain. ... Each petitioner operated under a bareboat charter, by which it took full control of the ship for 20 or 22 years as though it owned it, with the obligation afterwards to return the ship to the real owner. See G. Gilmore & C. Black, Admiralty §§ 4–1, 4–22 (2d ed. 1975). Each charterer assumed responsibility for the cost of any repairs to the ships. ...

The Stuyvesant sailed on its maiden voyage in late July 1977. On December 11 of that year, as the ship was about to enter the Port of Valdez, Alaska, steam began to escape from the casing of the high-pressure turbine. That problem was temporarily resolved by repairs, but before long, while the ship was encountering a severe storm in the Gulf of Alaska, the high-pressure turbine malfunctioned. The ship, though lacking its normal power, was able to continue on its journey to Panama and then San Francisco. In January 1978, an examination of the high-pressure turbine revealed that the first-stage steam reversing ring virtually had disintegrated and had caused additional damage to other parts of the turbine. The damaged part was replaced with a part from the Bay Ridge, which was then under construction. In April 1978, the ship again was repaired, this time with a part from the Brooklyn. Finally, in August, the ship was permanently and satisfactorily repaired with a ring newly designed and manufactured by Delaval.

The Brooklyn and the Williamsburgh were put into service in late 1973 and late 1974, respectively. In 1978, as a result of the Stuyvesant's problems, they were inspected while in port. Those inspections revealed similar turbine damage. Temporary repairs were made, and newly designed parts were installed as permanent repairs that summer.

When the Bay Ridge was completed in early 1979, it contained the newly designed parts and thus never experienced the high-pressure turbine problems that plagued the other three ships. Nonetheless, the complaint appears to claim damages as a result of deterioration of the Bay Ridge's ring that was installed in the Stuyvesant while the Bay Ridge was under construction. In addition, the Bay Ridge experienced a unique problem. In 1980, when the ship was on its maiden voyage, the engine began to vibrate with a frequency that increased even after speed was reduced. It turned out that the astern guardian valve, located between the high-pressure and low-pressure turbines, had been installed backwards. Because of that error, steam entered the low-pressure turbine and damaged it. After repairs, the Bay Ridge resumed its travels.

II

The charterers' second amended complaint, filed in the United States District Court for the District of New Jersey, invokes admiralty jurisdiction. It contains five counts alleging tortious conduct on the part of respondent Delaval and seeks an aggregate of more than $8 million in damages for the cost of repairing the ships and for income lost while the ships were out of service. The first four counts, read liberally, allege that Delaval is strictly liable for the design defects in the high-pressure turbines of the Stuyvesant, the Williamsburgh, the Brooklyn, and the Bay Ridge, respectively. The fifth count alleges that Delaval, as part of the manufacturing process, negligently supervised the installation of the astern guardian valve on the Bay Ridge. ...

The District Court granted summary judgment for Delaval, and the Court of Appeals for the Third Circuit, sitting en banc, affirmed. East River S.S. Corp. v. Delaval Turbine, Inc., 752 F. 2d 903 (1985). ...

III

* * *

We join the Courts of Appeals in recognizing products liability, including strict liability, as part of the general maritime law. ...

IV

Products liability grew out of a public policy judgment that people need more protection from dangerous products than is afforded by the law of warranty. See Seely v. White Motor Co., 63 Cal.2d 9, 15, 403 P.2d 145, 149 (1965). It is clear, however, that if this development were allowed to progress too far, contract law would drown in a sea of tort. See G. Gilmore, The Death of Contract 87–94 (1974). We must determine whether a commercial product injuring itself is the kind of harm against which public policy requires manufacturers to protect, independent of any contractual obligation.

A

The paradigmatic products-liability action is one where a product "reasonably certain to place life and limb in peril," distributed without reinspection, causes bodily injury. See, e.g., MacPherson v. Buick Motor Co., 217 N.Y. 382, 389, 111 N.E. 1051, 1053 (1916). The manufacturer is liable whether or not it is negligent because "public policy demands that responsibility be fixed wherever it will most effectively reduce the hazards to life and health inherent in defective products that reach the market." Escola v. Coca Cola Bottling Co. of Fresno, 24 Cal., at 462, 150 P.2d, at 441 (opinion concurring in judgment).

For similar reasons of safety, the manufacturer's duty of care was broadened to include protection against property damage. ... Such damage is considered so akin to personal injury that the two are treated alike. ...

In the traditional "property damage" cases, the defective product damages other property. In this case, there was no damage to "other" property. Rather, the first, second, and third counts allege that each supertanker's defectively designed turbine components damaged only the turbine itself. Since each turbine was supplied by Delaval as an integrated package, ... each is properly regarded as a single unit. "Since all but the very simplest of machines have component parts, [a contrary] holding would require a finding of 'property damage' in virtually every case where a product damages itself. Such a holding would eliminate the distinction between warranty and strict products liability." Northern Power & Engineering Corp. v. Caterpillar Tractor Co., 623 P.2d 324, 330 (Alaska 1981). The fifth count also alleges injury to the product itself. ... The fifth count thus can best be read to allege that Delaval's negligent manufacture of the propulsion system—by allowing the installation in reverse of the astern guardian valve—damaged the propulsion system. ... Obviously, damage to a product itself has certain attributes of a products-liability claim. But the injury suffered—the failure of the product to function properly—is the essence of a warranty action, through which a contracting party can seek to recoup the benefit of its bargain.

B

The intriguing question whether injury to a product itself may be brought in tort has spawned a variety of answers. At one end of the spectrum, the case that created the majority land-based approach, Seely v. White Motor Co., 63 Cal.2d 9, 403 P.2d 145 (1965) (defective truck), held that preserving a proper role for the law of warranty precludes imposing tort liability if a defective product causes purely monetary harm. ...

At the other end of the spectrum is the minority land-based approach, whose progenitor, Santor v. A & M Karagheusian, Inc., 44 N.J. 52, 66–67, 207 A. 2d 305, 312–313 (1965) (marred carpeting), held that a manufacturer's duty to make nondefective products encompassed injury to the product itself, whether or not the defect created an unreasonable risk of harm. . . . The courts adopting this approach . . . find that the safety and insurance rationales behind strict liability apply equally where the losses are purely economic. These courts reject the Seely approach because they find it arbitrary that economic losses are recoverable if a plaintiff suffers bodily injury or property damage, but not if a product injures itself. They also find no inherent difference between economic loss and personal injury or property damage, because all are proximately caused by the defendant's conduct. Further, they believe recovery for economic loss would not lead to unlimited liability because they think a manufacturer can predict and insure against product failure. . . .

Between the two poles fall a number of cases that would permit a products-liability action under certain circumstances when a product injures only itself. These cases attempt to differentiate between "the disappointed users . . . and the endangered ones," Russell v. Ford Motor Co., 281 Ore. 587, 595, 575 P.2d 1383, 1387 (1978), and permit only the latter to sue in tort. The determination has been said to turn on the nature of the defect, the type of risk, and the manner in which the injury arose. See Pennsylvania Glass Sand Corp. v. Caterpillar Tractor Co., 652 F. 2d, at 1173 (relied on by the Court of Appeals in this case). The Alaska Supreme Court allows a tort action if the defective product creates a situation potentially dangerous to persons or other property, and loss occurs as a proximate result of that danger and under dangerous circumstances. Northern Power & Engineering Corp. v. Caterpillar Tractor Co., 623 P.2d 324, 329 (1981).

We find the intermediate and minority land-based positions unsatisfactory. The intermediate positions, which essentially turn on the degree of risk, are too indeterminate to enable manufacturers easily to structure their business behavior. Nor do we find persuasive a distinction that rests on the manner in which the product is injured. We realize that the damage may be qualitative, occurring through gradual deterioration or internal breakage. Or it may be calamitous. Compare Morrow v. New Moon Homes, Inc., 548 P.2d 279 (Alaska 1976), with Cloud v. Kit Mfg. Co., 563 P.2d 248, 251 (Alaska 1977). But either way, since by definition no person or other property is damaged, the resulting loss is purely economic. Even when the harm to the product itself occurs through an abrupt, accident-like event, the resulting loss due to repair costs, decreased value, and lost profits is essentially the failure of the purchaser to receive the benefit of its bargain—traditionally the core concern of contract law. See E. Farnsworth, Contracts § 12.8, pp. 839–840 (1982).

We also decline to adopt the minority land-based view espoused by Santor . . . . Such cases raise legitimate questions about the theories behind restricting products liability, but we believe that the countervailing arguments are more powerful. The minority view fails to account for the need to keep products liability and contract law in separate spheres and to maintain a realistic limitation on damages.

C

Exercising traditional discretion in admiralty, ... we adopt an approach similar to Seely and hold that a manufacturer in a commercial relationship has no duty under either a negligence or strict products-liability theory to prevent a product from injuring itself.

"The distinction that the law has drawn between tort recovery for physical injuries and warranty recovery for economic loss is not arbitrary and does not rest on the 'luck' of one plaintiff in having an accident causing physical injury. The distinction rests, rather, on an understanding of the nature of the responsibility a manufacturer must undertake in distributing his products." Seely v. White Motor Co., 63 Cal.2d, at 18, 403 P.2d, at 151. When a product injures only itself the reasons for imposing a tort duty are weak and those for leaving the party to its contractual remedies are strong.

The tort concern with safety is reduced when an injury is only to the product itself. When a person is injured, the "cost of an injury and the loss of time or health may be an overwhelming misfortune," and one the person is not prepared to meet. Escola v. Coca Cola Bottling Co., 24 Cal.2d, at 462, 150 P.2d, at 441 (opinion concurring in judgment). In contrast, when a product injures itself, the commercial user stands to lose the value of the product, risks the displeasure of its customers who find that the product does not meet their needs, or, as in this case, experiences increased costs in performing a service. Losses like these can be insured. ... Society need not presume that a customer needs special protection. The increased cost to the public that would result from holding a manufacturer liable in tort for injury to the product itself is not justified. ...

Damage to a product itself is most naturally understood as a warranty claim. Such damage means simply that the product has not met the customer's expectations, or, in other words, that the customer has received "insufficient product value." See J. White & R. Summers, Uniform Commercial Code 406 (2d ed. 1980). The maintenance of product value and quality is precisely the purpose of express and implied warranties.[7] See UCC § 2-313 (express warranty), § 2-314 (implied warranty of merchantability), and § 2-315 (warranty of fitness for a particular purpose). Therefore, a claim of a nonworking product can be brought as a breach-of-warranty action. Or, if the customer prefers, it can reject the product or revoke its acceptance and sue for breach of contract. See UCC §§ 2-601, 2-608, 2-612.

Contract law, and the law of warranty in particular, is well suited to commercial controversies of the sort involved in this case because the parties may set the terms of their own agreements.[8] The manufacturer

---

7. If the charterers' claims were brought as breach-of-warranty actions, they would not be within the admiralty jurisdiction. ...

8. We recognize, of course, that warranty and products liability are not static bodies of law and may overlap. In certain situations, for example, the privity requirement of warranty has been discarded. ...

can restrict its liability, within limits, by disclaiming warranties or limiting remedies. See UCC §§ 2–316, 2–719. In exchange, the purchaser pays less for the product. Since a commercial situation generally does not involve large disparities in bargaining power, ... we see no reason to intrude into the parties' allocation of the risk.

While giving recognition to the manufacturer's bargain, warranty law sufficiently protects the purchaser by allowing it to obtain the benefit of its bargain. See White & Summers, supra, ch. 10. The expectation damages available in warranty for purely economic loss give a plaintiff the full benefit of its bargain by compensating for forgone business opportunities. ... Recovery on a warranty theory would give the charterers their repair costs and lost profits, and would place them in the position they would have been in had the turbines functioned properly. ... Thus, both the nature of the injury and the resulting damages indicate it is more natural to think of injury to a product itself in terms of warranty.

A warranty action also has a built-in limitation on liability, whereas a tort action could subject the manufacturer to damages of an indefinite amount. The limitation in a contract action comes from the agreement of the parties and the requirement that consequential damages, such as lost profits, be a foreseeable result of the breach. See Hadley v. Baxendale, 9 Ex. 341, 156 Eng. Rep. 145 (1854). In a warranty action where the loss is purely economic, the limitation derives from the requirements of foreseeability and of privity, which is still generally enforced for such claims in a commercial setting. See UCC § 2–715... .

In products-liability law, where there is a duty to the public generally, foreseeability is an inadequate brake. ... Permitting recovery for all foreseeable claims for purely economic loss could make a manufacturer liable for vast sums. It would be difficult for a manufacturer to take into account the expectations of persons downstream who may encounter its product. In this case, for example, if the charterers—already one step removed from the transaction—were permitted to recover their economic losses, then the companies that subchartered the ships might claim their economic losses from the delays, and the charterers' customers also might claim their economic losses, and so on. "The law does not spread its protection so far." Robins Dry Dock & Repair Co. v. Flint, 275 U.S. 303, 309 (1927).

And to the extent that courts try to limit purely economic damages in tort, they do so by relying on a far murkier line, one that negates the charterers' contention that permitting such recovery under a products-liability theory enables admiralty courts to avoid difficult line drawing. ...

In other circumstances, a manufacturer may be able to disclaim strict tort liability. See, e.g., Keystone Aeronautics Corp. v. R.J. Enstrom Corp., 499 F.2d 146, 149 (CA3 1974). Nonetheless, the main currents of tort law run in different directions from those of contract and warranty, and the latter seem to us far more appropriate for commercial disputes of the kind involved here.

D

For the first three counts, the defective turbine components allegedly injured only the turbines themselves. Therefore, a strict products-liability theory of recovery is unavailable to the charterers. Any warranty claims would be subject to Delaval's limitation, both in time and scope, of its warranty liability. ... The record indicates that Seatrain and Delaval reached a settlement agreement. ... We were informed that these charterers could not have asserted the warranty claims. ... Even so, the charterers should be left to the terms of their bargains, which explicitly allocated the cost of repairs. ...

Similarly, in the fifth count, alleging the reverse installation of the astern guardian valve, the only harm was to the propulsion system itself rather than to persons or other property. Even assuming that Delaval's supervision was negligent, as we must on this summary judgment motion, Delaval owed no duty under a products-liability theory based on negligence to avoid causing purely economic loss. ... Thus, whether stated in negligence or strict liability, no products-liability claim lies in admiralty when the only injury claimed is economic loss. ...

It is so ordered.

Notes

(1) **Hazardous Risks and Strict Tort Liability.** One court held that the line between tort and warranty liability should not be drawn in terms of the type of the loss, but should be determined rather by the nature of the defect and the type of risk it poses; thus, if a manufacturer so designs a product that a sudden, unexplained small fire spreads and destroys an expensive piece of equipment, a claim falls within the policy of tort law that manufacturers should not create safety hazards that pose a serious risk of harm to people and property. Pennsylvania Glass Sand Corp. v. Caterpillar Tractor Co., 652 F.2d 1165 (3d Cir.1981)

(2) **Disclaimers of Strict Tort Liability.** Courts in jurisdictions that permit buyers to recover for economic loss under the doctrine of strict tort liability have faced the further question of the effect of contract clauses purporting to modify or limit sellers' liability. One court held that it was permissible for sellers to contract out of strict tort liability, but a contract clause that disclaimed warranty liability would not be effective as a disclaimer of tort liability. Keystone Aeronautics Corp. v. R.J. Enstrom Corp., 499 F.2d 146 (3d Cir.1974).

SECTION 6. PRIVITY BETWEEN OWNER OR USER AND WARRANTOR

(A) DOMESTIC UNITED STATES LAW

(1) **Introduction.** Until now, we have considered the issue of sellers' responsibility for the quality of their goods in situations where

complaining buyers had bought the goods from sellers from whom they sought relief. (One significant exception: in *Hill v. BASF Wyandotte Corp.*, Section 3, supra, a farmer sought recovery not from his seller, but rather from the manufacturer of a herbicide.) In this section, we turn to the difficult legal issues that arise when owners of goods sue remote suppliers. The primary legal issue is whether such suits are possible even though there is no privity of contract between the parties.

Goods may be sold a number of times before reaching the ultimate owner or user. Chains of distribution link the sources of goods (e.g., manufacturers, growers, miners) and the eventual final users of those goods. Thus, a manufactured item may be sold by the manufacturer to a wholesaler, who in turn sells the item to a retailer, who then sells it to a customer.

One privity question arises when a buyer at the end of a chain of distribution sues a seller at or near the beginning of the chain. These problems are commonly characterized as issues of "vertical" privity.

A different set of problems, characterized as involving "horizontal" privity, arise when the last buyer in the chain of distribution of a product may not use the goods or may not fully consume them. The product may have been purchased as a gift; the owner-user would not be a buyer at all. A product bought by one family member may be used by other family members and guests. Partially used goods may re-enter the market as "trade-ins." Similar events occur regularly at the commercial level. (Recall the sale of the oil drilling rigs in *Universal Drilling Co.*, Section 3, supra.)

(2) Manufacturers' Advertisements as Express Warranties. One vertical privity issue, now quite well settled, permits retail buyers to enforce warranties made by manufacturers in advertising their products to the general public. A 19th century common-law contract principle established contractual relationships by treating some advertisements as "offers" that can be "accepted" by readers. The classic British case permitted recovery of a "reward" offered by the Carbolic Smoke Ball Company to any of their product's users who came down with one of the diseases supposedly prevented by the smoke. Carlill v. Carbolic Smoke Ball Co., [1893] 1 Q.B. 256 (C.A.1892). In 1932, this took on modern warranty form in Baxter v. Ford Motor Co., 168 Wash. 456, 12 P.2d 409 (1932) (statement in manufacturer's promotional literature that windshields were "shatterproof" held to create an express warranty to retail buyer). Consider again the decision in cases like *Hill* that the terms of the labeling on the package became a manufacturer's express warranty.

Problem 1. M, a manufacturer of building materials, markets its products through independent distributors. However, M sends sales engineers to construction companies to explain the uses of M's products and promote their purchase. Following such a visit by one of M's sales engineers, the B construction company buys M's roofing material from distributor, D. B claims that the roofing material does not have the qualities described by M's sales engineer, and sues M for breach of express warranty. What result in a state which adheres to traditional rules of privity? See Ruud, Manufacturers' Liability for Representations made by their Sales Engineers to Subpurchasers, 8 U.C.L.A.L.Rev. 251 (1961). For numerous ways of finding privity, see Gillam, Products Liability in a Nutshell, 37 Ore. L. Rev. 119, 153 (1958).

(3) **Assignment and Third Party Beneficiary Law.** The general rules on assignment and of third party beneficiaries, which permit contract litigation to proceed between persons who did not contract with each other, applies to transactions in goods. Article 2 of the Commercial Code codifies to some extent both assignment and third party beneficiary law. UCC 2–210, 2–318. Sharp conflicts of policy are reflected in the latter which offers states three choices.[1] Are these principles more likely relevant to horizontal or vertical privity issues?

Problem 2. M, a manufacturer of industrial machinery, sold a power lathe to B Manufacturing Company. E, an employee of B, suffered physical injuries as a result of a defect in the lathe. Under which, if any, version of UCC 2–318 would E be assured a direct cause of action against M?

Problem 3. M sold a machine to D, a distributor; D resold the machine to B Manufacturing Company. The machine exploded and caused a fire which damaged B's property and led to an expensive shutdown. Which, if any, version of UCC 2–318 would assure B a direct cause of action against M?

(4) **Manufacturer's Implied Warranties.** The most difficult vertical privity problem arises when retail buyers or other persons seek recovery from remote suppliers on a warranty theory other than breach of express warranty.

This issue was central to many of the cases in which consumers were injured by unwholesome foods or beverages. In permitting recovery, courts declared that vertical privity was not necessary in that limited category of cases. By 1960, William Prosser was able to write an extraordinarily influential article about the fall of the citadel of privity that had once shielded manufacturers from consumer suits. Prosser, The Assault Upon the Citadel (Strict Liability to the Consumer), 69 Yale L.J. 1099 (1960). In the same year, the New Jersey Supreme Court expanded the category of consumer products in which privity would not be required to include automobiles. Henningsen v. Bloomfield Motors, Inc., 32 N.J. 358, 161 A.2d 69 (1960). Two years later, the California Supreme Court announced strict tort liability. Greenman v. Yuba Power Products, Inc., 59 Cal.2d 57, 377 P.2d 897 (1963). Fundamental to the new tort was the explicit omission of any

---

1. UCC 2–318 as originally promulgated did not contain Alternatives B and C. What is now "Alternative A" was the only provision. In 1966, the Permanent Editorial Board added B and C.

requirement that consumer or user have had a contract with the seller or manufacturer.[2] See Restatement (Second) of Torts § 402A(2)(b).[3]

While the privity issue in personal injury cases is largely removed by the advent of strict tort liability, the issue remains a matter of considerable uncertainty and disagreement in warranty cases involving claims of economic loss.

MORROW v. NEW MOON HOMES, INC.

Supreme Court of Alaska, 1976.
548 P.2d 279.

RABINOWITZ, CHIEF JUSTICE.

This appeal raises questions concerning personal jurisdiction over, and the liability of, a nonresident manufacturer of a defective mobile home that was purchased in Alaska from a resident seller.

In October of 1969, Joseph R. and Nikki Morrow bought a mobile home from Golden Heart Mobile Homes, a Fairbanks retailer of mobile homes. A plaque on the side of the mobile home disclosed that the home had been manufactured in Oregon by New Moon Homes, Inc. The Morrows made a down payment of $1,800, taking out a loan for the balance of the purchase price from the First National Bank of Fairbanks. The loan amount of $10,546.49, plus interest of 9 percent per year, was to be repaid by the Morrows in 72 monthly installments of $190.13 each.

At the time of the purchase, the Morrows inspected the mobile home and noticed that the carpeting had not been laid and that several windows were broken. Roy Miller, Golden Heart's salesman, assured them that these problems would be corrected and later made good his assurances. Miller also told the Morrows that the mobile home was a "good trailer," " ... as warm as ... any other trailer." After the sale, Miller moved the Morrows' mobile home to Lakeview Terrace, set it up on the space the Morrows had rented, and made sure that the utilities were connected. Then the troubles started.

On the first night that the mobile home's furnace was in use, the motor went out and had to be replaced. The electric furnace installed by the manufacturer had been removed by someone who had replaced the original with an oil furnace. The furnace vent did not fit, and consequently the "stove pipe" vibrated when the furnace was running. Subsequent events showed the furnace malfunction was not the primary problem with the mobile home.

---

2. A curious factual coincidence links the New Jersey decision in *Henningsen* and the California decision in *Greenman*. In both cases, the product that caused injury was purchased as a gift and the person injured was the donee.

3. The drafters of § 402A issued a caveat on the horizontal privity question whether bystanders or others who were neither users nor consumers should be permitted to recover.

About four days after the mobile home had been set up, the Morrows noticed that the doors did not close all the way and that the windows were cracked. The bathtub leaked water into the middle bedroom. In March of 1970 when the snow on the roof began to melt, the roof leaked. Water came in through gaps between the ceiling and the wall panels, as well as along the bottom of the wallboard. A short circuit developed in the electrical system; the lights flickered at various times. When it rained, water came out of the light fixture in the hallway. Other problems with the mobile home included the following: the interior walls did not fit together at the corners; the paneling came off the walls; the windows and doors were out of square; the door frames on the bedroom doors fell off and the closet doors would not slide properly; the curtains had glue on them; and the finish came off the kitchen cabinet doors.

Despite all these problems, the Morrows continued to live in the mobile home and make the loan payments. Golden Heart Mobile Homes was notified many times of the difficulties the Morrows were having with their mobile home. Roy Miller, the Golden Heart salesman with whom the Morrows had dealt, did put some caulking around the bathtub, but otherwise he was of little assistance. Finally, sometime before April 1, 1970, Nikki Morrow informed Miller that if Golden Heart did not fix the mobile home the Morrows wanted to return it. Miller said the Morrows would "[h]ave to take it up with the bank." Subsequently, Golden Heart went out of business.

The First National Bank of Fairbanks was more sensitive to the Morrows' plight. Upon being informed by the Morrows that they intended to make no further payments on the mobile home, bank personnel went out and inspected the home several times. In addition, on May 27, 1970, the bank wrote to New Moon Homes, Inc. in Silverton, Oregon. Its letter informed New Moon of the problems the Morrows were having with their New Moon mobile home and asked whether New Moon expected to send a representative to Fairbanks since Golden Heart, the dealer, was no longer in business. Apparently, New Moon did not respond to the bank's letter.

A short time later the Morrows' counsel wrote a letter to New Moon Homes notifying New Moon that the Morrows intended to hold the company liable for damages for breach of implied warranties. About a month later the Morrows separated, with Nikki Morrow continuing to live in the mobile home. She continued to make payments to First National because she "couldn't afford Alaskan rents." Nikki Morrow eventually moved out of the mobile home but made no effort to sell or rent it because she considered it "not fit to live in." In October of 1971 the Morrows filed this action against both New Moon Homes and Golden Heart Mobile Homes, alleging that defendants had breached implied warranties of merchantability and fitness for particular purpose in manufacturing and selling an improperly constructed mobile home. The complaint further alleged that New Moon "is a foreign corporation doing business in the State of Alaska." Although the record does not disclose the method by which New Moon was informed of the pending action, apparently the Morrows served a copy of the summons and complaint upon the Commissioner of Commerce, who forwarded the papers to New Moon in Oregon. In its answer New Moon *inter alia* raised the "affirmative defenses" of lack of personal jurisdiction and improper service of process.

The case was tried in July of 1973. No attorney appeared on behalf of Golden Heart Mobile Homes, but the Morrows proceeded to present their evidence against New Moon because they were looking primarily to the manufacturer for recovery. The Morrows offered the testimony of four witnesses which tended to identify the mobile home in question as a New Moon home. Neither side presented any evidence concerning New Moon's business connections with Alaska or the circumstances under which the New Moon mobile home came into Golden Heart's possession. The superior court granted the Morrows a default judgment against Golden Heart, but dismissed their claim against New Moon "for both failure of jurisdiction and failure of privity of contract." The Morrows then appealed from that portion of the superior court's judgment which dismissed their claim against New Moon.

The heart of this appeal concerns the remedies which are available to a remote purchaser against the manufacturer of defective goods for direct economic loss. The superior court held that the Morrows had no legal claim against New Moon because they were not in privity of contract with New Moon. The first argument advanced here by the Morrows amounts to an end run around the requirement of privity. The Morrows contend that their complaint asserted a theory of strict liability in tort. They further argue that they should have prevailed irrespective of any lack of privity of contract between New Moon and themselves, because lack of privity of contract is not a defense to a strict tort liability claim.

* * *

... Under the Uniform Commercial Code the manufacturer is given the right to avail himself of certain affirmative defenses which can minimize his liability for a purely economic loss. Specifically, the manufacturer has the opportunity, pursuant to [UCC 2–316], to disclaim liability and under [UCC 2–719] to limit the consumer's remedies, although the Code further provides that such disclaimers and limitations cannot be so oppressive as to be unconscionable and thus violate [UCC 2–302]. In addition, the manufacturer is entitled to reasonably prompt notice from the consumer of the claimed breach of warranties, pursuant to [UCC 2–607(3)(a).]

In our view, recognition of a doctrine of strict liability in tort for economic loss would seriously jeopardize the continued viability of these rights. The economically injured consumer would have a theory of redress not envisioned by our legislature when it enacted the U.C.C., since this strict liability remedy would be completely unrestrained by disclaimer, liability limitation and notice provisions. Further, manufacturers could no longer look to the Uniform Commercial Code provisions to provide a predictable definition of potential liability for direct economic loss. In short, adoption of the doctrine of strict liability for economic loss would be contrary to the legislature's intent when it authorized the aforementioned remedy limitations and risk allocation provisions of Article II of the Code. To extend strict tort liability to reach the Morrows' case would in effect be an assumption of legislative prerogative on our part and would vitiate clearly articulated statutory rights. This we decline to do. Thus, we hold that the theory of strict liability in tort ... does not extend to the consumer who suffers only economic loss because of defective goods.

The principal theory of liability advocated by the Morrows at trial was that New Moon had breached statutory warranties which arose by operation of law with the manufacture and distribution of this mobile home. Specifically, the Morrows rely upon [UCC 2–314] and [UCC 2–315] of the Uniform Commercial Code as enacted in Alaska. The former section provides for an implied warranty of "merchantability" in the sale of goods governed by the Code; the latter establishes an implied warranty that the goods are fit for the particular purpose for which they were purchased. The superior court was of the view that these Code warranties operated only for the benefit of those purchasing directly from a manufacturer or seller. Since the Morrows were not in privity of contract with New Moon, the superior court concluded that a warranty theory based on [UCC 2–314] and [UCC 2–315] could not serve as a basis for liability. ...

It is equally clear that in this jurisdiction the Morrows, as immediate purchasers, can recover against their seller for breach of the Code's implied warranties. Indeed, this was the theory upon which the default judgment against Golden Heart Mobile Homes was predicated. The critical question in this case is whether the Morrows, as remote purchasers, can invoke the warranties attributable to the manufacturer which arose when New Moon passed title of the mobile home to the next party in the chain of distribution. In other words, do the implied warranties of merchantability and fitness run from a manufacturer only to those with whom the manufacturer is in privity of contract?

Although sometimes criticized, the distinction between horizontal and vertical privity is significant in this case. The issue of horizontal privity raises the question whether persons other than the buyer of defective goods can recover from the buyer's immediate seller on a warranty theory. The question of vertical privity is whether parties in the distributive chain prior to the immediate seller can be held liable to the ultimate purchaser for loss caused by the defective product. The Code addresses the matter of horizontal privity in [UCC 2–318], extending the claim for relief in warranty to any " ... person who is in the family or household of his buyer or who is a guest in his home if it is reasonable to expect that the person may use, consume, or be affected by the goods...." With regard to vertical privity, the Code is totally silent and strictly neutral, as Official Comment 3 to [UCC 2–318] makes eminently clear. The Code leaves to the courts the question of the extent to which vertical privity of contract will or will not be required.

This court has never previously confronted the question whether a requirement of privity of contract will preclude a purchaser from recovering against the original manufacturer on a theory of implied warranties. . . . [W]e expressly held in Clary v. Fifth Avenue Chrysler Center, Inc., 454 P.2d 244 (Alaska 1969), that a manufacturer is strictly liable in tort for personal injuries attributable to his defective goods. In approving a theory based on strict liability in tort, we stressed the efficacy, simplicity, and comprehensiveness of that theory. Appellees in *Clary* had urged this court to limit the consumer's source of redress to possible application of the statutory provisions governing sales warranties, particularly [UCC 2–313: Express Warranties]. This we declined to do. As we have noted, under the statutory scheme an injured consumer is required to give notice of the defect to the warrantor within a relatively short period of time, and potential liability may be circumscribed by express disclaimers from the manufacturer. The *Clary* court was concerned that such provisions might operate as a trap for the unwary, and it expressed a preference for a tort theory more solicitous of the needs of the consumer in the modern, prepackaged, mass merchandised market place. However, this preference was never intended to imply that reliance on the statutory warranty provisions was not available as an alternative vehicle for relief. There is nothing incompatible in affording parallel consumer remedies sounding in tort and in contract, and several jurisdictions which have adopted strict liability in tort also make available an implied warranty theory without regard to privity of contract.

The dispute here is whether the requirement of vertical privity of contract should be abolished in Alaska. This battle has already been waged in many jurisdictions, and the results are well known: the citadel of privity has largely toppled. The course of this modern development is familiar history and we need not recount it at length here. Contrived "exceptions" which paid deference to the hoary doctrine of privity while obviating its unjust results have given way in more recent years to an open frontal assault. The initial attack came in Spence v. Three Rivers Builders & Masonry Supply, Inc., 353 Mich. 120, 90 N.W.2d 873 (1958), but the leading case probably remains Henningsen v. Bloomfield Motors, Inc., 32 N.J. 358, 161 A.2d 69 (1960), in which the New Jersey Supreme Court held liable for personal injuries and property damages both the manufacturer of an automobile and the dealer who sold the vehicle. The rationale for the widespread abolition of the requirement of privity stems from the structure and operation of the free market economy in contemporary society; it was succinctly summed up not long ago by the Supreme Court of Pennsylvania [in Kassab v. Central Soya, 432 Pa. 217, 246 A.2d 848, 853 (1968)]:

> Courts and scholars alike have recognized that the typical consumer does not deal at arms length with the party whose product he buys. Rather, he buys from a retail merchant who is

usually little more than an economic conduit. It is not the merchant who has defectively manufactured the product. Nor is it usually the merchant who advertises the product on such a large scale as to attract consumers. We have in our society literally scores of large, financially responsible manufacturers who place their wares in the stream of commerce not only with the realization, but with the avowed purpose, that these goods will find their way into the hands of the consumer. Only the consumer will use these products; and only the consumer will be injured by them should they prove defective.

The policy considerations which dictate the abolition of privity are largely those which also warranted imposing strict tort liability on the manufacturer: the consumer's inability to protect himself adequately from defectively manufactured goods, the implied assurance of the maker when he puts his goods on the market that they are safe, and the superior risk bearing ability of the manufacturer. In addition, limiting a consumer under the Code to an implied warranty action against his immediate seller in those instances when the product defect is attributable to the manufacturer would effectively promote circularity of litigation and waste of judicial resources. Therefore, we decide that a manufacturer may be held liable for a breach of the implied warranties of [UCC 2-314] and [UCC 2-315] without regard to privity of contract between the manufacturer and the consumer.

The more difficult question before this court is whether we should extend this abolition of privity to embrace not only warranty actions for personal injuries and property damage but also those for economic loss. Contemporary courts have been more reticent to discard the privity requirement and to permit recovery in warranty by a remote consumer for purely economic losses. In considering this issue we note that economic loss may be categorized into direct economic loss and consequential economic loss, a distinction maintained in the Code's structure of damage remedies. One commentator has summarized the distinction:

> Direct economic loss may be said to encompass damage based on insufficient product value; thus, direct economic loss may be "out of pocket"—the difference in value between what is given and received—or "loss of bargain"—the difference between the value of what is received and its value as represented. Direct economic loss also may be measured by costs of replacement and repair. Consequential economic loss includes all indirect loss, such as loss of profits resulting from inability to make use of the defective product.

The claim of the Morrows in this case is one for direct economic loss.

A number of courts recently confronting this issue have declined to overturn the privity requirement in warranty actions for economic loss. One principal factor seems to be that these courts simply do not find the social and economic reasons which justify extending enterprise liability to the victims of personal injury or property damage equally compelling in the case of a disappointed buyer suffering "only" economic loss. There is an apparent fear that economic losses may be of a far greater magnitude in value than personal injuries, and being somehow less foreseeable these losses would be less insurable, undermining the risk spreading theory of enterprise liability.

Several of the courts which have recently considered this aspect of the privity issue have found those arguments unpersuasive. We are in agreement and hold that there is no satisfactory justification for a remedial scheme which extends the warranty action to a consumer suffering personal injury or property damage but denies similar relief to the consumer "fortunate" enough to suffer only direct economic loss.

. . .

The fear that if the implied warranty action is extended to direct economic loss, manufacturers will be subjected to liability for damages of unknown and unlimited scope would seem unfounded. The manufacturer may possibly delimit the scope of his potential liability by use of a disclaimer in compliance with [UCC 2–316] or by resort to the limitations authorized in [UCC 2–719]. These statutory rights not only preclude extending the theory of strict liability in tort, supra, but also make highly appropriate this extension of the theory of implied warranties. Further, by expanding warranty rights to redress this form of harm, we preserve " ... the well developed notion that the law of contract should control actions for purely economic losses and that the law of tort should control actions for personal injuries." We therefore hold that a manufacturer can be held liable for direct economic loss attributable to a breach of his implied warranties, without regard to privity of contract between the manufacturer and the ultimate purchaser.[42] It was therefore error for the trial court to dismiss the Morrows' action against New Moon for want of privity.

Our decision today preserves the statutory rights of the manufacturer to define his potential liability to the ultimate consumer, by means of express disclaimers and limitations, while protecting the legitimate expectation of the consumer that goods distributed on a wide scale by the use of conduit retailers are fit for their intended use. The manufacturer's rights are not, of course, unfettered. Disclaimers and limitations must comport with the relevant statutory prerequisites and cannot be so oppressive as to be unconscionable within the meaning of [UCC 2–302]. On the other hand, under the Code the consumer has a number of responsibilities if he is to enjoy the right of action we recognize today, not the least of which is that he must give notice of the

---

42. We recognize that the arguments against the abolition of privity are more compelling when the injury alleged is damages of a consequential nature many times the value of the manufacturer's product. See, e.g., Note, Economic Loss in Products Liability Jurisprudence, 66 Colum.L.Rev. 917, 965–66 (1965). We do not speak today to the issue of consequential economic loss, other than to note that [UCC 2–715] governs the recovery of such damages and requires, among other things, that said damages must have been foreseeable by the manufacturer. Adams v. J.I. Case Co., 125 Ill.App.2d 388, 261 N.E.2d 1 (1970).

breach of warranty to the manufacturer pursuant to [UCC 2–607]. The warranty action brought under the Code must be brought within the statute of limitations period prescribed in [UCC 2–725]. If the action is for breach of the implied warranty of fitness for particular purpose, created by [UCC 2–315], the consumer must establish that the warrantor had reason to know the particular purpose for which the goods were required and that the consumer relied on the seller's skill or judgment to select or furnish suitable goods. In the case of litigation against a remote manufacturer, it would appear that often it will be quite difficult to establish this element of actual or constructive knowledge essential to this particular warranty.

In the case at bar the trial judge failed to enter written findings of fact.... We cannot determine from the record whether the Morrows would have prevailed on a theory of breach of implied warranties had the trial court not erred in raising the barrier of privity. Trial was had over two years ago. We are therefore of the opinion that, if the dismissal for want of jurisdiction was also erroneous, a new trial is warranted at which the Morrows will have the opportunity to assert their warranty theories free from the confines of privity. It is to the jurisdictional ruling that we now turn.

...

... Consequently, we order that this cause be remanded for a new trial in which Morrows will have the opportunity to establish every element of their case, including personal jurisdiction over New Moon.

Reversed and remanded for a new trial in accordance with this opinion.

ERWIN, JUSTICE (concurring).

While I concur with the opinion, I would extend the concept of strict liability to cover "economic loss" rather than use the warranty theory advanced by the majority.

The history of products liability law does not justify a distinction between personal injury and property damage. The primary purpose of the strict liability rule is to insure that the costs of injuries resulting from defective products are borne by the manufacturers that put such products on the market rather than by the consumers who are powerless to protect themselves.

Those in favor of the dichotomy between "economic loss" and other types of damage argue that an abolition of the distinction would result in manufacturers being liable for damages of unknown and unlimited scope. This concept is embraced by the majority, which notes that the manufacturer who may now minimize liability by relying on certain provisions in the Uniform Commercial Code, would be unable to do so if the doctrine of strict liability were applied. In essence, this position intimates that manufacturers' rights under the Uniform Commercial Code should be maintained in order to assure the predictability of their potential liability.

... [T]he concerns expressed by the majority in this case would for all intents and purposes be eliminated if the notion of "defective" in the strict liability doctrine is viewed as co-extensive with the concept of "unmerchantability" in the implied warranty field. The term has been well defined by case law and has a fixed meaning so far as the Uniform Commercial Code is concerned.

If the doctrine of strict liability were adopted for cases such as the present one, the ordinary consumer, whose bargaining power is seldom equal to the manufacturers', would have the opportunity to bring an action against the original wrongdoer, instead of the local retailer who served as little more than a conduit for the defective product. ...

Notes

(1) **Sequential Actions or Direct Action.** No vertical privity problems arise if a retail buyer of a manufactured product brings suit against the dealer from whom the product was purchased. If the buyer's complaint is based upon the condition of the product as it left the plant of the manufacturer, the retailer will have a cause of action against its supplier, and so in sequence up the chain of distribution to the manufacturer, who will bear ultimate liability.

Two procedural devices facilitate such back-to-back law suits. Modern procedures permit impleader. See, e.g., Fed.R.Civ.P. 14. Less well known is the Code's statutory version of the device of vouching-in, provided by 2–607(5).

In light of this, what justifies permitting implied warranty actions by consumer buyers against remote manufacturers for the buyers' disappointment in the quality of their goods? Is the court's rationale in *Morrow* persuasive?

(2) **Contract Description and Merchantability.** When consumer buyers sue remote manufacturers for economic loss, the buyers are likely to rely principally on the warranty of merchantability as defined in UCC 2–314(2)(c)(not fit for the ordinary purposes for which such goods are used). What determines "such goods"? Suppose a manufacturer sold certain goods as "seconds." Thereafter some of the goods came into the possession of a consumer buyer who was not told that they were not regular merchandise. Is the manufacturer liable to the consumer buyer for the difference between the value of regular merchandise and the value of the goods that are "seconds"?

(3) **Change in Condition of the Goods After Manufacture.** For many reasons, goods can deteriorate during the time they are in the chain of distribution. In warranty of merchantability actions for economic loss by consumer buyers against remote manufacturers, who has the burden of proving the quality of the goods as they left the manufacturers' plants?

Recall in *Morrow* that the mobile home had been modified at some time after the sale by the manufacturer to change the heating system.

Is a manufacturer liable for modifications made by others? Suppose, for example, that a new car dealer agrees to sell a car from the dealer's inventory to a consumer buyer; the buyer, however, wants a car with a sun roof, which the seller agrees to install. Is the manufacturer of the car liable if the sun roof leaks?

Manufactured goods are commonly sold by manufacturers with the expectation that retail dealers or others will perform certain functions to make the goods ready for delivery to consumers. New car dealers undertake a large number of such tasks (the "dealer-prep" functions). Is a manufacturer liable for inadequate performance of these tasks by a retailer?

(4) **Measure of Ordinary Damages for Economic Loss.** Market value of a product at the retail level is normally considerably higher than the market value as the products first enter the chain of distribution. In a warranty action, a buyer's damages are measured by the value the goods would have had if they had been as warranted. UCC 2–714(2). If a remote manufacturer is held liable to a consumer buyer, which market level establishes the value of the goods as warranted?

(5) **Consequential Economic Losses.** In warranty actions by consumers buyers against remote manufacturers, can damages be recovered for buyers' consequential economic losses? Note the way the *Morrow* court dealt with this question. In what circumstances could a manufacturer, at the time of its sale of a product, have reason to know of the general or particular needs of an unknown consumer?

(6) **Warranty Disclaimers and Clauses Limiting Damages.** The *Morrow* court stated that its decision preserved manufacturers' statutory rights to define contractually their potential implied warranty liability to ultimate consumers. How would a manufacturer, who is making no express warranty to ultimate consumers, contract effectively with them? Must a disclaimer or damage limitation clause, to be binding on a consumer, be part of the retail contract with the consumer? Is a post-sale disclaimer or damage limitation clause binding? Recall UCC 2–316, 2–719; cf. *Hill v. BASF Wyandotte Corp.*

(7) **Notice of Breach to Remote Manufacturers.** The *Morrow* court stated that consumer buyers have responsibilities, not the least of which is the responsibility to give notice of breach to the manufacturer. Recall that the birth of strict tort liability for personal injury resulted from the failure of the Greenmans to give timely notice of breach to the manufacturer. Suppose a dissatisfied consumer gave timely notice to the retailer, but not to the remote manufacturer. Would the consumer be barred from any remedy against the manufacturer?

(8) **Statute of Limitations on Manufacturers' Liability.** The *Morrow* court stated that a consumer must bring action against a manufacturer within the time permitted by UCC 2–725. Under that provision, the period of limitations begins when tender of delivery is made. Does the statute run from the date of manufacturer's tender of delivery or from the date of the retailer's tender? See *Heller v. U.S.*

Suzuki Motor Corp., 64 N.Y.2d 407, 488 N.Y.S.2d 132, 477 N.E.2d 434 (1985)(statute runs from date of manufacturer's tender).

(9) Fitness for Particular Purpose. The *Morrow* court "decided" that a manufacturer may be held liable for breach of either the implied warranty of merchantability or the implied warranty of fitness for particular purpose. How would a consumer buyer communicate to the remote manufacturer the buyer's particular purpose for which the goods are required and be in a position to rely reasonably on the manufacturer's skill and judgment in selecting or furnishing suitable goods? If the consumer buyer communicated to the retailer, would a manufacturer be liable for the retailer's lack of skill or judgment in selecting the wrong goods?

Problem 4. A home owner, needing paint for a masonry wall, went to a local paint store and described the project to the salesperson. The salesperson recommended Pierce's shingle-and-shake paint. Following the recommendation, home owner bought and applied that paint to the masonry wall. The results were totally unsatisfactory. Is Pierce Co., the paint manufacturer, liable to the home owner? Cf. Catania v. Brown, 4 Conn.Cir. 344, 231 A.2d 668 (1967).

(10) Components Suppliers. The image of vertical privity has products moving down a chain of distribution from manufacturers to consumers. In many instances, however, the final product contains many components made by others and sold to the manufacturer. May consumer buyers recover from the even more remote suppliers of components to the remote manufacturers?

(11) Remote Sellers of Primary Goods. If the goods in question are primary goods, such as crude oil or tomatoes, should remote sellers or farmers be liable to ultimate buyers?

SZAJNA v. GENERAL MOTORS CORP.

Supreme Court of Illinois, 1986.
115 Ill.2d 294, 503 N.E.2d 760.

JUSTICE RYAN delivered the opinion of the court:

The plaintiff, John L. Szajna (Szajna), filed a suit in the circuit court of Cook County against the defendant, General Motors Corporation (GM), on his own behalf and on behalf of all others who bought 1976 Pontiac Venturas which were equipped with Chevette transmissions.

* * *

The following allegations were common to all three counts of Szajna's second amended complaint. In August 1976, he bought a 1976 Pontiac Ventura from Seltzer Pontiac, Inc. (Seltzer), in Chicago. Seltzer, as agent for GM, gave Szajna a folder which contained two

Sec. 6   *PRIVITY BETWEEN OWNER AND WARRANTOR*   199

warranties: one entitled a "Limited Warranty On 1976 Pontiac Car" and another entitled "1976 Pontiac Passenger Car Emission Control System." It was alleged that both warranties were made by GM to Szajna. It was also alleged that thousands of the cars sold as 1976 Pontiac Venturas, including Szajna's, were equipped with Chevette transmissions; that the use of Chevette transmissions in Pontiac Venturas necessitates higher amounts of repairs and that they have shorter service lives than do transmissions ordinarily used in Pontiac Venturas because the Chevette transmission was designed for use in a lighter weight car; that use of the Chevette transmission in Pontiac Venturas lessens the value of the cars; and that Szajna paid $375 to have the transmission in his car replaced.

The following allegations were also common to all three counts. GM manufactured, labeled and made available through its Pontiac Division the 1976 Pontiac Ventura. GM designed and engineered a transmission specifically for the 1976 Pontiac Ventura. "Through its brochures, parts catalogues and repair manuals, as well as through the release of automobile news and information from its public relations department," GM "advised the expert observers, testers and reporters of the nature of the '1976 Pontiac Ventura' model as including the transmission designed for that size of car." The public and Szajna, in buying the cars, relied on the experts and on GM for any noteworthy information on GM cars not readily observable. No information was given to the public or the experts that some of the 1976 Pontiac Venturas were equipped with Chevette transmissions.

Count I of Szajna's second amended complaint alleges breach of implied warranty under section 2–314 of the UCC. It alleges that 1976 Pontiac Venturas equipped with Chevette transmissions were not merchantable because they "would not pass without objection in the trade" under the contract description; "were not of fair average quality within the description, did not run within the variations permitted by the agreement of even kind and quality and did not conform to their labels" as Pontiac Venturas. (See Ill. Rev. Stat. 1975, ch. 26, pars. 2–314(2)(a), (b), (d), (f).) (The "description" referred to above was the name 1976 Pontiac Ventura.) Count I also alleges that the failure by GM to deliver 1976 Pontiac Venturas as warranted rendered them nonconforming goods for which Szajna and other purchasers could ... receive damages (Ill. Rev. Stat. 1975, ch. 26, par. 2–714).

Szajna also alleges in count I breach of implied warranty pursuant to section 110(d) of Magnuson–Moss, which provides that a consumer who is damaged by the failure of a supplier or warrantor to comply with any obligation under an implied warranty may bring suit for damages and other legal and equitable relief in any court of competent jurisdiction in any State. 15 U.S.C. sec. 2310(d)(1) (1976).

In dismissing count I of Szajna's second amended complaint, the trial court entered the following conclusions of law. First, privity of contract is a prerequisite in Illinois to a suit for breach of implied warranty alleging economic loss. Second, Magnuson–Moss, in permitting recovery for breach of implied warranty, incorporates State-law privity requirements. (15 U.S.C. sec. 2301(7) (1976).) Third, no privity of contract existed between Szajna and GM. Fourth, the limited written warranty extended by GM, although running to the ultimate purchaser, did not give rise to the implied warranty of merchantability. The appellate court, in essence, adopted the trial court's conclusions of law. It was of the opinion, however, that while Szajna and GM "were in privity for purposes of the provisions in the express limited warranty, they were not in privity for purposes of implied warranties, which were specifically disclaimed by the express warranty." Szajna v. General Motors Corp. (1985), 130 Ill.App. 3d 173, 177.

* * *

Magnuson–Moss, enacted by Congress in 1975, ... does not require that warranty be given, but if there is a *written* warranty, Magnuson–Moss imposes certain requirements as to its contents, disclosures, and the effect of extending a written warranty. ... No supplier may disclaim or modify an implied warranty, except a supplier giving a limited written warranty may limit the duration of an implied warranty to the duration of the written warranty if such limitation is conscionable and is clearly set forth (15 U.S.C. sec. 2308 (1976).) ... In this case we are concerned only with the question of whether, under Magnuson–Moss, Szajna can maintain an action based on an implied warranty against the manufacturer of the automobile. ... Section 2301(7) defines implied warranty as follows:

> The term "implied warranty" means an implied warranty arising under State law (as modified by sections 2308 and 2304(a) of this title) in connection with the sale by a supplier of a consumer product. (15 U.S.C. sec. 2301(7)(1976).)

Focusing on that part of the definition stating the term means "an implied warranty arising under State law," some authors maintain that if the law of the State holds that privity is essential to implied warranty, then an action such as is involved in our case cannot be maintained. (Miller & Kanter, *Litigation Under Magnuson–Moss: New Opportunities in Private Actions,* 13 U.C.C. L.J. 10, 22 (1980).) However, the definition also states that the term means an implied warranty arising under State law "*(as modified by sections 2308 and 2304(a) of this title).*" (Emphasis added.) (15 U.S.C. sec. 2301(7) (1976).) Section 2308 provides:

> No supplier may disclaim or modify (except as provided in subsection (b) of this section [limiting the duration of an implied warranty to the duration of a "limited" written warranty]) any implied warranty to a consumer * * * if (1) such supplier makes any written warranty to the consumer * * * or (2) at the time of sale, or within 90 days thereafter, such supplier enters into a service contract with the consumer which applies to such consumer product." (15 U.S.C. sec. 2308(a) (1976).)

Sec. 6   PRIVITY BETWEEN OWNER AND WARRANTOR

This section raises the question as to whether it modifies implied-warranty State-law provisions to the extent that any written warranty given by a manufacturer to a remote purchaser creates an implied warranty by virtue of Magnuson–Moss. At the very least we must acknowledge that the provisions of section 2308 clearly demonstrate the policy of Magnuson–Moss to sustain the protection afforded to consumers by implied warranties.

The Act broadly defines "consumer" in section 2301(3) as "a buyer (other than for purposes of resale) of any consumer product, any person to whom such product is transferred during the duration of an implied or written warranty * * * and any other person who is entitled by the terms of such warranty * * * or under applicable State law to enforce against the warrantor * * * the obligations of the warranty." (15 U.S.C. sec. 2301(3) (1976).) It has been suggested that this broad definition of "consumer" and the provisions of section 2310(d)(1) (15 U.S.C. sec. 2310(d)(1) (1976)), which section authorizes a "consumer" to maintain a civil action for damages for failure of a "supplier" or "warrantor" to comply with any obligation of a written or implied warranty, effectively abolish vertical privity. (See Comment, *Consumer Product Warranties Under the Magnuson–Moss Warranty Act and the Uniform Commercial Code,* 62 Cornell L. Rev. 738, 755–59 (1977).) We do not think we can focus on any one section of Magnuson–Moss but should read the sections referred to together to accomplish the purpose of Magnuson–Moss of furnishing broad protection to the consumer.

In resolving this murky situation we find helpful, and accept, Professor Schroeder's analysis and suggestion as a reasonable solution. In cases where no Magnuson–Moss written warranty has been given, Magnuson–Moss has no effect upon State-law privity requirements because, by virtue of section 2301(7), which defines implied warranty, implied warranty arises only if it does so under State law. However, if a Magnuson–Moss written warranty (either "full" or "limited") is given by reason of the policy against disclaimers of implied warranty expressed in Magnuson–Moss and the provisions authorizing a consumer to sue a warrantor, the nonprivity "consumer" should be permitted to maintain an action on an implied warranty against the "warrantor." (Schroeder, *Privity Actions Under the Magnuson–Moss Warranty Act,* 66 Calif.L.Rev. 1, 16 (1978).) The rationale of this conclusion, though not specifically articulated by Professor Schroeder in the article, would hold that under Magnuson–Moss a warrantor, by extending a written warranty to the consumer, establishes privity between the warrantor and the consumer which, though limited in nature, is sufficient to support an implied warranty under sections 2–314 and 2–315 of the UCC. The implied warranty thus recognized, by virtue of the definition in section 2301(7) of Magnuson–Moss, must be one arising under the law of this State. ... .

The appellate court in this case held that while the parties were in privity for purposes of the provisions of the express written limited warranty which General Motors had extended, they were not in privity for the purposes of implied warranty. (130 Ill.App. 3d 173, 177.) This holding is in conflict with our holding herein and will therefore be reversed.

* * *

Notes

(1) **Rationale.** The Illinois Supreme Court based its holding in *Szajna*, regarding privity in implied warranty claims, on a policy perceived to underlie the Magnuson–Moss Warranty Act. Is the court's reading of the federal statute persuasive? Should the court have based its holding on state law? Suppose a manufacturer of a consumer good makes an express warranty to retail consumers, but the express warranty is not a "written warranty" under the Magnuson–Moss Act. Would the Illinois court conclude that privity exists for purpose of enforcing the express warranty, but would not exist for purpose of enforcing the implied warranty of merchantability?

(2) **UCC 2–318; Non–uniform Variations.** In an omitted portion of *Szajna*, the Illinois court agreed with the *Morrow* court that the Commercial Code does not address the privity problems presented in those cases. Both states had adopted the version of that section now referred to as Alternative A. Do Alternatives B or C address the privity problems in *Morrow* or *Szajna?*

Several legislatures have found all of the Editorial Board's proposals unsatisfactory. Some have deleted Section 2–318 entirely; others have revised 2–318, usually to lower the privity barrier. In this area there is little uniformity of even the statutory text, and case-law development has been even more individualistic. Local variations can be found in Uniform Laws Annotated.

COLLINS COMPANY, LTD. v. CARBOLINE COMPANY

Supreme Court of Illinois, 1988.
125 Ill.2d 498, 532 N.E.2d 834.

JUSTICE STAMOS delivered the opinion of the court:

This cause is before us on a question of Illinois law certified by the United States Court of Appeals for the Seventh Circuit. The certified question is:

> In the absence of original contractual privity, does an express warranty extend to an assignee's right to sue for purely economic loss and consequential damages?

For the reasons that follow and with the qualifications noted, we answer the question in the affirmative.

FACTS ...

In March 1981, Chicago Title and Trust Company, as trustee (Chicago Title), and Wachovia Bank and Trust Company, N.A. (Wachovia), owned a warehouse in Elk Grove Village, Illinois. The owners contracted with Flexible Roof Contractors, a wholly owned division of Pureco Systems, Inc. (Pureco), to replace the roofing system at the warehouse. The roofing system was to be replaced with one manufactured by Carboline Company (Carboline).

In manufacturing and supplying the system, Carboline issued an express written warranty, warranting the installed system against leakage for 10 years from the date of completing the installation, which was stated in the warranty as March 17, 1981. The warranty also stated that final inspection of the installation by Carboline occurred on March 19, 1981, and that the warranty would be effective only upon Carboline's inspection and acceptance of the installation. The warranty copy attached to the complaint does not appear to bear a signature in behalf of Carboline, but in its answer Carboline admitted that it issued "to Wachovia Bank & Trust Co., N.A." a warranty as exemplified by the copy and that the warranty "speaks for itself."

The warranty contained numerous terms, limitations, and conditions and disclaimed any warranty of merchantability or of fitness for a particular purpose. It provided that Carboline's sole warranty obligation should be to repair roofing leaks caused by defects in the roofing material or by the roofing applicator's workmanship and that Carboline's financial liability for the repairs should not exceed "the owner's original cost" of the installed system.

* * *

The warranty did not specifically identify the warrantee. In a blank labeled "Project Name and Location," the following legend was inserted: "Jarvis Ave. Job—1441 Jarvis Ave. Elk Grove Village, IL." On a second, unlabeled blank line immediately below was inserted "Chicago Title & Trust Co., Ancillary Trustee/Trust Agreement # 09–64234." On a third blank line labeled "Owner" and appearing immediately below the second line, the name "Wachovia Bank & Trust Co., N.A." was inserted. As completed, the warranty form did not make clear whether the Chicago Title designation was meant to denote an additional "owner" or simply to further identify the "project name and location"; however, at the end of the form, in a blank labeled "OWNER ACCEPTANCE," the words "CT & T CO., as Trustee aforesaid" were inserted, followed by a signature and the designation "Vice President" under date of June 1, 1981. A warranty term provided that Carboline would not be liable under the warranty until "the owner" had accepted the roofing contractor's installation by signing the warranty form. Nowhere did the warranty state that it extended or was limited to the "owner," whoever or of whatever that might be. In fact, one term provided merely that the warranty should be void if reasonable care were not used "by the party occupying the building" in maintaining the roof.

It is also noteworthy that, despite the large number of terms and conditions expressed by the warranty form, no term forbade assignment of rights or obligations by any party.

In June 1984, Collins Company, Ltd. (Collins), acquired the warehouse building from Chicago Title and Wachovia. Beginning in or about May 1985, leaks developed in the roofing system, which have caused Collins to incur expense for temporary repairs, will require a complete replacement of the roofing system in the near future, and have interfered with the conduct of Collins' business. In 1986, Chicago Title and Wachovia assigned to Collins their rights under the warranty and any claims or rights they had against Pureco. The assignment was given in exchange for a covenant not to sue.

On March 6, 1986, Collins filed its three-count diversity complaint in the United States District Court for the Northern District of Illinois... .

In count I, Collins claimed $500,000 in damages from Carboline for breach of warranty. In that count, Collins asserted that the roofing system was defectively manufactured and installed and that Carboline was obliged under the warranty to replace the system and pay for any damages caused by leakage. Collins also asserted that it had relied on the warranty in deciding to purchase the building and that it had exercised due care in maintaining the roof. ...

As affirmative defenses, Carboline asserted that the warranty was not assignable and therefore denied that Chicago Title and Wachovia had made an assignment to Collins. Carboline also asserted that the warranty was not issued to Collins. In addition, Carboline asserted that Collins' damages against it, if any, were limited by the warranty terms and that the latter barred Collins' claim. Finally, Carboline asserted that the roof leaks and other damage claimed were caused not by a roofing system defect but by sources beyond Carboline's control for which Carboline has no liability.

* * *

[B]ecause it found that Collins was not in privity with Carboline, the district court granted Carboline's motion for judgment. ...

On appeal, the Seventh Circuit court requested that we consider the certified question as one that may be determinative of the cause. ... We accepted the certification, pursuant to our Rule 20.... .

OPINION

* * *

We ... hold that the assignee of a warrantee's rights under an express warranty, if the assignment is otherwise valid, succeeds to all those rights and thus stands in privity with the warrantor. ... Such an assignee's privity would generally enable it to sue for economic loss and consequential damages, just as an original contracting party might do.

* * *

We have previously stated that an express warranty is imposed by the parties to a contract and is part of the sale contract and that an action for breach of express warranty is an action ex contractu. ... It is clear that in its contractual nature an express warranty differs materially from an implied warranty. ...

An implied warranty is derived from the interplay of a transaction's factual circumstances with the foreseeable expectations of a buyer or other person who is protected by law in those expectations. ... This is a concept that the common law recognized long before promulgation of the UCC, albeit a concept that was originally rather limited in application. ... The implied warranty arises regardless of an affected seller's actual wishes.

By contrast, the warrantor is the master of the express warranty. ... The warranty arises only because the warrantor has willed it into being by making the requisite affirmation as part of a contract to which it is an adjunct. ...

In this difference between express and implied warranty can arguably be found justification for a differing treatment of the lack of privity when express-warranty claims are made by remote buyers or other persons. ...

While "[p]rivity requires that the party suing has some contractual relationship with the one sued" (Crest Container Corp. v. R.H. Bishop Co. (1982), 111 Ill.App. 3d 1068, 1076), privity accompanies a valid assignment of the contract. ...

Once made, an assignment puts the assignee into the shoes of the assignor. ... Because the assignor was in privity with the opposite contracting party, so is the assignee. ...

Despite Carboline's and the district court's reliance for a contrary conclusion on our decision in Szajna v. General Motors Corp. (1986), 115 Ill.2d 294, the holding of that case is in harmony with our decision today.

In Szajna, we were asked to abolish the privity requirement in suits to recover for economic loss when breach of an implied warranty is alleged. ... This we chose not to do, noting our previously expressed preference that recovery for economic loss be had within the framework of contract law. ...

In Szajna we thus declined to extend to subsequent nonprivity buyers the UCC's implied warranties in sales of new automobiles. ... In so declining, we referred to the General Assembly's failure to adopt more expansive versions of the UCC's section 2–318 that would expressly attenuate privity requirements, and we observed that the UCC's overall contractual orientation would accommodate only with some difficulty the further extension of implied warranties to nonprivity parties. ...

* * *

Neither do we decide today whether an express warranty such as the one here ... can actually be interpreted to run beyond its original holder even in the absence of formal assignment.... .

Our decision also potentially gives effect to the ostensible promise of performance made by Carboline in its warranty, instead of rendering the promise illusory on the happenstance basis of a transfer of the warranted goods before the end of the stated warranty period. After all, Carboline could have included a limitation on assignment in its express 10–year warranty if it had so desired. ...

In addition, though the vouching-in procedure established by section 2–607(5) of the UCC ... remains available in proper cases ..., our decision potentially avoids the need for any such circuitous litigation in this case.

* * *

In answer to the question certified by the United States Court of Appeals for the Seventh Circuit, we conclude that, because the assignee of an express warranty acquires privity with the warrantor by virtue of a valid assignment, the express warranty does therefore "extend to an assignee's right to sue for purely economic loss and consequential damages."

Notes

(1) **Horizontal or Vertical Privity; UCC 2–318.** Would the privity problem presented in this case be more properly characterized as vertical or horizontal privity? If the issue is one of horizontal privity, could the current owner of the warehouse recover under any version of UCC 2–318? (Recall that Illinois has enacted Alternative A.) If 2–318 does not permit recovery, does that indicate a legislative judgment that recovery should be denied?

(2) **Express and Implied Assignments.** The Illinois court reserved decision on the importance of the former owner's formal assignment of the roofer's repair warranty to the current owner of the warehouse. Should not transfer of a long-term roof warranty be implied in the sale of the building? Would the remaining years of that warranty be of value to the former owner?

(3) **Warranty to Original Owner Only.** Some sellers and manufacturers, who make repair or replace warranties, provide that the warranties extend to the first consumer purchaser only and do not extend to subsequent owners. Why would warrantors include such a limitation in their warranties? Are such provisions permitted under the Commercial Code? See UCC 2–318. Are such provisions permitted under the Magnuson–Moss Act? See 16 C.F.R. §§ 700.6(b), 701.3(a)(1).

If buyers of used goods could enforce express warranties, would they also be entitled to enforce implied warranties. See Bagel v. American Honda Motor Co., 132 Ill.App.3d 82, 477 N.E.2d 54 (1985)(second owner had no right to enforce implied warranty of merchantability); Johnson v. General Motors Corp., 349 Pa.Super. 147, 502 A.2d 1317 (1986)(widow of first consumer had no right to enforce implied warranty of merchantability).

(B) INTERNATIONAL SALES LAW

The Convention on International Sales of Goods has no specific provisions regarding privity of contract.

With regard to vertical privity, CISG provisions on the responsibilities of sellers and rights of buyers are drafted in terms of "the seller" and "the buyer" and "the contract," language which strongly implies a requirement of contractual privity. Suppose, however, that a manufacturer participates actively in marketing its products by providing dealers with the manufacturer's written "warranty" for delivery to buyers from those dealers. Even if it were held that the "warranty" created a contractual obligation to the ultimate buyers, should the rules of the Convention apply to that contractual relationship? See J. Honnold, Uniform Law for International Sales § 63 (2d ed. 1991).[4]

CISG lacks any provision relaxing privity requirements on the horizontal axis. Nothing comparable to UCC 2–318 exists in the Convention. Nor does CISG speak to assignments of unexecuted contracts. This may constitute a gap in the Convention for which no general principle is available under CISG 7(2). In that event, issues of assignability and recognition of third party beneficiaries would be governed by that domestic law "applicable by virtue of the rules of private international law."

Problem 5. A United States company enters into a contract to sell and deliver a quantity of crude oil to a French buyer in three months at a port to be specified by the buyer. Both France and the United States have ratified CISG. Before the date for delivery, the French buyer notifies the U.S. seller that it has assigned its rights to the crude oil to a British firm. The United Kingdom has not ratified CISG. Assuming that the assignment is valid, is the contract between the U.S. seller and British assignee governed by the Convention?

---

4. In the first edition of this commentary on the Convention, the author concluded that the language of CISG did not reach remote sellers. The point was reconsidered in the second edition in light of the possibility that manufacturers may not only participate in, but may in fact dominate the way in which its products are ultimately sold.

While flexible interpretation of CISG may be urged as a general matter, the Convention's provisions on scope of application should be construed to achieve maximum predictability. J. Honnold, Uniform Law for International Sales S 60.5. Would predictability of CISG's application be endangered by flexible reading of "the seller" to include a remote seller in appropriate cases?

Chapter 4

BUYERS' RESPONSIBILITY FOR THE PRICE

(A) DOMESTIC UNITED STATES LAW

A contract of sale is an exchange transaction with responsibility on both sellers and buyers. In the previous chapter we considered sellers' responsibility for the quality of the goods delivered. Buyers' responsibility, of course, is payment of the contract price. The legal issues concerning the price obligation, while fewer than those concerning quality of the goods, are nonetheless of great importance to sellers.

Amount of the Price; "Open" Price Terms. Karl LLewellyn wrote that "Price is the heart of the sales contract." K. Llewellyn, Law of Sales 1 (1930). "Price" is a necessary element for a "sale" under the Commercial Code. UCC 2–106. Nevertheless, parties to sales contracts often agree to the transaction without establishing the price to be paid. The Code declares that the price in such transactions is a "reasonable price at the time for delivery." UCC 2–305(1). What is the relationship between "reasonable price" and market value? To what extent does 2–305 state rules that mirror the probable actual intention of the parties? Most students have explored the meaning of this provision in the course on Contracts.

Price Terms in Long–Term Supply Contracts. In contracting for supply of goods over an extended period of time, parties may fix prices that turn out, later, to be greatly different from the market value of the goods at the time of expected performance. The party disadvantaged by the unexpected rise or fall in market values may seek to be relieved from its obligation to deliver the goods or to pay the contract price.

Problem 1. Aluminum Refining Company agreed to provide Wire Manufacturing Company with its requirements of aluminum over a twenty year period. The agreement established a base price subject to adjustment determined by changes in the Producers' Price Index, which tracks the change in prices of industrial commodities. Five years after the agreement, as a result of oil embargoes and related world developments, the price of energy, including electricity, rose dramatically. The aluminum refining process requires an extraordinary amount of electrical energy. As a result, price adjustments under the contract formula are inadequate to meet the sharply rising costs of Aluminum Refining Company, which faces the prospect of severe loss in performance of the balance of the contract. Wire Manufacturing Company, on the other hand, stands to receive refined aluminum at a cost well below current market prices for that material.

(a) On what legal grounds, if any, may Aluminum Refining Company properly cease performance? Does UCC 2–615 offer relief to seller? See Re Westinghouse Elec. Corp. Uranium Contracts Litigation No. 235 (E.D.Va. Oct. 27, 1978); Iowa Elec. Light and Power Co. v. Atlas Corp., 467 F.Supp. 129 (N.D.Iowa 1978), rev'd, 603 F.2d 1301 (8th Cir.1979); Missouri Public Service Co. v. Peabody Coal Co., 583 S.W.2d 721 (Mo.App.1979). Do the common-law rules of mistake have any application?

(b) If Aluminum Refining Company seeks a court order to reform the contract, what should be the result? See Aluminum Co. of America v. Essex Group, Inc., 499 F.Supp. 53 (W.D.Pa.1980), vacated, No. 80–1604 (3d Cir. Feb. 5, 1981).

For further reading on these and related matters, see Wladis, Impracticality as Risk Allocation: The Effect of Changed Circumstances Upon Contract Obligations for the Sale of Goods, 22 Ga. L. Rev. 503 (1988); Scott, Conflict and Cooperation in Long–Term Contracts, 75 Cal.L.Rev. 2005 (1987); Halpern, Application of the Doctrine of Commercial Impracticability: Searching for the "Wisdom of Solomon," 135 U.Pa.L.Rev. 1123 (1987); Hillman, Court Adjustment of Long–Term Contracts: An Analysis Under Modern Contract Law, 1987 Duke L.J. 1; Prance, Commercial Impracticality: A Textual and Economic Analysis, 19 Ind. L.J. 457 (1986); Gillette, Commercial Rationality and the Duty to Adjust Long–Term Contracts, 69 Minn.L.Rev. 521 (1985); Goldberg, Price Adjustments in Long–Term Contracts, 1985 Wis.L.Rev. 527; Trakman, Winner Take Some: Loss Sharing and Commercial Impracticability, 69 Minn.L.Rev. 471 (1985); Speidel, Court–Imposed Price Adjustments Under Long–Term Supply Contracts, 76 Nw. U.L.Rev. 369 (1981); Joskow, Commercial Impossibility, the Uranium Market and the Westinghouse Uranium Contracts Litigation, 6 J. Legal Studies 119 (1977).

Problem 2. Producer agreed to sell to Distributor specified quantities of natural gas for fifteen years. The agreement provided that Distributor could take gas as needed and pay the contract price, but if Distributor took less than the minimum annual amount, Distributor would pay the contract price for the difference. In the oil and gas industry, these agreements are commonly referred to as take-or-pay contracts. Two years after the agreement, Distributor's gas sales dropped sharply as a result of decline in oil prices making oil an attractive alternative to natural gas, successful energy conservation efforts, abnormally warm weather, and economic recession. Distributor was unable to sell the minimum annual quantities of natural gas specified in the agreement with Producer. On what legal grounds, if any, may Distributor be excused from the obligation to pay for that part of the annual minima it had not taken? Does UCC 2–615 have any applicability? See Golsen v. ONG Western, Inc., 756 P.2d 1209 (Okl.1988); Resources Investment Corp. v. Enron Corp., 669 F.Supp. 1038 (D.Colo.1987); Northern Indiana Public Service Co. v. Carbon

County Coal Co., 799 F.2d 265 (7th Cir.1986).[1]

Quality of the Money; "Legal Tender." Under general federal law, buyers meet their payment obligations if they deliver "legal tender."[2] For many reasons, buyers and sellers do not use, and do not expect to use "legal tender" in performance of the payment obligation of sales contracts.

(B) INTERNATIONAL SALES LAW

The nature of buyers' payment responsibility is less clear under international sales law than under domestic United States law. Part III, chapter III of the Convention on International Contracts for the Sale of Goods states buyers' obligation without indicating the kind of money that sellers must accept.

Article 54 states that "the buyer's obligation to pay the price includes taking such steps and complying with such formalities as may be required under the contract or any laws and regulations to enable payment to be made." To what kind of law or regulation does this provision refer?

"Open" Price Terms. In a contract governed by CISG, is an agreement with an "open" price term enforceable? Article 55 declares that "in the absence of any indication to the contrary, [the parties are considered] to have impliedly made reference to the price generally charged at the time of the conclusion of the contract for such goods sold under comparable circumstances in the trade concerned."

Note that the time chosen for price determination under CISG is different from that under UCC 2–305. In what setting would this departure be important? Which approach is more likely to reflect the parties' probable intentions?

Choice of Currency. In sales contracts between sellers and buyers from different nations, what determines the currency of payment? The agreement may provide expressly or by implication that the price is to be paid in U.S. dollars, Canadian dollars, Deutsche marks, Japanese yen, British pounds, or Soviet rubles, etc. If, however, the agreement lacks an express or implied term of this kind, what legal rule fills the gap? Statutes like the Legal Tender Act of the United

---

1. For further reading, see Farnsworth, Developments in Contract Law During the 1980's: The Top Ten, 41 Case Western L. Rev. 203, 213–216 (1990); Medina, McKenzie & Daniel, Take or Litigate: Enforcing the Plain Meaning of the Take–or–Pay Clause in Natural Gas Contracts, 40 Ark. L. Rev. 185 (1987); Comment, Take–or–Pay Provisions: Major Problems for the Natural Gas Industry, 18 St. Mary's L.J. 251 (1986).

2. "Legal tender" is defined in 31 U.S.C.A. § 5103:

United States coins and currency (including Federal reserve notes and circulating notes of Federal reserve banks and national banks) are legal tender for all debts, public charges, taxes, and dues. Foreign gold or silver coins are not legal tender for debts.

The constitutionality of this statute was upheld in The Legal Tender Cases, 110 U.S. 421, 4 S.Ct. 122, 28 L. Ed. 204 (1884).

States govern domestic transactions, but what rule of law applies in an international transaction?

One aspect of the real value of a payment is bound up in the issue of choice of currency.[3] All nations' currencies commonly fluctuate in value as against each other. Among the most important commercial markets are the markets for exchange of currencies. The value of one currency in terms of another changes with great rapidity. A currency is said to be "strong" or "weak" depending upon the amount of other currencies that can be bought with it. Recreational and business travellers are familiar with the daily variations at currency exchanges in airports and hotels. These reflect the movements of currency exchange rates in the major markets of the world.

If the date of payment under a sales contract is other than the date of the contract, the parties cannot know what the relative value of different currencies may be when the time for payment arrives. The longer the period of time before a payment is due, the greater becomes the uncertainty. Given a choice, buyers (or any debtors) would prefer to pay in a cheaper currency.[4] Sellers would prefer the opposite.

Restricted Convertibility; "Hard" and "Soft" Currencies. The major industrial nations of the world permit their currencies to "float" without significant legal restrictions. These currencies are the so-called "hard" currencies. Nations with weaker economies, however, tend not to permit free exchange of currencies because the international currency markets has limited demand for their domestic currencies. Such nations, which can acquire only limited amounts of the "hard" currencies through international sales of their domestic goods and services, often restrict the expenditure of the acquired "hard" currencies in order to meet the nation's priorities. Potential buyers in those countries, negotiating with foreign sellers, must obtain governmental permission to pay in "hard" currencies unless the sellers agree to accept a "soft" currency more easily available to the buyers.

National laws with respect to free convertibility of currency change over time.[5] A transactional risk for a seller is possible change in law

---

3. A payee who wants to spend the payment in a particular place, where one currency is the common medium of payment, will be less concerned with fluctuations in currency exchange rates if payment is made in the currency that the payee plans to spend. Thus, to the extent that a French seller spends the price received for goods sold to pay its employees and its domestic French suppliers in French francs, the value of the franc against other currencies is not important if the price is paid in francs. If, however, the price is paid in another currency, the French seller will suffer any loss or gain that occurs when the currency of payment is converted into French francs.

4. Vastly simplified, this difference underlay the great 19th century controversy over "free silver" in the United States. The bimetallism movement championed by William Jennings Bryan, who rode to prominence on the famous "cross of gold" speech, would have made payment of long term debt less onerous by deflating the value of the U.S. dollar.

5. The former nations of the Communist bloc, and particularly the Soviet Union, have faced or are facing the need to change their laws on convertibility in order to enter the free world market. Making this change is difficult because of the resulting upheavals in the domestic economies of those nations.

by the government of the buyer's country, restricting the buyer's ability to pay the price, when due, in the contractually required currency.

Chapter 5

EXECUTION OF SALES CONTRACTS: MANNER, TIME AND PLACE

SECTION 1. INTRODUCTION

Previous chapters were concerned with the "what" (title and quality and price) and the "who" (privity) of sales transactions. In this chapter we consider "when," "where," and "how" the parties execute the promises made in contracts of sale. Most sales involve physical handing over and receiving of goods. Title, a legal abstraction, cannot be delivered physically. However, sometimes title can be reified in a "document of title," a tangible thing that can be handed over to a buyer. Payment of the price may involve physical handing over of money, but payment commonly occurs with delivery of instruments that effect transfer to sellers of bank credits. How, where and when these steps take place can be as important to the parties as are issues of title, quality and price.

Agreed Terms and Default Rules. Buyers and sellers may fix the terms of manner, time and place of performance by agreement. Terms may be set by express agreement or by implication from trade usage, course of dealing, or course of performance. Agreed terms regarding execution may state specifically how, where and when each party is to perform, but it is not uncommon for agreements to confer on one party discretion to determine these matters unilaterally, perhaps within stated limits. Thus, the agreement may require seller to ship goods in March or April, with the exact date determined by the seller. Under domestic United States law, when an agreement "leaves particulars of performance to be specified by one of the parties, . . . specification must be made in good faith and within limits set by commercial reasonableness." UCC 2–311(1).

Buyers and sellers sometimes fail to agree, even by implication, on manner, time and place of each party's performance. To fill those gaps, domestic United States law and the Convention on International Sale of Goods set forth a number of default rules. In this sense, the law reduces the costs of transacting by providing standardized performance terms that become part of the sales contract.[1]

Two–Party Execution. Execution of sales contracts often is accomplished by buyers and sellers without the intervention of third parties. Sellers and buyers may meet for handing over of the goods

---

1. Recall the definition of "contract" in UCC 1–201(11): "the total legal obligation which results from the parties' agreement as affected by this Act and any other applicable rules of law."

and the money. In retail sales customers commonly go to stores to pick up and pay for goods. Sometimes, sellers, using their own employees or agents, take goods to buyers; dealers' delivery of home heating oil is an example.

Execution Through Third Parties: Carriers and Banks. In other commercial settings, particularly when the parties are at a distance from each other, they will authorize or require use of carriers to transport goods from sellers to buyers. In some settings, the parties will authorize or require that payment of the sales price be made by banks.

Remedies for Non–execution or Improper Execution. Contractual terms on how, when and where sales contracts are to be executed are enforceable obligations. A party who fails, without excuse, to meet an obligation when due is in breach of contract; the aggrieved party will have one or more legal remedies. The terms of parties' agreements or the law's default rules provide the normative standards against which to measure whether sellers' or buyers' acts or omissions were in breach of their obligation to execute sales contracts.

(A) DOMESTIC UNITED STATES LAW

Basic performance obligations and related default rules are stated by the Commercial Code. The Code provisions are found largely in Parts 3 and 5 of Article 2.

Section 2–301 of the Code states the general obligation of both parties:

> The obligation of the seller is to transfer and deliver and that of the buyer is to accept and pay in accordance with the contract.

Presumably "transfer" refers to title and "deliver" refers to goods. On the buyers' side, the general obligation to "pay" is coupled with the obligation to "accept" the goods. This purport of the obligation to "accept" is, on the surface, strange;[2] if sellers are paid, would they care whether buyers "accept" the goods? We defer further consideration of that matter until the next section.

The parties' 2–301 obligation is elaborated in the operational standards of *tender of delivery* and *tender of payment*. Tender connotes performance by the tendering party that satisfies its obligation and puts the other party in default if it fails to execute its obligation. See UCC 2–507(1) and 2–511(1). The Commercial Code's default rules on

---

2. Students should be cautious to avoid confusing "acceptance of goods" with the concepts of offer and acceptance familiar from general contract law and found in the Commercial Code in UCC 2–206 and 2–207. "Acceptance of an offer" is a way of describing formation of contracts. "Acceptance of goods" is a concept used in connection with buyers' performance of sales contracts. Referring to "acceptance" without indicating whether one is referring to acceptance of an offer or of goods can be confusing, but context usually indicates which type of acceptance is meant. See, e.g., UCC 2–310.

manner, time and place of the parties' obligations to execute sales contracts are based on the concept of tender.

(1) TWO–PARTY TRANSACTIONS

Manner of Sellers' Tender of Delivery of Goods. "Tender of delivery requires that the seller put and hold conforming goods at the buyer's disposition and give the buyer any notification reasonably necessary to enable him to take delivery." UCC 2–503(1). The "put and hold" formulation, which by implication excludes "let go," is the essence of the concept of tender of goods. Tender must be at a "reasonable hour" and tendered goods must be kept available for "the period reasonably necessary to enable the buyer to take possession." UCC 2–503(1)(a). "Tender" begins delivery, but effecting completed delivery usually requires buyers' response.

Place of Sellers' Tender. If the agreement is silent, the default rule establishes the place of delivery at a merchant seller's place of business. UCC 2–308(a). In this circumstance, a seller tenders by holding the goods at the place of business and notifying buyer that the goods are available.[3] Sellers may agree to take the goods to their buyers; in such transactions, the Code provides that buyers must furnish facilities reasonably suited to receipt of the goods.[4] UCC 2–503(1)(b).

Time of Sellers' Tender. Section 2–503(1)(a) provides that sellers' tender must be made at a reasonable hour and for a reasonable duration, but does not have a default rule for the date on which a seller is required to have the goods ready. The Code's answer is a "reasonable time" standard. UCC 2–309(1). Under this provision, a seller has some leeway before failure to tender delivery becomes a breach of contract. The outside limits of that period of time will be difficult to fix as an exact date.

Manner of Buyers' Tender of Payment. The Commercial Code refers to "tender of payment" in UCC 2–511, but does not define what constitutes such a tender. By analogy to tender of delivery, tender of payment occurs when a buyer "puts and holds" money or other instrument or payment device at the disposition of a seller. If a buyer tenders a personal check,[5] seller may insist on legal tender but must give buyer any additional time needed to procure it. UCC 2–511(2).

---

3. The Commercial Code has no provision declaring that buyers are contractually obligated to take possession of tendered goods. When sellers put and hold goods at buyers' disposition, in the overwhelming majority of transactions the buyers will dispose of them. They want to have possession of the goods they agreed to buy. That may explain why the Code is silent on the matter.

4. This provision on buyers' obligation is oddly located in a section defining the manner of sellers' tender of delivery. Comment 4 to 2–503 states that this obligation of the buyer is no part of the seller's tender.

5. Personal checks would likely be considered a means of payment "current in the ordinary course of business." UCC 2–511(2). A buyer's personal check is an order by the buyer to a designated bank to

Time and Place of Tender of Payment. Sales contracts are more likely to have express or implied terms regarding buyers' tender of payment than sellers' tender of delivery. Commonly, parties agree to a time of payment that involves sellers' extending credit to buyers or buyers' making "down payments." Other reasons also explain the greater prevalence of agreed payment terms. Nonetheless, many sales contracts are silent on the manner, time and place of buyers' performance. The Commercial Code provides the default rules that fill those gaps in agreements.

Several Commercial Code provisions indicate the default rule regarding time and place for buyers' performance of their payment obligation. A buyer's payment is due "at the time and place at which the buyer is to receive the goods...." UCC 2–310(a). Before paying, a buyer has the right to inspect the goods. UCC 2–513(1).

Tender of Delivery in "Lots." Ordinarily, sellers must tender all goods at once, but the Code provides for exceptions of partial deliveries.[6] If a seller properly delivers goods in installments, in the absence of agreement otherwise, a buyer must pay for each delivery if the contract price can be apportioned; otherwise the buyer can withhold payment until all the goods have been tendered. UCC 2–307.

To test your understanding of the performance rules, consider the following problems:

Problem 1. Wire Manufacturer ordered a quantity of certain copper from Copper Trading Co., which agreed to supply it. The sales agreement specified no delivery date. Manufacturer knew that Trading Co. would have to find a source of copper that met Manufacturer's needs, but assumed that no shortage of such copper existed. Trading Co. also assumed that it would have little difficulty locating the needed copper at a favorable price. Trading Co. discovers that the copper market is "tight" and spot prices are high. Trading Co. extends its search for copper to look for a relatively low price in the current market or, if necessary, to wait out what it hopes is a temporary peak in market prices.

(a) Manufacturer, whose inventory of copper is running low, demands that Trading Co. make immediate delivery. Trading Co. responds that it will deliver soon but gives no specific date.

---

pay money to a designated payee on demand. See UCC 3–104.

6. When a single article has been sold, delivery or tender of that article is the only performance possible. However, sometimes the goods sold are physically divisible into "lots." UCC 2–105(5). Under what circumstances may a seller make a proper delivery or tender of less than all of the goods? The agreement may provide for multiple deliveries. In the absence of express agreement, the circumstances may indicate that this is not only proper but necessary. For example, the buyer of a large quantity of bricks needed to construct a large building may lack space at the site to store all the bricks if delivered at one time; when both seller and buyer are aware of this, multiple deliveries are proper. The default rule, however, is that all the goods must be delivered or tendered in a single lot. UCC 2–307.

(i) As counsel for Manufacturer, advise it on when Trading Co. was or will be in default.

(ii) As counsel for Trading Co., advise it as to the outside limit of its time for performance without breach.

(b) Manufacturer declares Trading Co. in default and institutes legal action. Which party has the burden of proving that a reasonable time had elapsed before Manufacturer's decision?

Problem 2. Plastics agreed to manufacture and deliver 40,000 pounds of special high-impact polystyrene pellets at 19 cents a pound for Industries. Industries agreed to accept delivery at the rate of 1000 pounds per day as the pellets were produced. Two weeks after the June 30 agreement, Plastics notified Industries that it was ready to deliver. Industries telephoned to say that labor difficulties and vacation schedules made it impossible to receive any pellets immediately; in that conversation Plastics replied that it would complete production and that it hoped that Industries would start taking delivery soon.

(a) On August 18, Plastics wrote to Industries: "We produced 40,000 pounds of high-impact pellets to your special order. You indicated that you would be using 1,000 lbs. per day. We have warehoused these products for more than forty days. However, we cannot keep these products indefinitely and request that you begin taking delivery. We have done everything that we agreed to do." After another month, Industries has not taken any pellets. Plastics consults you for legal assistance. What advice would you give? Is UCC 2–610 applicable? Compare Multiplastics, Inc. v. Arch Industries, Inc., 166 Conn. 280, 348 A.2d 618 (1974).

(b) Suppose Plastics had consulted you before sending its August 18 letter. Would you have advised changes in the letter? Would you have set a specific date as a deadline for Industries to take delivery? Is UCC 2–311 helpful? Would you advise sending a written demand pursuant to UCC 2–609(1)?

Problem 3. Consumer and Car Dealer entered into a sales agreement for a new automobile. Three weeks after the agreement, Car Dealer notified Consumer that the specified car had arrived. Consumer went to Car Dealer's place of business, looked at and sat in the car, kicked the tires, lifted the hood and peered at the engine. Consumer asked for the keys in order to "take it for a trial" to see if the car performed satisfactorily. Car Dealer responded that Consumer could have the keys only after he had paid the price. Has Consumer had a reasonable opportunity to inspect? The Code declares that "tender of payment is a condition of the seller's duty to ... complete any delivery." UCC 2–507(1). Does this support Car Dealer's contention that Consumer's right to inspect includes only what Consumer can learn from examination of the goods while still in the Car Dealer's possession?

Problem 4. Recall the inspection arrangements in the flour sale transaction in *T.J. Stevenson & Son,* Chapter 3, section 2, supra. What determined this method of inspection? Which party must pay the expenses of such inspections? See UCC 2–513(2).

Problem 5. Builder, constructing a new house, ordered appliances from Dealer. The sales contract required Dealer to deliver the appliances to the construction site on February 1. Builder agreed to pay 30 days after delivery. When Dealer's truck arrived, after 5 p.m., all Builder's employees had gone for the night. Dealer's truck driver put the appliances into the garage and locked it. Were Dealer's actions in conformity with the requirements of UCC 2–503? See Ron Mead T.V. & Appliance v. Legendary Homes, Inc. 746 P.2d 1163 (Okl.App.1987).

(2) TRANSACTIONS USING CARRIERS TO DELIVER GOODS

We turn now to transactions in which sellers perform through an intermediary, a carrier, and the necessary adaptation of the law governing performance of sales contracts.[7] Sellers surrender physical possession of the goods to carriers who in turn surrender possession to buyers. The parties may include in their agreement terms regarding the manner, time and place of execution of contracts in which carriers provide transportation services. However, the Code provides default rules defining tender of delivery and payment in such transactions to fill gaps when agreements are silent.

When sellers are required or authorized by sales contracts to send goods by carrier, the Code recognizes two types of such contracts. Different tender rules apply to these types. If a seller is required to deliver the goods *at a particular destination,* the tender rules applicable to two-party transactions apply. UCC 2–503(3). If a seller is not required to deliver the goods at such destination another set of tender rules applies.[8] UCC 2–503(2) and 2–504.[9]

The Code's meaning of a sales contract requirement to deliver goods via carrier at a particular destination is found by considering other sections. Comment 1 to 2–504 declares that the general principles of the section cover the special cases of "F.O.B. point of shipment contracts." The Comment refers here to certain trade terms that

---

7. Goods move to their markets on trucks, railroads, airplanes, and ships whose owners sell this transportation service. Some carriers hold themselves out as available to the public; they are deemed "common carriers" and are regulated by federal and state laws. Others, "contract carriers," do not offer their services to the general public.

8. In the parlance of commercial law, the former are often called *destination contracts* and the latter *shipment contracts.* See Comment 1 to UCC 2–504.

9. On quick and careless reading, the phrase makes little sense. Would not every sales contract that requires a seller to ship via carrier be a destination contract? How can a seller send goods to the buyer via carrier without sending them to a named destination? If a seller is required to send the goods to a buyer at buyer's place of business or residence, would that not be sending them to a particular destination? Such questions misread the key language of the Code, which speaks of delivery at, not delivery to a particular designation.

parties to sales contracts commonly use in their agreements. The Code defines the meaning of these contract terms in UCC 2–319 and 2–320. Within those definitions, we find the manner, time and place of sellers' tender of delivery in transactions involving carriers' transport of the goods.

F.O.B. or Free on Board. Parties to sales contracts often use the F.O.B. term, or other similar terms, as convenient shorthand expressions. It is common in sales contracts contemplating land transport by rail or truck. To make sense an F.O.B. term must refer to a designated place where the goods are to be free on board. Choice of the place allocates between buyer and seller the carrier's charges to transport the freight; seller pays for the freight to the specified place.[10] More important for our present purposes, choice of place in an F.O.B. contract also defines sellers' tender obligations.[11]

F.O.B. terms are one of several common contract terms defining sellers' tender obligations. A wide variety of terms are used in contracts that contemplate deep water transportation, including F.A.S., F.O.B. vessel, C.I.F., C. & F., Ex Ship. Each of these is defined by the Commercial Code. UCC 2–319(1)(c) and (2), 2–320, 2–321, 2–322.

"At a Particular Destination" Contracts. If the parties use an F.O.B. term and designate "the place of destination," the Code characterizes this as a contract in which seller is required to deliver at a particular destination. A seller must, at its own expense, transport the goods to "*the* place of destination" and "*there*" tender delivery of the goods to the buyer. UCC 2–319(1)(b). The tender rules are otherwise comparable to rules for sellers' tender in simple, two-party transactions, UCC 2–503(3), except the place of tender is at the destination of the transportation. In all likelihood, the seller will not be "there" in person to put and hold the goods at buyer's disposition. This is effected by the carrier acting pursuant to seller's instructions.

"The Place of Shipment" Contracts. If the parties use an F.O.B. term and designate "the place of shipment," the Code characterizes this as a contract in which seller is *not* required to deliver at a particular destination. A seller "must at that place ship the goods in the manner provided in this Article (Section 2–504)."[12] Similar provisions are found in the UCC definitions of most deep water shipment terms.

Section 2–504(a) and (c) state two basic requirements. A seller must:

10. Costs of transportation will probably be borne ultimately by buyers. When, by contract, a seller bears the cost of freight, as in an F.O.B. Buyersville contract, its cost of performance is raised by that amount. In a rational business, costs will be reflected in the price of the goods. Thus, freight costs initially allocated to sellers are likely to be passed through to their buyers.

11. This explains why the Code describes an F.O.B. term as a "delivery term," UCC 2–319(1), and not "merely a price term." Comment 1.

12. The seller bears the expense of putting the goods into the possession of the carrier at the place of shipment; freight costs are added to the price of the goods as part of the buyer's obligation.

(1) put the goods in the possession of the carrier and make a contract for their transportation as may be reasonable having regard to the nature of the goods and other circumstances,[13] and

(2) promptly notify the buyer of the shipment.

If contracts with the carriers require them simply to deliver the goods to buyers, sellers complete their tender of delivery substantially before buyers receive the goods. For example, if the carrier is the U.S. Postal Service or Federal Express, a seller has made tender of delivery when the goods are mailed or handed over to the carrier. A similar result follows if the goods are shipped via a railroad or trucking line.

For a number of commercial reasons, sellers may hand over goods to carriers but not authorize the carriers simply to deliver the goods to buyers. Sellers may keep control of the carriers' duty to deliver after the goods have been shipped. This is feasible by use of the device of carriers' negotiable or "order" bills of lading. A bill of lading (originally a bill of "loading") is a document that a carrier (e.g., railroad, trucking company, ship owner, air freight carrier) issues when goods are delivered to it for shipment.[14] An "order" bill of lading typically provides:

> The surrender of this Original Bill of Lading properly indorsed shall be required before the delivery of the property.

This states a carrier's contractual duty to the shipper, but it also restates the carrier's legal duty, once it has issued an "order" bill, under federal or state law.[15]

---

13. Specifications and arrangements relating to shipment are at the seller's option unless otherwise agreed. UCC 2–311(2).

14. A bill of lading, in part, embodies the contract between the carrier and the shipper (often termed the *consignor*). A number of terms are printed on the front of printed bills of lading where terms describing specific shipments are filled in; the back contains more standard contract terms densely packed in small print. The bill of lading identifies the carrier receiving the goods, the shipper, the goods, the intended destination, the consignee, and possibly other terms. In this course, we are concerned with only those aspects of carriage contracts that are significant to the performance of sales transactions.

Carriers issue two kinds of bills of lading, the "order bill of lading" and the "straight bill of lading." Under the "straight" bill, the carrier undertakes to deliver the goods at the destination to a stated person, e.g., "to Buyer & Co." Under the "order" bill of lading, the carrier agrees to deliver *to the order of* a stated person, e.g., to "the order of Seller & Co."

When sales contracts use the trade terms, C.I.F. or C. & F., sellers are required to obtain negotiable bills of lading. UCC 2–320(2)(a); see also UCC 2–323(1).

15. The law governing interstate and export shipments is federal law, the 1916 Federal Bills of Lading (or Pomerene) Act, 49 U.S.C. App. §§ 81 to 124. Excerpts of the Pomerene Act are reprinted in an Appendix of this book. The most pertinent provisions are § 88(b)(carrier is bound to deliver goods under an order bill to one who surrenders the bill, properly indorsed, to the carrier, and § 90 (carrier is liable for delivery of the goods to a person not entitled thereto). See also §§ 89, 91.

The law governing intrastate carriage is state law, found in Article 7 of the Commercial Code. The relevant sections of Article 7 cover both bills of lading and their cousins, warehouse receipts. The legal responsibility of carriers (or warehousemen) to deliver is found in UCC 7–403 and 7–404. A key concept under the Code is "person entitled under the document," defined in 7–403(4), to whom the carrier must deliver under 7–403(1). Liability for failure to cancel an "order" bill of lading is stated in 7–403(3).

When a seller ships goods under an "order" bill of lading, UCC 2–504(b) adds a third requirement to seller's manner of execution of sales contracts. Seller must tender to buyer the bill of lading in a form that permits the buyer to obtain possession of the goods from the carrier. The Code provides that "tender [of such documents] through customary banking channels is sufficient." UCC 2–503(5). Through "banking channels" or otherwise, a seller can transmit documents to a buyer.

Time of Sellers' Tender. When sellers are authorized or required to ship goods to buyers via carriers, the matter of time of performance has multiple phases: when must seller deliver to carrier, when must seller give notice of shipment to buyer, and when must carrier deliver to buyer? If seller ships under an "order" bill of lading, when must seller tender that document?

If the sales contract is a "place of shipment" contract, it may provide that seller must ship within a stated time, but in the absence of agreement the reasonable-time standard would apply. UCC 2–309(1). Once a shipment is begun, notification to buyer must be made "promptly." UCC 2–504(c). Tender of any documents needed to obtain possession of goods must also be made "promptly" under UCC 2–504(b).

If the sales contract requires delivery at a particular destination, it may provide that seller must deliver there within a stated time, but again, in the absence of agreement, the reasonable-time standard would apply.

Manner, Time and Place of Buyers' Tender. The Commercial Code contains default rules for the manner, time and place of tender of payment when goods are delivered by carrier. Unless otherwise agreed, payment is due at the time and place at which the buyer is to receive the goods. UCC 2–310(a). This rule applies even though the place of shipment is the place of delivery, e.g., as in F.O.B. "the place of shipment" contracts.[16] Buyers ordinarily receive shipped goods at the termination of the carriage. Sellers may designate an agent to receive payment at that time and place, but in the absence of someone authorized to receive payment, buyers may send it to sellers. This is easily and commonly done by mailing checks.

The Commercial Code provisions create several difficult problems of construction. The Code gives some meaning to the distinction between "at a particular destination" contracts and other shipment contracts through the Code's definitions of certain common trade terms. If parties enter into contracts that authorize sellers to ship goods via carriers, but do not use the Code-defined trade terms, characterization of the contracts under UCC 2–503 and 2–504 poses difficulties.

---

16. This rule applies whether or not sellers ship goods under negotiable or "order" bills of lading. If seller tenders a document of title, "the buyer may inspect the goods after their arrival before payment is due unless such inspection is inconsistent with the terms of the contract (Section 2–513)." UCC 2–310(b). Some buyers agree to pay against tender of documents. We will consider those agreements in a later section.

Comment 5 to 2–503 declares that the drafters of the Code intentionally omitted the rule under prior uniform legislation that a contract term requiring a seller to pay the freight or costs of transportation was equivalent to an agreement to deliver to the buyer or at an agreed destination and regard the-place-of-shipment contract as "the normal one." The Comment continues:

> The seller is not obligated to deliver at a named destination ... unless he has specifically agreed so to deliver or the commercial understanding of the terms used by the parties contemplates such delivery.

Does the Comment go beyond the text of the Code? Does it provide a reasonable interpretation of the text? [17]

Problem 6. Buyer telephoned Catalogue Seller and ordered a compact disc player. In the conversation, Buyer said: "Please send the CD player by parcel post." Seller accepted the order without more being said about the price or delivery. Is the contract a place-of-shipment or at-a-particular-destination contract? Which party must pay the parcel post charges? See Pestana v. Karinol Corp., 367 So.2d 1096 (Fla.App. 1979).

Problem 7. National Heater Co., located in St. Paul, Minnesota, offered to sell heating units to Corrigan Co. to be used by the buyer in construction of an automobile plant in Fenton, Missouri. National Heater's written proposal of the terms of sale stated the price as $275,640, "F.O.B. St. Paul, Minn. with freight allowed." Corrigan then submitted a purchase order with the following: "Price $275,640—Delivered." National Heater sent an acknowledgment which included: "$275,640 Total Delivered to Rail Siding." Is the contract a place-of-shipment or at-a-particular-destination contract? See National Heater Co. v. Corrigan Co., 482 F.2d 87 (8th Cir.1973).

(3) TRANSACTIONS IN GOODS NOT TO BE MOVED

For many reasons, owners of goods, having put them into storage, may decide to sell them to buyers who want to keep the goods where they are. The person with custody of the goods, perhaps a warehouse operator, is characterized legally as a bailee. Performance rules for sales contracts in which goods are not to be moved require, in substance, that seller transfer to buyer the bailee's obligation to surrender the goods on demand. Such rules are provided in UCC 2–503(4) for transactions in which the parties have not specifically described the manner of sellers' performance.

---

17. The Permanent Editorial Board Study Group on UCC Article 2 stated:
Without FOB terms in the agreement, § 2–319(1), it is not clear when a seller who is authorized to ship goods is "required to deliver at a particular destination." § 2–503(3). Comment 5 to § 2–503 provides a rule for construction. [We recommend] that this rule of construction be placed in the text of either § 2–319(1) or § 2–503.

Preliminary Report 134 (1990). See also id. at 115.

An example of a market situation in which goods may be sold without intent to move them at the time of sale occurs in sales of propane and natural gas, which are held in huge underground storage facilities. Sellers and buyers perform contracts for sale of the goods by transfer to buyers of commitments to deliver by operators of the storage facilities. See., e.g., Commonwealth Petroleum Co. v. Petrosol International, Inc., 901 F.2d 1314 (6th Cir.1990).

An analogous transaction situation occurs when owners of goods, having put them into the possession of a carrier for transportation, decides to sell them to buyers. The carrier with custody of the goods is not generally characterized as a bailee and the goods are being moved as they are sold. While 2–503(4) is not literally applicable to transactions of goods sold in transit, seller's performance obligation must be to transfer to buyer the carrier's obligation to transport and deliver the goods.

In the oil business, crude oil in holds of supertankers moving across oceans is often bought and sold many times while the ships are en route.

Manner, Time, and Place of Sellers' Tender. Some bailees in possession of goods issue negotiable documents of title, similar to negotiable bills of lading issued by carriers, that control the right to obtain possession of the goods.[18] If goods are covered by such a document, seller performs its obligation under the sales contract by tendering the document. UCC 2–503(4)(a). The Code contains no provisions on the time or place for such tenders.

When goods are stored with a bailee who has not issued a negotiable document of title, tender occurs when seller's procure the bailee's acknowledgment of buyer's right to the goods. UCC 2–504(a). Sellers may tender by procuring that acknowledgment and notifying buyer or by giving buyer a document or written direction to the bailee to deliver goods to the buyer. The bailee's refusal to honor the document or direction "defeats" the tender. UCC 2–503(4)(b).

(B) INTERNATIONAL SALES LAW

The Convention on International Sale of Goods states the general obligation of buyers and sellers. Article 30 provides:

> The seller must deliver the goods, hand over any documents relating to them and transfer the property in the goods, as required by the contract and this Convention.

Article 53 is the reciprocal provision for buyers:

> The buyer must pay the price for the goods and take delivery of them as required by the contract and this Convention.

---

18. The governing law is Article 7 of the Commercial Code. The prototypical document of title issued by a bailee is a warehouse receipt. UCC 1–201(45), 7–202.

The Convention does not use the concept of *tender* for either party's performance.

Manner and Place of Delivery. Sales contracts between parties from different nations are highly likely to require use of carriers. Absent agreement on the nature of sellers' performance, sellers' obligation has the following three or four steps: Seller "must make such contracts as are necessary for carriage to the place fixed [by agreement] by means of transportation appropriate in the circumstances and according to the usual terms for such transportation." CISG 32(2). Seller must "hand ... the goods over to the first carrier for transmission to the buyer." CISG 31(a). If the goods are not clearly identified to the sales contract, by markings on the goods or by documents or otherwise, when handed over to the carrier, seller must give buyer notice of the consignment, CISG 32(1); the Convention does not require sellers to give notice of shipment in all transactions. Finally, seller "must ... hand over [to the buyer] any documents relating to [the goods]." CISG 30.[19]

Unlike the Commercial Code the Convention does not distinguish between place-of-shipment and at-a-particular-destination contracts. The latter are not contemplated, no doubt in light of prevailing mercantile practice.

> [E]ven when the seller undertakes to pay freight costs to destination under "C.I.F." and "C. & F." ... quotations, it has long been settled that the seller ... completes his delivery duties ... when the goods are (at the latest) loaded on the carrier.

J. Honnold, Uniform Law for International Sales § 209 (2d ed. 1991). Moreover, the Convention, unlike the Code, contains no provisions regarding the meaning of shipment terms.[20]

---

19. Sellers are bound to hand over documents relating to the goods "at the time and place and in the form required by the contract." CISG 34. The Convention has no default rule for when and where this is to occur.

20. By contract, parties to international sales contracts may refer to a set of trade terms promulgated by the International Chamber of Commerce (ICC), which are known as *Incoterms*. The ICC is a nongovernmental organization with members from 110 countries.

Incoterms, last revised in 1990, categorize shipping or delivery terms into four principal categories: main carriage paid by seller (e.g., Cost and Freight, CFR, or CIF), main carriage paid by buyer (e.g., FOB, FAS), departure terms (Ex Works), and arrival terms (e.g., Delivered Ex Ship or DES). *Incoterms 1990* do not use FOB other than at port of shipment. Departure terms do not oblige sellers to contract for carriage. The arrival term, DES, requires a seller to place the goods at the disposal of the buyer on board the vessel at the usual unloading point in the named port of destination.

During the drafting of the Convention, consideration was given to inclusion of a term that would have had the effect of incorporating trade terms in common usage, like *Incoterms*, into all international sales contracts. This proposal was opposed, in part because it would impose trade terms on a party, perhaps one from a developing country, whether or not it knew or ought to have known of them. The Convention's general provision on trade usage would direct tribunals to consider *Incoterms* if both parties knew or ought to have known of them. CISG 9(2). See J. Honnold, Uniform Law for International Sales § 118 and n. 5 (2d ed. 1991).

The Convention provides default rules for performance of contracts that do not involve carriage of goods. Seller's obligation to deliver consists of "placing the goods at the buyer's disposal at the place where the seller had his place of business at the time of the conclusion of the contract," CISG 31(c), unless the parties knew from the circumstances of the contract that the goods would be placed at buyer's disposal at another location. CISG 31(b).

The CISG has no provision regarding the manner of delivery of goods held in storage or in transit.[21]

Time of Delivery. The Convention looks to the parties' contract as the primary source of the time term. CISG 33(a). Often, international sales contracts specify a period of time within which delivery is to occur. The agreement may provide further how an exact date will be set by one or both of the parties. If a period of time is stated without more, CISG 33(b) states a default rule that permits the seller to choose to perform "at any time within that period unless circumstances indicate that the buyer is to choose a date." When the contract is silent on time, CISG 33(c) requires a seller to perform "within a reasonable time after the conclusion of the contract."

Problem 8. Seller and Buyer contracted for sale of 12,000 tons of sugar to be delivered at the port of Dunkirk in May or June 1986 on board one or more ships provided by Buyer. The contract required Buyer to give Seller not less than 14 days' notice of the vessels' readiness to load. The contract also incorporated by reference the Rules of the London Refined Sugar Association. One Rule stated: "the seller shall have the sugar ready to be delivered at any time within the contract period." Another Rule provided: "the buyer, having given reasonable notice, shall be entitled to call for delivery of the sugar between the first and the last working days inclusive of the contract period." A third Rule stated that the buyer was responsible for costs incurred by the seller if the nominated vessel did not present herself within five days of the date specified in the buyer's notice. On May 15, Buyer gave notice calling on Seller to load the sugar on board the *Naxos,* estimated to arrive in Dunkirk between May 29 and 31. The *Naxos* was at the dock in Dunkirk and ready to load on May 29. Seller informed Buyer that the sugar would be available on June 3. Under the CISG, was Seller then in breach of contract? See Compagnie Commerciale Sucres et Denrees v. C. Czarnikow Ltd. (*The Naxos*), [1990] 1 W.L.R. 1337 (H.L.), reversing [1989] 2 Lloyd's Rep. 462 (C.A.).[22]

***Nachfrist* Provisions.** The Convention permits either party to a sales contract to extend the time for sellers' performance beyond that

---

21. But see CISG 68 (risk of loss provision regarding goods sold while in transit).

22. Applying British domestic sales law, the House of Lords held that seller was bound to have the sugar ready for loading immediately upon the ship's arrival. Seller contended that the contract permitted commencement of loading within a reasonable time after the ship had arrived. The House of Lords construed the notice provision of the agreement and the Rules to require the seller to have the sugar at the dock, ready to be loaded, when the ship arrived.

required in sales contracts. The provisions derive from German law, where the word, "*Nachfrist*," is used. The dynamics of these provisions when exercised by buyers differ from the dynamics when exercised by sellers.

A seller may, even after the date for delivery, notify the buyer of intent to remedy a failure in performance and request additional time to do so.[23] The buyer may acquiesce or refuse seller's request, but if buyer does not respond within a reasonable time, seller may perform within the time indicated in its request. CISG 48(2).

The Convention provides that the buyer, too, "may fix an additional period of time of reasonable length for performance by the seller of his obligations." CISG 47(1). A commercial rationale for this provision is not quickly apparent; one can comprehend sellers needing and seeking additional time to remedy performance failures, but why would buyers thrust more time on sellers? As we will see in the next section, a *Nachfrist* notice "fixing" an additional but final period for performance plays an important role in the Convention's remedial system.

Buyers' Tender of Payment. The Convention does not have any provisions on the manner of buyers' payment beyond the requirement in CISG 54 that a buyer's obligation includes "taking such steps and complying with such formalities as may be required under the contract or any laws and regulations to enable payment to be made."

Time and Place of Buyers' Tender. Unless otherwise agreed, a buyer must pay when the seller places either the goods or documents controlling their disposition at the buyer's disposal in accordance with the contract and this Convention." CISG 58(1). If payment is to be made against the handing over of goods or of documents, a buyer must pay "at the place where the handing over takes place." CISG 57(1)(b). Otherwise, payment must be made "at the seller's place of business." CISG 57(1)(a).

Inspection of Goods Before Payment. Absent agreement to the contrary, buyers are not bound to pay the price until they have had opportunity to examine the goods. CISG 58(3).

SECTION 2. ACCEPTANCE, REJECTION, AND CURE; AVOIDANCE

(A) DOMESTIC UNITED STATES LAW

(1) ACCEPTANCE AND REJECTION

Buyers' Duty to Accept Goods. UCC 2–301 declares that buyers are obligated to "accept" goods delivered by sellers, and UCC 2–507(1)

---

23. Seller's notice alone that it will perform within a specified period of time is assumed to include a request. CISG 48(3).

states that: "tender entitles the seller to [buyer's] acceptance of the goods...." In this section, we consider the nature and significance of the obligation to accept goods.

Although not clearly stated, the Code's provisions cannot be read reasonably to impose on buyers the obligation to accept non-conforming goods or goods tendered in a manner, time or place that does not conform to sellers' obligation. Implicit in buyers' obligation is the condition that the tender and the tendered goods conform to the contract.

Buyers' Right to Reject Goods. The opposite of acceptance is rejection. Buyers may reject non-conforming goods or goods tendered other than in conformity with the contract. The provisions on rejection are found in UCC 2–601 and 2–612(2).

Significance of Acceptance or Rejection. Acceptance of goods is a significant legal watershed: at that moment the legal positions of a buyer and a seller change substantially. Acceptance precludes rejection. UCC 2–607(2). The buyer must pay at the contract rate for any goods accepted. UCC 2–607(3). If the buyer does not pay for accepted goods, seller has an action for the price. UCC 2–709(1)(a). In any subsequent litigation, such as an action for breach of warranty, the burden is on the buyer to establish any breach with respect to accepted goods. UCC 2–607(4). Acceptance of goods does not deprive buyers of monetary remedies if the goods do not conform to the requirements of the contract.[1] Unless time-barred under UCC 2–725 or barred for lack of notice under UCC 2–607(3)(a), aggrieved buyers may recover damages under UCC 2–714 and 2–715.[2]

Rejection of goods, if rightful, means that seller has failed to meet its obligation to make due tender of conforming goods. If seller does not make a conforming tender to "cure" whatever was amiss, UCC 2–508, buyer is released from obligation to pay the contract price, UCC 2–507(1), and is entitled to monetary remedies, which are catalogued in UCC 2–711. In addition to recovering any part of the contract price paid, UCC 2–711(1), buyer is entitled to damages measured by the cost of purchasing substitute goods ("cover") from another source, UCC 2–712, or by the differential between market price and contract price, UCC 2–713, together with incidental or consequential damages under UCC 2–715. Responsibility for disposition of rejected goods is on seller,

---

1. Nearly all the breach of warranty of quality cases and problems in Chapter 3 and breach of the warranty of title cases and problems in Chapter 2 involved buyers who had accepted goods. Significant exceptions were the sale of cattle in Wright v. Vickaryous, Chapter 2, and the Bolivian flour sale in T.J. Stevenson & Son v. 81,193 Bags of Flour, Chapter 3, section 2, supra.

2. Monetary relief under UCC 2–714 and 2–715 is not the sole remedy for aggrieved buyers. Some are empowered to revoke their acceptances. UCC 2–608. We consider revocation of acceptance in a subsequent section.

although some buyers have the right or duty to act on seller's behalf in disposing of them.[3]

Manner of Buyers' Acceptance of Goods. The Commercial Code has a three-pronged definition of how buyers' accept goods: (1) overt statements to sellers, (2) estoppel resulting from buyers' handling of the goods, and (3) lapse of time after delivery or tender of delivery. UCC 2–606(1).

In most ordinary commercial and consumer transactions, acceptance is the result of mere lapse of time. Sometimes a buyer may "signif[y] to the seller that the goods are conforming or that he will take them or retain them in spite of their non-conformity," UCC 2–606(1)(a), but, more likely, buyers' receive goods and simply say nothing to the seller about conformity or non-conformity.[4] Continued silence becomes "failure to make an effective rejection," UCC 2–606(1)(b), because "rejection of goods must be within a reasonable time after their delivery or tender." UCC 2–602(1).[5]

Time of Acceptance: Inspection of Goods Before Acceptance. Acceptance by signification or by lapse of time cannot occur until buyers have had "a reasonable opportunity to inspect" the goods. UCC 2–606(1)(a) and (b), 2–513(1). We considered, in Section 1, buyers' right to inspect before the obligation to pay matured. The same provisions of the Code condition both the obligation to accept and the obligation to pay with buyers' right to inspect. The Code declares that buyers may inspect goods "in any reasonable manner," UCC 2–513(1), but offers no criteria for determining what inspection methods are reasonable.

ZABRISKIE CHEVROLET, INC. v. SMITH, 99 N.J. Super. 441, 240 A.2d 195 (1968). Buyer, who had paid by personal check, discovered a non-conformity after driving 7/10 of a mile from dealer's showroom.

3. If a non-merchant buyer has taken possession of goods before rejecting them, buyer must hold the goods with reasonable care for a time sufficient to permit seller to remove them, UCC 2–602(2)(b), but has no further obligations with regard to the goods. UCC 2–602(2)(c). A merchant buyer in possession of rejected goods must follow seller's reasonable instructions. UCC 2–603(1). A merchant buyer in possession of perishable goods or goods whose market value may decline speedily, in the absence of seller's instructions, must make reasonable efforts to sell the goods for the seller's account. Id. If sellers give no instructions within a reasonable time after notification of rejection, buyers may store the goods, ship them back to sellers, or sell them for the sellers' accounts. UCC 2–604.

Resales of goods before rejection would normally constitute acceptances of the goods under the provision that an act inconsistent with sellers' ownership constitutes acceptance. UCC 2–606(1)(c). However, resale of rightfully rejected goods in conformity with the Code is neither acceptance nor conversion of them. UCC 2–603(3), 2–604.

4. Businesses courting good will sometimes inquire about customer satisfaction with the goods received. This may produce express responses, but thank-you notes or equivalent are not commonplace occurrences in marketplace transactions.

5. The third prong, "does any act inconsistent with the seller's ownership," UCC 2–606(1)(c), is based on buyers' conduct. Common acts that may fit this prong are buyers' consumption of the goods or transfer of them to a sub-purchaser.

Buyer stopped payment on the check. Seller contended that buyer had accepted the car and sued for the purchase price. In deciding the buyer had not accepted the car, the court concluded that buyer had not completed his inspection of it when he paid and drove it away: "To the layman, the complicated mechanisms of today's automobiles are a complete mystery. To have the automobile inspected [in the showroom] by someone with sufficient expertise to disassemble the vehicle in order to discover latent defects ... is assuredly impossible and highly impractical. ... Consequently, the first few miles of driving become even more significant to the excited new car buyer. This is the buyer's first reasonable opportunity ... to see if it conforms to what it was represented to be.... . How long the buyer may drive the new car under the guise of inspection is not an issue in the present case."

PLATEQ CORP. v. MACHLETT LABORATORIES

Supreme Court of Connecticut, 1983.
189 Conn. 433, 456 A.2d 786.

PETERS, JUDGE.

In this action by a seller of specially manufactured goods to recover their purchase price from a commercial buyer, the principal issue is whether the buyer accepted the goods before it attempted to cancel the contract of sale. The plaintiff, Plateq Corporation of North Haven, sued the defendant, The Machlett Laboratories, Inc., to recover damages, measured by the contract price and incidental damages, arising out of the defendant's allegedly wrongful cancellation of a written contract for the manufacture and sale of two leadcovered steel tanks and appurtenant stands. The defendant denied liability and counterclaimed for damages. After a full hearing, the trial court found for the plaintiff both on its complaint and on the defendant's counterclaim. The defendant has appealed.

The trial court, in its memorandum of decision, found the following facts. On July 9, 1976, the defendant ordered from the plaintiff two leadcovered steel tanks to be constructed by the plaintiff according to specifications supplied by the defendant. The parties understood that the tanks were designed for the special purpose of testing x-ray tubes and were required to be radiation-proof within certain federal standards. Accordingly, the contract provided that the tanks would be tested for radiation leaks after their installation on the defendant's premises. The plaintiff undertook to correct, at its own cost, any deficiencies that this post-installation test might uncover. The plaintiff had not previously constructed such tanks, nor had the defendant previously designed tanks for this purpose. The contract was amended on August 9, 1976, to add construction of two metal stands to hold the tanks. All the goods were to be delivered to the defendant at the plaintiff's place of business.

Although the plaintiff encountered difficulties both in performing according to the contract specifications and in completing performance within the time required, the defendant did no more than call these deficiencies to the plaintiff's attention during various inspections in September and early October, 1976. By October 11, 1976, performance was belatedly but substantially completed. On that date, Albert Yannello, the defendant's engineer, noted some remaining deficiencies which the plaintiff promised to remedy by the next day, so that the goods would then be ready for delivery. Yannello gave no indication to the plaintiff that this arrangement was in any way unsatisfactory to the defendant. Not only did Yannello communicate general acquiescence in the plaintiff's proposed tender but he specifically led the plaintiff to believe that the defendant's truck would pick up the tanks and the stands within a day or two. Instead of sending its truck, the defendant sent a notice of total cancellation which the plaintiff received on October 14, 1976. That notice failed to particularize the grounds upon which cancellation was based.[3]

On this factual basis, the trial court, having concluded that the transaction was a contract for the sale of goods falling within the Uniform Commercial Code, General Statutes §§ 42a–2–101 et seq., considered whether the defendant had accepted the goods. The court determined that the defendant had accepted the tanks, primarily by signifying its willingness to take them despite their nonconformities, in accordance with General Statutes § 42a–2–606(1)(a), and secondarily by failing to make an effective rejection, in accordance with General Statutes § 42a–2–606(1)(b). Once the tanks had been accepted, the defendant could rightfully revoke its acceptance under General Statutes § 42a–2–608 only by showing substantial impairment of their value to the defendant. In part because the defendant's conduct had foreclosed any post-installation inspection, the court concluded that such impairment had not been proved. Since the tanks were not readily resalable on the open market, the plaintiff was entitled, upon the defendant's wrongful revocation of acceptance, to recover their contract price, minus salvage value, plus interest. General Statutes §§ 42a–2–703; 42a–2–709(1)(b). Accordingly, the trial court awarded the plaintiff damages in the amount of $14,837.92.

. . .

Upon analysis, all of the defendant's claims of error are variations upon one central theme. The defendant claims that on October 11, when its engineer Yannello conducted the last examination on the plaintiff's premises, the tanks were so incomplete and unsatisfactory that the defendant was rightfully entitled to conclude that the plaintiff would never make a conforming tender. From this scenario, the defendant argues that it was justified in cancelling the contract of sale. It denies that the seller's conduct was sufficient to warrant a finding of

---

3. The defendant sent the plaintiff a telegram stating: "This order is hereby terminated for your breach, in that you have continuously failed to perform according to your commitment in spite of additional time given you to cure your delinquency. We will hold you liable for all damages incurred [sic] by Machlett including excess cost of reprocurement."

tender, or its own conduct sufficient to warrant a finding of acceptance. The difficulty with this argument is that it is inconsistent with the underlying facts found by the trial court. Although the testimony was in dispute, there was evidence of record to support the trial court's findings to the contrary. ... There is simply no fit between the defendant's claims and the trial court's finding that, by October 11, 1976, performance was in substantial compliance with the terms of the contract. The trial court further found that on that day the defendant was notified that the goods would be ready for tender the following day and that the defendant responded to this notification by promising to send its truck to pick up the tanks in accordance with the contract.

On the trial court's finding of facts, it was warranted in concluding, on two independent grounds, that the defendant had accepted the goods it had ordered from the plaintiff. Under the provisions of the Uniform Commercial Code, General Statutes § 42a–2–606(1), "[a]cceptance of goods occurs when the buyer (a) after a reasonable opportunity to inspect the goods signifies to the seller ... that he will take ... them in spite of their nonconformity; or (b) fails to make an effective rejection."

In concluding that the defendant had "signified" to the plaintiff its willingness to "take" the tanks despite possible remaining minor defects, the trial court necessarily found that the defendant had had a reasonable opportunity to inspect the goods. The defendant does not maintain that its engineer, or the other inspectors on previous visits, had inadequate access to the tanks, or inadequate experience to conduct a reasonable examination. It recognizes that inspection of goods when the buyer undertakes to pick up the goods is ordinarily at the seller's place of tender. See General Statutes §§ 42a–2–503, 42a–2–507, 42a–2–513; see also White & Summers, Uniform Commercial Code § 3–5 (2d Ed.1980). The defendant argues, however, that its contract, in providing for inspection for radiation leaks after installation of the tanks at its premises, necessarily postponed its inspection rights to that time. The trial court considered this argument and rejected it, and so do we. It was reasonable, in the context of this contract for the special manufacture of goods with which neither party had had prior experience, to limit this clause to adjustments to take place after tender and acceptance. After acceptance, a buyer may still, in appropriate cases, revoke its acceptance, General Statutes § 42a–2–608, or recover damages for breach of warranty, General Statutes § 42a–2–714. The trial court reasonably concluded that a post-installation test was intended to safeguard these rights of the defendant as well as to afford the plaintiff a final opportunity to make needed adjustments. The court was therefore justified in concluding that there had been an acceptance within § 42a–2–606(1)(a). A buyer may be found to have accepted goods despite their known nonconformity ... and despite the absence of actual delivery to the buyer. ...

. . .

Once the conclusion is reached that the defendant accepted the tanks, its further rights of cancellation under the contract are limited by the governing provisions of the Uniform Commercial Code. "The buyer's acceptance of goods, despite their alleged nonconformity, is a watershed. After acceptance, the buyer must pay for the goods at the contract rate; General Statutes § 42a–2–607(1); and bears the burden of establishing their nonconformity. General Statutes § 42a–2–607(4)."
.... After acceptance, the buyer may only avoid liability for the contract price by invoking the provision which permits revocation of acceptance. That provision, General Statutes § 42a–2–608(1), requires proof that the "nonconformity [of the goods] substantially impairs [their] value to him." ... On this question, ... the trial court again found against the defendant. Since the defendant has provided no basis for any argument that the trial court was clearly erroneous in finding that the defendant had not met its burden of proof to show that the goods were substantially nonconforming, we can find no error in the conclusion that the defendant's cancellation constituted an unauthorized and hence wrongful revocation of acceptance.

Finally, the defendant in its brief, although not in its statement of the issues presented, challenges the trial court's conclusion about the remedial consequences of its earlier determinations. Although the trial court might have found the plaintiff entitled to recover the contract price because of the defendant's acceptance of the goods; General Statutes §§ 42a–2–703(e) and 42a–2–709(1)(a); the court chose instead to rely on General Statutes § 42a–2–709(1)(b), which permits a price action for contract goods that cannot, after reasonable effort, be resold at a reasonable price.[19] Since the contract goods in this case were concededly specially manufactured for the defendant, the defendant cannot and does not contest the trial court's finding that any effort to resell them on the open market would have been unavailing. In the light of this finding, the defendant can only reiterate its argument, which we have already rejected, that the primary default was that of the plaintiff rather than that of the defendant. The trial court's conclusion to the contrary supports both its award to the plaintiff and its denial of the defendant's counterclaim.

There is no error.

---

19. ... It should be noted that § 42a–2–709(1)(b) is not premised on a buyer's acceptance. Instead, it requires a showing that the goods were, before the buyer's cancellation, "identified to the contract." In the circumstances of this case, that precondition was presumably met by their special manufacture and by the defendant's acquiescence in their imminent tender. See White & Summers, Uniform Commercial Code, § 7–5 (2d Ed.1980). The defendant has not, on this appeal, argued the absence of identification.

It should further be noted that § 42a–2–709(1)(b), because it is not premised on acceptance, would have afforded the seller the right to recover the contract price even if the trial court had found the conduct of the buyer to be a wrongful rejection (because of the failure to give the seller an opportunity to cure) rather than a wrongful revocation of acceptance.

Acceptance or Rejection of Goods Delivered by Carrier. In "at a particular destination" contracts, when sellers tender goods through carriers at the stated place, buyers accept or reject in response to such tenders in the same way as they perform the acceptance obligation in transactions performed without carriers. Within a reasonable time after tender, they must elect to accept or reject the goods. UCC 2–606(1)(b).

In "the place of shipment" contracts, tender may be completed before arrival of the goods, but the time period for a buyer to accept or reject does not begin to run until buyer has had an opportunity to inspect the goods. UCC 2–606(1)(b). Unless the agreement designates a different time and place, the inspection opportunity begins when the goods have arrived. UCC 2–513(1). Thus, within a reasonable time after arrival of the goods, buyers must elect to accept or reject the goods. UCC 2–606(1)(b).

In "the place of shipment" contracts, sellers must do more than deliver conforming goods; sellers are also required to make proper contracts for transportation and to give buyers prompt notice of shipment. Sellers' failure on either score is a ground for rejection "only if material delay or loss ensues." UCC 2–504.

Manner and Time of Buyers' Rejection of Goods. Rejection of goods is the antithesis of acceptance. It must be made before lapse of a reasonable time after tender or delivery. UCC 2–602(1). The only way for a buyer to reject effectively is to notify the seller seasonably. UCC 2–602(1). The Code does not prescribe the minimum content of an effective rejection notice, but does provide that certain buyers' failure to describe particular defects will preclude them from later relying on unstated defects to justify their rejection or to establish sellers' breach. UCC 2–605.[6]

Effective Rejection and Transfer of Possession. Rejection decisions may be, and frequently are, made at the time of sellers' tender of goods, with the result that buyers refuse to take possession of the tendered goods. However, buyers who take possession of goods, without signifying that they accept them, may thereafter elect to reject them. Refusals to take possession of tendered goods usually occurs in contexts that notify sellers of buyers' choice to reject. However, when change of possession occurs without buyers' choosing whether to accept or reject, what must buyers do to make an effective rejection? What must they do with the rejected goods in their possession? Consider the following problems.

Problem 1. Grain Supply and Miller made a contract for the sale to Miller of 1,000 bushels of wheat at $5.00 per bushel. The contract specified that the wheat would be delivered on June 1, and would be of No. 1 milling quality, free of weevil; Miller was to pay the price of

---

[6]. Compare the necessary content of buyers' notices to sellers with regard to non-conformity of accepted goods. UCC 2–607(3)(a) and Comment 4.

$5,000 within 60 days after delivery. On delivery of the wheat, Miller inspected the wheat and found that it was "crawling" with weevils and was totally unfit for milling; he instructed his manager to sell the wheat for chicken feed. The manager suggested that they get in touch with Supply and work out some adjustment. Miller, thoroughly disgusted with Supply's performance, said: "I'm not having anything more to do with that outfit. Just let them try to collect for this rotten stuff." The wheat, sold for chicken feed, brought only $2,000—a fair price under the circumstances. Three months later, Supply called Miller and reminded him that the bill was overdue. Miller said "You should know that I won't pay for such a rotten shipment," and hung up.

Supply brought an action to recover the contract price for the wheat. Miller counterclaimed on grounds of breach of express and implied warranty and demanded damages resulting from the necessity of purchasing the No. 1 wheat elsewhere at $6.00 per bushel.

(a) What result in Supply's action to recover the contract price? UCC 2–709, 2–606.

(b) What result in Miller's counterclaim for damages? UCC 2–607(3)(a); Economy Forms Corp. v. Kandy, 391 F.Supp. 944 (N.D.Ga. 1974). For criticism see 15 UCC L.Rev. 105 (1982); 61 N.Car.L.Rev. 177 (1982).

Problem 2. Assume that in Problem 1, when the wheat arrived on June 1, Miller wired Grain Supply, "Wheat defective. Holding you responsible." Supply did not respond. Miller stored the wheat in his warehouse, and two months later (on August 1) Miller wired Supply, "What do you want done with your weevily wheat?" Supply wired back, "You bought the wheat, and I expect you to pay your bill," and brought suit. Miller interposed all available defenses and counterclaims.

By the time of trial, the wheat, which at delivery had been worth $2,000 for chicken feed, had been further damaged by the weevils; and in the meantime the price level for feed grains had dropped so that the shipment was worth only $300.

(a) May Miller defeat the claim for payment of the price on the ground that he has made an effective rejection of the goods? See UCC 2–607(1), 2–606(1)(b), 2–602(1); Boysen v. Antioch Sheet Metal, 16 Ill. App.3d 331, 306 N.E.2d 69 (1974); Louis Sherry Ice Cream Co. v. Harlem River Consumers' Cooperative, 18 UCC Rep. 97 (Sup.Ct.N.Y.Co., 1975) (purchase of perishable commodity).

(b) Assume that the court finds that Miller's rejection was not effective. What judgment should be entered? Was Miller's brief wire of June 1 adequate to meet the requirements of UCC 2–607(3)(a)? (See Comment 4.) Who bears the loss from deterioration and price decline that occurred after delivery? See UCC 2–510(1), 2–606(1)(b), 2–714.

(2) RIGHTFUL REJECTION

One of most controverted issues in sales law is the standard for determining when buyers are entitled to reject goods that have been tendered or delivered. Sellers sometimes fail to carry out contract commitments, but margins of failure can be large or small. Do insignificant or minor failures justify rejections? Buyers dissatisfied with their bargains may be tempted to reject goods or tenders that are conforming, or almost so. A not surprising example occurs when the contract price for the goods is higher than the market price prevailing at the time of tender; a narrowly self-interested buyer will prefer to buy on the market and be relieved of the obligation to pay the higher contract price. These matters underlie the normative standards for rightful rejection.

The "Perfect Tender Rule." The basic standard that differentiates rightful from wrongful rejection is UCC 2–601.[7] In ordinary cases, a buyer is permitted to reject "if the goods or the tender of delivery fail in any respect to conform to the contract." Common legal usage refers to this standard as the "perfect tender rule."[8] Goods or the tender of delivery may fail to conform to the contract in many respects, but four tend to predominate: clouds on title, defects in quality, deficiencies or excesses in quantity, and late deliveries.

MOULTON CAVITY & MOLD, INC. v. LYN–FLEX INDUSTRIES, INC.
Supreme Judicial Court of Maine, 1979.
396 A.2d 1024.

DELAHANTY, JUSTICE.

Defendant, Lyn–Flex Industries, Inc., appeals from a judgment entered after a jury trial by the Superior Court, York County, in favor of plaintiff, Moulton Cavity & Mold, Inc. The case concerns itself with an oral contract for the sale of goods which, as both parties agree, is governed by Article 2 of the Uniform Commercial Code, 11 M.R.S.A. §§ 2–101 et seq. For the reasons set forth below, we agree with defendant that the presiding Justice committed reversible error by instructing the jury that the doctrine of substantial performance applied to a contract for the sale of goods. We do not agree, however, that based on the evidence introduced at trial defendant is entitled to judgment in its favor as a matter of law. The appeal is therefore sustained and the case remanded for a new trial.

An examination of the record discloses the following sequence of events: On March 19, 1975, Lynwood Moulton, president of plaintiff,

---

7. Buyers are permitted, of course, to accept goods known to be non-conforming. See UCC 2–607(2). There is no concept of wrongful acceptance.

8. Comment 2 to UCC 2–106(2)(definition of "conforming") states: "It is in general intended to continue the policy of exact performance by the seller of his obligations as a condition to his right to require acceptance."

and Ernest Sturman, president of defendant, orally agreed that plaintiff would produce, and defendant purchase, twenty-six innersole molds capable of producing saleable innersoles. The price was fixed at $600.00 per mold. Whether or not a time for delivery had been established was open to question. In his testimony at trial, Mr. Moulton admitted that he was fully aware that defendant was in immediate need of the molds, and he stated that he had estimated that he could provide suitable molds in about five weeks' time. Mr. Sturman testified that "I conveyed the urgency to [Mr. Moulton] and he said 'within three weeks I will begin showing you molds and by the end of five weeks you will have [the entire order].'"

In apparent conformity with standard practice in the industry, plaintiff set about constructing a sample mold and began a lengthy series of tests. These tests consisted of bringing the sample mold to defendant's plant, fitting the mold to one of defendant's plastic-injecting machines, and checking the innersole thus derived from the plaintiff's mold to determine if it met the specifications imposed by defendant. After about thirty such tests over a ten-week period, several problems remained unsolved, the most significant of which was "flashing," that is, a seepage of plastic along the seam where the two halves of the mold meet. Although characterized by plaintiff as a minor defect, Mr. Moulton admitted that a flashing mold could not produce a saleable innersole.

It was plaintiff's contention at trial, supported by credible evidence, that at one point during the testing period officials of defendant signified that in their judgment plaintiff's sample mold was turning out innersoles correctly configured so as to fit the model last supplied by defendant's customer. Allegedly relying on this approval, plaintiff went ahead and constructed the full run of twenty-six molds.

For its part, defendant introduced credible evidence to rebut the assertion that it had approved the fit of the molds. It also noted that Moulton's allegation of approval extended only to the fit of the mold; as Moulton conceded, defendant had never given full approval since it considered the flashing problem, among others, unacceptable.

On May 29, some ten weeks after the date of the oral agreement and five weeks after the estimated completion date, Mr. Sturman met with plaintiff's foreman at the Moulton plant. A dispute exists regarding the substance of the ensuing conversation. Plaintiff introduced evidence tending to show that at that time, Mr. Sturman revoked defendant's prior approval of the fit of the sample mold and demanded that plaintiff redesign the molds to fit the last. Testimony introduced by defendant tended to show that it had never approved the fit of the molds to begin with and that on the date in question, May 29, plaintiff's foreman indicated that plaintiff simply would not invest any more time in conforming the molds to the contract. Mr. Sturman met the next day with Mr. Moulton, and Moulton ratified the position taken by his foreman. Thereupon, Mr. Sturman immediately departed for Italy and arranged to have the molds produced by the Plastak Corporation, an Italian mold-making concern, at a cost of $650.00 per mold. Plaintiff later billed defendant for the contract price of the molds, deducting an allowance for "flashing and shut-off adjustments." Upon defendant's refusal to pay, plaintiff brought this action for the price less adjustments. Defendant counterclaimed for its costs in obtaining conforming goods to the extent that they exceeded the contract price.

At trial, plaintiff's basic theory of recovery was that it had received approval with regard to the fit of the sample mold, that in reliance on that approval it had constructed a full run of twenty-six molds, and that defendant had, in effect, committed an anticipatory breach of contract within the meaning of Section 2–610 by demanding that the fit of the molds be completely redesigned. On its counterclaim, and in response to plaintiff's position, defendant advanced the theory that plaintiff had breached the contract by failing to tender conforming goods within the five-week period mentioned by both parties.

After the presiding Justice had charged the jury, counsel for plaintiff requested at side bar that the jury be instructed on the doctrine of substantial performance. Counsel for defendant entered a timely objection to the proposed charge which objection was overruled. The court then supplemented its charge as follows:

> The only point of clarification that I'll make, ladies and gentlemen, is that I've referred a couple of times to performance of a contract and you, obviously, have to determine no matter which way you view the contract to be, and there might even be a possible third way that I haven't even considered, whether the contract whatever it is has been performed and there is a doctrine that you should be aware of in considering that. That is the doctrine of substantial performance.

> It is not required that performance be in any case one hundred percent complete in order to entitle a party to enforcement of their contractual rights. That is not to say within the confines of this case that the existence of flashing would be excused or not be excused. It is just a recognition on the part of the law when we talk about performance, probably if we took any contract you could always find something of no substance that was not completed one hundred percent. It is for you to determine that whether it has been substantially performed or not and what in fact constitutes substantial performance.

> In your consideration, and as I say in this case, that's not to intimate that something like flashing is to be disregarded or to be considered. It's up to you based upon facts.

The jury returned a verdict in favor of plaintiff in the amount of $14,480.82.

I

In Smith, Fitzmaurice Co. v. Harris, 126 Me. 308, 138 A. 389 (1927), a case decided under the common law, we recognized the then-settled rule that with respect to contracts for the sale of goods the buyer has the right to reject the seller's tender if in any way it fails to conform to the specifications of the contract. We held that "[t]he vendor has the duty to comply with his order in kind, quality and amount." Id. at 312, 138 A. at 391. Thus, in *Smith,* we ruled that a buyer who had contracted to purchase twelve dozen union suits could lawfully refuse a tender of sixteen dozen union suits. Various provisions of the Uniform Sales Act, enacted in Maine in 1923, codified the common-law approach. R.S. (1954) ch. 185, §§ 11, 44. The so-called "perfect tender" rule came under considerable fire around the time the Uniform Commercial Code was drafted. No less an authority than Karl Llewellyn, recognized as the primum mobile of the Code's tender provisions (see, e.g., W. Twining, Karl Llewellyn and the Realist Movement 270–301 (1973); Carroll, Harpooning Whales, of Which Karl N. Llewellyn is the Hero of the Piece; or Searching for More Expansion Joints in Karl's Crumbling Cathedral, 12 B.C.Indus. & Comm.L.Rev. 139, 142 (1970)), attacked the rule principally on the ground that it allowed a dishonest buyer to avoid an unfavorable contract on the basis of an insubstantial defect in the seller's tender. Llewellyn, On Warranty of Quality and Society, 37 Colum.L.Rev. 341, 389 (1937). Although Llewellyn's views are represented in many Code sections governing tender,[6] the basic tender provision, Section 2–601, represents a rejection of Llewellyn's approach and a continuation of the perfect tender policy developed by the common law and carried forward by the draftsmen of the Uniform Sales Act. See Official Comment, § 2–106; Priest, Breach and Remedy for the Tender of Nonconforming Goods Under the Uniform Commercial Code: An Economic Approach, 91 Harv.L.Rev. 960, 971 (1978). Thus, Section 2–601 states that, with certain exceptions not here applicable, the buyer has the right to reject "if the goods or the tender of delivery fail *in any respect* to conform to the contract... ." (emphasis supplied). Those few courts that have considered the question agree that the perfect tender rule has survived the enactment of the Code. Ingle v. Marked Tree Equipment Co., 244 Ark.1166, 428 S.W.2d 286 (1968); Maas v. Scoboda, 188 Neb. 189, 195 N.W.2d 491 (1972); Bowen v. Young, 507 S.W.2d 600 (Tex.Civ.App.1974). We, too, are convinced of the soundness of this position.

In light of the foregoing discussion, it is clear that the presiding Justice's charge was erroneous and, under the circumstances, reversibly so. The jury was informed that "[i]t is not required that performance be in any case one hundred percent complete in order to entitle a party to enforcement of their contractual rights." Under this instruction, the jury was free to find that although plaintiff had not tendered perfectly

---

6. See, e.g., §§ 2–508 (seller's limited right to cure defects in tender), 2–608 (buyer's limited right to revoke acceptance), and 2–612 (buyer's limited right to reject nonconforming tender under installment contract).

conforming molds within the agreed period (assuming the jury found that the parties had in fact agreed on a specific time period for completion) it had nevertheless substantially performed the contract within the agreed time frame and was merely making minor adjustments when defendant backed out of the deal. Had the jury been instructed that plaintiff was required to tender perfectly conforming goods—not just substantially conforming goods—within the period allegedly agreed to and had they been instructed that, under Section 2-711, the buyer has the absolute right to cancel the contract if the seller "fails to make delivery," a different verdict might have resulted. Indeed, the supplemental instruction tended to encourage the jury to resolve the question by deciding whether "flashing" was or was not a substantial defect:

> It is not required that performance be in any case one hundred percent complete in order to entitle a party to enforcement of their contractual rights. That is not to say within the confines of this case that the existence of flashing would be excused or not be excused. ... It is for you to determine ... whether [the contract] has been substantially performed or not and what in fact constitutes substantial performance.

We find unpersuasive plaintiff's argument that the presiding Justice's instruction merely informed the jury that if it found that defendant had committed an anticipatory breach of the contract then plaintiff was not thereafter required to complete its performance as a condition precedent to recovery under the contract. Such an instruction might well have been appropriate and would certainly have been supportable under the applicable law. Dehahn v. Innes, Me., 356 A.2d 711, 719 (1976) ("When the other party has already repudiated the agreement, a tender would be a futile act and is not required by law."); §§ 2–610, 2–704. However, an examination of the passage of the charge in question leads us to reject plaintiff's interpretation. Without informing the jury that it must first find that defendant had committed an anticipatory repudiation, the presiding Justice, without qualification, stated that "performance [need not] be ... one hundred percent complete in order to entitle a party to enforcement of their contractual rights." Furthermore, the court drew a distinction between substantial and insubstantial defects, a distinction which, on these facts and under plaintiff's interpretation of the charge, would have been completely irrelevant. Finally, both the presiding Justice and counsel for plaintiff referred to the instruction at side bar as an explanation of the "substantial performance" doctrine. In legal parlance, that doctrine requires a buyer, under certain circumstances, to accept something less than a perfectly conforming tender. See, e.g., Rockland Poultry Co. v. Anderson, 148 Me. 211, 216, 91 A.2d 478, 480 (1952) (construction contract); Jacob & Youngs, Inc. v. Kent, 230 N.Y. 239, 129 N.E. 889 (1921) (Cardozo, J.) (construction contract). As such, it has no application to a contract for the sale of goods, and the jury should not have been permitted to consider it.

II

In his testimony at trial, Mr. Moulton indicated that he was aware that to defendant time was a critical factor. He also stated that he had given defendant an estimated delivery date of five weeks from the date the contract was formed. On appeal, defendant takes the position that the parties agreed on a five-week time period for delivery and that plaintiff's failure to tender conforming goods after ten weeks constitutes a breach as a matter of law and precludes plaintiff from recovering under the contract.

We disagree. While on the one hand Mr. Sturman testified that Mr. Moulton had told him that the goods would be delivered in five weeks, on the other hand Mr. Moulton testified that it was clear that he was merely making an estimate. The testimony thus left the jury at liberty to decide the factual question of whether the five-week time period was an agreed delivery date and thus a term of the contract or merely an estimate. While the interpretation of unambiguous language in a written contract falls within the province of the court, Blue Rock Industries v. Raymond International, Inc., Me., 325 A.2d 66 (1974), questions of fact concerning the terms of an oral agreement are left to the trier of fact, Carter v. Beck, Me., 366 A.2d 520 (1976).

The entry is:

Appeal sustained.

New trial ordered.

Notes

(1) Substantial Performance. Most students will recall from general contract law that a party is entitled to the full contract price if it has substantially performed its contractual obligations. To the extent that less than exact performance has been rendered, the other party is entitled to recoupment in the amount of any damages. A leading contracts case is Judge Cardozo's opinion in Jacob & Youngs, Inc. v. Kent, 230 N.Y. 239, 129 N.E. 889 (1921)(the Reading pipe case), cited by the Maine court. See also Restatement (Second) of Contracts §§ 237, 241, which puts the same performance standard in terms of material failure. On request of seller's counsel, the trial court in *Moulton Cavity & Mold* framed the jury charge on the substantial performance standard. What argument could be made in support of the trial court's decision?

(2) History of the Perfect Tender Rule. Historians identify a mid–19th century British decision as the origin of the perfect tender rule. Bowes v. Shand, [1876] 1 Q.B.D. 470, [1877] 2 Q.B.D. 112, [1877] 2 App. Cas. 455. Professor Grant Gilmore said that the perfect tender rule in the United States dates from October 26, 1885, when the Supreme Court decided Norrington v. Wright, 115 U.S. 188, 6 S.Ct.12, 29 L.Ed. 366 (1885), and Filley v. Pope, 115 U.S. 213, 6 S.Ct. 19, 29 L.Ed. 372 (1885). See E. Peters, Commercial Transactions 33 (1971). A high (or low) water mark cited by Professor (now Connecticut Supreme Court Chief Justice) Peters was Frankel v. Foreman & Clark, 33 F.2d 83 (2d Cir.1929)(permitting rejection of a shipment of coats for trivial and inconsequential nonconformities in less than 2% of the coats). Id. at 34. For a comprehensive review of the perfect tender rule prior to the Commercial Code, see Honnold, Buyer's Right of Rejection, 97 U.Pa. L.Rev. 457 (1949).

(3) Retention of the Perfect Tender Rule in the Code. As the Commercial Code evolved, a major study was conducted under the aegis of the Law Revision Commission of the State of New York. The Commission recommended that "the right of rejection as stated in Section 2–601 be limited to material breach." The Editorial Board responsible for revising the Code following the New York study did not accept this recommendation. That Board relied on two grounds: "first, ... the buyer should not be required to guess at his peril whether a breach is material; second, ... proof of materiality would sometimes require disclosure of the buyer's private affairs such as secret formulas or processes." R. Braucher & E. Sutherland, Commercial Transactions 56 (1964). Are these reasons persuasive? In the pending revision of Article 2, would you recommend retention of UCC 2–601 in its present form? See Sebert, Rejection, Revocation, and Cure Under Article 2 of the Uniform Commercial Code: Some Modest Proposals, 84 Nw. L. Rev. 375 (1990); Lawrence, The Prematurely Reported Demise of the Perfect Tender Rule, 35 Kan. L. Rev. 557 (1987).

What arguments support favoring a liberal remedy of rejection rather than compelling aggrieved buyers to use price adjustments? Some of the considerations are canvassed in Honnold, Buyer's Right of Rejection, 97 U.Pa.L.Rev. 457, 466–72 (1949): e.g., (1) the hazard of securing redress when full cash payment is demanded on tender; (2) the difficulty in many cases of measuring, without controversy, the value of the deficiency in seller's performance. Do the rules of the Code fit these underlying interests as well as is feasible? See Peters, Remedies for Breach of Contracts Relating to the Sale of Goods Under the UCC, 73 Yale L.J. 199, 206–27 (1963); Miniter, Rejection, 13 Ga.L.Rev. 805 (1979); Priest, Breach and Remedy for the Tender of Nonconforming Goods; An Economic Approach, 91 Harv.L.Rev. 960 (1978); Schmitt & Frisch, 13 Toledo L.Rev. 1375 (1982).

(4) Installment Sales: A Different Set of Standards. The standards governing buyers' power to reject tendered goods change dramatically if the sales contract "requires or authorizes the delivery of goods in separate lots to be separately accepted," UCC 2–612(1), language which the drafters of the Code intended to have considerable breadth.[9]

---

9. Section 2–307 permits delivery in several lots "where the circumstances give either party the right to make or demand delivery in lots." The issue in 2–307, whether a seller may demand payment for partial deliveries, is not the same as the issue in 2–612(1), whether a seller may demand acceptance of partial deliveries. Comment 1 to 2–612 states that drafters of the Code intended to define installment contracts more broadly than did pre-Code law, and Comment 2 adds that provision

Such sales, termed "installment contracts," are not governed by the perfect tender rule in UCC 2–601. As each lot is tendered in a simple, two-party sale, a buyer may reject only if "the non-conformity substantially impairs the value of that installment and cannot be cured." UCC 2–612(2).[10]

Problem 3. Sellers can escape from the rigors of the perfect tender rule by eliciting from buyers express or tacit consent to divide full performance into more than one "lot." In making such arrangements, buyers may or may not be aware that they are surrendering a significant amount of leverage over the sellers when the time comes for performance. If you were counsel to a firm regularly engaged in selling or buying goods, what advice would you give on standard contracting terms?

Problem 4. Seller and Buyer have a long-term trading pattern whereby Buyer submits orders frequently for goods to be delivered some time later. Within the delivery time necessary for an order, Buyer usually makes one or more additional orders. Each purchase order results in a single delivery by Seller. Is Buyer's right to reject tendered goods governed by UCC 2–601 or 2–612(2)?

T.W. OIL, INC. v. CONSOLIDATED EDISON CO.

Court of Appeals of New York, 1982.
57 N.Y.2d 574, 457 N.Y.S.2d 458, 443 N.E.2d 932.

FUCHSBERG, JUDGE.

In the first case to wend its way through our appellate courts on this question, we are asked, in the main, to decide whether a seller who, acting in good faith and without knowledge of any defect, tenders nonconforming goods to a buyer who properly rejects them, may avail itself of the cure provision of subdivision (2) of section 2–508 of the Uniform Commercial Code. We hold that, if seasonable notice be given, such a seller may offer to cure the defect within a reasonable period beyond the time when the contract was to be performed so long as it has acted in good faith and with a reasonable expectation that the original goods would be acceptable to the buyer.

The factual background against which we decide this appeal is based on either undisputed proof or express findings at Trial Term. In January, 1974, midst the fuel shortage produced by the oil embargo, the plaintiff (then known as Joc Oil USA, Inc.) purchased a cargo of fuel oil whose sulfur content was represented to it as no greater than 1%.

---

for separate payment for each lot is not essential to an installment contract.

10. In an unusual "belt and suspenders" style of drafting, 2–612(2) continues to define circumstances in which a buyer "must accept an installment." Conceptually under the Code, buyers must accept goods that they may not reject. Therefore, the criteria for "may reject" should be the same as the criteria for "must accept." However, as stated the drafters failed to make the two clauses complementary. Consider a tender of non-conforming goods by a seller who has the ability to cure the non-conformity but who fails to give adequate assurance of doing so.

While the oil was still at sea en route to the United States in the tanker *M T Khamsin,* plaintiff received a certificate from the foreign refinery at which it had been processed informing it that the sulfur content in fact was .52%. Thereafter, on January 24, the plaintiff entered into a written contract with the defendant (Con Ed) for the sale of this oil. The agreement was for delivery to take place between January 24 and January 30, payment being subject to a named independent testing agency's confirmation of quality and quantity. The contract, following a trade custom to round off specifications of sulfur content at, for instance, 1%, .5% or .3%, described that of the *Khamsin* oil as .5%. In the course of the negotiations, the plaintiff learned that Con Ed was then authorized to buy and burn oil with a sulfur content of up to 1% and would even mix oils containing more and less to maintain that figure.

When the vessel arrived, on January 25, its cargo was discharged into Con Ed storage tanks in Bayonne, New Jersey. In due course, the independent testing people reported a sulfur content of .92%. On this basis, acting within a time frame whose reasonableness is not in question, on February 14 Con Ed rejected the shipment. Prompt negotiations to adjust the price failed; by February 20, plaintiff had offered a price reduction roughly responsive to the difference in sulfur reading, but Con Ed, though it could use the oil, rejected this proposition out of hand. It was insistent on paying no more than the latest prevailing price, which, in the volatile market that then existed, was some 25% below the level which prevailed when it agreed to buy the oil.

The very next day, February 21, plaintiff offered to cure the defect with a substitute shipment of conforming oil scheduled to arrive on the *S.S. Appollonian Victory* on February 28. Nevertheless, on February 22, the very day after the cure was proffered, Con Ed, adamant in its intention to avail itself of the intervening drop in prices, summarily rejected this proposal too. The two cargos were subsequently sold to third parties at the best price obtainable, first that of the *Appollonian* and, sometime later, after extraction from the tanks had been accomplished, that of the *Khamsin.*

There ensued this action for breach of contract, which, after a somewhat unconventional trial course, resulted in a nonjury decision for the plaintiff in the sum of $1,385,512.83.... To arrive at this result, the Trial Judge, while ruling against other liability theories advanced by the plaintiff, which, in particular, included one charging the defendant with having failed to act in good faith in the negotiations for a price adjustment on the *Khamsin* oil (Uniform Commercial Code, § 1–203), decided as a matter of law that subdivision (2) of section 2–508 of the Uniform Commercial Code was available to the plaintiff even if it had no prior knowledge of the nonconformity. Finding that in fact plaintiff had no such belief at the time of the delivery, that what turned out to be a .92% sulfur content was "within the range of contemplation of reasonable acceptability" to Con Ed, and that seasonable notice of an intention to cure was given, the court went on to hold that plaintiff's "reasonable and timely offer to cure" was improperly rejected (sub nom. Joc Oil USA v. Consolidated Edison Co. of N.Y., 107 Misc.2d 376, 390, 434 N.Y.S.2d 623[Shanley N. Egeth, J.]). The Appellate Division, 84 A.D.2d 970, 447 N.Y.S.2d 572, having unanimously affirmed the judgment entered on this decision, the case is now here by our leave....

In support of its quest for reversal, the defendant now asserts that the trial court erred (a) in ruling that the verdict on a special question submitted for determination by a jury was irrelevant to the decision of this case, (b) in failing to interpret subdivision (2) of section 2–508 of the Uniform Commercial Code to limit the availability of the right to cure after date of performance to cases in which the seller knowingly made a nonconforming tender and (c) in calculating damages on the basis of the resale of the nonconforming cargo rather than of the substitute offered to replace it. For the reasons which follow, we find all three unacceptable.

I

[The court rejected objection (a).]

II

We turn then to the central issue on this appeal: Fairly interpreted, did subdivision (2) of section 2–508 of the Uniform Commercial Code require Con Ed to accept the substitute shipment plaintiff tendered? In approaching this question, we, of course, must remember that a seller's right to cure a defective tender, as allowed by both subdivisions of section 2–508, was intended to act as a meaningful limitation on the absolutism of the old perfect tender rule, under which, no leeway being allowed for any imperfections, there was, as one court put it, just "no room ... for the doctrine of substantial performance" of commercial obligations (Mitsubishi Goshi Kaisha v. Aron & Co., 16 F.2d 185, 186 [Learned Hand, J.]; see Note, Uniform Commercial Code, § 2–508; Seller's Right to Cure Non–Conforming Goods, 6 Rutgers–Camden L.J. 387–388).

In contrast, to meet the realities of the more impersonal business world of our day, the code, to avoid sharp dealing, expressly provides for the liberal construction of its remedial provisions (§ 1–102) so that "good faith" and the "observance of reasonable commercial standards of fair dealing" be the rule rather than the exception in trade (see § 2–103, subd. [1], par. [b]), "good faith" being defined as "honesty in fact in the conduct or transaction concerned" (Uniform Commercial Code, § 1–201, subd. [19]). As to section 2–508 in particular, the code's Official Comment advises that its mission is to safeguard the seller "against surprise as a result of sudden technicality on the buyer's part" (Uniform Commercial Code, § 2–106, Comment 2; see, also, Peters, Remedies for Breach of Contracts Relating to the Sale of Goods under the

Uniform Commercial Code: A Roadmap for Article Two, 73 Yale L.J. 199, 210; 51 N.Y.Jur., Sales, § 101, p. 41).

Section 2–508 may be conveniently divided between provisions for cure offered when "the time for performance has not yet expired" (subd. [1]), a precode concept in this State (Lowinson v. Newman, 201 App.Div. 266, 194 N.Y.S. 253), and ones which, by newly introducing the possibility of a seller obtaining "a further reasonable time to substitute a conforming tender" (subd. [2]), also permit cure beyond the date set for performance. ...

Since we here confront circumstances in which the conforming tender came after the time of performance, we focus on subdivision (2). On its face, taking its conditions in the order in which they appear, for the statute to apply (1) a buyer must have rejected a nonconforming tender, (2) the seller must have had reasonable grounds to believe this tender would be acceptable (with or without money allowance), and (3) the seller must have "seasonably" notified the buyer of the intention to substitute a conforming tender within a reasonable time.

In the present case, none of these presented a problem. The first one was easily met for it is unquestioned that, at .92%, the sulfur content of the *Khamsin* oil did not conform to the .5% specified in the contract and that it was rejected by Con Ed. The second, the reasonableness of the seller's belief that the original tender would be acceptable, was supported not only by unimpeached proof that the contract's .5% and the refinery certificate's .52% were trade equivalents, but by testimony that, by the time the contract was made, the plaintiff knew Con Ed burned fuel with a content of up to 1%, so that, with appropriate price adjustment, the *Khamsin* oil would have suited its needs even if, at delivery, it was, to the plaintiff's surprise, to test out at .92%. Further, the matter seems to have been put beyond dispute by the defendant's readiness to take the oil at the reduced market price on February 20. Surely, on such a record, the trial court cannot be faulted for having found as a fact that the second condition too had been established.

As to the third, the conforming state of the *Appollonian* oil is undisputed, the offer to tender it took place on February 21, only a day after Con Ed finally had rejected the *Khamsin* delivery and the *Appollonian* substitute then already was en route to the United States, where it was expected in a week and did arrive on March 4, only four days later than expected. Especially since Con Ed pleaded no prejudice (unless the drop in prices could be so regarded), it is almost impossible, given the flexibility of the Uniform Commerical Code definitions of "seasonable" and "reasonable" ..., to quarrel with the finding that the remaining requirements of the statute also had been met.

Thus lacking the support of the statute's literal language, the defendant nonetheless would have us limit its application to cases in which a seller *knowingly* makes a nonconforming tender which it has reason to believe the buyer will accept. For this proposition, it relies almost entirely on a critique in Nordstrom, Law of Sales (§ 105), which rationalizes that, since a seller who believes its tender is conforming would have no reason to think in terms of a reduction in the price of the goods, to allow such a seller to cure after the time for performance had passed would make the statutory reference to a money allowance redundant.[8] Nordstrom, interestingly enough, finds it useful to buttress this position by the somewhat dire prediction, though backed by no empirical or other confirmation, that, unless the right to cure is confined to those whose nonconforming tenders are knowing ones, the incentive of sellers to timely deliver will be undermined. To this it also adds the somewhat moralistic note that a seller who is mistaken as to the quality of its goods does not merit additional time (Nordstrom, *loc. cit.*). Curiously, recognizing that the few decisions extant on this subject have adopted a position opposed to the one for which it contends, Con Ed seeks to treat these as exceptions rather than exemplars of the rule (e.g., Wilson v. Scampoli, 228 A.2d 848 (D.C.App.) [goods obtained by seller from their manufacturer in original carton resold unopened to purchaser; seller held within statute though it had no reason to believe the goods defective]; Appleton State Bank v. Lee, 33 Wis.2d 690, 148 N.W.2d 1 [seller mistakenly delivered sewing machine of wrong brand but otherwise identical to one sold; held that seller, though it did not know of its mistake, had a right to cure by substitution]).

That the principle for which these cases stand goes far beyond their particular facts cannot be gainsaid. These holdings demonstrate that, in dealing with the application of subdivision (2) of section 2–508, courts have been concerned with the reasonableness of the seller's belief that the goods would be acceptable rather than with the seller's pretended knowledge or lack of knowledge of the defect (Wilson v. Scampoli, supra; compare Zabriskie Chevrolet v. Smith, 99 N.J.Super. 441, 240 A.2d 195).

It also is no surprise then that the aforementioned decisional history is a reflection of the mainstream of scholarly commentary on the subject (e.g., 1955 Report of N.Y.Law Rev.Comm., p. 484; White & Summers, Uniform Commercial Code [2d ed.], § 8–4, p. 322; 2 Anderson, Uniform Commercial Code [2d ed.], § 2–508:7; Hogan, The Highways and Some of the Byways in the Sales and Bulk Sales Articles of the Uniform Commercial Code, 48 Cornell L.Q. 1, 12–13; Note, Uniform Commercial Code, § 2–508: Seller's Right to Cure Non–Conforming Goods, 6 Rutgers–Camden L.J. 387, 399; Note, Commercial

---

8. The premise for such an argument, which ignores the policy of the code to prevent buyers from using insubstantial remedial or price adjustable defects to free themselves from unprofitable bargains (Hawkland, Sales and Bulk Sales Under the Uniform Commercial Code, pp. 120–122), is that the words "with or without money allowance" apply only to sellers who believe their goods will be acceptable with such an allowance and not to sellers who believe their goods will be acceptable without such an allowance. But, since the words are part of a phrase which speaks of an otherwise unqualified belief that the goods will be acceptable, unless one strains for an opposite interpretation, we find insufficient reason to doubt that it intends to include both those who find a need to offer an allowance and those who do not.

Law—The Effect of the Seller's Right to Cure on the Buyer's Remedy of Rescission, 28 Ark.L.Rev. 297, 302–303).

White and Summers, for instance, put it well, and bluntly. Stressing that the code intended cure to be "a remedy which should be carefully cultivated and developed by the courts" because it "offers the possibility of conforming the law to reasonable expectations and of thwarting the chiseler who seeks to escape from a bad bargain" (op. cit., at pp. 322–324), the authors conclude, as do we, that a seller should have recourse to the relief afforded by subdivision (2) of section 2–508 of the Uniform Commercial Code as long as it can establish that it had reasonable grounds, tested objectively, for its belief that the goods would be accepted (ibid., at p. 321). It goes without saying that the test of reasonableness, in this context, must encompass the concepts of "good faith" and "commercial standards of fair dealing" which permeate the code (Uniform Commercial Code, § 1–201, subd. [19]; §§ 1–203, 2–103, subd. [1], par. [b]).[10]

. . .

Judgment affirmed.

Notes

(1) Sellers' Right to Cure Non–conforming Tenders. In a substantial departure from prior law, the Commercial Code authorizes sellers to make a second tender or delivery if the first is rightfully rejected. UCC 2–508(1).[11] To what extent does this power overcome the vices perceived by critics of the perfect tender rule?

Buyer was found to have reject the *Khamsin* oil rightfully, but its subsequent rejection of the *Appollonian* oil was wrongful. Thus buyer was in breach. We consider sellers' remedies for wrongful rejection later in this section.

(2) Repair as Cure. Quality defects can be cured by tender of substitute goods, as in *T.W. Oil,* and quantity shortfalls by tender of additional goods. In a sale of a manufactured product, is seller's undertaking to replace a defective component a cure under UCC 2–508(1)? Does it matter whether the seller is the manufacturer or only a dealer? Suppose that a new automobile is rejected for transmission failures and car dealer replaces the transmission in its own service department? See Zabriskie Chevrolet, Inc. v. Smith, 99 N.J. Super.

---

10. Except indirectly, on this appeal we do not deal with the equally important protections the code affords buyers. It is as to buyers as well as sellers that the code, to the extent that it displaces traditional principles of law and equity (§ 1–103), seeks to discourage unfair or hypertechnical business conduct bespeaking a dog-eat-dog rather than a live-and-let-live approach to the marketplace (e.g., §§ 2–314, 2–315, 2–513, 2–601, 2–608). Overall, the aim is to encourage parties to amicably resolve their own problems (Ramirez v. Autosport, 88 N.J. 277, 285, 440 A.2d 1345; compare Restatement, Contracts 2d, Introductory Note to chapter 10, p. 194["the wisest course is ordinarily for the parties to attempt to resolve their differences by negotiations, including clarification of expectations [and] cure of past defaults"]).

11. Are sellers authorized to make a third tender if the first two are rightfully rejected? A fourth?

441, 240 A.2d 195 (1968)(dealer's replacement did not effect cure). Should the possibility of cure by repair in sales of capital equipment be more liberal than in sales of consumer goods?

(3) Cure and Warranty Service. How does sellers' repair or replacement of rightfully rejected goods relate to sales contracts under which sellers undertake to repair or replace goods during a specified warranty period?

(4) Price Adjustment as Cure. In some trade settings, particularly sales of fungible goods, sellers offer take a lower price when goods may be rightfully rejected and buyers agree. Could a practice of this kind be the basis for concluding that trade usage permits sellers to cure defective tenders by price adjustment? Counsel for seller in *T.W. Oil* argued, in the trial court, that buyer should be held liable for breach of a duty to bargain in good faith for a price adjustment on the *Khamsin* oil. This argument was rejected by the trial court and is mentioned only in passing by the court of appeals. Does this argument have force under the present Code? Should the Code be amended to provide generally that sellers may cure by price adjustment?

MENDELSON–ZELLER CO. v. JOSEPH WEDNER & SON CO.

U.S. Department of Agriculture, 1970.
29 Agriculture Decisions 47, 7 UCC Rep. Serv. 1045.

FLAVIN, JUDICIAL OFFICER

PRELIMINARY STATEMENT

This is a reparation proceeding under the Perishable Agricultural Commodities Act, 1930, as amended (7 U.S.C. 499a et seq.) A timely complaint was filed in which complainant seeks reparation against respondent in the amount of $2,480.73 in connection with a shipment of cantaloupes and lettuce in interstate commerce.

A copy of the formal complaint and of the Department's report of investigation were served upon the respondent, and respondent filed an answer denying liability. The answer included a counterclaim for $2,892.73. Complainant did not file a reply to the counterclaim and therefore it is deemed to be denied pursuant to section 47.9(a) of the rules of practice (7 CFR 47.9(a)).

An oral hearing at the request of respondent was held at Pittsburgh, Pennsylvania, on July 30, 1969. Respondent was represented by counsel at the hearing. One witness appeared for respondent. Complainant filed a brief.

FINDINGS OF FACT

1. Complainant, Mendelson–Zeller Co., Inc., is a corporation whose address is 450 Sansome Street, San Francisco, California. At the time of the transaction involved herein, complainant was licensed under the act.

2. Respondent, Joseph Wedner & Son Co., is a corporation whose address is 2018 Smallman Street, Pittsburgh, Pennsylvania. At the time of the transaction involved herein, respondent was licensed under the act.

3. On or about March 7, 1968, in the course of interstate commerce, complainant contracted orally to sell to respondent, a mixed truckload of produce consisting of 25 cartons of cantaloupes Jumbo size 45 at $17.75 per carton, 85 cartons of cantaloupes Jumbo size 56 at $15.25 per carton, and 574 cartons of lettuce size 24 at $3.45 per carton, delivered Pittsburgh, Pennsylvania. The total delivered price for the truckload, including $15.00 for top ice, was $4,116.55. It was agreed that shipment would begin on March 8. The parties estimated that delivery would be in time for the market of Tuesday morning, March 12, 1968.

4. Complainant shipped the lettuce at 9:40 a.m. March 8, 1968, from El Centro, California, and the cantaloupes were shipped at 10:00 p.m. the same day from Nogales, Arizona, in a truck operated by Arkansas Traffic Service, Inc., of Redfield, Arkansas. At 12:00 a.m. March 12, the truck driver called respondent stating that the truck would arrive about 3:00 or 3:30 p.m. and requesting that respondent's men wait to unload the truck. Respondent checked with its men, who said they would not wait, and then told the truck driver to arrive at 3:00 a.m. the morning of March 13th.

5. The truckload of produce arrived at respondent's place of business at 5:00 a.m., March 13, 1968, approximately 103 hours after leaving Nogales, Arizona.

6. Respondent unloaded and sold the commodities and remitted the net proceeds in the amount of $1,635.82 to complainant.

7. The formal complaint was filed on August 1, 1968, which was within 9 months after accrual of the cause of action.

CONCLUSIONS

Complainant seeks to recover the full delivered price for the truckload of produce sold to respondent and respondent contends that it was justified in remitting only the net proceeds resulting from its resale of the produce. The only material factual dispute relates to whether a delivery time of 3:00 a.m. March 12, 1968, was specified as a condition of the delivered sale contract. Complainant contends that such time was not specified as a contract condition but was merely the estimated time of arrival assuming normal condition, and that a 48 hour leeway is allowable by custom in such cases.

On March 13, 1968, the day the truck actually arrived, respondent's Manager, Norman Wedner, wrote to complainant's Sales Manager, Mr. E. A. Melia, Jr., in part as follows:

> The truck of mixed lettuce and cantaloupes was due for the market of Tuesday morning at 3:00 AM March 12, 1968.

The truck driver called us at noon Tuesday and said he would be in at 3:00 or 3:30 PM Tuesday afternoon, and asked us to have the men wait to unload him. We held him on the phone and our warehouse men said they could not wait for him. We then told him to be at the warehouse at 3:00 AM Wednesday morning. He said fine, he would be there.

He didn't arrive until 5:00 AM Wednesday Mar. 13, 1968. The lettuce wasn't available for delivery until 6:30 AM, causing us to miss a large chain store order.

Complainant's Traffic Manager, John Monk testified by deposition and referred to an exhibit which he said was a correct copy of his notes concerning instructions for the shipment of the produce. The exhibit is entitled "Loading and Delivery instructions," and in part gives the following information: "Delivery Date *Tues* Time *3:30 AM.*" Mr. Monk stated that this exhibit reflected the estimated time of arrival and that he "was given no specific instructions as to actual time of delivery other than the delivery was to be planned so that if at all possible it would arrive in Pittsburgh on Tuesday morning." Complainant's Salesman, Irving Raznikov, stated that he was the actual recipient of the telephone order from Mr. Wedner. Although he stated that "Wedner requested a Tuesday a.m. arrival and I indicated to him that under normal circumstances there would be no problem with said delivery schedule," he also stated that he "stressed with Mr. Wedner that we could not and would not guarantee any specific arrival."

Respondent as the party alleging that a specified arrival time was a part of the contract of sale had the burden of proving by a preponderance of the evidence that its allegation was true. In view of the foregoing discussion we conclude that respondent has not met its burden of proof.

Section 2–309(1) of the Uniform Commercial Code provides that the time for delivery in the absence of an agreed time shall be a reasonable time. The load was tendered and accepted at 5:00 a.m. March 13, about 103 hours after the truck left Nogales, Arizona. Under the circumstances, we are unable to say the delivery was not within a reasonable time.

The failure of respondent to pay to complainant the full purchase price of $4,116.55 for the lettuce was in violation of section 2 of the act. Respondent has already paid net proceeds of $1,635.82 to complainant. Reparation should therefore be awarded to complainant for the balance of the purchase price of $2,480.73, with interest. In the absence of any breach of contract on the part of complainant, respondent's counterclaim should be dismissed.

ORDER

Within 30 days from the date of this order, respondent shall pay to complainant, as reparation, $2,480.73, with interest thereon at the rate of 6 percent per annum from April 1, 1968, until paid.

The counterclaim should be dismissed.

Notes

(1) **Delay in Sellers' Tender of Delivery.** This case illustrates how much economic significance can attach to time of performance. Buyer resold lettuce and cantaloupes after 5:00 a.m. for $1,635.82, less than half of the original contract price. Moreover, buyer claimed damages of nearly $2,900.00, presumably profit that buyer allegedly would have made on resale to the large chain store. Assuming that the resale was reasonable [12] and the amount of the alleged damages is not exaggerated, goods delivered at 3:00 a.m. were worth $5,000 more than goods delivered at 5:00 a.m.

Buyer took the position that it was relieved of obligation to pay the contract price to seller because of the produce was received after the time permitted under the contract of sale. Did buyer contend that seller was late in handing over the produce to the carrier? Could seller be responsible for the carrier's delay in delivering the produce to buyer? See UCC 2–503(3).

(2) **Contract Interpretation.** Buyer apparently contended that the delivery term in the "Loading and Delivery instructions" was binding upon the seller. Was this document part of the contract of sale? On what theory might it reflect on the sales contract? [13]

(3) **Construction of UCC 2–309.** When buyer's principal contract argument failed, the seller's performance obligation was found in the default rule of UCC 2–309. Do you agree with the judicial officer's application of that provision to the facts of this case? If the truck driver could have delivered on the afternoon of March 12, was it not reasonable to require the goods to be delivered at 3:00 a.m. the next morning, in time to make the prime market for that day?

(4) **Buyer's Rejection and Resale.** The Commercial Code imposes a duty on a merchant buyer, after rejection of perishable goods, to make reasonable efforts to sell them for the seller's account. UCC 2–603(1). If buyer in this case had rejected the produce, its actions would have been consistent with that duty. In interpreting the contract, the judicial officer concludes, in effect, that buyer lacked the right to reject the goods for late delivery.[14]

---

12. The opinion does not suggest that the buyer "dumped" the goods at less than their market value at the time of resale.

13. A different legal question is whether the terms of the document were part of the contract of carriage and binding on the carrier. Although the buyer was not a named party to the contract of carriage, the buyer might be able to seek a remedy from the carrier for its breach of that contract. Cf. UCC 2–722. In the principal case, of course, the carrier was not a party to the litigation.

14. The law governing the *Mendelson–Zeller* case is the Commercial Code supplemented by a federal statute, the Perishable Agricultural Commodities Act. 7 U.S.C. §§ 499a –499s. The act and regulations issued under it determine the obligations of parties to sales contracts. Many trade terms used in sales agreements for perishable agricultural commodities are specially defined in 7 C.F.R. § 46.43. Some trade terms preclude buyers from rejecting goods on arrival. Among them are "f.o.b. acceptance final," "rolling acceptance," and "pur-

Problem 5. S, a fruit dealer with a place of business in Georgia, and B, of Providence, R.I., made a contract for the sale and shipment to B of a carload of peaches, known as "fancy Belles and Thurbers" at $2.25 per basket; at the contract price a carload cost $986.75. On arrival of the car, B paid the freight and examined the car, and found the peaches were not the varieties ordered. The varieties shipped would sell for $50 less than those specified. B wired S rejecting the car and advising S to ship to Boston, since Providence could not use peaches of that quality. S answered: "Car yours. Care not what you do with it. Gave you best colored stock possible as ordered and hold you responsible for amount of draft." B reshipped to Boston and ordered a Boston commission merchant to dispose of the car. B tendered S the proceeds, $638.13, less expenses (freight to Boston $362.63, expense of unloading $13.44 and commission of Boston agent $44.67) a balance of $217.39. The market price had dropped before arrival.

S sued B for the contract price of $986.75. If there had been no market decline, should it make any substantial difference whether B is held to have "accepted"? Does the decline in the peach market make the question of "acceptance" important? See UCC 2–607; Descalzi Fruit Co. v. William S. Sweet & Son, 30 R.I. 320, 75 A. 308 (1910); Askco Engineering Corp. v. Mobil Chemical Corp., 535 S.W.2d 893 (Tex.Civ.App.1976). Might B have been required to resell? See UCC 2–603.

FERTICO BELGIUM S.A. v. PHOSPHATE CHEMICALS EXPORT ASSOCIATION, INC.

Court of Appeals of New York, 1987.
70 N.Y.2d 76, 517 N.Y.S.2d 465, 510 N.E.2d 334.

BELLACOSA, J.

A seller (Phoschem) breached its contract to timely deliver goods to a buyer-trader (Fertico) who properly sought cover (under the Uniform Commercial Code that means acquiring substitute goods) from another source (Unifert) in order to avoid breaching that buyer-trader's obligation to a third-party buyer (Altawreed). The sole issue involves the applicable principles and computation of damages for breach of the Phoschem–to–Fertico contract.

We hold that under the exceptional circumstances of this case plaintiff Fertico, as a buyer-trader, is entitled to damages from seller Phoschem equal to the increased cost of cover plus consequential and incidental damages minus expenses saved (UCC § 2–712[2]). In this case, expenses saved as a result of the breach are limited to costs or expenditures which would have arisen had there been no breach. Thus, the seller Phoschem is not entitled to a credit from the profits of a subsequent sale by the first buyer-trader Fertico to a fourth party

chase after inspection." See, e.g., L. Gillarde Co. v. Joseph Martinelli & Co., 169 F.2d 60 (1st Cir.1948), cert. denied, 335 U.S. 885 (1948).

(Janssens) of nonconforming goods from Phoschem. Fertico's letter of credit had been presented by Phoschem and honored so, under the specific facts of this case, Fertico had no commercially reasonable alternative but to retain and resell the fertilizer. This is so despite Fertico's exercise of cover in connection with the first set of transactions, i.e., Phoschem to Fertico to Altawreed. The covering buyer-trader may not, however, as in this case, recover other consequential damages when the third party to which it made its sale provides increased compensation to offset additional costs arising as a consequence of the breach.

In October 1978 appellant Fertico Belgium S.A. (Fertico), an international trader of fertilizer, contracted with Phosphate Chemicals Export Association, Inc. (Phoschem), a corporation engaged in exporting phosphate fertilizer, to purchase two separate shipments of fertilizer for delivery to Antwerp, Belgium. The first shipment was to be 15,000 tons delivered no later than November 20, 1978 and the second was to be 20,000 tons delivered by November 30, 1978. Phoschem knew that Fertico required delivery on the specified dates so that the fertilizer could be bagged and shipped in satisfaction of a secondary contract Fertico had with Altawreed, Iraq's agricultural ministry. Fertico secured a letter of credit in a timely manner with respect to the first shipment.* After Phoschem projected a first shipment delivery date of December 4, 1978, Fertico advised Phoschem, on November 13, 1978, that the breach as to the first shipment presented "huge problems" and canceled the second shipment which had not as of that date been loaded, thus ensuring its late delivery. The first shipment did not actually arrive in Antwerp until December 17 and was not off-loaded until December 21, 1978. Despite the breach as to the first shipment, Fertico retained custody and indeed acquired title over that first shipment because, as its president testified "[w]e had no other choice" ... as defendant seller Phoschem had presented Fertico's $1.7 million letter of credit as of November 17, 1978, and the same had been honored by the issuer... .

Fertico's predicament from the breach by delay of even the first shipment, a breach which Phoschem does not deny, was that it, in turn, would breach its contract to sell to Altawreed unless it acquired substitute goods. In an effort to avoid that secondary breach, Fertico took steps in mid-November to cover (UCC § 2–712) the goods by purchasing 35,000 tons of the same type fertilizer from Unifert, a Lebanese concern. The cost of the fertilizer itself under the Phoschem-to-Fertico contract was $4,025,000, and under the Unifert–to–Fertico contract $4,725,000, a differential of $700,000. On the same day Fertico acquired cover, November 15, 1978, Fertico's president traveled

* [A letter of credit is a commitment by a bank to pay a designated amount of money to a beneficiary of the letter of credit; the bank's obligation to pay is usually conditional upon the beneficiary's presentment of described documents. This device is commonly used in international sales as the means by which buyers pay the contract price for goods when sellers present to the banks documents indicating that the goods have been shipped. We consider this payment device further in Section 4. Eds.]

to Baghdad, Iraq, to renegotiate its contract with Altawreed. In return for a postponed delivery date and an additional payment of $20.50 per ton, Fertico agreed to make direct inland delivery rather than delivery to the seaport of Basra. Fertico fulfilled its renegotiated Altawreed contract with the substitute fertilizer purchased as cover from Unifert.

In addition to the problems related to its Altawreed contract, Fertico was left with 15,000 tons of late-delivered fertilizer which it did not require but which it had been compelled to take because Phoschem had received payment on Fertico's letter of credit. This aggrieved international buyer-seller was required to store the product and seek out a new purchaser. Fertico sold the 15,000 tons of the belatedly delivered Phoschem fertilizer to another buyer, Janssens, on March 19, 1979, some three months after the nonconforming delivery, and earned a profit of $454,000 based on the cost to it from Phoschem and its sale price to Janssens.

In 1981 Fertico commenced this action against Phoschem seeking $1.25 million in damages for Phoschem's breach of the October 1978 agreement. A jury returned a verdict of $1.07 million which the trial court refused to overturn on a motion for judgment notwithstanding the verdict. The Appellate Division vacated the damage award, ordered a new trial on the damages issue only and ruled, as a matter of law, (1) that the increased transportation costs on the Altawreed contract were not consequential damages; (2) that the higher purchase price paid by Altawreed to Fertico was an expense saved as a consequence of the Phoschem breach; and (3) that the Fertico damages had to be reduced by the profits from the Janssens' sale.... Fertico appealed to this court on a stipulation for judgment absolute. We disagree with propositions (2) and (3) in the Appellate Division ruling, and conclude that the Uniform Commercial Code and our analysis support a modification and reinstatement of $700,000 of the damage award in a final judgment resolving this litigation between the parties.

Failure by Phoschem to make delivery on the contract dates concededly constituted a breach of the contract.... The Uniform Commercial Code § 2–711 gives the nonbreaching party the alternative of either seeking the partial self-help of cover along with recovery of damages (UCC § 2–712), or of recovering damages only for the differential between the market price and the contract price, together with incidental and consequential damages less expenses saved (UCC § 2–713...). Fertico exercised its right as the wronged buyer-trader to cover in order to obtain the substitute fertilizer it required to meet its obligation under its Altawreed contract (see, UCC § 2–712, comment 1).

A covering buyer's damages are equal to the difference between the presumably higher cost of cover and the contract price, plus incidental or consequential damages suffered on account of the breach, less expenses saved (UCC § 2–712[2]). Fertico is thus entitled to a damage remedy under this section because its cover purchase was made in good faith, without unreasonable delay, and the Unifert fertilizer was a reasonable substitute for the Phoschem fertilizer....

Fertico's additional costs for delivering the fertilizer inland rather than at a seaport would usually constitute consequential damages because they resulted from Phoschem's breach, because Phoschem knew that Fertico would incur damages under its separate contract obligation and because the damages were not prevented by the cover (UCC § 2–715[2]). The increased costs attendant to the Altawreed contract are consequential damages because they did not "arise within the scope of the immediate [Phoschem–Fertico] transaction, but rather stem from losses incurred by [Fertico] in its dealings [with Altawreed] which were a proximate result of the breach, and which were reasonably foreseeable by the breaching party at the time of contracting".... Inasmuch as Altawreed compensated Fertico for the additional delivery costs, Fertico was insulated from any loss in that respect as a result of Phoschem's breach, thereby eliminating this category of potential damages. On this question of consequential damages, the Appellate Division was correct.

The additional compensation to Fertico, an international trader, from Altawreed is not, however, an expense saved as a consequence of the seller Phoschem's breach for which Phoschem is entitled to any credit (UCC § 2–712[2]). In most instances, and particularly in this case, saved expenses must be costs or expenditures which would be anticipated had there been no breach.... For example, if a seller were to breach a contract to deliver an unpackaged product to the buyer and the buyer were to cover with the same product prepackaged, the cost of packaging which the buyer would have had to perform is an expense saved as a consequence of the breach.... The increased remuneration from Altawreed was compensation for the additional shipment responsibilities incurred by Fertico, not a cost or expenditure anticipated in the absence of a breach, and therefore was erroneously analyzed and credited in Phoschem's favor by the Appellate Division.

The third prong of the damages analysis relates to the profit made from the independent sale of the Phoschem fertilizer to Janssens. The Appellate Division erred in offsetting this profit against the damages otherwise suffered since that court mistakenly concluded that the sale stemmed from and was dependent upon Phoschem's breach. This offset, on these peculiar facts, would severely disadvantage Fertico, a trader in fertilizer who both buys and sells, and who would have pursued such commercial transactions had there been no breach by Phoschem. It would be anomalous to conclude that had it not been for Phoschem's breach Fertico would not have continued its trade and upon such reasoning to counterpoise the profits from the Janssens' sale against the damages arising from Phoschem's breach. Inasmuch as the facts here are exceptional because Fertico met its subsale obligations with the cover fertilizer and yet acquired title and control over the late-delivered fertilizer from Phoschem, our decision does not fit squarely within the available Uniform Commercial Code remedies urged by the dissent. . . .

Fertico learned of Phoschem's breach after Phoschem had negotiated Fertico's $1.7 million letter of credit, which constituted complete payment for the first shipment. With no commercially reasonable alternative, Fertico took custody of the first shipment but canceled the second (UCC § 2–601[c]), having previously notified Phoschem of its breach (UCC § 2–607). The loss resulting to Fertico by having to acquire cover, even in the face of its acceptance of a late-delivered portion of the fertilizer, is properly recoverable under section 2–714[1]. . . . At the same time, Uniform Commercial Code § 1–106 directs that the remedies provided by the Uniform Commercial Code should be liberally administered so as to put the aggrieved party in as good a position as if the other party had fully performed. Had Phoschem fully performed, Fertico would have had the benefit of the Altawreed transaction and, as a trader of fertilizer, the profits from the Janssens' sale as well. "Gains made by the injured party on other transactions after the breach are never to be deducted from the damages that are otherwise recoverable, unless such gains could not have been made, had there been no breach" (5 Corbin, Contracts § 1041, at 256 . . .). Fertico's profit made on the sale of a nonspecific article such as fertilizer, of which the supply in the market is not limited, should not therefore be deducted from the damages recoverable from Phoschem. . . .

Fertico was concededly wronged by Phoschem's breach and Fertico resorted to Uniform Commercial Code remedies which are rooted in what we perceive to be the realities of the marketplace. Fertico did what reasonable traders would do and would like to do in mitigating risks inflicted in this case by Phoschem and in exerting its commercial resourcefulness. That is, it took steps to save its business, its customers, its good will and its deals and ultimately to also recover appropriate damages from a wrongdoer. That did not produce a "windfall" or a "double benefit" to the aggrieved party as the dissenting opinion asserts. The result we reach today countenances no such thing. On the contrary, to deprive the buyer-trader Fertico of its rightful differential damages of $700,000 and to credit this transactionally independent profit to Phoschem would perversely enrich the wrongdoer at the expense of the wronged party, a result those in the marketplace would find perplexing and a result which the generous remedial purpose of the Uniform Commercial Code does not compel or authorize. The dissent's characterization of the recovery by an injured party of damages for a breach of contract as a "benefit" is wrong, since that functionally attributes a kind of lien against the independently pursued benefit derived out of that separate transaction.

Accordingly, the order of the Appellate Division affirming liability but vacating, on the law, the damage award and remanding the matter for a new trial on the issue of damages, as appealed to this court on a stipulation for judgment absolute, should be modified and damages awarded to Fertico in the amount of $700,000 in accordance with this opinion.

TITONE, J. (dissenting).

At issue in this appeal is the relationship among the various remedies that article 2 of the Uniform Commercial Code provides for buyers aggrieved by sellers' defaults. Central to the analysis is the principle that the Code's remedies "shall be liberally administered to the end that the aggrieved party may be put in *as good a position* as if the other party had fully performed" (UCC § 1–106[1][emphasis supplied]). Here, the majority has concluded that the aggrieved buyer may retain both cover damages and the profit from the resale of the late-delivered goods, in effect, securing the benefit of its bargain twice. Since that result is not required by, and indeed is not even consistent with, the purpose of Code's generous remedial provisions, I must respectfully dissent.[1]

I begin with the premise that an aggrieved buyer who has purchased substitute goods and sued for "cover" damages under UCC § 2–712 has impliedly rejected the seller's nonconforming performance and, consequently, holds the seller's goods only as security for any prepayments made to the seller (see, UCC § 2–706[6]; § 2–711[3]). I find the contrary position—that an aggrieved buyer may compatibly resort to cover and also retain and resell the nonconforming goods for its own account—to be legally insupportable and economically unsound. . . . [F]rom an economic standpoint, the buyer receives the full benefit of his bargain when he obtains cover damages under UCC § 2–712. Allowing the buyer to retain and resell the goods in addition obviously leads to a windfall, since the buyer is receiving more than the benefit of the transaction it bargained for.

* * *

The majority has attempted to rationalize that result here by relying on a damages rule that has previously been applied only to aggrieved sellers. The rule permits a seller who regularly deals in goods of a particular type to sue the breaching buyer for lost profit even though the wrongfully rejected goods have been sold to another buyer without loss. The rule applies only where the seller has an unlimited supply of standard-price goods. . . . In those situations, "it may safely be assumed that" the seller would have made two sales instead of one if the buyer had not breached, and, consequently, it can fairly be said that the buyer's breach deprived the seller of an opportunity for additional profit. . . . Thus, traditional remedies such as resale or market price differential are "inadequate to put the seller in as good a position as

---

1. My disagreement with the majority lies only in its conclusion that the Appellate Division erred by offsetting Fertico's damage award against the profit Fertico obtained on the resale of Phoschem's goods. I agree completely with the majority's conclusion concerning the proper application of the $20.50 per ton additional reimbursement that Fertico obtained from Altawreed.

performance would have done," and the seller may sue for the lost profit (UCC § 2–708[2]).

The Code, however, does not contain an analogous provision allowing aggrieved buyers to recover profits from lost sales, and there is good reason for that omission, since neither of the conditions necessary for application of the sellers' lost-profit remedy may be satisfied in the case of an aggrieved buyer. ...

Indeed, this case illustrates the difficulty of applying the seller's lost-profit remedy to aggrieved buyers. Were it not for Phoschem's breach, Fertico would have delivered the 15,000 tons of fertilizer it had purchased from Phoschem to Altawreed and would have had to go into the marketplace again to acquire an additional 15,000 tons if it wished to make a second sale to Janssens. In this respect, Fertico's position here is really no different in principle from that of an aggrieved seller which had only one set of goods at its immediate disposal. In both instances, the breach of a prior agreement is what has made the goods available for a second sale.... . And, while a second sale may have been theoretically possible even without the breach, the uncertainties occasioned by the buyer/seller's need to return to the marketplace for more goods of the same kind preclude the assumption, implicit in the majority's holding ... that the second sale and its accompanying profit would have been made on the same terms even if no breach had occurred.

Finally, I cannot agree with the majority's reliance on the supposedly "exceptional" circumstance that Fertico both "met its subsale obligations with the cover fertilizer and * * * acquired title and control over the late-delivered fertilizer".... . First, the basis for and significance of the majority's conclusion that Fertico acquired title to the goods is left unclear. Certainly, the fact that Fertico had already paid for the goods cannot be controlling, since the Code clearly does not equate payment and receipt of the goods with passage of title. To the contrary, the Code expressly contemplates and accounts for these situations by permitting a wronged buyer who has rejected to retain and resell the goods in its possession to recover any down payment (UCC § 2–706[6]; § 2–711[3]). The Code also requires in these situations, however, that the buyer account to the breaching seller for any additional profit it has made on the resale (UCC § 2–706[6]). Nothing in the majority opinion satisfactorily explains why this remedy is insufficient.

Furthermore, the majority's emphasis on the asserted "exceptional facts" is unpersuasive because under the terms of the majority's holding the outcome in a given case would turn, in large measure, on the fortuity of which party had possession of the goods after the breach. In the case of a simple late delivery the buyer will ordinarily have possession after the breach. Under the majority's holding, that buyer may both obtain cover damages and resell the seller's goods, retaining any profit for itself. In the case of a complete failure to deliver, however, the seller will ordinarily have possession of the goods after the breach. .... [T]he repudiating seller may resell the undelivered goods in its possession for its own account.... Since I cannot agree with a rule of law that ultimately imposes a greater penalty on the less serious of two similar breaches, I dissent and vote to affirm.

CHIEF JUDGE WACHTLER and JUDGES SIMONS, KAYE and HANCOCK, JR., concur with JUDGE BELLACOSA; JUDGE TITONE dissents and votes to affirm in a separate opinion in which JUDGE ALEXANDER concurs.

Notes

(1) Anticipating Breach. The opinion states that seller bound itself contractually that fertilizer to be shipped by ocean carriers would arrive in Antwerp on or before November 20 (15,000 tons) and November 30 (20,000 tons). Before November 20, buyer cancelled the second shipment and purchased "cover" goods for both (35,000 tons). What justified buyer's actions? Was seller in breach on November 13? Had seller repudiated the contract with respect to a performance not yet due? See UCC 2–610. Were buyer's expectations of receiving due performance impaired such that buyer had the right to invoke UCC 2–609?

Could buyer have rightfully rejected the shipment that arrived on December 17? Would UCC 2–601 or 2–612(2) apply? What Code provisions might justify buyer's cancellation of the second shipment? See UCC 2–610, 2–612(3).

(2) Rejection of Goods Already Paid For; Buyers' "Security Interest." Why did the majority conclude that buyer's right to reject was not a commercially reasonable solution? As the dissent notes, the Commercial Code provides that a buyer who has paid some or all of the price has a security interest in rejected goods in its possession, UCC 2–711(3). A buyer may enforce its security interest by selling the goods. Why would this not be a practical alternative for buyers who rightfully reject goods already paid for?

(3) Construction of UCC 2–711(3). The majority and dissent disagree about the proper disposition of the profit made on a resale. If an aggrieved *seller* resells under UCC 2–706 for a higher price than the original contract price, it is entitled to keep any profit made. UCC 2–706(6). The dissent erroneously asserts otherwise, but may have had in mind that a secured creditor who forecloses on a security interest under UCC Article 9 must turn over to the debtor proceeds obtained in liquidating the collateral in excess of the amount due to the creditor. UCC 9–504(2). Section 2–711(3) authorizes a buyer to resell "in the manner of an aggrieved seller (Section 2–706)." Should this be construed to authorize buyers generally to retain proceeds of resale in excess of the amounts of claims against sellers? Should a different result follow if the buyer, as in this case, is a trader, who regularly buys and sells fertilizer?

(3) WRONGFUL REJECTION

Sellers' Remedies. If buyers reject wrongfully and have not paid the full contract price, sellers are entitled to remedies, catalogued in UCC 2–703.

The Code provides for two remedies based upon sellers' actual or possible substitute transactions. A seller may resell the goods and recover monetary damages measured by the differential between the contract price and the net proceeds of the resale, UCC 2–706, or measured by the difference between the contract price and the market price of the goods, UCC 2–708(1).

The Code permits sellers the equivalent of specific enforcement in only limited circumstances. If, after reasonable effort, a seller is unable to resell wrongfully rejected goods or the circumstances reasonably indicate that such effort would be unavailing, the seller may be entitled to recover the contract price. UCC 2–709(1)(b). If buyers are compelled to pay the price, they are entitled to receive the goods. UCC 2–709(2).

The "wild card" remedy available under the Code to aggrieved sellers is recovery of damages measured by the "profit" the seller would have made if buyer had fully performed. UCC 2–708(2). "Profit" under this section is akin to the accounting formula of contract price less variable costs-of-goods-sold; "overhead" or so-called fixed costs are not included as an expense in calculations of "profit."

APEX OIL CO. v. THE BELCHER CO. OF NEW YORK, INC.
United States Court of Appeals, Second Circuit, 1988.
855 F.2d 997.

WINTER, CIRCUIT JUDGE:

This diversity case, arising out of an acrimonious commercial dispute, presents the question whether a sale of goods six weeks after a breach of contract may properly be used to calculate resale damages under Section 2–706 of the Uniform Commercial Code, where goods originally identified to the broken contract were sold on the day following the breach. Defendants The Belcher Company of New York, Inc. and Belcher New Jersey, Inc. (together "Belcher") appeal from a judgment, entered after a jury trial before Judge McLaughlin, awarding plaintiff Apex Oil Company ("Apex") $432,365.04 in damages for breach of contract and fraud in connection with an uncompleted transaction for heating oil. Belcher claims that the district court improperly allowed Apex to recover resale damages and that Apex failed to prove its fraud claim by clear and convincing evidence. We agree and reverse.

BACKGROUND

Apex buys, sells, refines and transports petroleum products of various sorts, including No. 2 heating oil, commonly known as home heating oil. Belcher also buys and sells petroleum products, including No. 2 heating oil. In February 1982, both firms were trading futures contracts for No. 2 heating oil on the New York Mercantile Exchange ("Merc"). In particular, both were trading Merc contracts for February 1982 No. 2 heating oil—i.e., contracts for the delivery of that commodity in New York Harbor during that delivery month in accordance with the Merc's rules. As a result of that trading, Apex was short 315 contracts, and Belcher was long by the same amount. Being "short" one contract for oil means that the trader has contracted to deliver one thousand barrels at some point in the future, and being "long" means just the opposite—that the trader has contracted to purchase that amount of oil. If a contract is not liquidated before the close of trading, the short trader must deliver the oil to a long trader (the exchange matches shorts with longs) in strict compliance with Merc rules or suffer stiff penalties, including disciplinary proceedings and fines. A short trader may, however, meet its obligations by entering into an "exchange for physicals" ("EFP") transaction with a long trader. An EFP allows a short trader to substitute for the delivery of oil under the terms of a futures contract the delivery of oil at a different place and time.

Apex was matched with Belcher by the Merc, and thus became bound to produce 315,000 barrels of No. 2 heating oil meeting Merc specifications in New York Harbor. Those specifications required that oil delivered in New York Harbor have a sulfur content no higher than 0.20%. Apex asked Belcher whether Belcher would take delivery of 190,000 barrels of oil in Boston Harbor in satisfaction of 190 contracts, and Belcher agreed. At trial, the parties did not dispute that, under this EFP, Apex promised it would deliver the No. 2 heating oil for the same price as that in the original contract—89.70 cents per gallon—and that the oil would be lifted from the vessel Bordeaux. The parties did dispute, and vigorously so, the requisite maximum sulfur content. At trial, Belcher sought to prove that the oil had to meet the New York standard of 0.20%, while Apex asserted that the oil had to meet only the specifications for Boston Harbor of not more than 0.30% sulfur.

The Bordeaux arrived in Boston Harbor on February 9, 1982, and on the next day began discharging its cargo of No. 2 heating oil at Belcher New England, Inc.'s terminal in Revere, Massachusetts. Later in the evening of February 10, after fifty or sixty thousand barrels had been offloaded, an independent petroleum inspector told Belcher that tests showed the oil on board the Bordeaux contained 0.28% sulfur, in excess of the New York Harbor specification. Belcher, nevertheless continued to lift oil from the ship until eleven o'clock the next morning, February 11, when 141,535 barrels had been pumped into Belcher's terminal. After pumping had stopped, a second test indicated that the oil contained 0.22% sulfur—a figure within the accepted range of tolerance for oil containing 0.20% sulfur. (Apex did not learn of the second test until shortly before trial.) Nevertheless, Belcher refused to resume pumping, claiming that the oil did not conform to specifications.

After Belcher ordered the Bordeaux to leave its terminal, Apex immediately contacted Cities Service. Apex was scheduled to deliver heating oil to Cities Service later in the month and accordingly asked if it could satisfy that obligation by immediately delivering the oil on the Bordeaux. Cities Service agreed, and that oil was delivered to Cities Service in Boston Harbor on February 12, one day after the oil had been rejected by Belcher. Apex did not give notice to Belcher that the oil had been delivered to Cities Service.

Meanwhile, Belcher and Apex continued to quarrel over the portion of the oil delivered by the Bordeaux. Belcher repeatedly informed Apex, orally and by telex, that the oil was unsuitable and would have to be sold at a loss because of its high sulfur content. Belcher also claimed, falsely, that it was incurring various expenses because the oil was unusable. In fact, however, Belcher had already sold the oil in the ordinary course of business. Belcher nevertheless refused to pay Apex the contract price of $5,322,200.27 for the oil it had accepted, and it demanded that Apex produce the remaining 48,000 barrels of oil owing under the contract. On February 17, Apex agreed to tender the 48,000 barrels if Belcher would both make partial payment for the oil actually accepted and agree to negotiate as to the price ultimately to be paid for that oil. Belcher agreed and sent Apex a check for $5,034,997.12, a sum reflecting a discount of five cents per gallon from the contract price. However, the check contained an endorsement stating that "[t]he acceptance and negotiation of this check constitutes full payment and final settlement of all claims" against Belcher. Apex refused the check, and the parties returned to square one. Apex demanded full payment; Belcher demanded that Apex either negotiate the check or remove the discharged oil (which had actually been sold) and replace it with 190,000 barrels of conforming product. Apex chose to take the oil and replace it, and on February 23 told Belcher that the 142,000 barrels of discharged oil would be removed on board the Mersault on February 25.

By then, however, Belcher had sold the 142,000 barrels and did not have an equivalent amount of No. 2 oil in its entire Boston terminal. Instead of admitting that it did not have the oil, Belcher told Apex that a dock for the Mersault was unavailable. Belcher also demanded that Apex either remove the oil *and* pay terminalling and storage fees, or accept payment for the oil at a discount of five cents per gallon. Apex refused to do either. On the next day, Belcher and Apex finally reached a settlement under which Belcher agreed to pay for the oil discharged from the Bordeaux at a discount of 2.5 cents per gallon. The settlement agreement also resolved an unrelated dispute between an Apex subsidiary and a subsidiary of Belcher's parent firm, The Coastal Corporation. It is this agreement that Apex now claims was procured by fraud.

After the settlement, Apex repeatedly contacted Belcher to ascertain when, where and how Belcher would accept delivery of the remaining 48,000 barrels. On March 5, Belcher informed Apex that it considered its obligations under the original contract to have been extinguished, and that it did not "desire to purchase such a volume [the 48,000 barrels] at the offered price." Apex responded by claiming that the settlement did not extinguish Belcher's obligation to accept the 48,000 barrels. In addition, Apex stated that unless Belcher accepted the oil by March 20, Apex would identify 48,000 barrels of No. 2 oil to the breached contract and sell the oil to a third party. When Belcher again refused to take the oil, Apex sold 48,000 barrels to Gill & Duffus Company. This oil was sold for delivery in April at a price of 76.25 cents per gallon, 13.45 cents per gallon below the Belcher contract price.

On October 7, 1982, Apex brought this suit in the Eastern District, asserting breach of contract and fraud. The breach-of-contract claim in Apex's amended complaint contended that Belcher had breached the EFP, not in February, but in March, when Belcher had refused to take delivery of the 48,000 barrels still owing under the contract. The amended complaint further alleged that "[a]t the time of the breach of the Contract by Belcher the market price of the product was $.7625 per gallon," the price brought by the resale to Gill & Duffus on March 23. ... In turn, the fraud claim asserted that Belcher had made various misrepresentations—that the Bordeaux oil was unfit, and unusable by Belcher; and that consequently Belcher was suffering extensive damages and wanted the oil removed—upon which Apex had relied when it had agreed to settle as to the 142,000 barrels lifted from the Bordeaux. Apex asserted that as a result of the alleged fraud it had suffered damages of 2.5 cents per gallon, the discount agreed upon in the settlement.

The case went to trial before Judge McLaughlin and a jury between February 3 and February 13, 1986. As it had alleged in its pleadings, Apex asserted that its breach-of-contract claim was based on an alleged breach occurring *after* February 11, 1982, the day Belcher rejected the oil on board the Bordeaux. Judge McLaughlin, however, rejected this theory as a matter of law. His view of the case was that Belcher's rejection of the Bordeaux oil occurred under one of two circumstances: (i) either the oil conformed to the proper sulfur specification, in which case Belcher breached; or (ii) the oil did not conform, in which case Apex breached. Judge McLaughlin reasoned that, if Belcher breached on February 11, then it could not have breached thereafter. If on the other hand Apex breached, then, Judge McLaughlin reasoned, only under the doctrine of cure, see N.Y.U.C.C. § 2–508 (McKinney 1964), could Belcher be deemed to have breached. Apex, however, waived the cure theory by expressly disavowing it (perhaps because it presumes a breach by Apex). Instead, Apex argued that, regardless of whether the Bordeaux oil had conformed, Belcher's refusal throughout February and March 1982 to accept delivery of 48,000 barrels of conforming oil, which Belcher was then still demanding, had constituted a breach of contract. Judge McLaughlin rejected this argument, which he viewed as simply "an attempt to reintroduce the cure doctrine."

In a general verdict, the jury awarded Apex $283,752.94 on the breach-of-contract claim, and $148,612.10 on the fraud claim, for a total of $432,365.04. With the addition of prejudgment interest, the judgment came to $588,566.29.

Belcher appeals from this verdict. Apex has not taken a cross-appeal from Judge McLaughlin's dismissal of its post-February 11 breach theories, however. The parties agree, therefore, that as the case comes to us, the verdict concerning the breach can be upheld only on the theory that, if Belcher breached the contract, it did so only on February 11, 1982, and that the oil sold to Gill & Duffus on March 23 was identified to the broken contract.

DISCUSSION
* * *

Belcher's principal argument on appeal is that the district court erred as a matter of law in allowing Apex to recover resale damages under Section 2–706. Specifically, Belcher contends that the heating oil Apex sold to Gill & Duffus in late March of 1982 was not identified to the broken contract. According to Belcher, the oil identified to the contract was the oil aboard the Bordeaux—oil which Apex had sold to Cities Service on the day after the breach. In response, Apex argues that, because heating oil is a fungible commodity, the oil sold to Gill & Duffus was "reasonably identified" to the contract even though it was not the same oil that had been on board the Bordeaux. We agree with Apex that, at least with respect to fungible goods, identification for the purposes of a resale transaction does not necessarily require that the resold goods be the exact goods that were rejected or repudiated. Nonetheless, we conclude that as a matter of law the oil sold to Gill & Duffus in March was not reasonably identified to the contract breached on February 11, and that the resale was not commercially reasonable.

Resolving the instant dispute requires us to survey various provisions of the Uniform Commercial Code. ... The Bordeaux oil was unquestionably identified to the contract under Section 2–501(b), and Apex does not assert otherwise. Nevertheless, Apex argues that Section 2–501 "has no application in the context of the Section 2–706 resale remedy," because Section 2–501 defines identification only for the purpose of establishing the point at which a buyer "obtains a special property and an insurable interest in goods." N.Y.U.C.C. § 2–501. This argument has a facial plausibility but ignores Section 2–103, which contains various definitions, and an index of other definitions, of terms used throughout Article 2 of the Code. With regard to "[i]dentification," Section 2–103(2) provides that the "definition[ ] applying to *this Article* " is set forth in Section 2–501. Id. § 2–103 (emphasis added).

Section 2–501 thus informs us that the Bordeaux oil was identified to the contract. It does not end our inquiry, however, because it does not exclude as a matter of law the possibility that a seller may identify goods to a contract, but then substitute, for the identified goods, *identical* goods that are then identified to the contract. . . . Belcher relies upon Section 2–706's statement that "the seller may resell the *goods concerned,*" N.Y.U.C.C. § 2–706(1) (emphasis added), and upon Section 2–704, which states that "[a]n aggrieved seller . . . may . . . identify to the contract conforming goods *not already identified* if at the time he learned of the breach they are in his possession or control." Id. § 2–704(1) (emphasis added). According to Belcher, these statements absolutely foreclose the possibility of reidentification for the purpose of a resale. Apex, on the other hand, points to Section 2–706's statement that "it is not necessary that the goods be in existence or that any or all of them have been identified to the contract before the breach." Id. § 2–706(2). According to Apex, this language shows that "[t]he relevant inquiry to be made under Section 2–706 is whether the resale transaction is reasonably identified to the breached contract and not whether the goods resold were originally identified to that contract." Apex Br. at 25.

None of the cited provisions are dispositive. First, Section 2–706(1)'s reference to reselling "the goods concerned" is unhelpful because those goods are the goods identified to the contract, but which goods are so identified is the question to be answered in the instant case. Second, as to Section 2–704, the fact that an aggrieved seller may identify goods "not already identified" does not mean that the seller may not identify goods as substitutes for previously identified goods. Rather, Section 2–704 appears to deal simply with the situation described in Section 2–706(2) above, where the goods are not yet in existence or have not yet been identified to the contract. Belcher thus can draw no comfort from either Section 2–704 or Section 2–706(1). Third, at the same time, however, Section 2–706(2)'s reference to nonexistent and nonidentified goods does not mean, as Apex suggests, that the original (prebreach) identification of goods is wholly irrelevant. Rather, the provision regarding nonexistent and nonidentified goods deals with the special circumstances involving anticipatory repudiation by the buyer. See N.Y.U.C.C § 2–706 comment 7. Under such circumstances, there can of course be no resale remedy unless the seller is allowed to identify goods to the contract after the breach. That is obviously not the case here.

* * *

[F]ungible goods resold pursuant to § 2–706 must be goods identified to the contract, but need not always be those *originally* identified to the contract. In other words, at least where fungible goods are concerned, identification is not always an irrevocable act and does not foreclose the possibility of substitution. . . . Nevertheless, as [§ 2–706] expressly states, "[t]he resale must be *reasonably* identified as referring to the broken contract," and "every aspect of the sale including the method, manner, time, place and terms must be commercially reasonable." Moreover, because the purpose of remedies under the Code is to put "the aggrieved party . . . in as good a position as if the other party had performed," id. § 1–106(1), the reasonableness of the identification and of the resale must be determined by examining whether the market value of, and the price received for, the resold goods "accurately reflects the market value of the goods which are the subject of the contract." Servbest [Foods, Inc. v. Emssee Industries, Inc., 82 Ill.App. 3d 662,] 671, [403 N.E.2d 1], 8.

* * *

Apex's delay of nearly six weeks between the breach on February 11, 1982 and the purported resale on March 23 was clearly unreasonable, even if the transfer to Cities Service had not occurred. Steven Wirkus, of Apex, testified on cross-examination that the market price for No. 2 heating oil on February 12, when the Bordeaux oil was delivered to Cities Service, was "[p]robably somewhere around 88 cents a gallon or 87." (The EFP contract price, of course, was 89.70 cents per gallon.) Wirkus also testified on redirect examination that the market price fluctuated throughout the next several weeks:

Q. Sir, while you couldn't remember with particularity what the price of oil was on a given day four years ago, is it fair to say that prices went up and down?

A. Definitely that's fair to say.

Q. From day-to-day?

A. Yes.

Q. Towards the end of February prices went down?

A. That's correct.

Q. Then in early March it went back up?

A. In early March, yes.

Q. Then they went back down again towards the middle of March; isn't that correct?

MR. GILBERT: I object to the form of this, your Honor, on redirect.

THE COURT: Yes.

Q. Did they go back down in mid March, Mr. Wirkus?

A. My recollection, yes.

Q. In late March what happened to the price?

A. Market went back up.

Moreover, Wirkus testified that, on March 23, in a transaction unrelated to the resale, Apex purchased 25,000 barrels of No. 2 oil for March delivery at 80.50 cents per gallon, and sold an equivalent amount for April delivery at 77.25 cents per gallon. Other sales on March 22 and 23 for April delivery brought similar prices: 100,000 barrels were sold at 76.85 cents, and 25,000 barrels at 76.35 cents. The Gill & Duffus resale, which was also for April delivery, fetched a price of 76.25 cents per gallon—some eleven or twelve cents below the market price on the day of the breach.

In view of the long delay and the apparent volatility of the market for No. 2 oil, the purported resale failed to meet the requirements of Section 2–706 as a matter of law. ...

... Apex's only asserted justification, which the district court accepted in denying Belcher's motion for judgment notwithstanding the verdict, was that the delay was caused by continuing negotiations with Belcher. We find that ruling to be inconsistent with the district court's view that Belcher's breach, if any, occurred on February 11. The function of a resale was to put Apex in the position it would have been on that date by determining the value of the oil Belcher refused. The value of the oil at a later date is irrelevant because Apex was in no way obligated by the contract or by the Uniform Commercial Code to reserve 48,000 gallons for Belcher after the February 11 breach. Indeed, that is why Apex's original theory, rejected by the district court and not before us on this appeal, was that the breach occurred in March.

The rule that a "resale should be made as soon as practicable after ... breach," ... should be stringently applied where, as here, the resold goods are not those originally identified to the contract. In such circumstances, of course, there is a significant risk that the seller, who may perhaps have already disposed of the original goods without suffering any loss, has identified new goods for resale in order to minimize the resale price and thus to maximize damages. That was not the case in Servbest, for example, where the resale consisted of the first sales made after the breach. See 82 Ill.App. 2d at 675, 403 N.E.2d at 11. Here, by contrast, the oil originally identified to the contract was sold the day after the February 11, 1982 breach, and no doubt Apex sold ample amounts thereafter in the six weeks before the purported resale. ... Because the sale of the oil identified to the contract to Cities Service on the next day fixed the value of the goods refused as a matter of law, the judgment on the breach-of-contract claim must be reversed.

We turn finally to Apex's fraud claim. ... Belcher claims that the evidence was insufficient to support the jury's finding that Apex, in agreeing to the settlement with Belcher, had relied upon Belcher's misrepresentations in ignorance of their falsity and had suffered injury accordingly.

In support of the finding of reliance, Apex relies primarily, if not exclusively, upon the testimony of its president, Anthony Novelly. Novelly testified that he had delegated the task of negotiation to in-house counsel, Harold Lessner. Lessner nevertheless kept Novelly abreast of Belcher's various demands and representations because it was Novelly, as president, "who had to approve the settlement ultimately." To this effect, Novelly testified as follows:

Q. During your discussion with Mr. Lesner [sic], did he say anything to you concerning whether Belcher had used the oil?

A. No, he said the oil was off spec and not useable.

Q. He said that is what Belcher had told him?

A. Correct.

Q. During your conversation with Mr. Lesner [sic], did he tell you anything about whether Belcher was claiming damages, as a result of the delivery?

A. Yes, they were.

Q. And did you rely on all the matters that were conveyed to you in approving the settlement?

A. Yes, I did.

According to Apex, this testimony regarding its alleged reliance is "unrebutted." That may be true so far as other witnesses are concerned, but Novelly candidly modified his testimony on cross-examination as follows:

Q. At the time you approved the settlement, one of the terms was that Belcher was going to get a discount off the agreed price for the BORDEAUX oil of two and a half cents per gallon, is that correct?

A. Yes.

Q. Did you believe they were intitled [sic] to a two and a half cent per gallon discount based on the facts you know?

MR. WEINER: Objection.

THE COURT: Overruled.

A. Not really.

Q. You did not believe that?

A. No.

Q. Did you believe they were intitled [sic] to any discount?

A. I wouldn't have thought so.

Q. You agreed to the settlement for other reasons, did you not?

A. I agreed to the settlement to get the thing settled.

Q. You wanted to get it behind you, is that correct?

A. Yes.

Q. You had a number of items—

A. Whole bunch of them.

Q. You didn't like to leave all these open items?

A. I didn't want a mess hanging around.

Q. You wanted to get everything cleaned up?

A. That's correct.

Q. You had another idea—withdrawn. You had another motivation, didn't you sir?

A. Coastal [Belcher's parent] was a big company, I don't like to have problems with big companies. I try to settle things and avoid litigation.

Q. You want to get all the open items closed, for you to do business with Coastal and its subsidiaries, is that correct?

A. That is a good statement, yes.

* * *

Q. At the time you were discussing the settlement with Mr. Lesner [sic] or anybody else you talked about it with, did you have the belief that the oil delivered to Belcher aboard the BORDEAUX was in fact not useable by Belcher?

A. I never had that belief, no.

However much this display of refreshing candor ought to be rewarded, we must conclude that, in light of the concessions that Novelly was seeking a compromise of all outstanding disputes and did not believe Belcher's misrepresentations as to the oil delivered on February 11, a reasonable jury could not find by clear and convincing evidence that Apex believed and relied upon Belcher's misrepresentations.

Reversed.

Notes

(1) **Commodities Futures.** This case illustrates how products may be traded through "exchanges" that permit buyers and sellers to anticipate future deliveries of certain standardized products. Many participants in these futures markets have no expectation of either delivering or receiving goods under their contracts; before the closing date, these traders take offsetting buy-sell positions so that no performance occurs. These participants may be investors seeking profits from changes in market prices of the commodities or merchants "hedging" planned transactions against shifts in market prices. The buyer and seller in *Apex Oil* did not close out their positions and were "matched" by the N.Y. Mercantile Exchange as seller and buyer. Once "matched" the parties became obligated as if they had chosen to contract with each other. Thereafter, they negotiated a modification of the place of performance for part of the oil.

(2) **Construction of UCC 2–706 and 2–708.** Seller's counsel sought unsuccessfully to fix damages under UCC 2–706 by the March 23 sale to Gill & Duffus. When a seller claims but fails to qualify for relief under 2–706, may recovery be had under UCC 2–708(1)? Under 2–708(2)? See Comment 2 to UCC 2–706. Should a seller-plaintiff plead and seek to prove damages under all possible statutory provisions in the alternative?

Problem 6. Suppose seller in *Apex* had sought damages measured by UCC 2–708(1). Buyer counters that seller's damages should be measured, under UCC 2–706, by the price of the resale to Cities Service.

Is there any statutory basis for an argument that seller may not recover a larger amount under 2–708(1) than it would receive if damages were measured by 2–706? See Sebert, Remedies Under Article Two of the Uniform Commercial Code: An Agenda for Review, 130 U.Pa.L.Rev. 360, 380–383 (1981).

R.E. DAVIS CHEMICAL CORP. v. DIASONICS, INC.
United States Court of Appeals, Seventh Circuit, 1987.
826 F.2d 678.

CUDAHY, CIRCUIT JUDGE

Diasonics, Inc. appeals from the orders of the district court denying its motion for summary judgment and granting R.E. Davis Chemical Corp.'s summary judgment motion.... We ... reverse the grant of summary judgment in favor of Davis and remand for further proceedings.

I.

Diasonics is a California corporation engaged in the business of manufacturing and selling medical diagnostic equipment. Davis is an Illinois corporation that contracted to purchase a piece of medical diagnostic equipment from Diasonics. On or about February 23, 1984, Davis and Diasonics entered into a written contract under which Davis agreed to purchase the equipment. Pursuant to this agreement, Davis paid Diasonics a $300,000 deposit on February 29, 1984. ... Davis ... [subsequently] refused to take delivery of the equipment or to pay the balance due under the agreement. Diasonics later resold the equipment to a third party for the same price at which it was to be sold to Davis.

Davis sued Diasonics, asking for restitution of its $300,000 down payment under section 2–718(2) of the Uniform Commercial Code (the "UCC" or the "Code"). Ill. Rev. Stat. ch. 26, para. 2–718(2) (1985). Diasonics counterclaimed. Diasonics did not deny that Davis was entitled to recover its $300,000 deposit less $500 as provided in section 2–718(2)(b). However, Diasonics claimed that it was entitled to an offset under section 2–718(3). Diasonics alleged that it was a "lost volume seller," and, as such, it lost the profit from one sale when Davis breached its contract. Diasonics' position was that, in order to be put in as good a position as it would have been in had Davis performed, it was entitled to recover its lost profit on its contract with Davis under section 2–708(2) of the UCC. ...

The district court ... entered summary judgment for Davis. The court held that lost volume sellers were not entitled to recover damages under 2–708(2) but rather were limited to recovering the difference between the resale price and the contract price along with incidental damages under section 2–706(1). ... Davis was awarded $322,656, which represented Davis' down payment plus prejudgment interest less Diasonics' incidental damages. Diasonics appeals the district court's decision respecting its measure of damages as well as the dismissal of its third-party complaint.

II.

We consider first Diasonics' claim that the district court erred in holding that Diasonics was limited to the measure of damages provided in 2–706 and could not recover lost profits as a lost volume seller under 2–708(2). Surprisingly, given its importance, this issue has never been addressed by an Illinois court, nor, apparently, by any other court construing Illinois law. Thus we must attempt to predict how the Illinois Supreme Court would resolve this issue if it were presented to it. Courts applying the laws of other states have unanimously adopted the position that a lost volume seller can recover its lost profits under 2–708(2). Contrary to the result reached by the district court, we conclude that the Illinois Supreme Court would follow these other cases and would allow a lost volume seller to recover its lost profit under 2–708(2).

We begin our analysis with 2–718(2) and (3). Under 2–718(2)(b), Davis is entitled to the return of its down payment less $500. Davis' right to restitution, however, is qualified under 2–718(3)(a) to the extent that Diasonics can establish a right to recover damages under any other provision of Article 2 of the UCC. Article 2 contains four provisions that concern the recovery of a seller's general damages (as opposed to its incidental or consequential damages); 2–706 (contract price less resale price); 2–708(1) (contract price less market price); 2–708(2) (profit); and 2–709 (price). The problem we face here is determining whether Diasonics' damages should be measured under 2–706 or 2–708(2). To answer this question, we need to engage in a detailed look at the language and structure of these various damage provisions.

The Code does not provide a great deal of guidance as to when a particular damage remedy is appropriate. The damage remedies provided under the Code are catalogued in section 2–703, but this section does not indicate that there is any hierarchy among the remedies. One method of approaching the damage sections is to conclude that 2–708 is relegated to a role inferior to that of 2–706 and 2–709 and that one can turn to 2–708 only after one has concluded that neither 2–706 nor 2–709 is applicable.[6] Under this interpretation of the relationship be-

---

6. Evidence to support this approach can be found in the language of the various damage sections and of the official comments to the UCC. See § 2–709(3) ("a seller who is held not entitled to the price under this Section shall nevertheless be awarded damages for non-acceptance under the preceding section [§ 2–708]"); UCC comment 7 to § 2–709 ("if the action for the price fails, the seller may nonetheless have proved a case entitling him to damages for non-acceptance [under § 2–708]"); UCC comment 2 to § 2–706 ("failure to act properly under this section deprives the seller of the measure of damages here provided and relegates him to that provided in Section 2–708"); UCC comment 1 to § 2–704 (describes § 2–706 as the "primary remedy" available to a seller upon breach by the buyer); see also Commonwealth Ed-

tween 2–706 and 2–708, if the goods have been resold, the seller can sue to recover damages measured by the difference between the contract price and the resale price under 2–706. The seller can turn to 2–708 only if it resells in a commercially unreasonable manner or if it cannot resell but an action for the price is inappropriate under 2–709. The district court adopted this reading of the Code's damage remedies and, accordingly, limited Diasonics to the measure of damages provided in 2–706 because it resold the equipment in a commercially reasonable manner.

The district court's interpretation of 2–706 and 2–708, however, creates its own problems of statutory construction. There is some suggestion in the Code that the "fact that plaintiff resold the goods [in a commercially reasonable manner] does *not* compel him to use the resale remedy of § 2–706 rather than the damage remedy of § 2–708." Harris, A Radical Restatement of the Law of Seller's Damages: Sales Act and Commercial Code Results Compared, 18 Stan.L.Rev. 66, 101 n.174 (1965) (emphasis in original). Official comment 1 to 2–703, which catalogues the remedies available to a seller, states that these "remedies are essentially cumulative in nature" and that "whether the pursuit of one remedy bars another depends entirely on the facts of the individual case." See also State of New York Report of the Law Revision Comm'n for 1956, 396–97 (1956).[7]

Those courts that found that a lost volume seller can recover its lost profits under 2–708(2) implicitly rejected the position adopted by the district court; those courts started with the assumption that 2–708 applied to a lost volume seller without considering whether the seller was limited to the remedy provided under 2–706. None of those courts

---

ison Co. v. Decker Coal Co., 653 F.Supp. 841, 844 (N.D.Ill. 1987) (statutory language and case law suggest that "§ 2–708 remedies are available only to a seller who is not entitled to the contract price" under § 2–709); Childres & Burgess, Seller's Remedies: The Primacy of UCC 2–708(2), 48 N.Y.U.L.Rev. 833, 863–64 (1973). As one commentator has noted, 2–706 "is the Code section drafted specifically to define the damage rights of aggrieved reselling sellers, and there is no suggestion within it that the profit formula of section 2–708(2) is in any way intended to qualify or be superior to it." Shanker, The Case for a Literal Reading of UCC Section 2–708(2) (One Profit for the Reseller), 24 Case W. Res. 697, 699 (1973).

7. UCC comment 2 to 2–708(2) also suggests that 2–708 has broader applicability than suggested by the district court. UCC comment 2 provides: "This section permits the recovery of lost profits in all appropriate cases, which would include all standard priced goods. The normal measure there would be list price less cost to the dealer or list price less manufacturing cost to the manufacturer."

The district court's restrictive interpretation of 2–708(2) was based in part on UCC comment 1 to 2–704 which describes 2–706 as the aggrieved seller's primary remedy. The district court concluded that, if a lost volume seller could recover its lost profit under 2–708(2), every seller would attempt to recover damages under 2–708(2) and 2–706 would become the aggrieved seller's residuary remedy. This argument ignores the fact that to recover under 2–708(2), a seller must first establish its status as a lost volume seller. ...

The district court also concluded that a lost volume seller cannot recover its lost profit under 2–708(2) because such a result would negate a seller's duty to mitigate damages. This position fails to recognize the fact that, by definition, a lost volume seller cannot mitigate damages through resale. Resale does not reduce a lost volume seller's damages because the breach has still resulted in its losing one sale and a corresponding profit. ...

even suggested that a seller who resold goods in a commercially reasonable manner was limited to the damage formula provided under 2–706. We conclude that the Illinois Supreme Court, if presented with this question, would adopt the position of these other jurisdictions and would conclude that a reselling seller, such as Diasonics, is free to reject the damage formula prescribed in 2–706 and choose to proceed under 2–708.

Concluding that Diasonics is entitled to seek damages under 2–708, however, does not automatically result in Diasonics being awarded its lost profit. Two different measures of damages are provided in 2–708. Subsection 2–708(1) provides for a measure of damages calculated by subtracting the market price at the time and place for tender from the contract price.[9] The profit measure of damages, for which Diasonics is asking, is contained in 2–708(2). However, one applies 2–708(2) only if "the measure of damages provided in subsection (1) is inadequate to put the seller in as good a position as performance would have done...." Ill. Rev. Stat. ch. 26, para. 2–708(2) (1985). Diasonics claims that 2–708(1) does not provide an adequate measure of damages when the seller is a lost volume seller. To understand Diasonics' argument, we need to define the concept of the lost volume seller. Those cases that have addressed this issue have defined a lost volume seller as one that has a predictable and finite number of customers and that has the capacity either to sell to all new buyers or to make the one additional sale represented by the resale after the breach. According to a number of courts and commentators, if the seller would have made the sale represented by the resale whether or not the breach occurred, damages measured by the difference between the contract price and market price cannot put the lost volume seller in as good a position as it would have been in had the buyer performed. The breach effectively cost the seller a "profit," and the seller can only be made whole by awarding it damages in the amount of its "lost profit" under 2–708(2).

We agree with Diasonics' position that, under some circumstances, the measure of damages provided under 2–708(1) will not put a reselling seller in as good a position as it would have been in had the buyer performed because the breach resulted in the seller losing sales volume. However, we disagree with the definition of "lost volume seller" adopted by other courts. Courts awarding lost profits to a lost volume seller have focused on whether the seller had the capacity to supply the breached units in addition to what it actually sold. In reality, however, the relevant questions include, not only whether the seller could have

---

9. There is some debate in the commentaries about whether a seller who has resold the goods may ignore the measure of damages provided in 2–706 and elect to proceed under 2–708(1). Under some circumstances the contract-market price differential will result in overcompensating such a seller. See J. White & R. Summers, Handbook of the Law under the Uniform Commercial Code § 7–7, at 271–73 (2d ed. 1980); Sebert, Remedies under Article Two of the Uniform Commercial Code: An Agenda for Review, 130 U.Pa.L.Rev. 360, 380–83 (1981). We need not struggle with this question here because Diasonics has not sought to recover damages under 2–708(1).

produced the breached units in addition to its actual volume, but also whether it would have been profitable for the seller to produce both units. Goetz & Scott, Measuring Sellers' Damages: The Lost–Profits Puzzle, 31 Stan.L.Rev. 323, 332–33, 346–47 (1979). As one commentator has noted, under the economic law of diminishing returns or increasing marginal costs[,] ... as a seller's volume increases, then a point will inevitably be reached where the cost of selling each additional item diminishes the incremental return to the seller and eventually makes it entirely unprofitable to conclude the next sale. Shanker, supra, at 705. Thus, under some conditions, awarding a lost volume seller its presumed lost profit will result in overcompensating the seller, and 2–708(2) would not take effect because the damage formula provided in 2–708(1) does place the seller in as good a position as if the buyer had performed. Therefore, on remand, Diasonics must establish, not only that it had the capacity to produce the breached unit in addition to the unit resold, but also that it would have been profitable for it to have produced and sold both. ...

One final problem with awarding a lost volume seller its lost profits was raised by the district court. This problem stems from the formulation of the measure of damages provided under 2–708(2) which is "the profit (including reasonable overhead) which the seller would have made from full performance by the buyer, together with any incidental damages provided in this Article (Section 2–710), due allowance for costs reasonably incurred and due credit for payments or *proceeds of resale*" (emphasis added). The literal language of 2–708(2) requires that the proceeds from resale be credited against the amount of damages awarded which, in most cases, would result in the seller recovering nominal damages. In those cases in which the lost volume seller was awarded its lost profit as damages, the courts have circumvented this problem by concluding that this language only applies to proceeds realized from the resale of uncompleted goods for scrap. See, e.g., Neri [v. Retail Marine Corp.,] 30 N.Y.2d [393,] at 399 & n.2, 285 N.E.2d [311,] at 314 & n.2; see also J. White & R. Summers, Handbook of the Law under the Uniform Commercial Code § 7–13, at 285 ("courts should simply ignore the 'due credit' language in lost volume cases") (footnote omitted). Although neither the text of 2–708(2) nor the official comments limit its application to resale of goods for scrap, there is evidence that the drafters of 2–708 seemed to have had this more limited application in mind when they proposed amending 2–708 to include the phrase "due credit for payments or proceeds of resale." We conclude that the Illinois Supreme Court would adopt this more restrictive interpretation of this phrase rendering it inapplicable to this case.

We therefore reverse the grant of summary judgment in favor of Davis and remand with instructions that the district court calculate Diasonics' damages under 2–708(2) if Diasonics can establish, not only that it had the capacity to make the sale to Davis as well as the sale to the resale buyer, but also that it would have been profitable for it to make both sales. Of course, Diasonics, in addition, must show that it probably would have made the second sale absent the breach.

* * *

Notes

(1) **Subsequent decision:** On remand, Diasonics proved its average costs of manufacturing through expert testimony by accountants. It introduced evidence that the contract price was $1,500,000 but offered no specific evidence of the cost of manufacturing the equipment intended for Davis and resold to the third party. Using average cost data, the district court found that Diasonics profit would have been $453,000. The court of appeals affirmed. 924 F.2d 709 (7th Cir.1991).[15]

(2) **Construction of 2–708(2).** As indicated in the court's opinion, the academic debate about the proper reading of UCC 2–708(2) has been and continues to be vigorous. Some explanation must be found for the enormous difference in the amount of damages recoverable in a case like *Davis*, under 2–708(2) ($453,000), under 2–706 ($–0–), under 2–708(1) (probably $–0–). The remarkably laconic Comment to 2–708(2) gives no indication of appreciating the sheer force of this section. Much of the academic debate is in the mode of law-and-economics analysis, based upon models of "lost volume" sellers. Others argue that the basic remedial principle requires putting an aggrieved seller into as good a position as buyer's performance would have done, UCC 1–106, and that market-based damages under 2–706 and 2–708(1) fail to mirror full performance. In addition to the materials referred to by the court, see Sebert, Remedies Under Article Two of the Uniform Commercial Code: An Agenda for Review, 130 U.Pa.L.Rev. 360 (1981); Goldberg, An Economic Analysis of the Lost-Volume Retail Seller, 57 S.Cal.L.Rev. 283 (1984); Cooter and Eisenberg, Damages for Breach of Contract, 73 Cal.L.Rev. 1434 (1985); J. White & R. Summers, Uniform Commercial Code §§ 7–8 to 7–14 (3d ed. 1988); Scott, The Case for Market Damages: Revisiting the Lost Profits Puzzle, 4 U.Chi.L.Rev. 1155 (1990).

Although the 2–708 Comment states that the section is a rewriting of a provision in the Uniform Sales Act, that act had no provision comparable to UCC 2–708(2). The cited section, USA 64, provided generally for recovery of loss resulting in the ordinary course of events from buyer's breach (64(2)) and stated the specific formula of market-based damages in 64(3); it added in 64(4):

> (4) If, while labor or expense of material amount are necessary on the part of the seller to enable him to fulfill his obligations under the contract to sell or the sale, the buyer repudiates the contract or the sale, or notifies the seller to proceed no further therewith, the buyer shall be liable to the seller for no greater

---

15. The court of appeals remanded for further consideration of a contract term that buyer contended would have lowered the purchase price by a post-payment rebate of $255,000.

damages than the seller would have suffered if he did nothing towards carrying out the contract or the sale after receiving notice of the buyer's repudiation or countermand. The profit the seller would have made if the contract or the sale had been fully performed shall be considered in estimating such damages.

The Commercial Code revised the USA 64(4) allocation of risk if a manufacturing seller elects, upon repudiation, to complete the process. UCC 2–704(2). The manufacturer who exercises reasonable commercial judgment for the purposes of avoiding loss and "effective realization" is protected even if the value added thereby is less than the costs incurred.

Is it accurate to describe UCC 2–708 as a rewriting of USA 64?

(3) Revision of Article 2. The Permanent Editorial Board Study Group on UCC Article 2 recommended revision of UCC 2–708(2) to state, explicitly, that a seller may invoke the profit-measure of damages (1) when seller can show "lost volume," i.e., that but for the breach seller would probably have made two sales, or (2) or when a "middleman" seller reasonably stopped performance before the goods were obtained or a manufacturing seller stopped performance before the goods were completed. Preliminary Report 214–216 (1990). The Study Group recommended, further, that different measures be used for these two categories: The "due allowance ... due credit ..." clause should apply only to "stopped performance" cases and not to "lost volume" cases, but consideration should be given to economic analyses of declining margins of profit in multiple transactions. Id. 217–218. Do you agree?

(B) INTERNATIONAL SALES LAW

(1) BUYERS' AVOIDANCE FOR SELLERS' BREACH

The Convention on International Sale of Goods does not use the concepts of buyers' acceptance and rejection of goods and for the most part eschews any performance standard like the perfect tender rule. The Convention permits buyers to throw goods back on sellers on two grounds: (1) if sellers' performances are so deficient as to constitute "fundamental breach" as defined in CISG 25, or (2) if seller does not deliver goods within an extended time fixed by buyers under the *Nachfrist* provision of CISG 47. If either ground exists, a buyer may declare the contract avoided. CISG 49. For deficiencies that do not amount to "fundamental breach" or delays that are not within the *Nachfrist* provisions, buyers must take and keep or dispose of the goods. Buyers may, of course, seek monetary relief through price reduction or damages.

Buyers' exercise of the power to avoid contracts for fundamental breach is analogous to buyers' power to revoke acceptance under domestic United States law. We defer discussion of the manner, time, and effect of avoidance until the next section. We consider here the power to avoid for delay in performance.

Avoidance for Sellers' Late Performance. Sellers who deliver goods substantially after the time required for performance under the contracts may thereby commit fundamental breach. Aggrieved buyers may declare contracts avoided for fundamental breach whether the result of sellers' delay or other non-conformity.

However, the Convention underscores buyers' right to timely performance by sellers with additional provisions that do not depend upon fundamental breach. These provisions permit strict enforcement, not with regard to the time terms of the sales contracts, but rather with regard to the extensions of time that buyers can set under the Convention's *Nachfrist* provisions. Article 49(1)(b) empowers a buyer to avoid a sales contract if the seller has not delivered the goods within the "additional time" fixed by the buyer under CISG 47(1). In this facet of sellers' performance, buyers can effectively demand something akin to the exact performance of the perfect tender rule. Under what circumstances would buyers be specially concerned about the time of sellers' performance? See J. Honnold, Uniform Law for International Sales §§ 288, 305 (2d ed. 1991).

Time of Avoidance. The avoiding power of CISG 49(1)(b) is explicitly limited to cases of non-delivery. Once a seller has delivered, a buyer's power to throw the goods back on seller turns upon the degree of injury; buyer can avoid only for fundamental breach. Thus, here as elsewhere, CISG tends to restrict remedies for breach to monetary damages rather than permitting destruction of the duty to perform—a policy choice that responds to the waste that may result from contract-avoidance after extended international transport.

Manner of Avoidance. To avoid a contract under CISG 49(1)(b), a buyer must declare the contract avoided and give notice to the seller. CISG 26.

Effect of Avoidance. In cases of non-delivery, a buyer who declares the contract avoided is released from its obligations under the contract. CISG 81. Particularly, a buyer is released from the CISG 53 obligations to take delivery of the goods and pay the price. If buyer has already paid the price, it is entitled to restitution. CISG 81(2). Whether or not the price has been paid, buyer is entitled to damages. CISG 81(1). If the goods have arrived at their destination and placed there at buyer's disposal, even though the buyer has exercised the right to avoid the contract, the buyer must take possession of the goods on behalf of the seller, provided that this can be done without payment of the price and without unreasonable inconvenience or expense. CISG 86(2). Buyer must take steps to preserve the goods, CISG 87, and, under circumstances defined by the Convention, may or must sell them. CISG 88.

Problem 7. Assume the international sales transaction in *Fertico Belgium* had been governed by CISG. Would the *Nachfrist* provisions affect the outcome? Does CISG permit a buyer, who does not avoid the contract, to "cover" for a late delivery and recover damages? In calculating buyer's damages under CISG, would seller be entitled to a reduction for the amount of buyer's profit on resale of the late arriving goods?

(2) SELLERS' AVOIDANCE FOR BUYERS' BREACH

The Convention contains provisions that permit sellers to declare contracts avoided on grounds analogous to those that permit buyers to do so. CISG 64. Sellers' primary concern is, of course, payment of the price. Commonly in international sales, agreements provide that buyer must open bank letters of credit, to assure sellers of payment, before sellers ship the goods. (We have seen such a term in the *Fertico Belgium* case.) Failure of a buyer to obtain a letter of credit pursuant to its contract may, in some circumstances, constitute fundamental breach. Sellers, like buyers, may exercise a *Nachfrist* provision that fixes an additional time for buyers to meet their obligations regarding payment. CISG 63(1). If a buyer fails to act properly within that time, the seller may avoid the contract whether or not the delay constitutes fundamental breach. CISG 64(1)(b).[16]

SECTION 3. REVOCATION OF ACCEPTANCE

(A) DOMESTIC UNITED STATES LAW

Buyers who accepted non-conforming goods may still throw the goods back at sellers under the conditions set forth in UCC 2–608. Revocation of acceptance is a powerful legal tool in the hands of buyers. If justified in revoking acceptance buyers are entitled to recover the contract price and damages, UCC 2–711(1), measured by a substitute purchase, UCC 2–712, or by market prices, UCC 2–713. Further disposition of the goods becomes sellers' problem; revocation of acceptance gives buyers the same rights and duties with regard to the goods as if they had rejected them. UCC 2–608(3).

McCULLOUGH v. BILL SWAD CHRYSLER–PLYMOUTH, INC.
Supreme Court of Ohio, 1983.
5 Ohio St.3d 181, 449 N.E.2d 1289.

On May 23, 1978, appellee, Deborah A. McCullough (then Deborah Miller), purchased a 1978 Chrysler LeBaron from appellant, Bill Swad Chrysler–Plymouth, Inc. (now Bill Swad Datsun, Inc.). The automobile

---

16. In dealing with buyers' obligation to pay, CISG 64(1)(b) is not limited to contracts that contemplate payment by bank letter of credit.

The *Nachfrist* provision of 64(1)(b) refers not only to buyers' obligation to pay the price, but alternatively refers to the obligation to take delivery of the goods. This is a somewhat anomalous provision; a seller who is paid is not likely to be much concerned with the timeliness of buyer's taking delivery. For discussion of this aspect of CISG 64(1)(b), see J. Honnold, Uniform Law for International Sales § 354 (2d ed. 1991).

was protected by both a limited warranty and a Vehicle Service Contract (extended warranty). Following delivery of the vehicle, appellee and her (then) fiance informed appellant's sales agent of problems they had noted with the car's brakes, lack of rustproofing, paint job and seat panels. Other problems were noted by appellee as to the car's transmission and air conditioning. The next day, the brakes failed, and appellee returned the car to appellant for the necessary repairs.

When again in possession of the car, appellee discovered that the brakes had not been fixed properly and that none of the cosmetic work was done. Problems were also noted with respect to the car's steering mechanism. Again, the car was returned for repair and again new problems appeared, this time as to the windshield post, the vinyl top and the paint job. Only two weeks later, appellant was unable to eliminate a noise appellee complained of that had developed in the car's rear end.

On June 26, 1978, appellee returned the car to appellant for correction both of the still unremedied defects and of other flaws that had surfaced since the last failed repair effort. Appellant retained possession of the vehicle for over three weeks in order to service it, but even then many of the former problems persisted. Moreover, appellant's workmanship had apparently caused new defects to arise affecting the car's stereo system, landau top and exterior. Appellee also experienced difficulties with vibrations, the horn, and the brakes.

The following month, while appellee was on a short trip away from her home, the automobile's engine abruptly shut off. The car eventually had to be towed to appellant's service shop for repair. A few days later, when appellee and her husband were embarked on an extensive honeymoon vacation, the brakes again failed. Upon returning from their excursion, the newlyweds, who had prepared a list of thirty-two of the automobile's defects, submitted the list to appellant and again requested their correction. By the end of October 1978, few of the enumerated problems had been remedied.

In early November 1978, appellee contacted appellant's successor, Chrysler–Plymouth East ("East"), regarding further servicing of the vehicle. East was not able to undertake the requested repairs until January 1979. Despite the additional work which East performed, the vehicle continued to malfunction. After May 1979, East refused to perform any additional work on the automobile, claiming that the vehicle was in satisfactory condition, appellee's assertions to the contrary notwithstanding.

On January 8, 1979, appellee, by letter addressed to appellant, called for the rescission of the purchase agreement, demanded a refund of the entire purchase price and expenses incurred, and offered to return the automobile to appellant upon receipt of shipping instructions. Appellant did not respond to appellee's letter, and appellee continued to operate the car.

On January 12, 1979, appellee filed suit against appellant, East, Chrysler Corporation, and City National Bank & Trust Co., seeking rescission of the sales agreement and incidental and consequential damages. By the time of trial, June 25, 1980, the subject vehicle had been driven nearly 35,000 miles, approximately 23,000 of which were logged after appellee mailed her notice of revocation. The trial court dismissed the action as to East, the bank and Chrysler Corporation, but entered judgment for appellee against appellant in the amount of $9,376.82, and ordered the return of the automobile to appellant. The court of appeals subsequently affirmed, determining that appellee had properly revoked her acceptance of the automobile despite her continued use of the vehicle, which use the appellate court found reasonable.

The cause is now before this court pursuant to the allowance of a motion to certify the record.

LOCHER, JUSTICE.

The case at bar essentially poses but a single question: Whether appellee, by continuing to operate the vehicle she had purchased from appellant after notifying the latter of her intent to rescind the purchase agreement, waived her right to revoke her initial acceptance. After having thoroughly reviewed both the relevant facts in the present cause and the applicable law, we find that appellee, despite her extensive use of the car following her revocation, in no way forfeited such right.

The ultimate disposition of the instant action is governed primarily by R.C. 1302.66[UCC 2–608]. . . .

Appellant essentially argues that appellee's revocation of her initial acceptance of the automobile was ineffective as it did not comply with the mode prescribed for revocation in [UCC 2–608]. Specifically, appellant asserts that appellee's continued operation of the vehicle after advising appellant of her revocation was inconsistent with her having relinquished ownership of the car,[2] that the value of the automobile to appellee was not substantially impaired by its alleged nonconformities, and that the warranties furnished by appellant provided the sole legal remedy for alleviating the automobile's defects. Each of appellant's contentions must be rejected.

Although the legal question presented in appellant's first objection is a novel one for this bench, other state courts which have addressed the issue have held that whether continued use of goods after notification of revocation of their acceptance vitiates such revocation is solely dependent upon whether such use was reasonable. . . . Moreover, whether such use was reasonable is a question to be determined by the trier of fact. . . .

---

2. [UCC 2–608(3)] requires that a buyer who revokes his acceptance must treat the subject goods as if he had rejected them pursuant to [UCC 2–602]. Under [2–602(2)(a)], a buyer's continued exercise of ownership rights *vis-a-vis* the rejected goods is a wrong against the seller.

The genesis of the "reasonable use" test lies in the recognition that frequently a buyer, after revoking his earlier acceptance of a good, is constrained by exogenous circumstances—many of which the seller controls—to continue using the good until a suitable replacement may realistically be secured. Clearly, to penalize the buyer for a predicament not of his own creation would be patently unjust. As the court stated in Richardson v. Messina (1960), 361 Mich. 364, 369, 105 N.W.2d 153, 156:

> ... It does not lie in the seller's mouth to demand the utmost in nicety between permissible and impermissible use, for the perilous situation in which the purchaser finds himself arises from the imperfections of that furnished, for a consideration, by the seller himself. ...

In ascertaining whether a buyer's continued use of an item after revocation of its acceptance was reasonable, the trier of fact should pose and divine the answers to the following queries: (1) Upon being apprised of the buyer's revocation of his acceptance, what instructions, if any, did the seller tender the buyer concerning return of the now rejected goods? (2) Did the buyer's business needs or personal circumstances compel the continued use? (3) During the period of such use, did the seller persist in assuring the buyer that all nonconformities would be cured or that provisions would otherwise be made to recompense the latter for the dissatisfaction and inconvenience which the defects caused him? (4) Did the seller act in good faith? (5) Was the seller unduly prejudiced by the buyer's continued use. ...

It is manifest that, upon consideration of the aforementioned criteria, appellee acted reasonably in continuing to operate her motor vehicle even after revocation of acceptance. First, the failure of the seller to advise the buyer, after the latter has revoked his acceptance of the goods, how the goods were to be returned entitles the buyer to retain possession of them. ... Appellant, in the case at bar, did not respond to appellee's request for instructions regarding the disposition of the vehicle. Failing to have done so, appellant can hardly be heard now to complain of appellee's continued use of the automobile.

Secondly, appellee, a young clerical secretary of limited financial resources, was scarcely in position to return the defective automobile and obtain a second in order to meet her business and personal needs. A most unreasonable obligation would be imposed upon appellee were she to be required, in effect, to secure a loan to purchase a second car while remaining liable for repayment of the first car loan. ...

Additionally, appellant's successor (East), by attempting to repair the appellee's vehicle even after she tendered her notice of revocation, provided both express and tacit assurances that the automobile's defects were remediable, thereby, inducing her to retain possession. Moreover, whether appellant acted in good faith throughout this episode is highly problematic, especially given the fact that whenever repair of the car was undertaken, new defects often miraculously arose while previous ones frequently went uncorrected. Both appellant's and East's refusal to honor the warranties before their expiration also evidences less than fair dealing.

Finally, it is apparent that appellant was not prejudiced by appellee's continued operation of the automobile. Had appellant retaken possession of the vehicle pursuant to appellee's notice of revocation, the automobile, which at the time had been driven only 12,000 miles, could easily have been resold. Indeed, the car was still marketable at the time of trial, as even then the odometer registered less than 35,000 miles. In any event, having failed to reassume ownership of the automobile when requested to do so, appellant alone must bear the loss for any diminution of the vehicle's resale value occurring between the two dates.

[UCC 2–711(3)] provides an additional basis for appellee's retention after revocation of the automobile. A buyer who possesses, as appellee does in the instant action, a security interest in the rejected goods may continue to use them even after revoking his acceptance. .... Consequently, appellee's continued use of the defective vehicle was a permissible means of protecting her security interest therein.

Appellant maintains, however, that even if appellee's continued operation of the automobile after revocation was reasonable, such use is "*prima facie* evidence" that the vehicle's nonconformities did not substantially impair its value to appellee, thus precluding availability of the remedy of revocation. Such an inference, though, may not be drawn. As stated earlier, external conditions beyond the buyer's immediate control often mandate continued use of an item even after revocation of its acceptance. Thus, it cannot seriously be contended that appellee, by continuing to operate the defective vehicle, intimated that its nonconformities did not substantially diminish its worth in her eyes.

We must similarly dismiss appellant's assertion that, as appellee's complaints primarily concerned cosmetic flaws, the defects were trivial. First, the chronic steering, transmission and brake problems which appellee experienced in operating the vehicle could hardly be deemed inconsequential. Moreover, even purely cosmetic defects, under the proper set of circumstances, can significantly affect the buyer's valuation of the good. ...

Whether a complained of nonconformity substantially impairs an item's worth to the buyer is a determination exclusively within the purview of the factfinder and must be based on objective evidence of the buyer's idiosyncratic tastes and needs. ... Any defect that shakes the buyer's faith or undermines his confidence in the reliability and integrity of the purchased item is deemed to work a substantial impairment of the item's value and to provide a basis for revocation of the underlying sales agreement. Durfee v. Rod Baxter Imports, Inc. (Minn.1977), 262 N.W.2d 349, at 354; Asciolla v. Manter Oldsmobile–Pontiac, Inc., supra, 370 A.2d at 274. Clearly, no error was committed in finding that the fears occasioned by the recurrent brake failings, steering malfunctions and other mechanical difficulties, as well as the utter frustration caused by the seemingly endless array of cosmetic flaws, constituted nonconformities giving rise to the remedy of revocation.

. . .

Judgment affirmed.

HOLMES, J., dissents in part and concurs in part.

I concur in the syllabus law as set forth in this case, but would remand to the trial court for a determination of the amount due the dealer from the buyer as a setoff due to the buyer's use of the goods after revocation. Both the court of appeals and this court state that Swad should be entitled to such an offset against the judgment for the reasonable value of the use of the automobile after the revocation. However, both courts summarily dispense with such an offset by stating that Swad introduced no evidence to establish the reasonable value of the automobile's use.

The need for any such evidence when the appellant was asserting that the buyer had waived any right to revoke acceptance would, from the standpoint of trial procedure, have been highly questionable. The seller should be given an opportunity to present evidence of the reasonable value of such use, or the trial court should take judicial notice of the fair market value of the use of such an automobile.

Notes

(1) Substantial Impairment; Measure of Conforming Goods and Identity of Warrantor. Since the right to revoke acceptance is conditioned upon substantial non-conformity of the goods, it is necessary to begin with the measure of conforming goods. Revocations are most likely to involve dissatisfaction with the quality of the goods. Thus, the measure of conformity is found in express or implied warranties of quality. Identifying the warranty that was breached in *McCullough*, and further identifying the warrantor of the breached warranty, is not a simple matter.

The opinion notes, at the outset, that "the automobile was protected by both a limited warranty and a Vehicle Service Contract (extended warranty)," but does not indicate that either was breached. Is it likely that the revocation occurred during the active coverage of the extended warranty? If not, consider the limited warranty. The manufacturer is almost certain to have made the limited warranty. Is Chrysler Corporation a party to the case in the Ohio Supreme Court?

Only Bill Swad Chrysler–Plymouth is a defendant on appeal. For what quality warranty is the dealer responsible? If a dealer is not a cowarrantor of a manufacturer's limited warranty, the Magnuson–Moss Warranty Act does not foreclose the dealer from selling cars with a disclaimer of all implied warranties, including the warranty of merchantability. Typically, car dealers include such disclaimers in sales agreements with their customers, who are informed that the only quality warranties are those of the manufacturer or, in some instances, components suppliers (e.g., tires). If Bill Swad's agreement with McCullough contained such a disclaimer, what would be the measure of conforming goods vis-a-vis Bill Swad?

(2) Manner and Time of Buyers' Revocation of Acceptance. Revocation of acceptance occurs when buyers give notice of it to the sellers.[1] UCC 2–608(2). Buyers are not required to offer to hand back the goods to effect a revocation; buyers who have paid part or all of the price have security interests in the goods that entitle them to keep the goods and, if necessary, to sell them to recover the price paid. UCC 2–711(3), 2–608(3). The Code provides that buyers must act "within a reasonable time" after they discover or should have discovered the ground; the time is defined in part by deterioration in the condition of the goods not caused by their defects.

(3) Cure After Revocation. After buyers give notice of revocation of acceptance, do sellers have the right to cure? No such right is mentioned in UCC 2–608 and UCC 2–508, literally construed, is limited to cure after buyers' rejections.

> The issue is not novel. Numerous courts ... have confronted it and have generally agreed that in most circumstances the right to cure is lost once acceptance has occurred. The Mississippi [Supreme Court] decided otherwise in *Fitzner Pontiac–Buick–Cadillac, Inc. v. Smith,* [523 So.2d 324 (1988)], holding that the buyer of an automobile that had been plagued with infirmities since its purchase could not revoke unless the seller was first afforded an opportunity to cure.
>
> Undaunted by the reality that neither the language of the Code nor the weight of authority sanction this extension of the right to cure, the court reasoned that its holding was justified by the general policy of the law favoring the prevention of economic waste.

Frisch & Wladis, General Provisions, Sales, Bulk Transfers, and Documents of Title, 44 The Business Lawyer 1445, 1464 (1989). See also U. S. Roofing, Inc. v. Credit Alliance Corp., 228 Cal.App.3d 1431, 279 Cal.Rptr. 533 (1991).

The Permanent Editorial Board Study Group on UCC Article 2 recommended that 2–608 be amended to provide the seller with a right to cure only until the time for performance has expired. Preliminary Report 171 (1990).

(4) Buyers' Legal Actions Following Revocation. Buyers who revoke acceptance often find it necessary or desirable to bring law suits to obtain relief. Buyers who have paid all or part of the price may seek to recover those sums from the sellers. Even if, as in *McCullough,*

---

1. This is by inference from the actual language of the Code, which states that a revocation is "not effective until" a buyer gives notice. UCC 2–608(2).

buyer has a security interest in goods retained following revocation, buyer may elect not to resell the car and may choose instead to sue the seller (and others). What might induce buyers to seek recovery through litigation rather than by self-help relief through foreclosures of their security interests? See UCC 2–711(1).

(5) **Actions Against Manufacturers.** Buyers who revoke acceptance often elect to bring post-revocation legal actions against the manufacturers, in addition to or instead of suing the immediate sellers. McCullough did so; the trial court dismissed that part of buyer's case and apparently buyer did not appeal. Does UCC 2–608 contemplate or authorize revoking buyers to bring legal actions against manufacturers? Courts deciding the issue are sharply divided.[2] One set of commentators argues that revocation against remote sellers should be permitted:

> There is certainly nothing in Article 2 that would be inconsistent with such an approach. Moreover, the concept of "remote revocation" is gaining a foothold elsewhere. In the Magnuson–Moss Federal Warranty Act, a manufacturer who markets consumer products under a "full warranty" heading must permit the consumer/buyer to elect either a refund of the full purchase price or replacement goods if the product contains a "defect" or "malfunction" that cannot be cured after a "reasonable number of attempts" by the manufacturer. Thus, revocation against the remote manufacturer is a remedy under *federal* law in some situations. Similarly, a number of state legislatures are enacting "lemon" statutes that give revocation rights against the manufacturer of a defective motor vehicle without regard to limits in the written warranty accompanying the goods.

B. Clark & C. Smith, The Law of Product Warranties ¶ 7.03(3)(d) (1984). Cf. J. White & R. Summers, Uniform Commercial Code 376–77 (3d ed. 1988).

(6) **Actions Against Lenders.** Most retail car buyers pay part of the price at delivery (including, perhaps, the agreed value of a trade-in) but arrange to pay the balance of the price in installments over a period of years. Commonly, the loans that finance buyers' purchases are made by banks or finance agencies. We can infer that the buyer in *McCullough* entered into such an arrangement; one of the parties sued

---

2. *Compare* Andover Air Ltd. Partnership v. Piper Aircraft Corp., 7 U.C.C. Rep. Serv. 2d 1494 (D.Mass.1989); Gasque v. Mooers Motor Car Co., 227 Va. 154, 313 S.E.2d 384 (1984); Seekings v. Jimmy GMC of Tucson, Inc., 130 Ariz. 596, 638 P.2d 210 (1981); Edelstein v. Toyota Motors Distributors, 176 N.J. Super. 57, 422 A.2d 101 (1980); Conte v. Dwan Lincoln–Mercury, Inc., 172 Conn. 112, 374 A.2d 144 (1976); Voytovich v. Bangor Punta Operations, Inc., 494 F.2d 1208 (6th Cir.1974), *with* Gochey v. Bombardier, Inc., 153 Vt. 607, 572 A.2d 921 (1990); Ford Motor Credit Co. v. Harper, 671 F.2d 1117 (8th Cir.1982); Volkswagen of America, Inc. v. Novak, 418 So.2d 801 (Miss.1982); Murray v. Holiday Rambler, Inc., 83 Wis.2d 406, 265 N.W.2d 513 (1978); Volvo of America Corp. v. Wells, 551 S.W.2d 826 (Ky.App.1977); Durfee v. Rod Baxter Imports, Inc., 262 N.W.2d 349 (Minn.1977); Asciolla v. Manter Oldsmobile–Pontiac, Inc., 117 N.H. 85, 370 A.2d 270 (1977).

was a bank, presumably the bank to which buyer was obligated to make installment payments. What relief would buyers likely seek from lenders? Refund of previous payments? Release from obligation to pay future installments? Damages for breach of warranty?

The trial court dismissed the suit against the bank and apparently buyer did not appeal. Under what theory might a buyer's revocation of acceptance affect the buyer's rights against or obligations to a bank or finance company? See Smith v. Navistar International Transportation Corp., 714 F.Supp. 303 (N.D.Ill.1989) (manufacturer, financer, and dealer were part of one corporate family).

In retail installment-purchase transactions, typically the contract of sale provides for buyer's deferred payments; promptly after the sale, the retailer assigns the buyer's debt to a bank or finance company. Since 1975, a Federal Trade Commission rule requires sellers of consumer goods to insert into their contract documents a provision that makes lenders subject to all claims and defenses that buyers could assert against sellers. Preservation of Consumers' Claims and Defenses, 16 C.F.R. § 433. If buyers have claims or defenses against their immediate sellers, the lenders would be subject to them as well.[3] In such transactions, would lender be subject to buyers' claims or defenses against remote sellers?

(7) Use After Revocation and the Code. Did the *McCullough* court give adequate attention to the incorporation by 2–608(3) of the "rights and duties" applicable to rejection—particularly the prohibition by 2–602(2)(a) of "any exercise of ownership" and the duty under 2–602(2)(b) "to hold" the goods for the seller? See also 2–606(1)(c): "any act inconsistent with the seller's ownership."

Do these words indicate that the law-makers faced and decided the issues presented in the *McCullough* case? Do your answers lead to any conclusions concerning "literal reading" of Article 2? Have you encountered other statutes where a "literal" reading is more or less acceptable?

(8) Compensation for Use after Revocation. In Johnson v. G.M. Corp., 233 Kan. 1044, 668 P.2d 139 (1983), the buyers of a 1979 Chevrolet pick-up truck, after extended and unsuccessful attempts at repair, notified GM that they revoked acceptance and thereafter drove the truck an additional 14,619 miles. The court awarded the buyers a judgment for return of the price less an offset for the value of their use of the truck. In fixing the offset the court relied on a Federal Highway Administration Booklet, "Cost of Owning and Operating Automobiles and Vans 1982." How would the cost of operation compare with rental costs?

---

3. The rule provides that buyer's recovery against a lender "shall not exceed amounts paid by the debtor hereunder."

(9) Magnuson–Moss "Full" Warranties; "Lemon Laws." The Magnuson–Moss Warranty Act, in § 104(a)(4), permits consumers to elect a "refund" for a defective product if a "reasonable number of attempts" fail to remedy a defect or malfunction. However, this remedy depended on the granting of a "full" federal warranty. Most sellers of expensive goods that they do not want thrown back after acceptance have chosen to grant "limited" warranties.

A large number of states have enacted "lemon laws" that give special protection, including the right to revoke acceptance, when defects in motor vehicles are not corrected within a reasonable time. While non-uniform in their language, these statutes tend to allow consumers, for a limited period, to demand from manufacturers refund of the purchase price or a replacement car when the "same defect" continues to exist after four attempts to repair it or the car was out of service for 30 days during the year after it was sold. See C. Reitz, Consumer Product Warranties Under Federal and State Laws, ch. 14 (2d ed. 1987).

(B) INTERNATIONAL SALES LAW

The Convention on International Sale of Goods does not use the concept of buyers' acceptance and, therefore, has no provision for revocation of acceptance. The comparable CISG provisions are those permitting buyers to avoid contracts. As discussed in the previous section, CISG permits buyers to avoid contracts in two circumstances. We previously considered avoidance in connection with delays in performance in connection with CISG's *Nachfrist* provisions. In this section, we are concerned with buyers' right to avoid contracts, particularly contracts that have been executed, on the ground that the goods are non-conforming. The Convention relates this power to avoid to the concept of fundamental breach.

Avoidance for Fundamental Breach. The Convention's default performance rules contemplate that buyers must keep goods received unless sellers' performance failures constitute fundamental breach. A breach is "fundamental" if the detriment in performance substantially deprives the aggrieved party of what it was entitled to expect under the contract. CISG 25.

Manner of Avoiding. If goods received are so non-conforming that sellers' performance amounts to fundamental breach, buyers may declare contracts avoided. CISG 49(1). For a declaration of avoidance to be effective, it must be made by notice to the seller. CISG 26.[4]

Time of Avoidance. A buyer's time to decide whether to declare a contracted avoided for fundamental breach is determined by the time needed to discover the deficiency. Power to avoid for quality or quantity defects expires a reasonable time after buyer knew or ought to

---

4. Notices under the Convention are effective, whether or not received, if dispatched "by means appropriate in the circumstances." CISG 27.

have known of the breach. CISG 49(2)(b)(i). Power to avoid for late delivery that constitutes fundamental breach expires a reasonable time after buyer has become aware that delivery has been made. CISG 49(2)(a).

Effect of Avoidance. Avoidance of a contract generally releases both parties from their obligations under it. CISG 81(1). The aggrieved buyer is entitled to damages that have accrued prior to avoidance, id., but must account to the seller for benefits derived from the goods. CISG 84. A party who has performed the contract in whole or in part may claim restitution. CISG 81(2). A buyer who elects to avoid must be able generally to return the goods delivered substantially in the condition in which it received them. CISG 82(1). Exceptions exist (1) if buyer is unable to return the goods and the impossibility is not due to its act or omission, or (2) if the goods were sold in the normal course of business or consumed or transformed by the buyer before it discovered or ought to have discovered the lack of conformity, or (3) if the goods deteriorated or perished as a result of buyer's examination of them. CISG 46(2). A buyer must act, on behalf of the seller, to preserve goods in the buyer's possession or placed at its disposal at their shipping destination. CISG 86.[5] The buyer may warehouse the goods. CISG 87. A buyer need not return goods if seller fails to repay the price or the cost of preservation of the goods. CISG 88(1). If seller delays unreasonably in taking the goods back, buyer may sell them by any appropriate means, CISG 88(1), and must do so if the goods are subject to rapid deterioration or their preservation would involve unreasonable expense. CISG 88(2).

Cure of Non–conforming Deliveries. Without power to reject goods and only limited power to avoid, buyers are not in a strong position to use self-help to compel sellers to cure non-conforming deliveries. However, the Convention permits buyers to seek court orders compelling sellers to perform. CISG 46(1). Article 46 differentiates sharply between court orders to compel delivery of substitute goods and court orders to repair. Substitute goods may be ordered only if the deficiency in the original delivery was a fundamental breach. CISG 46(2). An order to repair is permitted unless repair is unreasonable in the circumstances. CISG 46(3).

The Convention's authorization of court-ordered relief may be of little value to buyers in the United States or other common-law nations where equitable relief, by injunction or specific performance, is denied if the aggrieved party has an adequate remedy at law, i.e. monetary damages. See, e.g., UCC 2–716. The Convention accepts that some nations' laws limit parties' access to specific relief. CISG 28.

---

5. Note that CISG 86 uses the word "reject" in connection with buyers' rights. That word does not appear elsewhere in the Convention. It does not have the connotation of "rejection" under domestic United States law. See J. Honnold, Uniform Law for International Sales § 455 (2d ed. 1991).

Sec. 3 REVOCATION OF ACCEPTANCE

Even if not faced with buyers' avoidance or not ordered to cure non-conforming deliveries, sellers may elect to try to remedy failures in their performances. Buyers must permit sellers to do so if the sellers act without unreasonable delay and without causing buyers unreasonable inconvenience. CISG 48(1). What might motivate sellers to act in this way?

Problem 1. Telecommunications Company (TCo) in an African country contracted to buy a high power microwave amplifier (HPA) from a United States supplier (SCo). The agreement contained extensive technical specifications for the HPA. The agreement provided, further, that SCo would install and test the HPA at the site in Africa within 15 months. When the HPA had been manufactured, TCo inspected it at the factory and found that it met the contract specifications. SCo installed the HPA in Africa. Before the HPA was operational, TCo again inspected the equipment and indicated that it was satisfactory. After six months of SCo's effort to get the HPA into service, SCo realized that it would not work because it had been designed for a grounded neutral power supply system, whereas the power supply at the site was an isolated neutral power system. The contract specifications were silent on the nature of the power supply. Rebuilding the HBA to operate with the available power supply would delay installation for more than a year. Assuming that TCo accepted the HPA, may it revoke its acceptance? See Awards of June 1984 and May 1985 in Case No. 4567, 11 Yearbook Commercial Arbitration 143 (1986).

Problem 2. Buyer and seller contracted for sale of a computer. Seller shipped the computer to buyer. On arrival, buyer discovered that three major components of the equipment were defective. Buyer immediately informed seller of the defects and of its election to avoid the contract. Seller wired back: "All defects can promptly and completely corrected. Will send top-level team next week." Assume that the deficiencies in the computer, as delivered, would constitute fundamental breach. If the seller has the ability to correct the problems without unreasonable delay and without causing buyer unreasonable convenience, may it do so despite buyer's declaration of avoidance? What is the meaning of "subject to article 49" in CISG 48(1)? See J. Honnold, Uniform Law for International Sales § 296 (2d ed. 1991)("The seller's right to cure should also be protected if, ... where cure is feasible, the buyer hastily declares the contract avoided before the seller has an opportunity to cure the defect. ... [W]here cure is feasible and where an offer of cure can be expected, one cannot conclude that the breach is "fundamental" until one knows the answer to this question: Will the seller cure?")

Problem 3. In performance of a contract for the sale of sugar with an average polarization of 78, seller shipped sugar which buyer tested and determined to average 73. Buyer immediately wired seller a notice that the sugar received did not conform to contract specifications on polarization. What purpose would this notice serve? Recall CISG

39(1). Would this notice constitute a declaration of avoidance? May sellers combine, in one communication, notice of a lack of conformity and declaration of avoidance? What content would such a communication have? Must a buyer use the word "avoid"?

Problem 4. Buyer received goods that are sufficiently deficient in quality that seller has committed a fundamental breach. Buyer sent notice to the seller specifying the lack of conformity (CISG 39) and declaring the contract avoided (CISG 26). One week later, buyer sought a court order directing the seller to deliver substitute goods on the ground that seller had delivered goods whose lack of conformity constitutes a fundamental breach and that buyer was entitled to "require" seller to deliver substitute goods under CISG 46(2). Seller counters that its obligations under the contract were released when buyer declared the contract avoided. Is seller correct? See J. Honnold, Uniform Law for International Sales § 440.2 (2d ed. 1991).

SECTION 4. PERFORMANCE AND THE CREDIT RISK

Introduction. Unless the parties to sales contracts tender and complete delivery and payment simultaneously, one incurs the credit risk inherent in having surrendered something of value without having received the expected thing of value. If a seller delivers goods without receiving the price, the seller has incurred a credit risk. Conversely, if a buyer pays the price without receiving goods, the buyer has incurred a credit risk.

In many commercial situations, one of the parties willingly and openly assumes the credit risk of performing first. Sales on short-term or long-term credit are common. The tremendous volume of domestic commercial credit is encouraged by highly organized channels for credit information and the transactional efficiency of delivery on open billing. An important asset of businesses who sell goods (or services) on credit is their accounts receivable, generated typically by delivering goods to buyers on terms that require payment at the end of the month, within 30 days of delivery, etc. Long-term credit sales tend to involve installment payment arrangements, familiar in consumer purchasing of automobiles and other relatively expensive durable goods.

Similarly, buyers' prepayments are commonly made in certain types of transactions. (In a service contract familiar to students, tuition is paid at the beginning of an academic term.) Sales contracts for goods to be manufactured by sellers are one of the most common settings in which buyers pay some of the price before delivery. "Down payments" are also found in other transaction situations.

The two principal topics for this section are: (1) How and to what extent do the default rules of performance supplied by law, i.e., gap-filling provisions that apply in the absence of agreement on the matter, impose credit risks on buyers or sellers who have not agreed to assume such risks? (2) What protections are available to parties exposed to loss from credit risk?

Credit risks generally fall into two categories: obligors who *cannot* or who *will not* perform. The former are sometimes thought of in terms of bankruptcy risk. The latter are a more commercial risk. Risk avoidance strategies do not distinguish between unable and unwilling promisors. However, the potential relief once a credit risk has materialized depends greatly on the distinction.

(A) DOMESTIC UNITED STATES LAW

(1) Simultaneous Exchanges. The Commercial Code's default rules on performance tend to avoid or minimize credit risk to either buyers or sellers through the complementary provisions of 2–507(1) and 2–511(1). Under the former, a buyer's duty to pay is conditional upon a seller's tendering delivery. Under the latter, a seller's duty to tender and complete delivery is conditional upon a buyer's tender of payment. These conditions can be satisfied if the parties tender their reciprocal performances simultaneously.

In face-to-face performances, the "put and hold" manner of tender of the goods and the price permits the parties to "let go" at the same time. Events at the check-out counter of a food store are an example of a relatively simple simultaneous exchange. In more complex transactions, simultaneous exchanges may occur at meetings scheduled for that purpose, sometimes called "closings." (This is a normal event in the performance of real estate sales contracts, contracts for the issuance of securities, and the like.)

(2) Sequential Exchanges. Simultaneous exchange is not feasible in some situations even though the parties may be in direct contact. Some sales contracts with a service component, such as contracts to sell and install goods, cannot be performed in the "put and hold" manner. The seller's performance necessarily occurs over a period of time. Simultaneous exchange of goods plus service for money is therefore impractical. The Commercial Code states no performance rule for this type of transaction. Common-law contract principles presumably would apply (UCC 1–103).

(3) Documentary Transactions. Face-to-face performance is not feasible when the goods are to be sent via carriers to buyers. In this transactional setting, however, the marketplace developed and the law reinforces a performance scenario that comes remarkably close to eliminating credit risk for either party in non-simultaneous performances. The Commercial Code assists sellers and buyers to set up simultaneous performances in the form of "documentary transactions," but the parties must agree to do so. This mode of performance is not prescribed by the Code as a default rule.

The parties to sales contracts who elect to enter into "documentary transitions" enlist the aid of carriers and banks to accomplish the result. Underlying the services of carriers and banks is the law of negotiable instruments and negotiable documents of title. The document of title is typically a negotiable bill of lading. The negotiable instrument is typically a negotiable draft ordering the buyer to pay the purchase price. With this mix of services and documents, sellers and buyers are able to effect simultaneous transfer of documents of title in exchange for payment of the price.

Negotiable Bills of Lading. In section 1, we considered the Code's default rules on the manner of sellers' performance of contracts in which they are authorized or required to ship goods by use of carriers. Carriers issue bills of lading upon receipt of goods from sellers in either "straight bill" or "order bill" form.[1] If sellers choose to take "order bills," carriers incur the contract duty, undergirded by federal or state statutes, to deliver the goods only to persons who duly present the "order bills." 49 U.S.C. App. 88 and 90, UCC 7–104(1)(a).

By keeping control of an "order bill" until buyer tenders payment of the price, a seller can avoid the credit risk of delivering without receiving payment. By keeping control of the money until seller tenders the "order bill," a buyer can avoid the credit risk of paying without receiving title to the goods and the power to get them from the carrier.

Negotiable Drafts. "Documentary transactions" commonly require a document, other than the negotiable bill of lading, to facilitate the transfer of the purchase price. For this purpose sellers and buyers use drafts (also known as "bills of exchange"). A draft is an instrument in which one party, the seller (the *drawer*), orders another party, the buyer (the *drawee*), to pay a specified amount of money, the contract price, at a specified time. A draft is drawn by the seller on the buyer for the amount of money due to the seller in exchange for the goods. Typically, the seller's draft will order buyer to pay the price when the draft is presented to buyer ("at sight"); drafts payable on demand are called "sight drafts." Drafts, like bills of lading, are negotiable if drawn in the required form. See UCC 3–104.[2]

Banks' Services. Sellers and buyers typically employ the services of banks to effect simultaneous exchange of the negotiable bill of lading and the contract price. A seller first delivers the goods to a carrier and obtains an "order bill of lading." Seller then prepares a "sight draft" for the price of the goods, attaches to it the "order bill," and delivers both documents to its local bank for transmission to the buyer "through banking channels."[3] The receiving bank forwards the documents

---

1. Trucking concerns have found it awkward to accept goods under order bills of lading because of lack of terminal facilities at the points of destination.

2. Drafts are one common form of negotiable instruments, which are governed by Article 3 of the Commercial Code.

3. Seller's actions comply with its performance obligations under UCC 2–308(c) and 2–503(5), which permit use of "customary banking channels," and with 2–504.

through the network of bank-to-bank relationships that exists for this, and many other purposes.[4] In due course, the draft and bill of lading arrive at a bank in buyer's city.[5] It is the function of that bank to effect the exchange of goods for money by turning over the bill of lading when buyer has paid the amount of the draft.[6] After payment is made, it is transferred back to seller's bank and eventually to seller, again through normal banking channels.[7]

Negotiation; Rights of Holders. Both the "order bill" and the negotiable draft move through these steps by the process of negotiation, not by mere transfer. "Holders" of negotiable documents of title or of negotiable instruments may receive greater legal protection than mere transferees. In Chapter 2, we noted that the concept of good faith purchase has developed in a wider setting than purchase of goods. Commercial law offers very significant legal protection to holders in due course of negotiable instruments, UCC 3–305, and to holders of negotiable documents of title to whom the documents have been duly negotiated.[8] 49 U.S.C. App. 111(b)[9]; UCC 7–502. These protections

---

4. Article 4 of the Commercial Code, supplemented by Article 3, governs bank deposits and collections. The bank taking the paper from seller is authorized to present the draft to buyer or to send it via another bank or banks to buyer. UCC 4–202(a)(1). Banks who handle the paper are agents and subagents of sellers. See UCC 4–201. Each bank that handles a seller's draft becomes a "collecting bank" (UCC 4–105(5)), with the duties set out in UCC 4–202, 4–501, and 4–503. The last bank in the chain is the "presenting bank." UCC 4–105(6).

5. Often the bank selected to make presentment is the bank with which the buyer has an ongoing banking relationship and which the buyer had told seller would be the appropriate bank to which documents should be forwarded.

6. Unless otherwise instructed, the bank presenting a "sight draft" is authorized to send buyer a written notice that it holds a draft for payment; buyer has three days to make payment. UCC 4–212. If, instead of sending notice, the bank presents the draft to buyer at its place of business or residence UCC 3–501(b)(1), 3–111. Payment is due no later than the third day following presentment. UCC 3–502(c). The bank may deliver the bill of lading accompanying the draft "only on payment." UCC 4–503(1).

An alternative transaction involves use of a "time draft," which orders a buyer to pay a specified time after presentment. A buyer's choices on presentment of a time draft are to accept or to dishonor the draft. See UCC 3–409, 3–413 (definition and operation of acceptance), 3–410 (acceptance varying draft), 3–502(c) (dishonor). Accepted "time drafts," known as "trade acceptances," tend to be marketable negotiable instruments. Sellers often sell accepted drafts before their due date, albeit for less than their face value; this process is often called "discounting" of drafts.

7. **Air Freight.** The speed of carriage of goods by air required adaptation of the method of issuing and transmitting bills of lading. Taking a bill of lading at the point of shipment and forwarding it through banking channels to the destination to be exchanged for the price would be too slow. A solution is found by using electronic communications. The Commercial Code permits a carrier, at the request of a consignor, to issue a bill of lading at the point of destination, UCC 7–305(1), and to deliver it to a local bank. Meanwhile, seller (or seller's bank) wires a draft on the buyer to the bank holding the bill. Within hours, the bank notifies buyer who pays the draft and obtains the bill.

8. Negotiable bills of lading issued by carriers engaged in interstate commerce are governed by the Pomerene Act. The most pertinent provisions on negotiation of these bills of lading is 49 U.S.C. App. 108. See Appendix to this casebook.

Comparable provisions on negotiation of bills of lading governed by Article 7 of the Commercial Code are found in UCC 7–501.

9. See Appendix to this casebook.

are often significant to buyers and sellers as well as to the banks whose services they use in carrying out "documentary transactions."

DIAGRAM OF A DOCUMENTARY TRANSACTION

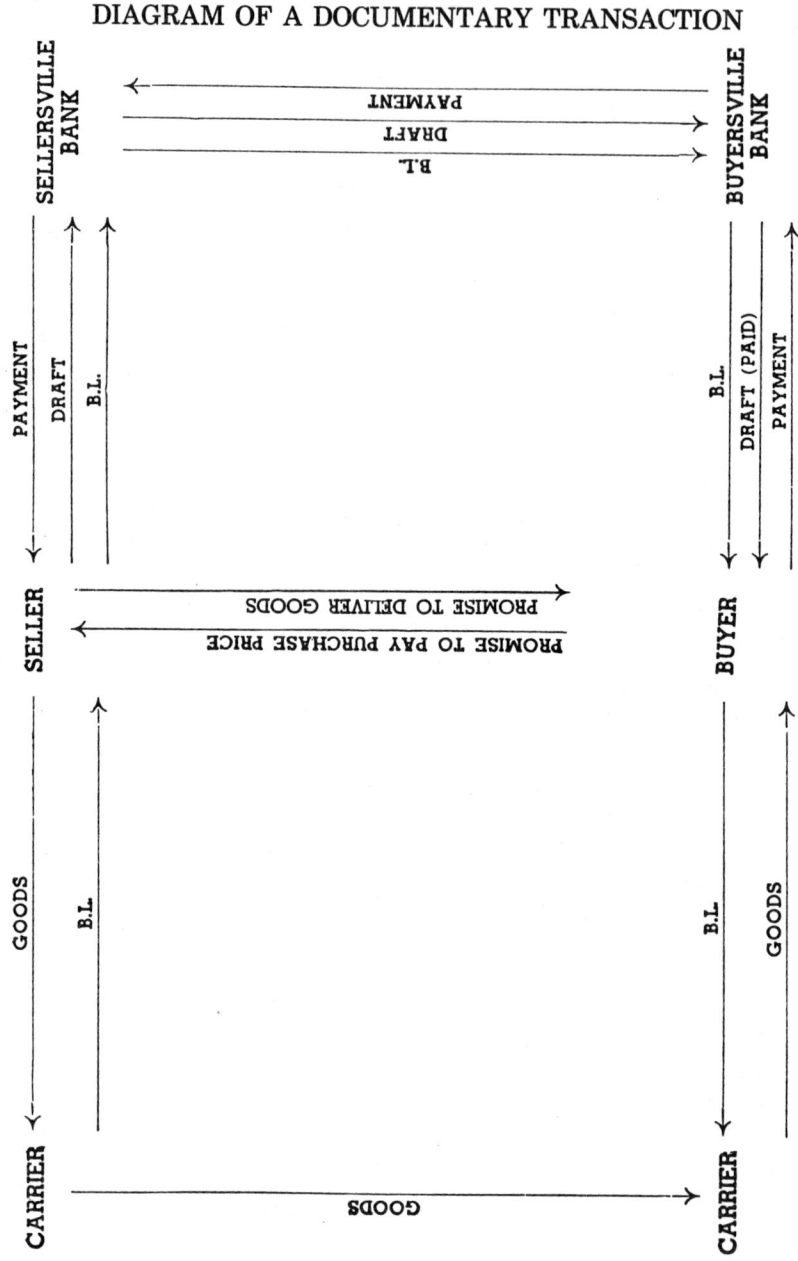

STEPS IN COLLECTION OF DOCUMENTARY DRAFT

PROMISE TO DELIVER GOODS

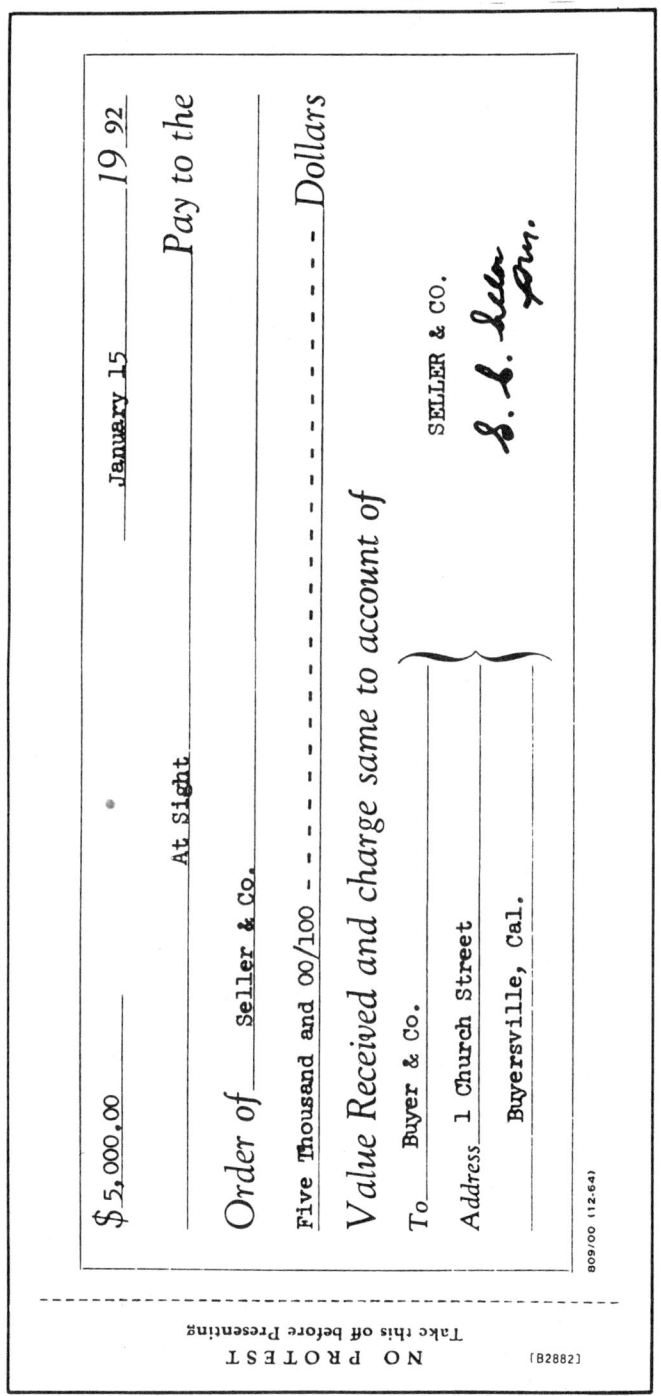

SIGHT DRAFT

EXECUTION OF SALES CONTRACTS

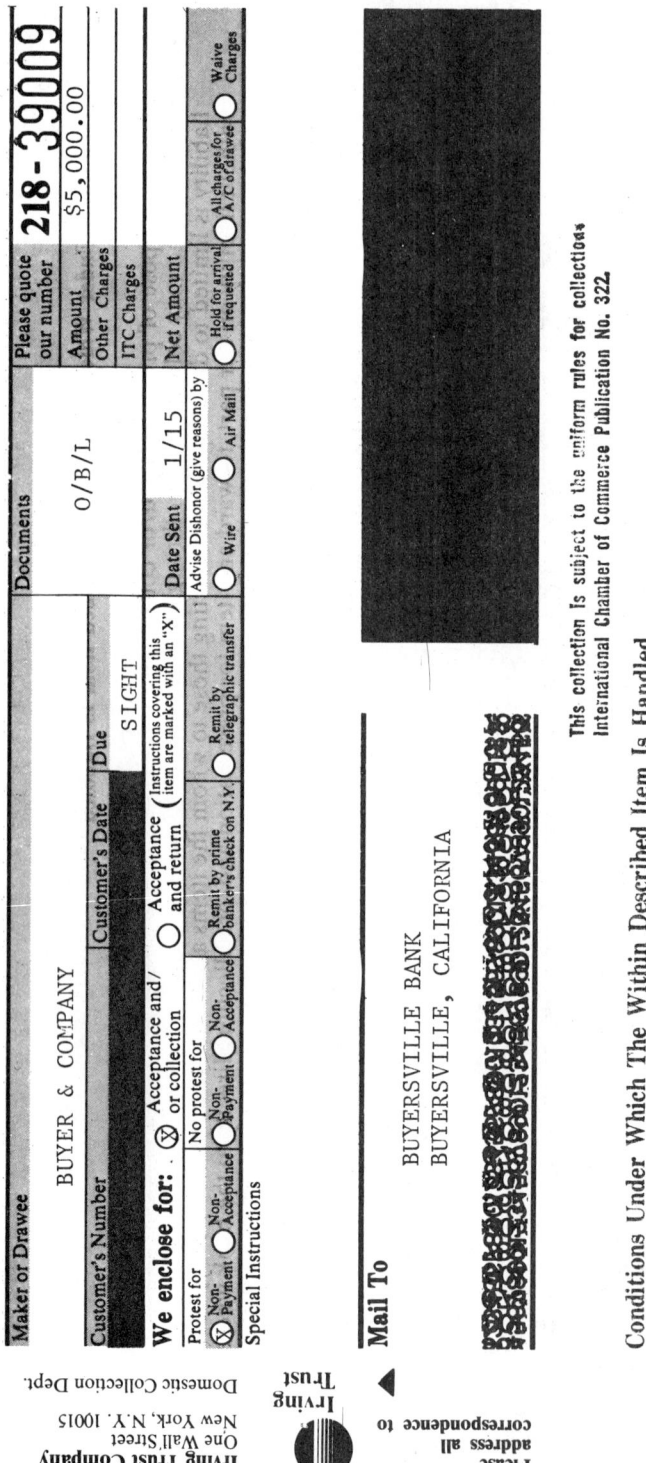

COLLECTION LETTER

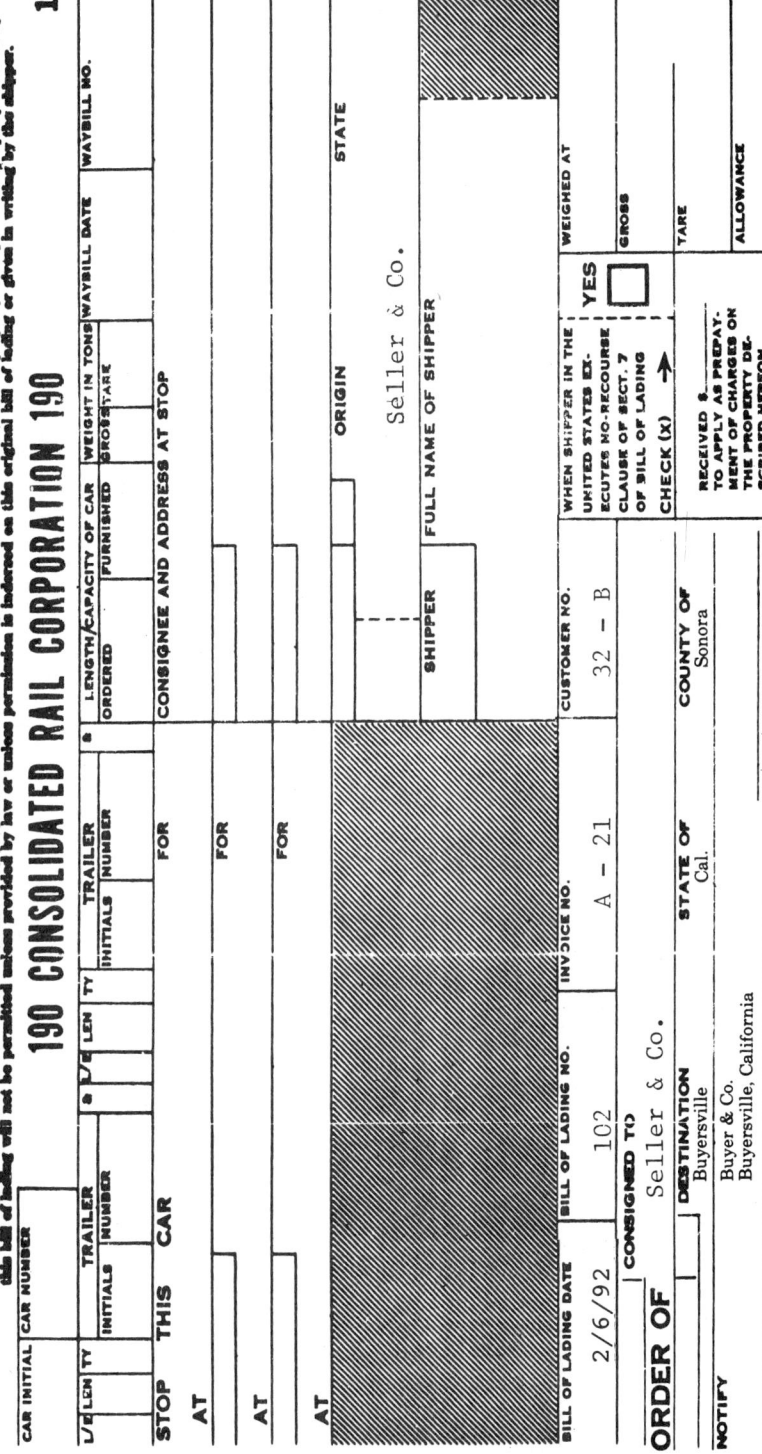

AT	STATE OF	COUNTY OF					NET
1 Church St., Buyersville, California							
ROUTE (FOR SHIPPER'S USE ONLY)		DELIVERY CARRIER					IF CHARGES ARE TO BE PREPAID WRITE OR STAMP HERE:
PC – C&NW – UP – SP		SP					"TO BE PREPAID"
			AGENT OR CASHIER				
			PER				
			(THE SIGNATURE HERE ACKNOWLEDGES ONLY THE AMOUNT PREPAID)				
			CHARGES ADVANCED				
			$				

NO. PKGS.	DESCRIPTION OF ARTICLES, SPECIAL MARKS AND EXCEPTIONS	COMMODITY CODE NO.	*	WEIGHT (SUBJECT TO COR.)	RATE	FREIGHT	ADVANCES	PREPAID
50 ctns.	Bags, paper			1,000 lbs.	$4.60	$46.00		$46.00

SHIPPER Seller & Co.	PER AGENT	PER
PERMANENT POST OFFICE ADDRESS OF SHIPPER	1 Main Street, Sellersville, N.Y.	

NEGOTIABLE BILL OF LADING
[*Printed on yellow paper; front*]

ENDORSEMENTS

CONTRACT TERMS AND CONDITIONS

NEGOTIABLE BILL OF LADING
[Reverse]

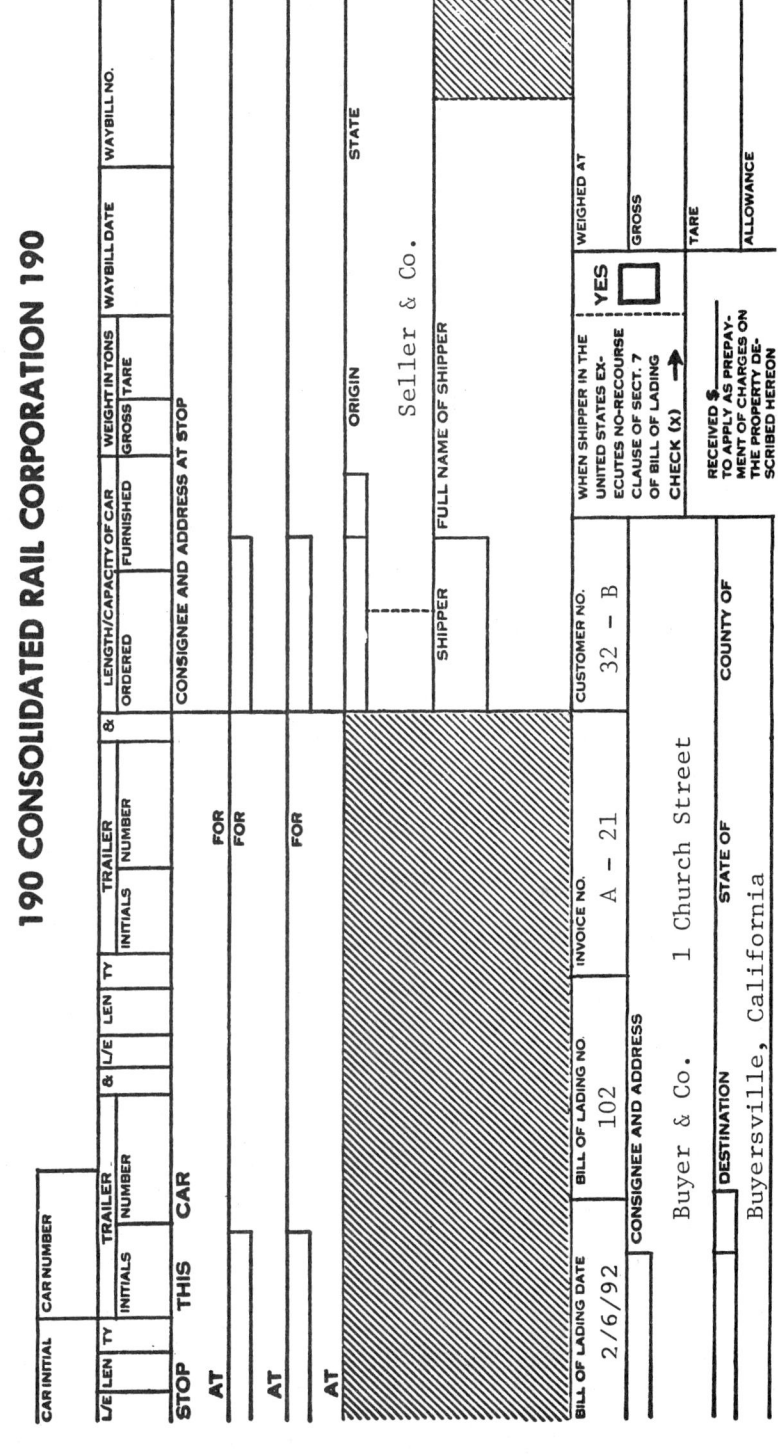

ROUTE (FOR SHIPPER'S USE ONLY)

PC – C&NW – UP – SP

DELIVERY CARRIER

SP

Subject to Section 7 of Conditions, if the shipment is to be delivered to the consignee without recourse on the consignor, the consignor shall sign the following statement: The carrier shall not make delivery of this shipment without payment of freight and all other lawful charges.

_____
Signature of Consignor

Note—Where the rate is dependent upon value, shippers are required to state specifically in writing the agreed or declared value of the property. The agreed or declared value of the property is hereby specifically stated by the shipper to be not exceeding

PER _____

*If the shipment moves between two ports by a carrier by water, the law requires that the bill of lading shall state whether it is "carrier's or shipper's weight."

SHIPPERS SPECIAL INSTRUCTIONS (INCLUDE ICING, VENTILATION, HEATING, MILLING, WEIGHING, ETC.)

NO. PKGS.	DESCRIPTION OF ARTICLES, SPECIAL MARKS AND EXCEPTIONS	COMMODITY CODE NO	*	WEIGHT (SUBJECT TO COR.)	RATE	AGENT OR CASHIER		NET	
						PER			IF CHARGES ARE TO BE PREPAID WRITE OR STAMP HERE:
						(THE SIGNATURE HERE ACKNOWLEDGES ONLY THE AMOUNT PREPAID)			"TO BE PREPAID"
						CHARGES ADVANCED $			
						FREIGHT	ADVANCES		PREPAID
50 ctns.	Bags, paper			1,000 lbs.	$4.60	$46.00			$46.00

THIS IS TO CERTIFY THAT THE ABOVE NAMED MATERIALS ARE PROPERLY CLASSIFIED, DESCRIBED, PACKAGED, MARKED AND LABELED, AND ARE IN PROPER CONDITION FOR TRANSPORTATION, ACCORDING TO THE APPLICABLE REGULATIONS OF THE DEPARTMENT OF TRANSPORTATION.   SIGNED

PER | AGENT

SHIPPER Seller & Co.

PERMANENT POST OFFICE ADDRESS OF SHIPPER   1 Main Street, Sellersville, N.Y.   PER

NON–NEGOTIABLE BILL OF LADING
[Printed on white paper; front]

CONTRACT TERMS AND CONDITIONS

Sec. 1. (a) The carrier or party in possession of any of the property herein described shall be liable as at common law for any loss thereof or damage thereto, except as hereinafter provided.

(b) No carrier or party in possession of all or any of the property herein described shall be liable for any loss thereof or damage thereto or delay caused by the act of God, the public enemy, the authority of law, or the act or default of the shipper or owner, or for natural shrinkage. The carrier's liability shall be that of warehouseman, only, for loss, damage, or delay caused by fire occurring after the expiration of the free time allowed by tariffs lawfully on file (such free time to be computed as therein provided) after notice of the arrival of the property at destination or at the port of export (if intended for export) has been duly sent or given, and after placement of the property for delivery at destination, or tender of delivery of the property to the party entitled to receive it, has been made. Except in case of negligence of the carrier or party in possession (and the burden to prove freedom from such negligence shall be on the carrier or party in possession), the carrier or party in possession shall not be liable for loss, damage, or delay occurring while the property is stopped and held in transit upon the request of the shipper, owner, or party entitled to make such request, or resulting from a defect or vice in the property, or for country damage to cotton, or from riots or strikes.

(c) In case of quarantine the property may be discharged at risk and expense of owners into quarantine depot or elsewhere, as required by quarantine regulations or authorities, or for the carrier's dispatch at nearest available point in carrier's judgment, and in any such case carrier's responsibility shall cease when property is so discharged, or property may be returned by carrier at owner's expense to shipping point, earning freight both ways. Quarantine expenses of whatever nature or kind upon or in respect to property shall be borne by the owners of the property or be a lien thereon. The carrier shall not be liable for loss or damage occasioned by fumigation or disinfection or other acts required or done by quarantine regulations or authorities even though the same may have been done by carrier's officers, agents, or employees, nor for detention, loss, or damage of any kind occasioned by quarantine or the enforcement thereof. No carrier shall be liable, except in case of negligence, for any mistake or inaccuracy in any information furnished by the carrier, its agents, or officers, as to quarantine laws or regulations. The shipper shall hold the carriers harmless from any expense they may incur, or damages they may be required to pay, by reason of the introduction of the property covered by this contract into any place against the quarantine laws or regulations in effect at such place.

Sec. 2. (a) No carrier is bound to transport said property by any particular train or vessel, or in time for any particular market or otherwise than with reasonable dispatch. Every carrier shall have the right in case of physical necessity to forward said property by any carrier or route between the point of shipment and the point of destination. In all cases not prohibited by law, where a lower value than actual value has been represented in writing by the shipper or has been agreed upon in writing as the released value of the property as determined by the classification or tariffs upon which the rate is based, such lower value plus freight charges if paid shall be the maximum amount to be recovered, whether or not such loss or damage occurs from negligence.

(b) As a condition precedent to recovery, claims must be filed in writing with the receiving or delivering carrier, or carrier issuing this bill of lading, within nine months after delivery of the property (or, in case of export traffic, within nine months after delivery at port of export) or, in case of failure to make delivery, then within nine months after a reasonable time for delivery has elapsed; and suits shall be instituted against any carrier only within two years and one day from the day when notice in writing is given by the carrier to the claimant that the carrier has disallowed the claim or any part or parts thereof specified in the notice. Where claims are not filed or suits are not instituted thereon in accordance with the foregoing provisions, no carrier hereunder shall be liable, and such claims will not be paid.

(c) Any carrier or party liable on account of loss or damage to any of said property shall have the full benefit of any insurance that may have been effected upon or on account of said property, so far as this shall not avoid the policies or contracts of insurance: Provided, That the carrier reimburse the claimant for the premium paid thereon.

Sec. 3. Except where such service is required as the result of carrier's negligence, all property shall be subject to necessary cooperage and baling at owner's cost. Each carrier over whose route cotton or cotton linters is to be transported hereunder shall have the privilege, at its own cost and risk, of compressing the same for greater convenience in handling or forwarding, and shall not be held responsible for deviation or unavoidable delays in procuring such compression. Grain in bulk consigned to a point where there is a railroad, public or licensed elevator, may (unless otherwise expressly noted herein, and then if it is not promptly unloaded) be there delivered and placed with other grain of the same kind and grade without respect to ownership (and prompt notice thereof shall be given to the consignor), and if so delivered shall be subject to a lien for elevator charges in addition to all other charges hereunder.

Sec. 4. (a) Property not removed by the party entitled to receive it within the free time allowed by tariffs, lawfully on file (such free time to be computed as therein provided), after notice of the arrival of the property at destination or at the port of export (if intended for export) has been duly sent or given, and after placement of the property for delivery at destination, or tender of delivery of or at place usually assigned for delivery of like property, subject to the tariff charges for storage and to carrier's responsibility as warehouseman, only, or has been made, may be kept in vessel, car, depot, warehouse, or place of delivery of the carrier, subject to a reasonable charge for storage and to carrier's responsibility as warehouseman, only, or at the option of the carrier, may be removed to and stored in a public or licensed warehouse at the place of delivery or other available place, at the cost of the owner, and there held without liability on the part of the carrier, and subject to a lien for all freight and other lawful charges, including a reasonable charge for storage.

(b) Where nonperishable property which has been transported to destination hereunder is refused by consignee or the party entitled to receive it, or said consignee or party entitled to receive it fails to receive it within 15 days after notice of arrival shall have been duly sent or given, the carrier may sell the same at public auction to the highest bidder, at such place as may be designated by the carrier: Provided, That the carrier shall have first mailed, sent, or given to the consignor notice that the property has been refused or remains unclaimed, as the case may be, and that it will be subject to sale under the terms of the bill of lading if disposition be not arranged for, and shall have published notice containing a description of the property, the name of the party to whom consigned, or, if shipped order notify, the name of the party to be notified, and the time and place of sale, once a week for two successive weeks, in a newspaper of general circulation at the place of sale or nearest place where such newspaper is published: Provided, That 30 days shall have elapsed before publication of notice of sale after said notice that the property was refused or remains unclaimed was mailed, sent, or given.

(c) Where perishable property which has been transported hereunder to destination is refused by consignee or party entitled to receive it, or said consignee or party entitled to receive it shall fail to receive it promptly, the carrier may, in its discretion, to prevent deterioration or further deterioration, sell the same to the best advantage at private or public sale: Provided, That if time serves for notification to the consignor or owner of the refusal of the property or the failure to receive it and request for disposition of the property, such notification shall be given, in such manner as the exercise of due diligence requires, before the property is sold.

(d) Where the procedure provided for in the two paragraphs last preceding is not possible, it is agreed that nothing contained in said paragraphs shall be construed to abridge the right of the carrier at its option to sell the property under such circumstances and in such manner as may be authorized by law.

(e) The proceeds of any sale made under this section shall be applied by the carrier to the payment of freight, demurrage, storage, and any other lawful charges and the expense of notice, advertisement, sale, and of other necessary expense and of caring for and maintaining the property, if proper care of the same requires special expense, and should there be a balance it shall be paid to the owner of the property sold hereunder.

(f) Property destined to or taken from a station, wharf, or landing at which there is no regularly appointed freight agent shall be entirely at risk of owner after unloaded from cars or vessels or until loaded into cars or vessels, and, except in case of carrier's negligence, when received from or delivered to such stations, wharves, or landings shall be at owner's risk until the cars are attached to and after they are detached from locomotive or train or until loaded into and after unloaded from vessels.

Sec. 5. No carrier hereunder will carry or be liable in any way for any documents, specie, or for any articles of extraordinary value not specifically rated in the published classifications or tariffs unless a special agreement to do so and a stipulated value of the articles are indorsed hereon.

Sec. 6. Every party, whether principal or agent, shipping explosives or dangerous goods, without previous full written disclosure to the carrier of their nature, shall be liable for and indemnify the carrier against all loss or damage caused by such goods, and such goods may be warehoused at owner's risk and expense or destroyed without compensation.

Sec. 7. The owner or consignee shall pay the freight and average, if any, and all other lawful charges accruing on said property; but, except in those instances where it may lawfully be authorized to do so, no carrier by railroad shall deliver or relinquish possession at destination of the property covered by this bill of lading until all tariff rates and charges thereon have been paid. The consignor shall be liable for the freight and all other lawful charges, except that if the consignor stipulates, by signature, in the space provided for that purpose on the face of this bill of lading, that the carrier shall not make delivery without requiring payment of such charges and the carrier, contrary to such stipulation, shall make delivery without requiring such payment, the consignor (except as hereinafter provided) shall not be liable for such charges. Provided, that, where the carrier has been instructed by the shipper or consignor to deliver said property to a consignee other than the shipper or consignor, such consignee shall not be legally liable for transportation charges in respect of the transportation of said property (beyond those billed against him at the time of delivery for which he is otherwise liable) which may be found to be due after the property has been delivered to him, if the consignee (a) is an agent only and has no beneficial title in said property, and (b) prior to delivery of said property has notified the delivering carrier in writing of the fact of such agency and absence of beneficial title, and, in the case of a shipment reconsigned or diverted to a point other than that specified in the original bill of lading, has also notified the delivering carrier in writing of the name and address of the beneficial owner of said property; and, in such cases the shipper or consignor, or, in the case of a shipment so reconsigned or diverted, the beneficial owner, shall be liable for such additional charges. If the consignee has given to the carrier erroneous information as to who the beneficial owner is, such consignee shall himself be liable for such additional charges. On shipments reconsigned or diverted by an agent who has furnished the carrier in the reconsignment or diversion order with a notice of agency and the proper name and address of the beneficial owner, and where such shipments are refused or abandoned at ultimate destination, the said beneficial owner shall be liable for all legally applicable charges in connection therewith. If the reconsignor or diverter has given to the carrier erroneous information as to who the beneficial owner or diverter shall himself be liable for all such charges.

If a shipper or consignor of a shipment of property (other than a prepaid shipment) is also the consignee named in the bill of lading and, prior to the time of delivery, notifies, in writing, a delivering carrier by railroad (a) to deliver such property at destination to another party, (b) that such party is the beneficial owner of such property, and (c) that delivery is to be made to such party only upon payment of all transportation charges in respect of the transportation of such property, and delivery is made by the carrier to such party without such payment, such shipper or consignor shall not be liable (as shipper, consignor, consignee, or otherwise) for such transportation charges but the party to whom delivery is so made shall in any event be liable for transportation charges billed against the property at the time of such delivery, and also for any additional charges which may be found to be due after delivery of the property, except that if such party prior to such delivery has notified, in writing the delivering carrier that he is not the beneficial owner of the property, and has given in writing to such delivering carrier the name and address of such beneficial owner, such party shall not be liable for any additional charges which may be found to be due after delivery to him of the property, but, if the party to whom delivery is made has given to the carrier erroneous information as to who the beneficial owner is, such party shall nevertheless be liable for such additional charges. If the shipper or consignor has given to the delivering carrier erroneous information as to who the beneficial owner is, such shipper or consignor shall himself be liable for such transportation charges, notwithstanding the foregoing provisions of this paragraph and irrespective of any provisions to the contrary in the bill of lading or in the contract of transportation under which the shipment was made. The term "delivering carrier" means the line-haul carrier making ultimate delivery.

Nothing herein shall limit the right of the carrier to require at time of shipment the prepayment of guarantee of the charges. If upon inspection it is ascertained that the articles shipped are not those described in this bill of lading, the freight charges must be paid upon the articles actually shipped.

Where delivery is made by a common carrier by water the foregoing provisions of this section shall apply, except as may be inconsistent with Part III of the Interstate Commerce Act.

Sec. 8. If the bill of lading is issued on the order of the shipper, or his agent, in exchange or in substitution for another bill of lading, the shipper's signature to the prior bill of lading as to the statement of value or otherwise, or election of common law or bill of lading liability, in or in connection with such prior bill of lading, shall be considered a part of this bill of lading as fully as if the same were written or made in or in connection with this bill of lading.

Sec. 9. (a) If all or any part of said property is carried by water over any part of said route, and loss, damage or injury to said property occurs while the same is in the custody of a carrier by water the liability of such carrier shall be determined by the bill of lading of the carrier by water (this bill of lading being such bill of lading if the property is transported by such water carrier thereunder) and by and under the laws and regulations applicable to transportation by water. Such water carriage shall be performed subject to all the terms and provisions of, and all of the exemptions from liability contained in the Act of the Congress of the United States, approved on February 13, 1893, and entitled "An act relating to the navigation of vessels, etc.," and of other statutes of the United States according carriers by water the protection of limited liability, as well as the following subdivisions of this section; and to the conditions contained in this bill of lading not inconsistent with this section, when this bill of lading becomes the bill of lading of the carrier by water.

(b) No such carrier by water shall be liable for any loss or damage resulting from any fire happening to or on board the vessel, or from explosion, bursting of boilers or breakage of shafts, unless caused by the design or neglect of such carrier.

(c) If the owner shall have exercised due diligence in making the vessel in all respects seaworthy and properly manned, equipped, and supplied, no such carrier shall be liable for any loss or damage resulting from the perils of the lakes, seas, or other waters, or from latent defects in hull, machinery, or appurtenances whether existing prior to, at the time of, or after sailing, or from collision, stranding, or other accidents of navigation, or from prolongation of the voyage. And, when for any reason it is necessary, any vessel carrying any or all of the property herein described shall be at liberty to call at any ports, in or out of the customary route, to tow and be towed, to transfer, trans-ship, or lighter, to load and discharge goods at any time, to assist vessels in distress, to deviate for the purpose of saving life or property, and for docking and repairs. Except in case of negligence such carrier shall not be responsible for any loss or damage to property if it be necessary or is usual to carry the same upon deck.

(d) General Average shall be payable according to the York-Antwerp Rules of 1924, Sections 1 to 15, inclusive, and Sections 17 to 22, inclusive, and as to matters not covered thereby according to the laws and usages of the Port of New York. If the owners shall have exercised due diligence to make the vessel in all respects seaworthy and properly manned, equipped and supplied, it is hereby agreed that in case of danger, damage or disaster resulting from faults or errors in navigation, or in the management of the vessel, or from any latent or other defects in the vessel, her machinery or appurtenances, or from unseaworthiness, whether existing at the time of shipment or at the beginning of the voyage (provided the latent or other defects or the unseaworthiness was not discoverable by the exercise of due diligence), the shippers, consignees and/or owners of the cargo shall nevertheless pay salvage and any special charges incurred in respect of the cargo, and shall contribute with the shipowner in general average to the payment of any sacrifices, losses or expenses of a general average nature that may be made or incurred for the common benefit or to relieve the adventure from any common peril.

(e) If the property is being carried under a tariff which provides that any carrier or carrier's party thereto shall be liable for loss from perils of the sea, then as to such carrier or carriers the provisions of this section shall be modified in accordance with the tariff provisions, which shall be regarded as incorporated into the conditions of this bill of lading.

(f) The term "water carriage" in this section shall not be construed as including lighterage in or across rivers, harbors, or lakes, when performed by or on behalf of rail carriers.

Sec. 10. Any alteration, addition, or erasure in this bill of lading which shall be made without the special notation hereon of the agent of the carrier issuing this bill of lading, shall be without effect, and this bill of lading shall be enforceable according to its original tenor.

EFFECTIVE JUNE 15, 1941

NON–NEGOTIABLE BILL OF LADING
[Reverse]

(1) THE SITUATION OF BUYERS

Documentary transactions in the form just described reduce the credit risk for buyer and sellers in many ways, but they leave buyers in a precarious position in a number of respects. The following problems are intended to examine the situation of buyers who are expected to pay the purchase price in exchange for a negotiable bill of lading.

Problem 1. Seller & Co. of Sellersville, N.Y., agreed to sell a large quantity of paper bags to Buyer & Co., of Buyersville, California, who agreed to pay $5,000.00, F.O.B. Buyersville. The parties agreed to a payment term: "sight draft against order bill of lading." Seller & Co. turned over the goods to Conrail and received a negotiable bill of lading made out to the order of Seller & Co. Seller & Co. prepared a draft for the purchase price, indorsed the bill of lading "in blank,"[10] and forwarded the draft and bill through Sellersville Bank to Buyer & Co.

(a) Before the goods have arrived in Buyersville, Buyersville Bank received the draft and bill of lading. Buyersville Bank promptly notified Buyer & Co. that it had a draft and bill of lading. Buyer & Co. refused to pay the draft on the ground that it had not had an opportunity to inspect the goods. Is Buyer & Co. permitted to refuse to pay pending arrival of the goods and inspection of them? See UCC 2–513(3)(b); see also 2–310(b).

(b) Assume that Buyer & Co. paid when the sight draft was presented and obtained the bill of lading. Subsequently, the railroad car containing the 50 cartons of paper bags arrived in Buyersville and the railroad so notified Buyer & Co.[11] Buyer & Co. surrendered the bill of lading and took possession of the goods. Upon opening the boxes, Buyer & Co. discovered that a large percentage of the paper bags had been improperly glued. May Buyer & Co. reject the goods under UCC 2–601? See UCC 2–512(2). If Buyer & Co. has the power to reject the goods, to what extent are buyer's rights affected by the fact that it has already paid the price?

(c) Assume that Buyer & Co. paid when the sight draft was presented and obtained the bill of lading. The goods did not arrive within the expected time. When buyer asked the railroad for information, the railroad disclosed that the car containing the goods had been attached to the wrong train in St. Louis. The goods arrived in Califor-

---

10. A negotiable document of title running to the order of a named person can be negotiated by indorsement and delivery. An indorsement "in blank" permits further negotiation by delivery alone. 49 U.S. Code App. 89(c); UCC 7–501(1). Negotiation of documents of title within banking channels is facilitated by "in blank" indorsements. This permits a document to move forward without the necessity that each bank sign it and identify the next bank in the chain.

11. Order bills of lading usually indicate the person to be notified upon arrival of the goods at their destination. (See the face of order bill of lading form in the prototype transaction.) The "notify" provision does not authorize the carrier to deliver goods to the party listed without surrender of the bill of lading.

nia three weeks later than anticipated. May Buyer & Co. reject the goods under UCC 2–601?

Rejection of Tender of Documents. In shipment contracts with negotiable bills of lading, buyers are first tendered documents that control the right to obtain possession of the goods from the carriers. Before seeing the goods, buyers accept or reject the tender of documents. Acceptance of a tender of the documents does not signify acceptance of the goods. Acceptance and rejection of goods by signification or lapse of time occurs only after buyers have had a reasonable opportunity to inspect them upon arrival. UCC 2–513(1).

Under UCC 2–601, a buyer may reject "the whole" if "the tender of delivery" fails in any respect to conform to the contract. Documents, like goods, may or may not conform to the contract; tendered documents must be in "correct" and "due" form. UCC 2–503(5), 2–504(b). The Code's most explicit reference to non-conformity of documents is found in the installment contract provision. UCC 2–612(2). The perfect tender rule is associated historically with cases in which buyers were tendered documents.

Contracting for Documentary Transactions. In the prototype transaction, buyer pays the price upon seller's tender of a negotiable bill of lading. Recall that this arrangement is not a default rule of performance; it result from the agreements of the parties. What terms in sales contracts are sufficient to commit buyers to pay at this stage in performance? See UCC 2–310, 2–513(3).

(a) A commonly used contract term is: "sight draft against order bill of lading." Does this satisfy the Code requirements?

(b) If a sales contract uses the term C.I.F. or C. & F., must the buyer pay the price upon tender of an order bill of lading? See UCC 2–320(4).

(c) If the sales contract uses the term F.O.B. Sellersville or F.O.B. Buyersville, must the buyer pay the price upon tender of an order bill of lading? What explains the difference between the F.O.B. term and C.I.F. or C. & F. terms? Is it significant that the latter are used most commonly in shipments by water? See Comment 4 to UCC 2–310. For other terms in contracts contemplating shipment by water, see UCC 2–319(4), 2–321, 2–322.

Inspection by Third Party. Parties to documentary transactions may agree that the goods will be inspected by a third party before shipment or at some point en route. The sales contract may specify that results of the inspection must be reflected in the inspector's certificate of quality which must be tendered to the buyer with the bill of lading. Recall the contractual arrangements for inspection in *T.J. Stevenson,* the case concerning sale of flour to the Bolivian government. And see UCC 2–513(4).

Inspection by Carrier. Carriers have some duties regarding the quality and quantity of goods not in packages or sealed containers.

Thus a carrier must ascertain the kind and quantity of bulk freight, and may be liable for misdescription or nonreceipt of the goods. 49 U.S.C. App. 100, 102, UCC 7–301(2). To protect themselves against claims that goods were damaged en route, carriers may add notes on bills of lading about the condition of the goods or packages.

In the paper bags transaction, would Buyer & Co. have a cause of action against the railroad for delivering goods that do not conform to the sales contract? Does the description of the goods in the bill of lading, "Bags, paper," create a basis for carrier liability for the quality of the goods? See UCC 7–301(1). Read again the RECEIVED paragraph at the head of the order bill of lading.

(2) THE SITUATION OF SELLERS

Sellers who engage in documentary exchange transactions incur certain risks of transaction failure. Vis-a-vis buyers, risk exists that buyers will not make payment against tender of documents. Sellers may want to stop the goods, then en route to buyers' locations, and either get them back or divert them to other destinations. Carriers permit consignors to modify the routing of goods, but sellers lose time and incur expenses in making these changes.

Sellers are dependent upon banks and carriers to carry out their respective services. If they should fail to do so, sellers might be deprived of their goods without having received the promised payments.

Problem 2. Buyer and Seller agreed on sale of a lathe No. 3X from Seller's current catalogue with payment to be made against documents. The next day, Seller delivered a No. 3X lathe to the railroad, obtained a bill of lading that calls for delivery to "order of Seller," indorsed the bill in blank, and gave it along with a sight draft drawn on Buyer to its local bank for transmittal to Buyer. The documents were forwarded to a bank in Buyer's city, which sent a notice to Buyer that it held these documents for Buyer's payment. Buyer ignored the notice. What is the nature of the bank's obligation?

(a) Has Buyer dishonored the draft by not responding to the bank's notice? See UCC 3–502(c)?

(b) Is the bank obliged to do more than inform Seller of a Buyer's dishonor? See UCC 4–503(2). What might be the reason for this provision?

Problem 3. Assume the same facts as above, except that the presenting bank gave Buyer the bill of lading in exchange for the Buyer's uncertified check in the amount of the draft. Before the Buyer's check was paid, Buyer obtained the lathe from the railroad and stopped payment on its check. See UCC 4–403(1). What are Seller's rights?

(a) Does Seller have a claim against the railroad? See 49 U.S.C. App. 89(c), UCC 7–404.

(b) Does Seller have a claim against the presenting bank? See UCC 4–202(a), 4–213, 4–103(e). And see Bunge v. First National Bank of Mount Holly Springs, 118 F.2d 427 (3d Cir.1941).

(c) Does Seller have a claim against its local bank for the actions of the presenting bank? See UCC 4–202(c) and Comment 4.

(d) Does Seller have a claim against Buyer? See UCC 2–301, 2–507. Of what practical value to Seller is 2–507(2)?

Problem 4. Assume the same facts as in the original problem, except that Buyer, without paying the draft or obtaining the bill of lading from the presenting bank, gets possession of the lathe from railroad. What are Seller's rights?

(a) Does Seller have a claim against the railroad? See 49 U.S.C. App. 88(b), 90; UCC 7–403(1). What would be the proper measure of damages? See Alderman Bros. Co. v. New York, etc. R. Co., 102 Conn. 461, 129 A. 47 (1925).

(b) Does Seller have a claim against any Bank?

(c) Does Seller have a claim against Buyer?

Sellers' Use of Drafts to Obtain Credit. Sellers engaging in documentary transactions sometimes seek to speed up the inflow of cash by getting the amount of the drafts, less a discount, from the banks who take them for presentation and collection. The context of documentary transactions gives banks reasonable assurance that credit extended to sellers will be repaid promptly from proceeds of the drafts. Moreover, the drafts are negotiable instruments on which the sellers are liable as drawers. UCC 3–414(b). Not uncommonly, therefore, banks taking drafts for collection will "discount" them. At the same time they also receive the "order bills" indorsed in blank.

(a) If a carrier delivers the goods to the wrong person under an "order bill," is the discounting bank entitled to a remedy against the carrier? See 49 U.S.C. App. 90, 91; UCC 7–403.

(b) Is the discounting bank liable to the buyer if the goods do not conform to the seller's obligations under the sales contract? See UCC 7–507, 7–508; cf. UCC 2–210(4).

Sellers may also "discount" drafts to anticipate payment when underlying documentary transactions require buyers to accept "time drafts" upon presentment rather than make immediate payment. Accepted drafts establish liability on both the drawer and the drawee/acceptor. UCC 3–409, 3–413, 3–414.

(3) SELLERS' POWER TO RECLAIM GOODS

Introduction. Sellers who delivered goods without being paid may, in some limited circumstances, reclaim the goods from their buyers. The power to reclaim is essentially lost in credit sales, i.e., transactions in which sellers voluntarily agree to deliver before payment.

One exception, introduced in Chapter 2, is sellers' power to rescind transactions induced by buyers' fraudulent misrepresentation. Rescission and its accompanying *in rem* remedies are associated with the law of torts and restitution as much as with contract law. Article 2 of the Commercial Code, which assumes the common-law power to rescind for fraud, also creates for sellers statutory power to reclaim in some circumstances. Effective exercise of that power reduces sellers' credit risk.

Problem 5. Buyer induces Seller to deliver goods on credit by promising to pay for them in 30 days. Shortly after delivering the goods, Seller discovers that Buyer is insolvent. May Seller recover the goods? See UCC 2–702(2). What difference, if any, would it make if:

(a) Two months prior to delivery Seller had received from Buyer its financial statement showing Buyer to be solvent?

(b) Two months prior to delivery Seller had received a report from a credit reporting agency erroneously showing Buyer to be solvent?

Problem 6. Buyer and Seller contract for sale of an antique brass chandelier. Seller delivers the chandelier in exchange for Buyer's personal check for the price, $7,500.00. Seller deposits the check the next day. A week later, Seller's bank informs Seller that the deposited check had been dishonored by Buyer's bank, that the provisional credit to Seller's account has been reversed, and that Seller's account has been charged a fee for the transaction. May Seller recover the chandelier? See UCC 2–507(2).

Originally, Comment 3 to UCC 2–507 declared that the ten day time limit for sellers' reclamation in UCC 2–702(2) is also applicable in here. That Comment was withdrawn by the Permanent Editorial Board in 1990. See PEB Commentary No. 1, Section 2–507(2):

> There is no specific time limit for a cash seller to exercise the right of reclamation. The right may be exercised as long as there has not been excessive delay causing inequitable prejudice to the buyer.

Is the 1990 commentary persuasive? Is it any more or less binding on a court than the original Comment?

Problem 7. A contract for sale between Seller in San Francisco and Buyer in New York calls for shipment of a carload of Sunkist oranges at $3000, f.o.b. San Francisco. Payment terms are: Cash 30 days after delivery. Seller ships oranges in conformity with the contract on a "straight bill of lading" naming buyer as consignee. After the carload arrives in the New York freight yards but before the oranges are unloaded, Seller learns that Buyer's creditors have begun to obtain judgments against Buyer and judicial liens against Buyer's property.

(a) Has Seller a chance to keep the oranges for itself? See UCC 2–705. Note the Code's extension of the grounds for stoppage beyond insolvency, for carload and similarly large shipments.[12]

(b) Assume Seller instructs the railroad not to deliver the oranges to Buyer but rather to transport them to another consignee in Philadelphia.

(i) If the railroad refuses to release the oranges to Buyer, would it be liable to Buyer for failing to honor the terms of its bill of lading? See UCC 7–403; UCC 7–303.

(ii) Under what circumstances, if any, may the railroad ignore Seller's instructions without incurring liability to Seller? See UCC 2–705; UCC 7–303. See also Butts v. Glendale Plywood Co., 710 F.2d 504 (9th Cir.1983) (carrier's rerouting of shipment to buyer's buyer, made at buyer's direction while goods still in transit, held to be "reshipment" under UCC 2–705(2)(c)).

(B) INTERNATIONAL SALES LAW

Introduction. Grappling with international sales transactions runs some of the hazards of navigating among icebergs. The elements, while broadly standardized, have infinite variations in particular transactions. In reported decisions of courts and arbitrators, many critical facts may be invisible. Seldom do these tribunals give the complete setting from which the controversies arose. To provide a basis for understanding the fundamental mechanics of international sales transactions, this section opens with a prototype transaction that follows the sale, step by step, through its most important stages.

Management of credit risk is more important in international sales transactions than in domestic transactions, where both seller and buyer are in the same country and subject to the same domestic laws. The marketplace developed a payment device, the bank letter of credit, which serves well the parties' needs to control credit risks in the performance of export-import sales.

As noted in previous sections, the Convention on Contracts for the International Sale of Goods has few provisions on the manner, time, and place for performance of buyers' payment obligation that are not dependent upon the agreement of the parties. However, the Convention contains a default rule that, absent agreement otherwise, buyers need not pay until they have had an opportunity to examine the goods. CISG 58(3). Agreement to pay before inspection may be inferred from agreement on "the procedures for delivery or payment." Id. If the contract involves carriage of goods, sellers may dispatch the goods on

---

12. Would you advise a seller to ship on credit to a shaky buyer in reliance on the seller's stoppage rights? Would sellers likely hear of insolvency during the time required for shipment? On the other hand, a lawyer would probably be liable for malpractice if a client presented the facts in the preceding Problem and the lawyer could think of no course of action other than taking a day or so to research the point.

terms whereby the goods, or documents controlling their disposition, will not be handed over to the buyer except against payment of the price. CISG 58(2). Since examination of goods can occur before they are "handed over" to buyers, Article 58(2) does not override 58(3).

The Convention makes no mention of payment by letter of credit. Parties who wish to use this payment device must do so by their agreement.

Agreements on payment terms, like other contract terms, may be express or implied. No implication arises from the parties' use of the ICC's *Incoterms,* which describe the buyer's payment obligation in documentary transactions to be: pay the price as provided in the contract of sale. However, common-law courts have long held that an obligation to pay against documents is implicit in international sales. The leading case is E. Clemens Horst Co. v. Biddle Bros., [1912] A.C. 18 (H.L.)(sale of hops shipped from San Francisco C.I.F to London, Liverpool, or Hull). Recall that this common-law rule was incorporated into the Commercial Code, which provides that contractual use of terms associated with water transport (C.I.F., C. & F., F.A.S., F.O.B. vessel) creates a duty on buyers to pay against documents. UCC 2–319(4), 2–320(4), 2–321(3).

(1) BALL BEARINGS FOR BRAZIL: A PROTOTYPE EXPORT TRANSACTION[1]

SKF Industries, Inc., is a Philadelphia manufacturer of ball and roller bearings. On December 4, 1983, SKF receives a letter from Companhia Importadora Brasileira, a distributor of bearings in Rio de Janeiro, Brazil (hereinafter called "Brasileira"), requesting a price quotation for 1200 ball bearings (catalogue number 187B) and 2400 roller bearings (catalogue number 839R). On December 15 SKF replies by letter (FORM 1) explaining the quotation as set forth in the enclosed proforma invoice (FORM 2).

---

1. Mr. B.A. Tassone, Director of International Marketing, and Mr. H.J. Gupfinger, Manager of Material Flow, SKF Industries, Inc., were exceedingly helpful in explaining their practices and in preparing the sample forms. Thanks are also owing to Mr. Robert S. Adamson, Assistant Vice President, Philadelphia National Bank, for preparing the letter of credit. Of course, any errors in presenting the transaction are my own responsibility.

SKF INDUSTRIES, INC.
INTERNATIONAL MARKETING/BEARINGS GROUP

December 15, 1983

Companhia Importadora Brasileira
Caixa Postal 10
Rio de Janeiro, Brazil

Re: CIB - 43H2

Gentlemen:

We are very pleased to acknowledge receipt of your above inquiry dated December 4 requesting our quotation on a total quantity of 3,600 ball and roller bearings.

We are attaching hereto our proforma invoice in quadruplicate showing the net price for each size, along with the total f.a.s. Philadelphia or New York City value. For your convenience, we have also estimated the insurance charges, ocean freight and handling charges as well as the consular fees. We have, therefore, arrived at a total estimated c.i.f. Rio de Janeiro value. We wish to call your attention specifically to the fact that our quotation is an f.a.s. Philadelphia or New York City quotation and the total c.i.f. value shown is simply as an estimated value which we have included for your convenience in obtaining your Import License and opening the Letter of Credit. The shipping and handling charges will be for your account and we will invoice the exact charges whether they are higher or lower than those estimated.

We have been able to quote a January delivery for both sizes, but have to point out that this promise is valid only if your firm order will be received by return air mail. Even though the delivery has been promised for January, we suggest that your Letter of Credit be valid until February 28, 1984, so that there will be no necessity to request an extension unless some unforeseen difficulties should arise. Needless to say, the Letter of Credit should be for a minimum of 10,950 United States dollars. As all of the bearings which you require are available for shipment in January, we have estimated shipping expenses for only one shipment. Therefore, it is not necessary to allow for partial shipments in the Letter of Credit.

We appreciate very much this opportunity of quoting and will look forward to the early receipt of your firm order.

Very truly yours,

E. L. Derry
E. L. Derry
General Supervisor

[D628]

FORM 1
LETTER TRANSMITTING QUOTATION

SKF INDUSTRIES, INC.
FRONT STREET AND ERIE AVENUE
PHILADELPHIA, PA. 19132

CABLE ADDRESS
"SKAYEF" – PHILADELPHIA

TELEX 83-4539

REFER CORRESPONDENCE TO
EXPORT SALES DEPT.
P.O. BOX NO. 6731
PHILADELPHIA, PENNA. 19132

OUR PROFORMA INVOICE
NUMBER: IA/100
DATE: 12/15/83

YOUR INQUIRY
NUMBER: CIB-43H2
DATE: 12/4/83

Companhia Importadora Brasileira

Caixa Postal 10

Rio de Janeiro, Brazil

ITEM NO.	MATERIAL SPECIFICATIONS		QUANTITY	PRICE		AVAILABILITY		WEIGHT
	MANUFACTURER'S PART NUMBER	SIZE DESCRIPTION		UNIT	TOTAL	STOCK		IN LBS.
1	187 B		1200	2.15	2,580.00		January	
2	839 R.		2400	3.37	8,088.00		January	

Os precos acima indicados sao os correntes no mercado de exportacao para qualquer pais.

Nao ha comissao.

Nao sao publicados catalogos e/ou lista de preco para o material acima indicado.

    Est. total net weight - 4520 lbs. - 2050 kilos
    Est. total gross weight - 5010 lbs. - 2272 kilos

        Schedule B Commodity Code - 7197010

TOTAL MAT'L. VALUE F.A.S. VESSEL PHILA. OR N.Y.C.	$10,668.00
ESTIMATED FREIGHT FORWARDER'S CHARGES	19.00
ESTIMATED CONSULAR CHARGES	58.00
ESTIMATED F.O.B. VESSEL	
ESTIMATED INSURANCE CHARGES	48.50
ESTIMATED TRANSPORTATION CHARGES	156.50
ESTIMATED C.I.F.	10,950.00

THIS OFFER SUBMITTED SUBJECT TO PRIOR SALE AND CONFIRMATION OF TERMS AND PRICES AT TIME OF RECEIPT OF ORDER.

INDUSTRIES, INC.

TERMS:
DELIVERY FAS VESSEL PHILADELPHIA/NEW YORK CITY
PAYMENT LETTER OF CREDIT

CONDITIONS: Prices shown are those in effect at time of quotation. Prices in effect at time of shipment will prevail.

**FORM 2
PROFORMA INVOICE**

TERMS AND CONDITIONS

Any order resulting from this quotation will be subject to the following conditions:

1. Delivery dates are approximate. Seller shall not be liable for any delay in, or inability to complete delivery because of any of the following causes: Acts of God; suspension or requisition of any kind; strikes or other stoppages of labor or shortage in the supply thereof; inability to obtain fuel, material or parts; fire, casualties or accidents; failure of shipping facilities; riot; or any cause, whether the same or a different character, beyond Seller's control.

2. Prices indicated are based on the prices in effect as of the date hereof. They are subject to change in accordance with the prices in effect as of the date of shipment.

3. Products are not returnable for credit or replacement, unless authorized in writing by Seller.

4. If, for any reason whatsoever, this order or any part thereof, is terminated by the Buyer, such termination shall be effected with the understanding that termination charges may result therefrom.

5. Orders for special products are subject to shipment of any overrun or underrun not to exceed 10%. The Buyer will pay, in full, for such overshipment, and in the event of an undershipment the Buyer will consider the order completed with such undershipment.

6. Goods manufactured by Seller shall conform to the description, shall be fit for the ordinary purposes for which such goods are used, and shall be free of defects in material and workmanship at time of shipment. THERE ARE NO WARRANTIES OF MERCHANTABILITY OR OTHERWISE, EXCEPT OF TITLE, WHICH EXTENDS BEYOND THAT STATED ABOVE.

7. Seller's liability and Buyer's remedy for breach of warranty or otherwise is expressly limited to the replacement of any products sold hereunder which Seller determines, by laboratory examination is non-conforming, provided said non-conforming products are returned F.O.B. Seller's warehouse within twelve (12) months of shipment hereunder. Seller retains the right to render credit for the purchase price in lieu of furnishing a replacement product.

8. IN NO EVENT SHALL SELLER BE LIABLE HEREUNDER OR OTHERWISE FOR LOSS OF PROFITS, SPECIAL, INCIDENTAL, OR CONSEQUENTIAL DAMAGES OF ANY KIND.

9. Shipments hereunder shall be at all times subject to the approval of Seller's Credit Department.

10. The terms and conditions on the face and reverse side hereof constitute the entire agreement between Buyer and Seller. No reference herein to Buyer's inquiry or order shall in any way incorporate different or additional terms or conditions which are hereby objected to. No modification hereto shall be binding upon Seller unless made in writing by Seller's authorized representative. Receipt of this acknowledgment by Buyer without prompt written objection thereto shall constitute an acceptance of these terms and conditions by Buyer.

[B2891]

[*Reverse*]

PROFORMA INVOICE

FORM 2

Examination of the proforma invoice will show that it contains all the particulars for the proposed shipment which are then known to SKF. (It will be useful to consider whether this communication constitutes an offer which, on acceptance, would create a binding contract. Compare the letter with the printed language in the bottom right-hand corner of the proforma invoice.)[2]

The Price Quotation: F.A.S. and C.I.F. One will note that the proforma invoice in the bottom left-hand corner has a blank after "TERMS: DELIVERY" and that SKF inserted the following: "F.A.S. PHILA/NEW YORK CITY". "F.A.S." stands for "Free Along Side"; this means that the seller will be responsible for the cost and risks of bringing the goods "Along Side" an overseas vessel at the stated location: the buyer bears the costs and risks from that point.[3] Therefore, under this quotation the Brazilian buyer will understand that its total costs will include not only the quoted F.A.S. price of $10,668, but also freight charges from Philadelphia to Brazil, the cost of insurance and any other expenses of bringing the goods into Brazil.

It is necessary to pause in the description of this transaction to note that instead of quoting a price "F.A.S. Philadelphia," the price might have been quoted "C.I.F. Rio de Janeiro." The initials "C.I.F." stand for "Cost, Insurance, and Freight" and mean, among other things, that in exchange for this stated price the seller undertakes not only to supply the goods ("cost") but also to obtain and pay for insurance and bear the freight charges to the stated point.[4] In spite of the widespread use of C.I.F. quotations in foreign trade, sellers in the position of SKF often prefer to quote on a F.A.S. basis since this relieves them of the burdens and hazards of variations and fluctuations in freight and insurance costs for shipments to widely scattered points. This preference is reflected in the "F.A.S." quotation in the transaction which we are following. (Note the explanation in the second paragraph of the letter in FORM 1.)

Buyer's Purchase Order. In response to SKF's letter of December 15, on January 5, Brasileira sent SKF the Buyer's Purchase Order that follows (FORM 3).

---

2. If the seller were a middleman purchasing goods for export could he safely leave the transaction open at this point?

3. See International Chamber of Commerce's INCOTERMS F.A.S.; UCC 2–319(2).

4. See International Chamber of Commerce's INCOTERMS C.I.F.; UCC 2–320. From the fact that the contract price includes the freight, do not leap to any conclusion about who has the risk of loss.

COMPANHIA IMPORTADORA BRASILEIRA

Caixa Postal, 10   Fone 2-1881   End. Teleg. ROLESFER

RIO DE JANEIRO, BRAZIL

EXPORT SALES
DATE REC'D DISTRIBUTORES DIRETOS
JAN 10 1984 REGULAMENTOS

Pedido No. (Order):	42

Fornecedor: S K F Industries, Inc.
(Supplier)
Data (Date): 5/1/84

Endereço: P.O.Box 6731 - Philadelphia 32, Pa. USA
(Address)
Banco (Bank): Advise

Condições Pagamento: Irrevocable Letter of Credit
(Payment Terms)
Marca (Shipping Mark): C.I.B.

Embarque: Ship to Rio de Janeiro
(Shipment)
Rio de Janeiro

Embarcador: Pierce-Byron, Inc., 325 Chestnut St., Phila., PA
(Forwarder)

Declaração Consular: Rolamento de esfera, rolete cone ou agulhas para mancal
(Consular Declaration)

Licença de Importação No. DG-59/10000   **Valór (Value):** $10,950.00   **Validade (Validity):** 2/28/84
(Import License)

Seguro: Against all usual risks including theft and   **Embalagem (Packing):** Packing export
(Insurance) marine up to clients warehouse. in wood cases

[B29l3]

Item No.	Quant.	DESIGNAÇÃO (Part No.)	DENOMINAÇÃO (Description)	Desconto (Discount)	Preço Unitário (Unit Price)	Imp. Total (Amount)
01	1,200	187-B	Bearings	US $ NETTO	2.15	2,580.00
02	2,400	839-R	Bearings	"	3.37	8,088.00
					F.A.S.	10,668.00
			Insurance Fee			48.50
			Documentation & Expenses			19.00
			Consular Fee on Invoice			52.00
			Consular Fee on Bill of Lading			6.00
			Ocean Freight			156.50
					Total C.I.F.	10,950.00

COMPANHIA IMPORTADORA BRASILEIRA

Juan Cordova Hernandez
Director Comercial

[B2914]

**FORM 3
BUYER'S PURCHASE ORDER**

The Letter of Credit. The proforma invoice (FORM 2), which SKF enclosed with its letter of December 15, under "TERMS ... PAYMENT" contained the notation "Letter of Credit". Letters of credit play a central role in most exporting transactions and deserve careful attention. In following the domestic documentary transaction between Sellersville, New York and Buyersville, California, Sec. A, supra, we saw that one way for a seller to be assured of payment is to ship goods under a negotiable bill of lading and arrange for a bank in buyer's city to hold the bill of lading until the buyer pays the draft. In the usual foreign sale (and in some domestic sales) this arrangement for securing payment of the price is not adequate. For example, in our current SKF export it probably will not be advisable for SKF to allow payment to be delayed until the bearings reach Brazil. Under such an arrangement Brasileira might reject the bearings in Rio de Janeiro; at this point substantial shipping costs would have been incurred and the bearings would be at a location where it might be awkward and expensive for the seller to arrange for redisposition. Of course, the seller would have a claim against the buyer for this loss, but litigation is always hazardous and in a foreign country the hazards multiply. Moreover, in dealing with the many countries which control foreign exchange, it may be difficult to get the local money converted into usable dollars.

In some situations, sellers may need assurance of payment even before the time for shipment. This problem arises in contracts (either foreign or domestic) which call for the manufacture of goods to the buyer's specifications (electric generators; locomotives; steel girders to be cut in non-standard lengths). In these contracts the seller will need firm assurance of payment before it starts to manufacture.

Strong protection against these hazards can be created if the contract provides that, at a specified point in the transaction before the seller incurs costs it cannot readily recoup, the buyer must establish an irrevocable letter of credit. By such a letter of credit, a bank promises to honor the seller's draft for the price; in our export transaction the bank's promise will be conditioned upon seller's presenting specified documents, one of which will be a negotiable bill of lading evidencing shipment of the goods.

Although the proforma invoice did not so specify, SKF will expect the letter of credit to be "confirmed" by a local bank in the United States. (Cf. UCC 2–325.) It is easy to see why SKF wants the undertaking by a bank of known solvency and responsibility. But why does the local bank only "confirm," rather than "issue," the letter of credit? The answer arises from this practical consideration: the bank that issues a letter of credit needs assurance that it will be reimbursed by the buyer, on whose behalf it pays the seller. The Philadelphia bank will probably not know the Brazilian buyer, and cannot be sure of reimbursement. But the buyer's own bank (Banco do Brasil) can take steps to minimize or remove these hazards. As we shall see, it will receive the negotiable bill of lading controlling the goods which will provide security for the customer's obligation to reimburse the bank; in addition, the buyer's own bank can judge whether security is needed before it issues the letter of credit.

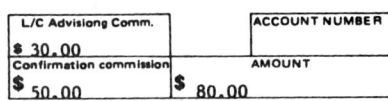

		L/C Advising Comm.	ACCOUNT NUMBER
		$ 30.00	
		Confirmation commission	AMOUNT
		$ 50.00	$ 80.00

IRREVOCABLE DOCUMENTARY CREDIT

OUR CREDIT NO.	CR NO-CORRESPONDENT	DATE	EXPIRY DATE	LETTER OF CREDIT AMOUNT
E 4450	164	JAN.11,1984	FEB.28,1984	US$10,950.00

BENEFICIARY

SKF INDUSTRIES, INC.
PHILADELPHIA, PA.

CORRESPONDENT

BANCO do BRAZIL S.A.
RIO de JANEIRO, BRAZIL

Gentlemen:

We are instructed by the above correspondent to advise you that they have opened their irrevocable credit in your favor for account of <u>COMPANHIA IMPORTADORA BRASILEIRA, CAIXA POSTAL 10, RIO de JANEIRO, BRAZIL</u> available by your drafts on THE PHILADELPHIA NATIONAL BANK AT SIGHT accompanied by the following documents:

1. FULL SET OF CLEAN ON BOARD OCEAN BILLS OF LADING STATING "FREIGHT PREPAID" MADE OUT TO ORDER OF BANCO do BRAZIL S.A.
2. INSURANCE POLICY OR CERTIFICATE COVERING MARINE AND WAR RISK.
3. PACKING LIST.
4. COMMERCIAL INVOICE IN SEXTUPLICATE OF WHICH THREE COPIES MUST BE LEGALIZED BY THE BRAZILIAN CONSUL AND VISAED BY THE LOCAL CHAMBER OF COMMERCE.

COVERING: 1200 BALL BEARING NO. 187-B AND 2400 ROLLER BEARINGS NO. 839-R.
          TOTAL VALUE $10,950.00 CIF RIO de JANEIRO
          IMPORT LICENSE DC-59/10000 EXPIRES 2/28/84

SPECIAL INSTRUCTIONS:

A. ALL DRAFTS SO DRAWN MUST BE MARKED "DRAWN UNDER ADVICE NO. E 4450/164".

SHIPMENT FROM: PHILADELPHIA   TO: RIO de JANEIRO

PARTIAL SHIPMENTS: ARE NOT PERMITTED   TRANSHIPMENTS: ARE NOT PERMITTED

THE ABOVE CORRESPONDENT ENGAGES WITH YOU THAT ALL DRAFTS DRAWN UNDER AND IN COMPLIANCE WITH THE TERMS OF THIS CREDIT WILL BE HONORED ON DELIVERY OF DOCUMENTS AS SPECIFIED IF PRESENTED AT THIS OFFICE ON OR BEFORE THE EXPIRATION DATE SHOWN ABOVE.

IF DESIRED, DRAFTS AND DOCUMENTS MAY BE PRESENTED AT PHILADELPHIA INTERNATIONAL BANK, 55 BROAD STREET, NEW YORK, N.Y. 10004.

[Letter of Credit continued on next page]

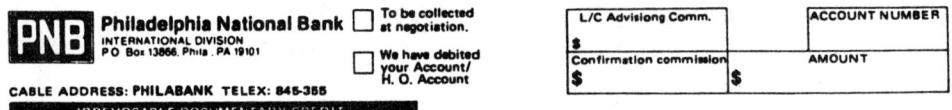

ATTACHED TO AND FORMING PART OF DOCUMENTARY CREDIT NO. E4450 DATE: JANUARY 11,1984
CR. NO. CORRESPONDENT 164

DOCUMENTS MUST CONFORM STRICTLY WITH THE TERMS OF THIS CREDIT, IF YOU ARE UNABLE TO COMPLY WITH ITS TERMS, PLEASE COMMUNICATE WITH YOUR CUSTOMER PROMPTLY WITH A VIEW TO HAVING THE CONDITIONS CHANGED. THIS WILL ELIMINATE DIFFICULTIES AND DELAY WHEN YOUR DOCUMENTS ARE PRESENTED FOR NEGOTIATION.

X   WE CONFIRM THIS CREDIT AND THEREBY UNDERTAKE THAT ALL DRAFTS DRAWN IN ACCORDANCE WITH TERMS THEREOF WILL BE DULY HONORED ON PRESENTATION.

ALL DRAFTS AND DOCUMENTS MUST INDICATE THE REFERENCE NUMBER OF THE CORRESPONDENT BANK AND THE REFERENCE NUMBER OF THE PHILADELPHIA NATIONAL BANK.

Carrie Cash
AUTHORIZED SIGNATURE

EXCEPT SO FAR AS OTHERWISE EXPRESSLY STATED, THIS DOCUMENTARY CREDIT IS SUBJECT TO THE "UNIFORM CUSTOMS AND PRACTICE FOR DOCUMENTARY CREDITS: (1974 REVISION), INTERNATIONAL CHAMBER OF COMMERCE, PUBLICATION NO. 290.

[D630]

FORM 4
LETTER OF CREDIT

Sec. 4   *PERFORMANCE AND THE CREDIT RISK*   323

By this process, something remarkable happens: large hazards inherent in a transaction between a seller and a remote buyer can be reduced almost to the vanishing point by breaking the transaction into steps, and by assigning each step to a party who is in a position to avoid mishap. Thus, the seller is assured of payment by the engagement of the confirming Philadelphia bank; the Philadelphia bank is assured of reimbursement by the undertaking of the issuing Brazilian bank; this Brazilian bank can take steps to assure reimbursement by its local customer. Unhappily, as will soon be seen, not every risk can be removed. But the success of these arrangements is shown by their widespread use by sellers and by the minimal rates charged by banks for the risks which remain.[5]

To meet SKF's letter of credit requirements, Brasileira requests its local bank, Banco do Brasil, to arrange for the issuance of a letter of credit which will comply with the terms of the proforma invoice. Brasileira will sign a detailed Application and Agreement for Commercial Credit prepared by the bank.[6] Banco do Brasil, after approving Brasileira's credit standing, transmits a letter of credit by cable to the Philadelphia confirming bank. The Philadelphia bank then delivers to SKF a document (FORM 4) advising SKF that Banco do Brasil has opened a described letter of credit in favor of SKF and adding the Philadelphia bank's confirmation. (See the end of FORM 4.)

By this arrangement, SKF, the beneficiary of the credit, is assured of payment of its sight drafts drawn on the local Philadelphia bank in the amount of the total cost of the sale, provided it presents the documents called for in the letter of credit. An examination of this letter of credit also reveals that the bill of lading is to be consigned to the "order of Banco do Brasil," thereby giving this bank control over the goods, with the consequent security for its claim against the buyer which has already been discussed.

5. In domestic or import letters of credit, an American bank might typically charge an opening commission of $20 and, for negotiations, ¼% (minimum of $10 for clean drafts and $30 for documentary drafts). A typical commission for accepting an export letter of credit would be 1½% (rate varying with risk; minimum $50), and for confirming a foreign letter of credit ¹⁄₁₀% (minimum $50). For paying under an export letter of credit, the charge might be ¹⁄₁₀% ($35 minimum).

6. A typical American bank's Application and Agreement for Commercial Letter of Credit calls for the buyer to specify which documents should be required by the Letter of Credit, and other essential information such as the amount and expiration date of the credit. The form of agreement then contains two or more closely-printed pages of provisions most of which are designed to assure the bank of reimbursement from its customer for the bank's outlays under the credit in spite of various mishaps. The form also may provide that, except for points covered by the agreement, the operation of the credit will be governed by the Uniform Customs and Practice for Commercial Documentary Credits (1983 Revision in force from 1 October 1984).

This Application, of course, governs only the relationship between the bank and its customer requesting the credit (Brasileira). The obligation of the bank to the beneficiary (SKF) will be governed by the terms of the Letter of Credit which the bank thereafter issues.

CUSTOMER		CUSTOMER ORDER NO.		SKF ORDER NO.		SHPT. NO.
Companhia Importadora Brasileira		CIB-43H2		W-77		1
ADDRESS		CUSTOMER ORDER DATE	CUSTOMER NO.		DATE	
Caixa Postal 10		1/5/84	88831		1/12/84	
Rio de Janeiro, Brazil		TERRITORY NO.		IND. NO.		
		824	X4	100		
SOLD TO		OF Caixa Postal 10				
Companhia Importadora Brasileira		Rio de Janeiro, Brazil				
TERMS		EXPORT LICENSE				
Letter of Credit		G-DEST				
IMPORT LICENSE		LETTER OF CREDIT				
DG-59/10000 expires 2/28/84		No. E 4450/164 expires 2/28/84				

MARKS AND CASE NUMBERS	QUANTITIES		DESCRIPTION OF GOODS	SELLING PRICE	
	ORDERED	SHIPPED		UNIT	TOTAL
	1,200	1,200	187-B Bearings	2.15	2,580.00
	2,400	2,400	839-R Bearings	3.37	8,088.00
					10,668.00

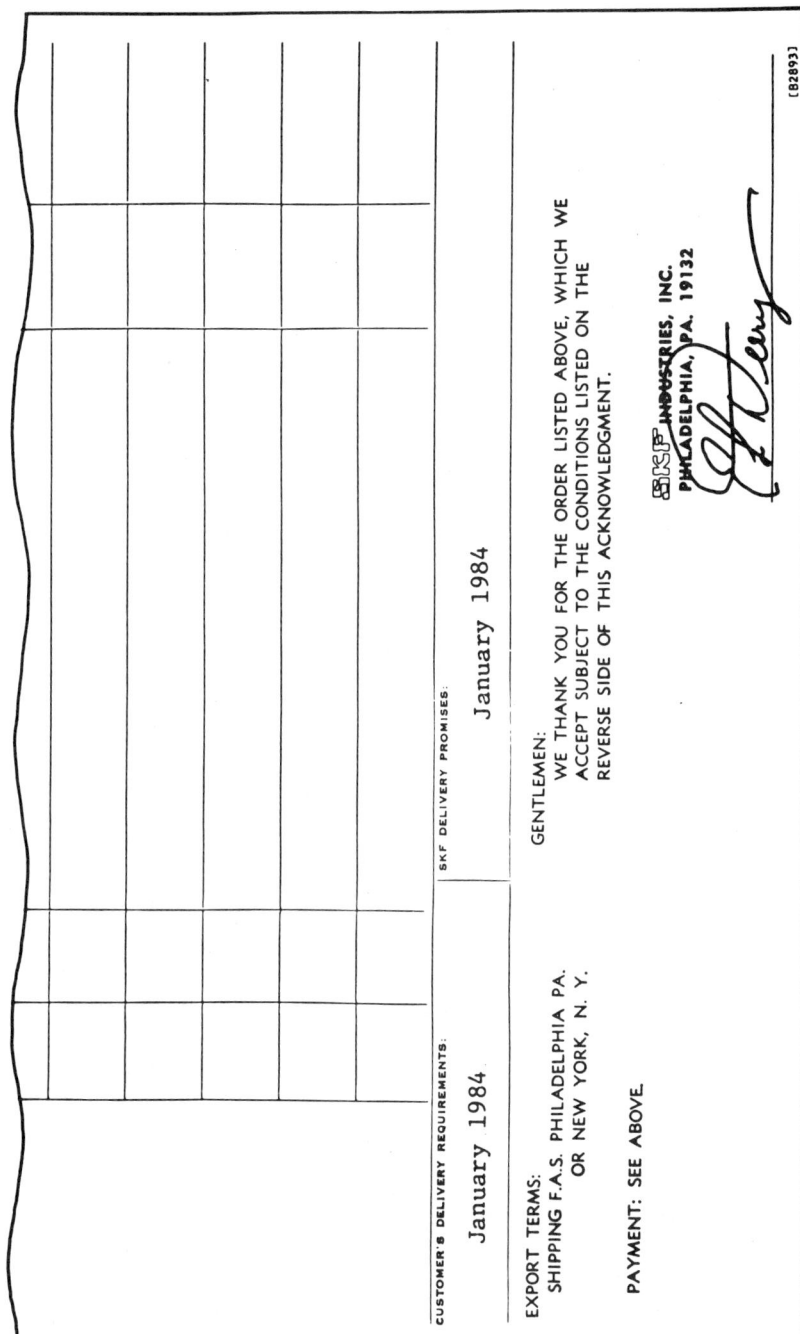

FORM 5
ORDER ACKNOWLEDGEMENT
[*The reverse side of this form is the same as the reverse side of Form 2*]

SKF INDUSTRIES, INC. FRONT STREET AND ERIE AVE. PHILADELPHIA, PA. 19132 P.O. BOX 6731	CUSTOMER ORDER NO. NUMERO DE PEDIDO DEL CLIENTE CIB-43H2	SKF ORDER NO. NUMERO DE PEDIDO DE SKF ~~XMX~~ W-77	SHPT. NO. DESPACHO 1
	EXPORT SALES DEPT. CABLE ADDRESS "SKAYEF"	SKF INVOICE DATE FECHA DE LA FACTURA 1/12/84

SOLD TO VENDIDO A	Companhia Importadora Brasileira	OF DE Caixa Postal 10 Rio de Janeiro, Brazil
TERMS PLAZOS	Letter of Credit	FAS/▇ Philadelphia
IMPORT LICENSE LICENCIA DE IMPORTACION	DG-59/10000 expires 2/28/84	LETTER OF CREDIT CARTA DE CREDITO No. E 4450/164 expires 2/28/84

MARKS AND CASE NUMBERS MARCAS Y NUMEROS DE CAJA	QUANTITY SHIPPED CANTIDAD EMBARCADA	DESCRIPTION OF GOODS "ROLAMENTOS COMPLETOS DE ESFERAS" DESCRIPCION DEL MATERIAL		SELLING PRICE PRECIO DE VENTA	
				UNIT UNIDADES	TOTAL TOTAL
C.I.B. RIO DE JANEIRO #1/25	1,200 2,400	187-B 839-R	Bearings Bearings	US$ 2.15 3.37	US$ 2,580.00 8,088.00 10,688.00
		Consular Fees			58.00
		Freight Forwarders Chrgs.			19.00
		Insurance Charge			48.50
		Transportation Charge			156.50
				TOTAL C.I.F.	10,950.00

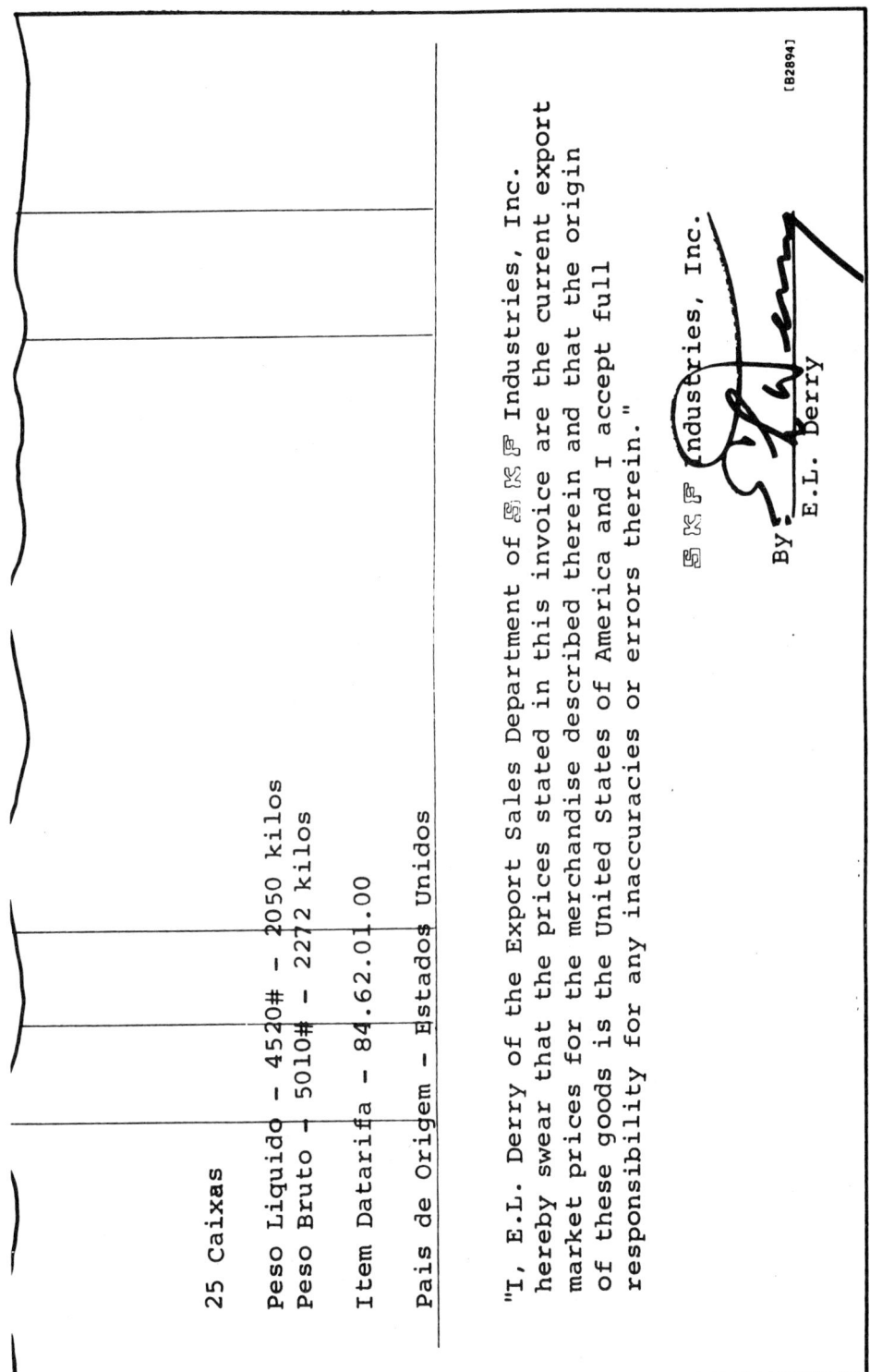

FORM 6
COMMERCIAL INVOICE

Acceptance; Shipment. On receipt of the confirmed letter of credit, SKF sends Brasileira its Order Acknowledgment (FORM 5). This document repeats the description and price of the goods which had also appeared on the proforma invoice and states the number and expiration date of the letter of credit. Note the provision in the lower right hand corner that the buyer's order is accepted, "Subject To The Conditions Listed On The Reverse Side Of This Acknowledgment." (Note especially the conditions dealing with the effect of contingencies beyond the seller's control, fluctuations in the price of the goods, and liability for defective merchandise.)

The arrival of the letter of credit is the "go ahead" signal for SKF to make the shipment. SKF then prepares the Commercial Invoice (FORM 6) which provides a complete record of the transaction and is an important source of information to such interested parties as a bank discounting a draft or an underwriter extending insurance. Note that all data on the commercial invoice conforms to that found in the other shipping documents. By scanning it, one should be able to form a complete picture of the nature of the packing (number of packages, weights, etc.), the commodities being shipped, and the value of the shipment.

As the time for actual shipment of the bearings approaches, SKF contacts Pierce–Byron Inc., the forwarder who will act as the agent of the shipper in attending to the details of shipment and further documentation. Since SKF is located in a port city there are no problems regarding inland transportation to the port of export. SKF sends shipping instructions to Pierce–Byron that inform the forwarder that to comply with the requirements of the letter of credit, the bill of lading must be drawn to the "order of Banco do Brasil." In addition to these shipping instructions, SKF also sends its forwarder copies of the commercial invoice, a packing list and a Shipper's Export Declaration (a Department of Commerce form designed to give the government data from which foreign trade statistics can be compiled). When the forwarder receives these documents, it takes over all further documentation as the agent of the shipper; the latter merely has to dispatch the goods from the factory in accordance with the forwarder's instructions.

In shipments to many countries one of the documents specified in the letter of credit will be a "Consular Invoice," which is required by the buyer's government for foreign customs and statistical purposes. In the case of Brazil, such a separate invoice is not necessary. Instead, a notarized statement is set forth at the end of the Commercial Invoice (FORM 6, supra) and this document is visaed by the Brazilian consul in Philadelphia.

MOORE McCORMACK LINES, Incorporated

COMBINED TRANSPORT PORT TO PORT BILL OF LADING

NOT NEGOTIABLE UNLESS CONSIGNED "TO ORDER"

SHIPPER/EXPORTER
SKF INDUSTRIES, INC
1100 FIRST AVENUE
KING OF PRUSSIA, PA 19406

DOCUMENT NO.

EXPORT DEC. NO.

EXPORT REFERENCES

CONSIGNEE / ORDER OF
BANCO DO BRAZIL, S.A.
RIO DE JANEIRO, BRAZIL

FORWARDING AGENT - REFERENCES
PIERCE BYRON, INC.
325 CHESTNUT ST. PHILA., PA

MMC NO.

POINT AND COUNTRY OF ORIGIN

NOTIFY PARTY
COMPANHIA IMPORTADORA BRASILEIRA
CAIXA POSTAL 10
RIO DE JANEIRO, BRAZIL

DOMESTIC ROUTING/EXPORT INSTRUCTIONS
DELIVERY TO STEAMER
BY DELAIR TRUCKING CO.

ONWARD INLAND ROUTING

PRECARRIAGE BY
PACKER AVENUE

PLACE OF RECEIPT

EXPORTING CARRIER (SHIP)
S/S MORMACOAK

USA FLAG
AM

PORT OF LOADING
PHILA., PA

PORT OF DISCHARGE
RIO DE JANEIRO

PLACE OF DELIVERY

[*Ocean Bill of Lading continued on following pages.*]

MARKS AND NUMBERS	NO. OF PKGS.	SHIPPERS DESCRIPTION OF PACKAGES AND GOODS	GROSS WEIGHT KILOS	POUNDS	MEASUREMENT
C.I.B. RIO DE JANEIRO #1/25	25	(TWENTY-FIVE) CASES OF: STEEL AND ROLLER BEARINGS "IMPORT LICENSE DG-59/10000 EXPIRES FEBRUARY 28, 1984" LETTER OF CREDIT NO E4450/164 "EVIDENCING SHIPMENT OF 1200 BALL BEARINGS NO 187-B AND 2400 ROLLER BEARINGS NO 839-R" FREIGHT PREPAID "ON BOARD" JANUARY 12, 1984 "O R I G I N A L"	2272 KGS	5010 LBS	

PARTICULARS FURNISHED BY SHIPPER OF GOODS

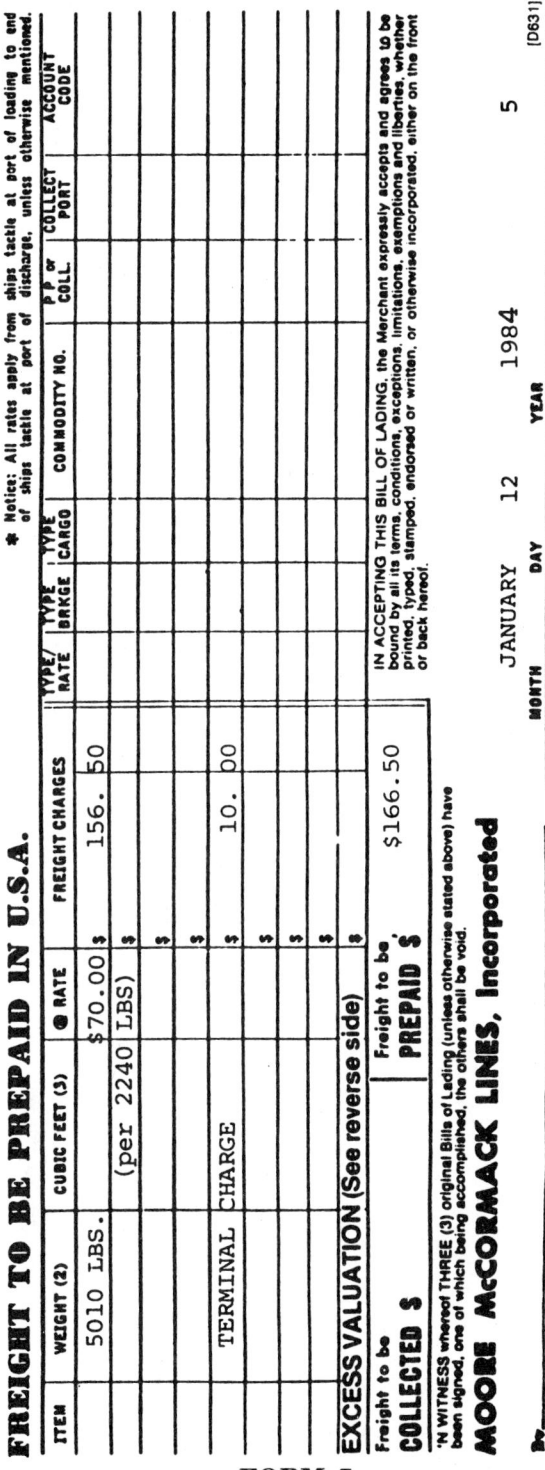

**FORM 7
OCEAN BILL OF LADING**
[*Front; reverse on following pages*]

SHORT FORM BILL OF LADING

Received the Goods, or containers, vans, trailers, vehicles, transportable tanks, flats, palletized units, skids, platforms, frames, cradles, slingloads or other packages said to contain the Goods herein mentioned in apparent external good order and condition, except as otherwise indicated herein, to be transported to the port of discharge named herein and/or such port or place as authorized or permitted hereby or so near thereunto as the vessel can get, lie and leave, always in safety and afloat under all conditions of tide, water and weather and there to be delivered to the Merchant or on-Carrier on payment of all charges due thereon.

This short form Bill of Lading issued for the Merchant's convenience and at its request instead of the Carrier's regular long form Bill of Lading, shall have effect subject to the provisions of the United States Carriage of Goods by Sea Act approved April 16, 1936 or, if this Bill of Lading is issued in any other locality where there is in force a compulsorily applicable Carriage of Goods by Sea Act, Ordinance or Statute of a nature similar to the International Convention for the Unification of Certain Rules Relating to Bills of Lading, dated at Brussels, August 25, 1924, it shall be subject to the provisions of said Act, Ordinance or Statute and rules thereto annexed.

All the terms and conditions of the Carrier's regular long form Bill of Lading, including any clauses presently being printed, typed, stamped, endorsed or written thereon, are incorporated herein by reference with the same force and effect as if they were written at length herein, and all such terms and conditions so incorporated by reference are agreed by Merchant to be binding and to govern the relations, whatever they may be, between all who are or may become parties or holders of this Bill of Lading or owners of the Goods, or containers or other packages covered thereby, as fully as if this Bill of Lading had been prepared on the Carrier's regular long form Bill of Lading.

At all times when the Goods, or containers or other packages are in the care, custody or control of a participating Carrier, such Carrier shall be entitled to all the rights, privileges, liens, limitations of and exonerations from liability, granted or permitted to such participating Carrier under its Bill(s) of Lading, tariff(s) and law compulsorily applicable, and nothing contained in this Bill of Lading shall be deemed a surrender thereof by such participating Carrier.

Each Carrier shall, subject to the terms and conditions of this Bill of Lading and the applicable tariffs, laws, rules and regulations, be responsible for any loss or damage to the Goods, or containers or other packages only during the time the Goods, or containers or other packages are in its actual care, custody and control, except as otherwise expressly provided herein.

In making any arrangement for transportation by participating Carriers of the Goods, or containers or other packages carried hereunder, either before or after ocean carriage, it is understood and agreed that the ocean Carrier acts solely as agent of the Merchant, without any other responsibility whatsoever as Carrier for such transportation.

The Merchant's attention is directed to the fact that the Carrier's regular long form Bill of Lading contains a number of provisions giving the Carrier and participating Carriers certain rights and privileges and certain exemptions and immunities from and limitations of liability additional to those provided by the said United States Carriage of Goods by Sea Act, 1936 and/or Convention and/or such other Act, Ordinance or Statute as may be applicable and, in addition, extends the benefit of its provisions to-stevedores and other independent contractors. The Carrier's regular long form Bill of Lading is on file with the Federal Maritime Commission and Interstate Commerce Commission in Washington, D.C. and copies can be obtained from the Carrier or from the Federal Maritime Commission or, if covering Intermodal Transporation, from the Interstate Commerce Commission if applicable.

In case of any loss or damage to or in connection with Goods exceeding in actual value the equivalent of $500 lawful money of the United States, per package, or in case of Goods not shipped in packages, per shipping unit, the value of the Goods shall be deemed to be $500 per package or per shipping unit. The Carrier's liability, if any, shall be determined on the basis of a value of $500 per package or per shipping unit or pro rata in case of partial loss or damage, unless the nature of the Goods and a valuation higher than $500 per package or per shipping unit shall have been declared in writing by the shipper before shipment and inserted in this Bill of Lading, and extra freight or charge paid. In such case, if the actual value of the Goods per package or per shipping unit shall exceed such declared value, the value shall nevertheless be deemed to be declared value and the Carrier's liability, if any, shall not exceed the declared value and any partial loss or damage shall be adjusted pro rata on the basis of such declared value.

The words "shipping unit" shall mean and include physical unit or piece of cargo not shipped in a package, including articles or things of any description whatsoever, except Goods shipped in bulk, and irrespective of weight or measurement unit employed in calculating freight charges.

Where containers, vans, trailers, vehicles, transportable tanks, flats, palletized units, skids, platforms, frames, cradles, sling-loads and other such packages are not packed by the Carrier, each individual such container, van, trailer, vehicle, transportable tank, palletized unit, skid, platform, frame, cradle, sling-load and other such package, including in each instance its contents, shall be deemed a single package and Carrier's liability limited to $500 with respect to each such package.

A signed original Bill of Lading, duly endorsed, must be surrendered to the Carrier on delivery of the Goods, or container or other packages.

All agreements with respect to the Goods, or containers or other packages carried hereunder are superseded hereby and none of the terms hereof shall be deemed waived or surrendered unless in writing and signed by a duly authorized agent of the Carrier.

[D632]

FORM 7
OCEAN BILL OF LADING
[*Reverse*]

SKF then sends the cases of bearings by truck to the pier where they are delivered to the ocean carrier's receiving clerk who signs a dock receipt. The dock receipt is a form, supplied by the ocean carrier, which contains information relevant to the shipping of the bearings, such as the number of the pier and (if known) the name of the ship. The dock receipt is non-negotiable; as its name suggests, when signed by the receiving clerk, the dock receipt serves as a temporary receipt for the goods until they are loaded on board.

The S.S. Mormacoak is soon ready to receive cargo. When the bearings are loaded on board, the steamship line issues a Bill of Lading (FORM 7, supra) which, to comply with the letter of credit, is "CONSIGNED TO ORDER OF *Banco do Brasil.*" The bill of lading is initially prepared by the forwarder on a form supplied by the ocean carrier; it sets forth the markings and numbers of the packages, a description of the goods, and the number and weight of the packages. The reverse side of the bill of lading states that the goods are "Received for Shipment," but a statement "FREIGHT PREPAID *ON BOARD*" is initialed by a representative of the steamship line after loading. (Note carefully this indorsement; the distinction between a "Received for Shipment" and an "on board" bill of lading may be important. See infra.) The forwarder delivers the bill of lading and the commercial invoice to SKF.

Insurance. It was noted above that in this transaction the price was quoted "F.A.S. Philadelphia," whereas in many overseas transactions the price is quoted as "C.I.F". One of the important differences between these two forms of quotation relates to the handling of insurance. Under the C.I.F. quotation the seller is obliged to obtain and pay for insurance on the shipment. Receiving this insurance coverage is, of course, important to the buyer; to assure this the letter of credit under C.I.F. transaction would require the seller to present an appropriate insurance policy covering the shipment, along with the shipping and other documents, when seller presents its draft to the bank for payment.

The present F.A.S. transaction of itself imposes no such obligation. However, one will note that the letter of credit (FORM 4) requires SKF to present "Insurance Policy or Certificate covering marine and war risk." If there were no letter of credit, the buyer might arrange independently for insurance. But a bank issuing a letter of credit needs insurance to protect its interest in the goods as security for the buyer's obligation to reimburse the bank for its payments under the credit. As the first step towards complying with this requirement, you may have noted that on the proforma invoice SKF computed an "estimated value—C.I.F. which included an item for "estimated insurance charges" of $48.50.

A STOCK COMPANY
MARINE INDEMNITY INSURANCE COMPANY OF AMERICA
Wm. H. McGEE & CO., Inc., Managers, 4 World Trade Center, New York, N.Y. 10048

SPECIAL CARGO POLICY
R-32251 OC 970788
In correspondence refer to these letters and numbers

SUM INSURED	ASSURED'S REFERENCE	PLACE AND DATE
$ 10,950.00	CIB-43H2	KING OF PRUSSIA, PA 19406 JANUARY 12, 1984

Company, in consideration of an agreed premium and subject to the terms and conditions below and on the reverse hereof or stamped or endorsed hereon, does insure

SKF INDUSTRIES, INC.

the sum of TEN THOUSAND NINE HUNDRED FIFTY AND 00/100 US Dollars

TWENTY-FIVE (25) CASES CONTAINING: STEEL BALL AND ROLLER BEARINGS GROSS WT: 5010 LBS

valued at sum insured, to be shipped subject to an "Under Deck" Bill of Lading unless otherwise specified hereon,
S.S MORMACOAK   or other vessel, and connecting conveyances   B/L date JANUARY 12, 1984
and from PHILADELPHIA, PA USA   via
   RIO DE JANEIRO, BRAZIL

MARKS AND NUMBERS
C.I.B.
RIO DE JANEIRO #1/25
IMPORT LICENSE DG-59/10000
EXPIRES FEBRUARY 28, 1984
L/C NO E 4450/164

Loss, if any, payable to the order of the Assured.

—————————— SPECIAL TERMS AND CONDITIONS ——————————

SHIPMENTS ON DECK, AIR CARGO and MAIL or PARCEL POST SHIPMENTS, when insured under this Policy are subject to average terms and conditions specified in clauses 18, 19 and 20 hereof. SHIPMENTS SUBJECT TO AN "UNDER DECK" BILL OF LADING AND SHIPMENTS IN CONTAINERS SUBJECT TO AN "UNDER DECK" BILL OF LADING OR A BILL OF LADING WHICH DOES NOT DISCLOSE THE NATURE OF STOWAGE ARE INSURED:—

Machinery, Tools, Ball Bearing Parts, Factory Instruments, Steel and Raw Materials incidental to the business of the Assured are insured:—

To cover against all risks of physical loss or damage from any external cause or spontaneous combustion (excepting such risks as are excluded by the F. C. & S. Warranty and S. R. & C. C. Warranty in this policy) irrespective of percentage.

This Insurance is also subject to the following American Institute Clauses current on the date of issuance of this policy:—
MARINE EXTENSION CLAUSES   S. R. & C. C. ENDORSEMENT   WAR RISK INSURANCE

When goods are so destined this Insurance is subject to:—
SOUTH AMERICAN 60 DAY CLAUSE

ORIGINAL — DUPLICATE UNPAID

This Policy not transferable unless countersigned by an authorized representative of this Company or the Assured
Countersigned: SKF Industries, Inc.
P. Cassola

IN WITNESS WHEREOF, this Company has executed and attested these presents.

_____ Secretary   _____ President

(D833)

FORM 8

MARINE INSURANCE POLICY
[Continued on following pages]

This insurance is against the perils of the seas, fire, assailing thieves, jettisons, barratry of the master and mariners, and all other like perils, losses or misfortunes that have or shall come to the hurt, detriment or damage of the property insured hereunder or any part thereof except as otherwise provided for herein.

TERMS AND CONDITIONS REFERRED TO ON THE FACE OF THIS POLICY

AMERICAN INSTITUTE CARGO CLAUSES (February, 1949)
(F. C. & S. Warranty October, 1949)

1. **WAREHOUSE TO WAREHOUSE CLAUSE:** [illegible body text]

2. **CRAFT, &c. CLAUSE:** [illegible]

3. **DEVIATION CLAUSE:** [illegible]

4. **F. P. A. CLAUSE:** [illegible]

5. **WAREHOUSING & FORWARDING CHARGES, TOTALLY LOST PACKAGES ETC.:** [illegible]

6. **LABELS CLAUSE:** [illegible]

7. **MACHINERY CLAUSE:** [illegible]

8. **G/A CLAUSE:** General Average and Salvage Charges payable according to United States laws and usage, or as per Foreign Statement and/or as per York-Antwerp Rules (as prescribed in whole or in part) if in accordance with the Contract of Affreightment.

9. **EXPLOSION CLAUSE:** [illegible]

10. **SHORE CLAUSE:** [illegible]

11. **BILL OF LADING, &c. CLAUSE:** [illegible]

12. **INCHMAREE CLAUSE:** [illegible]

OTHER TERMS AND CONDITIONS OF THIS POLICY

18. **SHIPMENTS ON DECK:** [illegible]

19. **AIR CARGO:** [illegible]

20. **MAIL AND PARCEL POST SHIPMENTS:** [illegible]

21. **G/A CONTRIBUTORY CLAUSE:** This Company shall be liable for only such proportion of General Average and Salvage Charges as the sum hereby insured (less Particular Average, if any, for which this Company is liable hereunder) bears to the contributory value of the property hereby insured.

22. **GROUNDING IN CANALS, HARBORS, ETC.:** Grounding in canals, harbors or tidal rivers not to be deemed a stranding, but this Company shall be liable for any damage or loss which may be proved to have resulted therefrom and which would be recoverable if caused by stranding.

23. **FUMIGATION CLAUSE:** [illegible]

24. **GRAIN LOADING WARRANTY:** [illegible]

25. **LOSS INSURANCE:** [illegible]

26. **SUE AND LABOR:** [illegible]

27. **NOTICE OF LOSS:** [illegible]

FORM 8

MARINE INSURANCE POLICY

[*Reverse*]

SKF, like most sellers who ship goods abroad, has an "open" policy of insurance which covers all goods in transit from warehouse to warehouse plus 30 days; the premiums depend on the volume of shipments reported to the insurer and covered by the policy. SKF fills out a Marine Insurance Policy (FORM 8) stating the necessary details of the specific shipment. Since the insurance policy will pass through various hands which may need its protection, the policy provides that it "does insure SKF Industries, Inc., For account of whom it may concern ... Loss, if any, payable to assured *or order*." The policy will be countersigned by the insurance company to provide evidence to third persons of its obligation under the policy.

Payment; the Draft. The Philadelphia bank stated in its letter that the estimated C.I.F. price of $10,950 would be "available by your drafts on us at sight" when accompanied by the listed documents. SKF accordingly draws a sight draft for $10,950 on the Philadelphia bank (FORM 9, infra). The draft together with the commercial invoice (in sextuplicate), insurance certificate (original and duplicate), full set of ocean bills of lading (three originals) and the packing list (original and duplicate) are presented to the Philadelphia bank. When the bank receives these documents it issues its bank draft to SKF's order for $10,950 and transmits the documents by air mail to Banco do Brasil, which will reimburse the Philadelphia bank.

The documents, sent by air mail, will reach the Brazilian bank well ahead of the ocean shipment. The time for the release of the documents to buyer and its reimbursement to the bank will depend upon the arrangement which was made between the bank and buyer when the letter of credit was initially established. If the buyer plans to resell the bearings, it may not be able to reimburse the bank until the goods arrive and it resells the goods. In this event, the Brazilian bank may need to take further steps to secure its claim against the buyer. Happily, such added complications need not concern us now.

$ 10,950.00   PHILADELPHIA, JANUARY 12   1984

AT SIGHT _____ PAY TO THE ORDER OF

SKF INDUSTRIES, INC.

TEN THOUSAND NINE HUNDRED FIFTY-----------00/100 DOLLARS

THE PHILADELPHIA NATIONAL BANK
DRAWN UNDER ADVICE NO. E 4450/164   SKF INDUSTRIES, INC.

To FOR THE ACCOUNT OF: COMPANHIA
IMPORTADORA BRASILEIRA, CAIXA   /s/ Lincoln Kaiser
POSTAL 10, RIO DE JANEIRO
BRAZIL

FORM 86 1/70   [D634]

FORM 9
DRAFT

(2) RESPONSIBILITY OF BUYERS AND SELLERS WHO AGREE TO DOCUMENTARY SALES USING LETTERS OF CREDIT

Sales Contracts' Provisions for Letters of Credit. The Convention on Contracts for International Sales of Goods is silent on payment devices; it does not set a default rule that buyers must open letters of credit nor the terms of satisfactory letters of credit.

Sellers who wish to be paid by letter of credit must obtain not only their buyers' contract commitment to do so, but must also establish in the sales contract what will be the nature and terms of those letters of credit. Buyers who agree to pay by letter of credit are also concerned about the letter of credit terms because buyers want to assure, insofar as feasible, that they will receive the contracted for goods after the letters of credit have been paid. To do this, buyers need to establish the conditions on the banks' duty to pay that tend to show sellers have performed before banks are permitted and required to pay under their letters of credit; a prime condition usually is a bill of lading or comparable shipping document that shows that seller has delivered the goods to a carrier. The conditions, initially agreed upon in the sales contracts, later become the conditions in the banks' commitment letters.

Sellers typically require buyers to open letters of credit for an amount in excess of the contract price so that sellers can recover incidental expenses incurred on buyers' behalf. Sellers typically require that letters of credit be issued or confirmed before shipping the goods; if a seller must specially manufacture or procure the goods to be delivered, the seller may negotiate to require the buyer to open a letter of credit well before the estimated date for shipment of the goods to buyer. If the date of shipment is uncertain at the time of the sales contract, the parties may negotiate for the length of time during which a letter must remain open. Sellers typically do not identify banks that must be the issuing bank or the confirming bank, but they may specify that buyers use banks of recognized standing in the banking community. If sellers do not negotiate for the commitment of local banks as confirming banks, enforcement of the issuing banks' obligation may require litigation in foreign countries.[1] Sellers who want a local bank's commitment must negotiate buyers' obligation to obtain a letter of credit from an issuing bank that will, in turn, secure a confirming bank.[2] Finally, the sales contract determines whether a letter of credit

---

1. See Pacific Reliant Industries, Inc. v. Amerika Samoa Bank, 901 F.2d 735 (9th Cir.1990)(Oregon seller of building materials to Samoa buyer agreed to letter of credit issued by Samoan bank; seller's suit to enforce the credit in Oregon federal district court dismissed for lack of personal jurisdiction over the bank).

2. In making its commitment to the beneficiary of a confirmed credit, the confirming bank is relying entirely on the credit of the issuing bank. This works better when the banks have a continuing relationship. "It is customary that the issuing bank requests a bank of its choice to advise and, as the case may be, to confirm its credit to the beneficiary." ICC,

is required under the Uniform Customs and Practices for Documentary Credits (UCP).[3]

Problem 8. A contract for the sale of 3000 tons of Brazilian groundnuts called for shipment from Brazil for Genoa between February 1 and April 30, at the option of the sellers. The contract further provided: "Payment: By opening of a confirmed, irrevocable, divisible, transmissible and transferable credit opened in favour of the sellers and utilisable by them against delivery of the following documents." The buyer established a letter of credit on April 22. The seller had already resold the goods on the ground that the credit was established too late in the light of the seller's privilege to ship in February or March. Seller sued the buyer for damages. What evidence of custom and what arguments concerning seller's need for the letter of credit would be relevant? See Pavia & Co. v. Thurmann–Nielsen, [1952] 1 All Eng.L.R. 492 (C.A.).

If the buyer has the obligation to arrange for shipping and has the privilege of selecting the date for shipment within a designated period, may the buyer delay establishing the letter of credit until the end of the period? What would be the effect of a showing by seller that it was customary in this trade to use the letter of credit in order to raise funds to pay the seller's supplier? See Ian Stach, Ltd. v. Baker Bosly, Ltd., [1958] 1 All E.R. 542 (interesting and instructive opinion by Diplock, J., on the practical problems presented by using the ultimate buyer's letter of credit to finance "a string of merchants' contracts between the manufacturer or stockist and the ultimate user"); 108 L.J. 388 (1958).

Once sales contracts have set the nature and terms of letters of credit that buyers must obtain and that sellers must accept in the performance of their contracts, those undertakings can and do give rise to disputes between sellers and buyers over the sufficiency and timeliness of buyers' performance. If buyer fails seasonably to furnish an agreed letter of credit, what are the consequences on seller's obligations to perform and on seller's right to remedy? Domestic United States law, the Commercial Code, declares that the buyer is in breach. UCC 2–325(1). Would the same result follow under CISG?

Revocable Letters of Credit. Banking practice developed two types of letters of credit, revocable and irrevocable. Issuing banks and their customers choose whether the customers have power to revoke without the consent of the beneficiaries of the credits. As between sellers and buyers, revocable letters of credit are akin to buyers' personal checks; payment can be stopped by instructions to the bank.

Case Studies on Documentary Credits, Case 26, p. 39 (J. Dekker 1989).

3. The Uniform Customs and Practices for Documentary Credits, promulgated by the International Chamber of Commerce, are discussed below in the materials dealing with the responsibility of banks under their letters of credit.

Thus, revocable letters of credit are not satisfactory to sellers who want to be free of credit risk. If a sales contract requires only that buyer furnish a letter of credit, does buyer meet that obligation by obtaining a revocable letter of credit? Domestic United States law, the Commercial Code, declares that buyer must provide an irrevocable letter of credit. UCC 2–325(3). Would the same result follow under CISG?[4]

Bankers' Acceptances and Letters of Credit. If the buyer in the letter of credit transaction does not wish to pay upon presentment, a slightly different transaction may be arranged. The seller will draw a time draft rather than a sight draft on the issuing bank, which will accept it, return it to the seller, and release the documents to the buyer on open credit or perhaps against trust receipts. The buyer has its goods; the seller has a "banker's acceptance" which can easily be discounted; the issuer has lent its credit but has paid no money. Before the maturity date of the draft, the buyer will place the necessary funds in the hands of the issuing bank. See also: P. Oppenheim, International Banking 195–96 (4th ed. 1983).

Among the cases that follow, many are transactions in which sellers agreed to bankers' acceptances rather than insisting upon immediate payment under sight drafts. As a result, buyers learned about the nature of sellers' performances before the credits had been paid and took action to prevent payment altogether or to prevent the proceeds of payment from reaching sellers.

"Back-to-Back" Credits. Assume that Buyer agrees to buy a large shipment of goods from Seller, and establishes a letter of credit covering the purchase with Seller as beneficiary. Seller will buy goods to fill this contract from Distributor. Distributor requires cash for the goods and Seller lacks sufficient cash until it delivers to Buyer. Can the assurance of payment under the letter of credit give Seller the credit it needs to make the purchase? (Distributor may face the same credit problem in arranging a purchase from Manufacturer. Indeed, in some cases a long string of transactions needs to be financed on the strength of the letter of credit established by the ultimate buyer.)

A dilemma appears. The initial letter of credit from Buyer to Seller needs to be utilized as a source of credit before Seller gets the goods; on the other hand, tender of these goods is a condition of the bank's obligation to pay. Ingenious attempts to answer this problem have produced the so-called "back-to-back" credits. The bank which has issued the initial credit to Seller issues a second letter of credit to Distributor, contingent on Distributor's presenting documents which either satisfy the initial letter of credit or which can readily be made to satisfy the letter of credit, as by getting a new bill of lading evidencing shipment from Seller to Buyer. Distributor is thus assured of payment; and credit strain on Seller and the bank are avoided since Distributor will not be paid until (a) Seller's right to obtain funds under the credit,

---

4. A similar, but quite different question arises of interpreting a letter of credit that does not declare whether or not it is revocable.

and (b) the bank's right to reimbursement from Buyer have both been established.

Added flexibility may be achieved if the rights under a letter of credit may be assigned. In this area, as in others, there is possible conflict between the Code and the ICC Uniform Customs if the latter's language is given its full, literal sweep. Article 54 of the Uniform Customs provides: "A credit can be transferred only if it is expressly designated as 'transferable' by the issuing bank." UCC 5–116(1) establishes a similar rule as to "the right *to draw* under a credit." But subsection (2) states: "Even though the credit specifically states that it is nontransferable or nonassignable the beneficiary may before performance of the conditions of the credit assign his *right to proceeds*." The balance of the subsection contains interesting rules regulating such assignments. Compare UCC 2–210(2) and 9–318(4) which similarly invalidate "restraints on alienation" of the right to receive cash proceeds.

(3) RESPONSIBILITY OF BANKS UNDER THEIR LETTERS OF CREDIT

The commercial linchpin in setting up sales transactions using letters of credit is the degree of certainty with which parties can expect that the banks, particularly confirming banks, will pay when drafts are presented to them. From sellers' perspective, that translates into the question of ease of enforcement of the banks' commitments. Sellers' aim is to divorce the banks' duty to pay from any question of sellers' performance on the underlying sales contracts beyond presentation of documents. From buyers' perspective, the question is whether they can effectively "stop payment" by the banks. Buyers' aim is to retain some control over the banks' paying in the event that sellers are seen to be defaulting on their obligations to deliver the goods. The clash between these two objectives is addressed in the law and practice governing banks' obligations under their letters of credit.

The ICC Uniform Customs and Practice for Documentary Credits (UCP). About 1930, the international banking community began to promulgate rules to harmonize the issuance and performance of letters of credit. Published by the International Chamber of Commerce, the Uniform Customs and Practice or UCP have been revised a number of times, and most recently in 1992.[5] The UCP, adhered to by banks in over 145 nations, are practically universal in application. Bankers from throughout the world have been organized by the ICC into a Commission on Banking Technique and Practice which issues opinions on interpretation of the UCP and, through a group of experts, responds to queries about the UCP.[6]

---

[5]. The 1983 version of the UCP are found in ICC Brochure No. 400. See also M. Davis, The Documentary Credits Handbook (1988).

[6]. Opinions of the Banking Commission are published regularly by the ICC. See

A common practice emerged whereby banks issuing or confirming letters of credit referred explicitly to the UCP. See, e.g., Form 4 in the Prototype transaction.

The UCP do not deal with the rights or obligations of parties to the contracts underlying letters of credit. "Credits, by their nature, are separate transactions from the sales or other contract(s) on which they may be based and banks are in no way concerned with or bound by such contract(s), even if any reference whatsoever to such contract(s) is included in the credit." UCP 1983, Article 3.

UCP provisions are not laws. They are standard contractual terms adopted by the international banking community and enforceable only as terms of contracts. In common-law courts, banks that issue or confirm letters of credit might argue that their promises to the beneficiaries of the credits are unenforceable for want of consideration. Domestic United States law, the Commercial Code, responded that no consideration is necessary. UCC 5–105.

UCC Article 5; New York Exclusion. Drafters of the Commercial Code elected to attempt to codify the law on letters of credit by including in the Code Article 5 on that subject. Prior to that time, letters of credit had not been subject to statutory enactment in the United States or elsewhere. Article 5 differs from the UCP in a number of respects. When the Commercial Code was presented to the states for enactment, in New York there was concern about displacement of the UCP. Much letter of credit practice, particularly in international sales, was centered in that state. New York eventually adopted the Commercial Code, but added a non-uniform provision, 5–102(4), rendering the entire article inapplicable to a letter of credit if by its terms or by agreement, course of dealing or usage of trade the letter of credit is subject in whole or in part to the UCP. The Permanent Editorial Board for the Commercial Code reacted vigorously (Report No. 2 (1964)):

PERMANENT EDITORIAL BOARD COMMENT

Reasons for Rejection. The New York Clearing House Association (NYCHA) in its report of December 1, 1961 recommended the entire elimination of Article 5 on letters of credit. The above variation in Section 5–102(1), as the Code was enacted in New York, represents a continuation of the views of the NYCHA. Article 5 is still printed as a part of the Code but the variation as enacted provides that "Article 5 does not apply to a letter of credit or a credit if by its terms or by agreement, course of dealing or usage of trade such letter of credit or credit is subject in whole or in part to the Uniform Customs and Practice for Commercial Documentary Credits fixed by the Thirteenth or by any subsequent Congress of the International Chamber of Com-

---

ICC Publications 371, 399, 434 and 469. For a set of responses to recent queries, see Case Studies on Documentary Credits: Problems, Queries, Answers (J. Dekker, 1989).

merce" (Uniform Customs). This point of view and the action in New York constitutes a sufficiently fundamental departure from the Code that it needs to be dealt with on fundamental lines.

1. The underlying and basic concept behind the NYCHA position is that there should be no legislation in the letter of credit field. The reasoning is that it is better for banks, if not for all interested parties, to have the determination of rights and duties of parties under letters of credit left to the present combination of case law, Uniform Customs, agreements, practices and customs in the field.

This underlying point of view is contrary to the fixed policy of the sponsoring organizations of the Uniform Commercial Code, long considered and carefully determined. The Editorial Board sees no good reason to reverse this policy. ...

2. A second basic position taken by the NYCHA is that most letters of credit finance international shipments of merchandise and are, therefore, international in character, with the result that there should be no unilateral legislation on the subject in the United States. Conversely, the NYCHA appears to contend that the only controlling rules governing letters of credit should be international rules. The NYCHA further contends that if one or more American states sees fit to enact statutory legislation in this field, other countries may do likewise to the detriment of the United States.

The Editorial Board considers this view to be totally unrealistic. Carried to its logical conclusion, under this view no court in the United States should render a decision in a letter of credit case because such a decision, which clearly creates law in the United States, is unilateral. An equally logical extension of the same argument is that there should be neither statutory law nor case law in the United States in any international field because such law is necessarily unilateral.

Assuming that letters of credit are used preponderantly to finance international shipments of goods, in the absence of a world order and world courts, the problems of society and commerce can only be solved by the various instrumentalities of law available in the several sovereign nations. The great preponderance of what law there is today controlling international transactions is exactly "unilateral" law, established either by courts or legislatures, in independent, sovereign nations. Recognizing the imperfections in this process, the conflict of laws questions arising from it, and the uncertainties and confusion involved in it, this process has done fairly well to establish rules of law and, in any event, absent a world order and world courts, it is all that society has except for a very limited number of treaties. ...

3. The third basic position taken by the NYCHA is that, recognizing the need of some rules as to "international" letters of credit, the Uniform Customs which are now in existence, and have been for twenty or more years, fill all needs and work well.

The Editorial Board approves of the effort to provide rules governing letters of credit by way of the drafting and promulgation of the Uniform Customs. The Editorial Board considers that the Uniform Customs contribute materially to the aggregate body of rules making more definite and certain letter of credit operations. However, the Board does not agree that the Uniform Customs constitute the only set of rules and guide lines that are available and needed.

Of paramount importance is that the Uniform Customs do not have the status of "law." Not being law they are subject to all of the weaknesses and vicissitudes of what they purport to be, namely, "customs." Have they been accepted by, are they binding upon, all interested parties? ...

4. A fourth basic position advanced by the NYCHA is that the Uniform Customs have preempted the field of rules dealing with letters of credit and, consequently, no state legislation can or should be enacted in this field. The argument is that New York and the other several states must have either the Uniform Customs or Article 5; they cannot have both.

The Editorial Board cannot agree with this reasoning. A fundamental concept of the Code as a whole is that there can be a set of statutory rules (with varying degrees of completeness of coverage) in the fields of the different articles but there is also room and need for customs, course of dealing, usages of trade, agreement of parties and business practices. See Sections 1–102(2)(b), 1–205, 4–103 and 5–102(3). The Code also recognizes the need of supplementary principles of law other than the specific terms of the Code itself. See Sections 1–103, 9–104 and 9–203(2). ...

5. The Editorial Board considers that the attempt, through the New York variation in Section 5–102(4), to find a compromise between the Code position on Article 5 and that of the NYCHA, is highly confusing, unwise and potentially productive of substantial litigation. Of first importance, the New York variation adopts the mutually exclusive concept that if the Uniform Customs in any way apply, then Article 5 is totally inapplicable. Aside from the general wisdom of any state legislature's enacting comprehensive and serious legislation, all of which can be rendered completely nugatory by the election of individual persons, the Board considers that the determination of when a credit is "by agreement, course of dealing or usage of trade ... subject in whole or in part to the Uniform Customs ..." will be a matter of great difficulty. The added New York language is almost a direct invitation to litigation. If Article 5 and the Uniform Customs overlap only to the extent of, let us say, 25% of their respective provisions and, of such overlapping, the rules of Article 5 and the Uniform Customs are, in substance, the same, with inconsistency occurring in only two instances, the Board entirely fails to see why, whether there is a large or trifling application of the Uniform Customs, Article 5 should be ren-

dered totally inapplicable. The Board considers the New York variation both unacceptable and unsound.

PETRA INTERN. BANKING CORP. v. FIRST AMER. BANK OF VA.
United States District Court, Eastern District of Virginia, 1991.
758 F. Supp. 1120.

ELLIS, UNITED STATES DISTRICT JUDGE.

This dispute grows out of the use of two documentary letters of credit to finance the purchase of T-shirts by a Virginia corporation from the manufacturer in Amman, Jordan. In essence, following the delivery of poor quality T-shirts, the purchaser refused to pay the issuing bank and the issuing bank then refused to pay the confirming bank, which had honored drafts drawn under the letters of credit. The purchaser and the issuing bank rely on their receipt of technically nonconforming documents under the letters as grounds for nonpayment. The purchaser and the manufacturer settled their dispute over the poor quality T-shirts, but the remaining parties were not able to resolve their differences. Thus, here the confirming bank seeks recovery against the issuing bank and the purchaser for payments it made under the letters of credit, and the issuing bank seeks recovery against the purchaser for any sums it must pay to the confirming bank.

Before the Court are cross-motions for summary judgment. The motions raise, inter alia, the seldom litigated issue of what remedy an account customer has when an issuing bank inadvertently accepts nonconforming documents under a letter of credit. All material facts are undisputed. These facts, the terms of the letters of credit, other relevant contractual agreements, and existing law require that defendant First American Bank, the issuer of the letters, reimburse the confirming bank for payments made under the letters, and that First American Bank's account customer, the purchaser of the T-shirts, reimburse First American. Both First American and the purchaser, by failing to object to documentary inconsistencies in timely fashion, have waived their right to do so. All other issues raised in this case with the exception of costs and attorney's fees are also disposed of on summary judgment.

Facts

In 1987 Dameron International, Inc., a Virginia corporation ("Dameron"), purchased T-shirts from National Marketing–Export Co. ("National Marketing") of Amman, Jordan. To facilitate the transaction, Dameron sought issuance of two letters of credit by First American Bank of Virginia ("First American"). To this end, Dameron executed two documents, each entitled Application and Agreement for International Commercial Letter of Credit ("the Agreements"), and signed two commercial notes, each in the amount of $135,000.00, to secure the letters of credit. Richard Pitts, the president of Dameron, and his wife, son, and daughter-in-law, executed continuing guaranties to further secure any debts of Dameron owed to First American. First American issued its Irrevocable Letters of Credit Nos. 1–629 and 1–630 ("the Letters"), each for $135,000, on December 17, 1987. The Letters stated that they were issued "in favor of National Marketing-Export Co.," of Amman, Jordan and "for the account of Dameron Intl., Inc." of McLean, Virginia. The Letters authorized drafts to be drawn on First American within thirty days of submission to First American of specific, listed documents. At the request of National Marketing and National's bank in Jordan, Petra Bank, the Letters were amended on December 22, 1987, to provide that drafts under the Letters could be drawn directly on Petra International Banking Corporation of Washington, D.C. ("PIBC"), Petra's American affiliate. In the vernacular of letters of credit transactions, PIBC became a "confirming bank," First American an "issuing bank," Dameron the "account customer," and National Marketing the "beneficiary" of the Letters.

When initially issued, the Letters required that an "inspection certificate from [an] independent inspector certifying number and quality of pieces per sample" of the T-shirts be among the documents presented for payment. This provision subsequently was amended to require both a certificate from a specific independent inspection company and a "statement by the beneficiary," National Marketing, attesting to the quality of the T-shirts.

Dameron received several T-shirt shipments from National Marketing in 1988. Several corresponding payments were made under the Letters by PIBC to National Marketing. In late September 1988, another shipment was begun and National Marketing made a demand for payment under the Letters. This demand was relayed from Petra Bank in Amman to PIBC as two documentary time drafts drawn against the Letters in the aggregate amount of $95,904. PIBC sent a telex to First American on October 7, 1988, noting certain discrepancies between the documents submitted and those required by the Letters, including the fact that the certificate from the independent inspection company was missing. First American forwarded PIBC's telex to Dameron, which waived the discrepancies listed by PIBC on condition that the drafts were drawn 150 days from the date of the bill of lading, i.e., from the date of shipment. First American sent a telex message to PIBC on October 19, 1988, stating "ACCOUNT PARTY HAS WAIVED ALL DISCREPANCIES PROVIDED DRAFTS ARE DRAWN AT 150 DAYS BILL OF LADING." First American sent a second telex message on October 24, 1988, stating in relevant part: "DISCREPANCIES HAVE BEEN WAIVED BY A/P [i.e., Dameron]. PLEASE ACCEPT DRAFT AND FORWARD DOCS TO US." Between receipt of the first and second telexes, on October 21, 1988, PIBC discounted and accepted the documentary time drafts. On October 25, 1988, PIBC sent a telex to First American that confirmed receipt of First American's telex of

October 24th, informed First American that the drafts had been accepted with the proviso that they be drawn 150 days from the date of the bill of lading, i.e., on February 21, 1989, and transmitted the documents to First American. First American forwarded the documents to Dameron shortly after receiving them. Dameron kept the documents and took possession of the T-shirts. On November 16, 1988, First American sent an acknowledgement letter to PIBC stating that the documentary drafts for $95,904 were "accepted and, at maturity, we will remit proceeds according to your cover letter."

Dameron was dissatisfied with the quality of the T-shirts received from National Marketing. It undertook negotiations with National concerning the $95,904 payment. As the February 21, 1989 deadline for drawing on the time drafts approached, Dameron requested that First American obtain an extension of payment. First American then sent a telex to PIBC requesting an extension to May 21, 1989. The telex stated that National Marketing had agreed to this delay in receiving payment. PIBC informed First American that it would delay and refinance the payment provided that First American pay interest during the delay at the prime rate plus two percent. Dameron and First American agreed. As the new May 21, 1989 deadline drew near, Dameron requested that First American seek an additional extension of thirty days. First American requested the extension, explaining that "SPECIAL ARRANGEMENTS REGARDING THESE PAYMENTS WERE MADE BY BUYERS AND SELLERS ALLOWING THE 30 DAY EXTENSION." PIBC agreed to this second extension on the condition that it continue to receive interest at prime plus two percent, and First American and Dameron accepted this requirement.

In June or July, 1989, Richard Pitts informed First American that Dameron did not want to pay National Marketing because of the poor quality of the T-shirts. William von Berg of First American informed Pitts that First American would be obligated to pay under the Letters unless the bank were sued by Dameron and enjoined from doing so. While the parties are uncertain as to when this conversation occurred, it is clear that in late June, when Dameron requested a third extension, Dameron and National Marketing continued to be hopeful that they would settle their differences concerning the $95,904. Dameron planned to obtain additional T-shirts of suitable quality from National at a reduced price, and it so informed First American. On June 20, 1989, Richard Pitts requested that First American seek a third extension. On the same day, Bassem Farouki, the principal of National Marketing, informed PIBC that Dameron would be requesting an additional thirty-day extension. Although PIBC initially took the position that First American should finance Dameron, it eventually agreed to an extension to July 21, 1989, under the same interest payment conditions as were attached to the previous two extensions.

Dameron's negotiations with National Marketing did not bear fruit. On July 20, 1989, Dameron obtained an Order of Attachment from the Fairfax County Circuit Court, directing First American not to pay PIBC under the Letters. First American claims that it did not immediately learn of the existence of the writ. Nevertheless, First American did not pay PIBC on July 21, 1989. Rather, on that day, at Dameron's request, First American requested an extension of payment to the following week. PIBC responded by demanding payment. Payment was not made. Instead, on July 28th, First American informed PIBC that it had been enjoined by the Fairfax County Circuit Court from making payments under the Letters until further notice.

From July 20, 1989 until April 13, 1990, Dameron pursued a law suit against National Marketing in the Fairfax County Circuit Court. In the course of this litigation, and more than one year after its receipt of the documents, Dameron noticed and then informed First American that the "Statement of the Beneficiary" was not among the documents that First American forwarded pertaining to the $95,904 shipment. First American informed Dameron that it had forwarded all documents it had received. The absence of the Statement of the Beneficiary from the documents was not noted as a discrepancy by PIBC or First American when each had examined the documents. Both Dameron and First American agree that the Statement of the Beneficiary was never among the documents presented by National Marketing to PIBC, and that PIBC, First American, and Dameron each inadvertently failed to notice the missing Statement of the Beneficiary when each received the documents.

Dameron and National Marketing eventually settled their suit. Dameron kept the T-shirts, but received an undisclosed amount of cash from National Marketing related, it appears, to the shipment here at issue and to other shipments and disputes between the parties. The precise terms of the settlement remain confidential and have not been disclosed to the Court. On April 13, 1990, the Fairfax County Circuit Court vacated the Order of Attachment. On the same day, PIBC requested payment from First American of $95,904 of principal and $14,079.24 of interest. First American has refused to make the payment, relying primarily on PIBC's alleged failure to note the missing Statement of the Beneficiary. Dameron, in turn, has refused to reimburse First American if payment is made under the Letters, despite having signed the Agreements and commercial notes, kept the documents accompanying the relevant drafts, taken possession of the T-shirts, and recovered settlement compensation from National Marketing. The Pitts, in turn, have refused First American's demands for reimbursement under the Continuing Guarantees.

* * *

I. First American's Obligation to Pay PIBC

PIBC requests summary judgment on Count I of its Complaint, which alleges that First American wrongfully refused to honor the Letters and pay the $95,904 plus interest to PIBC. First American contends that PIBC's failure to note the missing Statement of the

Beneficiary relieves it of any obligation to honor the drafts drawn under the Letters. The threshold issue is the choice of governing law. The Letters state on their face that they are to be governed by the Uniform Customs and Practices for Documentary Credits (1983 Revision), International Chamber of Commerce Publication No. 400 ("the UCP"). Given this, the Court finds that the UCP should be applied in this case. Neither PIBC nor First American objects to application of the UCP, though they differ in interpreting its provisions.

The pertinent UCP provision is Article 16, which states that if an issuing bank desires to "refuse documents," it must do so "without delay" by stating the discrepancies it has found and "holding the documents at the disposal of, or ... returning them to, the presentor (remitting bank or the beneficiary, as the case may be)." If the issuing bank fails to perform these requirements, it "shall be precluded from claiming that the documents are not in accordance with the terms and conditions of the credit." [26] Numerous courts have held that Article 16 and its predecessor, Article 8 of the 1974 UCP, preclude an issuing bank from asserting the noncompliance of documents presented by a beneficiary where the bank delays in raising this claim. Bank of Cochin v. Manufacturers Hanover Trust Co., 808 F.2d 209 (2d Cir.1986), a case precisely on point, presents a striking example of this principle in operation between an issuing and a confirming bank. There, the issuing bank, on the very day of its receipt of a documentary draft from the confirming bank, telexed its intention to dishonor the draft. But the issuing bank did not supply the confirming bank with a reason for

---

26. The full text of Article 16 of the UCP is as follows:

(a) If a bank so authorized effects payment, or *incurs a deferred payment undertaking,* or accepts or negotiates *against documents which appear on their face to be in accordance with the terms and conditions of a credit,* the party giving such authority *shall be bound* to reimburse the bank which has effected payment, or incurred a deferred payment undertaking, or has accepted or negotiated, and *to take up the documents.*

(b) If, upon receipt of the documents, the issuing bank considers that they appear on their face not to be in accordance with the terms and conditions of the credit, *it must determine, on the basis of the documents alone, whether to take up such documents, or to refuse them* and claim that they appear on their face not to be in accordance with the terms and conditions of the credit.

(c) The issuing bank shall have *a reasonable time* in which to examine the documents and to determine as above whether to take up the documents or to refuse the documents.

(d) *If the issuing bank decides to refuse the documents it must give notice to that effect without delay* by telecommunication or, if that is not possible, by other expeditious means, to the bank from which it received the documents (the remitting bank), or to the beneficiary, if it received the documents directly from him. *Such notice must state the discrepancies* in respect of which the issuing bank refuses the documents *and must also state whether it is holding the documents at the disposal of, or is returning them to, the presentor* (remitting bank or the beneficiary, as the case may be). The issuing bank shall then be entitled to claim from the remitting bank any refund of any reimbursement which may have been made to that bank.

(e) *If the issuing bank fails* to act in accordance with the provisions of paragraphs (c) and (d) of this article and/or fails *to hold the documents at the disposal of,* or to return them to, *the presentor, the issuing bank shall be precluded from claiming that the documents are not in accordance with the terms and conditions of the credit.*

(Emphasis added.)

the dishonor until twelve-to-thirteen-days later. This delay, the Court found, violated Article 8(d)'s command that an issuing bank intending to dishonor a documentary draft "notify [the confirming bank] 'expeditiously' and 'without delay' of specific defects and of the disposition of the documents, and ... precluded [the issuing bank] from asserting noncompliance...." Id. at 213. The same result should obtain here because the issuing bank's notice was delayed even longer than in Bank of Cochin. In the instant case, First American received the documents on or about October 25, 1988. Not only did it fail to note any discrepancies or to hold the documents at PIBC's disposal, it transferred the documents to its account customer and formally notified PIBC on November 16, 1988 that "the transaction was accepted and, at maturity, we will remit proceeds...." First American did not mention any discrepancies to PIBC until more than one year after receipt of the documents. In the interim, it made several promises to pay in exchange for extensions of time. First American is therefore precluded by Article 16 from asserting noncompliance.

First American seeks to avoid application of Article 16 by arguing that Article 16 applies to drafts passing from beneficiaries or advising banks to issuing banks, but not to drafts passing from confirming banks to issuing banks. In support, First American points to Virginia Code § 8.5–107(2), which states that a confirming bank "becomes directly obligated on the credit to the extent of its confirmation, *as though it were its issuer* and acquires the rights of an issuer." (Emphasis added.) From this, First American argues that it should be viewed as PIBC's account customer in the transaction at issue, while PIBC should be deemed to be the issuing bank subject to Article 16. It is true that PIBC, upon becoming a confirming bank, has the rights and duties of an issuing bank and is therefore subject to Article 16. It is also true that First American may be viewed as PIBC's customer. Even so, neither of these points changes First American's status as an issuing bank nor relieves it from its Article 16 duties. In short, as one or more confirming banks are inserted in the chain between the original issuing bank and the beneficiary, each bank, including the original issuer, is an issuing bank subject to Article 16. This conclusion finds support in the language of Article 16 and makes good commercial sense. On its face, Article 16 uses broad language, the plain meaning of which covers documentary draft transfers between confirming and issuing banks. Sensible policy considerations support this construction. To hold otherwise and accept First American's reading of Article 16 would render the UCP devoid of standards governing transactions between confirming and issuing banks. This would make no business sense. For similar reasons, the Court rejects First American's odd claim that PIBC's acceptance of the documentary drafts before First American had received and reviewed the documents should absolve First American of its obligation to honor the draft.[32] Finally, even if the Court were to

---

32. Under the scheme of Article 16, it appears that a confirming bank becomes obligated to pay a documentary credit when it transfers documents on to the issu-

find that First American should be treated as a "customer" of PIBC, First American would still be liable for the reasons given below in Part III for holding Dameron liable to reimburse First American.

* * *

III. Dameron's Obligation to Reimburse First American

Having found that PIBC has a legal right to payment from First American, ... the Court turns next to First American's claim that Dameron must reimburse it for any amount it must pay PIBC under the Letters. First American relies on the Agreements executed by Dameron to obtain the Letters. In the Agreements, Dameron pledged to indemnify First American for the latter's acts with respect to the Letters as long as such acts were taken in good faith. And, First American correctly notes that Dameron has not shown any bad faith on the part of First American with respect to accepting the documents. Dameron argues, however, that the good faith standard in the Agreements violates Virginia law and hence is void. Therefore, Dameron continues, First American's failure to note the missing Statement of the Beneficiary, though not a breach of good faith, nevertheless relieves Dameron of any obligation to reimburse First American.

It is not necessary to reach the unsettled, thorny question whether the Agreements, which appear to be standard form contracts employed by First American, violate Virginia law. Even assuming first that the Agreements run afoul of Virginia law, next that First American is obligated, as Dameron contends, by Virginia Code § 8.5–109(2) to "examine documents with care so as to ascertain that on their face they appear to comply with the terms" of the Letters, and finally that First American breached this duty by failing to note the absence of the Statement of the Beneficiary, the Virginia UCC and the common law of letters of credit still bar Dameron's claim because Dameron accepted the documents and used them to gain control of the T-shirts. Under these circumstances, Dameron cannot rely on documentary discrepancies to avoid honoring its Agreements with First American.

The Agreements between First American and Dameron state that they shall be governed by Virginia law. Title 8.5 of Virginia's UCC, which pertains to Letters of Credit, contains no provision governing an account customer's remedies for wrongful honor by an issuing bank.

ing bank. The confirming bank may, if it finds discrepancies, dishonor a documentary draft and return the documents to the beneficiary or to a prior confirming or advising bank in the chain of transfer. The confirming bank, like the issuing bank, appears to be required to accept or reject the documents "on the basis of the documents alone." Article 16(b). It is not permitted to pass them on perfunctorily to the issuing bank to obtain that bank's opinion on the documents' compliance with the letter of credit. If it could so operate, it would be no more than an advising bank. Furthermore, First American can claim no harm from PIBC's acceptance of the draft before First American received the documents. Under Article 16, First American was still entitled to review the documents upon receipt and to reject and return them as nonconforming to PIBC. ...

Section 8.5–102(3), however, frankly admits that Title 8.5 "deals with some but not all of the rules and concepts of letters of credit...." The section invites the application of "rules or concepts ... developed prior to this act or ... hereafter" to "a situation not provided for ... by this title." Id. ... Thus, in ascertaining Dameron's remedies as an account customer for First American's wrongful honor, this Court is directed by Virginia law to apply the "fundamental theory" of letters of credit and the "canon of liberal interpretation" in Virginia Code § 8.1–102. ...

A review of the few existing, apposite cases indicates that under the common law of letters of credit an account customer, by accepting documents from the issuing bank and subsequently "surrendering the documents [to shippers or customs officials] and accepting a substantial portion of the goods ... waives its right to seek strict enforcement of the letter of credit." Dorf Overseas Inc. v. Chemical Bank, 91 A.D.2d 895, 457 N.Y.S.2d 513, 514 (N.Y. App.Div.1983). This result "is the only one consistent with principle and common sense." H. Harfield, Bank Credits and Acceptances 107 (5th ed. 1974). Fundamental to letter of credit transactions is the principle that both the letter of credit and also the separate agreement between account customer and issuing bank are transactions in documents entirely independent from the underlying sale of goods. ... An account customer, if it desires to claim discrepancies, has a duty to return documents to the issuing bank rather than use them to obtain control over the goods. The documents provide some compensation to a bank which has inadvertently honored nonconforming documents. "The bank's loss will be the amount of the payment which it has made under the credit less any amount which it may realize from disposition of the documents which it has purchased." Id. at 105. The result is equitable. The beneficiary/seller is paid by the bank for the goods; the bank owns the documents and title to the goods; and the account customer has avoided paying for goods that, because of discrepancies in the documents, it feared accepting. This rule also avoids the inequitable result of a windfall for the account customer in the form of obtaining goods never paid for. While some commentators have favored less stringent rules with respect to an account customer's acceptance of documents,[42] the rule just stated has

---

42. Harfield, quoted in the text, presents the most in-depth analysis found of an account customer's remedies for an issuing bank's inadvertent acceptance of nonconforming documents. Harfield's conclusion, discussed supra, is that an account party must reject and return nonconforming documents within a reasonable period or be deemed to have waived its right to object to documentary inconsistencies. ... Some commentators have favored other rules.

In an early treatise, Finkelstein contended that an account customer should be able to accept nonconforming documents, reimburse the issuing bank, but deduct any direct or consequential damages flowing from the bank's acceptance of nonconforming documents. Finkelstein likened this to a buyer's ability to keep nonconforming goods, retain its right of action against the seller for breach of contract, and recover consequential damages. Finkelstein, Legal Aspects of Commercial Letters of Credit 195–97 (1930). ...

More recently, Kozolchyk took a middle ground between Finkelstein and Harfield. Kozolchyk, Commercial Letters of Credit in the Americas 322–26 (1966). Kozolchyk ... believed ... that an account customer

gained the widest acceptance in American case law and best reflects the fundamental theory underlying letters of credit.

The undisputed facts of this case are that shortly after October 25, 1988, First American transferred the documents at issue to Dameron. Dameron did not note any discrepancies; rather, it used the documents to take possession of the T-shirts. Until July 1989, when it brought suit against National Marketing, Dameron attempted to sell the T-shirts, apparently with disappointing results, and to work out a deal with National to compensate Dameron for the nonconforming goods. On three occasions during this period, Dameron pledged to reimburse First American for honoring the drafts related to the T-shirts in exchange for extensions of time for payment. Furthermore, Dameron obtained a court order attaching payment of the drafts, which order was not lifted until Dameron had settled its law suit with National Marketing. The terms of this settlement have been kept confidential by Dameron, although it stated that it received some monetary compensation under the settlement. It is reasonable to assume that a portion of the settlement was intended to compensate Dameron for the substandard quality of the T-shirts. Not until approximately a year or more after receipt of the documents and goods, did Dameron raise the issue of the missing Statement of the Beneficiary. The undisputed facts therefore show that Dameron delayed informing First American of any discrepancies for more than a reasonable period of time. It failed to return the documents to First American and instead took control of the goods. By these acts, Dameron waived its right to reject nonconforming documents and bound itself to reimburse First American for the amount of the drafts. ... First American's cross-claim against Dameron should be granted, and Dameron will be ordered to reimburse First American for the amount of the drafts plus interest.

* * *

might be permitted to receive "direct and foreseeable" damages, and urged American courts to adopt the practice found in some other countries of permitting an account customer to accept documents while expressly reserving a right of action against the bank for document inconsistencies. Id. at 316, 324. See also J. White and R. Summers, Handbook of the Law Under the Uniform Commercial Code § 19–8 at 864–65 (3d ed. 1988) (suggesting that an account customer might recover damages pertaining to defective goods from an issuing bank that wrongfully honors a draft, but providing no case law or reasons for this conclusion and observing that "because customers are so infrequently successful in suing issuing banks for wrongful honor, the law here is quite undeveloped"); Dolan, The Law of Letters of Credit para. 9.03 at 9–35, 9–36 (1984) (observing merely that disputes between issuing banks and account parties should be governed by "contract remedy rules" unless such rules are inadequate).

...

[E]ven if the Court were to accept the notion that an account customer should be able to accept documents and goods and then sue for direct damages resulting from a bank's acceptance of nonconforming documents, it would not permit Dameron to reduce the payment owed to First American by any damages stemming from National Marketing's delivery of faulty goods. Such damages stem from the seller's breach, not First American's. Moreover, even if the court were to hold that an account customer could receive damages from the issuing bank stemming from the receipt of faulty goods, Dameron has already been compensated for such receipt through its settlement with National Marketing. There is no reason in this case for Dameron not to reimburse First American for the full amount First American paid for the goods.

Notes

(1) Nature of Terms Conditioning Banks' Obligations. In theory, the parties to letter of credit transactions could make any fact or event the condition that unlocks a bank's duty to pay or accept a demand for payment. Banking practice, however, strongly favors limiting the fact or event to the presentation of described documents. UCP Article 4 declares: "In credit operations all parties deal in documents, and not in goods, services and/or other performances to which the documents may relate." For example, parties to a sales contract may agree that goods must be shipped by conference line vessels but should not expect a bank to verify that this has occurred. The ICC experts advise: "It should be remembered that banks are to check documents, not facts. Therefore the condition ... should be expressed as a requirement for a certificate of the carrier that the vessel is a conference line one." ICC Case Studies on Documentary Credits 20 (J Dekker 1989).

The parties in *Petra* established a documentary requirement that seller provide its statement that the goods shipped were of the quality of the samples on which buyer had relied. This statement, which the court refers to as the Statement of the Beneficiary, was not presented to the banks. Of what value to buyer would such statement be?

(2) Bills of Lading: "Clean" and "Foul." Bills of lading are obviously important to buyers concerned that payments may be made for goods not shipped. Letters of credit usually call for "clean" bills of lading; in any event, such a requirement may be implied. British Imex Industries Limited v. Midland Bank Limited, [1958] 1 Q.B. 542. If a carrier receives a shipment in torn or leaky cartons, it will note that fact on the bill of lading to protect itself from the claim that it damaged the goods. A bill of lading with such a notation is not "clean," and a bank need not pay under a letter of credit when such bills of lading are tendered.

Article 34 of the 1983 ICC Uniform Customs deals with this question as follows:

> a. A clean transport document is one which bears no superimposed clause or notation which expressly declares a defective condition of the goods and/or the packaging.
>
> b. Banks will refuse transport documents bearing such clauses or notations unless the credit expressly states the clauses or notations which may be accepted.

Suppose that a bill of lading covering a shipment of oil well casing and tubing is tendered under a letter of credit. In the bill of lading the phrase "in apparent good order and condition" has been deleted and the following inserted: "Ship not responsible for kind and condition of merchandise." The bill also bears the stamped notation, "Ship not responsible for rust." If the ICC Uniform Customs are applicable, may the bank decline to pay under the letter of credit? See Liberty National Bank & Trust Co. v. Bank of America National Trust &

Savings Association, 218 F.2d 831 (10th Cir.1955), affirming 116 F.Supp. 233 (W.D.Okl.1953).

Problem 9. Seller, in London, agreed to sell "Coromandel groundnuts" to a Danish buyer. Pursuant to the contract Bank opened a letter of credit in Seller's favor. Seller tendered documents to Bank which conformed to the letter of credit except that the bill of lading described the goods as "machine shelled groundnut kernels" instead of "Coromandel groundnuts." The invoice described the goods in the manner called for in the letter of credit. The war intervened, and Bank refused to honor Seller's draft because of the discrepancy between the bill of lading and the letter of credit. In action by Seller against the Bank, Seller proved that in the London produce market the two terms referred interchangeably to the same commodity. What result? See Rayner & Co. v. Hambros Bank, [1942] 2 All E.R. 694 (C.A.). Compare UCC 5–109(1) (preamble) with paragraph (1)(c) of that section. But cf. Temple–Eastex Inc. v. Addison Bank, 672 S.W.2d 793, 38 UCC Rep. 971 (Tex.1984) (letter of credit called for presentation of "draft" but plaintiff presented demand letter; presentation was consistent with banking practice).

The 1983 UCP provide in Article 41(c):

The description of the goods in the commercial invoice must correspond with the description in the credit. In all other documents the goods may be described in general terms not inconsistent with the description of the goods in the credit.

In the above problem, were the goods described in "general terms" in the bill of lading? Will the distinction drawn by the Uniform Customs, Art. 41 be binding under the Code? See UCC 5–109.

(3) Bills in a Set. A practice of carriers' issuing bills of lading in a set of parts grew up in overseas transportation in an era when the transmission of any document across the ocean was more hazardous than it is today. To cope with the risk of non-arrival of the documents, each part of the set could be sent separately. If only one part arrived, the carrier would honor it. Bills of lading in a set are now governed by UCC 7–304, which limits their issuance to overseas transportation. Once bills of lading are issued in more than one copy, the separate parts can be negotiated to different persons. Some of the problems associated with this possibility are addressed in 7–304(3) and (5).

When sellers and buyers have agreed to payment by letter of credit, the question arises of the banks' treatment of bills in a set when only one part of the set is presented for payment. Commercial banking practice developed whereby issuing or confirming banks would pay against presentation of part of the set, even though the letter of credit presentation of the "full set," provided the presenting bank agreed to indemnify the paying banks against loss. In a World War II era case, an issuing bank in New York refused to pay against part of the set. The Court of Appeals held that the bank's refusal was wrongful:

It is absolutely to the expeditious doing of business in overseas transactions in these days when one part of the bill of lading goes by air and another by water. Unless an indemnity can be substituted for the delayed part, not only does quick clearance of such transactions become impossible but also the universal practice of issuing bills of lading in sets loses much of its purpose.

Dixon, Irmaos & Cia. v. Chase National Bank, 144 F.2d 759, (2d Cir.1944), cert. denied, 324 U.S. 850 (1945). The *Dixon* case was sharply criticized and defended. Backus & Harfield, Custom and Letters of Credit: The Dixon, Irmaos Case, 52 Colum.L.Rev. 589 (1952); Honnold, Letters of Credit, Custom, Missing Documents and the Dixon Case: A Reply to Backus and Harfield, 53 Colum.L.Rev. 504 (1953).

The 1983 Uniform Customs and Practices provide, in Article 26(iii), that banks will accept a transport document which "consists of the full set of originals issued to the consignor if issued in more than one original." The ICC group of exports, responding to an inquiry about how to determine the number of parts to a set, replied that the number of originals must be ascertainable from each copy of the bill of lading itself. ICC Case Studies on Documentary Credits 82 (J. Dekker 1989).

The Commercial Code took account of bills in a set only in Article 2. Tender rules, as between seller and buyer, are set forth in UCC 2–323(2). The Code takes no position as to whether banks are subject to a similar rule under letters of credit. Cf. UCC 5–113.

UNION EXPORT CO. v. N.I.B. INTERMARKET, A.B.

Supreme Court of Tennessee, 1990.
786 S.W.2d 628.

DROWOTA, C.J.

This case involves an international letter of credit. Union Export Company (Union) had First American National Bank (First American) issue an irrevocable letter of credit in the amount of $345,000 to N.I.B. Intermarket, A.B. (N.I.B.), a Swedish exporter, to insure payment for calcium chloride that Union had purchased from N.I.B. In this appeal, First American argues that the Court of Appeals erred in affirming the Chancellor's issuance of a permanent injunction enjoining First American from paying a draft drawn pursuant to the letter of credit. Union also appeals, arguing that the injunction was proper but that it was error for the Court of Appeals to remand the case to the trial court for a determination of whether a Swedish bank, to whom the draft had been negotiated before it was presented to First American, was a holder in due course. For the reasons that follow, we reverse the decision of the Chancellor and the Court of Appeals.

I.

Union commenced this action against N.I.B. and First American, seeking, as to N.I.B., damages for breach of contract, and, as to First American, a temporary restraining order and a permanent injunction barring First American from honoring a $345,000 letter of credit issued on Union's account in favor of N.I.B., as well as attachment of any proceeds of the letter of credit owing to N.I.B. The trial court granted Union a temporary restraining order on April 29, 1987, and a preliminary injunction on June 17, 1987.

Thereafter, First American filed its answer and a counterclaim in which it sought to have the preliminary injunction vacated. First American also sought a judgment against Union for Union's reimbursement obligation once First American paid the draft it had accepted under the letter of credit.

Union then moved for a partial summary judgment against First American, requesting that the injunction in its favor be made permanent. First American also filed a motion for summary judgment, in which it alleged that Union owed it reimbursement for Union's liability under the letter of credit.

The Chancellor held a hearing on both motions for summary judgment, after which he granted Union's motion, permanently enjoining First American from making any payment under the letter of credit. In so doing, the trial court found that there was fraud in the underlying transaction, that fraudulent documents had been presented to First American, and that the fraud perpetrated by N.I.B. entitled Union to have payment of the draft drawn under the letter of credit permanently enjoined under Tenn. Code Ann. § 47–5–114(2).

First American subsequently moved to alter or amend the judgment and also sought an indemnity bond from Union in the amount of $345,000 plus ten percent (10) interest from June 18, 1987, payable in the event that Union succeeded in its appeal. The Chancellor denied this motion.

First American then appealed to the Court of Appeals. The Court of Appeals sustained the Chancellor's provision of injunctive relief but ordered that the case be remanded to the trial court and that an attempt be made to join Skanska Banken, a Swedish bank, a claimant to First American's enjoined acceptance, as a party. The Court of Appeals held that if Skanska could prove it were a holder in due course, then, under § 47–5–114(2)(a) the injunction must be vacated.

II.

The facts in this case are undisputed. Sometime prior to August 26, 1986, Union, a Nashville based company, agreed to purchase 1500 metric tons of calcium chloride, a chemical used in snow removal, from N.I.B., a Swedish exporter. In order to guarantee payment, Union had First American issue N.I.B. an irrevocable letter of credit in the amount of $345,000. The letter of credit required the presentment of a draft payable 150 days after sight along with certain other documents.

On December 1, 1986, First American received from Skanska Banken (Skanska) a $345,000 time draft, drawn and endorsed in blank by N.I.B., together with other documents, all of which complied with the letter of credit. First American accepted the draft on December 1, 1986 by affixing its signature thereto, and on the next day, December 2, sent notice of its acceptance by Telex to Skanska. The acceptance had a maturity date of April 30, 1987.

Upon receiving notice of the acceptance, Skanska made two loans to N.I.B. totaling $345,000, taking as security N.I.B.'s claim under the letter of credit.

In February, 1987, Union notified First American that the shipment of chemicals it purchased from N.I.B. was defective. Because First American indicated it would pay its acceptance when it matured, Union commenced this action.

III.

A commercial letter of credit transaction involves three separate contractual relationships: (1) the underlying contract between the buyer (in this case, Union) and the seller (N.I.B.); (2) the agreement between the issuer (First American) and its customer (Union) in which the issuer agrees to issue the letter of credit in return for the customer's promise to reimburse it and pay a commission; and (3) the letter of credit itself which is an engagement by the issuer that it will honor drafts presented by the beneficiary or a transferee beneficiary upon compliance with the terms and conditions specified in the letter of credit. ...

The fundamental principle governing these transactions is the doctrine of independent contracts, which provides that the issuing bank's obligation to honor drafts drawn on a letter of credit by the beneficiary is separate and independent from any obligation of its customer to the beneficiary under the sale of goods contract and separate as well from any obligation of the issuer to its customer under their agreement. ...

In the case at bar, both the trial court and the Court of Appeals found that the injunction against payment under the letter of credit was proper under the limited exception to the doctrine of independence found at Tenn. Code Ann. § 47–5–114(2) ... .

Under the general rule the issuer must honor the draft when the documents presented comply with the terms of the letter of credit. Tenn. Code Ann. § 47–5–114(1). Under this limited exception of § 5–114(2), however, when a required document does not conform to the necessary warranties, is forged, is fraudulent, or there is fraud in the transaction, an issuer acting in good faith is not required to, but may honor a draft drawn under a letter of credit if the documents presented appear on their face to comply with the terms of the letter of credit. In addition, a court may enjoin an issuer from honoring such a draft if the issuer fails to do so on its own. Tenn. Code Ann. § 47–5–112(2)(b). ... Notwithstanding this exception, if the person presenting a draft drawn on a letter of credit is a holder in due course (Tenn. Code Ann. § 47–3–302), the issuer must pay the draft, whether or not it has notice of forgery or fraud. Tenn. Code Ann. § 47–5–114(2)(a) ... .

In this case, the element of fraud is undisputed. For this reason, the Chancellor enjoined payment under Tenn. Code Ann § 5–114(2)(b). The Court of Appeals remanded for a determination of whether Skanska, to whom the draft had been negotiated, is a holder in due course, and thus entitled to the proceeds under Tenn. Code Ann. § 5–114(2)(a) despite the element of fraud.

First American appeals this decision, arguing that the injunction is inappropriate regardless of whether or not Skanska is a holder in due course because the injunction was issued after First American accepted the time draft, and thus was untimely under Tenn. Code Ann. § 47–4–303.

Tenn. Code Ann. § 47–4–303(1) provides in relevant part:

(1) Any ... legal process served upon ... a payor bank, *whether or not effective under other rules of law* to terminate, suspend, or modify the bank's right or duty to pay an item or to charge the customer's account for the item, comes too late to so terminate, suspend or modify such right or duty if the ... legal process is received or served and a reasonable time for the bank to act thereon expires or the setoff is exercised after the bank has done any of the following: (a) accepted or certified the item. [Emphasis added.]

Acceptance is defined in § 47–3–410(1) as:

(1) Acceptance is the drawee's signed engagement to honor the draft as presented. It must be written on the draft, and may consist of his signature alone. It becomes operative when completed by delivery or notification.

In the case at bar, it is undisputed that First American is the payor bank, and that it accepted the draft within the meaning of Tenn. Code Ann. § 47–3–410(1) prior to the issuance of legal process. Union argues that the injunction was timely, because Tenn. Code Ann. § 47–5–114(2)(b) provides that "a court ... may enjoin such honor," and "honor" is defined in the general definitional section of the U.C.C. as "to pay or to accept and pay." Tenn. Code Ann. § 47–1–201(21). Thus, there is an apparent conflict between Tenn. Code Ann. § 47–5–114(2)(b) and Tenn. Code Ann. § 47–4–303 under the facts of this case.

Article 4 of the U.C.C. governs bank deposits and collections. U.C.C. § 47–4–101. Section 102 of article 4 specifically provides that if provisions in article 4 conflict with those in article 3 then article 4 governs, but in the event article 4 provisions conflict with article 8, then article 8 governs. There is no provision in the Code providing which article would apply in the event of a conflict between articles 4 and 5.

In First Commercial Bank v. Gotham Originals, Inc., 475 N.E.2d at 1260, the New York Court of Appeals held that § 4–303 governed. It relied on the express language of § 4–303(1), which states "whether or not effective under other rules of law" legal process is not effective under the specified circumstances. The Court found further support from the language of § 5–102(3) and comment (2) thereto, on the limited controlling authority of article 5.

The facts in Gotham Originals are similar to the facts in the present case. The issuing bank accepted two drafts drawn under a letter of credit. The drafts were payable after sight in 60 days. After acceptance, but before payment, the customer discovered fraud in the transaction, and the trial court enjoined the issuer from payment. The intermediate appellate court reversed and vacated the injunction, and the Court of Appeals affirmed, both acting under § 4–303.

In addition to holding that § 4–303 prevailed by its own terms, the Court noted the following policy reason supporting the result:

> Important policy considerations suggest the result also. Letters of credit provide a quick, economic and predictable means of financing transactions for parties not willing to deal on open accounts by permitting the seller to rely not only on the credit of the buyer but also on that of the issuing bank. By its terms, the credit often reflects a conscious negotiation of risk allocation between customer and beneficiary and its utility rests heavily on strict adherence to the agreed terms and the doctrine of independent contract (see, J. White & R. Summers, Handbook on Uniform Commercial Code § 18–1, at 704–08[2d ed.]). It is this predictability of credit arrangements which permits not only the financing of sale of goods transactions between widely separated parties in different jurisdictions but also has permitted the development of a market in trade or bankers' acceptances of time drafts. Once a draft payable in the future is accepted by a bank, it becomes known as a bankers' acceptance, and such acceptances can be, and regularly are, sold in conjunction with letter of credit transactions to obtain financing prior to the date of maturity in a market sanctioned by the Federal Reserve Board (see, 12 U.S.C. § 372; PLI, Letters of Credit and Bankers' Acceptances 231–34, 236). If the courts intervene to enjoin issuing banks from paying drafts they have previously accepted they seriously undermine this market and limit the use of acceptances as a financing tool.

Id. at 1261.

The same policy considerations apply in Tennessee. We therefore hold that, under Tenn. Code Ann. § 47–4–303(1), Union's injunction against payment of the time draft drawn pursuant to the letter of credit was untimely because it was issued after First American had already accepted the draft. We therefore reverse the decision of the Court of Appeals, and we order the injunction vacated.

IV.

Union next argues that, should the injunction be vacated, the proceeds owing to N.I.B. under the letter of credit are subject to attachment since they represent personal property of either legal or equitable nature. Tenn. Code Ann. § 29–6–132. Attachment of the proceeds would also enable Union to obtain Tennessee jurisdiction over N.I.B. as an out-of-state defendant pursuant to Tenn. Code Ann. § 29–6–101(1).

For the same reasons we above vacated the injunction against payment of the draft drawn under the letter of credit, we now hold that Union is not entitled to an attachment of the letter of credit's proceeds. The attachment issued after First American accepted the draft, and thus is invalid under Tenn. Code Ann. § 47–4–303.

Accordingly, the judgment of the Court of Appeals is reversed, and the trial court's injunction against the payment of the accepted time draft drawn pursuant to Union's letter of credit is hereby vacated. Costs will be taxed to Union Export Company.

Notes

(1) "Holder in Due Course" Protection for Collecting Banks. In the *Union Export* case the bank collecting the seller's draft argued that UCC 5–114(2)(a) barred injunctive relief on the ground that the collecting bank "had taken the draft under conditions that would make it a holder in due course."

UCC 5–114(2)(a) carries "holder in due course" protection beyond that conferred by Article 3. Under 3–305 a holder in due course of an instrument (e.g., a draft) is protected against claims to that instrument and defenses of the obligor. In other words, a bank collecting a draft would be protected against ownership claims to *the draft* and defenses of the obligor. UCC 5–114(2)(a) goes further since the bank that issues a letter may not be a party to the draft drawn by the seller. In *Union Export,* the bank which had issued the letter of credit accepted the draft when it was presented. By that acceptance, the bank became a party to the draft, indeed became the primary party obligated *on the draft.* UCC 3–413. The provision in 5–114 applies to an issuing bank's liability on its *letter of credit* undertaking even though the bank is not a party to the draft.

This extension of the concept of holder in due course accounts for the fact that 5–114(2)(a) does not state that the negotiating bank has the rights of a holder in due course; instead, 5–114(2)(a) protects a bank which has taken the draft under circumstances that "*would* make it a holder in due course," and extends that type of protection to cut off defenses under a different instrument—the letter of credit.

This extension might be justified on the ground that the issuing bank has promised, under specified circumstances, to honor a draft drawn by the seller; thus the issuing bank might be analogized to a bank that "certifies" a check by putting its signed "acceptance" on the check; the certifying bank then becomes a party to the check and is subject to the rights of a holder in due course.

There remain questions of policy as to whether a collecting bank should be given the immunity from injunctive relief granted by 5–114(2)(a). To qualify for this immunity the collecting bank must have given value (3–303)—either by "discounting" the draft or by taking the draft as security for an antecedent debt the seller owed to the bank. And the collecting bank must have taken the draft in "good faith" (UCC 3–302(a)(2)(ii), 1–201(19)).

(2) Attachment of Proceeds of Letters of Credit. The buyer in *Union Export* proceeded on two remedial paths: injunction against the bank to stop payment or seizure of the proceeds of the bank's payment before transmission to the seller. The Tennessee court held that the injunction remedy was untimely because Skanska was a holder in due course of the draft accepted by First American. The court then summarily rejected buyer's alternative remedy of attachment of the proceeds *after* First America had paid; the court explains that "the same reasons" apply. Given the seller's fraud, why are the funds that represent the purchase price not subject to attachment? See also the decision of the French Cour de Cassation in SA Discount Bank v. Teboul, Recueil, 1982, 382 (attachment of funds at intermediary bank was violation of French Civil Code Article 1134 and of Article 3 of the UCC); see Goldman, The Applicable Law: General Principles of Law— the *Lex Mercatoria*, in Contemporary Problems in International Arbitration 119 (J. Lew ed. 1987).

ANDINA COFFEE, INC. v. NATIONAL WESTMINSTER BANK, USA

Supreme Court of New York, Appellate Division, First Department, 1990.
160 A.D.2d 104, 560 N.Y.S.2d 1.

MILONAS, J.

Plaintiff Andina Coffee, Inc., a New York corporation, was engaged in the importation of coffee from defendant Gonchecol, Ltda., at one time a major Colombian exporter of coffee. To pay for its purchases, Andina delivered to Gonchecol letters of credit which it obtained from a number of commercial banks in New York, including defendants National Westminster Bank USA (NatWest) and Cooperatieve Centrale Raiffeisenboerenleenbank B.A. (Rabobank). As the beneficiary of the letters of credit, Gonchecol apparently used all or some of the funds to borrow money from defendant Banco Credito y Commercio de Colombia

(BCCC) and other Colombian banks in order to finance its business operations. In June 1986, BCCC advanced $2,100,000 to Gonchecol in exchange for which it was to be reimbursed through a $2,100,000 check drawn on a Panamanian bank. However, Gonchecol's check bounced, and BCCC was left with an unpaid $2,100,000 loan. According to NatWest and Rabobank, this event could only have served to confirm what BCCC had already learned from its own sources; that is, that Gonchecol had already lost millions of dollars and was experiencing severe financial difficulties. As was the situation with most of the moneys made available by BCCC to Gonchecol, the source of repayment would have to be proceeds from the letters of credit provided to Gonchecol from the issuing banks.

Beginning in May of 1986, coffee financed under the various letters of credit, which were to be paid on the presentation of interior truck bills of lading, failed to materialize. Consequently, representatives of the New York banks were dispatched to Colombia in August of 1986 when it was discovered that Gonchecol had caused fraudulent truck bills of lading to be furnished for large quantities of coffee which were, in fact, never shipped, thereby resulting in substantial financial losses to New York banks. The four letters of credit involved here are the last outstanding instruments which were not drawn against prior to the disclosure of the exporter's dishonest practices. In that regard, NatWest and Rabobank had each supplied two of the letters of credit, one for $2,104,000 and the other three in the amount of $1,000,000, pursuant to which they agreed to make payment upon the presentation within a specified period of time of drafts and certain documents, among which were to be the "original railroad and/or truck bill of lading." The bill of lading was supposed to show that the coffee was actually in existence, that it had left the control of the growers and that it was in the hands of the shipper and en route from the interior of Colombia to a seaport.

On July 9, 1986, 15 days after BCCC had already advanced $2,100,000 to Gonchecol against the latter's bad check, it received from NatWest a letter of credit in the amount of $2,104,000. The following day, almost six weeks before the earliest possible date for presentment under that instrument, BCCC accepted from Gonchecol its draft and accompanying documents. These documents included truck bills of lading which were dated August 22, 1986, almost six weeks after the date submitted to BCCC, and purported to show that 8,000 bags of coffee had been delivered to a trucking company for transport to a Colombian port. BCCC sent the draft and documents to NatWest with a cover letter dated July 15, 1986. By telex dated July 22, 1986, NatWest advised BCCC that it would not pay under the letter of credit because of four enumerated discrepancies in the documents, including the fact that the draft and documents were presented prior to the earliest date mentioned in the letter of credit and that the truck bills of lading were postdated.

BCCC thereupon requested that the bills of lading and other documents be returned to it by mail. It then reviewed the documents received under the other three letters of credit and perceived that the bills of lading in those instances were similarly postdated. Consequently, it sent all of the bills of lading back to Gonchecol so that the exporter could revise the dates to comply with the letters of credit. Indeed, some of the changes were made twice in an attempt to bring the documents into conformity with both the form and date mandates of the letters of credit. Thus, it appears that the documents were designed more to effect payment under the letters of credit than to reflect accurately the business transactions that they were intended to evince. In any event, by the time that the documents had been altered and realtered, the full extent of Gonchecol's fraud had been detected, and payment was rejected by NatWest and Rabobank on the ground that, in part, the bills of lading were postdated and fraudulent.

The instant appeal concerns respective motions and cross motions for summary judgment with respect to the letters of credit. The Supreme Court, in granting BCCC's cross motion for summary judgment and denying the motions of NatWest and Rabobank for the same relief, was persuaded that BCCC took the drafts for value, in good faith and without any knowledge of any fraud defenses and was, therefore, a holder in due course entitled to payment under the letters of credit. In the view of the court, there is no evidence to support the assertions by NatWest and Rabobank that BCCC possessed actual knowledge of Gonchecol's fraud and that it did not accept the drafts in good faith. Finally, the court concluded that the "transactions involved in this case must be considered against a background of haphazard permissive and careless negotiations and payment of prior letters of credit by the issuing banks over a year and a half period. First of all, it is not denied that the same discrepancies alleged in the documents submitted by BCCC were the same one [sic] which the banks had accepted for the aforementioned period .... Secondly, it cannot be denied that the letters of credit involved are not based upon underlying arms-length transactions." The court proceeded to criticize the issuing banks for assuming a high risk by merely demanding trucking bills of lading rather than on-board bills of lading, since it "appears that the port forwarder and the trucking company were all part of Gonchecol's enterprises and that the importer, Andina Coffee, Inc., although a separate corporate entity, belonged to the same overall organization as the exporter."

Yet, notwithstanding the questionable nature of the financing arrangement undertaken by NatWest and Rabobank, and, certainly, the record is replete with indications of dubious business judgment by the various issuing banks, the soundness of the lenders' financial practices is not at issue here. What is crucial is whether BCCC accepted drafts drawn upon letters of credit "under circumstances which would make it a holder in due course" (Uniform Commercial Code 5–114[2][a]). ...

The mere fact that the documents presented in connection with the letters of credit may have been complete forgeries and that no coffee was delivered to the trucker for export is insufficient to avoid payment under the letter of credit .... What is critical is whether the bills of lading complied with the requirements of the letters of credit or whether BCCC possessed actual knowledge of the fraud ... or otherwise acted in bad faith. ... Thus, according to the Court of Appeals in First Commercial Bank v. Gotham Originals, Inc., 64 N.Y.2d [287], at 295:

> But when a required document does not conform to the necessary warranties or is forged or fraudulent or there is fraud in the transaction, an issuer acting in good faith may, but is not required to, refuse to honor a draft under a letter of credit when the documents presented appear on their face to comply with the terms of the letter of credit. ... Notwithstanding this exception, if the person presenting a draft drawn on a letter of credit is a holder in due course ..., the issuer *must* pay the draft, whether it has notice of forgery or fraud or not.

It is settled that New York law mandates strict compliance with the terms of a letter of credit .... The postdating of bills of lading is not only a departure from the requirements of the letters of credit but also constitutes a form of fraudulent practice. Contrary to the Supreme Court's characterization that the objections to the accompanying documents raised by NatWest and Rabobank were frivolous and highly technical, the discrepancies were, in reality, material. At the very least, they would have had the effect of concealing the actual shipment dates (even assuming that they had represented genuine, and not fictitious, transactions) and, in fact, did not, as required by the letters of credit, "evidence shipment" of the coffee. Further, while there is authority that by its previous acceptance of nonconforming documents, as admittedly occurred herein, the issuing bank does not waive the right to reject future defects ... and the preclusion rule contained in the UCP (Uniform Customs and Practice for Documentary Credits) is by no means absolute, at most the failure to assert an objection on a previous occasion presents a question of fact as to whether there was a waiver ....

Unless the postdating was expressly allowed under the letters of credit, and there is no indication that this is the situation, or the parties' prior course of conduct conclusively demonstrates otherwise, the documents provided under the letters of credit did not comply with the terms thereof, and BCCC may not compel payment. Equally significant is the BCCC's apparently active role in obtaining the revisions of the documents, particularly after it was confirmed with definite proof of Gonchecol's financial instability in the form of a bad check, raises questions of fact as to whether it was acting in good faith and without actual knowledge of the exporter's fraud. The record of the present matter clearly presents sufficient unresolved matters precluding summary judgment as to whether BCCC participated in a scheme whereby the bills of lading were altered simply to render them in conformity with the letters of credit. Once it has been "shown that a defense exists a person claiming the rights of a holder in due course has the burden of establishing that he or some person under whom he claims is in all respects a holder in due course" (Uniform Commercial Code 3–307[3]). Since NatWest and Rabobank have demonstrated a viable defense with respect to the letters of credit, BCCC must now prove that it is a holder in due course, and, consequently, summary judgment in its favor is not warranted.

(4) "STANDBY" (OR "GUARANTY") LETTERS OF CREDIT

New Wine in Old Bottles. The classical letter of credit is a device for routine, safe exchange; something of value, usually a negotiable bill of lading controlling the delivery of goods, is exchanged for cash. In recent years, banks have been issuing "Letters of Credit" that promise to pay large sums on the presentation of pieces of paper that are scarcely marketable—statements of non-performance or default. Even when the "Letter of Credit" does not mention default but instead promises payment on presentation of a certificate of *performance* (e.g., the completion of a building project), in actual operation the bank is asked to pay only when a party who was expected to pay (e.g., the one for whom a building was constructed) fails to do so. The fact that the bank's obligation is normally used only when something goes wrong has led these devices to be called "standby" or "guaranty" letters of credit.

Standby letters of credit are used in sales transactions. But whereas it is the seller who is the beneficiary of the ordinary documentary letter of credit, it is the buyer who is the beneficiary of the standby letter of credit. The standby letter may be given to secure performance by the seller and, if the buyer has paid something in advance, to secure the buyer's advance.

The label "Letter of Credit" and statements in the instrument that payment is to be made in presentation of a draft accompanied by a "certificate" or other "document" (no matter how worthless) respond to the fact that many state laws prohibit banks from guaranteeing debts. However, there seems to be need for such undertakings, and the volume and form of these instruments have multiplied. See Baird, Standby Letters of Credit in Bankruptcy, 49 U.Chi.L.Rev. 130 (1982); Verkuil, Bank Solvency and Guaranty Letters of Credit, 25 Stan.L.Rev. 716 (1973); Symposium: Letters of Credit and Standbys, 24 Ariz.L.Rev. 235–369 (1982).

GROUND AIR TRANSFER, INC. v. WESTATES AIRLINES, INC.
United States Court of Appeals, First Circuit, 1990.
899 F.2d 1269.

BREYER, CIRCUIT JUDGE.

The two parties before us—Westates and Charter One—signed a "charter air service" contract. As the contract required, Charter One arranged for a bank to issue a $50,000 "standby" letter of credit in Westates' favor, a letter designed, in part, to make certain Westates would not suffer harm should Charter One fail to carry out its contractual obligations. ... Subsequently, a dispute arose; each party claimed the other broke the contract.

Westates, the beneficiary of the letter of credit, would now like to "call" the letter, thereby obtaining the $50,000, which it hopes to keep, at least while the courts litigate the parties' various "breach of contract" claims. The federal district court, however, has issued an injunction, forbidding Westates to call the letter of credit.

Westates appeals from the issuance of the injunction. It says that the law prohibits a court from enjoining a call on a standby letter of credit, at least in a typical case, where the beneficiary's position in the underlying contract dispute is colorable and where the beneficiary can satisfy the terms that the letter of credit itself sets forth as conditions for its call. ... We agree with Westates that the record before us indicates that this case presents the typical commercial circumstances (in respect to the underlying contract, the dispute, and the letter of credit), in which commercial law, as embodied in the Uniform Commercial Code, prohibits an injunction. ... Consequently, we reverse the district court.

I.

Background

We set forth several background circumstances so that the reader can see that this case (as far as the record here reveals) is one in which commercial law normally would prohibit an injunction. That is to say, the underlying contract is a simple, typical commercial contract; Westates' claim that Charter One broke the contract is at least "colorable"; and Westates seems able to satisfy the terms that the letter of credit itself sets forth as conditions for its call.

1. *The contract.* Westates provides airplanes and related services for charter flights. Charter One sells charter flights to travelers. In mid–1989 Westates and Charter One signed a contract under which Westates promised to provide planes and crews for Charter One's new service between Providence, Rhode Island, and Atlantic City, New Jersey, and also (by later amendment to the contract) for its new service between Worcester, Massachusetts, and Atlantic City. The contract required Charter One to pay Westates each month a fee calculated on the basis of the number of hours flown, with a minimum fee of about $105,000 (based on 70 hours flown), which was increased to about $209,000 (150 hours flown) when the Worcester service was added. The contract contained a special "default" clause, which says,

> upon any default by Charter One as defined in this agreement, Westates may immediately terminate all service. ... Westates shall immediately notify Charter One of the default. ... If the default is not cured by Charter One within ten (10) days from the

date of mailing the *notice of default,* Westates shall have the right to immediately declare Charter One's default to be a material breach of this agreement and declare this agreement to be terminated without further notice to Charter One.

(Emphasis added.) The contract also required speedy transmission of each monthly payment. It said that late payment was "considered a default."

2. *The contract dispute.* Each party now says that the other party broke this contract. The record reveals a dispute that began in August 1989, when the contract was less than one month old. Charter One's president says that Westates' owner called him and threatened to cancel the contract unless Charter One would pay a higher minimum fee. Charter One refused. Westates then sent Charter One a "ten day default" notice, under the contract's special "default" provision. The "ten day notice" said that Westates would not provide planes for Charter One's Worcester/Atlantic City service after September 4. Westates, even before September 4, provided only one plane, rather than two planes (as the contract required), but Westates says that maintenance problems, not contract-cancellation efforts, were responsible.

Subsequently, Westates, apparently under pressure from Charter One, changed its mind about cancelling the contract. Charter One's attorney wrote to Westates suggesting that "Westates reconsider its decision to cancel the contract and instead perform its obligations as required." The letter adds:

> Please advise the undersigned by close of business on Wednesday, August 30, 1989, whether Westates intends ... cancellation of the Worcester program. If we do not hear from [you] ... by that time, we will assume that Westates does not intend to abide by its contract, and Charter One will take such measures as are necessary to protect its rights.

On August 30 a Westates attorney, in California, called Charter One's attorney, in Washington, D.C. She says that she told Charter One that Westates indeed intended to abide by the contract and that it rescinded its cancellation. She did not call, however, until 3 p.m. California time, which was 6 p.m. Washington, D.C., time. Charter One then decided that it would not go through with the contract; and it wrote back to Westates that Westates' call had come "too late" (apparently meaning that the call had arrived after "close of business"). The letter added that Charter One would therefore "reject your verbal offer to rescind cancellation of the Worcester program...."

Westates then stopped providing Worcester/Atlantic City service. It continued, however, to provide Providence/Atlantic City service. In mid-September Charter One withheld about $32,000 from the monthly fees due Westates for that Providence service. Westates said that the contract did not permit Charter One to withhold this money. On September 22 it sent Charter One another "ten day default" notice. After ten days it cancelled the contract.

The parties have not yet litigated the merits of their contract disputes. We therefore need not decide whether Westates did, or did not, break the contract in mid-August, or whether it successfully reinstated the contract on August 30, or whether, irrespective of the status of the Worcester/Atlantic City portion of the contact, the Providence/Atlantic City portion remained in effect, or whether Charter One did, or did not, have the right to withhold $32,000 in mid-September. We need only decide that the record, so far, indicates that Westates' position, in respect to the contract dispute, is not obviously without merit, that its position is "colorable," and that, in arguing that it was entitled to receive the $32,000 and (not having received the money) to send a "ten day default" letter, Westates is not acting "fraudulently."

3. *The letter of credit.* The letter of credit here at issue is a typical, commercial letter designed to guarantee a beneficiary against harm caused by a contractual "default." The air service contract described above requires Charter One to arrange for a "letter of credit" as a "default guarantee." It says specifically in the section dealing with "default" that

> Charter One must provide Westates with a Irrevocable Letter of Credit acceptable to Westates in the amount of $50,000. ...

It adds that:

> Upon termination of the agreement by Westates ... it is agreed that Westates may take the irrevocable Letter of Credit as liquidated damages for the breach of this agreement by Charter One.

Charter One arranged for a Michigan bank to issue the letter. The letter itself says that Westates may "call" the letter and obtain the money by asking the bank for the money and providing the bank with a copy of the ten day default notice. It reads:

> the credit amount is available to you [Westates] by your drafts on us at sight accompanied by: Dated notarized copy of the ten (10) day notice described in [the Westates/Charter One contract].

The record indicates that Westates can easily meet the terms in this letter of credit. It can provide the bank with a draft and with the "dated notarized copy of the ten ... day notice" that it sent to Charter One on September 22.

II.

Ordinary Principles of Commercial Law

As we have previously explained, parties to commercial contracts often arrange for "standby" or "guarantee" letters of credit. The beneficiary of such a letter typically wants to make certain that, if the other party to the contract defaults, the beneficiary can gain access to a secure fund of money which he can use, say, to satisfy the other party's debt to him (if he is a "seller"), or to purchase a substitute performance (if he is a "buyer"). He may also wish to make certain that, should any contractual dispute arise, it will "wend [its] way towards resolution with the money in [his] pocket, rather than in the pocket" of his adversary. Itek [Corp. v. First National Bank of Boston], 730 F.2d [19], at 24. In order to permit the parties to agree to achieve these objectives, courts have typically considered the letter of credit as "independent" of the contract. That is to say, they have considered it a separate agreement with, say, the issuing bank, that permits the beneficiary to present the documents that satisfy the "call" conditions, and that requires the bank to honor the letter when the beneficiary does so. ... Whether in satisfying those conditions—say, as here, by presenting a draft and a copy of a ten day notice—the beneficiary is, or is not, violating the terms of some other document, such as an underlying contract, is normally beside the point, for to prevent the beneficiary from obtaining the money while the court decides the "underlying contract" question may deprive the beneficiary of the very benefit for which he bargained, namely that any such underlying contract dispute will be "resolved while he is in possession of the money." Itek, 730 F.2d at 24 ... . That is why the Uniform Commercial Code explicitly states that an "issuer must honor a ... demand for payment which complies with the terms of the relevant contract regardless of whether the ... documents conform to the underlying contract ... between the customer and the beneficiary." U.C.C. § 5–114(1), Cal.Com. Code § 5114(1) (West 1989). And, that is why the U.C.C. narrowly circumscribes the circumstances under which a court can enjoin the issuer from making such a payment. See U.C.C. § 5–114(2). Courts have also proved about as reluctant to issue injunctions against beneficiaries calling, as against issuers paying, letters of credit. ... Given the policy reasons against enjoining payment, the random happenstance as to whether beneficiary or issuer is within the court's jurisdiction, and the practical fact that, in any such case, the real parties in interest are likely the contracting parties (with issuing bank as neutral observer), the roughly parallel reluctance to enjoin both issuer and beneficiary is understandable. ...

We have said throughout that courts may not "normally" issue an injunction because of an important exception to the general "no injunction" rule. The exception, as we also explained in Itek, 730 F.2d at 24–25, concerns "fraud" so serious as to make it obviously pointless and unjust to permit the beneficiary to obtain the money. Where the circumstances "plainly" show that the underlying contract forbids the beneficiary to call a letter of credit, Itek, 730 F.2d at 24; where they show that the contract deprives the beneficiary of even a "colorable" right to do so, id. at 25; where the contract and circumstances reveal that the beneficiary's demand for payment has "absolutely no basis in fact," id.; ... where the beneficiary's conduct has " ' "so vitiated the entire transaction that the legitimate purposes of the independence of the issuer's obligation would no longer be served," ' " Itek, 730 F.2d at 25 ...; then a court may enjoin payment. The Uniform Commercial Code, as adopted in most states, says:

Unless otherwise agreed when documents appear on their face to comply with the terms of a credit but a required document ... is forged or fraudulent or there is fraud in the transaction: ...

(b) [except in certain circumstances listed in subsection (a) not here applicable] an issuer acting in good faith may honor the draft or demand for payment despite notification from the customer of fraud, forgery or other defect not apparent on the face of the documents *but a court of appropriate jurisdiction may enjoin such honor.*

U.C.C. 5–114(2) (emphasis added).

The "fraud" exception does not apply in this case, however, for the record shows nothing "fraudulent" about Westates' demand for payment, nor did the district court find to the contrary. As our earlier discussion of the contract dispute makes clear, ... the record reveals that Westates' claims and defenses are, at the least, "colorable."

...

III.

California Law

California letter of credit law quite obviously differs from the norm in one important respect, but in a respect that must make a court more reluctant, not less reluctant, to issue an injunction. When California adopted the Uniform Commercial Code, it consciously refused to adopt the language permitting an injunction that we underlined when we quoted U.C.C. 5–114(2) .... By omitting this language, California underscored the principle of the "independence" of the letter of credit. The California Code's drafters explicitly stated that the U.C.C.'s "provision for a protective injunction was omitted because: 'By giving the courts power to enjoin the honor of drafts drawn upon documents which appear to be regular on their face, the Commissioners on Uniform State Laws do violence to one of the basic concepts of the letter of credit, to wit, that the letter of credit agreement is independent of the underlying commercial transaction.'" Cal.Com. Code § 5114, comment 6 (West 1989) .... Thus California would seem even more hostile than the typical state to an injunction in the circumstances before us.

...

[W]e do not believe the California Supreme Court would permit an injunction where other states (applying the traditional "fraud" exception) would not do so. After all, California's state legislature has altered the U.C.C. to make it more difficult in California than elsewhere to enjoin an issuer's payment of a letter of credit; to make it significantly easier than elsewhere to enjoin a call by a beneficiary would undercut that underlying legislative policy.

For these reasons the judgment of the district court is

Reversed.

Notes

(1) Independence From Underlying Transactions. The "standby" credit, which in fact (though not in form) is used when there is default in the underlying transaction, places heavy strain on the classic doctrine that the letter of credit is "independent" from the contractual obligations of the parties. See, for example, Roman Ceramics Corp. v. Peoples National Bank, 714 F.2d 1207 (3d Cir.1983). A letter of credit called for the bank to pay S on S's certification that invoices for S's sales to B had not been paid. The bank refused to pay on the basis of evidence from B that the invoices covered by the bank had been paid. A majority of the court, per Garth, J., ruled that the demand for payment was "fraud in the transaction" under UCC 5–114(2)(b); a dissent, by Adams, J., argued that there was no fraud, and that sustaining the bank's refusal (in contrast to an injunction against payment) further impaired the certainty of payment needed in commercial transactions. See Bank of Newport v. First National Bank & Trust Co., 687 F.2d 1257 (8th Cir.1982) (refusal by issuing bank); Becker, Standby Letters of Credit, Will the Independence of the Credit Survive? 13 U.C.C.L.J. 335 (1981).

(2) General References. See J. Dolan, The Law of Letters of Credit: Commercial and Standby Credits (1984); H. Harfield, Bank Credits and Acceptances (5th ed.1974). For a shorter treatment, see H. Harfield, Letters of Credit (1979). For a comparative work, see B. Kozolchyk, Commercial Letters of Credit in the Americas (1966).

Chapter 6

RISK OF LOSS

SECTION 1. INTRODUCTION

The Problem. Casualty to goods—as by fire, theft, or flood—may occur at any one of several stages in the performance of the sales contract. The casualty may occur on the seller's premises, either after the making of a contract for the sale of specific (identified) goods or after the seller has identified goods as those intended for performance of the contract. More frequently, the loss occurs while the goods are in transit or after their arrival but before the buyer takes possession. Problems can arise even after the buyer receives the goods if casualty occurs during a period of testing or inspection, or following the buyer's rejection (or revocation of acceptance) of the goods on the ground that they were not in conformity with the contract.

Dispute between the seller and buyer is often avoided by the availability of insurance coverage, and sometimes by the legal responsibility of the carrier for damage occurring during transit. Even in these situations, problems may arise as to whether the seller or the buyer has the responsibility to take over and salvage damaged goods, press a claim against the insurer or carrier, and bear any loss from inadequacy in insurance coverage or from limitations on the liability of the carrier. The point at which the risk of loss passes is thus of greater practical significance than would be indicated by the volume of litigation.

In addition, rules on risk of loss may determine whether the seller has performed its warranty and other contractual obligations. Suppose, for instance, that a contract calls for No. 1 wheat and that water damage during the rail shipment makes the wheat grade only No. 4; in such a case the rules on risk of loss in transit will determine whether the buyer has a claim against the seller for breach of contract. Anglo-American statutory formulations do not bother to express this obvious relationship between rules on risk and warranty; the Convention on International Sale of Goods is more articulate: "The seller is liable ... for any lack of conformity which exists at the time when the risk passes to the buyer, even though the lack of conformity becomes apparent only after that time."[1]

Historical Background; Early Common Law. English law, at an early stage, seemed to conclude that risk of loss did not pass to the buyer until the goods were delivered to it. Such was the view expressed in the thirteenth century by Bracton in De Legibus, " ...

---

1. CISG 36(1); see also CISG 36(2), 66.

because in truth, he who has not delivered a thing to the purchaser, is still himself the lord of it;" Bracton illustrated the point with the death of an ox and the burning of a house prior to delivery to the purchaser.[2]

Long before the first codification of English sales law, a different approach had developed. This change probably was not designed to accelerate the transfer to the buyer of risk of loss, but rather to strengthen the buyer's remedies against the seller and against third persons who may attempt to take the goods. The difficulty stemmed from the fact that the buyer had no common law remedy to take the goods from a recalcitrant seller, or from third persons (such as the seller's creditors), unless the buyer could be said to have "property" or "title." A claim for damages against a seller who is plagued by creditors is, of course, of little value; what is needed is a remedy to seize the goods, or a legal claim (e.g., for conversion) against a third person who is not judgment-proof. There is evidence that, to mitigate this deficiency in the common law remedial system, courts at an early date developed the view that when a contract is made for the sale of specific (identified) goods, the buyer thereupon has the "property."[3]

Once it was concluded that the buyer had "property" in the goods, it seemed to follow that it bore the risk if "its" goods were destroyed. The famous 1827 King's Bench decision in Tarling v. Baxter involved the sale of a stack of hay which burned prior to the time for delivery and payment.[4] The opinion by Bayley, J., opened with the basic premise: "It is quite clear that the loss must fall upon him in whom the property was vested at the time when it was destroyed by fire." All that remained was to find where "the property" was located. The answer was that "the property" vested in the buyer when the contract was made, even though the buyer did not have possession and would not have even the right to possession until it paid (or tendered) the price. The opinion recognized that more was at stake than risk of loss: "*All* the consequences resulting from the vesting, of the property follow, *one* of which is, that if it be destroyed, the loss falls upon the vendee." (Emphasis added.) As we have seen, the other consequences included the strong proprietary remedies given to the buyer.[5]

---

2. Bracton, De Legibus, Twiss Ed.1878, Ch. XXVII, p. 493. Compare Glanville, Laws and Customs (Cir.1187–89) Book X, Ch. XIV, 216 (Beames ed. 1900). The joint treatment of goods and realty did not survive later developments in the common law, but to some extent has persisted in civil law formulations.

3. Holdsworth, History of English Law 355–56 (3d ed. 1923). Holdsworth suggests that such remedies led to "the doctrine that a contract of sale of specific goods passes the property in the goods." See also: Blackburn, The Contract of Sale 188–189 (1845); 2 Pollock & Maitland, History of English Law 210 (2d ed. 1898); P. Atiyah, The Rise and Fall of Freedom of Contract 103, 106 (1979) (present ownership, with possession postponed, used as tool for effective future planning).

4. 6 B & C 360, 108 Eng.Rep. 484 (K.B. 1827).

5. Another remedial consequence was that the seller could recover the full price from the buyer in an action of debt, as contrasted with a damage claim in assumpsit. The action of debt was reserved for executed transactions in which the defendant had received a quid pro quo. But this requirement was met by the conclusion that the buyer had the "property" even though it did not have the goods.

"Property" and Risk in the Sale of Goods Act and the Uniform Sales Act. The use of the "property" concept was brought to the New World as part of the common-law heritage, and dominated the handling of sales problems in both England and the United States long before the onset of codification. Chalmers conscientiously transcribed the case-law rules in preparing the (British) Sale of Goods Act (1893)—a set of rules which is on the statute-books in substantial parts of the world.[6] Under Section 20, unless the parties have agreed otherwise, when "the property" in goods "is transferred to the buyer, the goods are at the buyer's risk whether delivery has been made or not." Under Section 17, where there is a contract for the sale of "specific or ascertained" goods, the property is transferred when the parties so intend. Section 18 lays down five rules (when no different intention appears) "for ascertaining the intention of the parties as to the time at which the property in the goods is to pass to the buyer." Rule 1 codifies the approach of Tarling v. Baxter:

> Where there is an unconditional contract for the sale of specific goods, in a deliverable state, the property in the goods passes to the buyer when the contract is made, and it is immaterial whether the time of payment or the time of delivery, or both, be postponed.

In preparing the Uniform Sales Act, Professor Williston closely followed the British model. The general rule that risk of loss passes when "the property" is transferred was placed in Section 22; the rules for ascertaining the parties' intent appear in Article 19—with the rule of the Tarling Case reproduced as Rule 1.[7] The Uniform Sales Act retained the crucial role of "property" in other settings. For example, under Section 66, where the property has passed, the buyer may "maintain any action allowed by law to the owner of goods of similar kind when wrongfully converted or withheld;" under Section 63(1) the seller may bring an action to recover the price (as contrasted with damages for breach of contract) where "the property has passed to the buyer." Thus, the solution of a variety of sales problems under the Uniform Sales Act was entangled with the question whether "the property" in the goods remained with the seller or whether "it" had passed to the buyer.

Difficulty With the "Property" Concept; The Code. "Property" in goods is, of course, a legal conclusion and can serve as a tool for decision only when it is implemented by rules referring to events, such as the making of a contract, completion of an agreed performance, delivery to a carrier, or receipt by a buyer. The "property" concept thus was highly malleable, and probably would have served as well as

---

6. E.g., the provinces of Canada other than Quebec, Australia, New Zealand, India, Pakistan, Singapore, Nigeria, Ghana, Kenya, and various other jurisdictions where the common law tradition was established.

7. The Uniform Sales Act made a significant (and unfortunate) deviation from the British Act by adding as Rule 5 a provision holding risk in transit on the seller where the contract "requires the seller to deliver the goods to the buyer ... or to pay the freight or cost of transportation to the buyer. ..."

any other label for the development of rules addressed to a single problem such as risk of loss. Difficulty, however, developed because this one concept was employed to solve different problems which sometimes called for different solutions. For instance, as we have noted, there was reason to speed the passage of "property" to the buyer to provide him with effective remedies against a recalcitrant seller. Very different practical considerations bear on the question as to who should bear casualty loss while the goods are still held by the seller. The use of "property" in sales law thus suffered from a difficulty that has arisen in various parts of the legal structure when a single concept is pressed into service to solve disparate problems.

The most radical departure of the Sales Article of the Code from the approach of the Uniform Sales Act is the Code's virtual abandonment of "property" (or "title") as a vehicle for deciding sales controversies. Instead, the Code provides separate rules to govern risk, replevin rights, recovery of the full price, and other problems which the Uniform Sales Act referred to the "property" concept. Professor Williston characterized this step as "the most objectionable and irreparable feature" of the Sales Article; even apart from other objections, this was sufficient reason for rejecting Article 2.[8] Most students have come to a different conclusion.[9] The crucial test, of course, is the appropriateness of the Code's rules for concrete situations.[10]

1980 Convention on International Sales of Goods. The Convention provisions on risk of loss are found in Chapter IV. The most important articles are 67 and 69. Article 67 applies when the sales contract involves carriage of goods; the special situation of goods sold while in transit is covered in Article 68. Article 69 applies when the sales contract requires the buyer to come for the goods. For a useful account of the Convention's rules, see Roth, The Passing of Risk, 27 Am.J.Comp.L. 291 (1979).

SECTION 2. CASUALTY IN TWO-PARTY TRANSACTIONS

(A) DOMESTIC UNITED STATES LAW

Introduction. We begin with the structure of the Commercial Code's provisions allocating risk of loss in two-party transactions, sales in which delivery of the goods occurs without the use of third-party carriers. The nature of the problem and the basic rules can be seen in the following problem, which is suggested by the facts of the famous English case of Tarling v. Baxter, discussed in Section 1, supra.

---

8. See Williston, The Law of Sales in the Proposed Uniform Commercial Code, 63 Harv.L.Rev. 561, 569–71 (1950).

9. Corbin, The Uniform Commercial Code—Sales; Should it be Enacted? 59 Yale L.J. 821, 824–27 (1950); Latty, Sales and Title and the Proposed Code, 16 Law & Contemp.Prob. 3 (1951). Some interesting comparisons are provided by Tanikawa, Risk of Loss in Japanese Sales Transactions, 42 Wash.L.Rev. 463 (1967).

10. See White, Evaluating Article 2 of the UCC: A Preliminary Empirical Expedition, 75 Mich.L.Rev. 1262 (1977).

Problem 1. John Smith, a dairy farmer, usually grows a small amount of alfalfa hay to feed to his dairy cows. This summer his alfalfa field did unusually well and he found he had a stack of hay he did not need. On June 1, a neighbor, Brown, came and looked at the stack of hay in Smith's field, and a contract was made for the sale of the stack to Brown for $400; Brown was to pay for the hay and remove it during the first week in July. On June 15, the stack burned.

(a) Smith sues Brown to recover the agreed price of $400. What result? See UCC 2–509; 2–104(1) and the *Martin* case, infra. Would the result be different if the seller was the Smith Alfelde Company?

(b) At the trial, Smith's lawyer calls Smith to the stand and asks questions that would elicit testimony that Brown specifically requested and received assurances that Smith "would hold the hay in the pasture for Brown and would not sell it to anyone else." Brown's lawyer objects to the evidence as irrelevant. Smith's lawyer answered that the evidence was relevant to show that Brown had received the goods under UCC 2–509(3). What ruling? See UCC 2–103(1)(c).

(c) Suppose the fire had occurred on July 10? See UCC 2–503, 2–510.

MARTIN v. MELLAND'S INC.
Supreme Court of North Dakota, 1979.
283 N.W.2d 76.

ERICKSTAD, CHIEF JUSTICE.

The narrow issue on this appeal is who should bear the loss of a truck and an attached haystack mover that was destroyed by fire while in the possession of the plaintiff, Israel Martin (Martin), but after certificate of title had been delivered to the defendant, Melland's Inc. (Melland's). The destroyed haymoving unit was to be used as a trade-in for a new haymoving unit that Martin ultimately purchased from Melland's. Martin appeals from a district court judgment dated September 28, 1978, that dismissed his action on the merits after it found that at the time of its destruction Martin was the owner of the unit pursuant to Section 41–02–46(2), N.D.C.C. (Section 2–401 U.C.C.). We hold that Section 41–02–46(2), N.D.C.C., is inapplicable to this case, but we affirm the district court judgment on the grounds that risk of loss had not passed to Melland's pursuant to Section 41–02–57, N.D.C.C. (Section 2–509 U.C.C.).

On June 11, 1974, Martin entered into a written agreement with Melland's, a farm implement dealer, to purchase a truck and attached haystack mover for the total purchase price of $35,389. Martin was given a trade-in allowance of $17,389 on his old unit, leaving a balance owing of $18,000 plus sales tax of $720 or a total balance of $18,720. The agreement provided that Martin "mail or bring title" to the old unit to Melland's "this week." Martin mailed the certificate of title to Melland's pursuant to the agreement, but he was allowed to retain the use and possession of the old unit "until they had the new one ready." The new unit was not expected to be ready for two to three months because it required certain modifications. During this interim period, Melland's performed minor repairs to the trade-in unit on two occasions without charging Martin for the repairs.

Fire destroyed the truck and the haymoving unit in early August, 1974, while Martin was moving hay. The parties did not have any agreement regarding insurance or risk of loss on the unit and Martin's insurance on the trade-in unit had lapsed. Melland's refused Martin's demand for his new unit and Martin brought this suit. The parties subsequently entered into an agreement by which Martin purchased the new unit, but they reserved their rights in any lawsuit arising out of the prior incident.

The district court found "that although the Plaintiff [Martin] executed the title to the ... [haymoving unit], he did not relinquish possession of the same and therefore the Plaintiff was the owner of said truck at the time the fire occurred pursuant to [UCC 2–401]."

Martin argues that the district court erroneously applied ... [§ 2–401 U.C.C.], regarding passage of title, to this case and that ... [§ 2–509 U.C.C.], which deals with risk of loss in the absence of breach, should have been applied instead. Martin argues further that title (apparently pursuant to [UCC 2–401(1)]) and risk of loss passed to Melland's and the property was then merely bailed back to Martin who held it as a bailee. Martin submits that this is supported by the fact that Melland's performed minor repairs on the old unit following the passage of title without charging Martin for the repairs. Melland's responds that [UCC 2–401(2)], governs this case and that the district court's determination of the issue should be affirmed.

One of the hallmarks of the pre-Code law of sales was its emphasis on the concept of title. The location of title was used to determine, among other things, risk of loss, insurable interest, place and time for measuring damages, and the applicable law in an interstate transaction. This single title or "lump" title concept proved unsatisfactory because of the different policy considerations involved in each of the situations that title was made to govern. Furthermore, the concept of single title did not reflect modern commercial practices, i.e. although the single title concept worked well for "cash-on-the-barrelhead sales," the introduction of deferred payments, security agreements, financing from third parties, or delivery by carrier required a fluid concept of title with bits and pieces held by all parties to the transaction.

Thus the concept of title under the U.C.C. is of decreased importance. The official comment to Section 2–101 U.C.C. [§ 41–02–01, N.D.C.C.] provides in part:

> The arrangement of the present Article is in terms of contract for sale and the various steps of its performance. The legal consequences are stated as following directly from the contract and action taken under it without resorting to the idea of when proper-

ty or title passed or was to pass as being the determining factor. The purpose is to avoid making practical issues between practical men turn upon the location of an intangible something, the passing of which no man can prove by evidence and to substitute for such abstractions proof of words and actions of a tangible character. Uniform Commercial Code (U.L.A.) § 2–101.

Section 41–02–46, N.D.C.C. (§ 2–401 U.C.C.), which the district court applied in this case, provides in relevant part:

> Each provision of this chapter with regard to the rights, obligations and remedies of the seller, the buyer, purchasers or other third parties applies irrespective of title to the goods except where the provision refers to such title. Insofar as situations are not covered by the other provisions of this chapter and matters concerning title become material the following rules apply ...

[UCC 2–509] is an "other provision of this chapter" and is applicable to this case without regard to the location of title. Comment one to Section 2–509 U.C.C. provides that "the underlying theory of these sections on risk of loss is the adoption of the contractual approach rather than an arbitrary shifting of the risk with the 'property' in the goods."

. . .

Before addressing the risk of loss question in conjunction with [UCC 2–509], it is necessary to determine the posture of the parties with regard to the trade-in unit, i.e. who is the buyer and the seller and how are the responsibilities allocated. It is clear that a barter or trade-in is considered a sale and is therefore subject to the Uniform Commercial Code. ... It is also clear that the party who owns the trade-in is considered the seller. [UCC 2–304] provides that the "price can be made payable in money or otherwise. If it is payable in whole or in part in goods each party is a seller of the goods which he is to transfer."

. . .

Martin argues that he had already sold the trade-in unit to Melland's and, although he retained possession, he did so in the capacity of a bailee (apparently pursuant to [UCC 2–509(2)]). White and Summers in their hornbook on the Uniform Commercial Code argue that the seller who retains possession should not be considered bailee within Section 2–509:

> "The most common circumstance under which subsection (2) will be applied is that in which the goods are in the hands of a professional bailee (for instance, a warehouseman) and the seller passes a negotiable or a non-negotiable document of title covering the goods to the buyer. That case is simple enough. One question remains, however. Can the seller ever be a 'bailee' as the word is used in subsection (2)? The facts in a pre-Code case ... well illustrate the problem. There seller had reached an agreement with buyer for the sale of a colt. The parties had agreed that the

seller would hold the colt for the buyer and, depending upon the terms of the payment of the price, would or would not charge him a fee for stabling the colt. The colt was killed without any fault on the part of the seller, and the seller sued the buyer for the purchase price. In such a case the seller could certainly argue that he was a bailee and that risk had passed since he had acknowledged the buyer's 'right' to possession of goods under (2)(b). The case would be a particularly appealing one for that argument if the seller were receiving payment from the buyer for the boarding of the horse.

We believe that such an interpretation of the word bailee should be rejected by the courts, and except in circumstances which we cannot now conceive, a seller should not ever be regarded as a bailee. To allow sellers in possession of goods already sold to argue that they are bailees and that the risk of loss in such cases is governed by subsection (2) would undermine one of the basic policies of the Code's risk of loss scheme. As we have pointed out, the draftsmen intended to leave the risk on the seller in many circumstances in which the risk would have jumped to the buyer under prior law. The theory was that a seller with possession should have the burden of taking care of the goods and is more likely to insure them against loss.

If we accept such sellers' arguments, that is, that they are bailees under subsection (2) because of their possession of the goods sold or because of a clause in the sale's agreement, we will be back where we started from, for in bailee cases the risk jumps under (2)(b) on his 'acknowledgment' of the buyer's right to possession. By hypothesis our seller has acknowledged the buyer's right and is simply holding the goods at buyer's disposal. Thus, to accomplish the draftsmen's purpose and leave risk on the seller in possession, we believe that one should find only non-sellers to be 'bailees' as that term is used in 2–509(2). Notwithstanding the fact that a seller retains possession of goods already sold and that he has a term in his sale's contract which characterizes him as a "bailee" we would argue that he is not a bailee for the purposes of subsection (2) of 2–509 and would analyze his situation under subsection (1) or subsection (3) of 2–509." J. White & R. Summers, Handbook of the Law Under the Uniform Commercial Code, 144–45 (1972) ...

It is undisputed that the contract did not require or authorize shipment by carrier pursuant to [UCC 2–509(1)]; therefore, the residue section, subsection 3, is applicable:

> In any case not within subsection 1 or 2, the risk of loss passes to the buyer on his receipt of the goods if the seller is a merchant; otherwise the risk passes to the buyer on tender of delivery.

Martin admits that he is not a merchant; therefore, it is necessary to determine if Martin tendered delivery of the trade-in unit to Melland's. Tender is defined in [UCC 2–503(1)] ... .

It is clear that the trade-in unit was not tendered to Melland's in this case. The parties agreed that Martin would keep the old unit "until they had the new one ready." ...

We hold that Martin did not tender delivery of the trade-in truck and haystack mover to Melland's pursuant to (§ 2–509 U.C.C.); consequently, Martin must bear the loss.

We affirm the district court judgment.

Notes

(1) Insurance Coverage. Comment 3 declares that the underlying theory of UCC 2–509(3) is based on expectations as to casualty insurance coverage on the goods. Merchants, it is said, can be expected to have effective coverage on merchandise in their possession, while buyers cannot be expected to have insurance on property purchased but not yet delivered. This follows from standard fire and casualty insurance policies, sold to business concerns, that provide coverage for specified buildings including, generally, all contents. Policies typically include expressly "property sold but not removed."[1] Does either the text of 2–509(3) or the Comment's theoretical explanation state or imply the further rule that merchant-sellers may obtain relief for the loss from their insurance carriers primarily or exclusively?

(2) Effect of Casualty on Parties' Contract Obligations: UCC 2–613. The Commercial Code does not declare, in 2–509, that sellers are discharged of obligation to deliver because certain goods have been lost or damaged while the risk of loss was on sellers. Under contracts of sale, there are a number of possibilities that bear on the question of discharge. (a) The goods lost or damaged were the only goods that the seller might have tendered properly under the contract. (b) The goods lost or damaged were part of a supply of substitutable goods, any of which the seller might have tendered properly under the contract, but the seller had identified the specific goods lost or damaged as those it planned to deliver. (c) The goods lost or damaged were among a supply of substitutable goods, but the seller had not yet identified any specific goods lost or damaged as those it planned to deliver. Should seller be discharged from its contractual obligation in any or all of these circumstances?

The Code provides a partial answer in UCC 2–613, which provides that contracts may be totally or partially "avoided" depending upon the degree of the physical loss. When contracts are avoided, according to Comment 1, the parties are relieved from obligation. Section 2–613 fits, to large extent, the first of the three circumstances we hyothesized. Would 2–613 apply on the facts of *Martin?*[2] If so, did Melland's have a

---

1. In recent years, business concerns have had access to even broader insurance coverage through "multiple line" or "package" policies.

2. Query: Could Melland's Inc. argue persuasively that Martin's allowing the insurance coverage to lapse was a "fault" that should deprive him of the protection of 2–613?

claim against Martin for breach of his promise to deliver the haystack mover? What line of reasoning leads to the conclusion that Melland's should be excused from performing its promise to deliver the new haystack mover? If Martin had not allowed the insurance coverage to lapse and tendered the insurance proceeds plus $18,720 (the agreed cash balance owed) to Melland's, could Melland's refuse to deliver the new haystack mover without being in breach of contract?

What happens to the contract obligations of sellers who have incurred risk of loss but whose contracts are not avoided under 2–613? See UCC 2–615.

(3) **Insurance Carrier Subrogation.** A seller who suffers loss or casualty to goods on which it has effective insurance coverage is likely to submit a claim under the insurance policy even if the risk of loss has passed to the buyer. If an insurance company pays a claim, may it seek to be subrogated to seller's claim for the price under UCC 2–709(1)? Would seller be entitled to the proceeds of the policy from the insurance company and recovery of the price from the buyer? Should it matter whether the buyer has caused the loss or casualty? These interrelated questions have been answered most clearly in the context of real property transactions. In an executory contract, if only the vendor has effective insurance on property that suffers loss or casualty after risk of loss has passed to the vendee, the vendor's insurance should ultimately benefit the vendee. See R. Keeton & A. Widiss, Insurance Law 324 (1988).

(4) **Insurance at Less Than Market Value.** Typically, insurance companies do not insure goods for the full market value. When insureds do not retain significant risk, the insurers face what is commonly called moral hazard. Thus sellers who recover on their insurance policies are likely to receive less compensation than they would have received from their buyers under the sales contracts. On what theory is the difference between insured coverage and contract price (or market value) allocated between sellers and buyers? See UCC 2–510(1) and (3)?

(5) **Risk of Loss in Non–merchant Seller Transactions.** The most natural transactional description of the parties in the *Martin* case would characterize the farmer, Martin, as the buyer, and the dealer, Melland's Inc., as the seller. In trade-in transactions, however, each party is both a seller and buyer of the separate goods involved. See UCC 2–304(1). For purposes of risk of loss analysis under UCC 2–509(3), would the owner of a good being traded in be a merchant? UCC 2–104(1). If not, is the contention plausible that he had made a tender of delivery to the dealer who was not yet prepared to tender the reciprocal performance? UCC 2–503(1), 2–511(1).

How should UCC 2–509(3) be applied when trade-in equipment is lost or damaged after contract but before completed performance? Is the underlying theory that allocates risk on expectation of insurance coverage appropriate in this context? Would it be reasonable to fashion a risk of loss rule on the expectation that non-merchant sellers of trade-in goods will have fire and casualty insurance coverage on things of sufficient value to be worth trading in? Does 2–509(3) permit such a rule to be fashioned?

In *Martin*, the farmer had effective insurance at the time of contract, but allowed that insurance to lapse. Whatever the general rule on risk of loss for trade-ins, should a decision to drop coverage, without notifying the dealer, affect the allocation of risk of loss in this particular situation?

Problem 2. S Company made a contract for the sale to B of a specified machine tool which S had been using in its manufacturing operations; prior to this transaction S had never sold a machine tool. The contract permitted B to remove the tool within a month. One week after the contract was made, the tool was destroyed by a fire in S's plant. Both S and B are insured under the standard fire policy. How should the interests of the parties be adjusted?

The Permanent Editorial Board Study Group on UCC Article 2 recommended that the Commercial Code be revised to eliminate the distinction between merchant and non-merchant sellers. "We assume that the non-merchant seller in possession will be in a much better position than the buyer to obtain insurance." Preliminary Report 148 (1990).

UNITED AIR LINES, INC. v. CONDUCTRON CORP.

Appellate Court of Illinois, First District, 1979.
69 Ill.App.3d 847, 26 Ill.Dec. 344, 387 N.E.2d 1272.

GOLDBERG, PRESIDING JUSTICE:

United Air Lines, Inc. (plaintiff), brought an action for breach of contract against Conductron Corporation, McDonnell Douglas Electronics Company, a subsidiary of McDonnell Douglas Corporation, and McDonnell Douglas Corporation (defendants). ... The case involves sale by defendants to plaintiff of an aircraft flight simulator. This machine was destroyed by fire while on plaintiff's property. [At the time of the fire, plaintiff had paid $1,043,434.33 as partial payment of the purchase price. Plaintiff sought recovery of its payments, liquidated damages for defendants' breach of contract, and interest.] The trial court entered summary judgment in favor of plaintiff for $1,326,573.20. Defendants appeal.

Defendants contend that the trial court erred in entering summary judgment for plaintiff because the risk of loss of the simulator was upon plaintiff at the time of its destruction. ...

Plaintiff contends that at the time the simulator was destroyed the risk of loss was upon defendants. In this regard, plaintiff urges that defendants defaulted under the terms of the contract by failing to deliver a conforming aircraft flight simulator; this default was never cured; the simulator was never accepted by plaintiff because of its deficiencies and plaintiff at all times retained the right of rejection. . . .

Many of the facts which appear from the pleadings, interrogatories, depositions, and affidavits are undisputed. The purchase agreement between plaintiff and defendants, some 65 pages in length, was executed on December 30, 1966. The agreement contains 19 articles and was supplemented by a number of change orders. It required defendants to deliver a Boeing 727 digital flight simulator to plaintiff on January 13, 1968. A flight simulator is a highly sophisticated electromechanical device operated by computers. It is designed to simulate the experiences of a pilot in the cockpit of a jet airplane during flight. As flight simulators are used for training pilots, they must meet the requirements necessary for approval by the Federal Aviation Administration (FAA). The contract so provided. In addition the contract provided that the simulator would conform to plaintiff's specifications.

The original contract provided for inspection and testing of the simulator by plaintiff at defendants' plant prior to its shipment to plaintiff's Flight Training Center in Denver, Colorado. The defendants agreed to correct any deficiency or discrepancy appearing from such inspection. The agreement further provided that when delivery of the simulator was made title would pass to plaintiff but that such delivery would not constitute acceptance of the simulator by plaintiff. Final acceptance by plaintiff was subject to satisfactory completion and also to certification by the FAA.

Defendants failed to complete fabrication of the simulator by the agreed upon date. This resulted in a request by plaintiff that the simulator be delivered to the plaintiff's training center in Colorado for the testing process which, under the original agreement, could have been completed at defendants' plant. On February 20, 1969, the parties entered into a modification of the contract referred to as Change Order Number 3. This order provided for disassembly of the machine, its delivery to plaintiff by common carrier not later than February 28, 1969, and reassembly by defendants on plaintiff's premises not later than March 15, 1969. From July 1, 1969 to August 1, 1969, the simulator was to be available to plaintiff for demonstration purposes and for correction by defendants of deviations noted by plaintiff in the above mentioned testing. The documents stated that in the event the defendants were unable satisfactorily to correct all deviations prior to November 1, 1969, the plaintiff would have the right to cancel the agreement and receive a refund of all payments made to the defendants as buyer plus liquidated damages. The Change Order also gave plaintiff the right to use the simulator for personnel training purposes.

While the simulator was still in possession of defendants upon their facilities, plaintiff's personnel noted some 647 deficiencies in its operation. These difficulties were recorded and reported to defendants by means of written reports referred to as "squak sheets." The simulator was delivered to plaintiff's facility and was reassembled by defendants on March 14, 1969, in accordance with Change Order Number 3. Since the machine had not received FAA approval, it could not be used as an aircraft flight simulator. It was used for training purposes to acquaint and familiarize pilots with instrument location in the cabin of a Boeing 727 aircraft.

On April 18, 1969, the simulator was tested for 10 hours by two of plaintiff's test pilots. About 10 p.m. a fire was discovered in the machine. The simulator was substantially damaged. The origin of the fire is unknown. After the fire, plaintiff requested that defendants dismantle and ship the simulator back to their plant for repairs at plaintiff's expense. On May 16, 1969, plaintiff notified defendants that they considered there was a breach by defendants of the warranties contained in the purchase agreement. On June 4, 1969, the parties amended the agreement by Change Order Number 4. This document provided that the plaintiff would receive $60,000 as liquidated damages for the late delivery of the simulator to be deducted from the remaining payments due defendants. Plaintiff commenced this action on May 11, 1973, seeking rescission of the contract and damages. On January 28, 1977, plaintiff filed Count VII as an amendment to the complaint. This amendment alleged that the risk of loss of the simulator was upon defendants at the time it was destroyed.

... Summary judgment in favor of plaintiff was entered by the trial court based on the theory that the simulator had never been accepted by plaintiff and, therefore, the risk of loss remained upon defendants. The order allowed plaintiff $1,043,434.33 as a refund of partial payments made, $60,000 as liquidated damages for delay and prejudgment interest of $223,138.78; a total of $1,326,573.20. No issue is raised on computation of these damages.

...

III.

We turn next to the merits of summary judgment in favor of plaintiff based on the theory that defendants should bear the risk of loss for the destruction of the simulator. ...

To evaluate the risk of loss issue, attention must be given to the impact of both the Uniform Commercial Code and the contract terms. Section 2–510 of the Code (Ill.Rev.Stat.1977, ch. 26, par. 2–510(1)), provides:

> (1) Where a tender or delivery of goods so fails to conform to the contract as to give a right of rejection the risk of their loss remains on the seller until cure or acceptance.

Few cases involve this section of the Code and those that do merely cite the Code with little explanation. ... The official Uniform Commercial Code Comment provides some guidance by stating that the purpose of this section is to make clear that "the seller by his individual action cannot shift the risk of loss to the buyer unless his action conforms with all the conditions resting on him under the contract." (S.H.A. ch. 26, par. 2–510(1) at page 398.) Of primary importance, then, is the determination of whether or not the simulator so failed to conform to the contract provisions as to vest the right of rejection in plaintiff and whether or not there was acceptance of the simulator by plaintiff.

The purchase agreement provided in part that the simulator would "accurately and faithfully simulate the configuration and performance of ..." a certain specified Boeing aircraft and that final acceptance of the simulator would be "subject to satisfactory completion of the reliability demonstration requirements ..." and to Federal Aviation Administration certification. The affidavit of John Darley, an employee of plaintiff who tests and evaluates flight simulators to determine whether they meet plaintiff's and the FAA specifications, states that the simulator at no time met those requirements and that plaintiff was never able to begin acceptance testing. His affidavit states clearly that the machine was destroyed by fire "before that time when United [plaintiff] was to begin acceptance testing ... ." The affidavit of Phil C. Christy, employed by plaintiff as a technical assistant regarding simulators, reaffirms that as late as February 1969 there were "numerous discrepancies" in the operation of the simulator. These affidavits stand uncontradicted by counteraffidavit. Therefore they "are admitted and must be taken as true." ... On February 23, 1977, J.M. Gardner, Director of Contracts & Pricing for defendant McDonnell Douglas Electronics Company wrote a letter to plaintiff's attorney in which he stated that the simulator was "destroyed prior to final acceptance."

Defendants contend that Change Order Number 3, which provided for delivery of the simulator at plaintiff's training center in Denver, resulted in waiver of plaintiff's right to object to predelivery nonconformities. We reject this contention. The Change Order simply provides that the testing and inspection, which under the original agreement would have occurred at defendants' plant, would take place in Denver. Sections of the original agreement which provide that delivery does not constitute acceptance remain unchanged by this Change Order Number 3. Also, the language of the Change Order that testing and inspection would be completed in Denver and that the seller would have access to the simulator to demonstrate compliance are inconsistent with the idea that plaintiff had waived the right to object to nonconformity of the simulator.

Defendants do not contest the fact that there were technical difficulties with the simulator, as evidenced by the hundreds of discrepancy reports, actually 645, prepared by plaintiff's employees during the testing period. Instead, defendants stress the complex nature of the device and urge that plaintiff accepted the simulator despite its manifest deficiencies. In support of this contention defendants look to the six week period of inspection of the simulator in Denver and cite Uniform Commercial Code section 2–606 (Ill.Rev.Stat.1977, ch. 26, par. 2–606), which provides:

Acceptance of goods occurs when the buyer

(a) after a reasonable opportunity to inspect the goods signifies to the seller that the goods are conforming or that he will take or retain them in spite of their non-conformity; or

(b) fails to make an effective rejection (subsection (1) of Section 2–602), but such acceptance does not occur until the buyer has had a reasonable opportunity to inspect them; or

(c) does any act inconsistent with the seller's ownership; but if such act is wrongful as against the seller it is an acceptance only if ratified by him.

Defendants thus wish this court to hold that plaintiff had a reasonable opportunity to inspect the simulator and to reject it prior to its destruction. This approach completely ignores the terms of the contract. The purpose of the Uniform Commercial Code is set forth in section 1–102 (Ill.Rev.Stat.1977, ch. 26, par. 1–102), which states that the provisions of the act may be varied by agreement. This court expressed the same principle in First Bank & Trust Co., Palatine v. Post (1973), 10 Ill.App.3d 127, 131, 293 N.E.2d 907, 910, where we stated:

[t]he Uniform Commercial Code was enacted to provide a general uniformity in commercial transactions conducted in this state and was never intended to be used by courts to create a result that is contrary to the clearly understood intentions of the original parties.

The clear intent of the parties before this court, as stated in the purchase agreement, was that physical delivery of the simulator and payments received by the defendants were not to constitute acceptance of the simulator. Acceptance was to be predicated on successful completion of acceptance testing and also upon receipt of FAA certification. The contract terms definitely anticipated and sanctioned use of the simulator by plaintiff to enable it to determine whether this complex and expensive device met the contract specifications. If use of goods is necessary to allow proper evaluation of them, such use does not constitute acceptance. . . .

This record shows that the simulator at no time conformed to the specifications agreed to in the purchase agreement and it remained nonconforming until its destruction. Although plaintiff had use and possession of the simulator for six weeks that arrangement was expressly sanctioned by the contract to allow testing. Retention of the simulator for testing purposes did not constitute acceptance so as to shift the risk of loss to the plaintiff. The simulator was destroyed before completion of acceptance testing and before receipt of FAA certification. Both were conditions precedent to acceptance of the simulator. In this situation the risk of loss remained on the defendants as seller. On the issue of risk of loss, there is no genuine issue regarding any material fact. On the contrary, in our opinion, plaintiff's right to summary judgment in this regard is clear beyond question. We conclude that the plaintiff is entitled to summary judgment as a matter of law.

. . .

Judgment affirmed.

Notes

(1) Risk of Loss After Buyers Have Received Goods. Assuming that UCC 2–509(3) governs passage of the risk of loss on the facts of *United Air Lines,* the merchant-seller provision provides that risk passes to the buyer on "receipt of the goods." "Receipt" means "taking physical possession" of goods. UCC 2–103. Without referring to 2–509, the court analyzed the case not in terms of buyer's receipt of the simulator, but in terms of buyer's acceptance of it. On what basis could the court determine that risk of loss remained upon sellers until buyer accepted the simulator? Should UCC 2–509(3) be read to mean that risk of loss passes to a buyer only upon receipt of *conforming* goods? See the caption to UCC 2–509 and UCC 1–109.

The court in *United Air Lines* based its opinion on UCC 2–510(1). Does this section apply to the facts of that case? When Conductron delivered the simulator to United Air Lines pursuant to Change Order Number 3, did the parties expect that it would conform to the contract requirements? Was Conductron then in breach? Was Conductron in breach when the fire occurred on April 18? If Conductron was not in breach, is UCC 2–510 pertinent? (We consider UCC 2–510 further after the following case.)

If neither 2–509(3) nor 2–510(1) is applicable, what risk of loss rule does apply?

(2) Alternative Analysis Under UCC 2–711(1). Why should risk-of-loss analysis be used at all in a case like *United Air Lines?* Buyer seeks to recover so much of the price as has been paid plus damages, remedies available under UCC 2–711(1) "where the seller fails to make delivery ... or the buyer rightfully rejects [the goods]." United Air Lines would not accept the fire-damaged simulator; if Conductron tendered the simulator in that condition, United Air Lines would certainly reject it. If Conductron fails to tender a conforming simulator within the time permitted under the contract, it will have failed to make delivery. Is application of UCC 2–711(1) affected by risk-of-loss rules?

Problem 3. B agreed to buy a mobile home of S. In accordance with the agreement, S put the mobile home in place on B's lot and made the sewer and gas connections. B moved into the home. S had not yet made the furnace and electrical hook-ups when a gas explosion and an ensuing fire destroyed the mobile home. Who bears the loss? See Southland Mobile Home Corp. v. Chyrchel, 255 Ark. 366, 500

S.W.2d 778 (1973); William F. Wilke, Inc. v. Cummins Diesel Engines, Inc., 252 Md. 611, 250 A.2d 886 (1969).

Problem 4. The S Chevrolet Company delivered a car to B under a "Conditional Sales Contract." B paid S $700 in cash and in the contract agreed to pay the balance of $1500 in 15 monthly installments. The contract provided that S held a security interest in the car which S could exercise to enforce its right to receive payment. In addition, the contract provided:

> It is expressly understood and agreed that the title to the above-described automobile shall remain in the seller until the aforesaid sums of money shall be paid as herein provided, and that the seller may at any time, either personally or by agent, using so much force as is necessary, enter in or upon the premises where said automobile may be, with or without the issuance of any writ of replevin, and take possession of said automobile on default in any of the payments herein provided or on failure to comply with one or all of the conditions of this contract.

A month after delivery, the car is wrecked beyond repair without any fault by B. Must he continue to make the payments to S? Does the language of the Conditional Sales Contract evidence an intent by the parties to exercise their power, under UCC 1–102(3), to vary by agreement the Code's rules on risk of loss? Can the policy of the Code be drawn, by analogy, from Sections 2–505; 2–509(1)(a); 1–201(37) (second sentence)? What, apart from constructional aids in the statute, is the most sensible reading of this language? (In actual practice, unless there has been some mishap in the drafting, printing or assembling of the form, the contract will say in so many words that the buyer bears all casualty risks.)

RON MEAD T.V. & APPLIANCE v. LEGENDARY HOMES, INC.

Oklahoma Court of Appeals, Division Three, 1987.
746 P.2d 1163.

HANSEN, PRESIDING JUDGE

Plaintiff, Ron Mead, is a retail merchant selling household appliances. Defendant, Legendary Homes, is a home builder. Defendant purchased appliances from Plaintiff for installation in one of its homes. The appliances were to be delivered on February 1, 1984. At five o'clock on that day the appliances had not been delivered. Defendant closed the home and left. Sometime between five and six-thirty Plaintiff delivered the appliances. No one was at the home so the deliveryman put the appliances in the garage. During the night someone stole the appliances.

Defendant denied it was responsible for the loss and refused to pay Plaintiff for the appliances. This suit resulted.

After a non-jury trial the court issued a "Memorandum Opinion" finding § 2–509 of the Uniform Commercial Code, 12A O.S. 1981 controlled. This section provides: "The risk of loss passes to the Buyer on his receipt of the goods." The trial court found Defendant had not received the goods, thus the risk of loss remained with Plaintiff. Plaintiff appeals the judgment rendered in favor of Defendant.

* * *

Plaintiff ... submits the trial court erred in concluding Plaintiff did not establish usage of trade in leaving appliances unattended at a building site. The trial court found the record was void of any evidence which would show the method of delivery used by Plaintiff was pursuant to a "course of dealing" between the parties which would waive or excuse the requirements of 12A O.S. 1981 § 2–503.

Section 1–205(2) defines "usage of trade" as any "practice or method of dealing having such regularity of observance in a place, vocation or trade as to justify an expectation that it will be observed with respect to the transaction in question." Although there was testimony some builders allow deliveries to be made to unattended job sites, nothing indicated such practice was uniformly observed after working hours unless specifically agreed to by the parties.

Although there was conflicting testimony between witnesses whether Defendant advised Plaintiff to deliver the appliances before noon, nothing appears in the record to indicate there was any agreement the appliances would be accepted after hours.

Section 2–103 defines "receipt" of goods as taking physical possession of them. We agree with the trial court "(t)he act by the deliveryman of placing the goods in an unlocked garage, in a house under construction, and then locking the door did not give the Buyer the opportunity to take physical possession (of them)."

Credibility of witnesses and weight and value to be given to their testimony is for the trial court on waiver of a jury, and conclusions there reached will not be disturbed on appeal, unless appearing clearly to be based upon caprice or to be without any reasonable foundation. Accordingly, the trial court is affirmed.

* * *

HUNTER, J. and BAILEY, J. concur.

Notes

(1) Basis of the Decision: Analytical Confusion. The problem presented in this case can be analyzed in three ways: under the Commercial Code's rules for tender of delivery or under the Code's two rules allocating risk of loss. The Oklahoma courts, and presumably the lawyers arguing the case, did not resolve which of these standards they were applying.

If seller had not made a tender of delivery, buyer had no duty to pay the price. UCC 2–507(1). Seller tried and failed to establish a course of dealing or trade usage that permitted tender of delivery by the method it employed. Thus, buyer's duty to pay the price never matured.

Alternatively, the case can be analyzed under the risk of loss rules in 2–509(3). Since seller unquestionably was a merchant, risk of loss would pass only on receipt of the goods. The appellate court, citing 2–103, concludes that "receipt" had not occurred. Seller's action for the price depends on risk of loss passing. 2–709(1)(a). Absent receipt, risk of loss did not pass, and the price action must fail.

A third line of analysis has been offered:

> Although the court manages to properly conclude that the risk of loss had not passed to the buyer, it does so despite misapplication of the Code's risk of loss provisions. Both the trial court and the court of appeals incorrectly cited section 2–509 as the controlling section. Because of the improper tender by the seller, the risk of loss issue in this case should have been resolved by application of section 2–510(1). Regardless of whether the goods have been received, under section 2–510(1) the buyer does not bear risk of loss where the tender is so nonconforming as to give a right of rejection. ... One must wonder how this case would have ended if, all other things being the same, the court had decided that the buyer had received the goods. In view of the court's apparent ignorance of both section 2–510 and the immateriality of the possession issue, it would seem that, notwithstanding the defective tender, the seller would have wrongfully prevailed.

Frisch and Wladis, Uniform Commercial Code Annual Survey: General Provisions, Sales, Bulk Transfers, and Documents of Title, 44 Bus. Law. 1445, 1467 (1989).

Query: Which, if any, of these lines of analysis is correct?

(2) Proposed Repeal of UCC 2–510. The Permanent Editorial Board Study Group on UCC Article 2 found numerous flaws in 2–510 and recommended that it be repealed. Preliminary Report 149 (1990). The Study Group noted that the section requires no showing of any causal connection between the breach and the loss and may allocate risk from the party in the best position to insure the goods to the party who is not. Moreover, the Study Group declared, the section is "complex, incomplete and difficult to apply." Id. See also Howard, Allocation of Risk of Loss Under the UCC: A Transactional Evaluation of §§ 2–509 and 2–510, 15 U.C.C.L.J. 334 (1983).

(3) Sellers' Price Action. The remedy sought in *Ron Mead* was the contract price for the appliances. On what basis could seller seek to recover the price of the stolen appliances? See UCC 2–709(1)(a). Could seller argue successfully that it was entitled to the price on the ground that the appliances were "conforming goods" even though the manner of their tender did not conform to the contract?

MULTIPLASTICS, INC. v. ARCH INDUSTRIES, INC.

Supreme Court of Connecticut, 1974.
166 Conn. 280, 348 A.2d 618.

BOGDANSKI, J.

The plaintiff, Multiplastics, Inc., brought this action to recover damages from the defendant, Arch Industries, Inc., for the breach of a contract to purchase 40,000 pounds of plastic pellets. From a judgment rendered for the plaintiff, the defendant has appealed to this court.

The facts may be summarized as follows: The plaintiff, a manufacturer of plastic resin pellets, agreed with the defendant on June 30, 1971, to manufacture and deliver 40,000 pounds of brown polystyrene plastic pellets for nineteen cents a pound. The pellets were specially made for the defendant, who agreed to accept delivery at the rate of 1000 pounds per day after completion of production. The defendant's confirming order contained the notation "make and hold for release. Confirmation." The plaintiff produced the order of pellets within two weeks and requested release orders from the defendant. The defendant refused to issue the release orders, citing labor difficulties and its vacation schedule. On August 18, 1971, the plaintiff sent the defendant the following letter: "Against P.O. 0946, we produced 40,000 lbs. of brown high impact styrene, and you have issued no releases. You indicated to us that you would be using 1,000 lbs. of each per day. We have warehoused these products for more than forty days, as we agreed to do. However, we cannot warehouse these products indefinitely, and request that you send us shipping instructions. We have done everything we agreed to do." After August 18, 1971, the plaintiff made numerous telephone calls to the defendant to seek payment and delivery instructions. In response, beginning August 20, 1971, the defendant agreed to issue release orders but in fact never did.

On September 22, 1971, the plaintiff's plant, containing the pellets manufactured for the defendant, was destroyed by fire. The plaintiff's fire insurance did not cover the loss of the pellets. The plaintiff brought this action against the defendant to recover the contract price.

The trial court concluded that the plaintiff made a valid tender of delivery by its letter of August 18, 1971, and by its subsequent requests for delivery instructions; that the defendant repudiated and breached the contract by refusing to accept delivery on August 20, 1971; that the period from August 20, 1971, to September 22, 1971, was not a commercially unreasonable time for the plaintiff to treat the risk of loss as resting on the defendant under General Statutes § 42a–2–510(3), and that the plaintiff was entitled to recover the contract price plus interest.

General Statutes § 42a–2–510, entitled "Effect of breach on risk of loss," reads, in pertinent part, as follows: "(3) Where the buyer as to conforming goods already identified to the contract for sale repudiates or is otherwise in breach before risk of their loss has passed to him, the seller may to the extent of any deficiency in his effective insurance coverage treat the risk of loss as resting on the buyer for a commercially reasonable time." The defendant contends that § 42a–2–510 is not applicable because its failure to issue delivery instructions did not constitute either a repudiation or a breach of the agreement. The defendant also argues that even if § 42a–2–510 were applicable, the period from August 20, 1971, to September 22, 1971, was not a commercially reasonable period of time within which to treat the risk of loss as resting on the buyer. The defendant does not claim that the destroyed pellets were not "conforming goods already identified to the contract for sale," as required by General Statutes § 42a–2–510(3), nor does it protest the computation of damages. With regard to recovery of the price of goods and incidental damages, see General Statutes § 42a–2–709(1)(a).

The trial court's conclusion that the defendant was in breach is supported by its finding that the defendant agreed to accept delivery of the pellets at the rate of 1000 pounds per day after completion of production. The defendant argues that since the confirming order instructed the defendant to "make and hold for release," the contract did not specify an exact delivery date. This argument fails, however, because nothing in the finding suggests that the notation in the confirming order was part of the agreement between the parties. Since, as the trial court found, the plaintiff made a proper tender of delivery, beginning with its letter of August 18, 1971, the plaintiff was entitled to acceptance of the goods and to payment according to the contract. General Statutes §§ 42a–2–507(1), 42a–2–307.

The defendant argues that its failure to issue delivery instructions did not suffice to repudiate the contract because repudiation of an executory promise requires, first, an absolute and unequivocal renunciation by the promisor, and, second, an unambiguous acceptance of the repudiation by the promisee. .... Anticipatory repudiation is now governed by General Statutes §§ 42a–2–609 to 42a–2–611, which in some respects alter the prior law on the subject. The present case does not involve repudiation of an executory promise, however, since the defendant breached the contract by failing to accept the goods when acceptance became due.

The defendant next claims that the plaintiff acquiesced in the defendant's refusal to accept delivery by continuing to urge compliance with the contract and by failing to pursue any of the remedies provided aggrieved sellers by General Statutes § 42a–2–703. In essence, the defendant's argument rests on the doctrines of waiver and estoppel, which are available defenses under the Uniform Commercial Code. General Statutes §§ 42a–1–103, 42a–1–107, 42a–2–209; Mercanti v. Persson, 160 Conn. 468, 477–79, 280 A.2d 137 .... . The defendant has not, however, shown those defenses to apply. Waiver is the intentional relinquishment of a known right. ... Its existence is a question of fact for the trier. ... The trial court did not find that the plaintiff intentionally acquiesced in the defendant's breach of their agreement, thereby waiving its right to take advantage of that breach. Indeed, the plaintiff's repeated attempts to secure compliance seem inconsistent with the possibility of waiver. ...

Nor has the defendant made out a case of estoppel. "The two essential elements of estoppel are that 'one party must do or say something which is intended or calculated to induce another to believe in the existence of certain facts and to act on that belief; and the other party, influenced thereby, must change his position or do some act to his injury which he otherwise would not have done.' Dickau v. Glastonbury, 156 Conn. 437, 441, 242 A.2d 777; Pet Car Products, Inc. v. Barnett, 150 Conn. 42, 53, 184 A.2d 797." Mercanti v. Persson, supra, 477. Neither element of estoppel is present in the record of this case. The plaintiff's requests for delivery instructions cannot be said to have misled the defendant into thinking that the plaintiff did not consider their contract breached. In fact, General Statutes § 42a–2–610, entitled "Anticipatory repudiation," specifically provides that the aggrieved seller may "resort to any remedy for breach as provided by section 42a–2–703 ..., even though he has notified the repudiating party that he would await the latter's performance and has urged retraction." Although the present case is not governed by General Statutes § 42a–2–610, that section does demonstrate that the plaintiff's conduct after the defendant refused to accept delivery was not inconsistent with his claim that the contract was breached.

The remaining question is whether, under General Statutes § 42a–2–510(3), the period of time from August 20, 1971, the date of the breach, to September 22, 1971, the date of the fire, was a "commercially reasonable" period within which to treat the risk of loss as resting on the buyer. The trial court concluded that it was "not, on the facts in this case, a commercially unreasonable time," which we take to mean that it was a commercially reasonable period. The time limitation in § 42a–2–510(3) is designed to enable the seller to obtain the additional requisite insurance coverage. ... The trial court's conclusion is tested by the finding. ... Although the finding is not detailed, it supports the conclusion that August 20 to September 22 was a commercially reasonable period within which to place the risk of loss on the defendant. As already stated, the trial court found that the defendant repeatedly agreed to transmit delivery instructions and that the pellets were specially made to fill the defendant's order. Under those circumstances, it was reasonable for the plaintiff to believe that the goods would soon be taken off its hands and so to forego procuring the needed insurance.

We consider it advisable to discuss one additional matter. The trial court concluded that "title" passed to the defendant, and the defendant attacks the conclusion on this appeal. The issue is immaterial to this case. General Statutes § 42a–2–401 states: "Each provision of this article with regard to the rights, obligations and remedies of the seller, the buyer, purchasers or other third parties applies irrespective of title to the goods except where the provision refers to such title." As one student of the Uniform Commercial Code has written: "The single most important innovation of Article 2[of the Uniform Commercial Code] is its restatement of ... [the parties'] responsibilities in terms of operative facts rather than legal conclusions; where pre-Code law looked to 'title' for the definition of rights and remedies, the Code looks to demonstrable realities such as custody, control and professional expertise. This shift in approach is central to the whole philosophy of Article 2. It means that disputes, as they arise, can focus, as does all of the modern law of contracts, upon actual provable circumstances, rather than upon a metaphysical concept of elastic and endlessly fluid dimensions." Peters, "Remedies for Breach of Contracts Relating to the Sale of Goods Under the Uniform Commercial Code: A Roadmap for Article Two," 73 Yale L.J. 199, 201.

There is no error.

In this opinion the other judges concurred.

(B) INTERNATIONAL SALES LAW

Two-party transactions may occur in international sales. The Convention on International Sale of Goods establishes risk of loss rules for this type transaction in Article 69. The general principle is that risk passes when a buyer "takes over the goods." CISG 69(1). This phrase is more clear in its connotation of positive buyer action than is the Code's "receipt." Recall, for example, the conceptual difficulty posed in the *United Air Lines* case. Moreover the Convention standard applies to all sellers. The Convention does not contemplate non-merchant sellers.

The Convention also addresses the possibility that buyers, having opportunity to do so, will fail to "take over" goods. Although the Convention does not generally use the concepts of tender of delivery, it incorporates a similar idea here only for the purpose of allocating risk of loss to such buyers. Risk of loss thus remains on sellers until buyers' failure to take over goods placed at their disposal is breach of contract.

The Convention explicitly relates buyers' duty to pay to the risk of loss rules. Buyers' duty to pay is not discharged if casualty or loss occurs after risk of loss has passed. CISG 66. An inference can be drawn that payment obligations are discharged if risk of loss had not passed.[3] The Convention has no counterpart provision that relates sellers' duty to deliver to the rules of risk of loss. However, the Convention provides broadly that sellers (and buyers) may not be liable for failures to perform if the failures were due to impediments beyond their control. CISG 79.[4]

---

3. Under CISG 66, a buyer is discharged from the obligation to pay the price if the loss or damage is due to an act or omission of the seller.

4. CISG 79 adds other conditions that sellers must meet to be protected from liability.

Problem 5. On June 1, Seller handed over goods to Buyer. Buyer's inspection on June 2 disclosed that the goods were not in conformity with the contract. On June 3 a fire in Buyer's warehouse injured the goods.

(a) Buyer claims damages from Seller for the non-conformity of the goods and for the injury to the goods. What result under CISG? See CISG 36(1), 69(1), 74.

(b) Buyer contends that the non-conformity was so substantial as to constitute a fundamental breach and, on June 4, declares the contract avoided. Assuming that Buyer is correct in characterizing the non-conformity as a fundamental breach, to what remedies is Buyer entitled under CISG? See CISG 70, 81, 84. See also J. Honnold, Uniform Law for International Sales § 383 (2d ed. 1991).

SECTION 3. CASUALTY DURING SHIPMENT

(A) DOMESTIC UNITED STATES LAW

Introduction. In many sales transactions, sellers are authorized or required to ship goods to buyers via carriers. While en route, goods may of course suffer loss or damage. The principal subject in this Section is the allocation of risk of such losses between sellers and buyers. A subordinate question is the extent of the carriers' liability for goods that suffer casualty while in their possession.

Shipment and Destination Contracts. In Chapter 5, we learned that sales contracts that contemplate delivery of goods by carrier are generally characterized as place-of-shipment or at-a-particular-destination contracts. In the former, the cost of transportation is borne by the buyer; in the latter, freight charges are paid by seller. Risk of loss is allocated in the same characterization. UCC 2–509(1).

Under UCC 2–319, sales contracts that use the F.O.B. term are shipment contracts if the term is F.O.B. the place of shipment; seller bears the risk of putting the goods into the carrier's possession. UCC 2–319(1)(a). Risk passes when the goods are duly delivered to the carrier. UCC 2–509(1)(a). Conversely, if the contract term is F.O.B. the place of destination, seller must at its own risk transport the goods to that place. UCC 2–319(1)(b). Risk passes when the goods are there duly tendered. UCC 2–509(1)(b).

Shipping terms commonly associated with water transport pose difficult problems for risk of loss. Even though the price includes the cost of transportation, sellers expressly bear the risk of putting the goods into the carriers' possession, loading the goods on board, or delivering them alongside a vessel, as the terms require. UCC 2–319(1)(b) and (2), 2–320(2) and (3). Contracts that use the terms F.O.B. vessel or F.A.S. can be recognized as shipment contracts; thus the risk passing provision of UCC 2–509(1)(a) applies. However contracts that use the terms C.I.F. and C. & F. cannot easily be characterized as shipment contracts. Nor is it plausible to construe them as destination contracts with risk passing at the place of destination.[1] A different result follows if the term used is "delivery ex-ship." UCC 2–322.

Risk of loss and contract performance problems tend to arise when sales contracts are ambiguous as to whether they are shipment or destination contracts.

Problem 1. Seller Manufacturing Company, in Sellersville, Pennsylvania, has distributed a catalogue giving descriptions and prices for a line of garden tractors which Seller makes and sells. Buyer Garden Supply Company, in Birmingham, Alabama, an enterprise with stores in various cities in Alabama, wired Seller, "Please ship to us in Birmingham, 10 Garden Tractors, Catalogue No. 103X, priced at $1,430 each." Seller replied: "Order accepted. Tractors being shipped this week." Neither the catalogue nor the correspondence dealt with methods or costs of delivery.

Seller promptly hauled the 10 garden tractors in his truck to the freight station of the Conrail Railroad in Sellersville and delivered them to the freight agent in the freight yards. Seller received a "straight" (non-negotiable) bill of lading providing that the goods were "Consigned to Buyer Garden Supply Co., Birmingham, Ala." Freight costs of $310 were noted on the bill of lading as "C.O.D." (Collect on Delivery).

One of the tractors was stolen from the Conrail freight yard in Sellersville. Another was damaged in a freight car en route to Birmingham.

(a) Buyer paid for eight tractors, but refused to pay for the tractor that was stolen or for the damaged tractor. Seller sues for the price of the two tractors. Buyer interposes all available defenses to the price action and, in addition, counterclaims for the freight costs of $610 which he had to pay the railroad in order to receive delivery of the tractors. What result? See UCC 2–509, 2–504, 2–709(1)(a); Pestana v. Karinol Corporation, infra.

(b) Suppose Seller's truck had overturned and burned while the tractors were being taken from Seller's factory to the freight yards. May Seller recover the price for the tractors destroyed by fire?

PESTANA v. KARINOL CORP.
District Court of Appeal of Florida, Third District, 1979.
367 So.2d 1096.

HUBBART, JUDGE.

This is an action for damages based on a contract for the sale of goods. The defendant seller and others prevailed in this action after a non-jury trial in the Circuit Court for the Eleventh Judicial Circuit of Florida. The plaintiff buyer appeals.

---

1. The Code provision on the C.I.F. term imposes a duty on sellers to contract for casualty insurance for the benefit of the buyers. UCC 2–320(2)(c).

The central issue presented for review is whether a contract for the sale of goods, which stipulates the place where the goods sold are to be sent by carrier but contains (a) no explicit provisions allocating the risk of loss while the goods are in the possession of the carrier and (b) no delivery terms such as F.O.B. place of destination, is a shipment contract or a destination contract under the Uniform Commercial Code. We hold that such a contract, without more, constitutes a shipment contract wherein the risk of loss passes to the buyer when the seller duly delivers the goods to the carrier under a reasonable contract of carriage for shipment to the buyer. Accordingly, we affirm.

A

The critical facts of this case are substantially undisputed. On March 4, 1975, Nahim Amar B. [the plaintiff Pedro P. Pestana's decedent herein] who was a resident of Mexico entered into a contract through his authorized representative with the Karinol Corporation [the defendant herein] which is an exporting company licensed to do business in Florida and operating out of Miami. The terms of this contract were embodied in a one page invoice written in Spanish and prepared by the defendant Karinol. By the terms of this contract, the plaintiff's Amar agreed to purchase 64 electronic watches from the defendant Karinol for $6,006. A notation was printed at the bottom of the contract which, translated into English, reads as follows: "Please send the merchandise in cardboard boxes duly strapped with metal bands via air parcel post to Chetumal. Documents to Banco de Commercio De Quintano Roo S.A." There were no provisions in the contract which specifically allocated the risk of loss on the goods sold while in the possession of the carrier; there were also no F.O.B., F.A.S., C.I.F. or C & F terms contained in the contract. See §§ 672.319, 672.320, Fla.Stat. (1977). A 25% downpayment on the purchase price of the goods sold was made prior to shipment.

On April 11, 1975, there is sufficient evidence, although disputed, that the defendant Karinol delivered the watches in two cartons to its agent American International Freight Forwarders, Inc. [the second defendant herein] for forwarding to the plaintiff's decedent Amar. The defendant American insured the two cartons with Fidelity & Casualty Company of New York [the third defendant herein] naming the defendant Karinol as the insured. The defendant American as freight forwarder strapped the cartons in question with metal bands and delivered them to TACA International Airlines consigned to one Bernard Smith, a representative of the plaintiff's decedent, in Belize City, Belize, Central America. The shipment was arranged by Karinol in this manner in accord with a prior understanding between the parties as there were no direct flights from Miami, Florida to Chetumal, Mexico. Mr. Smith was to take custody of the goods on behalf of the plaintiff's decedent in Belize and arrange for their transport by truck to the plaintiff's decedent Amar in Chetumal, Mexico.

On April 15, 1975, the cartons arrived by air in Belize City and were stored by the airline in the customs and air freight cargo room. Mr. Smith was duly notified and thereupon the plaintiff's decedent made payment on the balance due under the contract to the defendant Karinol. On May 2, 1975, Mr. Smith took custody of the cartons after a certain delay was experienced in transferring the cartons to a customs warehouse. Either on that day or shortly thereafter, the cartons were opened by Mr. Smith and customs officials as was required for clearance prior to the truck shipment to Chetumal, Mexico. There were no watches contained in the cartons. The defendant Karinol and its insurance carrier the defendant Fidelity were duly notified, but both eventually refused to make good on the loss.

The plaintiff Pedro P. Pestana, as representative of the Estate of Nahim Amar B., deceased, filed suit against the defendant Karinol as the seller, the defendant American as Karinol's agent freight forwarder, and the defendant Fidelity as the defendant Karinol's insurer. The complaint alleged that the defendant Karinol entered into a contract to ship merchandise from Miami, Florida to Chetumal, Mexico with the plaintiff's decedent, that the defendant American as freight forwarder and agent of the defendant Karinol accepted shipment of such merchandise, that the merchandise was lost, stolen or misplaced while in the care and custody of the defendant Karinol and the defendant American, that the defendants Karinol and American failed to make delivery to the plaintiff's decedent at Chetumal, Mexico, and that there existed a liability policy with the defendant Fidelity for the benefit of the plaintiff's decedent. The complaint sought damages together with court costs and reasonable attorneys fees. All the defendants duly filed answers to the complaint wherein liability was denied. The defendant Karinol filed a cross-complaint against the defendant American. The trial court after a non-jury trial found for all of the defendants in this cause. This appeal follows.

B

There are two types of sales contracts under Florida's Uniform Commercial Code wherein a carrier is used to transport the goods sold: a shipment contract and a destination contract. A shipment contract is considered the normal contract in which the seller is required to send the subject goods by carrier to the buyer but is not required to guarantee delivery thereof at a particular destination. Under a shipment contract, the seller, unless otherwise agreed, must: (1) put the goods sold in the possession of a carrier and make a contract for their transportation as may be reasonable having regard for the nature of the goods and other attendant circumstances, (2) obtain and promptly deliver or tender in due form any document necessary to enable the buyer to obtain possession of the goods or otherwise required by the agreement or by usage of the trade, and (3) promptly notify the buyer of the shipment. On a shipment contract, the risk of loss passes to the buyer when the goods sold are duly delivered to the carrier for shipment to the buyer. §§ 672.503 (Official U.C.C. comment 5), 672.504, 672.509(1), Fla.Stat. (1977). . . .

A destination contract, on the other hand, is considered the variant contract in which the seller specifically agrees to deliver the goods sold to the buyer at a particular destination and to bear the risk of loss of the goods until tender of delivery. This can be accomplished by express provision in the sales contract to that effect or by the use of delivery terms such as F.O.B. (place of destination). Under a destination contract, the seller is required to tender delivery of the goods sold to the buyer at the place of destination. The risk of loss under such a contract passes to the buyer when the goods sold are duly tendered to the buyer at the place of destination while in the possession of the carrier so as to enable the buyer to take delivery. The parties must explicitly agree to a destination contract; otherwise the contract will be considered a shipment contract. §§ 672.319(1)(b), 672.503 (Official U.C.C. comment 5), 672.509(1), Fla.Stat. (1977) . . . .

Where the risk of loss falls on the seller at the time the goods sold are lost or destroyed, the seller is liable in damages to the buyer for non-delivery unless the seller tenders a performance in replacement for the lost or destroyed goods. On the other hand, where the risk of loss falls on the buyer at the time the goods sold are lost or destroyed, the buyer is liable to the seller for the purchase price of the goods sold. White and Summers, Uniform Commercial Code 134 (1972).

C

In the instant case, we deal with the normal shipment contract involving the sale of goods. The defendant Karinol pursuant to this contract agreed to send the goods sold, a shipment of watches, to the plaintiff's decedent in Chetumal, Mexico. There was no specific provision in the contract between the parties which allocated the risk of loss on the goods sold while in transit. In addition, there were no delivery terms such as F.O.B. Chetumal contained in the contract.

All agree that there is sufficient evidence that the defendant Karinol performed its obligations as a seller under the Uniform Commercial Code if this contract is considered a shipment contract. Karinol put the goods sold in the possession of a carrier and made a contract for the goods safe transportation to the plaintiff's decedent; Karinol also promptly notified the plaintiff's decedent of the shipment and tendered to said party the necessary documents to obtain possession of the goods sold.

The plaintiff Pestana contends, however, that the contract herein is a destination contract in which the risk of loss on the goods sold did not pass until delivery on such goods had been tendered to him at Chetumal, Mexico—an event which never occurred. He relies for this position on the notation at the bottom of the contract between the parties which provides that the goods were to be sent to Chetumal, Mexico. We cannot agree. A "send to" or "ship to" term is a part of every contract involving the sale of goods where carriage is contemplated and has no significance in determining whether the contract is a shipment or destination contract for risk of loss purposes. ... As such, the "send to" term contained in this contract cannot, without more, convert this into a destination contract.

It therefore follows that the risk of loss in this case shifted to the plaintiff's decedent as buyer when the defendant Karinol as seller duly delivered the goods to the defendant freight forwarder American under a reasonable contract of carriage for shipment to the plaintiff's decedent in Chetumal, Mexico. The defendant Karinol, its agent the defendant American, and its insurer the defendant Fidelity could not be held liable to the plaintiff in this action. The trial court properly entered judgment in favor of all the defendants herein.

Affirmed.

Notes

(1) Allocation of Freight Costs as Allocation of Risk of Loss. If freight from Sellersville to Buyersville is $12 per ton, quotations of "$100 F.O.B. Sellersville," "$112 F.O.B. Buyersville," and "$112 F.O.B. Sellersville, freight allowed" all have the same effect with respect to the buyer's costs. However, the first and third allocate transit risk to the buyer, while the second allocates transit risk to the seller. It seems likely that the parties, in negotiating the contract, are more likely to concentrate on immediate cost and return factors rather than on the relatively unusual feature of risk of loss. Hence, there is ground for skepticism that choice among the above forms of quotation reflects an express agreement as to risk.

Price quotations that include freight may, on occasion, be employed to meet competition from a seller that is close to the buyer. If a seller wishes to be in a position to quote prices that include freight, but with transit risk allocated to the buyer, how could the order forms be structured? Would it be adequate to include a form clause dealing with risk of loss? Since negotiating agents cannot be expected to remember technical instructions, should the form include a special notation at the point where the price is to be inserted? What would you recommend?

(2) Policy Considerations Relevant to Risk Allocation Rules. Comment 5 to UCC 2–503 regards the "shipment" contract as normal and the "destination" contract as a variant. Under UCC 2–509(1) the "normal" shipment contract places transit risks on the buyer. Are there considerations of policy that bear on this result?

In considering risk allocation while the seller remains in possession, we asked whether the seller or the buyer has the better opportunity to guard against casualty and to insure against loss. Are these considerations significant in transportation cases? It has been suggested that the seller should bear transit loss since he is in a better position to select and bargain with the carrier. In evaluating this argument would it be relevant to inquire into the amenability of railways, truckers and ocean carriers to negotiate concerning the terms and conditions for transport?

Would it be relevant to consider which party can more readily cope with the consequences of transit damage? At which point in the transaction will transit damage be discovered? Is the seller or the buyer in a better position to salvage the goods, assess the damage, and press a claim against the carrier or insurer? Would the answer be the same for (a) raw materials, such as cotton shipped to a textile manufacturer and (b) a complex machine manufactured by the seller?

Note that considerations of policy as to who can most efficiently handle transit losses is relevant not only in the construction of ambiguous contracts but also in the process of negotiating and drafting contract provisions.

Problem 2. Seller agreed to sell Buyer an accumulation of brass scrap, with terms "f.o.b. Seller's city, payable by sight draft on arrival." Seller shipped and took a bill of lading running to "Seller or order." The brass was stolen during transit. Must Buyer pay the price? Does the fact that the bill of lading is a "document of *title*" and ran in Seller's name affect the risk of loss? See UCC 2–509(1)(a) ("even though the shipment is under reservation").

What considerations of policy underlie this result? (Suppose that the bill of lading is to be transferred to the buyer in exchange for payment while the goods are in transit.)

Problem 3. Seller in Seattle and Buyer in Boise made a contract calling for Seller to ship Buyer one hundred bags of "No. 1 Cane Sugar," F.O.B. Seattle. When the shipment was unloaded at Buyer's place of business Buyer inspected the sugar and immediately wired Seller "Sugar grades No. 2, will hold you responsible for reduced value of shipment." The next day the sugar was destroyed by a fire in the buyer's warehouse.

(a) On the above facts, who has risk of loss? See UCC 2–510(1), 2–606(1)(a).

(b) Suppose the buyer had wired: "Sugar grades No. 2. Will reject sugar unless you allow price reduction of 50 cents per hundredweight." If the casualty occurred before Seller replied, who would bear the risk?

Problem 4. Seller is a sugar refiner located in San Francisco; Buyer is a Boston candy manufacturer. Seller and Buyer made a contract for the sale to Buyer of 1000 tons of No. 1 beet sugar at $160 per ton. The contract terms were "C.I.F. Boston, ocean carriage via the Panama Canal. Shipment during June; payment 60 days after arrival of ship in Boston."

During the ocean voyage, water leaked into the hold and seriously damaged half of the sugar. On arrival Buyer noticed not only the water damage, but also concluded that the sugar had been poorly refined and that it contained excessive impurities, so that the sugar graded No. 2 and was unsuitable for use in making candy. The sugar undamaged by water would bring $110 per ton; the water-soaked sugar was worthless. Buyer rejected the entire shipment and refused to pay the price.

(a) Seller sues for the price, and claims that the sugar conformed to the contract when it was loaded on board in San Francisco. Seller also contends that, in any event, the loss from the water damage fell on the Buyer, and that the Buyer may not reject since he cannot return the goods to the Seller in the same condition as when risk of loss passed to the Buyer. What result? See UCC 2–320, 2–509, 2–510, 2–601, 2–709(1)(a).

(b) Assume that Seller delivered No. 1 sugar to the ocean carrier, but had completed delivery to the ship on July 3. As in the above problem, the sugar is seriously damaged in transit by ocean water. Seller sues Buyer for the price. What result?

Note: Liability of Domestic U.S. Carriers

Rail and Truck. Uniform bills of lading used by rail carriers in this country contain the following provision:

> Sec. 1(a) The carrier or party in possession of any of property herein described shall be liable as at common law for any loss thereof or damage thereto, except as hereinafter provided.
>
> (b) No carrier or party in possession of all or any part of the property herein described shall be liable for any loss thereof or damage thereto or delay caused by the Act of God, the public enemy, the authority of law, or the act or default of the shipper or owner, or for natural shrinkage. The carrier's liability shall be that of warehouseman, only, for loss, damage, or delay caused by fire occurring after the expiration of the free time allowed by tariffs lawfully on file (such free time to be computed as therein provided) after notice of the arrival of the property at destination or at the port of export (if intended for export) has been duly sent or given, and after placement of the property for delivery at destination, or tender of delivery of property to the party entitled to receive it, has been made. Except in case of negligence of the carrier or party in possession (and the burden to prove freedom from such negligence shall be on the carrier or party in possession), the carrier or party in possession shall not be liable for loss, damage, or delay occurring while the property is stopped and held in transit upon the request of the shipper, owner, or party entitled to make such request, or resulting from a defect or vice in the property, or for country damage to cotton, or from riots or strikes.

The liability "as at common law" to which the bill of lading refers is one of absolute responsibility for the safety of the freight.[2]

---

2. See Guandolo, Transportation Law 934 (2d ed. 1973); Miller, Law of Freight Loss and Damage Claims § 101 (2d ed. 1961). Carrier liability for human cargo is lighter, and is limited to negligence. What might explain the difference?

The bills of lading issued by truck carriers employ the same language as that quoted above, but add at the end exculpation from liability for delay resulting from highway obstruction or impassability, etc., unless the carrier is negligent.

A general *caveat* is necessary with respect to the dollar amount of recovery. Examination of the bills of lading discloses the provision that goods are

> RECEIVED, subject to the classification and tariffs in effect on the date of issue of this Bill of Lading.

The "classifications" are set forth in a thick book which lists the myriads of things which may be hauled by a railroad, and classifies them for rate purposes. These classifications are filed with the Interstate Commerce Commission and are part of the rate structure; the carrier may not deviate from them, under penalty of the stern rules against discrimination. Some of the items are classified under rates with sharply limited liability. Owners of valuable goods have to their dismay learned of these limitations buried in the book on freight classification.

Air Carriers. The liability of carriers of air freight for shipments within the United States has not been fully developed. The problem is, however, minimized since the tariffs filed by domestic air carriers with the Civil Aeronautics Board, which the airbills incorporate, assume virtually absolute liability, subject to a monetary limit based on weight; responsibility for value exceeding the limit calls for added charges.

Note: Insurers v. Carriers

As we have seen, the seller or the buyer may have insurance that covers damage to the goods that occurs during transit. In cases where rules of law provide that the carrier is also responsible for the damage, interesting jockeying for position has occurred to determine whether the loss should fall ultimately on the insurer or on the carrier. The situation has been summarized by Professors Robert E. Keeton and Alan I. Widiss as follows:

Claims Against Common Carriers

> For many years insurers and common carriers (such as truckers and railroads) engaged in an extended struggle with regard to the insurers' assertion of claims against carriers for damage to goods covered by insurance obtained by shippers. The following description of some main events in this struggle indicates the nature of the controversy and its relation to subrogation.
>
> One of the early events in the conflict was the adoption by carriers of a bill-of-lading clause giving a carrier the benefit of insurance effected by a shipper. Insurers responded to this clause in the bill-of-lading with a policy clause providing for nonliability of an insurer upon shipment under a bill of lading that gave a carrier

the benefit of a shipper's insurance. Since carriers then had nothing to gain and shippers had much to lose by retention of the clause previously used in bills of lading, the carriers modified the bill-of-lading clause to give a carrier the benefit of any insurance effected on the goods so far as this did not defeat the insurer's liability. This strategic retreat by the carriers still left the insurers with a problem. If an insurer paid a shipper, would it be a "volunteer" and therefore not entitled to subrogation to the shipper's claim against the carrier? If it did not pay the shipper, how could it maintain good business relations with an insured who wanted prompt payment from somebody and did not like waiting for the carrier and insurer to resolve a dispute as to ultimate responsibility for the loss? To avoid this problem, insurers resorted to loan receipts: an insurer paid a shipper an amount equal to the promised insurance benefits, but the transaction was cast as a loan repayable out of the prospective recovery from the carrier. The effectiveness of a loan receipt in preserving rights against a common carrier has been recognized in a number of judicial decisions. Thus, at least as reflected in such precedents, the insurers prevailed in the struggle with carriers over form provisions concerning responsibility for losses of insured property during shipment. And this result is also fortified by decisions that a "benefit of insurance" clause in a bill of lading is invalid under statutory prohibitions against rate discrimination, since a carrier would be receiving greater compensation from a shipper who had insurance than from one who did not.

R. Keeton & A. Widiss, Insurance Law 250–251 (1988).[3]

(B) INTERNATIONAL SALES LAW

Introduction. Risk of loss rules for international sales are provided in Articles 67 and 68. Compare these articles with the provisions in UCC 2–509(1) and 2–510. See Berman & Ladd, Risk of Loss or Damage in Documentary Transactions Under the Convention on the International Sale of Goods, 21 Cornell Int'l L.J. 423 (1988).

Problem 5. In April, Continental entered into a contract with the Commodity Credit Corporation (C.C.C.), to sell cement to C.C.C. for delivery to Vietnam. The prices were quoted "CFR" Vietnam. Simultaneously with the signing of the contract, Continental entered into a contract with a company in Taiwan to supply the concrete; the Taiwanese supplier shipped the goods with States Marine Lines, Inc. On May 28, the shipping line announced that war risk surcharges would be added to freight costs; for this contract the surcharges amounted to $371,000. Who bears the burden of the surcharges?

---

3. Copied with permission of the authors and of the West Publishing Company.

Does CISG allocate the responsibility to purchase casualty insurance on goods in transit? If the sales contract incorporates *ICC Incoterms* (1990), use of the term, CFR,[4] (cost and freight to a named port of destination), means (p. 44):

> The seller must ... contract on usual terms at his own expense for the carriage of the goods to the named port of destination by the usual route in a seagoing vessel (or inland waterway vessel as appropriate) of the type normally used in the transport of goods of the contract description, [but seller has] no obligation [as to purchase of insurance]

If the parties use the term, CIF, *Incoterms* 1990 has a different set of sellers' obligations (pp. 50, 52):

> The seller must ... obtain at his own expense cargo insurance as agreed in the contract, that the buyer, or any other person having an insurable interest in the goods, shall be entitled to claim directly from the insurer and provide the buyer with the insurance policy or other evidence of insurance cover.
>
> The insurance shall be contracted with underwriters or an insurance company of good repute and, failing agreement to the contrary, be in accordance with the minimum cover of the Institute Cargo Clauses (Institute of London Underwriters) or any similar set of clauses. ... When required by the buyer, the seller shall provide at buyer's expense war, strikes, riots and civil commotion risk insurances if procurable. The minimum insurance shall cover the price provided in the contract plus ten per cent (i.e. 110%) and shall be provided in the currency of the contract.

Problem 6. Seller in San Francisco made a contract with Buyer in Bombay for the sale of a machine to Buyer. The contract included the provision: "Price $10,000. CIF Bombay." The machine was damaged during the ocean voyage. Who bears the risk of loss?

For purposes of applying CISG 67(1), is Seller "bound to hand [the goods] over at a particular place," i.e., Bombay? Compare CISG 31.

The matter is dealt with more clearly if the parties have incorporated the *ICC Incoterms* into their sales contracts. *Incoterms* (1990) specify when risk of loss passes in three categories of common shipping terms, which the ICC categorizes as "F" terms, "C" terms, and "D" terms. The "F" category are the terms in which the contract price does not include cost of carriage (e.g., FOB or FAS). In the "C" category are terms under which sellers must paid the costs of carriage (e.g., CFR and CIF). Under any of the "F" or the "C" terms of CFR and CIF, risk of loss passes at the time of shipment. A different result follows if the parties use other "C" terms, such as CPT (carriage paid to place of

---

4. *Incoterms* (1990) does not use the term, C. & F., found in UCC 2–320, 2–321. The ampersand, which could be replaced by an "A", would be confusing in international usage. In French, the English "insurance" translates to "assurance." Without knowing which language is implied, use of CAF creates unnecessary ambiguity. Thus the ICC uses CFR in lieu of C. & F.

destination) or CIP (carriage and insurance paid to place of destination) or "D" terms, such as DES (delivered ex ship), DEQ (delivered ex quay), and DDP (delivered duty paid). Sellers bear risk of loss until the goods are delivered at the specified place.

Precision in Defining the Moment of Risk Passing. Loading and offloading goods pose special risks of damage to the goods in that process. Allocation of this risk of loss between buyer and seller requires precision in knowing exactly when risk passes.

In an FOB vessel contract, for example, risk passes when the goods pass the ship's rail. This traditional usage is retained in *ICC Incoterms* (1990) at 38. The same point is designated in CFR and CIF contracts. Id. at 46, 52. In an FAS contract, risk passes when the goods have been placed alongside the vessel on the quay or in lighters. Id. at 32.

Use of other terms puts the moment of risk passing when goods are delivered into the possession of carriers, including delivery to a terminal facility, e.g., FCA (free carrier). Id. at 26–28. In the "D" terms, sellers bear the risks of offloading under the term, DEQ (delivered ex quay), but not under DES (delivered ex ship). Id. at 74, 82.

RHEINBERG–KELLEREI GMBH v. VINEYARD WINE CO., 53 N.C.App. 560, 281 S.E.2d 425 (1981). Rheinberg, a West German wine importer, and Vineyard, a North Carolina wine distributor, made a contract for Rheinberg to sell 620 cases of wine to Vineyard. The contract called for Rheinberg to ship the wine to Vineyard, and on 29 November 1978 Rheinberg delivered a container containing the wine to a shipping company for shipment to Wilmington, Delaware, freight payable by Vineyard at destination. Early in December the shipment left Germany via the M.S. Munchen, which in mid-December was lost in the North Atlantic with all hands and cargo. The sales contract provided: "Insurance to be covered by purchaser." Rheinberg notified Sutton, its agent, of the shipment, and forwarded shipping documents to a correspondent bank in Charlotte, North Carolina. Vineyard received no notice of the shipment until after the ship and cargo had been lost.

Vineyard refused to pay for the wine, and Rheinberg sued for the price in a North Carolina court. The case was litigated under domestic United States law.

Judgment for the defendant was affirmed by the Court of Appeals. The transfer of risk of loss to buyer was negated by UCC 2–504(c) since the seller did not "promptly notify the buyer of the shipment." It would not be practical "to attempt to engraft into [2–504] a rigid definition of prompt notice ... which must be determined on a case-by-case basis, under all the circumstances." However, in this case Vineyard was not notified "within the time in which its interest could have been protected by insurance or otherwise"; the notice had not been "prompt."

Queries: The opinion did not discuss the ambiguities latent in the last phrase of UCC 2–504(c): "if material loss or delay *ensues.*" On these facts, would loss have "ensued" from the failure to notify if the buyer was covered by insurance under a blanket policy? Or did loss "ensue" from the loss at sea of the ship and cargo? Who should have the burden to show that loss had "ensued"?

How would the case be decided if CISG were the applicable law?

Note: Liability of Carriers in International Transport

Liability of Ocean Carriers. The development of liability of ocean carriers is a story of sharp international bargaining; an early phase involved the conflict between British case-law enforcing standard bill of lading clauses that disclaimed carrier liability, and American case-law that invalidated clauses that exempted the carrier from responsibility for negligent loss or damage to cargo.

Attempts to solve the problem by international agreements at Liverpool in 1882 and at Hamburg in 1885 failed to satisfy American shipper interests. There ensued the so-called Harter Act, which was enacted by Congress in 1893, 46 U.S.C. §§ 190–95. This Act drew a distinction between the obligation of the carrier to "exercise due diligence to make the ... vessel in all respects seaworthy and properly manned, equipped and supplied" and the freedom from liability for "damage or loss resulting from faults or errors in navigation or in the management of said vessel. ..." Sections 1 and 2 limited the power to contract out of the responsibility which the Act imposed. Australia, Canada and New Zealand copied this legislation, but England kept its rules permitting further limitation of liability, even as applied to American bills of lading.

The Hague Rules. Further attempts for agreement finally culminated, at the Fifth International Conference on Maritime Law held in Brussels in 1924, in an international convention usually called the "Hague Rules." The United States Government and many other countries signed this Convention. However, ratification by the United States Senate was delayed until 1936, and was then given in connection with the enactment by Congress of the Carriage of Goods by Sea Act, 1936, 46 U.S.C. §§ 1300–15. This Act followed the language of the 1924 Brussels Convention, with a few minor modifications. The Brussels Convention has now been ratified by most of the important commercial countries. United States coastwise shipping (e.g., Seattle to San Diego) and some aspects of international shipping are subject to the Harter Act which, at significant points provides stronger legal protection for cargo. See Gilmore and Black, Admiralty 145 (2d ed. 1975).

One accustomed to the heavy responsibility of domestic rail carriers will be surprised at the rules which govern ocean carriers. For example, Article 4 the Brussels Convention (as embodied in Section 4(2) of the Carriage of Goods by Sea Act) sets forth a "catalogue" of seventeen grounds for exempting the carrier from liability. This article provides in part:

> Neither the carrier nor the ship shall be responsible for loss or damage arising or resulting from—
>
> (a) Act, neglect, or default of the master, mariner, pilot or the servants of the carrier in the navigation or in the management of the ship;
>
> (b) Fire, unless caused by the actual fault or privity of the carrier;
>
> (c) Perils, dangers, and accidents of the sea or other navigable waters; ..."

The Hamburg Rules. The special exemptions for the carrier in The Hague Rules of 1924 were virtually eliminated from the United Nations Convention on the Carriage of Goods by Sea, finalized in 1978 at Hamburg ("The Hamburg Rules"). For discussion and text of the Convention see Symposium, UNCITRAL's First Decade, 27 Am. J.Comp.L. 353–419 (discussion), 421–440 (text). The United States was one of the twenty-seven States that signed the Convention, but ratification by the United States and several other signatories has been delayed by opposition from ocean carriers. Contrast: Moore, The Hamburg Rules, 10 J.Mar.L. & Comm. 1 (1978) (objections to Convention) with Selvig, 12 id. 299 (1981) (sympathetic analysis). See also Donovan, The Hamburg Rules: Why a New Convention on Carriage of Goods by Sea, 4 Maritime Lawyer 1 (1979); Sweeney, 7 J.Mar.L. & Comm. 69, 372, 487, 617 and 8 id. 167 (1975–76) (comprehensive review drafting history); S. Mankabady (Ed.), The Hamburg Rules on Carriage of Goods by Sea (1978); Honnold, International Regulation of Maritime Transportation (Sweeney, ed., 1978) at 365–374. Impetus for ratification has resulted from the reliance on the Hamburg rules in preparing the U.N. Convention on International Multimodal Transport of Goods (1980). See Selvig, Mar.Ins. No. 44 (1979); Mankabady, 2 Int.Contr.L. & Fin.Rev. 233 (1981); 15 J.World Tr.L. 283 (1981).

The twentieth ratification needed to bring the Hamburg Convention into force occurred on October 7, 1991; the Convention will enter into force for these twenty States on 1 November 1992. With few exceptions, the initial parties to the Convention are small, developing countries. However, the Convention's impending entry into force has stimulated consideration in additional States. Thus, a British solicitor wrote in 1991:

> The claim that the Hamburg Rules overly favour cargo owners is predictable, ... but so far as the effect of the Rules is concerned it does not bear close scrutiny. This is no system of strict carrier liability, it has, at its core, the principle of liability based on carrier fault. It is true that in general carrier fault is presumed but this is subject to important exceptions. The imposition of the burden of proof upon carriers (except in the case of fire, an important

> exception) is hardly an unbearable burden as they will be in a position to control the carriage and ascertain the cause of any loss. They need only show that they were not negligent. ... Despite its weaknesses, an international momentum now seems to be developing which will lead to the Convention's operation in the near future and it is quite possible that its acceptance by a major trading nation would give it the critical mass it needs to overthrow the ancient regime based on the Hague Rules.

Waldron, The Hanburg Rules—A Boondoggle for Lawyers?, [1991] J. Bus. Law 305, 318–319.

Marine Insurance. Problems resulting from the restricted responsibility of the ocean carrier may be solved but are not necessarily simplified by a marine insurance policy. For instance, one of the common and important clauses in marine policies is "free of particular average" (F.P.A.): hardly a word in this phrase means what a layman would suppose. "Free of" means without insurance coverage; "average" is a corruption of a French term (derived from the Arabic) which means loss or damage; "particular average" refers to partial losses which are not "general." (But a "general average" or loss does not mean total loss, but rather (roughly speaking) those losses incurred when some part of a marine venture is sacrificed to save the rest, as when part of a cargo is jettisoned to lighten a ship in peril.) The point of this illuminating explanation is to suggest that even in dealing with marine policies a specialist is needed. See Gilmore & Black, Admiralty 76–79 (2d ed., 1975); MacDonald, Practical Exporting and Importing 318–31 (1959).

Liability of Air Carriers. Rules for liability for international air shipments were prescribed by the Warsaw Convention of 1929. The Convention has now been accepted by the United States and over 90 other countries. Article 20 of this Convention in part provides (in translation):

> (1) The carrier shall not be liable if he proves that he and his agents have taken all necessary measures to avoid the damage or that it was impossible for him or them to take such measures.

> (2) In the transportation of goods and baggage the carrier shall not be liable if he proves that the damage was occasioned by an error in piloting, in the handling of the aircraft, or in navigation and that, in all other respects, he and his agents have taken all necessary measures to avoid the damage.

Article 22 sets forth monetary limits on damage awards. The most controversial limits apply to recovery for personal injury and death—issues that are not relevant here. Unless damage to cargo is caused by wilful misconduct, recovery was initially limited to approximately $16 per kilogram—a figure that was augmented by devaluation of the dollar.

Continuing dissatisfaction with the Convention brought about its revision by the Guatemala City Protocol of 1971. Should this agreement go into effect, air carriers would no longer have the benefit of the exceptions for errors in piloting, and the like, set forth in Article 20(2), above. Under this revision, Article 20 would provide:

> In the carriage of cargo the carrier shall not be liable for damage resulting from destruction, loss, damage or delay if he proves that he and his servants and agents have taken all necessary measures to avoid the damage or that it was impossible for them to take such measures.

The Guatemala City Protocol would raise the maximum liability for personal injury and wrongful death but the limits on liability for cargo would be preserved, subject to unlimited liability for losses resulting from certain intentional or reckless conduct of the carrier. See S. Sorkin, How to Recover for Loss or Damage to Goods in Transit §§ 9.15–9.21, 13.08 (1978, with supplements). The Protocol has not been acted upon by the U.S. Senate.

*

Appendix

FEDERAL BILLS OF LADING ACT
TITLE 49 UNITED STATES CODE APP.

§ 88. Duty to deliver goods on demand; refusal

A carrier, in the absence of some lawful excuse, is bound to deliver goods upon a demand made either by the consignee named in the bill for the goods or, if the bill is an order bill, by the holder thereof, if such a demand is accompanied by—

    (a) An offer in good faith to satisfy the carrier's lawful lien upon the goods [for freight and other charges];

    (b) Possession of the bill of lading and an offer in good faith to surrender, properly indorsed, the bill which was issued for the goods, if the bill is an order bill; and

    (c) A readiness and willingness to sign, when the goods are delivered, an acknowledgment that they have been delivered, if such signature is requested by the carrier.

In case the carrier refuses or fails to deliver the goods, in compliance with a demand by the consignee or holder so accompanied, the burden shall be upon the carrier to establish the existence of a lawful excuse for such refusal or failure.

§ 89. Delivery; when justified

A carrier is justified, subject to the provisions of sections 90–92 of this title, in delivering goods to one who is—

    (a) A person lawfully entitled to possession of the goods, or

    (b) The consignee named in a straight bill of lading, or

    (c) A person in possession of an order bill for the goods, by the terms of which the goods are deliverable to his order; or which has been indorsed to him, or in blank by the consignee, or by the mediate or immediate indorsee of the consignee.

§ 90. Liability for delivery to a person not entitled thereto

Where a carrier delivers goods to one who is not lawfully entitled to the possession of them, the carrier shall be liable to anyone having a right of property or possession in the goods if he delivered the goods otherwise than as authorized under subdivisions (b) and (c) of section 89 . . . .

§ 91. Liability for delivery without cancellation of bill

Except as provided in section 106 of this title [permitting carriers' to dispose of goods to collect the freight or other charges], and except where compelled by legal process, if a carrier delivers goods for which an order bill had been issued, the negotiation of which would transfer the right to the possession of the goods, and fails to take up and cancel the bill, such carrier shall be liable for failure to deliver the goods to anyone who for value and in good faith purchases such bill, whether such purchaser acquired title to the bill before or after the delivery of the goods and notwithstanding delivery was made to the person entitled thereto.

§ 108. Negotiation of order bill of lading by indorsement

An order bill may be negotiated by the indorsement of the person to whose order the goods are deliverable by the tenor of the bill. Such indorsement may be in blank or to a specified person. If indorsed to a specified person, it may be negotiated again by the indorsement of such person in blank or to another specified person. Subsequent negotiation may be made in like manner.

§ 111. Title and right acquired by transferee of ordinary bill

A person to whom an order bill has been duly negotiated acquires thereby—...

(b) The direct obligation of the carrier to hold possession of the goods for him according to the terms of the bill as fully as if the carrier had contracted directly with him.

INDEX

References are to Pages

ACCEPTANCE OF GOODS
Buyer's duty to accept, 227–228
Failure to make effective rejection, 229–233
Legal effect of acceptance, 227
Obligation to pay at contract rate, 227
Remedies for breach of warranty, 227
Signification by buyer, 229–233

ACTION FOR THE PRICE
Accepted goods, 227
After risk of loss passed, 393–394

AGENCY
Agent's authority, 44
Nemo dat maxim, 46

ARBITRATION
International transactions, 96–103

ASSIGNMENT BY BUYER
See Privity

AVOIDANCE
Cure for non-conforming deliveries, 288–289
Effect of avoidance, 288
Fundamental breach, 276–277, 287
In international transaction, 276–278, 287–290
Late delivery, 277

BANKS
 See Letters of Credit
Bank's duty re presentment of documentary drafts, 307–308
Role in documentary transactions, 292–293

"BATTLE OF THE FORMS"
Warranty disclaimer, 115–119

BILLS OF LADING
Basic terms, 220–221
Bills in a set, 357–358
"Clean" and "foul", 356–357
Negotiable bills, 292
Negotiation of bills, 293
Specimen forms, 297, 304

BUYER IN ORDINARY COURSE OF BUSINESS
 See also Good Faith Purchaser

BUYER IN ORDINARY COURSE OF BUSINESS—Cont'd
Under UCC, 49

CARRIERS
See also Bills of Lading
Hague Rules, 410–411
Hamburg Rules, 411–412
Liability for casualty to or loss of goods, 405–407, 410–413
Role in documentary transactions, 292–297, 305–306

CONSTRUCTION OF CISG
See Interpretation of CISG

CONSTRUCTION OF UCC
See Interpretation of UCC

COVER
In anticipation of late delivery, 252–259
Measure of buyer's damages, 227

CREDIT RISK
Documentary transactions, 291–292
Simultaneous exchanges, 291

CRIME
Criminal fraud, 45, 48
Criminal's power to convey, 44–45, 47–48
Larceny, burglary, robbery, 45, 47–48

CURE
After rejection, 242–247
Price adjustment as cure, 248
Repair as cure, 247–248

DAMAGES AFTER WRONGFUL REJECTION
See also Resale, Profit
Basic rules, 227–228, 260–269

DAMAGES AFTER RIGHTFUL REJECTION OF GOODS
See also Cover
Basic rules, 227

DAMAGES FOR BREACH OF WARRANTY
Basic rules, 57–58, 96
Burden of proof, 92–95
Buyer's lost profit, 90–92
Consequential damages, 89–90, 123–132

DAMAGES FOR BREACH OF WARRANTY
—Cont'd
Market formula applied, 80–88

DELIVERY
See Tender of Delivery; Time Term
Delivery in international sales, 223–225
Late delivery, 252–259, 277
Nachfrist provision, 225–226

DESTINATION CONTRACT
Defined, 218–219
Place of tender, 219

DISCLAIMER OF WARRANTY
"As-is" sale, 110–113
Basic rules, 104–105, 142–143
Conspicuous, 105–110
Implied disclaimer, 104, 115–119
Mention merchantability, 105–110
Post-contract disclaimer, 140–141
Under MMWA, 170–171
Warranty and disclaimer in same contract, 104

DOCUMENT OF TITLE
See Bills of Lading; Warehouse Receipt

DRAFTS
Bank's duty on presentment, 307–308
Discounting by bank, 308, 342
Function in documentary transactions, 292
Specimen form, 295, 339

ENTRUSTING TO MERCHANT
Buyer in ordinary course of business, 49
Factor's Acts, 46–47
Under UCC, 49–52

EXCUSE
Casualty to identified goods, 383–384

EXPRESS WARRANTY OF QUALITY
Buyer's reliance, 55, 76–78
Compared with mistake, 79
Compared with other warranties, 56–57
Compared with tortious misrepresentation, 70–75, 78–79
Conflicting descriptions of goods, 80
Manufacturer's warranty to ultimate buyer, 134–139
Oral warranties, 88, 114–115, 137–138
Part of the basis of the bargain, 70–75, 76
Relates to goods, 70–75, 76
Seller's intent, 54–55
Seller's opinion, puffing, 70–76
Warranty and disclaimer: interpretation, 104

FITNESS FOR PARTICULAR PURPOSE
Applied, 88–89
Compared with other warranties, 56–57

FRAUD
Buyer who assumes false identity, 45, 48
Buyer who intends not to pay, 45

FUNDAMENTAL BREACH
See Avoidance

GOOD FAITH LESSEE
Compared with good faith purchase, 48, 52

GOOD FAITH PURCHASE
See also Agency; Crime; Fraud
Basic principles, 45–48
Entrusting, 48–52
Factor's Acts, 46–47
International sales, 53
Market overt, 46
Voidable title, 47

GOOD FAITH PURCHASER
Buyer in ordinary course of business, 48–52
Holder in due course of negotiable instrument, 358–363
Holder of duty negotiated document of title, 293–294

HOLDER IN DUE COURSE
Notice of defense, 364
Of negotiable instrument, 358–363
Under letter of credit, 363–364

HOLDER OF DULY NEGOTIATED DOCUMENT OF TITLE
Rights of holder, 293–294

INSPECTION
Before purchase, 104
Condition of duty to pay, 221, 226, 228–229
Independent inspector, 58–63, 306
In documentary transactions, 305–306
Payment against documents, 306
Post-delivery inspection, 229–233

INSURANCE
Marine insurance, 334–337, 412
Risk of loss in sales transactions, 383, 384
Subrogation to buyer's claim, 105–109

INTERPRETATION OF CISG
General principles, 32–34
Good faith, 34, 36
Party autonomy, 34–35
Promotion of uniformity, 35–36
Regard for international character, 35–36

INTERPRETATION OF SALES CONTRACTS
Bargain in fact, 63, 69, 104, 109, 113
Course of dealing, 23–24, 119–123
Usage of trade, 23–24, 115–119

INTERPRETATION OF UCC
Definitions, 30
Good faith, 24
Official comments, 5, 28–30
Property concept, 37, 375–378
State enactment, 19–20
Supplementary laws, 23
Theories of interpretation, 25–28
Unconscionability, 24, 132–134, 140–141

INDEX

References are to Pages

LETTERS OF CREDIT
Back-to-back credits, 342–343
Defects in documents, 347–358
Fraud by seller, 358–363
Sales contract terms for, 340–342
Specimen form, 320–322
Stand-by credits, 369–374
Terms of credits, 356
Time drafts under, 342, 347–355

LIMITATION OF DAMAGES CLAUSE
Basic rules, 104–105, 142–143
Conspicuous, 105–110
Post-contract provision, 140–141
Repair or replace: failure, 123–134
Unconscionable, 132–134, 140–141
Under MMWA, 171–172

MAGNUSON–MOSS WARRANTY ACT (MMWA)
Creation of privity, 198–202
Disclaimer of implied warranty, 170–171
Federal court jurisdiction, 172–177
Limitation of damages clause, 171
Limited and full warranties, 169–170
Limited duration of implied warranty, 171–172
Right to attorney's fees and costs, 172
Scope, 167–168, 172–177

MERCHANTABLE QUALITY
Compared with other warranties, 56–57
Fair average quality, 68–69
Fitness for ordinary purpose, 67
Label on product, 79–80
Pass without objection, 67–68

MONEY
Hard and soft currencies, 210–212
Legal tender, 210

NOTICE OF BREACH
Condition of buyer's warranty recovery, 143–149, 159–163
Limited duration of implied warranty with MMWA, 171–172
Manufacturer's warranty, 197

PAROL EVIDENCE RULE
Manufacturer's representative's warranties, 138–140
Seller's oral warranties, 114–115

PAYMENT
   See Tender of Payment
Inspection before payment, 221, 226
Payment in international sales, 226

PERFECT TENDER RULE
See Rejection of Goods

PRICE
Restitution on buyer's breach, 270
Seller's right to recover, 227, 393–394

PRICE TERM
Open price term, 208, 210

PRICE TERM—Cont'd
Price in long-term contract, 208
Take-or-pay contract, 209

PRIVITY
Assignment by buyer, 187, 202–206
International sales, 207
Manufacturer's advertisement, 186
Manufacturer's implied warranty, 188–198
Manufacturer's representative's warranties, 186–187
Third-party beneficiary, 187, 202, 206

PRODUCT LIABILITY
Early development, 164–165
Personal injury under MMWA, 172
Restatement (2d) Torts § 402A, 165, 178
Strict tort liability, 165–167

PROFIT
Measure of seller's damages, 270–276

RECLAMATION OF GOODS
Seller's right to reclaim, 308–310

REFUND OF PRICE
Under "full" MMWA warranty, 169–170

REJECTION OF DOCUMENTS
Documentary transaction, 233, 306

REJECTION OF GOODS
Buyer's responsibility for rejected goods, 228, 251–252
Buyer's right to reject, 227
Defect in document of title, 233
Installment transactions, 241–242
Legal effect of rejection, 227
Perfect tender rule, 235–241
Remedies after rightful rejection, 227
Remedies after wrongful rejection, 227–228, 260–269
Substantial performance, 235–241
Untimely notice of shipment, 233

REMEDIES
See Action for the Price; Cover; Damages after Rightful Rejection of Goods; Damages after Wrongful Rejection; Damages for Breach of Warranty; Profit; Reclamation of Goods; Resale

REPAIR OR REPLACE OBLIGATION
Consequential damages, 123–134, 134–139, 141–142
Failure of essential purpose, 123–132
Magnuson–Moss Warranty Act, 168–169

RESALE
Measure of seller's damages, 260–269

REVOCATION OF ACCEPTANCE
Action against lender, 285–286
Action against remote manufacturer, 285
Cure after revocation, 284
Offset for buyer's use, 286–287

INDEX

References are to Pages

REVOCATION OF ACCEPTANCE—Cont'd
Substantial impairment of value, 278–284
Use after revocation, 278–284, 286

RISK OF LOSS
Early development, 375–378
Effect of buyer's breach, 394–397
Effect of seller's breach, 391–393, 404–405
Goods delivered but not received, 391–393
Goods in possession of buyer, 385–391, 394–397
Goods in possession of carrier, 398–405
Goods in possession of seller, 379–385
Hague Rules, 410–411
Hamburg Rules, 411–412
In international transactions, 397–398, 402–410
Insurance coverage, 383, 384
Liability of carrier, 405–407, 410–413

SCOPE OF CISG
"Contracting States", 31
"Goods", 31
Goods and real property, 32
Mixed goods and services, 31–32
Parties in different states, 30–31

SCOPE OF UCC ART. 2
"Goods", 9–10
Goods and real property, 21–22
Mixed goods and services, 10–16, 229–233
"Sale", 9, 37

SHIPMENT CONTRACT
Defined, 218–219
Place of tender, 219

SIGNIFICANT PERSONS IN HISTORY OF COMMERCIAL LAW
Judah P. Benjamin, 2
Mackensie Chalmers, 26–27, 377
Grant Gilmore, 4, 46
Karl Llewellyn, 2, 4, 27
Lord Mansfield, 2
Joseph Story, 3
Samuel Williston, 4, 33, 55, 377–378

SPONSORS OF UNIFORM INTERNATIONAL SALES LAW
Hague Conference (ULIS), 7
UNCITRAL (CISG), 7–8

SPONSORS OF UNIFORM LAWS IN U.S.
American Law Institute, 4, 19
Nat'l Conf. of Commissioners on Uniform State Laws, 4, 19

STATUTE OF FRAUDS
Common law, 21
UCC Art. 1, 21
UCC Art. 2, 16–17, 20–21

STATUTE OF LIMITATIONS
Basic rules, 149, 163
Future performance warranty, 149–159
Limited duration of implied warranty under MMWA, 171–172
Manufacturer's implied warranty, 197–198
Under MMWA, 149–159

STRICT TORT LIABILITY
Disclaimer of tort liability, 185
Early development, 164–165
Personal injuries, 164–167
Property damage, 177–178, 178–185
Relation to warranty, 164–167, 178–185
Restatement (2d) Torts § 402A, 165

TENDER OF DELIVERY
Basic rules, 214–215
Delivery in lots, 216

TENDER OF PAYMENT
Basic rules, 214–215, 221–222

THIRD PARTY BENEFICIARY
See Privity

TIME TERM
In absence of agreement, 248–251
Nachfrist provision, 225–226

UNIFORM CUSTOMS AND PRACTICE FOR DOCUMENTARY CREDITS (UCP)
New York provision re UCC Article 5, 344–347
Promulgated by Int'l Chamber of Commerce, 343–344

WAREHOUSE RECEIPT
In documentary transactions, 222–223

WARRANTY OF QUALITY
Basis in sales contract, 63, 69, 104, 109, 113
Caveat emptor, 54
CISG warranty, 96
Early development, 54–56
Types of UCC warranties, 56–57

WARRANTY OF TITLE
Auction sale, 39–41, 42
Claims of encumbrancers, 39–41
Claims of prior owners, 38
Cloud on title, 41
Export restriction, 42–43
"Good title", 38, 52
Infringement of intellectual property right, 38, 43
Lessee's protection, 43–44
Quiet possession, 41–42
Sheriff's sale, 42